EPICS AND HEROES

in China's Minority Cultures

Edited by

Mineke Schipper and Hubin Yin

Guangxi Normal University Press

Guangxi and Beijing

Contents

Preface

Many people deserve thanks, because without them this co-operative project would not have been possible. I will express my thanks to them in the process of sketching the history of the present book which dates back to 1999-2000, when Professor Yang Enhong was in the Netherlands as a visiting scholar of the International Institute of Asian Studies based in Leiden in the Netherlands. She first introduced me to Professor Yang Yi, the Director of the Chinese Academy of Social Sciences in Beijing who expressed his wish for our co-operation, while visiting the University of Leiden. Already at that occasion, he strongly expressed the idea of co-operation between scholars of the Chinese Academy with scholars in the field of intercultural research in comparative literature in The Netherlands. My being invited to visit the Chinese Academy can certainly be seen as a follow up of this and other contacts I had with Prof. Yang Yi to whom we are all very grateful, as participants in this intercultural project.

Prof. Yang Enhong was the first to launch the idea for our co-operation on the particular topic of "Epics and Heroes" while she was a visiting scholar in Leiden, and she deserves our gratitude for it. We were in close contact during her research stay as a fellow of the Asia Institute in Leiden in 1999, when she co-organised the international congress for Tibetologists. She invited me to present a workshop on intercultural literary studies and oral literature at that congress. It appeared that most Tibetologists were not really used to doing research from an intercultural perspective, nor to reflect on the similarities and differences of their specific literatures in a wider comparative context. However, they saw the relevance and asked me to commit myself to a follow up, as they now felt that such an approach would not only yield new insights into Tibetan literature but also be enriching for comparative literature. Research about Tibetan epics throws new light upon the comparative study of the epic worldwide, and the other way round. This also holds for other oral genres such as creation myths, proverbs, animal stories, etc.

Over many years, the Institute of Ethnic Literatures of the Chinese Academy of Social Sciences had been working extremely hard in transcribing material on all China's minority Literatures. However, its researchers had less been involved in exchanging the results of their respective efforts among scholars specialized in the various cultures in China, or in comparing their own work with results transcribed and studied elsewhere in the world. Our new comparative project aimed, first, at exploring the possibilities for the intercultural study of minority literatures in China; second, to introduce the results of the project into the international comparative literature research community. And Professor Yang Enhong was very much aware of the great rewards to be gained from both.

During her stay in Leiden I had frequent dialogues and very interesting exchanges of ideas with Prof. Yang Enhong who asked me whether I would be willing to come to Beijing and give some lectures at the Institute as a preparation for more comparative study of China's rich and diverse oral literatures and cultures. Initially I was hesitant, because I am not a Sinologist after all. But she appeared to be very insistent, arguing that, thanks to my theoretical schooling and my research and training in the field of Intercultural Literary Studies, and as a specialist in African oral traditions and written literatures over the years, I had gained important insights in the phenomenon of oral traditions and their relations to transcribed or written texts, and the mutual connections and dialectics of both. As a follow up, the Institute of Ethnic Literatures of the Chinese Academy of Social Sciences sent me an invitation letter expressing its wish for me to share my "outsider's" knowledge with Chinese colleagues and to co-operate in a new project, as part of the Institute 's initiative to pay more attention to intercultural research, which had been my field of research and interest over the years.

The Institute recommended that in the co-operation project my contribution would consist of presenting information on comparative research in the field of o-ral literature from an intercultural perspective in September 2001, and to advise on the programming and preparation for the next year's extended workshop on "Epics and Heroes in Chinese Minority Cultures" which I was invited to attend in order to comment on scholars' contributions to that workshop in October 2002.

Right from the beginning, both the Chinese Academy of Social Sciences and its Institute of Ethnic Literatures, on the one hand, and the Royal Netherlands Academy of Sciences and its China Committee on the other hand have been extremely supportive of this project, and deserve our heartfelt thanks. I want to express my profound gratitude to both institutions for their moral and material support to my travels to and stays in China and those of my Chinese colleagues Yang Enhong and Yin Hubin allowing them to stay here in the Netherlands as visiting scholars. Without the existing agreements between the two institutions this fruitful co-operation would not have been possible at all.

Thanks to the generosity of the Royal Netherlands Academy of Sciences' extra funds for translation and copy-editing, it has been possible to engage two indispensable very hardworking people whose names need to be praised here: first, Xiaohong Zhang who has finished writing her doctoral dissertation here in Leiden and who was marvellous in polishing and copy-editing the English language papers; and, second, Thera Giezen who worked extremely hard in correcting the typography of the manuscript and who was also absolutely essential and ingenious in finding the correct names, titles, places and dates in footnotes and bibliography. Special thanks, ladies, for your wonderful hard work and for your indestructible cheerfulness, against all time pressure and fatigue. You were exemplary and admirable. And thanks to Professor Bi Xun for patiently sending us indispensable Kazak transcriptions. Special thanks also go to Ms. Zhou Xiang and Song Ying who were of great help in the process of finalising the Chinese version of the papers.

Dr. Chao Gejin had been involved in the co-ordination of the second workshop in Beijing in 2002, and we had discussed the preparation of this volume at the time. Regrettably, due to other urgent obligations, he has not been able to co-edit the book with me. In his place he delegated Dr. Yin Hubin, who came to The Netherlands in the spring of 2004, and it was a pleasure working with him in great co-operation, in spite of the innumerable problems of translation and communication that had to be solved. In this book, Dr. Yin Hubin has been responsible for editing the Chinese version included in this book, whereas I have been responsible for the English version. We both want to thank once more all contributors to this volume who have worked so hard on their papers in spite of all the difficulties due to geographical distance, language transcription problems, lurking deadlines and other pressures. It is our hope that thanks to all our common efforts the eloquence of narrators and singers of fascinating epics in various languages of China's rich cultures, as discussed in this book, will become better known, so that new dimensions will be added to the comparative perspectives on epics worldwide.

Mineke Schipper and Hubin Yin

Notes on Contributors

Mineke Schipper is professor of Intercultural Literary Studies at the University of Leiden in The Netherlands. She is the author of numerous books including *Never Marry a Woman with Big Feet*. *Women in Proverbs from Around the World* (2004); *Imagining Insiders*. *Africa and the Question of Belonging* (1999); *Unheard Words*. *Women and Literature in Africa*, *The Arab World*, *Asia*, *The Caribbean*, *and Latin America* (1985) and *Realism*. *The Illusion of Reality in Literature* (1979). She has also published two novels.

Yang Enhong currently serves as Senior Researcher and Director of the Division of Tibetan literature at the Institute of Ethnic Literature of the Chinese Academy of Social Sciences. While performing fieldwork in the borderlands of Tibet, Sichuan, and Qinghai, she closely studied performances by singers of the Gesar epic and has since published widely in this field. She is the author of *Investigations and Researches into Singers of the 'Gesar' Epic* (1995) and *'Gesar'*: *A Heroic Epic from Chinese Ethnic Minority Traditions* (1990).

Li Lianrong (brtson-vgrus-rgya-mtsho) is Assistant Researcher at the Institute of Ethnic Literature of the Chinese Academy of Social Sciences, where he focuses on the Tibetan *Gesar* epic. After completing his doctoral dissertation *On the Making and Development of 'Gesar' Epic Studies in China*: 1959-1996, he began researching the texts and performances of *Gesar*. He has recently published papers entitled *The Theoretical Construction of 'Gesar' Studies*: *Early Chinese Scholarship* (2001) and *History and the Tibetan 'Gesar' Epic* (2001).

Zhalagaa's research presently centers on historical literature derived from *The Secret History of the Mongolian*. He is Senior Researcher at the Institute of Ethnic Literature of the Chinese Academy of Social Sciences. As the author of many articles on Mongolian literature and the relations between Mongolian and Han literatures, he has written *A Storied Building with a Single Floor*: *Weeping for the Red Pavilion*, *and Dream of the Red Chamber* (1984), *The Chronicle of Yinjiannasi's Life* (1991), and *A Critical Biography of Yinjiannasi* (1994).

Siqinbatu is Associate Professor at the Institute of Ethnic Literature of the Chinese Academy of Social Sciences. His research field is Mongolian literature and religion. Dr. Siqinbatu has published books entitled ' *Jangar*' *and Mongolian Religious Culture* (1999), *Study of Mongolian Myths I*: *Origin and Development of Mongolian Myths* (1992), *Study of Mongolian Myths II*: *Preservation and Evolution of Mongolian Myths* (1992), *Study of Mongolian Myths III*: *The Values and Significance of Mongolian Myths* (1992), *Introduction to the Cult of Trees among Altaic Language-Speaking Peoples* (1990), *About the Problems of the Function of Mongolian Buddhist Myths* (1989) and *Jangar Kahan's Palace and Shamanism* (1999).

Adil Zhumaturdi is a scholar of Kirghiz nationality in Xinjiang Uygur Autonomous Region of China. He is now Associate Researcher at the Society for the Study of Folk Literature and Arts in Xinjiang. Dr. Adil Zhumaturdi is specialized in the field of *Manas* studies. His main recent publications include: *Critical Biography of Famous Manaschi Jusup Mamay* (2002), *Ethnography of the Kirghiz Nationality* (2004), *Manaschi's Image as a Shaman* (2004), *A Comparative Study in the Origin Epic ' Er Töshtük'* (2003), *The Relationship of the ' Manas' Epic and the Persian Language 'Jāmi' al- Tawārīkh' by Rashīd al-Dīi fadl allah in the 16th Century* (2002), *The Artistic Features of the ' Manas' Epic Sung Texts Performed by Jusup Mamay* (2000).

Lang Ying is Senior Researcher and Deputy Director at the Institute of Ethnic Literature of the Chinese Academy of Social Sciences. Her extensive work on Uygur and Turkic literature and northern Chinese epic studies is reflected in the following samples of her works: ' Manas ' : *A Hero Epic from Chinese Ethnic Minority Traditions* (1990), ' Manas ' : *Comments and Analysis* (1991), ' Kudatku Bilik ' [*Wisdom of Felicity and Happiness*] *and Oriental-Western Cultures* (1992) and *On the ' Manas ' Epic* (1990).

Huang Zhongxiang is Associate Professor at the Institute of Ethnic Literature of the Chinese Academy of Social Sciences. His PhD. dissertation is entitled *Kazak Vocabulary and Culture*. His special field is the folk literature of Turkic speaking peoples in Xinjiang. He is skillful in many languages such as Kazak, Uygur, Kirghiz, Uzbek, etc. From the 1980s on, he has carried out intensive field work in the areas of Turkic-speaking peoples in Xinjiang, Qinghai, Gansu, and Henan, and has collected a large amount of first-hand materials. Dr. Huang's recent papers mainly concern the relationship of language and culture in the case of the Kazak nationality: *Shamanistic Ideas as Seen Through the Epics of the Kazak Nationality* (2002), *Characteristics of Kazak Proverbs and Animal Husbandry Culture* (1999) *and Kazak Proverbs and Eating Culture* (1997).

Liu Yahu is Senior Researcher of the Institute of Ethnic Literature at the Chinese Academy of Social Sciences. His research field is mainly on epics and the literary relationships of ethnic nationalities in the southern China. Prof. Liu Yahu's main publications include: *The History of Literary Relationship for the Nationalities in China* (volume of southern China, 1997), *Aesthetic Study of Legends about Scenery of Guangxi* (1994), *On the Southern Epics* (1999).

Yin Hubin is Senior Researcher at the Institute of Ethnic Literature of the Chinese Academy of Social Sciences, where his primary field of study is oral poetic theory, oral tradition and folk religion in northern China. His recent papers include: *Homer and the Singer of Tales in Our Era : Translation Notes on ' The Singer of Tales'* by *A . B . Lord* (2003), *Oral Poetics and Ethnography* (2002) and *On Parry-Lord Oral Poetics* (2002). He has recently published a book entitled *Classical Canon and Oral Tradition : A Historical Glossary of Epic Studies in the 20th Century* (2002).

I
Epics and Their Heroes.
An Intercultural Approach to Oral Literatures

Mineke Schipper

Abstract: Theoretical frames, concepts and tools are indispensable for the description, the analysis and the comparison of literatures. Comparative studies can be divided into historically related traditions (contact relations and one way or mutual influences), and historically unrelated traditions (typological relations) revealing the relative uniqueness or universality of cultural phenomena, e. g. genres such as creation myths, epics, tragedies or novels. Intercultural research involves elements from more than one culture. In this essay some of the most frequent aspects and issues to be dealt with in the intercultural study of epics will be discussed: formal and thematic elements related to the text as well as features (referred to in the text) related to the cultural context.

Key words: comparative literature, intercultural approaches, genre classifications, the genre of the epic

1
Understanding Each Other's Cultures

All over the world, we can assume (though not prove), cultures have literature in the form of poetry and storytelling. More specifically, all peoples have sought explanations for the secrets and mysteries around them presented in the form of origin myths. That is one genre we find all over the world. Myths change and they

1

provoke debates, confrontations, reconciliations; and they produce new myths or variations of myths; they also resurrect old myths. In the debate, arguments develop in favor of the myths as well as going against them, and the debate can lead to versions that are the very opposites of the original ones.

This also happens in the epic. In order to survive people develop helpful strategies, and manipulate their own traditions to make the best of life given the circumstances. Cultural norms are indeed transmitted in oral traditions, but they do change with history; they are reflected upon from different perspectives and they are sometimes questioned. Cultural norms and roles are not fixed forever in a petrified past. But the past as it is expressed in literature's legacies has to be studied over and again.

If we want to know whom we are as human beings worldwide, we have to know who our forefathers and foremothers were, culturally speaking. And we have to know the stories they told and the songs they sang, in order to select from our common legacy the oral and written literatures we want to pass on to our children, and the ones we want to question, or rather to abandon and to forget. Oral as well as written stories from the past teach us where we come from as men and women, as people from different cultures. Selecting and transcribing or transmitting their favorite stories, people choose their own predecessors, not only as storytellers and authors, but also as listeners, readers, cultural critics and academics.

To what extent are those stories marked by human similarities or by cultural differences? In order to answer such questions we have to study literature comparatively. Intercultural comparison deals with a large variety of cultures and languages. How is it possible that we are able to understand texts originating from all sorts of "foreign" cultures? In my own research and teaching in different parts of the world, I have often been amazed about the ease with which audiences are able to understand oral texts from other cultures, countries and continents than their own: in China, for example, an audience had no difficulty in understanding proverbs or creation myths from Africa or Europe when I quoted them, in spite of largely different contexts of origin and also the other way round.

Individual people and societies have ideals about life and events, about how people should behave and what things should ideally look like. Such ideals are expressed in language, and literature teaches people how these ideals can be realized. Texts, oral as well as written, also present deviations from such ideals as problematic and often also as blameworthy. Three interrelated fields are thus connected: social norms and values, language, and people's minds. People's universal ideals are represented in a specific text as a *specific* ideal, by means of particular words and syntax. Their universality comes about thanks to people's commonalities on the biological, psychological, and cultural levels. An ideal becomes specific in its cultural context because it represents a particular, local, form of the general ideal underlying and motivating the text concerned. Ideals make use of contrasts and comparisons. Most oral texts can be divided into *ideal-confirming* and *ideal-disconfirming* messages. The former express what the ideal is or how to attain it, while the latter express the ideal only indirectly, by describing some deviation from the ideal concerned. The ideal and its opposite are often presented in one and the same text. In epics, for example, different characters represent an ideal and its opposite. Ideals become more prominent by narrators telling people what should not be thought or done or expected. In oral traditions, that which is considered as "not done" necessarily leads to a condemnable situation, from the perspective of the narrator who wants to get this message across to his audience.

Although matters are much more complicated than I am arguing here, in oral literature information associated with general transcultural ideals does provide a basis for assembling an intercultural understanding of the oral text. Cherished ideals are part of people's memory, so much so that, most of the time, audiences are no longer consciously aware of them.

The question is then, where do those ideals come from? Are they learned through socialization, as the cultural view would argue? This occurs, of course, but it leaves out biology as well as individual experience of the physical world.

Everyday knowledge develops within a socio-cultural context, and social realities are expressed in people's local verbal culture. On the other hand, people are gifted with human cognitive qualities. Both these factors, the cognitive as well as the cultural, serve as the source of ideals, and the main ideals are more likely to be universal than to be culturally based.

Comparative studies are complex, and intercultural comparison is a problematic topic. The majority of books on comparative literature in the Western world deal exclusively with Western literature and cultural traditions.

Theoretical frames, concepts and tools are indispensable for the description, the analysis and the comparison of literatures. If they come from a specific cultural context, they need to be critically checked and adapted (or rejected for that matter) when applied elsewhere.

Comparative studies can be divided into: 1) historically related traditions (contact relations and one way or mutual influences); 2) historically unrelated traditions (typological relations). In the latter case one can gain insight in the relative uniqueness or universality of cultural phenomena, e. g. texts of a certain kind such as creation myths, epics, tragedies or novels.

What is the use, what are the (im)possibilities of intercultural comparison? Immediately, a number of other worrisome questions creep up. Aren't we too biased to understand other cultures? Are there any common patterns at all or are these simply products of our own projections and assumptions? Is it possible to search for universal laws of literary creation?[1] Generally speaking, there are two extreme attitudes: one rejecting as a principle all and any form of comparison and the other the naive comparatist who does not see any problem. In between lies the field of those who are convinced and who have experienced that a comparative approach is relevant and worthwhile. Intercultural comparison should preferably be practiced in co-operation with specialists who work in and on the respective cultures, and

---

[1]   I have dealt with some of these questions elsewhere, e. g. Mineke Schipper, *Beyond the Boundaries*: *African Literature and Literary Theory*, London: Allison & Busby, 1989.

whenever possible there ought to be close co-operation with scholars belonging to the cultures concerned.

Intercultural research is research involving elements from more than one culture. These include, for example, concepts or methods from one culture that are used in the study of another culture. This immediately poses a problem: where does the other culture start? The delimitation of culture varies with one's perspective. The demarcation line between cultural insiders and outsiders can be very subjective, and in our times of globalization they are more problematic than ever. In each case it is necessary to specify the cultural criteria one is following. Intercultural studies oblige researchers to take into account their own legacy of taking things for granted, as well as constantly to raise questions about the possible cultural restraints of their own visions and knowledge. An intensive interdisciplinary discussion is taking place on the danger of authoritarian science in the hierarchical relations between subject and object, between "scribers" and "described". This problematic relationship occurs in all disciplines of the human sciences, from history to anthropology, from sociology to literary theory and comparative literature. And no clearcut solution seems at hand.

2
Comparative Perspectives on Epic Traditions:
Some Guidelines

The aim of our project has been to study the epic as an established genre in Chinese minority cultures. The book addresses an interested readership unfamiliar with those minority cultures, either in China or outside. How to study texts from widely different cultures comparatively? Comparison requires comparable data. Therefore, let us look into some of the most frequent aspects and issues to be dealt with in the study of epics across the world. Epics can be roughly defined as long heroic poems originally transmitted by narrators, bards or singers in oral performances. In such oral "texts", we can distinguish elements and features related to the text itself, and features referring to the cultural context.

Storytelling is a way to transmit values and to satisfy the need for detail. How can we know whether the text is directing or manipulating us into taking for granted certain kinds of information? How can we recognize ways of knowing other than our own? In seeking to respond to such questions, we need to focus on the subject of the text and ask a few questions:

- Who is the hero in the text concerned? What are his qualifications and his actions? Is the hero glorified or vilified? By whom and why?
- What are the other characters doing? Are they acting individually or as a group? Are they acting in accord with each other or are they opposed to each other's interests?

Such questions are relevant in our attempts to gain insight in the complexity of intercultural comparison in general, and in the cultural construction of human relations. How then to study texts comparatively from widely different cultures, and how to find comparable data? We can distinguish elements and features related to the text itself, and features (referred to in the text) related to the cultural context. The following practical points might be a useful framework for intercultural comparative research in the field of oral texts and, in our case, for studying the epic cross-culturally. First, we'll look at the epic as a transcribed text.

I . The Epic Text

a. *Formal features*, i.e. striking use of language or specific language devices. A text may contain a number of fixed formulas, e.g. for the beginning or the end ("Once upon a time" etc) or other formulas, a series of lines or some striking expressions; proverbs; riddles; metaphors; repetitions with a difference; songs; word play; rhythm; rhyme; a clear alternation of narrative "prose" passages and "poetry". In this book, many such poetic devices have been referred to, for example in Yang Enhong's discussion of the Tibetan *Gesar* Epic, and Adil Zhumaturdi presents the Kirghiz Manas epic as formulaic in structure as well as in content.

b. *Relations with the audience as mentioned in the transcribed text*. A narrator may directly address the audience as a whole, or specific people in the audience (a wizard or a guest or a foreigner, or an accompanying musician). Also: the reactions, comments, interventions of the audience – have they been included in the text or simply been omitted or ignored in the transcription?

c. *Genre and type of story*. Is it an epic or a tale? Here, Huang Zhongxiang compares the two in his thematic analysis of Kazak heroic narratives. Why is a narrative to be defined as an epic, and what does the role of the hero contribute to the story's belonging to the genre of the epic? Are there any local classifications within the culture concerned? How to relate such genre classifications to "the epic" as a genre? (See also below under Ⅱ).

d. *Thematics*. Are there specific thematic conventions related to the genre of the epic? What about thematic cycles? Is the local setting the unifying theme or is a heroic character the unifying theme of the epic concerned?

e. *Characters*: First of all, there is the hero or there are several heroes, and there is a pattern that can be found in epics from different parts of the world, as discussed and demonstrated by numerous scholars: The life of the hero is an important common feature to be examined in comparing epic texts across cultures. Points to be checked are, for example:

- Birth, life, and possibly also death of the hero
- A special (noble or royal?) origin and a miraculous or strange birth
- The hero's extraordinary childhood characterized by extreme difficulties or a-mazing miracles, a childhood in which he is made invulnerable or, on the contrary, solves personal problems due to opponents
- Heroes perform extraordinary acts and overcome terrible dangers
- Important heroes have formidable adversaries: who are they and what hap-

pens to them ultimately?

- What is the role of religion and magic in the hero's adventures?
- Does the hero become invulnerable by some rite or medicine?
- The hero's visit to the netherworld deserves special attention
- After his adventures, the hero often seems to be destined to become a king
- Are there specific other characters associated with the text as an epic? (e.g. gods, demons, a shaman, men, women, children, animals – a (Kazak) speaking or flying horse, for example – magic objects or other objects that play a significant role, etc.

How are the characters, and especially the hero, represented in their various roles? What are the norms and social (im)possibilities in the text for both sexes? How does the hero relate to other characters, such as his brothers or sisters, his mother or stepmother, his wife, a shaman etc.: positive versus negative? Heroic versus ordinary? Respecting the norm versus breaking the norm? Dominant versus submissive? And so forth. All such points can be checked as to their presence and poetic effect in epics from around the world.

f. *Time*: What kind of time is referred to? Is it mythical time (as the beginning of time, time "in the making", the beginning of the world in preparation); human time; "magical" time (as delayed or still time), determined or undetermined time? The end of creation means the establishing of the human time order. Human ancestors in myths differ from gods in that death has been sent to the world of the humans in the course of or after creation, or as part of the human time order. Indications of time can be found in every text, such as "In the beginning of time" or "Once upon a time", etc.

g. *Space*: In a story an event always takes place "somewhere". An event always means the crossing of a border between two spaces or situations.

- How is the place or the space described? As familiar or strange, as good and comforting or as evil and threatening?

- Does the action, do the characters move from one space to another? E. g. from the place where the gods live to the human space? Or from heaven to the underworld? Or, if the action takes place on earth, from the town to the wilderness or the faraway mountains, and vice-versa?

The process of bringing order to a space or a country where chaos used to reign or was created by an evil character (m/f) is no less reflected in epics than in other stories, legends, animal stories and fairy tales.

A space will indeed be presented as either familiar or "strange": our village, the forest, the savannah, the desert, the water (a sea, a river), the sky/ the air, a hollow or shadowy tree, a mountain, a house or hut, a temple. There are also the familiar or "strange" landscapes, there is the other, after-or nether-world, or the in-between space (earthly paradise, fairyland etc.).

It is important to notice which epic characters (m/f) are allowed to enter which spaces or places, and also which actions are associated with specific places. The access to certain spaces will partly define the character's heroic roles and extraordinary actions.

h. *Objects*: Familiar or strange? This question can be answered at several levels: in the epic, characters can consider an object as "special", because it contains supernatural power. It can also be presented as a special object, because it is foreign to the cultural context in which the story originates.

II. The Epic in the Context of the Literary Field

There are two contexts to be distinguished: the literary context and the social context. Here, the literary context refers here to a text's network of relations with other texts in the same culture. An oral or written text has always relationships with other versions of the same text in the same time/place and with earlier versions of the same text that have been transmitted from one generation to the next, whether they have been transcribed earlier or not (as far as we can know). A text is always situated vis-à-vis other versions and variants of the same text. It is not always possible to find exact data about this issue. Sometimes variants of the same story exist in a culture nearby or even far away, as in the case of the Tibetan *Gesar* epic and the Mongolian *Geser* discussed by Zhalagaa in this volume. Studying a variety of versions can be extremely interesting and insightful. On the other hand, in the local context, different storytellers in the same village may tell a story or sing a song in different ways, introducing different characters and adding or omitting parts of the plot. This may even hold for one and the same bard.

An oral text not only relates to versions of the same epic but also to other epics and genres. If we define a genre as a series of works with common characteristics, then we should take into account that classifications of oral and written texts are being made within and across cultures. A story may swallow and digest other genres such as riddles or proverbs. An epic may "borrow" aetiological stories or historical chronicles, and so forth. A text performance is sometimes reserved to a particular group of storytellers (professional bards, priests, hunters, men only or women only). Or a text is special because of the exclusive occasion associated with the telling: at a funeral or after the harvest, for example. Local classifications may be based on such criteria: hunter's stories, harvest stories and so forth. The intercultural classification of genres will always remain a serious problem.

Different texts within the same culture complement each other. Comparing classifications within and across cultures throws new light on to the similarities, differences and overlaps between various genres. A classification from outside can be helpful as well as confusing because of scholars' sometimes uncritically taking for granted certain criteria, whether their own culture's or outsiders' cultural criteria.

III. The Epic in the Socio-Cultural Context

Oral literature has a social function. In the course of the story, certain characters break the established social and cultural norms, but towards the end of the story the norms are usually reconfirmed. Social and cultural elements from the context are the bricks that build the house of the story. They refer to everyday reality, geographical surroundings, social organization, etc. On the other hand, stories can also be meant to manipulate the audience so as to serve certain interests. There are always signs in stories indicating whose interests are served, especially when we are asking the earlier mentioned critical questions. Stories, however, cannot be taken literally. They are mostly inventions, even though people experience certain myths or legends or genealogies as "real events". Stories refer to reality but not in a direct way. It is important to have information about the local context explaining customs, traditions, events, social relations and so forth, as some scholars in this book carefully did. On the other hand, there are always elements in stories that are alien to the context and deviant from or inexistent in everyday reality, and those are often the elements that especially tend to intrigue and fascinate local audiences.

Ⅳ. Across Epic Contexts

Across cultural contexts epics share a special style of composition as well as striking thematic similarities, as, among others, the Indian scholar Nabaneeta Dev Sen has argued in her book Counterpoints.[1] Indeed, the use of fixed formulas, songs and themes such as meetings, departures, festivities, challenges, battles and victories—used as pegs to hang long stories on, are features and devices used in oral traditions everywhere. Of course, such devices are also being used in written texts, but in written literature the variation possibilities are much wider and less coercive.

One of the points of earlier international discussion has been whether an epic is only an epic when it has been molded into poetry. The problem here is: how to define poetry? A clear-cut distinction between prose and poetry is not possible or is at least very problematic. In oral literature in general, prose and poetry

---

[1]   Nabaneeta Dev Sen, *Counterpoints*: *Essays in Comparative Literature*, Calcutta: Prajña, 1985.

meet, mix, and overlap through rhythm, music and song. There is more a gradual than a fundamental difference between prose, poetry and drama in an oral performance, an idea that has changed the perspective on what has to be defined as prose or poetry in the Western world. Looking back at the European medieval situation reveals that the term poetry was applied to literature in general. It was only in the eighteenth century that in England poetry and prose came to be distinguished and opposed to each other as metrical versus non-metrical. This prose versus poetry distinction, the use of speech and/or song modes or a combined use of both has been referred to in various essays in this book, and reflects that different cultures have their own unique ways of performing epics in China's minority cultures.

In oral performances, music often plays a crucial role. In various cultures, epics are partly told, and partly sung. The musical accompaniment is strongly associated with emotions provoked by what the soul of poetry is. Bards often emphasize that they find it difficult or even impossible to perform without music. The fact that the living unity between telling and music is much more seriously studied today will certainly open new perspectives and produce new insights into the artificial distinction between prose and poetry.

Whenever epics have been transcribed literally, one finds sometimes remarks such as: 'Hé harpist, you are slowing down my words' or: 'If you speed up the strings, I am not able to speak', or: 'Sleep has made your eyes heavy! Pay attention to the rhythm'.[1] Such warnings are being addressed to the musicians accompanying the narration. They make clear that the rhythm is indispensable to the narrator's being able to keep the track of the story. The music supports the performance and unites the lose ends.

Long compositions – epics usually count thousands of lines – cannot do without formulas. In fact they consist of fixed structural elements such as formulas al-

---

[1] See for example Isidore Okpewho, *The Epic in Africa*: *Toward a Poetics of the Oral Performance*, New York: Columbia University Press, 1979: 60-61.

ternating with improvisations. In the *Rāmāyana* Dev Sen found the same formula techniques as those detected in Western epics by Parry, Lord and Bowra[①]. Sometimes two or three variations on the same theme constitute repetitions to build up tensions in the story (e.g. in *Beowulf* where two struggles against evil are taking place, or in *Gilgamesh* where the hero gets two chances to gain eternal life. The same holds for Odysseus' adventurous meeting with Calypso and Circe respectively). Those are all examples of thematic repetition used as a device to build up tension. Similar devices have been described and can be found in the various contributions to this book on Mongolian, Tibetan, Kirghiz, Kazak and Tyva epics as well.

Life and death of the hero are at the center of the epic, in spite of differences in time and culture. If we want to map out the main characteristics of epic heroes, we have to wonder whether the hero is always a man; or are there also female heroes? The details of origin and birth inevitably stress the outstanding personality of the hero and so does the death of the hero: paradoxically, an epic hero seems to mostly gain immortality among humans because of his untimely dramatic death.

Two last remarks: first, as far as epics are concerned, in the oral presentation one may discover several styles: next to the speech mode, there are the recitation mode and the song mode. The more emotional, the more musical, seems to be the rule: in the Congolese Nyanga epic whose hero is called Mwindo, there is a formula, which goes as follows: 'Mwindo threw sweet words into his mouth and sang.' The singing always seems to happen at dramatic moments in the story.

Second, much more than in the past, attention is being paid or has to be paid to the bards who are often highly gifted performers, although there are also mediocre artists. Researchers have to study and compare their qualities and personalities, interview them, and try to discover the secrets of their artistic back-

---

① Albert B. Lord, *The Singer of Tales*, Cambridge, Mass.: Harvard University Press, 1960; Cecil Maurice Bowra, *Heroic Poetry*, London: Macmillan, 1961; Milman Parry, *The Making of Homeric Verse*: *The Collected papers of Milman Parry*, edited by Adam Milman Parry, Oxford: Clarendon Press, 1971.

ground, to what extent are their qualities determined by their cultural traditions or by their individual talents. Tibetologist Professor Yang Enhong, who has contributed to this book, often told me about the spectacular talents of the old and time-honored Tibetan bard Sam-Grubb.

The field of intercultural comparison is rich and varied, and time has come to bring the rich harvests of local in-depth research together, so as to study this artistic wealth comparatively. The harvest of carefully collected epics sung and told in Chinese minority cultures have been patiently transcribed by scholars over the years. Their analysis will throw new light on to the extraordinary artistic legacies of gifted epic oral narrators and performers from the past as well as the present.

3
Intercultural Comparison in an Age of Globalization

Comparison requires comparable data, as we said earlier. Before going into that question we must first look into the advantages and disadvantages of "close reading" and "distant reading" in comparative literature. Both have advantages, both need each other, and there is no need anymore to settle the controversy between the two. Close reading has the advantage of looking close at an oral or written text in the context of a particular culture. Distant reading

> allows you to focus on units that are much smaller or much larger than the text: devices, themes, tropes – or genres and systems. And if, between the very small and the very large, the text itself disappears, well, it is one of those cases when one can justifiably say, Less is more. If we want to understand the system in its entirety, we must accept losing something. [1]

In order to keep data comparable, a brief but practical rule should be that "the

---

[1]   Franco Moretti, "Conjectures on World Literature," *New Left Review* Jan.-Feb. 2000: 57.

larger the geographical space one wants to study, the smaller should the unit of analysis be".[1] In other words, if we want to study exclusively one epic in depth, we can thoroughly examine the whole text, but we cannot ask intercultural questions about the hero and his opponents, we cannot compare epic themes or the importance of travelling in epics, or generally, we cannot study the genre of the epic as it exists in widely different cultures. The unifying theme of the hero in the epic makes it particularly well suited for intercultural comparison.

Literary theory has a long and respectable experience of studying Western written texts, but, with the exception of some individual researchers, it has only been at a relatively late stage that it has begun to look beyond its own Western horizon. The concept of cultural relativism was brought into literary studies towards the end of the 1960s, but today we need solid new attempts to approach the subject of comparative literature from a global viewpoint.

In literary theory, several attitudes vis-à-vis literature from cultures other than one's own prevail. The most cautious attitude is one of extreme relativism: I keep away from other cultures, because in relation to them I am an outsider. This attitude may have reactionary motives, or be caused by indifference, or suffocating modesty. Conversely, the exclusive right to study their own culture may also be claimed by insiders on the grounds that outsiders are incapable of doing so, a regrettable reaction to equally regrettable hierarchical misconceptions and denigratory statements. The result is, in both cases, a form of academic apartheid.

Intercultural literary theory deals with oral and written literatures from different cultures. In addition, texts, genres, or movements can be compared, or ideas studied about specific literatures that have connections with more than one culture. The varying relationships and the differing points of view involved in this can be complex, but their existence cannot be denied without doing injustice to the insights into the literatures in question.

---

[1] Ibid. 61.

For me, studying African literature and living in Africa for a number of years has been an extraordinary eye-opener to intercultural literary studies. First of all, it made clear how problematic our preconceived ideas about culture are likely to be. I became aware of how much I myself was culturally biased in my perspective on the world at large. The new questions I started to ask have proved to be very enlightening for my study of literature in general and for my intercultural perspectives on comparative literature in particular. The same holds for the Chinese scholars doing research in minority cultures. They have knowledge of more than one culture, and such knowledge has added new dimensions to their perspectives on the world of culture we share as humans.

In all contexts, the cultural criteria employed in the research have to be carefully established. In these matters, it is of importance to view culture as a construction, which never stands apart from the people who see it as their reality, a valid reality to the people concerned. This may hold in particular for minority cultures.

Depending on people's interests and depending on the realities they have in mind, every history has to begin with a specification of time and space, and history, of course, includes literary history and comparative literature.

Cultural references in and about literary works contain a wealth of information about cultures and societies. Whether authors, audiences and researchers express approval or rejection, in all cases their reactions generate cultural meanings reflecting the perspectives and contexts of the respective authors, readers, and researchers.

Oral literature has started to play an ever more important, and therefore more institutionalized, role in the study of literature. The Intercultural Studies Committee of the International Comparative Literature Association (ICLA) has committed itself, only very recently (in August 2000 in Pretoria), to pay more attention to the study of oral literature, which in the past had been seriously neglected as a field of research by the Association. In the context of globalization today, new genres, such as pop songs, are easily digested and processed into existing traditional forms whenever there is a need for it. Also, as soon as oral texts are being transcribed or translated, one is immediately confronted with intercultural questions; intercultural literary theory has indeed a formidable task in the field of oral literature. Again, the study of the epic as a central genre in Chinese minority cultures will represent an extraordinary enrichment of the intercultural field of epic research.

To what extent have the different disciplines been able to solve the problem of cultural differentness in research and scholarship, and to what extent has some progress been made in clearing the way for this cross-cultural academic debate? Our task as critical readers is then to critically identify texts. How can we know whether the text is manipulating us into accepting certain kinds of information simply because it is compatible with our own background knowledge? How can we recognize other ways of knowing? In seeking to respond to such questions, we need to focus on the subject of the text.

Simple questions-such as: Who is speaking? Who is seeing? Who is acting in this text? -continue to be relevant and need to be posed critically in *all* contexts. These three questions can be amended in a number of ways. They can be asked in the negative form: Who is *not* speaking, who does not have the right to speak in the text? Who is *not* seeing or not allowed to see (which means: Whose perspective is *not* represented?), and who does *not* act? Who is passive or powerless to act or to take the initiative? Who must submit to the acts of others? The next questions focus on the object of the three basic activities: *What* is the speaker saying? What kind of action is he or she taking? What does he or she consider worth including in the story? What is "naturally" omitted from it? What kinds of opinion are expressed and to what extent are they consistent with other (expressed or silenced) opinions? What are the characters doing? Are they acting individually or as a group? Are they acting in accord with each other or are they opposed to each other's interests? Such questions, which make it possible for us to gain insight into the power effect of the master discourse, are equally relevant to theory, to literature, and to the daily news as reported in the print media or on television. They are also relevant in our attempts to gain insight in the complexity of texts dealing with intercultural relations, and of texts dealing with gender, class or race relations.

Opting for intercultural comparison, we miss something – especially the connotative meanings the local context would provide – but we also gain something. What we gain is new insight into humankind's universals and differences in literary genres, and into the extent to which human cultures have given birth to similar literary forms and ideas cross-culturally.

Winding up, then, two main phenomena need to be taken into account in the intercultural study of comparative literature: on the one hand there are the literatures marked by mutual influences resulting from intercultural contacts, and on the other hand there is the typological comparison: looking for similarities and differences in genres (without cultural contact): myth, epic, proverb, legend etc., which can be looked for globally.

In the academic village of our time, the challenge is to no longer confine our research to our own academic office or cultural garden. In the study of texts, theories and disciplines, intercultural communication in the broadest sense has become inescapable. For this reason, genuine co-operation and dialogue with researchers from different backgrounds is fundamental. In-depth local approaches and intercultural comparative approaches are important and needed. All those who specialize in the study of a culture or sub-culture need a good dose of modesty. Nevertheless, one does not have to be a crocodile to swim in the waters of a culture other than one's own, just as one does not have to be a woman to engage in women's studies, or a member of the culture one happens to be studying.

Being an outsider is not necessarily negative. In fact, Michael Bakhtin underscores the way in which the outsider-status can be a powerful factor in understanding.

A meaning only reveals its depth once it has encountered and come into contact with another, foreign meaning: they engage in a kind of dialogue, which surmounts the closedness and onesidedness of these particular meanings, these cultures. We raise new questions for a foreign culture, ones that it did not raise itself; we seek answers to our own questions in it; and the foreign culture responds to us by revealing to us its new aspects and new semantic depths. [1]

The reverse is also true, as a dialogical intercultural encounter is mutually enriching by its very nature. As far as the intercultural study of literature is concerned, we could quote the Swahili proverb from East Africa, which goes thus: "Knowledge is like an ocean; it needs many arms to embrace it." Or, as an old Chinese saying puts it: "The wisdom that does not increase by the day, diminishes by the day."

References:

Bakhtin, Michail M. *Speech Genres and Other Late Essays*. Translated by Vern W. McGee. Edited by Caryl Emerson and Michael Holquist. Austin: University of Texas Press, 1986.

Bowra, Cecil Maurice. *Heroic Poetry*. London: Macmillan, 1961.

Dev Sen, Nabaneeta. *Counterpoints*: *Essays in Comparative Literature*. Calcutta: Prajña, 1985.

Lord, Albert B. *The Singer of Tales*. Cambridge, Mass.: Harvard University Press, 1960.

Moretti, Franco. "Conjectures on World Literature." *New Left Review* Jan.-Feb. 2000.

Okpewho, Isidore. *The Epic in Africa*: *Toward a Poetics of the Oral Performance*. New York: Columbia University Press, 1979.

Parry, Milman. *The Making of Homeric Verse*: *The Collected Papers of Milman Parry*. Edited by Adam Milman Parry. Oxford: Clarendon Press, 1971.

Schipper, Mineke. *Beyond the Boundaries*: *African Literature and Literary Theory*. London: Allison and Busby, 1989.

---

[1] Michail M. Bakhtin, *Speech Genres and Other Late Essays*, translated by Vern W. McGee, edited by Caryl Emerson and Michael Holquist, Austin: University of Texas Press, 1986: 7.

II
Characteristics of the Tibetan Oral Tradition.
The Example of the *King Gesar* Epic

Yang Enhong

Abstract: A writing system has been created since the Tubo period (600-800 AD) in the Tibetan society. At the same time, Buddhism was introduced and eventually obtained its predominant position; the political system of the unification of religion and politics was formatted. Because of Buddhist influence, men of letters of this period had their works composed in the combined form of literature, history and philosophy, and they had created a model of source-tracing chronological narration. The combination of verse and prose can be considered to be the major and most commonly used form in the Tibetan narrative tradition. It has been widely used in epics, narrative poems, folktales, and Tibetan opera up to date. *Biography of King Gesar* has inherited the traditional Tibetan poetical meter and rhythm scheme. Oral transmission is the earliest and most vigorous form throughout the Tibetan traditional culture. Even after the invention of writing, the form of oral transmission has always been in use. The artists of storytelling and singing have been drawing on the tradition of religious classics to spread their epic songs. The time-honored tradition of oral transmission and the cultivation of a people's good memorization mechanisms may cast light on the secret why ballad singers can memorize the long epic.

Key words: Tibetan narrative tradition, oral transmission, *King Gesar* epic

Tibetans living in the unique environment of the Tibet Plateau have a written history of fifteen hundred years, and have undergone a five thousand-year-long process of human reproduction, which has laid a solid and rich cultural foundation for Tibetans. Here I will trace down the roots of the talking-and-singing of the *King Gesar* epic and the Tibetan oral tradition.

The Tibetan ethnic group is an industrious and valiant one. The Tibetan ancestors had been living on the Tibet Plateau in remote antiquity. According to recent archaeological findings in Tibet, there are traces of the Paleolithic Period in Shan Rtsa county of Nag Chu area, in the counties of Rtsaw Phug and Spu Hreng of Mngav Ris area and in the county of Ding Ri of Gzhis Ka Rtse area; cultural traces of the Mesolithic Period and the Neolithic Age can be found across Tibet.[①] Tibetans have become who they presently are through their strenuous fight with the harsh natural environment and through their integration with neighboring tribes.

In their long struggle against nature, optimistic and enterprising Tibetans have created a plateau culture—the rich and profound Tibetan culture with its unique historical sediments, social experience and spiritual feelings. According to traditional Tibetan classification, the Tibetan culture can be divided into five major sciences: technology (*bzo rig pa*), medical science (*gso ba rig pa*), rhyme scheme (*sgra rig pa*), logic (*tsha ma rig pa*), and Buddhism (*nan don rig pa*), and five minor sciences: rhetoric (*snyan ngag*), ornate diction (*mngon brjod*), prosody (*sdeb sbyor*), drama (*zlos gar*) and astrology (*skar rtsis*). The two classifications are lumped together under the heading of rig gnas che chung lnga in the Tibetan language. Literature is not independently classified, because of the historically determined combination of literature, history, and philosophy in the long Tibetan historical process.

Since the Tubo creation of the writing system for the Tibetan society, its thread of literary development is as follows: the Tubo period (from the 7th to the

---

① Don Sgrub Dbang Spon, *History of the Tibetan Cultural Development*, Lanzhou: Gansu Education Publishing House, 2001: 64-143.

9th centuries) was the brewing and embryonic stage of the classical Tibetan literature; the separatist period (from the 9th to the 13th centuries) was its rising and formative stage; the time after the unification of the country by the Yuan Dynasty witnessed its prime development stage.[1] Since the Tubo period and the introduction of Buddhism, a local political power with a unification of religion and politics has emerged and obtained dominance in Tibetan society through a long-term fight with the Bon, the indigenous religion.[2] Buddhist influence was powerful, and Buddhist temples were scattered everywhere. At the temples monks were educated not only in religious knowledge but also in astronomy, medicine, logic, history, languages and literature, which made many monks well-versed intellectuals who were doctors, historians, linguists, astronomers and writers all at once. Since the 11th century, the phenomenon that Buddhist monks were concurrently men of letters characterized the then literary circles. Up till the 17th century, Tibetan writers had been invariably Buddhist monks. Given the fact that monks had been receiving education at the temple for a long time, their knowledge and their outlook on life, values, aesthetic orientations and creative methods were all restricted by Buddhism. Therefore, most of their works were a mixed bag of literature, history and philosophy, which constitutes an important characteristic of the classical Tibetan literature.

One characteristic of Tibetan classical literature is that stylistically it mixes prose with verse, i.e. the style of talking and singing, be they biographies, poems, admonitory poems, fables, or novels and dramas of later periods, differing only in terms of the different genres' respective proportions of prose and verse. These two characteristics are omnipresent in the Tibetan folk literary works, i.e. even narratives are intersected with verse for expressive purposes, and long

---

[1] Tong Jinhua, *Tibetan Classical Literature*, Changchun: Jilin Education Publishing House, 1989: 5.

[2] Bon religion, also called "Bon Po religion", used to be called the "black religion", because the followers of this sect wear black monastic habits. The Bon religion is an animistic belief, the objects of worship include the sky, the earth, the sun, the moon, mountains, lakes, the sea, animals, etc. Bon had been the prevailing religion in Tibet before Buddhism was introduced.

poems and lyrics also include prose-style explanations or plot introductions. This combination of prose and verse can be considered the major and most commonly used form in the Tibetan narrative tradition.

1
The Origin of the Tibetan Narrative Tradition

The aforesaid combination of prose and verse can be traced back and evidenced by Tibetan historical records preserved in Dun Huang in which the form of combined prose and verse was applied appropriately from biographies of *btsan po*[①] to oracle inscriptions. This shows that the combined style became widespread as early as the Tubo period (600-800 AD). For instance, in the *btsan po* biographies, the *btsan po* Srong Btsan Sgam Po[②] recited the following poems to his minister:

After taking an oath, the *btsan po* sings loudly:

From today on,
You shall not desert me,
And I will not give you up!
If I abandon you,
You will be blessed by Heaven!
If you abandon me,
I will punish you!

---

① The *btsan* are a group of spirits who control the sky in Tibetan Bon religion. The *btsan* travel on wild horses through forests and over mountains, killing with their arrows everything that moves. In ancient Tibet, the ruler, who was considered to be a representative of the *btsan*, had the title of *btsan po*.

② Srong Btsan Sgam Po (617? -650?), founder of the Tubo kingdom, united for the first time the many tribes inhabiting the Tibet plateau in the 7th century. He also made Lhasa the capital. Both deeds contributed to social progress in Tibet.

When the singing is over, the minister named Dbavs Dbyi Tshab replies in singing. It goes:

My superior is you, btsan po,
Small as I am, I will put you on my shoulders. [1]

About thirty paragraphs of oracle inscriptions have been found in the Dun Huang records. Each paragraph includes two parts, the first part being the text of the oracle inscriptions in verse and the second a prose-style explanation of the materialized contents of the oracle inscriptions. For example:

Oh,
Sons and offspring are like treasures,
Golden river surges,
Running water meanders,
The enemy flees,
The status is rising on a daily basis,
This is a sign of happiness. [2]

What follows the above-cited oracle inscriptions is a prose-style explanation to the lyrical lines:

This divinatory symbol is one response to sightseeing. If the virtuous divinities or goddesses who travel by land or water on a sightseeing tour should be properly worshipped, the person who divines on housing or life span will see all his wishes fulfilled. If someone divines on business, he will make profits; if he divines on a faraway man, that wandering man will return

---

[1] Wang Yao and Chen Jian, trans., *Dunhuang Tubo Lishi Wenshu* [*The Tubo Historical Texts in Dunhuang*], Beijing: Minzu Publishing House, 1980: 63.

[2] Tong Jinhua, *Tibetan Folk Literature*, Lhasa: Tibetan People's Publishing House, 1991: 193.

home; if he divines on an ill man, the patient will recover from his illness; if he divines on fortune, he will become very rich; if he divines on the enemy, there will be no enemy; if he divines on a child, he will get one. All divination is auspicious with this divinatory symbol.[①]

Later, the style of admonitory poems by Mi La Ras Pa (1040-1123) – a monk of the Bkav Brgyud,[②] a sect of Tibetan Buddhism that has exerted a significant impact on the Tibetan literary history – was quite popular on the grassroots level. Though named poetry, an admonitory song comprises verse singing and prose narrating by turns; the poetic part makes use of the multi-paragraphic and cyclic rhyme scheme of Tibetan folk songs and free meter is employed to sing the Bkav Brgyud sect's doctrines and approaches, to admonish people to discipline themselves in solitude, and to embark on self-salvation. The prose part is supposed to narrate the plot's advance. This style has inherited the tradition of combining prose with verse, as in biographies of *btsan po* of the Tubo period. With respect to meter, the admonitory song has developed on the basis of the pattern of four six-syllable lines into a multi-paragraphic, cyclic new form, each paragraph having an equal number of lines and each line an equal number of syllables (i. e. six, seven or eight syllables).

A New Feast for Wise Men by Dpav Wo Gtsug Lag Vphreng Wa (1504-1566) is a famous book rich in material, examples and quotations and detached in argumentation. The history recorded in this book is mingled with myths, legends and stories, which can be seen as a combination of literature and history. Its body features as verse with nine syllables in each line. A prose-style explanation is appended to the poem, thus manifesting itself as a style of combined prose and verse.

---

① Ibid. 193.

② In Tibetan language *bkav brgyud* means "Buddhist language transmission", which was translated into "oral transmission" in Chinese. The *bkav brgyud* sect was also called "white religion", because the Buddhist monks of this sect wore white monastic habits.

A Chronicle of Tibetan Kings and Subjects by Blo Bzang Rgya Mtsho (1617-1682), the fifth Dalai Lama during the 17th century, is a history book combining prose with verse. Its author was famous for utilizing the *sngan ngag* style.[1] Under the influence of *Mirror of Rhetoric*, *A Chronicle of Tibetan Kings and Subjects* contains elements of prose narration apart from its elegant and refined poems. Due to the influence of biographic literature, the famous 16th century historical work *A New Feast for Wise Men*, the 17th century biographic literary work *Life of Pho Lho Nas and Gzhon Nu Dar Med*, the first Tibetan novels written in the 18th century still could not break with the traditional Tibetan style of combined prose and verse, although they had extricated themselves from the time-honored symbiosis of literature and history and had embarked on the road of "pure literature".

The traditional style of combined prose and verse is a commonplace form in the Tibetan oral literature and drama and widely used in epics, narrative poetry, stories and Tibetan opera to this day. It incorporates prose's rich narrativity, conciseness and clarity with verse's musicality and expressiveness. Prose is employed in epics to unfold stories and to connect them, while verse, with its rhythmic musical devices, produces drastic artistic effects in setting off protagonists' psychological activities and in playing up settings as well as battling scenes' fierceness and grandeur.

To sum it up, the combination of prose and verse is a key and simultaneously a main form of expression in Tibetan literature. It originated in oral tradition and has been enriched and somewhat transformed by men of letters of different periods through their creativity. It has become a literary style with different charac-

---

[1]   Since the 13th century, *Mirror of Rhetoric* [*Kavyadarsa*], a book on the theory of poetic rhetoric written by Dandin, an Indian scholar and palace poet in the 7th century, has been translated, explained, revised and supplemented by many Tibetan scholars and has become a theoretical work on Tibetan literature and rhetoric of itself. In Tibetan, *Mirror of Rhetoric is snyan ngag me long*. *Snyan ngag* means "elegant language" or "beautiful articles and poems" and *me long* means "mirror". Poems composed in accordance with this theory are called *sngan ngag* poems.

teristics and exerted certain influence on oral literature. This age old narrative form has been existent in Tibet for nearly two thousand years and has made an enormous impact on literary creation by later generations.

2
Traditional Tibetan Poetical Meter and the Rhythm Scheme of *King Gesar*

Tibetan culture has a multitude of historical records, diversified oral literary forms and written works. The *Gesar* epic is just like a seedling that has grown into a giant, luxuriant tree by drawing on the rich Tibetan traditional culture. We have good reasons to say that *King Gesar* is a work indigenous to the vast Tibet Plateau and in line with Tibetan literature, in terms of form and content and of narrative and rhetoric tradition. These inherent connections are traceable in many works.

A chronological narration that connects the beginning with the end is a common rule observed by famous masters of different dynasties when they composed their works. When it comes to narrating history, all classical works start with accounts of the formation of the universe. Considering that the introduction of Indian Buddhism induced the ancient saying that 'the Tibetan ethnic group comes from the south', all classical works first tell of the stories about former Indian kings and the history of Buddhism created by Sakyamuni, and then narrate the inheritance of Tibetan *btsan po*, struggles between Buddhism and Bon, the history of Mongolian kings, the history of kings of the central areas, etc. This has become a narrative pattern to be employed by later generations in the Tibetan society.

The *King Gesar* epic has also been modeled on this pattern. The layout of each part of the epic as well as singers' talking and singing commences with the formation of heaven and earth (or the formation of the Ling State, so to speak), and the narration advances in a chronical fashion: his birth, his growth, his rise to the throne through horse-racing, his many conquests and his return to Heaven after his fulfillment of earthly missions. The epic consists, of course, of many parts; each part forms an independent unit and can be told and sung separately. The story-telling of each independent part also follows a chronological order. Characters usually initiate their narration by introducing themselves, names of places, names of horses and names of the songs and melodies. An embryonic form of this kind can be found in the biographies of *btsan po* amidst the Dun Huang records:

Do you want to know the name of the *btsan po*?	kye rje vi ni mtshan ba vdi
I am Khri Srong Btsan.	khri vi ni srong btsan zhig
Do you want to know the name of this minister?	blon gyi ni mying ba vdi
He is Stong Rtsan Yul Sung.	stong rtsan ni yul zung zhig
Do you want to know the name of the steed?	chibs kyi ni mying ba vdi
It is Engul Bu Gtsang Gtsang;	rngul bu ni gtsang gtsang lta
Engul Bu Gtsang Gtsang is a fine horse.	gtsang gtsang ni yang yang lta[①]

In the *Gesar* epic, such a self-introduction is an indispensable part of the sung text, for instance:

This place, if you do not know,	sa vdi dang sa ngo ma shes na
Is the right corner of the slow-running Yellow River,	rma klung dal vbebs gyas zur dang
Is the left side of the Snake-Headed	ri sbrul mgo vdra bavi gyon zur na

---

① Wang Yao and Chen Jian, trans., *Dunhuang Tubo Lishi Wenshu* [*The Tubo Historical Texts in Dunhuang*], Beijing: Minzu Publishing House, 1980: 79.

Mountain,

Is the Hell transfigured from Jo Ru.	dpon jo ru sprul bavi srin gling red
I, if you do not know,	bu nga dang nga ngo ma shes na
Am minister Tsha Zhang Vdan Ma.	blon tsha zhang vdan ma spyang khra zer
I am a small chieftain of the tribe of Mu Ba.	gling chung rgyud mu bavi blon chung yin[①]

3

The Traditional Tibetan Poetic Form and Meter

Tibetan poems are a well-developed genre. The neat and antithetic four-line and six-syllable form can be found in the earliest Dun Huang records, which shows that during the Tubo period folk songs of this style called *gzhas* were widespread. The love songs composed by Tshangs Dbyas Rgya Mtsgo (the sixth Dalai Lama, 1683-1706) adopted this *gzhas* song form and left far-reaching influence among the people. The multi-paragraphic and cyclic poetic form called *glu* was created on this basis. The production and spread of religious admonitory poems composed by the monk Mi La Ras Pa who employed the *glu* form also exerted great influence on poetry of later generations. The above-mentioned standarized form of Tibetan poetry is widely employed in Tibetan oral literature, such as Tibetan dramas, long narrative poetry and even in some stories, which is as well manifest in *King Gesar*.

Multi-paragraphic and cyclic admonitory poetry takes in many elements from folk songs, such as a white male lion residing on the snow mountain, vultures hovering over the cliffs, fierce tigers occupying the forest and golden-eyed fish

---

① Dkon Mchog Tshe Stan, *Subdue Demons and Monsters* [Tibetan], Lanzhou: Gansu People's Publishing House, 1980: 117-118.

swimming in the sea. The first paragraphs are metaphorical while the last paragraph is realistic:

If I, a white lion on top of the snow mountain,	gangs stod kyi seng ge dkar mo nga,
Do not wander round the vast snow mountain,	gangs stod yongs la mi vphyo ru,
My mane will not become full-fledged,	gyu ral legs po rgyas dus med,
Ras Chung shall go to Tibet instead of staying here,	ras chung mi sdod dbus la vgro,
I request my lord's approval.	da res bla mas bkav gnang zhu.
If I, a vulture on top of the rocky cliff,	brag stod kyi bya rgyal rgod po nga,
Do not take flight in the blue sky,	nam vphang mthon po mi gcod du,
My wings will hardly grow strong,	gshog drug legs po rgyas dus med,
Ras Chung shall go to Tibet instead of staying here,	ras chung mi sdod dbus la vgro,
I request my lord's approval.	da res bla mas bkav gnang zhu.
If I, a spotted tiger in the forest,	nags gseb kyi stag gu ri bkra nga,
Do not wander round the forest,	nags khrod yong la mi vphyo ru,
My stripes will not glow,	gra vdzum legs po rgyas dus med,
Ras Chung shall go to Tibet instead of staying here,	ras chung mi sdod dbus su vgro,
I request my lord's approval.	da res bla mas bkav gnang zhu.
If I, a golden-eyed fish in the sea,	mtsho dkyil gyi nya mo gser mig nga,

Do not swim round the great gulf,	mtsho mthav yong la mi rgyu ru,
My golden eyes will hardly grow well,	gser mig legs po rgyas dus med,
Ras Chung shall go to Tibet instead of staying here,	ras chung mi sdod dbus su vgro,
I request my lord's approval.	da res bla mas bkav gnang zhu.
If I, Ras Chung Rdor Grags Nga of Gung Thang,	gung thang ras chung rdor grags nga,
Do not travel round all the places,	rgyal khams yong la mi vgro ru,
My words will not take effect,	nyams rtogs bzang po rgyas dus med,
Ras Chung shall go to Tibet instead of staying here,	ras chung mistod dbus su vgro,
I request my lord's approval.	da res bla mas bkav gnang zhu. [1]

This admonitory poem has five paragraphs, each paragraph having five lines and each line seven syllables. The first four paragraphs metaphorically present the white lion, the vulture, the spotted tiger and the goldfish, and the last paragraph reads realistic. The first line in each paragraph ends with *nga* ("me"), the last three syllables in the third line are all *rgyas dus med* ("hardly thorough"); the fourth and fifth lines of each paragraph repeat the same ending – 'Ras Chung shall go to Tibet instead of staying here, I request my lord's approval' – which creates a strong artistic appeal with its rhyming, orality and repetition.

King Gesar bears formal and thematic resemblance to such multi-paragraphic and cyclic poetry. It contains three paragraphs, each paragraph having three lines and each line eight syllables:

---

[1] *Biography of Mi La Ras Pa and His Admonitory Poems* [Tibetan], Xining: Qinghai Minzu Publishing House, 1981: 736.

White lions on top of the snow moun-tain,	stod gangs dkar rtse movi send ge de
To have the mane fully-fledged,	mgo gyu ras sngon po rgyas yod na
You'd better live in the mountain in-stead of on the plain.	khyod thang la ma vbab gangs stod zungs
Spotted tigers in the forest,	nag rgya rdzong dkyil gyi stag phrug
To have the smiling stripes grow well,	stag vdzum drug ri mo rgyas yod na
You'd better live in caves instead of going out.	phyi gzan la ma chastshang sgo zungs
Golden-eyed fish in the deep sea,	dmav rgyal mtshovi klong gi gser nya de
To have the golden scale grow well,	nya gser mdog khrab ri rgyas yod na
You'd better live in the sea instead of on the seashore.	chu mtsho mthav ma bskor mtsho dkyil bsdod[①]

This three-paragraph poem has eight syllables in each line, which formally develops further than admonitory poetry. The first and second lines in each paragraph have end-rhymes: the last syllable of each line is *de* ("that"), while all the second lines end with *rgyas yod na* ("grow well").

---

① Wang Yinuan, *The Part of Subduing Demons and Monsters*, Lanzhou: Gansu People's Publishing House, 1985: 7-8 (translation by Wang Yinuan).

A comparative look draws attention to the two above-mentioned poems' similarities and mutual influences and to the sharp contrast between the neatly and antithetically authored poetry and the free derivations from the folklorist talking and singing. The timing of the appearance of admonitory poetry (11th and 12th centuries) and the spreading of *King Gesar*[①] *basically coincided. Evidently, the* two works were born against the same cultural backdrop, and carried influences by folk songs and mutual influences.

Take for example the Gansu version of *Bdud Vdul* (Subdue Demons and Monsters).[②] There are six places with similar metaphors, but all the places reveal variations, apart from the above-mentioned multi-paragraphic and cyclic sung text. For instance, there are eight lines in each of the three paragraphs (pp. 13-14) with the lion and the tiger as metaphors; there are four lines in each of the two paragraphs (p. 16) with the lion and the tiger as metaphors; there are four lines in each of the three paragraphs (p. 19), with the lion, the tiger and the golden-eyed fish as metaphors; there are four lines in each of the five paragraphs (pp. 134-135) with the roc bird, the green-manned lion and the spotted tiger as metaphors; there are five lines in each of the three paragraphs (p. 89) in which the jade dragon, the male lion and the wild bull serve as metaphors; there are two lines in each of the five paragraphs (p. 88) and the lion, the wild bull, the hawk, the tiger and the whale are metaphors.[③]

When Gesar was to set out on an expedition to the Devil State, he entrusted his beloved concubine Vbrug Mo with all state affairs, singing all along while entrusting Vbrug Mo with item by item: the silk storehouse, the jewelry storehouse, the castle, the precious Buddha statues, conch shell, Buddhist sutras,

---

① It is generally held by scholars that *Biography of King Gesar* appeared in the 11th century and that it has been developing into its present form through a long time of circulation among the people. According to ballad singers, Gesar was born in 1038, around the same time as Mi La Ras Pa.

② Wang Yinuan, *The Part of Subduing Demons and Monsters*, Lanzhou: Gansu People's Publishing House, 1985.

③ See appendix I for a translation.

the horse farm, the cattle farm, the sheep farm, accounting office, and so on. In the nine-paragraph sung text, the last two lines of each paragraph are the same: 'I give you all this and I will reclaim it all when I come back' (ngas bcol dus kha tshang cha tshang yin, tshur len dus sprod rgyu yod ni gyis). [1] This performance has inherited the traditional multi-paragraphic, cyclic and repeatable poetic form, and is easy to read aloud.

Since the introduction of *Mirror of Rhetoric* in the 13th century to Tibet in the form of free translation, many Tibetan scholars have been researching on and writing monographs to annotate the original text of *Mirror of Rhetoric*. Some rhetorical devices developed out of the Sanskrit-specific structure and phonetics that were at odds with the attributes and structures of the Tibetan language have been eliminated, while the metrical characteristics of Tibetan poetry have been supplemented and summarized. These meters are well utilized and developed in the *King Gesar* epic. For instance, *sngan ngag* is a form of repetition that occurs in the same place of different lines or in different places of the same line in a one-paragraph poem, whereas *King Gesar* uses the multi-paragraphed and cyclic style repetition in various places of a word, a phrase, or even, a whole line. According to Tong Jinhua:

> This kind of repetition is cyclic in phonology and melody, harmonious and melodious; and is modulating in tone, sonorous and forceful, thus adding boundless musical beauty to the poems. In terms of artistic atmosphere, such repetition works to deepen ideas and to intensify emotions, thus creating lingering artistic feelings. It is easy to read aloud, to memorize, and to be spread and to influence, and therefore it has become the most characteristic and privileged meter of Tibetan poetry. [2]

---

[1] Dkong Mchog Tshe Stan, *Subdue Demons and Monsters* [Tibetan], Lanzhou: Gansu People's Publishing House, 1980: 33-36.

[2] Tong Jinhua, *A Study on the Tibetan Literature*, Beijing: China Tibetology Publishing House, 1992: 381.

This form of repetition includes repetition at the beginning, in the middle and at the end of a sentence, repetition in every other sentence, and the repetition of a complete line. Here is only a brief introduction.

Monosyllabic repetition at the end of the sentence in the Tibetan original, such as:

There are few well-doers who point to the right way,	lam drang bor ston pavi dam pa *dkon*
There are few pure-minded Buddhist followers,	sems gcig tu gnas pavi sgom pa *dkon*
There are few friends always with a sense of shame,	khrel phyi thag ring bavi grogs po *dkon*
There are few honest merchants,	tshong drang por gtam pavi khe ba *dkon*
There are few followers whose *belief* remains steadfast,	sems mos pa mi vgyur slob ma *dkon*
There are few harmonious and peaceful husbands and wives.	gnas gcig tu mthun pavi bzav tshang *dkon*[1]

Multi-syllabic repetition occurs at the end of the sentence, such as:

The sun and the moon in the east,	shar nyi zla *da la la*
Rain and cloud in the south,	lho na char sprin *da la la*
Shadow in the west,	nub na gribs so *da la la*
Cold wind in the north,	byang na skyi ser *da la la*

---

[1] Dkon Mchog Tshe Stan, *Subdue Demons and Monsters* [Tibetan], Lanzhou: Gansu People's Publishing House, 1980: 85-86 (italics here and everywhere else by me [YE]).

| Lamas read sutras, | pha bla mavi gsum chos *da la la* |
| Good officials deliver speeches... | dpon bzang povi zhal gsung *da la la*[1] |

Repetition occurs at the beginning of every other sentence, such as:

Extremely intelligent sages,	*ha cang* shes rab che mkhan po
Will do harm to the country if they act recklessly,	bya ba mang na rang nyid vphung
Well-known great kings,	*ha cang* rgyal po grags chen po
Will do harm to the country if they entertain foolish ideas,	dran rgyu mang na rgyal srid nyams
Overtly hedonistic monks,	*ha cang* longs spyod sgrub mkhan po
Will suffer if they do not know how to save up,	gsog ma shes na rang gi gshes
Crapulent eaters,	ha cang zas la dad che bas
Will get poisoned if without self-restraint.	za ma shes na dug du vgyur[2]

The following rhetorical device is manifest in the epic: the last syllable of the preceding sentence constitutes the beginning of the following one, thus engendering the flow of language, well-knit, vivid and fluent. For example:

---

[1] Ibid. 61. *Da la la* is an adjective and is used to vivify the first part. Its meaning is as follows: The sun and the moon in the east are bright, the rain and cloud in the south are jumbled, the shadow in the west is dark, the cold wind in the north is cold, Lamas recite scriptures loudly and good officials speak gently.

[2] Ibid. 127-128.

The snow mountain is on top of the valley,

phu gsum dkar yag *gang* kyi ri

To which male lions in the snow mountain are often attached,

gang la dung *seng* vkhor bavi ri

And they shake their green mane in the snow mountain.

seng la gyul ral rgyal bavi ri

The green mountain is twined with sandalwood,

sked gsum tsan dan *nags* kyi ri

To which fierce tigers are often attached,

nags la rgua stag vkhor bavi ri

And they, with stripes, reflect prosperity of the mountain.

stag la vdzum drug rgyas pavi ri

The mountain is surrounded by furrows and watery fields,

mdav gsum chu ma *zhing* gi ri

Fertile farmland produces good harvests,

zhing la vbras drug smin pavi ri

Dark-haired people are attached to the mountain grown with grains.

vbras la dbu nag vkhor bavi ri

The mountain is surrounded by slow-running waters,

mthal gsum *chu* bo chab kyi ri

To which goldfish in the water are often attached,

chu la gser *nya* vkhor bavi ri

Goldfish jump in the waters of the mountain.

nga la gser gshog rgyas bavi ri

The mountain is the place where the three tribes of the Ling State took

gling la *sde* gsum chags pavi ri

shape,

To which tribal heroes are often at-   *sde* la *dpav* brtul vkhor bavi ri
tached,

And heroes demonstrate their military   *dpav* la rtsal dtug cdzoms pavi
might there.   ri[1]

The above rhetoric device is as follows: the fifth, or the second, the third and the fourth syllables of the first line of each paragraph are the beginning of the next line; likewise, the third or the fourth syllables of the second line are the beginning of the third line. Lines constructed in this way read wellknit and coherent. Second, the fifteen lines of the five cyclic paragraphs each end with the rhyming *ri* ("mountains"). Third, the second line of each paragraph ends with *vkhor bavi ri* ("ring-like mountains"), and the third line with *rgyal* (*rgyas*) *bavi* (*pavi*) ri ("prosperous mountains"), constituting a tri-syllable repetition at the end.

In *King Gesar*, animals are personified. For instance, a dialogue between the red-crowned crane (*khrung khrung*, transliteration in Tibetan) and the soul-depositing bird (*shang shang*, transliteration in Tibetan) is very characteristic. Each sentence ends with *khrung khrung* and *shang shang*, which is inclined to dramatization. For instance:

This place, if you do not know,   sa vdi yi sa ngo ma shes na khrung
khrung

Is the life mountain of the Demon   bdud kyi bla ri mthon po nas
. State,   khrung khrung

Is the pinnacle of the nine-pinnacled   lcags ra rtse dguvi rtse mo red

---

[1]   Grags Pa, *Conquering the Northern King Klu Btsan*, Beijing: Minzu Publishing House, 1997: 15. To reflect the style that the end of the preceding line is the beginning of the following and to reflect the regularity, literal translation is employed.

castle.	khrung khrung
I, the crane, if you do not know,	bya nga dang nga ngo ma shes na khrung khrung
Am from Mount Meru.	ri rgyal lhun povi khang rdzong naskhrung khrung
Am a blood sister of the golden-winged roc,	bya khyung chen rgyal povi sring mo redkhrung khrung
Am from the colorful place in the east,	shar khra mo gling gi sa cha naskhrung khrung
Am from the crystal palace of the Yellow River,	rma rdzong shel dkar lhun po nas khrung khrung
Am a white crane,	bya vdab chags khrung khrung dkar mo yinkhrung khrung
Am the soul-depositing bird of Me Bzav...	sman me bzav a vbum bla bya yinkhrung khrung... [①]

When the crane finishes its 114-line *khrung khrung* song, the soul-depositing bird replies with another song ending with *shang shang* at the end of each line (143 lines altogether):

...	...
I, the bird, if you do not know,	bya nga dang nga ngo ma shes na nishang shang
In the great India in the west,	nub phyogs rgya gar yul chen na nishang shang
In the middle of the vast divine sea,	mtsho rab lha chen po yi dkyil ni shang shang

①   Dkon Mchog Tshe Stan, *Subdue Demons and Monsters* [Tibetan], Lanzhou: Gansu People's Publishing House, 1980: 140-146.

In the cool, refreshing and beautiful wonderland,	dwang bsil gyu yi lha chab nang ni shang shang
There is the palace of the lukewarm Dragon King,	ma dros klu yi gzal med khang nishang shang
In this fine and beautiful palace,	pho brang mdzes sdug khang bzang dbus ni shang shang
I, the soul-depositing bird, live.	shang shang tevu rgyal bzhugs sa yod ni shang shang.[1]

The *King Gesar* epic has inherited the characteristics of traditional Tibetan meter. Due to its time-honored spreading on the grassroots level, many ballad singers have been able to enrich and diversify it with talking and singing elements. It has thus become even more alive and more accessible to ordinary people, and continues to have a strong vitality.

4
The History and Tradition of Tibetan Oral Knowledge Transmission

With respect to the lineage of the Tibetan traditional culture, oral transmission has been the earliest and most vigorous form. Even after the invention of writing, oral transmission has always been in use. It can be traced back to the teaching of the Bon sutras. Masters transmitted the knowledge to their disciples and fathers to their sons, the latter of which is called *uni-transmission*. In the aftermath of the warfare between Buddhism and the Bon, the Bon was subjected to persecution. Bon followers made wider use of this form of transmission in order to preserve its doctrines. The extant main Bon classics, such as *Zhang Zhung Document* and *Gzi Brjid*, had been first preserved by Bon monks through oral transmission and were

---

① ibid. 146-153.

later documented.

There are quite a few Buddhist classics that have been memorized through oral transmission. For instance, during the period of Khri Lde Gtsug Brtsan,[1] the two officials Bran Ka Mu Le Ko Shan and Gnyags Dznua Na Ku Ma Ra were sent to go on a pilgrimage for Buddhist sutras in India. When the two officials arrived at Gandisê Mountains, they chanced upon two senior Indian monks – Sangs Rgyas Gsang and Sangs Rgyas Zhi Ba – practicing Buddhism and meditating. They memorized the classics that the two Indian monks had learnt by heart and presented them to King Rgyal Po upon their return.[2] These classics include *Section of Sutric Parts*, *Nobel Golden Light Scripture*, *Supreme Yoga Tantra*, and *Action Tantra*.[3]

The Bkav Rgyud sect originated in the 12th century. The word *bkav* means Buddhist language, while *rgyud* means succession. The sect advocates the tradition that masters teach their disciples by oral and aural means, focusing on practicing Tantra. The well-known Mi La Ras Pa, a great master of the Bkav Rgyud sect, once practiced the oral transmission of Tantra in front of the statue of Mar Pa, the founder of the Bkav Rgyud sect. *Biography of Mi La Ras Pa* accounts vividly for the experience of his success in practicing Buddhism and how he started preaching scriptures after having been mentally tormented by the master Mar Pa who refused to instruct him the scriptures given his previous misbehavior of inflicting incantation upon the innocent. The book registers on many occasions the experience of oral transmission from Mar Pa to his disciples.

Sangs Rgyas Rgyal Mtshan (1452-1507), author of this biography, also wrote *Biography of Mar Pa*. He provided a specific account at the end of book, saying

---

[1]   Khri Lde Gtsug Brtsan was ruler of Tibet during the years 705-755 AD. He married Princess Jincheng from the Tang Dynasty. He made great effort to develop Buddhism, invited the Chinese Buddhist monks to translate the Buddhist scripture, and had supported many Buddhist monks in his kingdom.

[2]   Dung Dkar Rinpoche, *On the System of Unification of the Church and the State in Tibet*, Beijing: Minzu Publishing House, 1981: 17.

[3]   Ibid.

that the life and deeds of Mar Pa were first orally transmitted and later documented into a book: originally they were Mi La Ras Pa and Mar Pa Gog Log, two pupils of Mar Pa, who orally transmitted the life and deeds of Mar Pa to Nga Rdzong Bstan Pa, pupil of Mi La Ras Pa; Mi La Ras Pa also transmitted the oral knowledge to his favored pupil Ras Chung. Later on, Ras Chung and Nga Rdzong Bstan Pa consulted each other and compiled the oral tradition into a book. Sangs Rgyas Rgyal Mtshan based his biography on that book, and simultaneously absorbed other elements that had been orally transmitted by other pupils of Mar Pa. This illustrates that oral transmission is a very important way of instruction in the succession of the Bkav Rgyud sect.

It is said that the doctrine of the Indian Tantra, particularly the doctrine of the supreme Yoga, was transmitted from heaven to earth through the following three trails: *rgyal bavi dgongs brgyud* (the lineage of Buddha's commandments), *rig vdzin brda brgyud* (the lineage of sages' signals) and *gang zag snyan khung du brgyud* (the lineage of individual listening). Another tripartite form of transmission emerging later – i.e. *bkav vbabs lung bstan gyi brgyud pa* (the lineage of receiving commandments and predicts), *las vphro gter gyi brgyud pa* (the lineage of karmic hidden scriptures) and *smon lam gtad rgyal brgyud pa* (the lineage of stamped praying) – were accepted and used to transmit knowledge in Tibet by the Rning Ma sect. [1]

The lineage of Buddha's commandments (*rgyal bavi dgongs brgyud*) is both the starting point and the ultimate law of Buddhist doctrines. It refers to the Tantra that Buddha demonstrates in the secluded Buddhist domain. The lineage of sages' signals (*rig vdzin brda brgyud*) points to the way of instructing not through the

---

[1] *Rning ma means* "the old" or "ancient" in Tibetan. The Rning Ma sect is the earliest Buddhist sect in the religious history of Tibet. There are two main systems of transmission in this sect. One is the direct teaching of the classical scriptures; the other is by way of unearthening the hidden scripture. The followers of the sect wear red monastic habits, and therefore this sect used to be called "red religion". The Buddhist monks of the sect can get married, engaged in routine work, and are not confined to the monastary or the temple.

easy-to-understand oral language but through the media of signals, signs or symbols. The lineage of individual listening (*gang zag snyan khung du brgyud*) refers to oral and aural transmission from masters to pupils; the mission of transmitting the doctrines is completed through oral communication.

The *Tibetan Book of the Dead*, a widespread sutra to this day, is said to contain the teachings of the Buddha himself. It is said that it was buried by Padmasambhava, was re-discovered by treasure-hunter Karma Gling Pa, and began to be spread outside only after uni-transmission had been practiced for three generations. [1] Padmasambhava came to Tibet to preach in the latter half of the 8th century. There was a 600-700 year lag between the burial of the book by Padmasambhava, Karma Gling Pa's re-discovery and its eventual diffusion after three generations of uni-transmission. During this long period of time, especially in the 14th century, the oral and aural transmission was still in use.

The appearance of treasure-hunting ballad singers had to do with the Rning Ma sect. Gu Ru Rgyal Mtshan in Mgo log is a monk of the Rning Ma sect. [2] Such treasure-hunting ballad singers have transmitted the epic through the inheritance of classics as practiced in the Rning Ma sect. According to the Rning Ma sect, Gesar is the reincarnation of the great master Padmasambhava, and it is therefore natural that the treasure-hunting technique is used to transmit *Biography of King Gesar*.

The oral-and-aural transmission used to preserve classics is still extant. The time-honored tradition of oral transmission and the cultivation of a people's strong memorization mechanisms may cast light on the secret why ballad singers can memorize the long epic.

The epic *Biography of King Gesar* has been spread among people for about one

---

[1] Shen Weirong, "Rediscovering Karma Gling Pa and *Zhi khro dgongs pa rang grol gyi chos skor*," *A New Feast for Wise Men*, 2 vols., Shijiazhuang: Hebei Education Publishing House, 2000: II 69-91.

[2] Gung Bzang Ni Ma, a later famous treasure-hunting master from Seda county of Ganzi Prefecture, Sichuan, was active in Tibetan areas in the early 20th century and was a hereditary treasure-hunting master of the Rning Ma sect. He discovered many classics and was as well a treasure-hunting ballad singer of *Biography of King Gesar*. The copies of the epic that were discovered and written by him are very popular in Gansu and Qinghai provinces.

thousand years, notably through the medium of oral transmission. For instance, the so-called charismatic singers, the most outstanding of ballad singers, transmit ballads by oral and aural means. They all live in the pastoral areas of the Tibet Plateau where epics are widespread.[①] Though such areas are scattered in different provinces and regions, it is not difficult to tell from the map that they share region-specific characteristics, i.e. the bordering areas between Tibet, Qinghai, Gansu and Sichuan. These areas enjoy the following common characteristics. First, it is in these areas where the epic is widespread and the Kang-and-Anduo-speaking people live. Second, they are far away from Lhasa – the hinterland of Tibet – where the Dge-lugs-pa sect is the ruling power of unified religion and politics, and located in the frontier of Tibet where the Rning Ma sect, the Bkav Rgyud sect and the Bon concentrate and that enjoys relative ideological autonomy. Third, these areas are pilgrims' must access to the sacred place of Lhasa and the hinterland of Tibet, and are important for the exchange between Tibetans and other ethnic groups in the hinterland of China. Given all these accounts, the age-old oral transmission has been preserved and developed in the aforesaid areas up till now.

As a carrier of the essence of Tibetan popular culture, *Biography of King Gesar* not only epitomizes the tradition and the wisdom of an ethnic group but also represents the Tibetan oral narrative tradition, from which we can trace down the development and evolution of the Tibetan oral tradition and the ancient cultural origins of the Tibet Plateau.

The emergence and the development of this unique Tibetan oral tradition depend on Tibet's unique cultural and natural environment, particularly on the spiritual demands of the Tibetan herdsmen and recipients and on other aesthetic criteria that have taken shape over hundreds of years. However, this tradition, which has been the basis of the *King Gesar* epic, does not stay stagnant but rather mutates with

---

① For example in areas such as the prefectures of Nag Chu, Mngav Ris, Chab Mdo in Tibet, Mgo Log and Yul Shul in Qinghai province, Hainan Tibetan Autonomous Prefecture, Gannan Tibetan Autonomous Prefecture in Gansu province, Ganzi and Aba Tibetan Autonomous Prefecture in Sichuan province and Diqing Tibetan Autonomous Prefecture in Yunnan province.

the advance of time, as I will explore in another paper.

References:

Biography of Mi La Ras Pa and His Admonitory Poems [Tibetan]. Xining: Qinghai Minzu Publishing House, 1981.

Dkon Mchog Tshe Stan. *Subdue Demons and Monsters* [Tibetan]. Lanzhou: Gansu People's Publishing House, 1980.

Don Sgrub Dbang Spon. *History of the Tibetan Cultural Development*. Lanzhou: Gansu Education Publishing House, 2001.

Dung Dkar Rinpoche. *On the System of Unification of Religion and State in Tibet*. Beijing: Minzu Publishing House, 1981.

Grags Pa. *Conquering the Northern King Klu Btsan*. Beijing: Minzu Publishing House, 1997.

Shen Weirong. "Rediscovering Karma Gling Pa and *Zhi khro dgongs pa rang grol gyi chos skor*." *A New Feast for Wise Men*. 2 Vols. Shijiazhuang: Hebei Education Publishing House, 2000: Ⅱ 69-91.

Tong Jinhua. *Tibetan Classical Literature*. Changchung: Jilin Education Publishing House, 1989.

_____. *Tibetan Folk Literature*. Lhasa: Tibetan People's Publishing House, 1991.

_____. *A Study on the Tibetan Literature*. Beijing: China Tibetology Publishing House, 1992.

Wang Yao and Chen Jian, trans. *Dunhuang TuboLishi Wenshu* [*The Tubo Historical Texts in Dunhuang*]. Beijing: Minzu Publishing House, 1980.

Wang Yinuan. *The Part of Subduing Demons and Monsters*. Lanzhou: Gansu People's Publishing House, 1985.

Appendix 1[①]

(1) Three paragraphs with three lines in each paragraph and eight syllables in each line:[②]

---

① In this book, appendices contain either large illustrative text samples which further illuminate the previous paper's arguments or they provide extra information regarding text editions and other publicatons.

② See for the Tibetan original the Chinese part of the present book.

The white lion living on top of the snow mountain,

To have its jade mane grow well,

Had better live in the mountain instead of going down to the plain.

The spotted tiger in the forest,

To have its smiling stripes grow well,

Had better live in caves instead of going out.

The golden-eyed fish in the deep sea,

To have its golden scale grow well,

Had better live in the sea instead of on the seashore.[1]

(2) Three paragraphs with four lines in each paragraph. Each line has eight syllables:

The male lion king on top of the snow mountain,

Does not show its plentiful green mane,

When going down from the mountain to the plain,

The green mane might be damaged.

The spotted tiger in the vast forest,

Does not show its full-fledged smiling stripes,

When going out to look for food,

The smiling stripes might be damaged.

The golden-eyed fish in the deep sea,

---

[1] Dkon Mchog Tshe Stan, *Subdue Demons and Monsters* [Tibetan], Lanzhou: Gansu People's Publishing House, 1981: 8-9.

Does not show its six full-grown fins,

When swimming to the seashore,

The golden eyes might be damaged.[1]

(3) Three paragraphs with five lines in each paragraph and eight syllables in each line:

There is a jade dragon in the high blue sky,

Living in the thick purple-clouded castle,

Bellowing with a terrible roar to show its might,

Throwing out its reddish and arrow-like long tongue,

Smashing the red rock and the hawk's nest.

There is a male lion in the corner of the snow mountain,

Living on top of the snow mountain to defend the solid castle,

Draping its jade mane to show its might,

Roaring valiantly to shake the earth,

Swallowing fierce animals with bared fangs.

There is a wild bull on the high multi-colored rocky mountain,

Living on top of the mountain to defend the castle,

Rubbing its horns to produce dust and fog,

Sharpening its feet to show its power,

Killing the enemies once they appear.[2]

(4) Three paragraphs with eight lines in each paragraph and eight syllables in each line:

---

①   Ibid. 19.

②   Ibid. 89-90.

In the crystal palace on top of the snow mountain,

There is the snow-white lion with jade mane.

It is king of all animals,

It is powerful like a hero.

But looking upward at the clouds,

A blue dragon roars to shock the world.

If the lion should be killed by the blue dragon,

Its jade mane has grown in vain.

In the green sandalwood below,

The fierce tiger has its smiling stripes like flames.

It is king of all four-legged animals,

With radiantly smiling stripes.

But looking downward at the village,

There is a long-tailed and bearded old dog.

If the tiger should be killed by the old dog,

It is shameful of it to have six kinds of smiling stripes.

In the Lion-Dragon-Tiger Palace in the Ling State,

The male lion king has a bright golden scale.

You are king of dark-haired people,

You are a hero who can subdue four demons.

Please look westward at the Demon State,

The dying old devil is Klu Btsan.

If you should be killed by him,

It is shameful even if you wear a golden armor. [1]

---

[1] Ibid. 14.

(5) Five paragraphs with two lines in each paragraph and eight syllables in each line:

The crystal-like snow mountain becomes beautiful
Only when a white lion strolls around.

The patterned rock becomes well-decorated
Only when a red-horned wild bull saunters there.

The mountain becomes high and steep
Only when a white-chested hawk flies in the blue sky.

The vast forest becomes imposing
Only when a red tiger strolls around.

The boundless ocean becomes awesome
Only when there is a huge whale in it.[1]

(6) Five paragraphs with four lines in each paragraph and seven syllables in each line:

The brave man of unusual strength on the white side,
Wins the fight to defend the sacred white conch castle.
All devils on the black side
Are completely defeated in the demon castle in Ngam.

The red roc flying in the sky,
Wins the victory on top of Mount Meru.

---

[1]　Ibid. 88.

The amphibious black poisonous snake
Is completely defeated in the deep darkness.

The powerful white lion with green mane,
Wins the victory on top of the snow mountain.
The weak winged owl
Is completely defeated among withered trees.

The tiger with smiling stripes,
Wins the victory in the sandalwood.
The piercing-furred hedgehog
Is completely defeated by the frozen dark water.

I, Gesar incarnated from god,
Win the victory in the place of dark-haired people.
The old black sheperd dog, minister of the Demon State,
Is completely defeated in the dirty mire.[1]

Appendix II[2]

Today I will entrust state affairs
To my concubine Chung Ma.
I have silks in all colors outside
And jewelry inside.
I want to entrust all to her
And I will reclaim all later.

There are thirteen piles of compressed tea in the warehouse,

---

[1] Ibid. 134-135.
[2] The Tibetan original can be found in the Chinese part of the present book.

There are warehouses for jewelry, tophi and agate outside,
There are also piles of Chinese tea from different places,
I entrust all when I entrust them
And I will reclaim all later.

In the high Lion-Dragon-Tiger Palace,
There are six white Gling castles,
They are not to be dispersed outside like beads,
And not to be broken inside like eggshells,
I entrust them safe and sound
And I will reclaim all later.

At the back of the warehouse,
There are gold Sakyamuni statues,
Emerald statues,
And Bodhisattva statues made of white conch.
I entrust them completely
And I will reclaim all later.

At the back of the warehouse,
There are Buddhas of Longevity made of coral,
White umbrellas and conch shells,
Long spears with supernatural power,
Conch shell trumpets,
And the radiant and rare state seal.
I entrust them completely
And I will reclaim all later.

In the innermost place of the secrete warehouse,
There are crystal bowls for white rice,

Golden bottles for sweet water,

And there is the precious-tiger-box of the guardian king of the North.

I entrust them completely

And I will reclaim all later.

In the sacred palace above the tea city,

There are precious bottles available,

Bkav bgyur and bstan vgyur scriptures

Written with golden, silver and cinnabar powder,

And treasure-boxes full of documents and religious decrees.

I entrust them completely

And I will reclaim all later.

The furrow to the left is the horse-farm,

The furrow to the right is the cattle-farm,

The furrow in the middle is the sheep-farm.

I entrust them completely

And I will reclaim all later.

The big tents in Thang Shom Gong Dgu in the Ling State,

Are called big tents where wishes can come true,

And are also called roc-flying tents.

All the tent ropes and poles,

All instruments inside and outside,

I entrust them completely

And I will reclaim all later. [1]

---

[1]　Dkon Mchog Tshe Stan, *Subdue Demons and Monsters* [Tibetan], Lanzhou: Gansu People's Publishing House, 1981: 33-36.

III

The *Gesar* Epic.
Some Remarks on its Transmission and Diffusion in Tibet

Li Lianrong

Abstract: This paper deals with the issues of the *Gesar* epic and its transmission and diffusion in Tibet through a variety of materials. Since the 1940s scholars have pointed out that the singing form of *Gesar* is being spread and distributed only in the northern part of Tibet. Why is *Gesar* not sung in the southern part? Are there any other forms of transmission and dissemination in the southern part apart from singing? To investigate the major epic-spreading areas and its forms of transmission is crucial to our understanding of the epic's form of existence and development, as well as to our analysis of the compositional structure of the Tibetan culture. This kind of investigation is also crucial to our search for the reasons why the epic is not sung in the southern part of Tibet. In this paper I will look into the legends and the history of the clans mentioned in the epic and find out the main areas where the epic is spread and the routes it has traveled. In addition, a comparison is made between the singing tradition of the epic and other singing traditions in Tibet in order to find out the characteristics of both the singing tradition of the epic and its transmission.

Key words: *Gesar* epic, singing tradition, transmission

1

Research Background

The regional transmission and diffusion of the *Gesar* epic has become a hot topic in *Gesar* studies at the beginning of the 21th century. This has to do, in my opinion, not only with the internal development of Chinese scholarship on *Gesar* but also with the ongoing developmental project on exploring the western areas of China. Particularly after the *Gesar* epic was placed on the list of annual commemorate projects for 2002-2003 by UNESCO in 2002, the combination of the state-sponsored protection of the non-material cultural heritage and the demand for development through culture in the western region has, without doubt, stimulated this research project. [①]

I went to Tibet, the main inhabiting area for Tibetans, [②] in August 2002, to survey the efforts to rescue and collect epic literatures. After some time, I found an interesting phenomenon: generally speaking, there are distinctive differences in the mode of production and life style between the northern and southern parts of Tibet. Tibet is divided into two areas by the 30-degree line of northern latitude. In the northern part, yak, horse and sheep raising constitutes the main mode of production and life style, whereas in the southern part agriculture and forestry constitute the mainstay. At the same time, I have discovered that the singing form of *Gesar* is spread and distributed only in the northern part, especially in the present-day administrative prefectures of Chab Mdo, Nag Chu and Mngav Ris. Why is *Gesar* not sung in the southern part, and particularly not in the Yarlung Zangbo

---

①   An evident example of this is that in 2002 a series of activities was held to celebrate and commemorate the *Gesar* epic, which has aroused the attention of all media. An eye-catching piece of news reads: "It has been decided by experts and scholars that east Tibet is the birthplace of the epic" (Yuan Jian in New Chinese Network, 10 July 2002). On the commemorative activities, see Li Lianrong, "A Summary of the Symposium on the Gesar Epic in the Tibet Region." China's Tibet 4 (2002): 15-17.

②   The word Tibet mentioned in this paper refers to the present administrative division.

River area, the Tibetan cultural cradle, i.e. the present Lhog Kha, Gzhis Ka Rtse and Nying Khri, including Lhasa? Are there other forms of transmission and dissemination in the southern part apart from singing?

In fact, this is not a new discovery by any means, but a phenomenon already well known to scholars specializing in *Gesar* studies.[①] For a long time, we have accepted the theory that this epic has been widespread in the entire area where Tibetans live and that this Central Asian epic has even reached Siberia in the north, the bordering areas around Mount Qomolangma in the south, Kashmir in the west and the areas inhabited by various ethnic groups in the southwest of China. However, *Gesar* studies in the 21th century have shown, that this generalization somewhat covers up or overlooks our understanding of subtle differences in the major epic-spreading areas and its main forms of transmission. I think, therefore, that to investigate the major areas and forms of transmission is key to our understanding of the epic's form of existence and development, as well as to our analysis of the compositional structure of the Tibetan culture. This kind of investigation is also crucial to our search for the reasons why the epic is not sung in the southern part of Tibet.

I have been attracted to the "old" issue of the transmission and dissemination of the epic after I discovered that the epic is not sung in the southern part of Tibet— the birthplace of Tibetan culture. I am not going to talk about the origins and formation of the epic here. My view is that the origin and formation of the epic are a very complicated issue and that we cannot deal with it by relying blindly on one single point of the epic or on one single historical document. A hot debate with regard to this controversy went on in China in the 1950s and 1960s. Some scholars argued for a comprehensive view to look into this issue and that it should be ad-

---

① Descriptions in the paper "*Gesar*: The Epic Tradition of Tibetan People" by Samten G. Karmay are typical: 'The centre of the dissemination of the Gesar epic in Tibet lay in the regions of the mountain *A-myesr* Ma-chen in Amdo, north-eastern Tibet and that of the eastern part of Khams.' (Samten G. Karmay, "*Gesar*: The Epic Tradition of the Tibetan People," *The Arrow and the Spindle*: *Studies in the History, Myths and Beliefs in Tibet*, Kathmandu: Mandala Book Point: 465).

dressed only on the basis of results of research on other issues. [1]

2

Outlines of *Gesar* Scholarship at Home and Abroad

Since the "discovery" of the epic by foreign scholars, the exploration of its main spread areas has been entangled with questions about the origin and formation of this epic and some other issues.

According to materials now available, the first version of the *Gesar* epic that was introduced to foreign countries at the end of the 18th century is of a Mongolian origin. [2] Before the early 20th century, when A. H. Francke[3] recorded the Tibetan version in La Dwags, there were two views regarding the origin and spread of the Mongolian version of the epic. One view was that the epic originated and spread in the Mongolian region; the other view contended that the epic was closely related to Tibet. Since the Tibetan version was made public, A. H. Francke's view that the epic originated in Tibet has won the support of many scholars. It has been widely acknowledged that the epic is spread mainly in Tibet, especially after Alexandra David-Neel and Lama Yongden in the 1930s recorded the rather complete *Gesar* spread in the Khams area in the east of Ti-

---

[1] See Huang Jingtao, "Introduction to *Gesar* 4 – *A Battle between Hor and Ling*," *Biography of King Gesar*: *The War between Hor and Ling*, Shanghai Wenyi Publishing House, 1962.

[2] My knowledge of research achievements by foreign scholars mainly comes from the following works: (1) R. A. Stein, *Studies of Epics and Ballad Singers in Tibet*, Lhasa: Tibet People's Publishing House, 1993; (2) M. P. Khomonov, *The Buryat Heroic Epic 'Geser'*, edited by the Institute of Literature Research of IMASS, translated by Has, Huhhot: Inner Mongolian Academy of Social Sciences, 1986; (3) S. Yu. Nekliudov, *Epics of the Mongolian People*, translated by Xu Changhan, Gao Wenfeng and Zhang Zizhi, Huhhot: Inner Mongolian People's Publishing House, 1991.

[3] A. H. Francke, *A Lower Ladakhi Verion of the 'Kesar' Saga*, translated by Peng Gonghou in *The Monthly Journal of the Society of Studying Khams-pa and Tibet* 4-16 (1947-1948).

bet. Some Soviet scholars once challenged the theory that the epic had originated in Tibet, [2] but their position was soon revised by Tsendiin Damdinsuren's two important publications. [3] Notwithstanding the differences in the conclusions of the two works, both argue that Tibet is the area where the epic originated and spread, and that the epic is mostly transmitted in the eastern part of Tibet. Ever since, foreign scholars have reached a basic consensus: The epic is mainly spread or originated in Tibet, particularly in east Tibet. [4]

When foreign scholars come to assert that east Tibet is the main area of the epic's transmission, since the 1940s, Chinese scholars, too, have proposed that the epic originated and spread in east Tibet, and even inferred that the epic could not be transmitted in the Dbus Gtsang area because of the restrictions of the Dge-lugs-pa sect. [5] In the 1980s, some scholars thought that it was possible that the epic had migrated from Dbus Gtsang towards the southeast. [6] But on the

[1] David-Neel, Alexandra and Lama Yongden, *A Record of Super Hero Gesar from Gling*, edited by Yang Yuanfang, translated by Chen Zongxiang, Beijing: Institute of Nationality Studies, Southwestern Institute of Nationalities, 1984.

[2] Academician S.A. Kozin pointed out that the epic originated in Inner Mongolia or was created by Mongolians living in Tibet. See S.A. Kozin, *The 'Geser' Epic: Story about the Gracious Geser Mergen-Khan* [Russian], Moscow: Academy of Sciences of the USSR, 1935; and *The Epic of the Mongolian People* [Russian], Moscow: Academy of Sciences of the USSR, 1948.

[3] Tsendiin Damdinsuren, *Historical Roots of the 'Gesar' Epic* [Russian], Moscow: Academy of Science of the USSR, 1957; and *A Study of the Tibetan Epic and Ballad Singers* [French], Paris: French University Presses, 1959.

[4] Today almost all scholars agree with Geoffrey Samuel. See for his views "The *Gesar* Epic of East Tibet," eds. José Ignacio Cabezón and Roger R. Jackson, *Tibetan Studies: Studies of Genre*, Ithaca, New York: Snow Lion, 1996: 358-367.

[5] Ren Naiqiang, "A Brief Introduction to *Gesar*," *A Public Opinion of Frontier Politics* 4, 5 and 6 (1944), quoted from *Collected Papers on Gesar Studies*, edited by Jiangbian Jiacuo, Chengdu: Sichuan Nationalities Publishing House, 1986: 1-13; Xu Guoqiong, "The Tibetan Epic *Biography of Gesar*," *Literary Review* 6 (1959), quoted from *Collected Papers on Gesar Studies*, edited by Jiangbian Jiacuo, Chengdu: Sichuan Nationalities Publishing House, 1986: 32-47.

[6] Xie Jisheng, "The Southeastward Movement of the Area of Spread of the Gesar Epic and a Preliminary Exploration of the Causes," *Gesar* Studies, 6 vols., Beijing: China Folk Literary and Art Publishing House, 1988: III 339-351.

whole, it is a shared view that the epic originated in east Tibet and later spread in other directions.[1] In fact, traditional Tibetan works, such as *Rlang kyi po ti bse ru* of the 14th century, support the argument that the epic has been transmitted in the eastern part of Tibet.

Rich collections of materials on *Gesar* have been rediscovered in recent years, and, with the development of other realms of Tibetology, a new generation of *Gesar* scholars has emerged. Since the 1990s, they have also focused their attention on the eastern part of Tibet where the epic is still sung. With regard to this issue, these younger scholars have come to the following three conclusions. First, *Gesar* was a historical figure living in the 11th century, or the first *rab byung* (cycle of sixty years) of the Tibetan calendar. In the epic his life and deeds have been cast into a literary form. This view is basically inherited from traditional scholars. Second, *Gesar* has been transmitted in the eastern part of Tibet. Third, with regard to the origin of the epic, one view is that it appeared in the 11th century and another is that it appeared during the Tubo period (600-800 AD) or even earlier.[2]

In general, scholars have based their identification of the epic's spread on the following two aspects: first, on documentations of later periods relevant to the epic or to the characters in the epic; and second, on contents such as places and ethnic groups mentioned in the epic. Some scholars have been researching on the

---

[1] Wang Yinuan, "The Tibetan *Gesar* Epic," *Journal of the Central College of Nationalities* 2 (1979), quoted from Zhao Bingli, ed., *A Collection of Papers on Gesarology*, 5 vols., Lanzhou: Gansu Minzu Publishing House, 1990-1998: I 338-343; Jiangbian Jiacuo, *A Primary Exploration of Gesar*, Xining: Qinghai People's Publishing House, 1986; Yang Enhong, "On the Spread of *Biography of King Gesar*," *Studies of Ethnic Literature* 5 (1989): 37-41.

[2] See Gcod Pa Don Grub and Rta Mgrin, *A Fresh Look at 'Gesar'* [Tibetan], Xining: Qinghai Nationality Publishing House, 1995; Blo Gros Rgya Mtsho, *Legends of the Traces of 'Gesar'* [Tibetan], Lhasa: Tibet Minzu Publishing House, 1994; Rnam Rgyal, "The Origin of the Gesar Epic and Its Historical Connotation," *Tibetan Studies* Feb. 2001: 27-39 and "To Adhere to Historical Materialism and to Deepen Studies of *Gesar*," *Tibetan Studies* Apr. 2002: 5-9; and Dpav Lo, "New Exploration of the Early Location of the Ling State and Other Relevant Historical Issues," *Tibetan Studies* Apr. 1999: 59-68.

role played by ballad singers in spreading the epic, but not enough attention has been paid to the relations between ballad singers and the areas of transmission. Scholars of earlier periods, especially those scholars who first took notice of the Mongolian version of the epic, have argued for the later appearance of the epic in the light of its linguistic features. S. A. Kozin was an example. [1] Along this line of thinking, all evidence tends to point in the direction that the epic originated in Tibet.

Using the above-mentioned research results as a point of departure, I think that we should approach the question of the origin and dissemination of the epic from a different angle. I also think that, in order to bring about a new understanding, it is necessary to proceed with our survey from three other perspectives. First, we should go back to and regard the Dun Huang documents as materials with certain historical authenticity (instead of tracing *Gesar*'s historical origin from documentations of later periods), consult on the legends and history of the clans mentioned in the epic and find out the main areas and routes of the epic's transmission. Second, a comparison should be made between the singing tradition of the epic and other singing traditions in Tibet in order to find out the characteristics of the singing tradition of the epic and the characteristics of its spread. Last, we should proceed from the content and structure of the epic to find out the relations between the myths in the epic and the cultures where *Gesar* is spread and performed. At the same time we should look into the formation of the main structure of the epic to explain the reasons for its transmission, spread areas and expansion. A combined analysis may help us to explain why the epic does not have a singing pattern in the southern part of Tibet. This paper makes tentative efforts to compare the singing tradition of the epic and the singing tradition in Tibet.

---

[1] See for example S. A. Kozin, *The ' Geser' Epic: Story about the Gracious Geser Mergen-Khan* [Russian]. Moscow: Academy of Sciences of the USSR, 1935.

3

The Singing Tradition and the Spread of the Epic

When talking about the general characteristics of Russian epics, Vladimir Propp said: 'Musical, vocal performance is so essential to it [Russian epic poetry] that works not meant to be sung do not qualify as epic.'[1] This remark about the importance of musical performance is applicable to Tibetan epics as well. Singing endows epics with life and therefore the music of an epic constitutes an insepara-ble part of the epic. Then, what does it mean that the *Gesar* epic has been ex-tant without a singing pattern in the southern part of Tibet?

I . Introduction

The singing tradition of every ethnic group has its own characteristics that, his-torically speaking, cannot take form overnight and have been undergoing change up to the present day. Admittedly however, just like humankind and other species that have their unique genetic patterns, ethnic cultures have genetic pat-terns of their own. As for the genetic pattern of the Tibetan singing tradition, I think that there are similarities as well as differences due to the complexity of the formation of the Tibetan culture and history. Or, it is fair to say that there exist many local cultural genetic patterns alongside one shared genetic pattern. The proportion of similarities seems to be bigger due to the long-term historical and cultural interactions.

It is said that the Tibetan culture is largely made up of the tribal cultures of four or six clans. Presumably in ancient times, there were more than these six clans on the Tibet Plateau. Some scholars argue that the Tibetan culture and singing tradittition have a history of more than three thousand years. Their view is

---

[1] Vladimir Propp, *Theory and History of Folklore*, Minneapolis: University of Minnesota Press, 1993: 150.

based on the history of two main clans of the Tibetan culture: Yar Klung's Rgyal Rabs and Zhang Zhung's Rgyal Rabs. ① Does this mean that the other four clans did not have their cultures and singing tradition, or not even a history? Documentations cannot be silenced in this regard. I think therefore that we should broaden our understanding of the Tibetan culture and should not limit ourselves to Mount Gandisê and the Yarlung Zangbo River flowing there. It is true that this area is the main birthplace of both the Tibetan culture and the local state of power that finally completed the task of unifying the Tibet Plateau. But we must also examine, in a scientific and objective manner, the source of ancient Tibetan culture.

Let me make a brief introduction to the heroes and the Ldong clan, one of the four or six big clans in Tibetan history that appear in the *Gesar* epic. The first records of the Ldong clan appeared in the Dun Huang documents in Tibetan. According to the Dun Huang documents now available, the document with records of the Ldong clan is Piliot Tibet (P.T.) 1287. The fourth paragraph of this document mentions that after Khri Slon Btsan conquered the Zing Po Rje in the north, he occupied a vast area. He ordered that the area of Ngas Po where the Zing Po Rje stayed be renamed Vphan Yul. ② The document goes on: At a big feast thrown by the *btsan po* to his ministers, Khyung Po Spung Sad sang a song to boast of his own achievements: 'Lho and Rngegs were conquered by Vphan and Se and Khyung were at the disposal of the Vphan' (Lho rngegs ni vphan gyi snon, se khyung ni vphan gyis btab). ③ When the singing was over, the *btsan po* hoped that officials from the two tribes of Lho and Rngegs could stand up in re-

---

① Zhol Khang Bsod Names Dar Rgyas thinks that the first king Gnyav-khri-btsan-po of the Spur Rgyal Rabs in Tibet has a history of 2.100 years whereas the Zhang Zhung's Rgyal Rabs has a history of only more than 800 years (Zhol Khang Bsod Names Dar Rgyas, *A Brief History of Tibetan Music* [Tibetan], Lhasa: Tibet People's Publishing House, 1992: 48).

② Lines 184-185, see Wang Yao and Chen Jian, trans., *Dunhuang Tubo Lishi Wenshu* [*The Tubo Historical Texts in Dunhuang*], revised and enlarged version, Beijing: Minzu Publishing House, 1992: 44.

③ Lines 227-228, see Wang Yao and Chen Jian, trans., *Dunhuang Tubo Lishi Wenshu* [*The Tubo Historical Texts in Dunhuang*], revised and enlarged version, Beijing: Minzu Publishing House, 1992: 47, see also Appendix 2 in the same book (photocopy of the original): 1565.

sponse, but no one did. At that moment, Zhang Snang Pe Vu Zur Vbreng Po also sang a song at the request of Khri Slon Btsan. He eulogized the chancellors of the Myang and Dbavs clans who contributed to the conquest of the northern Zing Po Rje as well as the might of the Yar Klung tribe, singing: 'Lho and Rngegs were suppressed by Vphan and the Ldong and Tong were at the disposal of the Vphan' (Lho rngegs ni vphan gyi snon, ldong tong ni vphan gyis btab). [1] A paragraph of the sung text about the sister of Srong Btsan Sgam Po who married Zhang Zhung goes: 'Ah, there is a wild yak in the pastoral area in the north. It is a stud yak. To kill this wild yak of the north, some people from the Pu Nas should shout, the Ldong and Tong were conquered by Vphan, there were flag-wavers in Mdav Nas, there were Sha and Spug in the Skyivi Ni River, there were stone throwers in the central area and there were Lho and Rngegs in Yar Klung' (Kye byang vbrog ni ya bi na, pho mvi ni gchig pa, byang vbrog ni vbrong dgum na, pu nas ni kus vdebs pav, ldong thong ni vpan gyis thob, mdav nas ni gyab vdor ba, skyivi ni sha dangs spug, dbus nas ni dpor vphen ba, yar gyi ni lho dang rngegs...'). [2] From the above-quoted passage we can tell that the "author" of the sung text lived around the 6th or 7th century but the content reflected in the sung text does not quite reflect the reality of that period. These "histories" concern the gradual rise and development of the Yar Klung tribe. Therefore, they have a markedly legendary character and abound in metaphors.

With respect to the sung text, it seems that the sister of Srong Btsan Sgam Po tried to enhance the morale and ambitions and hoped that the *btsan po* could conquer the *mi-lu* and wild horse tribes of Zhang Zhung, the way he had done

---

[1]   Ibid. 48; 1565, line 239 in the original document.

[2]   Ibid. 58. 1573, lines 412-414 in the original document. For the translation I have made use of the following works: (1) Wang Yao and Chen Jian, trans., *Dunhuang Tubo Lishi Wenshu* [*The Tubo Historical Texts in Dunhuang*], revised and enlarged version, Beijing: Minzu Publishing House, 1992: 163 and 168; (2) *Ariane Macdonald, An Examination and Explanation of the Dun Huang Historical Document on Tubo*, translated by Geng Sheng, Xining: Qinghai People's Publishing House, 1991: 69, 71 and 74; (3) I have also asked for help from the two associate research fellows Nor Bu Rgya Mtsho and Dkon Mchog Skyabs at the Tibet Academy of Social Sciences.

with the wild yak tribe in the north. In Macdonald's account, the way of hunting and capturing wild yaks perhaps applied to the conquest of Zhang Zhung.[①] But in my view, the wild yaks here most probably refer to the Ldong and Tong tribes in the north instead of the Zhang Zhung tribe. Metaphors in the documentations of that and later periods show that the area around Mount Gandisê was the place for *mi-lu* (a kind of deer) and wild horses and that the northern part was the habitat of wild yaks. Therefore, the main theme of the aforesaid sung text by the sister of Srong Btsan Sgam Po is the victory of Vphan over the Ldong and Tong. Many scholars agree that Vphan refers to the Yar Klung tribe. But where then were the geographical location of the Ldong and Tong? Many scholars have reckoned with the Yar Klung area. But according to the aforesaid sung text, they lived in the upper reaches of the Skyivi Ni River, the area around Mount Gnyan Chen Thang La or the Thang La area. This means that there were two powerful tribes in the Byang Thang grassland in the vast north: the Ldong and the Tong. They must be the clan named "wild yak tribe". Such a conjecture corresponds to the above-mentioned sung text by Zhang Snang: 'The top of Mount Thang La has been whittled flat and put under the foundation of Mount Sham Po; Yu Sna castles and villages have been conquered and been supplemented to Pying Ba' (Thang la ni rtse bchad ching, sham po ni rmed duva bsnan, yu sna vi ni mkhar pab, pying ba vi ni snon du bgyid).[②] In academic circles, it is generally held that the Zing Po Rje Stag Ska Bo, living in Nyen Kar, and the Khri Pangs Sum, living in Yu Sna, together formed the Sum Pa tribe.[③] This view, however, has

---

① Macdonald, Ariane, *An Examination and Explanation of the Dun Huang Historical Document on Tubo*, translated by Geng Sheng, Xining: Qinghai People's Publishing House, 1991: 74.

② The original text is not included in *Dun Huang Historical Document on Tubo*, but taken from Ariane Macdonald, *An Examination and Explanation of the Dun Huang Historical Document on Tubo*, translated by Geng Sheng, Xining: Qinghai People's Publishing House, 1991: 71.

③ Wang Yao and Chen Jian, trans., Appendix 2 of *Dunhuang Tubo Lishi Wenshu* [*The Tubo Historical Texts in Dunhuang*], revised and enlarged version, Beijing: Minzu Publishing House, 1992: 47; 1561, lines 118-119 in the original document.

been challenged.① What is certain is that the Ldong and Tong were the nomadic tribes near Mount Thang La and were conquered by the Yar Klung tribe. After Khri Slon Btsan conquered the Zing Po Rje, the latter fled to the Dru Gru area further north. This shows, on the one hand, that the Zing Po Rje and Dru Gru maintained close relations and on the other hand, that the north (possibly including the areas to the south and north of the present day Kunlun Mountains) must have been a vast area in the eyes of the Yar Klung tribe. According to some scholars, the Dangxiang mentioned in the Chinese documentations correspond to the "Dongqiang" or "Dongxiang" in the Tibetan documentations.② I find it not baseless. But I don't think that the word "Dangxiang" was a term referring to the Khams Pa people of later periods; it should have its origin in the Tubo period or even earlier. In view of the sung text by Zhang Snang of the Khri Slon Btsan period, the conquest of the Ldong and Tong tribes by the Yar Klung tribe might refer to the victory over the Zing Po Rje. In Chinese documentation, for instance in the "Biography of Xiyu" in *Xin Tang Shu* and *Jiu Tang Shu*, the Dangxiang are given a prominent position in the introduction. It is said:

It is another name for the Xiqiang of the Han dynasty. The tribe became weak during the Wei and Jin dynasties. It defeated the Dangchang and Dengzhi during the Zhou dynasty and the Dangxiang began to have their own territory. The tribe occupied the ancient Xizhi area and neighbored on Songzhou in the east, Yehu in the west, Chongsang and Misang in the south and Tuyuhun in the north.③

---

① Ibid. 188, note 68; Tshong Kha Dbyang Grub Sgam Po, "Relations Between Sum Pa and Tubo and other Neighboring Regimes," *Tibetan Studies* 3 (1992): 51.

② Nam Mkhavi Nor Bu holds the view that the word "Dongxiang" is a term used by the Khams Pa people for the Dongba people in the north. The pronunciation of "Dongxiang" differs from "Dongqiang" used in the Dbus Gtsang area. In the Chinese documents the Dongba are called "Dangxiangqiang". See Nam Mkhavi Nor Bu, *Ancient Tibetan History*, Chengdu: Sichuan Minzu Publishing House, 1990: 127.

③ Ouyang Xiu and Song Qi [Song Dynasty], *Xin Tang Shu. Xi Yu Shang. Dang Xiang*, Beijing: Zhonghua Book Company, 1975, CCXXII 6214.

It is said in *Beishi* [*Annals of the Northern Dynasties*] and "Biography of Dangxiang" in *Sui Shu* [*Annals of the Sui Dynasty*]: 'Dangxiangqiang people are descendants of Sanmiao. They have branches named Dangchang and Bailang and they call themselves the Mihou (macaque) people.'[1] From the above-mentioned records we can see that the area occupied by the Dangxiang was at first confined to Mount Kunlun and the Xizhi River. This means that Mount Kunlun (including the area of Yehu in Xinjiang) was the starting point of the Dangxiang westward immigration. They inhabited an area stretching from Tuyuhun in the north (surrounding the Qinghai Lake and the area to the northeast of the lake), to Mount Thang La or Mount Gnyan Chen Thang La in the south,[2] and they roved around towards the east along the Tongtian River and the Xizhi River (the upper reaches of the Yellow River) in the direction of the area of Songpan. They picked up in Rma Yul (i.e. Mgo Log) and became powerful there. A faction of the Dangxiang continued to move to the east along the Maqu River (the Yellow River) and eventually established the Western Xia Dynasty.[3] It is even possible

[1] Li Yanshou [Tang Dynasty], *Beishi* [*Annals of the Northern Dynasties*], 10 vols., Beijing: Zhonghua Book Company, 1974: X 3192; and Wei Zheng and Linghu De |Tang Dynasty], *Suishu* [*Annals of the Sui Dynasty*], 6 vols., Beijing: Zhonghua Book Company, 1973: VI 1845.

[2] The Nag Shod corridor running from the west to the east between the area to the south of Mount Thang La and the area to the north of Mount Gnyan Chen Thang La or the Nag Chu River valley might have been the area for the nomadic Tong Sum Pa to rove around.

[3] In the Tibetan documents of later periods, the Ldong are always related to the Mi Nyag and the Mi Nyag are said to be a tribe of the Tong. The Western Xia State was established by the Mi Nyag tribe, a part of the Dangxiang tribe. The state is called "Mi Nyag" in Chinese documents. In extolling the ancestors of the Western Xia State, *a Poem to Eulogize Ancestors* (*A Paean of the Sacred Root of the Xia*) sings: 'The original town we black-haired people built with stones is on the river side of Damo, the hometown of our red-faced ancestors is by the side of a white river and that is the Mi Nyag State in the highland' (Bai Bin, *Studies of the History of Dangxiang*, Changchung: Jilin Education Publishing House, 1989: 89-90). The Mi Nyag were a part of the Tubo tribe; see Ouyang Xiu and Song Qi [Song Dynasty], *Xin Tang Shu. Xi Yu Shang*. Dang Xiang, Beijing: Zhonghua Book Company, 1975, CCXXII 6215: 'Their land is occupied by the Tubo. People living on this land become slaves of the Tubo and the name of their tribe is changed into Mi Nyag.'

that the Dangxiang roved westward and had contacts with the Zhang Zhung culture in Mngav Ris. The war between the wild horses and wild yaks tribes recorded in the Dun Huang documents implied to a certain extent the wars between the
two tribes. [1]

We know that, like all other cultures in the world, the Tibetan culture originated on the banks of big rivers. But it differs from other world cultures because
it has also incorporated elements of many cultures affiliated with high mountains
and big lakes. This exceptional phenomenon is due to its ecological environment. Within the whole Tibetan living area, there are various geographical areas
that have been shaped by their environmental surroundings of famous rivers,
mountains and lakes. For instance, Mount Gandisê and Lake Ma Phang Gyu Mtsho are the symbols of the Zhang Zhung culture, Mount Yar La Sham Po and the
Yarlung Zangbo River are the symbols of the Yar Klung culture, Moung Thang
La is the mark of the Ldong and Tong culture, and so on. I believe, therefore,
that the Ldong and Tong had a singing tradition as old as the Yar Klung and
Zhang Zhung traditions. Many issues concerning the *Gesar* epic can be solved if
a direct comparison could be made between the singing tradition of Ldong-Dangx-
iang-Mi Nyag and the epic performance of *Gesar*. But in restrospect, there are
few ancient documents that deal exclusively with these two clans and we can only
rely on the documents that mainly treat of the Yar Klung tribe to analyze the
singing tradition of this tribe. Of course, these documents include contributions
made by the singing tradition of the Ldong and Tong.

---

[1] See F.W. Thomas, "The End of Glorious Times, the Tragedy between Horses and Yaks," translated by
Li Youyi and Wang Qingshan, *Folk Literature from Northeast Tibet*, Chengdu: Sichuan Nationalities
Publishing House, 1989: 17-34.

Ⅱ. The Singing Tradition in Tibet

In the earliest singing tradition, the *Gesar* epic was closely related to folk songs. [①] But during the Yar Klung's Rgyal Rabs and even the whole Tubo period, records of its own typical folk songs were hardly seen, let alone the pure singing tradition of other tribes. Documents of later periods show that in the early period of the Yar Klung tribe, the administrative records were mainly written in the styles of *sgrung* (comparable to contemporary epics or stories), *ldevu* (comparable to riddle songs) and *bon* (of the Bon religion). [②] Songs were not mentioned in the records, but from the law of literary development we know that songs often constitute a most important part of the popular tradition. I think therefore that the three above-mentioned forms of expression-*sgrung*, *ldevu* and *bon* – must be regarded as forms of songs, or combinations of songs and dialogues. In fact, records of these three forms were basically characteristic of songs. There were songs and dialogues in *sgrung*. It was said that *ldevu* was in a way similar to riddle songs. The form of expression of *bon* also had the characteristics of songs, i.e. recital. So it is fair to say that songs were widely applied in all aspects.

Apart from these three forms characteristics of songs, dialogues between different characters basically make most of the form of singing except for accounts of activities, i.e. the mode of expression of *mgur glu*, as in the Dun Huang documents on the Yar Klung-Tubo dynasty. As some studies show, *mgur* and *glu*

---

① The present Tibetan singing tradition should also include the singing of Tibetan opera. The formation of this form of art was based on folk songs. It matured and acquired firm characteristics under the influence of other cultures and arts of later periods; see Liu Zhiqun, *Tibetan Opera and Tibetan Folklore*, Lhasa: Tibet People's Publishing House; Shijiazhuang: Hebei Juvenile Publishing House, 1999. The Tibetan folk song tradition has always been closely combined with singing and dancing. It has always been closer related to epic singing than to opera. Therefore, the following discussion of the Gesar epic is based mainly on folk songs.

② Dpav Wo Gtsug Lag Vphreng Wa, *A New Feast for Wise Men*, Beijing: Minzu Publishing House, 1986: 165.

were created by people living in antiquity and closely related to religion. *Mgur glu was used to extol various gods and had its own "god of songs"*.[1] *Don Grub Rgyal also thought that mgur glu* originated in the Yar Klung area where, at that time, the meanings of *mgur*, *glu* and *mchid* were basically identical. Later, because of the need for religious publicity, these folk songs were reworked and since then the meanings of *mgur* and *glu* have changed. *Mgur* became a honorific form of *glu* and *mgur* came to mean "songs" exclusively claimed by religious circles. Especially after Mar Pa and Mi La Ras Pa of the Bkav Brgyud sect began to use *mgur* on a wide scale, its religious character became firmly established. *Glu* was widely used among the people in folk songs. However, on the basis of an extensive study, Don Grub Rgyal pointed out the divergence of the folk songs at a later stage of their development:

1. In the central Dbus Gtsang area, there were two types of popular songs: *gzhas* songs with four sentences in one paragraph and six syllables in each sentence and *tshig rgyag* songs of antiphonal style with four sentences and six syllables. 2. *Glu songs* of the three-paragraph-four-sentence-eight-syllable style and glu shags songs of antiphonal style with four sentences and eight syllables in each sentence were spread in the Mdo Smad area. 3. *La gzhas* songs of the style of two-paragraph-four-sentence and seven or eight syllables in each sentence expresssing love were popular in Mdo Khams.[2] Don Grub Rgyal also provided in his study a detailed account of the characteristics of the development of *mgur glu* of later periods.

It is clear that the *mgur glu* recorded in the Dun Huang documents and the folk songs of the *gzhas* style prevailing in the Dbus Gtsang area in later periods were closely related. They were identical in terms of the number of syllables and had similar rhymes and modes of expression. But *mgur glu* as recorded in the Dun Huang documents was very different from the folk songs of the *glu* style,

---

[1] Don Grub Rgyal, *Origin and Development of Admonitory Poems*, Beijing: Minzu Publishing House, 1985: 9-11.

[2] Ibid. 21-24.

popular in the Mdo Smad and Mdo Khams areas. From my point of view, these stylistic differences, in all probability, stem from the contexts of different clan cultures out of which the variants of the *glu* style were born. Though formerly linked to folk songs from the Dbus Gtsang area, the folk songs from Mdo Smad and Mdo Khams had been subjected to cultural interaction for several hundred years or even up to a thousand years by the Tubo period. Like the workings of the aforesaid ethnic cultural genetic patterns, I think that there were fundamental differences between the two styles of *glu* based in different geographical areas. Although folk songs together with their words and phrases are constantly evolving, they reflect the rhyme of a culture. This internal rhyme manifests itself externally in the number of words, rhyme forms and rhyme schemes, just like the ancient poems with five or seven characters, *jueju* and *lüshi*, of a Han origin represent the cultural rhyme of the Han people. Therefore, an ethnic group will eventually form a relatively stable structure in its folk songs that mirrors the rhyme of this particular group. We may infer that the singing of folk songs of the *gzhas* style, popular in the Dbus Gtsang area, inherited many rhyme and expressive forms of the Yar Klung Rgyal Rabs, reflecting the tribe per se or even representative of an agricultural culture. The folk songs in Mdo Smad and Mdo Khams, on the other hand, mirror the rhyme of the nomadic Ldong and Tong tribes. These stable elements constitute the genetic patterns of various ethnic cultures. In this respect, it can be argued that the Tibetan culture is pluralistic.

What follows is a tentative analysis of the distribution of two kinds of folk songs that represent two folk song traditions in Tibet: folk songs of the *gzhas* style and that of the *glu* style. The glu style folk songs such as *la-gzhas* and *sgor-bro* predominate the vast pastoral area in the north, whereas the many kinds of folk songs of the *gzhas* style, such as *gzhas-chen*, *sgor-gzhas*, *nang-ma*, *stod-gzhas* and *chang-gzhas*, mainly scatter in Lhasa and in the vast agricultural area to the south of Lhasa.① The cultural characteristics correspond to the mode of production and life style in the Tibetan area: animal husbandry is the main mode of production and life style in the northern part where folk songs of the *glu* style are popular, whereas in the southern part agriculture as a mode of production and life style, and folk songs of the *gzhas* style prevail.

Some scholars have pointed out, that the *glu* style constitutes the basis for the singing of the *Gesar* epic. We have discussed earlier that the *glu*-style folk songs are transmitted among the Nordic nomads. This corresponds to the fact that the *Gesar* epic has been transmitted and sung in areas inhabited by nomadic tribes.

An examination of the distribution of epic singers in the 1990s in the Tibetan area exhibits the transmission and dissemination of the epic in the singing form in the whole Tibetan area, and also proves that the epic is being sung and spread in the northern part and even in Mdo Smad and Mdo Khams. The *glu*-style folk songs are also most popular in these northern areas. It is evident that there is an east-and-west corridor for the epic singing, with as the center Mount Thang La and Mount Gnyan Chen Thang La (especially along the direction of the chains of Mount Thang La). This basically corresponds to the map of nomadic routes of the

---

① According to *A Collection of Chinese Ballads – The Tibetan Volume*, the present popular Tibetan folk songs are divided into 12 kinds: 1. *sgor-gzhas*; 2. *gzhas-chen*; 3. *sgor-bro*; 4. *ral-pa*; 5. *nang-ma*; 6. *stod-gzhas*; 7. *chang-gzhas*; 8. *la-gzhas*; 9. *byid-pavi-gzhas*; 10. *life songs*; 11. *work songs*; 12. *Gesar* epic and its singing; see Organizing Committee of *A Collection of Chinese Ballads – The Tibetan Volume*, comp., *A Collection of Chinese Ballads – The Tibetan Volume*, Beijing: China IS-BN Center, 2001: 1-33. It needs to be added that folk songs of the *sgor-gzhas* and *sgor-bro* forms constitute an art typical of the Tibetan culture, i.e. a combination of singing, dancing and music. This art might be an artistic form enjoyed by all clans on the Tibet Plateau (including those who have moved eastward and evolved into other ethnic groups). The same form of transmission can be found among the descendants of the Tuyuhun people in the north, i.e. the present-day ethnic group of the Tu, the ethnic groups of the Naxi, the Qiang, the Pumi and so on. But the singing in performance is conducted according to the particularity of the folk songs of each individual ethnic group, just like the distinct difference between the northern and southern parts of Tibet. For the many differences between the folk songs of the glu and gzhas styles, see *A Collection of Chinese Ballads – The Tibetan Volume* mentioned above.

two clans of the Ldong and Tong mentioned above, especially in the case of the Ldong clan with its eastward expansion. Proceeding from Mount Gnyan Chen Thang La and Mount Thang La eastward up to the present area near Sanjiangyuanbei in Yul Shul county in Qinghai province, we can see two different routes. One route goes to the south along the Jinshajiang River; the other route reaches today's Ningxia in the north along the Rma Chu River. Further westward the route reaches the Balti people in La Dwags along the open Byang Thang praire between Mount Rang Kunlun and Mount Rang Gandisê. The survey we have hitherto conducted basically backs up our schematization of the existence of the singing form of the epic in the whole Tibetan region. Meanwhile, this also shows that our conjecture about the Ldong and Tong clans and their singing tradition can hold water.

A survey of the present distribution of *Gesar* singers in Tibet shows that the singing form of the *Gesar* epic is spread out in the nomadic area in the northern part. We can see that in the nomadic corridor between Mount Thang La in the north and Mount Gnyan Chen Thang La in the south (extended westward in the area between Mount Kunlun and Mount Gandisê), there is a large number of ballad singers who recite and sing this great epic. To our knowledge, there are more than forty ballad singers who recite and sing more than ten parts of the epic.[①] Famous ballad singers who can sing more than forty parts mostly come from Dpal Pa county of Chab Mdo district (singer Grags Pa), Steng Chen county (singer Bsang Grub) and Sog county of Nag Chu (singer Gyu Sman and Chos Grags). These areas have been inhabited by the Ldong and Tong clans since ancient times.

Apart from the transmission and dissemination of the *Gesar* epic in the singing form, other forms of transmission and dissemination also exist. We shall now look at those other forms of the spreading of the *Gesar* epic in Tibet.

---

①   Tshe Dbang Vgyur Med, "The Rescue Work of the Tibetan *Gesar* and A Prospective Research Summary," *Tibetan Studies* 4 (2002): 4.

Two points need to be elucidated. First, all forms of transmission, except singing, are widely spread in the whole Tibetan region, but only a small part in the south is sketched here due to the limited scope of this study. Second, the forms of legend and "relics about scenery" take a large share in the nomadic area in the north. We can tell from the map that the epic's transmission and dissemination are multi-dimensional, but singing as a main form of spread is widespread only in the northern part; the epic is also spread in the south, but there is a fundamental change in the form of spread. So, we venture to propose that the nomadic area in the north is the area of the earliest transmission and dissemination of the epic. The southern part began to pick up the transmission and dissemination of the epic only later.

Furthermore, in terms of the characteristics of the music of the epic, we can tell from historical records of later periods that at the celebration of the completion of the Bsams Yas Gtsug Lag Khang temple during the Tubo period, all people, including the king, Buddhist masters and translators, the queen, princes and officials, sang tuned songs suitable to their respective status. This kind of tunes bears resemblance to the ones sung by various figures in *Gesar*, on the basis of which other relevant issues, such as the timing of the epic's appearance can be determined.[①] I think that these conjectures are debatable. First, these records were discovered only from the 14th century on, when the epic had already been widespread, and it is possible that the records and the singing in *Gesar* bore cross-references. Second, as has been pointed out by some scholars, even if these tunes were extant in earlier periods, they might have been mere

---

①   Spen Rdor talks about this issue in his papers on the music of the epic "On the Historical Evolution and the Artistic Characteristics of the Talking-and-Singing Music of the Tibetan Heroic Epic Gesar," *On Contemporary Tibetan Music*, Lhasa: Tibetan People's Publishing House, 1993: 373-389; and "On the Musical Art of the *Gesar* Epic," *Tibetan Studies* 4 (2002): 25-30. In these papers he quotes and points out thirteen names of tunes sung after the completion of the Bsams Yas Gtsug Lag Khang temple *in Bkav thang sde lnga-btshun mo bkavi thang yig* (*The Crown Princess' Doctrine in the Five Kind of Doctrines*) and twenty names of tunes in *Rgyal rabs gsal bavi me long* (*The King-Lineage's Bright Mirror*). He has also found over fifty names of tunes in *Gesar — Becoming King through Horse-Racing*.

music for voices used to express feelings without a particular name.[①] *In recent years*, some scholars have conducted studies on the characteristics of the epic singing in Amdo and Khams Pa areas and pointed out that the tune of *Gesar* is constituted by repeating a basic musical form several times or infinitely. This relatively stable structural form is a one-part musical form with two phrases and two periods. It forms a structural whole with a mutual contrast between adjacent phrases, and with replies and supplements to finish with the musical content. The music for voices is simple. In intervals, four notes form one scale, and only the end of the third bar and the first tone of the fourth bar form a three-scale tone, all of which are typical of a chanting tune.

All in all, the epic seated in the Tibetan singing tradition is characteristic of the nomadic culture in the north; the singing tradition based on folk songs of the northern part has been restricted in the epic's southward spreading due to differences in ethnic rhymes or in culture. The form of epic singing does not spread in the southern farm fields of Tibet, except for the silent growth of the epic's content. Therefore, changes have taken place in terms of the form of dissemination.

---

① Mireille Helffer said: 'Some explanations are given to the names of tunes that appear in *The Chapter of Horse-Racing* and Tibetans themselves also provide some notes and explanations, but they are still difficult to understand···' ("A Study of the Songs in Biography of *the Tibetan King Gesar – The Chapter of Horse-Racing*," Zhao Bingli, ed., *A Collection of Papers on Gesarology*. 5 Vols. Lanzhou: Gansu Nationalities Publishing House, 1990-1998: V 3565. From the viewpoint of Ma Chengfu, the so-called names of the tunes of epic-singing are non-existent, which means that the epic does not have fixed names for tunes as drama does; there are only some adjectives for the expression of feelings. But the music for voices in the epic is indeed the main characteristic of the epic singing. At first it might be that the language and tone are highly exaggerated, like an emphasis in recital, and that there is even only one phrase. The peculiarity of singing in this manner is that, no matter how the tone changes, the basic structural pattern of the tone of *Gesar* cannot be made prominent, that means that "glu a la lha mo a la len, glu tha la la lha mo tha la len" plays a role (Ma Chengfu, "On the Analysis of Music Tones of the *Gesar* Epic," *Tibetan Art Studies* 4 (2002): 30-31).

4
Conclusion

Let us return to our initial question. By raising this issue, my intention was to obtain a simple answer by means of surveying Tibetan documentation and reality. However, while consulting many tangled historical documents and a variety of religious biases concerning the "origins and development" of the epic, I have found that this issue involves many other relevant topics. Many issues have been covered up by the already-fabricated beautiful "myths", and even our contemporaries are unwilling to unveil the already unfolding reality and truth. Take for example the pluralistic origin of the Tibetan culture. It is directly related to our previous debate on the Tibetan origin. One hypothesis advances that Tibetans came from the north: Tibetans originated in the ethnic group of Qiang. Another says that Tibetans came from the south: they have their roots in India. The widely recognized hypothesis insists that the area of Yar Klung be the birthplace of Tibetans. These hypotheses, and even historical records, are mixed with all kinds of feelings that have nothing to do with academic research or objective facts. Likewise, regarding the issue of the origin of the Tibetan culture, there are also obviously fabricated beautiful 'myths that monkeys are the ancestors of the six ethnic groups'.[1] The so-called four or six ethnic groups argued for in documents of later periods did not necessarily emerge during the Tubo period and it is even possible that they emerged in the 9th to the 12th century, during the cultural rebuilding from division to reunification.[2] Implicitly, this points to the pluralistic origin of the Tibetan culture. How can the Tibetan culture of the whole

---

[1]   Sa Skya Bsod Nams Rgyal Mtshan, *Rgyal rabs gsal bavi me long* [*King-Lineage of Ancient Tibet*: *The Bright Mirror*], Beijing: Nationalities Publishing House, 1982: 49-54.

[2]   The practice to turn traditional clans into families may find its counterpart in the origin of the four castes in India, as in the story "The Fairy Gautama" (Wei Ran ed., "The Fairy Gautama," *A Buddhist Story with Illustrations*, Chengdu: Sichuan Literature and Art publishing House, 2001: 9-11).

Tibet Plateau be covered if only the Yar Klung valley is regarded as the historical starting point of the Tibetan culture? I think that we should study closely the Dun Huang records, take documents of later periods (those of the Bon and Buddhism) as our references, and combine Chinese documentations and records of other ethnic groups, especially myths and legends of the ethnic groups that have emigrated from the Tibet Plateau, and archaeological findings in order to understand the sources of the Tibetan culture and its early cultural history on the Tibet Plateau.

As to the question why the *Gesar* epic is not sung in the Yar Klung area, many scholars, particularly those who base their analysis on Tibetan documents, contend that this is a valueless or even naive issue. In many cases, the reason why they stick to this position is, that they do not seem to be very eager to shatter religious beliefs and the various "myths" fashioned by the Yar Klung's Rgyal Rabs. In my opinion, this borders on narrow nationalism. For instance, the *Gesar* academic circles take an extremely negative stance towards the argument by R. A. Stein that the name "*Gesar*" comes from the outside.[1] In fact, we have not found any good reason yet to refute this argument. Their unwillingness simply results from certain nationalistic sentiments, or even from the narrow vision of some scholars themselves.

Proceeding from the Tibetan records, it seems that the name "*Gesar*" might come from Caesar of Fulin[2] and a comparison of historical records shows that there is some similarity between the two. Or, Ling *Gesar* was *Gesar* Dmag Gi Rgyal Po[3] or Khrom *Gesar*.[4] This is not impossible, because historical records show that the Ldong clan was living in the northern part of Tibet. According to

---

[1] See R. A. Stein, *Studies on the Epic and the Bard in Tibet* [French], Paris: French University Presses, 1959.

[2] Fulin: the East Roman Empire.

[3] Gesar Dmag Gi Rgyal Po: a king famous for his mighty army.

[4] Khrom is a place or city-state mentioned in Tibetan historical records. According to some scholars like R. A. Stein, Khrom might be Rome.

Chinese documentations, the Dangxiang people occupied a vast area as far as to Yehu in the west and were descendants of Sanmiao. The Zing Po Rje in the upper reaches of the Lhasa River fled to Dru Gu in the north after their defeat, and in many cases, the names Dru Gu and Khrom refer to the same place – the northern part of Tibet. Documents of later periods even talk about the Ldong as a different ethnic group. All this seems to suggest that this *Gesar* Dmag Gi Rgyal Po or Khrom *Gesar* is the later Ling *Gesar*. [①] The Dangxiang were originally a different group that was capable of fighting against the Yar Klung tribe on the Tibet Plateau or in the area including Xinjiang, but later the rising Yar Klung tribe conquered them. The Dangxiang people's eastbound migration led to the change of the name of their habitat and of their ethnic group, "Khrom" thus changed into "Ling". Linguistically speaking, "Khrom" denotes "market" in colloquial Amdo, but more often "stud ram". According to some surveys, ram heads were worshipped in the many early frescos in Kuche (Qiuci) in Xinjiang and in today's Tibetan areas in Amdo and Khams Pa. Even in the Dbus Gtsang area, ram heads are regarded as auspicious decorations. [②] In addition, yak heads are also very popular decorations in these areas. It is therefore possible that the powerful *Gesar* Dmag Gi Rgyal Po tribe in the northern part had blood relations with the Ldong clan, or even with Ling *Gesar*.

Proceeding from the issue that the epic is not sung among the Yar Klung tribe, we tend to draw a conclusion that the Ldong clan in the epic was a powerful nomadic tribe living in the north, based on the sketches of the early history or legends of the Ldong clan as recorded in the epic. The Ldong clan was once conquered by and at the disposal of the southern Yar Klung tribe with a developed agriculture. The Ldong tribe might have been the first ethnic group that spread and sang the epic if the epic had not been reworked and distorted by scholars and ballad singers. The tribe constituted a source of the ancient epic in its earliest

---

① R. A. Stein, *Ancient Tribes along the Sichuan, Gansu and Tibet Corridor*, translated by Geng Sheng, Chengdu: Sichuan Minzu Publishing House, 1992: 53-54.

② Nor Bu Rgya Mtsho, *A New Linguistical Exploration*, Beijing: Minzu Publishing House, 2002: 45-46.

form. The thesis of some scholars (both traditional and modern) that the epic came into being during the 11th century is perhaps based on the fact that the main structure of the epic took shape then. It is plausible that this was a big cooperative compilating activity of traditional scholars (religious followers) and epic singers, comparable to the compilation of the Greek and Indian epics. Therefore, in the 11th century, the whole framework and the main structure of the epic were established and its contents permeated into the "major legacy"[①] or the entire legacy of the whole Tibetan region. The epic began to be widely disseminated with a certain missionary zeal ever since. But the formation of the epic must have taken a very long time. The main structure also went through a long formation period lasting from the 9th to at least the 12th century. But one thing is certain: Present studies show that the epic prevailed first in the eastern part of Tibet and that only later it was gradually spread in all other directions.

In addition, we have also examined the characteristics of the Tibetan singing tradition and detected that the singing tradition in the nomadic area to the north of the Yar Klung valley is different in nature from that recorded in the Dun Huang documents and even from that in the Yar Klung area of later periods. We have found that the singing in the Yar Klung area of later periods clearly had inherited the singing characteristics of the Tubo dynasty recorded in the Dun Huang documents as regards the folk songs of the *gzhas* style prevailing in the southern part and other relevant singing traditions. Many singing traditions with the *glu*-style folk songs as a main form are popular in the northern part including Mdo Smad and Mdo Khams. The *Gesar* epic is representative of this tradition. The singing traditions are marked by the distinctive cultural characteristics of other tribes, particularly of nomadic tribes. Therefore, we venture to say that the differences between the two singing traditions have limited to a certain degree the spread of the singing form of the epic to the south. Other forms of transmission

---

①   Engels said that Homeric epics are the main legacy that the Greeks have brought from the barbarous to the civilized age. See Friedrich Engels, *The Origin of the Family*, *Private Property and the State*, Beijing: People's Publishing House: 1972: 24.

and dissemination of the epic are clearly discernible in the southern part of Tibet. Similar examples can be found in the Amdo area where the epic is popular. In the agricultural area of Amdo, and especially in the bordering areas where different ethnic groups concentrate, the talking form of the epic is to be heard more often.[1]

The form of the epic's transmission, or the form of cultural spreading, then, is more restricted than the spreading of its content. Our argument springs from our survey of the areas and forms of the *Gesar* epic's spreading in the Tibetan region.

References:

Bai Bin. *Studies of the History of Dangxiang*. Changchung: Jilin Education Publishing House, 1989.

Blo Gros Rgya Mtsho. *Legends of the Traces of 'Gesar'* [Tibetan]. Lhasa: Tibet Minzu Publishing House, 1994.

Damdinsuren, Tsendiin. *The Historical Roots of the 'Gesar' Epic* [Russian]. Moscow: Academy of Science of the USSR, 1957.

_____. *A Study of the Tibetan Epic and Ballad Singers* [French]. Paris: French University Presses, 1959.

David-Neel, Alexandra and Lama Yongden. *A Record of Super Hero Gesar from Gling*. Edited by Yang Yuanfang. Translated into Chinese by Chen Zongxiang. Beijing: Institute of Nationality Studies, Southwestern Institute of Nationalities, 1984.

Also published as: *La vie surhumaine de Guésar de Ling, le héros thibétain, racontée par les bardes de son pays*. Paris: Adyar, 1931.

The Superhuman Life of Gesar *of Ling, the Legendary Tibetan Hero, as sung by the bards of his country*. London: Rider, 1931.

Don Grub Rgyal. *Origin and Development of Admonitory Poems*. Beijing: Minzu Publishing House, 1985.

Dpav Lo. "New Exploration of the Early Location of the Ling State and Other Relevant His-

---

[1] Xu Guoqiong, *On-the-spot Investigation Report on 'Gesar'*, Kunming: Yunnan People's Publishing House, 1989: 60.

torical Issues." *Tibetan Studies Apr*. 1999: 59-68.

Dpav Wo Gtsug Lag Vphreng Wa. *A New Feast for Wise Men*. Beijing: Minzu Publishing House, 1986.

Engels, Friedrich. *The Origin of the Family*, *Private Property and the State*. Beijing: People's Publishing House, 1972.

Originally published as: *Der Ursprung der Familie*, *des Privateigenthums und des Staats*: *im Anschluss an Lewis H. Morgan's Forschungen*. Zürich-Hottingen: Schweizerische Genossenschaftsbuchdruckerei, 1884.

English translation: *The Origin of the Family*, *Private Property and the State*. Translated by Ernest Untermann. Chicago, C.H. Kerr & Co., 1910.

Francke, A.H. *A Lower Ladakhi Verion of the 'Kesar' Saga*. Translated by Peng Gonghou in *The Monthly Journal of the Society of Studying Khams-pa and Tibet* 4-16 (1947-1948).

Originally published as: A Lower Ladakhi Verion of the 'Kesar' Saga. Calcutta: Royal Asiatic Society of Bengal, 1905.

Gcod Pa Don Grub and Rta Mgrin. *A Fresh Look at 'Gesar'* [Tibetan]. Xining: Qinghai Nationality Publishing House, 1995.

Helffer, Mireille. "A Study of the Songs in *Biography of the Tibetan King Gesar – The Chapter of Horse-Racing*." Zhao Bingli, ed. *A Collection of Papers on* Gesarology. 5 Vols. Lanzhou: Gansu Nationalities Publishing House, 1990-1998: V 3556.

Huang Jingtao. "Introduction to *Gesar 4 – A Battle between Hor and Ling*." *The Biography of King Gesar: The War between Hor and Ling*. Shanghai: Shanghai Literature and Art Publishing House, 1962: 4.

Jiangbian Jiacuo. *A Primary Exploration of Gesar*. Xining: Qinghai People's Publishing House, 1986.

Karmay, Samten G.. "*Gesar*: The Epic Tradition of the Tibetan People." *The Arrow and the Spindle*: *Studies in History*, *Myths and Beliefs in Tibet*. Kathmandu: Mandala Book Point, 1998: 465-471.

Khomonov, M.P. *The Buryat Heroic Epic 'Geser'*. Edited by the Institute of Literature Research of IMASS. Translated by Has. Huhhot: Inner Mongolian Academy of Social Sciences, 1986.

Originally published as: *Buryatsky geroichesky êpos 'Geser'*: *Ekhirit-bulagatsky variant*. U-lan-Ude: Buryatskoe knizhnoe izdatel'stvo, 1976.

Kozin, S.A. *The 'Geser' Epic: Story about the Gracious Geser Mergen-Khan* [Russian].
  Moscow: Academy of Sciences of the USSR, 1935.

———. *The Epic of the Mongolian People* [Russian]. Moscow: Academy of Sciences of the
  USSR, 1948.

Li Lianrong. "Summary of the Symposium on the *Gesar* Epic in the Tibet Region." *China'
  s Tibet* 4 (2002): 15-17.

Li Yanshou [Tang Dynasty]. *Beishi* [*Annals of the Northern Dynasties*]. 10 Vols. Beijing:
  Zhonghua Book Company, 1974.

Liu Zhiqun. *Tibetan Opera and Tibetan Folklore*. Lhasa: Tibet People's Publishing House;
  Shijiazhuang: Hebei Juvenile Publishing House, 1999.

Macdonald, Ariane. *An Examination and Explanation of the Dun Huang Historical Document on Tubo*. Translated by Geng Sheng. Xining: Qinghai People's Publishing
  House, 1991.

Originally published as: *Essai sur la formation et l'emploi des mythes politiques dans la religion royale de Sron-bcan Sgam-po*. Paris: Librairie d'Amérique et d'Orient, 1971.

Ma Chengfu. "On the Analysis of Music Tones of the *Gesar* Epic." *Tibetan Art Studies* 4
  (2002): 30-31.

Nam Mkhavi Nor Bu. *Ancient Tibetan History*. Chengdu: Sichuan Minzu Publishing House,
  1990.

Nekliudov, S. Yu. *The Heroic Epic of the Mongolian People*. Translated by Xu Changhan,
  Gao Wenfeng and Zhang Zizhi. Huhhot: Inner Mongolian People's Publishing House,
  1991.

Originally published as: *Geroichesky èpos mongol' skich narodov: Ustnye i literaturnye
  tradicii*. Moskva: Glavnaja redakcija Vostochnoj literatury, 1984.

Nor Bu Rgya Mtsho. *A New Linguistical Exploration*. Beijing: Minzu Publishing House,
  2002.

Organizing Committee of *A Collection of Chinese Ballads – The Tibetan Volume*. *A Collection
  of Chinese Ballads – The Tibetan Volume*. Beijing: China ISBN Center, 2001.

Ouyang Xiu and Song Qi [Song Dynasty]. *Xin Tang Shu. Xi Yu Shang. Dang Xiang*.
  Beijing: Zhonghua Book Company, 1975.

Propp, Vladimir. *Theory and History of Folklore*. Minneapolis: Minnesota Press, 1993.

Ren Naiqiang. "A Brief Introduction to Gesar." *A Public Opinion of Frontier Politics* 4, 5,
  and 6 (1994). Quoted from *Collected Papers on Gesar Studies*. Edited by Jiangbian Ji-

acuo. Chengdu: Sichuan Nationalities Publishing House, 1986: 1-13.

Rnam Rgyal. "The Origin of the Gesar Epic and Its Historical Connotation." *Tibetan Studies Feb*. 2001: 27-39.

_____. "To Adhere to Historical Materialism and to Deepen Studies of *Gesar*". *Tibetan Studies Apr*. 2002: 5-9.

Samuel, Geoffrey. "The *Gesar* Epic of East Tibet." José Ignacio Cabezón and Roger R. Jackson, eds. *Tibetan Literature*: *Studies in Genre*. Ithaca, New York: Snow Lion, 1996: 358-367.

Sa Skya Bsod Nams Rgyal Mtshan. *Rgyal rabs gsal bavi me long* [*King-Lineage of Ancient Tibet*: *The Bright Mirror*]. Beijing: Nationalities Publishing House, 1982.

Spen Rdor. "On the Historical Evolution and the Artistic Characteristics of the Talking-and-Singing Music of the Tibetan Heroic Epic *Gesar*." *On Contemporary Tibetan Music*. Lhasa: Tibetan People's Publishing House, 1993: 373-389.

_____. "On the Musical Art of the *Gesar* Epic." *Tibetan Studies* 4 (2002): 25-30.

Stein, R. A. *Studies of Epics and Ballad Singers in Tibet*. Lhasa: Tibet People's Publishing House, 1993.

Originally published as: *Recherches sur l'épopée et le barde au Tibet*. Paris: Presses universitaires de France, 1959.

_____. *Ancient Tribes Along the Sichuan*, *Gansu and Tibet Corridor*. Translated by Geng Sheng. Chengdu: Sichuan Minzu Publishing House, 1992.

Originally published as: *Les tribus anciennes des marches sino-tibétaines*: *légendes*, *classifications et histoire*. Paris: Presses universitaires de France, 1961.

_____. *Studies of Epics and Ballad Singers in Tibet*. Lhasa: Tibet People's Publishing House, 1993.

Thomas, F. W. "The End of Glorious Times, the Tragedy between Horses and Yaks." Translated by Li Youyi and Wang Qingshan. *Folk Literature from Northeast Tibet*. Chengdu: Sichuan Nationalities Publishing House, 1989: 17-34.

Tshong Kha Dbyang Grub Sgam Po. "Relations between Sum Pa and Tubo and other Neighboring Regimes." *Tibetan Studies* 3 (1992): 51.

Tshe Dbang Vgyur Med. "The Rescue Work of the Tibetan *Gesar* and A Prospective Research Summary." *Tibetan Studies* 4 (2002): 1-4.

Wang Yao and Chen Jian, trans. *Dunhuang Tubo Lishi Wenshu* [*The Tubo Historical Texts in Dunhuang*]. Revised and enlarged version. Beijing: Minzu Publishing House,

1992.

Wang Yinuan. "The Tibetan *Gesar* Epic." *Journal of the Central College of Nationalities* 2 (1979). Quoted from Zhao Bingli, ed. *A Collection of Papers on Gesarology*. 5 Vols. Lanzhou: Gansu Minzu Publishing House, 1990-1998: I 338-343.

Wei Ran, ed. "The Fairy Gautama." *A Buddhist Story with Illustrations*, Chengdu: Sichuan Literature and Art Publishing House, 2001: 9-11.

Wei Zheng and Linghu De [Tang Dynasty]. *Suishu* [*Annals of the Sui Dynasty*]. 6 Vols. Beijing: Zhonghua Book Company, 1973.

Xie Jisheng. "The Southeastward Movement of the Area of Spread of the *Gesar* Epic and a Preliminary Exploration of the Causes." *Gesar Studies*. 6 Vols. Beijing: China Folk Literary and Art Publishing House, 1988: III 339-351.

Xu Guoqiong. *On-the-Spot Investigation Report on 'Gesar'*. Kunming: Yunnan People's Publishing House, 1989.

_____."The Tibetan Epic *Biography of Gesar*." *Literary Review* 6 (1959). Quoted from *Collected Works on Gesar Studies*. Edited by Jiangbian Jiacuo. Chengdu: Sichuan Nationalities Publishing House, 1986: 32-47.

Yang Enhong. "On the Spread of *Biography of King Gesar*." *Studies of Ethnic Literature* 5 and following issues (1989).

_____. *Folk God of Poetry*: *A Study on the Ballad Singers of 'Gesar'*. Beijing: China Tibetology Publishing House, 1995.

Yuan Jian. "It has been decided by experts and scholars that east Tibet is the birthplace of the epic." *New Chinese Network*, 10 July 2002.

Zhol Khang Bsod Names Dar Rgyas. *A Brief History of Tibetan Music* [Tibetan]. Lhasa: Tibet People's Publishing House, 1992.

IV

Mongolian *Geser* and Tibetan *Gesar*.
A Comparative Study of Three Texts

Zhalagaa

Abstract: The texts of the epics *Geser / Gesar*, [①] popular among the Mongolian and Tibetan ethnic groups, share a common origin and subject matter, but their independent values cannot be negated for this reason. This paper attempts to make a comparative study of three typical texts: the Tibetan (*Guide Chapter-based*) *Gesar*, the Mongolian (*Beijing Version*) *Geser* and the Mongolian (*Pajie Version*) Geser, to further explore the cultural connotations of epics in our search for particular national spirits and aesthetic ideals embodied in epics originating from different ethnic groups.

Key words: epic *Geser / Gesar*, Mongolian and Tibetan cultures, comparative study

This research project on the relationship between the Mongolian *Geser* and the Tibetan *Gesar* merits attention in studies of literary relations among various ethnic groups in China. *Geser* and *Gesar* not only have the same heroes but also the same basic narrative frameworks. This means that the two epics stem from the same origin. The transmission processes of *Geser* and *Gesar* have reflected long-standing historical, literary and cultural relations between the Mongolian and Tibetan ethnic groups.

---

① The Mongolian epic *Geser* and the Tibetan epic *Gesar* are put together as *Geser / Gesar* or *Gesar / Gesar*.

The texts of the epics *Geser* and *Gesar*, popular in the Mongolian and Tibetan cultures, share a common origin and the same subject matter, but their independent values cannot be negated for that matter. The epic is a mirror of national spirits of a particular ethnic group. Epics, in whatever form or however similar in subject matter, embody specific cultural connotations of a particular ethnic group once they have been created or recreated by folk artists and intellectuals from that ethnic group; what they extol is the national spirits of their ethnic group. The similarities in the epics' heroes and narrative frameworks are just superficial phenomena when compared with the national spirits as manifest in the epics. It is the cultural connotations of the epics underlying the surface that demonstrate the national spirits and aesthetic ideals embodied in.the epics of various ethnic groups.

This paper attempts to make a comparative study of the Mongolian *Geser* and the Tibetan *Gesar* on the basis of three representative texts, i. e. the Tibetan *Guide Manuscript with Separate Chapters for Biography of King Gesar* (*Guide Chapter-based ' Gesar'*), the Mongolian *Beijing Block Print Version for Biography of Geser* (*Beijing Version ' Geser'*) and the Mongolian *Pajie Version ' Geser'*.[1] The Tibetan *Guide Chapter-based ' Gesar'* is a hand-written copy and it is so named because it was first found in Guide, Qinghai Province. The whole book consists of five chapters. The famous late Tibetologist Wang Yinuan said: 'The Yellow sect of Lamaism of Tibet is mentioned many times in the original chapter-based text, and therefore this book might have been completed after the Yellow sect of Lamaism was established in the 15th century.'[2] The Mongolian *Beijing Version ' Geser'*, also called *Biography of Geser Khan*, was block printed and published in Beijing in 1716. Consisting of seven chapters, it is the first

---

[1]   In different sources the titles of the above three *Geser/Geser* texts may differ from our usage. In this research I stick to the names *Guide Chapter-based ' Gesar'*, *Beijing Version ' Geser'* and *Pajie Version ' Geser'*.

[2]   Wang Yinuan and Hua Jia, trans., Preface by the translators of *Biography of Gesar* (*Guide Manuscript with Separate Chapters*), Lanzhou: Gansu People's Publishing House, 1981: 3.

printed text of *Geser* discovered so far and it is of special significance in the transmission history of *Geser*. Pajie was a well-known Mongolian oral artist in the 20th century. The *Geser* he used to sing occupies an important place in the history of the development of Mongolian epics and can also be regarded as a representative version of the talking-and-singing texts of the Mongolian *Geser*. Pajie was an extremely gifted master of language. When performing *Geser*, he told and sang long narrative stories called "the Mongolian version of stories" (bensen ülger[①]), such as *Shuo Tang Wu Zhuan*, *Heroes of the Marshes* and *The Romance of the Three Kingdoms*.[②]

1

An important characteristic of the Tibetan *Gesar* is that the dialogues the heroes exchange often adopt the form of singing when stories are being told. Proceeding from present scholarship on *Gesar*, this is an outcome of the influence of dramas, and thus called the 'dramatic tendency of epics' talking-and-singing'.[③] This dramatic tendency finds echo in the Guide *Chapter-based 'Gesar'*. With view to a few other Chinese translations of the Tibetan Gesar, we find that the

---

① *Bensen ülger* (text tales) are a variety of *huurchi*. The *Huur* (*huqin*) is a four stringed instrument popular among the Mongolian. A *hurchi* is a *huqin* player. *Huurchin ülger* denotes all kinds of stories narrated by the artist, who tells a story while playing the *huur* with changeable melodic sounds. *Huurchi ülger* mainly comprises stories based on real life in Inner Mongolia. *Bensen ülger*, in its original sense, should also include the original stories in Chinese, popular in Mongolian areas. Many masters of *bensen ülger* know Chinese and the stories they sing often come directly from the Chinese originals. Having said that, however, for most artists, the original copies they rely on are bensen *ülger* in Mongolian.

② The three works to be compared here are the following editions: the Tibetan *Guide Chapter-based 'Gesar'* (*Biography of Gesar*) has as the written text (master copy) for comparison *Biography of Gesar* (*Guide Sub-section*), translated by Wang Yinuan and Hua Jia with the first edition published in 1981; the Mongolian *Beijing Version 'Geser'* has as master copy *Arban jug-un ejen Geser hagan-u tuguji* [*Biography of the Holy King Geser Khan of Ten Directions of Space*], first edition published in 1993; *the Pajie Version 'Geser* has as master copy the collated copy of Dorunga, first edition published in 1989.

③ Yang Enhong, *Folk God of Poetry*: *A Study on the Ballad Singers of 'Gesar'*, Beijing: China Tibetology Publishing House, 1995.

form of prose, rather than verse, is normally used when stories are being told.

The Mongolian Geser can be divided into three styles. First, prose is the most commonly used style, whereas verse is seldom used in the *Beijing Version 'Geser'*. Nevertheless, verse is dominant, and there is basically no prose narration in the *Pajie Version 'Geser'* and the Buryat Abay Geser – the two other versions of the text. Third, the combination of prose and verse is applied, for example in *Jamling sengchin-u namtar* (Biography of the Great King of Lion in the Southern Continent). In comparison, written texts mostly adopt the prose style, while in oral performance artists often make use of verse or a combined prose and verse style. During *Geser* performances by Mongolian oral artists, the dialogues between heroes are often presented in verse. Moreover, when talking and singing verse-style dialogues, artists are inclined to show off their talent in singing. However, this verse presentation is sung by the artist, but not by the characters of the epic; the presentation per se does not embody any intrinsic dramatic element. The tradition of dialogues in the verse form has a very long history in Mongolian literature. As early as the 13th century, verse was already used skillfully to represent dialogues between heroes in the great work *Secret History of Mongolia*. When narrating stories of *Geser*, Mongolian artists often use prose. Meanwhile, these artists often insert congratulations and hymns as well as proverbs into the singing and talking of the text. Better aesthetic effects are achieved by means of verse. The above-mentioned stylistic differences are of great significance in the various Mongolian Geser versions, e.g. the Mongolian *Jamling sengchin-u namtar* (Biography of the Great King of Lion in the Southern Continent)[1] still adopts the style of combined prose and verse, which is similar to the Tibetan text: Prose is used when stories are told and verse is mostly used in the dialogues between the heroes. Furthermore, dialogues between heroes in the verse form are also called "singing" in the Mongolian *Jamling sengchin-u namtar* (Biography of the Great King of Lion in the Southern Continent). This seemingly simple appellation shows that this copy originates from a translation of the Ti-

---

[1]   *Jamling sengchin-u namtar* [*Biography of the Great King of Lion in the Southern Continent*] [Mongolian], edited and annotated by U. Shinebayar, Huhhot: Inner Mongolian Science and Technology Publishing House, 1988.

betan *Gesar* epic.

The *Beijing Version* ' *Geser* ' takes the prose style, and the *Pajie Version* ' *Geser* ' the verse style, in contradistinction to the combined prose and verse style of the Tibetan *Guide Chapter-based* ' *Gesar* '.

As to oral transmission, the Mongolian *Geser* and the Tibetan *Gesar* have their own characteristics. The Mongolian *Geser* has been transmitted mainly through the teachings of masters to their disciples. All artists have their own masters. They learn from them basic skills needed for performance, including playing musical instruments, learning to sing tunes, studying synopses of different stories and a great quantity of formulas to improvise and expand the synopses into epic narratives. The oral transmission process of the Tibetan *Gesar* is quite different. Tibetan artists usually do not have their own masters. They obtain epic talking and singing skills on their own through a long exposure to the broad cultural contexts where epic talking-and-singing has emerged and evolved. By their own accounts, artists are divided into five types in the light of their different ways of acquiring performance skills, namely, "charismatic" artists, *Thos-sgrung* artists, *gTer-'don* artists, *Don-sgrung* artists and *pra-phab* artists. *Thos-sgrung* means "listening" or "hearing" in Tibetan. *Thos-sgrung* artists listen to others telling the story and are then able to tell it themselves. *gTer-'don* in Tibetan means "one who digs for the story of *Gesar*". *gTer-'don* artists are bards who dig out hidden teachings or treasures. In Tibetan *Don-sgrung* means "to chant". *Don-sgrung* artists, or artists "inspired to chant", have two characteristics: First, they are literate and able to chant from a book; second, their vocal abilities are fairly good and their chanting is magnificent. *Pra-phab* is a Bon technical term in Tibetan. When sorcerers are subduing gods or working divination, they are able to see good or ill luck by looking into a bronze mirror. The entire process is referred to as "circular light." This particular method came to be used by artists telling the epic. Standing before the audience, the narrator places a bronze mirror on a pile of fragrant eucalyptus, and, after reading scripture and praying, begins to sing facing the bronze mirror. It is said that he can see all the exploits of Gesar in this mirror. The *pra-pha* artists, or artists by "circular light", often say that they themselves do not understand Gesar at all, but are able to sing his story to the audience from the contents revealed to them in the mirror. If they do not have the bronze mirror to gaze into, they cannot tell any part of the story. However, if another person looks into it, all he or she will see is his or her own reflection. People explain this by maintaining that it is not their "predestination"; only those who are "fated" are able to view King Gesar's exploits in the bronze mirror.

Data available at this stage have confirmed that southeast Qinghai and northeast Tibet is the original center for the talking and singing of the Tibetan *Gesar*. The center for the talking and singing of the Mongolian *Geser* was located in the three east leagues of the Qing dynasty, i.e. Jirim league, Juud league and Jusad league. Utter differences in the performance tradition and in the form of transmission, plus the far distance between the centers of *Geser* and *Gesar* of the two ethnic groups, make us believe that it was impossible for artists from these two ethnic groups to establish direct and extensive exchanges between the various talking-and-singing forms of the epics, that is, the ontological form of epics. As far as the epics of *Geser* and *Gesar* are concerned, the links between the two ethnic groups must have been mainly established through the written epic texts, that is, the non-ontological form of epics.

2

Instead of making a comprehensive comparison of the above-mentioned three texts, this paper will focus on the story of the engagement between Geser (Gesar) and Rogmo Gova (called Zhumao in Wang Yinuan's translation). I will limit myself to a few selected examples so as to reach a preliminary understanding of the relations and differences between the two epics. My first step is to compare the *Guide Chapter-based 'Gesar'* and the *Beijing Version 'Geser'*. My second step is to compare the *Beijing Version 'Geser'* and the *Pajie Version 'Geser'*.

To begin with, here is a synopsis of the story of the *Guide Chapter-based 'Gesar'*: Skay Lo Sdon Pa, a headman, had three daughters who had been engaged to the three kings Stag-gzig-nor-rdzong, Ba-Da-Hor-gyi and Gru-gu-gyuri-rgyal-po respectively. One day, the three girls went to Gro-mavi-mtso in the gLing area to dig fern. When crossing a river, they were stopped by Te Pe Rdag Galng lying on the little bridge. This Te Pe Rdag Galng was the incarnation of Gesar. At that time he was still a poor child and he had just received this piece of Gro-mavi-mtso from his uncles. To cross the river, the three girls first offered him the buttered barley flavor (*rTsam-Pa*) they brought, but he did not let them cross. The three girls had to go to the river hand-in-hand. Te Pe Rdag Galng threw a stone into the river and the water swelled up to the waist of the girls. At the request of the younger sisters, Zhumao, the eldest girl, proposed to give to Te Pe Rdag Galng the gem on her head and asked Te Pe Rdag Galng to let them go. Te Pe Rdag Galng threw another stone into the river, and the water swelled up to their neck. The girls were neither able to advance nor to retreat. At the request of the younger sisters, Zhumao proposed to marry herself to Te Pe Rdag Galng for his consent to let them cross the river. Only then Te Pe Rdag Galng agreed.

The parents of the three girls were very angry when they learned that their eldest daughter married herself to the poor Te Pe Rdag Galng. Zhumao did not regret though. Her mother said: 'You married yourself off on the way without permission. You chose walnut peel instead of walnut kernel. You, silly girl, have ruined your happy fate.' Zhumao replied: 'I married myself at my free will on the way. I have chosen walnut kernel but not walnut peel. I, Skay Lo Sdon Pa, will have good fortune.' When Stag-gzig-nor-rdzong came to welcome the bride, Zhumao had just one request: she asked him to drink a gourd ladle of wine without touching it with his fingers, tongue, lips or teeth. Stag-gzig-nor-rdzong failed to do so, but Te Pe Rdag Galng succeeded. Zhumao brought Te Pe Rdag Galng home on the back of her horse. Te Pe Rdag Galng tore his boots into pieces that night and pretended having been swallowed by a wolf. He left Zhumao's house

and revealed his true identity in the company of many heavenly troops and generals. Zhumao woke up only to find that her husband had been eaten by a wolf and
was persuaded by her mother to become a nun in a temple. Gesar ordered his
subordinates to bring Zhumao back after he was enthroned.

The following is the corresponding story in the *Beijing Version* ' *Geser* ': At
that time, Rogmo Gova, daughter of Sengeslu Khan, was old enough to be married, but she still had not found a good Hubilgan[①] husband. She summoned
three excellent arrow-shooters, three smart wrestlers, a sage lama and many followers. She learnt that there were thirty Hubilgan heroes in Töbed and thought
that there would be some good men among them. She ordered that a gathering of
ten thousand people be organized and so it happened. Ju-ru, the incarnation of
Geser, came to the gathering. On the way, Ju-ru on foot asked his uncle
Chotong on horseback to let him sit on the hip of the horse, but was rejected.
When the ten thousand people got together, Rogmo Gova stood up and said:
'When I was born, a rhinoceros was rejoicing on the right eaves, and a deer was
rejoicing on the left. There was sunshine even without the sun, and rainfall even
without clouds... The goddess that fulfills these nine auspiciousnesses is me,
Rogmo Gova.' She then introduced the wrestlers and arrow-shooters she had
brought along, and said that she would marry the one who could defeat them.
None of the thirty Hubilgan heroes could defeat the warriors coming with Rogmo
Gova. Ju-ru stood up at that time, and proposed to have a try. The lama with
Rogmo Gova said: 'None of the thirty Hubilgan heroes could win and how can
you?' The lama, however, agreed at the request of Ju-ru. Ju-ru threw away the
first wrestler a thousand times farther than the reach of eyesight, threw away the
second wrestler two thousand times farther than the reach of eyesight and threw
away the third wrestler three thousand times farther than the reach of eyesight.

---

①   *Hubligan* is transliterated from the Tibetan word *sprua-sku* (the Living Buddha reincarnation system).
Originally, *hubilgan* referred to the rank of the reincarnation of Living Buddhas in Mongolian areas.
Later, the word was used in governmental documents of the Qing dynasty concerning the reincarnation
system for the Living Buddhas.

Later, he won in the arrow-shooting contest. Looking at Ju-ru with a running nose, Rogmo Gova got very sick and put forward a new term: She would marry the man who could grasp the ribs of seventy sheep with one hand and a wine jar with the other and distribute the ribs and wine to everyone present in the twinkle of her turning around. No one succeeded, and Ju-ru wanted to try. Rogmo Gova disgusted the running nose of Ju-ru, but agreed to let him have a try given the fact that those present insisted. Ju-ru completed all the requirements in the split second when she turned around. Rogmo Gova wanted to repudiate the marriage and escaped with her followers. While she was fleeing, she asked her people to see if Ju-ru was following them and they saw nothing. When she was about to re-laxe, her followers said: 'Ah, he is on the hip of your horse.'

When she came home, her parents also complained that she had brought home such a son-in-law. Her father took a whip to graze the horses, her brother took his bow and arrows to herd the sheep, her mother went out with anger and all servants expressed their dissatisfaction. Ju-ru said many fine words. The parents came home in the evening, got angry with Rogmo Gova and kept Ju-ru under a wok. Ju-ru walked out of the wok during the night and killed a sheep. After he had finished eating, he gave the leftovers to the dogs. He covered his leather coat with sheep blood and lay down in the field. In the morning, Rogmo Gova's parents saw him and said: 'Your good husband was eaten by dogs and you will bear future disasters.' Rogmo Gova felt very sad and thought: 'How sinful I am and I don't even know if he is alive.' She went out to look for Ju-ru who had then turned into the shape of a horse herdsman. Rogmo Gova asked him whether he had seen Ju-ru. The answer of the horse herdsman was negative. He also said that he had learned that people of the Ling State were coming for revenge when they were told that the Rogmo Gova family had fed Ju-ru to dogs by. Rogmo Go-va walked and cried and then she met Ju-ru who had turned into a shepherd. The shepherd repeated what the horse herdsman had said. Rogmo Gova thought that she had got into big trouble, and she would rather die now than be condemned to death by her parents. She let go her horse and ran towards a river. She felt somebody was holding the horse's tail. Looking back, Rogmo Gova saw that it was Ju-ru with a running nose. Ju-ru got onto the back of the horse together with Rogmo Gova, but disgusted by his snivel, Rogmo Gova asked him to ride the horse facing the rear. Ju-ru had to walk on foot. He was kicked down by the running horse and pretended to have died. Rogmo Gova asked him to stand up and Ju-ru said that he could not ride the horse facing the rear. Rogmo Gova a-greed to let him ride the horse facing the front. When they got home, Rogmo Go-va's maternal uncle and aunt also came. They said: 'Our niece is a goddess and we wonder what a husband she has got.' Rogmo Gova's parents brought Ju-ru a bowl of fried wheat, and then hid him. But when learning that people were talking about him, Ju-ru came out with a running nose and put some wheat on his snivel. Rogmo Gova's maternal uncle and aunt were very angry to see him and went away with the horses. Ju-ru seized back the horses. A few days later, Ju-ru told Rogmo Gova that he would go back. When going out, he turned him-self into the sons of Chontong Noyan and Badmarag and came back to sound out on Rogmo Gova. Rogmo Gova tacitly agreed to marry them if they should kill Ju-ru. Ju-ru criticized her for being disloyal to him. On the third day, Ju-ru changed into the thirty brave warriors of Töbed and, waving swords and spears, asked Rogmo Gova's father if he would marry his daughter to Ju-ru. Being afraid of the thirty warriors, the father not only agreed to marry his daughter to Ju-ru, but also moved the whole family to Töbed.

The above two paragraphs are the respective outlines of the story that Gesar/Geser married Rogmo Gova in the *Guide Chapter-based 'Gesar'* and the *Beijing Version 'Geser'*. So much space is devoted here to describe the same story from the two epics for the sake of comparison. In fact, even those who have not read the original texts can get some initial impression of the differences and common points between the two epics.

3

A comparison between the corresponding stories in the *Guide Chapter-based* '*Gesar*' *and the Beijing Version* '*Geser*' may shed light on some similarities as well as on some substantial differences.

First, the names of the main heroes are the same, and the narrative frameworks and the settings are identical, all exemplary of the links. The common ground of the large narrative frameworks includes the following points. First, the stories tell about the marriage between Geser/Gesar and Rogmo Gova/Zhumao. Second, the parents are not happy with the daughter's marriage proposal. Third, the marriage finally materializes with Geser's/Gesar's efforts.

However, there are more dissimilarities than similarities. First, the motives of the two stories are not the same. In the *Guide Chapter-based* '*Gesar*', the direct motif of the story is not the issue of marriage, but of Zhumao and her sisters' confrontation with Gesar when crossing the river. In the *Beijing Version* '*Geser*', however, the direct cause of the story is that Rogmo Gova wanted to select a husband.

Second, in the *Guide Chapter-based* '*Gesar*', Zhumao was forced to agree to marry Gesar, in order to save the lives of her sisters. Her sisters would not have asked her to marry Gesar if the river water had not swelled up to their necks. And Zhumao, who had already been engaged with Stag-gzig-nor-rdzong, would not have proposed to marry the poor Gesar. In the *Beijing Version* '*Geser*', there is no such plot as the one featuring in the *Guide Chapter-based* '*Gesar*'. In the *Beijing Version* '*Geser*' too, Rogmo Gova was forced to marry Geser, but she had not been engaged with another man. To find an ideal husband, she had her concrete requirements. She was forced to marry Geser precisely because the latter won the wrestling and the arrow-shooting contest and fulfilled all the terms she had put forward. The difference in this episode discloses a profound cultural content. Wrestling, arrowshooting and horseraces are three time-honored traditional men's games in Mongolian culture. It is common that a man wins a girl's love and her hand in marriage by being victorious in the wrestling and arrow-shooting contest.

Third, in the *Beijing Version 'Geser'*, after getting home, Zhumao argued with her mother in an antiphonal style whether she should be married to Gesar. Stag-gzig-nor-rdzong and others led a congregation of ten thousand people and horses to greet her as the bride, but Zhumao cleverly refused Stag-gzig-nor-rdzong. Instead, Zhumao brought Gesar home enthusiastically, and received him warmly. The *Beijing Version 'Geser'* contains plots absent from the *Guide Chapter-based 'Gesar'*. For instance, Rogmo Gova put forward conditions for selecting a husband on her own, took to the road with her arrow-shooters and introduced herself to the crowd before the start of the contest. Geser's uncle Chotong also wanted to take part in the contest. Geser appeared before Rogmo Gova with a running nose, and Rogmo Gova wanted to escape the marriage after Geser won the contest; Rogmo Gova's maternal uncle and aunt came to inspect the husband of their niece. Geser put Rogmo Gova to the test twice and so on.

Fourth, the aforesaid corresponding episodes also reveal differences in terms of representations of the characters. In the *Guide Chapter-based 'Gesar'*, Zhumao is depicted as a virtuous and kindhearted woman, as manifest in the aforesaid plot. She could sacrifice herself to save her sisters. At the request of her sisters, she asked Gesar to let them cross the river in exchange of her clothes, her jewelry and even herself. She did not despise the poor nor favor the rich when choosing a husband. She was persistent in love. She kept her promise when her mother criticized her for having married herself to the poor Gesar. When Stag-gzig-nor-rdzong came to greet the bride, she raised conditions that the former could not fulfill, thus turning down the marriage arranged by her parents. Finally she brought Gesar home.

In the *Beijing Version 'Geser'*, Rogmo Gova is depicted as a heroine of exceptional ability, as in the parallel plot above. Rogmo Gova was the daughter of a Khan and nine good signs manifested themselves at her birth. To marry an ideal husband, she did not wait for parental arrangement, but traveled around with three wrestlers and arrow-shooters in her search for an invincible hero. Her speech before the contest started off reflects her outstanding bearing and charm.

The above-mentioned parallel plots reveal that Rogmo Gova and Zhumao were apparently not of the same type. Zhumao was reserved, self-contented, but could be disobedient in given circumstances. Rogmo Gova was not very loyal to Geser, and failed to pass Geser's two tests. These are signs, which foreshadows later developments of the relevant plots. In the sixth chapter of the *Beijing Version* 'Geser', Mangus (a demon) turned into a Hubilgan lama who came to kill Geser. Rogmo Gova was tempted by the jewelry of Mangus, betrayed Geser and helped Mangus to change Geser into a donkey.[①]

In the *Beijing Version* 'Geser', the image of Geser is depicted with personal characteristics different from that of Gesar in the *Guide Chapter-based* 'Gesar'. Geser in the *Beijing Version* 'Geser' is depicted as humorous and amusing. He always had a running nose, constituting the main reason why Rogmo Gova disliked him. When Rogmo Gova rode the horse and fled, Geser sat on the hip of the horse, quiet and composed. When Rogmo Gova's maternal uncle and aunt came to see him, he did not hide himself as required, but instead came out and put some fried wheat on his snivel. When he was covered under a wok by his parents-in-law, he ran out during the night, killed and ate a sheep and pretend-

---

① Prof. Wang Yinuan explores the relations between the Mongolian *Geser* and Tibetan *Gesar* through a comparison of the differences and similarities between the *Mongolian Beijing Version* 'Biography of King Geser' and the *Guide Chapter-based* 'Gesar' in "After Reading the *Mongolian Beijing Block Print Version for* 'Biography of Geser.'" He remarks: 'The first chapter of the *Beijing Block Print Version for* 'Biography of King Geser' includes the main plots of the first three chapters of the Guide Text, ... that Geser killed the magic tiger in the north in the second chapter of the *Beijing Block Print Version for* 'Biography of King Geser' cannot be found in the Guide Text or Ladak Text. ... In the sixth chapter of the *Beijing Block Print Version for* 'Biography of King Geser', Geser was turned into a donkey by the demon in the disguise of a lama and such a plot is absent from the Tibetan text.' (Wang Yinuan, "After Reading the *Mongolian Beijing Block Print Version for* 'Biography of Geser,'" *Folk Literature Forum* 2 (1982): 15-19. The paper was later republished in Zhao Bingli, ed. *A Collection of Papers on Gesarology*. 5 Vols. Lanzhou: Gansu Minzu Publishing House, 1990-1998: II 1097-1098).

ed having been devoured by dogs. When Rogmo Gova found him and asked him to go home with her, he pretended having been kicked to death by the horse and laid on the ground just because he was not allowed to ride the horse... All these sketches work to visualize Gesar's humorous and funny disposition.

A further comparison of other plots may reveal many more discrepancies. Let us take two more examples. First, the episode in which Geser/Gesar decided to descend to the world from Heaven. In the *Guide Chapter-based 'Gesar'*, Gesar was the youngest son of the God of Heaven and a contest among the three princes decided that he should be the one to descend to the world. In the *Beijing Version 'Geser'*, Geser was the second son of the God of Heaven and was asked to descend to the world because he was the better arrow-shooter and wrestler. Amin-sahigchi ("Life Cherisher" or "Self-Defender"), the eldest son of the God of Heaven, first recommended his younger brother Uilbotgchi ("Successful Accomplisher"), which was the original name of Geser in Heaven, saying:

I do not mean to speak evil of my younger brother, but Uilbotgchi is able to accomplish all things successfully. At the Nadam fair in Brahma attended by seventeen gods, a contest in arrowshooting and wrestling was held and no one could defeat this Uilbotgchi. He is the most capable. Here, at the Nadam fair with thirty-three gods participating, no one could defeat him in arrowshooting and wrestling. In the world of man as well as in the sea where Nadam fairs were also organized by various dragon kings, still no one could win him. Uilbotgchi has acquired all kinds of abilities. How can we escape our [mission] of descending to the world only because we are the sons of Heaven! [①]

So, before the Nadam fair held by Rogmo Gova, Geser was said to have taken

---

① *Arban jug-un ejen Geser hagan-u tuguji* [*Biography of the Holy King Geser Khan of Ten Directions of Space*], Huhhot: Inner Mongolian People's Publishing House, 1993: 4.

part four times at Nadam fairs, two in Heaven, one in the sea and one in the world of man. In the eyes of the author of the *Beijing Version* 'Geser', Nadam, a favorite entertainment of the Mongolian people, is omnipresent in Heaven, on the land and in the sea. Such a profound love for Nadam springs, of course, from the cultural psychology of the Mongolian ethnic group. The Nadam and the plot of wrestling and arrow-shooting contests constructed in the *Beijing Version* 'Geser' reflect Mongolian cultural elements on the one hand, and echo the plot that Geser was good at arrow-shooting and wrestling upon his descent to the human world on the other hand. His previous performance in Heaven laid ground for Geser's later victory in the wrestling and arrow-shooting contest in the plot of fighting to obtain Rogmo Gova as a bride.

Second, the fact that Geser is constructed as the second son of the God of Heaven in the *Beijing Version* 'Geser'-vis-à-vis Gesar as the youngest son in the *Guide Chapter-based* 'Gesar' – is related to the literary tradition as it has developed in Mongolian culture. In ancient Mongolian practice, the youngest son had the right of succession. To put it differently, the right of property inheritance resided with the youngest son called *Otchigin*. In *Secret History of Mongolia*, when Genghis Khan executed enfeoffment (i. e. investing the nobility with hereditary titles, territories, and other property) he attached special importance to the *Otchigin* of his brothers and the *Otchigin* of his sons. Under the influence of other ethnic groups, the eldest son came into inheritance in some areas. In the *Beijing Version* 'Geser', if the God of Heaven wanted to send one of his three sons to the world, he should send the eldest or the second son in accordance with the older Mongolian tradition, and the second or the third son according to newer customs. When the envoy of the God of Heaven asked for the opinion of Uilbotgchi, i.e. Geser, he remarked:

Am I not a son of the God of Heaven? I am not a living being in the world of man. I cannot be seated on the emperor's throne, which should belong to my elder brother Aminsahigchi! As for those younger than me, there is

Teguschogtu and what has the whole matter to do with me![1]

Here, Uilbotgchi/Geser, who had elder and younger brothers, had bitter complaints about his own position in the family. This shows that the author of the epic has taken into account the tradition of family relations of the Mongolian ethnic group. The dispatch of the second son Uilbotgchi (i.e. the later Geser) is a desirable comprise between the older and the newer social customs.

All these examples illustrate there are similarities in terms of the basic narrative framework, alongside the significant differences in cultural connotations, in the ways how things are handled and in the character of the heroes, if we compare the *Beijing Version 'Geser'* and the Guide Chapter-based 'Gesar. These differences demonstrate that both the *Guide Chapter-based 'Gesar'* and the *Beijing Version 'Geser'* are works embodying the attributes of the literary and cultural traditions to which they belong.

4

The *Pajie Version 'Geser'* includes thirteen chapters. In terms of the origin of the plot, the first seven chapters come from the *Beijing Version 'Geser'* while the last six chapters come from the *Longfusi Version 'Geser'*. Concerning the story in which Rogmo Gova and Geser became husband and wife, the *Pajie Version 'Geser'* subsumes three sections, namely the twenty-second, twenty-third and twenty-fourth sections of the first chapter. The titles are *Asking Rogmo Gova to Be his Wife*, *Rogmo Gova Makes a Fool of Herself* and *Testing the Mood of Rogmo Gova* respectively. The three sections have about 1,900 verse lines. The *Pajie Version 'Geser'* originates from the *Beijing Version 'Geser'*, but there are slight variations. For example, singers omitted the part that Rogmo Gova told about the nine auspicious signs at her birth and added direct praises of her beau-

---

① Ibid. 3.

ty. As far as other plots are concerned, there are almost no changes, and this makes it difficult to detect differences between the talking-and- singing transcripts of the artists and the original written texts, on the basis of the synopses. I attempt here to extract and translate some episodes as concrete examples for the sake of comparison:

The golden world, / huge and vast. / The masses, / diverse and many. / Chotong's feast is over, / lama Choristung is gone. / The story I am going to tell, / will start elsewhere. / In the hometown of the hero Ju-ru, / to the west and north, / there are people from a small state, / living happily and calmly. / The King is called Sengeslu, / the Queen is Badmarag. / The King and the Queen / have a lovely daughter. / She excels all girls, / she is a true fairy maiden. / She is rare in the golden world, / she is said to be the reincarnation of Guanyin [Avalokiteśvara]. / She is rare in the universe and man's world, / she is the reincarnation of Handima. / Father and mother / call her Rogmo Gova. / The appearance of this girl / can be briefed here: Her beautiful and mellow face / turns pale ten thousand suns. / Her dignified and gentle disposition / can melt iron and steel. / Her delicate and pretty looks / turn pale hundred thousand suns. / Her elegant and earnest heart / can melt metal and stone. / Everyone likes her when they see her, / old people have compassion for her. / Children like her when they see her, / boys love her when they see her. / Truly virtuous and capable, / such a good girl.

This girl has grown up to / the age to fathom the future. / She does not obey her father, / she does not follow her mother's will. / She now will marry: whoever can defeat those three wrestlers, / can outdo those three arrow-shooters, / whoever can be settled on by the aged lama, / handsome and virtuous, / strong, brave and clever, / a man of good fortune. / She wants to entrust herself to him, / she wants to be his wife. / The young

Rogmo Gova / now for that purpose is leading her father's Sengesluna, / world famous, / three great wrestlers, / three smart arrow-shooters, / under the protection of the omniscient, / senior lama, / as well as all maids, / many servants, / and luggage and tents, / and going on a long journey.

All states and areas nearby, / have been visited, / wherever they go and live, / contests and jubilant feasts are held. / The man they search for / has not been found. / Even a fairy maiden is helpless, / and ceaseless walking in this way will defame! / The delicate child Rogmo Gova has no ideas and becomes downhearted, / and embarks on the way for her hometown. / But as to that kind of things, / who knows how strange. / On the way, / they meet some travelers, / as the old saying puts: 'The persons one meets on the way, / have a hundred days lot'. / They are talking about / how busy they run about, / and so on, / one traveler says: 'I learnt that, / to the east, / ten or five days away, / there is the location of three tribes, / and there are thirty heroes. / Their superb capability and strength, / in the universe, / are truly rare. / Your three outstanding wrestlers, / and three smart arrow-shooters / go to the hometown of the three tribes, / and have a contest with the thirty heroes, / isn't it possible?' / The teller goes away unbothered, / the listener is left puzzled. / The lovely Rogmo Gova / says when hearing this: 'Let's go now.' / The goal of the journey is not the hometown, / walking towards the east. / Ten or nine days are not long, / they have come to the living quarters of the three tribes. / Coming to the surrounding area of the three tribes, / the pretty Rogmo Gova looks into the distance: between the vast and beautiful grassland, / there are many magnificent yurts. / The beautiful pastureland is really fertile! / Five kinds of animal groups are scattered on the grassland. / Brave warriors and heroes shuttle back and forth, / all kinds of weapons are shining. / Songs of happy reunions are melodious. / Here is the rejoicing and happy place! / The sage lama is struck dumbfounded, /

the three smart arrow-shooters are greatly amazed, / the three rash wrestlers are in admiration, / immediately set a camp on the river bank. / The girl Rogmo Gova looks into the distance untiringly, / with waves roaring at the bottom of her heart. / She has come here with the desire to look for a husband, / and she wants to issue a public notice among the people. / The traveler from afar stays here, / everybody knows this the next morning. / A few young people from that tribe they met yesterday, / come to inquire about the traveler in the morning. / They get the incantation of the Buddha A-ti-sha[①] from the old lama, / run away when they learn about the purpose of the girl. / Doesn't the talking of many people run faster? / Isn't it novel that a husband is to be selected through men's skills? / In two days' time before the third day comes, / a stir has been effected among the people at the hometown of the three tribes.[②]

This is the beginning of the story of how Rogmo Gova selected her husband through a wrestling and arrow-shooting contest in the *Pajie Version 'Geser'*. It consists of verses, in both story-telling and dialogues between heroes. Verse can be considered stylistically characteristic of the epic. There are about 40.000 verse lines in total in the *Pajie Version 'Geser'*; it is quite challenging to represent so long an epic all in verse. Its style can be traced back to the same origin as that of traditional Mongolian heroic epics. This shows, on the one hand, the language talent of individual singers, and, on the other hand, that in the long process of transmission, the epic has been repeatedly refined through continuous efforts of various generations of artists.

The above long extract from the *Pajie Version 'Geser'* corresponds to the following paragraph in the *Beijing Version 'Geser'*:

---

① A-ti-sha (Atiśa, 982-1055) was a Buddhist scholar at Vikramashila University in India. His Buddhist monastic name is Dipamkaraśrijñāna. He came to Tibet at the invitation of the king to overcome the damage done by Langdama and helped found the Kadam traditon.

② *Pajie Version 'Geser'*, edited by Dorunga, Beijing: Minzu Publishing House, 1989: 205-210.

At that time, Rogmo Gova, daughter of Sengeslu Khan, reached the right age to marry, but she had not found a reincarnated person for a good husband. Therefore, she summoned three smart arrow-shooters, three superb wrestlers, a sage lama and many attendants. She had learnt that there were thirty reincarnated heroes in Töbed and thought that there must be some eligible men, and thus came here with her people. She announced that a gathering of ten thousand people were to be held. And ten thousand people were gathered together. [①]

The above quotation from the *Pajie Version 'Geser'* contains 138 verse lines in total, whereas the Chinese translation of the corresponding plot in the *Beijing Version 'Geser'* has only 128 characters. The difference in the length of the two texts is significant. It can be said that it mirrors the major difference between the written text and the orally transmitted epic.

The sung text of the artists' performance is much more enlarged than the master copy, for the following reasons. First, talking and singing has filled in many gaps of the written text with enriched details. A comparison of the two texts reveals that there are many additional details in the oral sung text. For instance, in the *Beijing Version 'Geser'*, there are no such details as the group's encounter with travelers and their turning away from homeward to the direction of Töbed under the strangers' guidance. Meanwhile, in the Beijing Version 'Geser', there are no such details as the travelers traveling 'all the states and areas nearby' before going to Töbed. The addition of these details works to enrich the contents of the story and reform the dull synopsis, elegant and imposing but void of daily flavors and legendary colors. The artist used verse lines to describe the abundance and beauty of the locality when Rogmo Gova and her followers reached the three

---

① *Arban jug-un ejen Geser hagan-u tuguji* [*Biography of the Holy King Geser Khan of Ten Directions of Space*], Huhhot: Inner Mongolian People's Publishing House, 1993: 51.

tribes of Töbed as well as their amazement at the sight of the local scenery. These accounts not only expand the scope of the story, but are also indirect compliments to the hometown of the artist, i.e. the Mongolian grassland. For example, when Rogmo Gova and her followers came to the three tribes of Töbed, the local young people whom they had met on the previous day paid them a visit next morning; this plot is an addition. Young people of all times are most active and most readily receptive to new things and new people. Logically, then, the young people of the three tribes of Töbed first greeted these outsiders. The Mongolian grassland, vast in area and sparse in population, was hospitable to guests. The young people met the guests on the previous day and rushed to approach them again next morning, which is reminiscent of the hospitality of the local people. Artists are good at tapping into day-to-day life for details to be added to epic narratives. These added details in the *Pajie Version* ' *Geser* ' can also be regarded as the artists' unique understanding and interpretation of the epic. This understanding and interpretation of the details finds echo in the Mongolian culture and tradition that have fostered these artists, as well as in the artists' artistic insight into life and in their gifted talent.

Second, commendatory, metaphoric and adjective verse lines are added. For instance, in the written text in the *Beijing Version* ' *Geser* ', there is no such a plot as to describe the appearance and manners of Rogmo Gova. But when the artist talks and sings, about twenty lines are added to eulogize the extraordinary beautiful and graceful manners of Rogmo Gova. The artist employs many adjectives and metaphors to depict her charming appearance and graceful manners, such as ' the reincarnation of Guanyin [Avalokiteśvara]', ' turns pale the sun', ' melt metal and stone' and so on, thus leaving a deep impression on the audience. And, for another example, when talking about Rogmo Gova's search for a husband, adjective phrases such as ' extraordinarily handsome', ' vigorously healthy' and ' with good fortune' are used.

Third, the use of repetition is another key reason why the scope of the epic has undergone expansion. For instance, when describing the looks of Rogmo Gova, the artist is not satisfied with the phrase 'turn pale ten thousand suns', and then adds that her beautiful appearance 'turns pale hundred thousand suns'. When talking about the temperament of Rogmo Gova, expressions such as 'can melt iron and steel' and 'can melt metal and stone' are used. These are redundant metaphors. These redundant metaphoric verse lines can enhance the presentational effect, but do not add to the content. For example, the metaphors like 'the reincarnation of Avalokitesvara [Guanyin]' and 'the reincarnation of Handima' employed to represent Rogmo Gova's appearance and manners are similar in content, and can thus be seen as redundant figures of speech. Redundant repetition can hardly produce any aesthetic effect in written prose. However, when the artist performs, in verse, with fluctuating moods and the accompaniment of melodious songs and musical instruments, an entirely different feeling is naturally aroused. This is the fundamental difference between the appreciation of an epic's oral performance and the reading of a written text. It is up to individual readers' creative reading to actualize written epics' aesthetic effect. Nevertheless, the uniformed written text turns into a piece of cubic art with multi-dimensional aesthetic effects in the process of appreciating an artist's talking and singing of the epic. For an excellent artist, the written epic only provides him with a format, the one that gathers together all kinds of relevant information he has hitherto inherited. What he sings and talks manifests the true art of what is called "epics".

It is characteristic of Mongolian epics to repeat certain age-old formulas with or without variations, in accordance with the already established aesthetic patterns. These formulas include the audience's aesthetic psychological model, namely its unique ways of understanding certain things. As an art emerging in an oral culture, epics can be understood and accepted by a particular audience group only if they fit in with their aesthetic psychological model. The verse lines considered redundant by contemporary people often constitute what most clearly reflects the early features of epics.

We can see from the above comparison that, first and foremost, the major links between the Mongolian heroic epic *Geser* and the Tibetan *Gesar* are based on the written texts. Within the scope of the oral talking and singing activities, the epics from the two ethnic groups have been evolving on their own in the specific historical contexts and in line with the specific literary and artistic traditions to which they belong. Second, there are parallels and similarities between the *Guide Chapter-based 'Gesar'* and *the Beijing Version 'Geser'* in the light of the narrative framework, although there are many substantial differences. Third, in the process of transformation from the *Beijing Version 'Geser'* to the *Pajie Version 'Geser'*, the epic *'Geser'* has likewise undergone qualitative changes both in artistic form and in aesthetic ideals.

Therefore, comparisons between the written texts, between the written text and artists' oral sung texts, and between the epics' contents or between their artistic forms all show that there are not only inseparable links between the Mongolian *Geser* and the Tibetan *Gesar* but also fundamental differences resulting from different ethnic cultures with distinctive characteristics. It is tempting to regard them as the same work or as different branches of the same work, with respect to the basic narrative framework or to the narrative origin. However, they are not identical works when viewed from the perspective of cultural tradition, aesthetic connotations, and the styles of talking and singing the epics. Such an insight not only conforms to the true picture of the epics but also reflects the brilliance, grandeur and richness of the *Geser/Gesar* epics as a whole.

References:

Arban jug-un ejen Geser hagan-u tuguji [*Biography of the Holy King Geser Khan of Ten Directions of Space*]. Huhhot: Inner Mongolian People's Publishing House, 1993.

Jamling sengchin-u namtar [*Biography of the Great King of Lion in the Southern Continent*] [Mongolian]. Edited and annotated by U. Shinebayar. Huhhot: Inner Mongolian Science and Technology Publishing House, 1988.

Pajie Version 'Geser'. Edited by Dorunga. Beijing: Minzu Publishing House, 1989.

Wang Yinuan. "After Reading the *Mongolian Beijing Block Print Version for 'Biography of Geser.'*" *Folk Literature Forum* 2 (1982): 15-19; and Zhao Bingli, ed. *A Collection of Papers on Gesarology*. 5 Vols. Lanzhou: Gansu Minzu Publishing House, 1990-1998: II 1097-1098.

——and Hua Jia, trans. Preface by the translators of *Biography of Gesar* (*Guide Manuscript with Separate Chapters*). Langzhou: Gansu People's Publishing House, 1981.

——trans. *Biography of Gesar* (*Guide Manuscript with Separate Chapters*). Lanzhou: Gansu People's Publishing House, 1981.

Yang Enhong. *Folk God of Poetry*: *A Study on the Ballad Singers of 'Gesar'*. Beijing: China Tibetology Publishing House, 1995.

V

The Tyva Kezer and Legend of Genghis Khan's Punitive Expedition Against Tangut[①]

Siqinbatu

Abstract: The world famous *Geser* epic (*Gesar* in Tibet) originated among the Mongolian and Tibetan ethnic people and thereafter has spread to various Chinese ethnic groups and foreign nations. No doubt, the stories of Geser that have spread overseas from their places of origin have taken root, flourished and formed different ideologies and artistic features in the particular cultural and historical contexts of these countries, thus taking on unique value in *Geser* studies.

Keywords: Tyva *Kezer*, Mongolian *Geser*, legend of Genghis Khan's Punitive Expedition Against Tangut, intercultural comparative research

1

During my stay at the State University of Mongolia as a senior visiting scholar from September 2002 to February 2003, I obtained by luck a version of The *Biography of Geser* (*Achiti Kezer-Mergen*) based on folk stories from the Tyva Republic in the Russian Federation. There are close ties between the Tyva *Kezer* and the Mongolian *Geser*. Nonetheless, there are many differences between them. This is particularly the case with Chapter Nine of the written version I used, which has no parallel story in the Mongolian Geser. The present paper

---

① The Tyva call Geser (Gesar) Kezer.

conducts a comparison between *Achiti Kezer-Mergen Khan*, *the Son of the God Kurbustu in the Tyva Kezer* and the legend of Genghis Khan's Punitive Expedition Against Tangut as recorded in Mongolian historical documents. The paper comes to the conclusion that the Mongolian *Geser* was spread to Tyva and became the Tyva *Kezer* some three hundred years ago, which was possible as a result of the historically induced close ties in politics, economy and culture between Tyva and Mongolia. The route by which the legend of Genghis Khan traveled and turned into the Tyva *Kezer* was possibly as follows: there was a separate legend, or perhaps an epic, of Genghis Khan who conquered Tangut in the past. The story or the epic once spread widely in both Tyva and Mongolia. On the Mongolian part, historians took up the story in historical documents by in the 17th century, while in Tyva, it spread orally and gradually mingled into the *Kezer* epic.

The world famous epic *Geser* (*Gesar* in Tibet) that originated among Mongolian and Tibetan ethnic groups has spread not only to other Chinese ethnic groups but also to countries like Mongolia, Afghanistan, Pakistan, the Russian Federation and others. It has become an important part of the spiritual legacies of these countries. No doubt, the stories of *Geser* that have spread overseas from their places of origin have taken root, flourished and formed different ideologies and artistic features in the particular cultural and historical contexts of these countries, thus taking on unique value in Geser studies.

During my stay at the State University of Mongolia as a senior visiting scholar from September 2002 to February 2003, I obtained by luck a version of *The Biography of Geser* (*Achiti Kezer-Mergen Khan*)[1] *which is based on folk stories from the Tyva Republic of the Russian Federation. Considering that few people in China, within or outside academic circles, know the Tyva Kezer, I translated* it into Mongolian. The book is composed of nine chapters. The first, the fifth, the seventh and the eighth chapters were all narrated in 1953 by Bayan-Balbyr, a famous epic artist in Toju (Tyva Republic, Russian Federation). Ondar-Dan-

[1] Edited and annotated by D.S. Kuular, Kyzyl: Tyva Publishing House, 1963.

dar, a famous artist in Chöön-Khemchik narrated chapter six in 1961 and the well-known local actor Tülüsh-Baazanggai from Ulug-Khem told chapter nine in 1951. The nine chapters are:

Chapter One   Achiti Kezer-Mergen Descends to this World

Chapter Two   Achiti Kezer-Mergen Defeats Monster Mangus Black Tiger in the North

Chapter Three   Achiti Kezer-Mergen Goes to Kidat to Persuade Kümbe Khan

Chapter Four   Achiti Kezer-Mergen Defeats Twelve-Headed Manggys Orunzaa

Chapter Five   Three Khans: Shara-Kherti, Sagaan-Kherti and Kara-Kherti in Shara-Khöl

Chapter Six   Achiti Kezer-Mergen Eliminates Fifteen-Headed Lang-Dolba Khan

Chapter Seven   Achiti Kezer-Mergen Cracks down on Adygyr-Kara Manggys

Chapter Eight   Achiti Kezer-Mergen Goes to the Residence of Hades Erlik-Lovung Khan to Save His Own Mother

Chapter Nine   Achiti Kezer-Mergen Khan, Son of the God Kurbustu

It is said that all Tyva epic artists believe that the stories about Kezer Khan they tell come originally from the Mongolians. Some of the artists narrate *Kezer* in the form of prose, some sing it in poetry and others hold a Mongolian copy in their hand and translate it to the audience.[1] It is evident that there is a close relationship between the Tyva *Kezer* and the Mongolian *Geser*. Nonetheless, I located many differences between them when I translated the Tyva Kezer. They manifest themselves in different plots of the same stories and in varying degrees of complexity of the same plot leading to completely different stories. This is particularly the case with Chapter Nine, i.e., the story narrated by Tülüsh-Baazanggai from Ulug-Khem in 1951, which has no correspondence in the Mongolian *Geser*.

---

[1] D.S. Kuular, *Achiti Kezer-Mergen*, Kyzyl: Tyva Publishing House, 1963: 10.

Its main plot reminded me of a legend about Genghis Khan. I will leave large-scale comparative research to the future, and will confine myself here to a comparison between *Achiti Kezer-Mergen Khan*, *Son of the God Kurbustu* in the Tyva *Kezer* and the legend of Genghis Khan's Punitive Expedition Against Tangut.

The historical figure Genghis Khan is sometimes identified with the epic personage Geser in Geser studies. S.A. Kozin, a famous Russian scholar in Mongolian studies, suggests that the hero Jangar in the *Jangar* epic of the Mongolian Oyrat, the hero Geser in the *Geser* epic and the historical figure Genghis Khan in *Secret History of Mongolia* are all the same person. He believed that *Secret History of Mongolia* is a long narrative poem about Genghis Khan. In the later half of the 14th century, the narrative legend should have developed into an epic, but the process let up for a time because of the fast disintegration of the empire and the expansion of Buddhist power in Mongolia. The evolving epic of Genghis Khan became the *Geser* epic in east Mongolia and *Jangar* in the west of the country.[1] This line of argument was subjected to strong criticism from the academic world, which Kozin accepted. I mention this fact here just to clarify that my line of research is different from his. I do not attempt to prove that the whole *Kezer* epic is about the history of Genghis Khan, but only to elucidate that there are parallels in motifs and plots between one *Kezer* story and the legend of Genghis Khan's punitive expedition against Tangut recorded in Mongolian historical documents.

2

Frankly speaking, the Tyva *Kezer* under scrutiny is not a story with outstanding artistic characteristics; it looks rather simple and rudimentary in terms of plots. But it is this simple and rudimentary story that provides us with a very significant subject for research. To give the reader an idea of the story and for clarity's sake

---

[1] S.A. Kozin, *The Epic of the Mongolian People*. Moscow: Academy of Sciences of the USSR, 1948: 194, 244, 246 and S. Yu. Nekliudov, *Epics of the Mongolian People*, translated by Xu Changhan, Gao Wenfeng and Zhang Zizhi. Huhhot: Inner Mongolian University Publishing House, 1991: 32-34.

in the comparative studies to come, I will first sketch the synopses of *Achiti Kez-er-Mergen Khan*, *Son of the God Kurbustu*, as told by Tülüsh-Baazanggai: Achiti Kezer-Mergen, son of the god Kurbustu issues an order to the whole country, forbidding people to smoke and drink. But soon afterwards, his country suffers from unprecedented drought. Rivers dry up, leaving not even a blade of grass or any livestock on the land intact, and all properties are gone. One day, Kezer runs into an old man when he goes hunting in a place where there is plenty of water and fresh pasture grounds with more than sixty goats. Kezer asks him which Khan's subject he is. The old man says he is a subject of Achiti Kezer-Mergen. Then Kezer asks why the place is not affected by the drought, but, instead, has plenty of water and lush pasture. The old man tells him this is because he secretly does not stop smoking and drinking for a single day. On hearing this, Kezer announces to abate the prohibition of smoking and drinking. As expected, it is effective. Since then, his country has favorable weather for crops, and his people live and work in peace and happiness. Kezer appoints the old man as a minister and asks him to handle affairs that his three hundred thirty-six ministers failed to handle for three years. The old man spends only three hours settling them down.

One day Kezer Khan goes hunting with the old man. Seeing fresh blood of games gushing out onto the snow into beautiful patterns, he asks the old man whether there is a beauty with snow-white skin and blood-red cheeks. The old man confirms this and tells him that the beauty Tongulak Sagaan Kadyn lives in the West under the rule of Khögdüüle Khan. Kezer then inquires about the Khan's strength and will. The old man says neither his strength nor his will is dreadful. But the Khan has seven red dogs that can foretell the enemy's trace from afar and will attack and kill the enemy. Kezer decides to loot the beauty and sets out with his three hundred thirty-six ministers and the old man. When they halt in a place on the way, Kezer looks around for a long time, extolling: 'The rich living here enjoy themselves to the full and the poor who can bury their corpses here also enjoy themselves to the full. It is really a fertile and beautiful place. '

All the ministers follow suits, but the old man keeps silent. When they arrive at Khögdüüle Khan's territory, the seven red dogs discover Kezer Khan from afar and pounce at him. Kezer Khan destroys all of them, occupies Khögdüüle Khan's palace, kills him in spite of his imploring and captures his wife. On their way back, Kezer Khan and his people are stationed at the place they have praised on their way to Tongulak-Sagaan Kadyn. At night, Kezer tries to make love with Khögdüüle Khan's wife. Unexpectedly, she cuts off his whole penis with a pair of scissors, and then kills him. The subjects of Khögdüüle Khan and Kezer Khan return to their own homes. The three elder sisters of Kezer Khan come and sprinkle sacred water on their younger brother's corpse. Kezer Khan comes back to live, saying: 'How come I have slept so soundly?'

Admiring the old man's wisdom, he confers on him the name Saryyl Ugaan ("Wise Man") and asks him to inspect the country to find out what is lacking. Saryyl Ugaan finds out that nothing is lacking except the Kangyr-Baazyn trees (trees symbolizing good fortune). Kezer Khan orders to plant these trees and his people enjoy a happier life each day as the trees grow up.

The story can be divided into three parts with three different subjects. Part one tells of how Kezer Khan issues a prohibition on smoking and drinking and terminates it afterwards. The second part tells of how Kezer Khan conquers Khögdüüle Khan, captures his wife, is killed by her, and comes back to life again. The third one tells of how Kezer Khan orders to plant Kangyr-Baazyn trees and makes his people live and work in peace and happiness.

The story has two distinctive characteristics. First, it is quite unique and novel. Although the Tyva *Kezer* originates from the Mongolian *Geser*, this story does not exist in any of the known ancient and modern written or oral Mongolian versions of *Geser*, including the ones of the Oyrat and Buryat. Second, in the story, the image of the wise old man seems more outstanding than that of Kezer Khan. Nonetheless, the excellent achievements of Kezer Khan function as links of the narrative chain, which is also one of the story's characteristics. However, the second part of the story, i. e. Kezer conquers Khögdüüle Khan and takes hold of the latter's wife, constitutes the main thread of the narrative.

The following points lie at the core of the story:

1. Someone recommends Khögdüüle Khan's wife to Kezer Khan, saying her beauty is matchless and advising Kezer Khan to capture her.
2. Khögdüüle Khan has seven red dogs with the ability of foretelling the enemy's trace from afar and attacking and killing the enemy.
3. Kezer Khan halts on the way and praises the place.
4. Kezer Khan kills Khögdüüle Khan in spite of his imploring and seizes his wife.
5. On the way back home, Khögdüüle Khan's wife Tongalak-Sagaan Kadyn cuts off Kezer Khan's penis with a pair of scissors.
6. Kezer Khan is killed at the place that he has admired and extolled.

The plot, i. e the old man's recommendation of Khögdüüle Khan's wife as a matchless beauty and his suggestion that Kezer Khan should go and get her, initiates later narrative development. To seize the beauty is the only reason for Kezer Khan to launch a war.

3

Now, let us examine the Mongolian story similar to the aforesaid one, that is, the legend of how Genghis Khan conquers Tangut (the Western Xia regime from 1038 to 1227), as recorded in Mongolian historical documents. The story is not identical in the various documents, and so there are many editions of the story per se. In order to expose the reader to the similarities between these editions and the Tyva story, I first introduce the edition that is the closest to the Tyva one, and then give a sketch of other editions. This layout is meant to display the characteristics of the spreading and mutation of the legends about Genghis Khan in different periods.

In Mongolian historical documents, the story most similar to the Tyva Kezer first appeared in *Compendium of Mongolian Golden History* by an anonymous writer and later in Lubsandanjin's *Mongolian Golden History*, Sagang Sechen's *Origin of Mongolia*, *History of Ancient Mongolian Khans' Origin*, *History of Asaragchi*, *The Golden Wheel with Thousand of Spokes*, *Crystal Mirror* and many other Mongolian historical documents. The following is the story *from Compendium of Mongolian Golden History*.

His Majesty, emperor Genghis Khan of the Mongolians, conquers Han territory and takes over the throne of the Jin ruler. On hearing the news, Sidurgu Khan of Tangut is scared and sends Dordung, son of Bayan Sardager, as an envoy and swears 'To be your right flank and pay tribute to you.' After he presents the memorial to his Majesty and is about to leave, Dordung says: 'Your Majesty is the son of Heaven, your empress excels ours. She is brilliant even in the evening without candle light.'[1] Dordung departs after having said this. It so happens that his Majesty has chosen Yabug-a's wife Mungulun Khow-a of the Taichigut tribe as his imperial concubine.

On hearing Dordung's remarks, Yabug-a reports to the emperor: 'Compared to my wife Mungulun Khow-a, Lady Khurbeljin Khow-a, the imperial concubine of Sidurgu Khan of Tangut and the daughter of a Han sage Zhang Jiani, is more brilliant, for she even does not need a candle to show her brilliance. Why don't you, your Majesty, take her as your imperial concubine?' Thus, his Majesty sends an envoy to Sidurgu Khan, declaring: 'I'll go on a punitive expedition against Sartagul Irgen [nations, mainly muslim, in Central Asia], you must dispatch troops!' Sidurgu Khan, however, says: 'How can you proclaim yourself a Khan since you have not taken possession of all territories; why do you still need

---

[1] There is an inaccuracy in the original Mongolian here. In other Mongolian documents it is: 'Your Majesty is the son of Heaven, but your empress is not as good as ours.'

assistance if you have proclaimed yourself a Khan?' He refuses to dispatch troops. On hearing this, his Majesty swears: 'I'll give up my precious life rather than let you go!'...[1] He then gives order to go on the punitive expedition against Tangut.

Sidurgu Khan's black-mouthed-and-yellow-haired dog can predict omens. If it barks peacefully and calmly, there will be no enemy; its yapping indicates there are enemies. His Majesty sets up battle flags and banners and sets out for a three-year-long expedition. Knowing his Majesty has gone on the expedition, the dog yaps for three years. 'My dog is old, for there is no sign of an enemy,' says Sidurgu Khan, not at all on alert.

His Majesty sets out with Yisui Khadun on the punitive expedition. Seeing the spur of Mount Muna, he issues an imperial edict, 'To live in solitude in the time of turmoil and to go pasture in the time of peace. We should hunt elks here to console our old age'...[2] He orders to go hunting on Mount Khangai, stating: 'If wolves and deer enter into the hunting ground, don't shoot; if a black man with curly hairs riding on an ashen horse comes, capture him alive.' Wolves and deer enter into the hunting ground, but they are set free. But the man riding on the ashen horse is captured alive when he arrives.

The man does not answer the question with whom he is affiliated and is sent to his Majesty. In answering his Majesty's question, he says: 'On hearing that the emperor of the Mongolians dispatches troops, Sidurgu Khan sent out spies. No horse can catch up with the ashen horse Khusbolat, but now it is captured and all its hoofs seem to have fallen off. I am the all-powerful Khar-a Butung who has won all others, but I have been captured by you now and I am afraid I will lose my head.'

His Majesty asks again: 'Your Khan is said to be Khubilkhan. Tell me the truth!' Khar-a-Butung says: 'He can metamorphose into a black patterned viper

---

[1]   The fairy tale that God bestows nectar wine on Genghis Khan is omitted here.

[2]   The legend that his Majesty asks Khasar, his brother, to shoot the ferocious fish hawk is omitted here.

in the morning. You cannot catch him then, nor can you when he transfigures into a spotted tiger at noon. Only when he changes into a good-looking naive child and sits down in reunion with his imperial concubine at night can you catch him.' The man is freed afterwards.

Then his Majesty arrives at Tangut...[1] He turns into a phoenix when Sidurgu Khan metamorphoses into a viper, into a lion when Sidurgu transfigures into a tiger, into an old man when Sidurgu becomes a child, and captures him. After being captured, Sidurgu Khan pleads: 'Don't kill me. I'll catch Venus to dispel omens and a comet to wipe out disasters. If you still want to kill me, your life will be endangered, or your offspring will be ruined.' His request is not granted, but neither shooting nor chopping can take his life. 'Shooting and chopping will not hurt my body,' says Sidurgu Khan, 'I have hidden a patterned bellyband in my boots. Strangle me with it.' The bellyband is taken out. While being strangled, Sidurgu Khan says again: 'If I am strangled to death, all your offspring will be strangled to death like me. Examine my wife Khurbeljin Khow-a from head to toes.' He dies after having said this.

His Majesty gets Lady Khurbeljin Khow-a. Her beauty dazzles everyone, from the emperor to every subject of the country. The Lady says: 'My looks have been contaminated by your soldiers. I was more beautiful than how I look now. If I can take a bath, I will become more attractive.' Believing her, his Majesty sends her to the water. The Lady arrives by the water and writes down a message on the tail of a blue peacock: 'I am going to die in the water. Don't go downstream to look for my corpse, but upstream.' She throws herself into the water and dies after having left the message to her father. Her father goes upstream to look for her corpse according to his daughter's instruction and finds it. Everybody takes a leather bag to get soil, and spreads soil on her body to bury her. The tomb is named Temur Olkhu and the river Khadun Gool ("Lady River").

---

[1]   The legend that his Majesty asks Khasar to shoot Sidurgu Khan's epidemic-spreading witch is omitted here.

After the hunting, his Majesty goes to his summer resort at Liupanshan Mountain, and falls seriously ill in Lingzhou City...[1] and dies on July 12, 1227 at the age of 67.

The Khan's corpse is carried back on a funeral cart...[2] The cart gets stuck in deep mud to the level of its wheels when it arrives at Muna and can't be pulled out by any livestock...because the Khan has once praised the place when passing by. It is said that he issued a suspicious imperial edict to leave there the clothes he wore, the house he dwelled in and one sock. His body is buried at Mount Gurhan Khaldun, but it is also said that it is buried at Yekhe Utuk between Altay Mountain and Khentei Mountain.[3]

The recorded historical event concerning Genghis Khan's conquest of Tangut works to piece together many related legends and stories. Most of them do not exist in *Secret History of Mongolia*, a book finished soon after the death of Genghis Khan. Here we leave out some of the legendary stories so as to get a clearer picture of Genghis Khan's conquest of Tangut. Here is a summary of the points that facilitate our textual analysis:

1. There are two reasons for Genghis Khan to go on a punitive expedition against Tangut. First, Sidurgu Khan of Tangut takes back his words in defiance against Genghis Khan. Secondly, someone recommends the beauty of Lady Khurbeljin Khow-a, wife of Sidurgu Khan. To seize this beautiful woman is the other important reason for Genghis Khan to dispatch troops.
2. Sidurgu Khan's well-known black-mouthed-and-yellow-haired dog can predict omens. Sidurgu Khan possesses various extraordinary powers as well as a ferocious fish hawk and an epidemic-spreading witch. All this sets off Genghis

---

[1]   A conversation between Genghis Khan and his ministers during his serious illness is omitted here.

[2]   Warrior Khilugedei's mourning and anthem to Genghis Khan made during the escort of Genghis Khan's hearse are omitted here.

[3]   *Chinese Version of 'Compendium of Mongolian Golden History'*, translated by Zhu Feng and Jiajingyan, Huhhot: Inner Mongolian Publishing House, 1985: 23-25.

Khan's extraordinary capabilities. In fact, these motifs serve the purpose of making Sidurgu Khan a devil, the one likening the devil Mangus in Mongolian epics.

3. Genghis Khan issues an imperial edict when seeing Mount Muna on the way to Tangut: 'To live in solitude in the time of turmoil and to go pasture in the time of peace. We should hunt elks here to console our old age.'

4. Genghis Khan kills Sidurgu Khan and seizes his wife in spite of his urgent imploring.

5. Before his death, Sidurgu Khan reminds Genghis Khan to examine his wife's body carefully.

6. Genghis Khan passes away during the punitive expedition against Tangut. His hearse gets trapped at the place he has once praised; so eight forever-solid white vaults have to be built there to keep his body as well as the articles he once used.[1]

4

A comparison of the two stories sheds light on their differences. First, the story from the Tyva Kezer is a purely epic one, while the one from Mongolian historical documents is a "historical story" told as history. The ways of narrating the beginning and the ending differ completely. The story of *Kezer* starts with the only reason for Kezer to go on a punitive expedition against Khögdüüle: to loot a beautiful wife. It is an epic beginning familiar to the Altaic language-speaking peoples. While in the Mongolian historical documents, the major reason for Genghis Khan to go on a punitive expedition against Sidurgu Khan is the fact that the latter time and again defies Genghis Khan's commands, although he pledges allegiance to Genghis Khan. Sidurgu Khan's beautiful wife is also mentioned to

---

[1] The place, located in Ordos, is consecrated to Genghis Khan's horse gears, battle banners, his empress and concubines. People hold memorial ceremonies for him here, so it is not proper to call it Genghis Khan's mausoleum.

indicate the plot of the looting of a wife, but it is not treated as a key reason in the narrative. This is the biggest difference between an epic and a historical story. At the end of *Kezer*, Kezer Khan's three sisters revive him with sacred water after he has been murdered, and Kezer Khan and his subjects live a happy life again. This is also a common ending of Altaic epics, but there is no such ending concerning the historically documented legend of Genghis Khan's conquest of Tangut.

The differences in the beginning and the ending of the stories lead to the essential thematic discrepancies of the two stories. The theme of *Kezer* is a marriage by capture, often traceable in Altaic epics; the one in Mongolian historical documents is a military conquest. If comparing the plots, the similarities between them are conspicuous too. The six main plots about Genghis Khan's punitive expedition against Tangut listed above run parallel to the six plots in the overall narration of the Tyva *Kezer*, although the characters are different and there are variations in details.

As far as the first plot is concerned, the wise man in the Tyva *Kezer* reports to Kezer that the beauty of Khögdüüle Khan's wife Tungalak Tsagaan is matchless, while in the legend of Genghis Khan, the envoy Dordung of Sidurgu Khan points to Yabug-a's wife, who in turn, reports to Genghis Khan that the beauty of Sidurgu Khan's wife is unrivalled. This recommendation is an important reason for Kezer Khan or Genghis Khan to start a war. The two plots differ in that in the Tyva Kezer, the beautiful woman is the only reason, while in the legend of Genghis Khan, it is merely one of the important reasons, but not the only one to go to war. According to the Mongolian historical documents, there is a more important reason for Genghis Khan to launch the war, that is, Tangut Sidurgu Khan's breach of the agreement and breaking his own pledge in open defiance against Genghis Khan. I will come back to the intriguing question why there is such a record in ancient Mongolian historical documents.

As to the second plot, the enemy of both Kezer and Genghis Khan owns a dog that can predict omens. Although the dogs are named differently and pertinent details vary, the dog's featuring constitutes a shared motif. Both stories present the unusual dog as an indicator of the crisis-ridden country of Khögdüüle Khan and Sidurgu Khan respectively. The legend of Genghis Khan even surpasses *Kezer* at this point. Sidurgu Khan owns not only the dog that can predict omens, but also an evil fish hawk and an epidemic-spreading witch.

With regard to the third plot, the correspondence between the two stories is very obvious too. The resemblance is particularly clear when linking the third with the sixth plot. In the third plot, both Kezer and Genghis Khan find a place during their expedition, which they admire and extol, while in the sixth plot, they happen to be at the same place on their way back home. Because Kezer Khan is murdered at that location, he is also buried there; Genghis Khan's hearse gets trapped when it arrives there. Eight forever-solid white vaults are built to symbolize that Genghis Khan was buried in the place and way of his choosing. Moreover, Kezer's compliments to the place and Genghis Khan's to Mount Muna convey similar meanings. Let us compare:

The rich living here enjoy themselves to the full and the poor that can bury their corpses here also enjoy themselves to the full. It is really a fertile and beautiful place.

as recorded in the Tyva *Kezer*.

To live in solitude in the time of turmoil and to go pasture in the time of peace. We should hunt elks here to console our old age.

as recorded in *Compendium of Mongolian Golden History*, Lubsandanjin's *Mongolian Golden History and History of Asaragchi Nerutu-Yin Teukhe* with anonymous authorship.

The meaning of the poem in various Mongolian historical documents is hard to understand. But it clears up when we consult the *Origin of Mongolia*:

To live in solitude in times of turmoil and to go pasture in times of peace.
Elks should be multiplied here; the old should rest here.

Apart from the praise for Mount Muna, the poem reveals Genghis Khan's intention to be buried there. The poem in the Tyva *Kezer* seems to express the same
intention. It echoes Kezer's death at the place that he once praised. Likewise,
Genghis Khan's hearse is trapped and the eight white vaults are built at the
place that once drew his admiration.

With regard to the fourth one, the basic plots of both stories coincide, although the Tyva *Kezer* is much simpler in detail while the legend of Genghis
Khan is quite complicated. According to the latter, Kezer Khan kills Khögdüüle
Khan and captures his wife; Genghis Khan kills Sidurgu Khan and seizes his wife
in spite of Sidurgu Khan's urgent imploring.

As far as the fifth plot is concerned, there is no corresponding plot in the story
from *Mongolian Golden History* and the Tyva *Kezer*. But interestingly, Sidurgu
Khan reminds Genghis Khan of examining his own wife carefully before his
death. The story does not clarify what it means and what hides in her body.
Sidurgu Khan dies, and there is no follow-up. His warning sounds very meaningful, but remains mystically unresolved. This episode is beyond comprehension
without consultation of other ancient Mongolian historical documents. However,
History of Ancient Mongolian Khans' Origin and other Mongolian historical documents reveal the enigma. According to the story from *History of Ancient Mongolian Khans' Origin*, before being killed, Sidurgu Khan warns Genghis Khan to
examine carefully the body of his own wife, Khurbeljin Khow-a Khadun.
Genghis Khan seizes his wife. Later on, the woman writes to her father when going to take a bath in the Khara Muren River ("Black River"), telling him that
she is going to die by drowning herself in the river and that her corpse can be
found only by going upstream instead of downstream. She ties the letter to the
neck of her father's bird and sends out the message. She returns to Genghis

Khan and hides a pair of scissors in the most private place of her body and hurts the emperor's penis. Then she runs away to the Khara Muren River and drowns herself. Since then, the Mongolians have changed the name Khara Muren to Khadun Gool ("Lady River").[1] Similar accounts are traceable in Sagang-Sechen's *Origin of Mongolia*,[2] Jimbadorji's *Crystal Mirror*,[3] Dharm-a's *Alran Khurdum minan Khegegesu*[4] and others.

From my point of view, the stories from *History of Ancient Mongolian Khans' Origin*, *Origin of Mongolia*, *History of Asaragchi*, *Crystal Mirror* and others are integral as far as the plot in case is concerned. While in the anonymous writer's *Compendium of Mongolian Golden History* and in Lubsandanjin's *Mongolian Golden History*, the plot is deleted on purpose. I think there are three reasons to justify the deletion. First, the pertinent writers might have believed that such an incident would discredit the image of Genghis Khan. Second, they might have doubted the authenticity of the plot. Among the Mongolians there goes a saying about the death of Genghis Khan, in which he falls off a horse when hunting and dies.[5] The third reason is that the writers' sources for the history of Genghis Khan's conquest of Tangut were of two kinds. One source consisted of ancient historical documents and the other of legends spread among the people. When these two sources contradicted, they had to omit one of them. This kind of processing may very well lead to incoherence or other textual gaps. It illustrates that the part narrating about Genghis Khan's illness and death is not coherent.

So far, we discern that the two stories corres pondas regards the fifth plot. The

---

[1] *History of Ancient Mongolian Khans' Origin*, annotated by Uljiit, Beijing: Ethnicity Publishing House, 1983: 89-90. The ancient Mongolians called the river Yellow River. The Mongolians still call the Yellow River Khadun Gool.

[2] Sagang Sechen, *Origin of Mongolia*, annotated by Khukhe-undur, Beijing: Ethnicity Publishing House, 1987: 101-130.

[3] Jimbadorji, *Crystal Mirror*, annotated by Liu Jinsuo, Beijing: Ethnicity Publishing House, 1984: 419.

[4] Dharm-a, *Alran Khurdum minan Khegegesu*, annotated by Choiji, Huhhot: Inner Mongolian People's Publishing House, 1987: 57-58.

[5] *History of Asaragchi*, annotated by B. Bagana, Beijing: Ethnicity Publishing House, 1984: 57-58.

story of *Kezer* conquering Khögdüüle Khan is identical or similar to the one of Genghis Khan's conquest of Tangut in many important respects, and even the concrete remarks made by the characters correspond. This fact indicates that the two stories are homologous, i.e., the legend of Genghis Khan has been interwoven with the Tyva *Kezer*.

5

The above discussion has validated the statement that there exists a significant correspondence between the story *Kezer* and Genghis Khan's punitive expedition. Then how did the legend of Genghis Khan get interwoven with the Tyva *Kezer*? Was the epic of Genghis Khan's conquest of Tangut once spread in Tyva? Bearing these questions in mind, we have hitherto dealt with the legend of Genghis Khan from two angles. Through an analysis of the legends about Genghis Khan's conquest of Tangut as recorded in Mongolian historical documents after the 17th century, we have found that the legend itself has many characteristics of a heroic epic, including traditional epic subject matter, plots and motifs. But those subject matter, plots and motifs with epic features do not exist in the documents from the 13th and 14th centuries. This indicates that they came into being around the 15th to the 17th centuries and were absorbed into Mongolian historical documents.

Genghis Khan's conquest of Tangut is a real historical event, and it was documented in *Secret History of Mongolia* after Genghis Khan had passed away. Genghis Khan had gone on punitive expeditions twice. He attacked Tangut for the first time on the way back from his punitive expedition against the Jin. Burkhan, King of Tangut, surrendered to Genghis Khan and swore fealty to him. Genghis Khan then withdrew his troops. Later, Genghis Khan went on a punitive expedition against Sartagul Irgen and sent an envoy to order Burkhan to dispatch troops to form the right flank. But Burkhan not only refused to send armies, but also spoke insolently against Genghis Khan in contempt. So, Genghis Khan went on a punitive expedition against Tangut seven years after his first expedition to conquer Central Asia and Europe.

During the march Genghis Khan went hunting, fell down from his horse and was hurt. Genghis Khan persuaded Burkhan to surrender, but one of Burkhan's subordinates refused and was then smashed. On seeing that he was at a disadvantage, Burkhan wanted to surrender. Genghis Khan accepted this and conferred on Burkhan the name Sidurgu.

Genghis Khan gave the order to kill Sidurgu and Tangut became extinct.[1] Rashid-Ad-Din, a Persian historian, added some legendary contents when writing about this historical event in *Collection of History* edited in the early 14th century, which basically tallied with the records in *Secret History of Mongolia*. The most remarkable addition is about Genghis Khan getting a revelation in a dream on his way to Tangut. He knew that he was approaching death, and made his will. According to Secret History of Mongolia, it was during the expedition against Sartagul Irgen that he took his favored concubine's advise and made a will in which he appointed his successor.[2]

This historical event has been twisted in the 17th century Mongolian historical documents. First, the theme of marriage by capture is added on top of the theme of going on a punitive expedition. The image of Genghis Khan possesses more features of an epic hero. As stated above, the image of Sidurgu Khan retains more characteristics of a Mangus in epics. Sidurgu Khan owns a dog that is able to predict the future as well as an evil fish hawk and a witch that Genghis Khan wipes out. All these motifs and plots are well-founded in Mongolian epics. When it comes to the execution of Sidurgu Khan, all chopping and shooting fail. So Sidurgu Khan says: 'Shooting and chopping will not hurt my body. I have hidden a patterned bellyband in my boot. Strangle me with it.' The antagonists in Mongolian epics are as impenetrable as Sidurgu Khan. In a similar vein, the an-

---

[1]　*Secret History of Mongolia*, edited and annotated by Eldengtei and Oyundalai. Huhhot: Inner Mongolian People's Publishing House, 1980, sections 249, 256, 265, 267 and 268.

[2]　Ibid. sections 254 and 255.

tagonists instruct how to eliminate themselves. Even some verses retain a strong epic flavor. For instance, after being captured, the spy of Sidurgu Khan says: 'No horse can catch the ashen horse Khusbolat, but now it is captured and all its hoofs seem to have fallen off. I am the all-powerful Khar-a Butung that has won all the others, but I have been defeated by you and I am afraid I will lose my head.' Usually we can only find such words in an epic.

These textual fragments show that the heroic epics modeled on the historical event of Genghis Khan's conquest of Tangut used to be very popular. Such epics might very well have come out between the 14th and the 16th centuries. Up to the 17th century, Mongolian historians absorbed these epics as historical data into their compilation.

This observation is of utmost importance. It reflects not only some of the traces of Mongolian epics' emergence, their development and spreading, but also the interaction between Mongolian epics and historiography. In the past we only acknowledged theoretically that there are genealogical links in terms of genre and subject matter between Mongolian historical documents and epics, but we failed to prove that the documents take in textual scraps from actual epic materials. If our research stands to future testimony, its findings are meaningful for us to understand how Mongolian nomadic historians have compiled history books.

6

Finally I want to discuss why the epic of Genghis Khan could spread to the Tyva.

The key to this question is to deepen our understanding of the Tyva *Kezer* and its tradition, as well as the historical and cultural links between the Tyva and the Mongolians. It is common belief among the Tyva epic performers that *Kezer* is a Mongolian epic.[①] This opinion is for the most part accountable, because the nine stories of *Kezer* that I translated, all correspond to the Mongolian *Geser* except

---

① D.S. Kuular, *Achiti Kezer-Mergen*. Kyzyl: Tyva Publishing House, 1963: 9.

for the story under scrutiny. Aside from minor differences, some of the stories correspond in full to the Mongolian *Geser*. Therefore, it is fair to say that the Mongolian *Geser* was spread to the Tyva and transformed into the Tyva *Kezer*. Then, when was the Mongolian *Geser* spread to the Tyva? D.S. Kuular believes that this process can be divided into two periods. The first period was prior to the publication of the Beijing block print of *Geser* in 1716, when the Mongolian story *Geser* was spread among the Tyva by oral and aural means, because of the close cultural relationship between Tyva and Mongolia. The second period was in the wake of the publication of the block print in 1716 when *Kezer* was widely spread in the region of Tyva. The remnants of the printed *Geser* that were discovered by V.V. Radlov at Kara Kul ("Black Lake"), a most remote area surrounded by high mountains, can evidence this periodization.[1] So, it is certain that *Kezer* has spread to Tyva for some 300 years.

Although Mongolian *Geser* spread to Tyva and developed into the Tyva *Kezer*, the transformation process gets entwined with the Tyva traditional culture, thus taking on dinstinctive cultural features. Most amazingly, the name of Geser is closely related with the historical figure Genghis Khan. In Tyva, many people believe that Kezer and Genghis Khan are the same person and that their story manifests an event that really happened in the past, thus simply calling the *Kezer* epic *The Biography of Kezer-Genghis Khan*. In the meantime, *Water Channel of Kezer-Genghis Khan*, *Damb of Kezer* as well as the other historical legends widely circulating in Tyva have provided ground for the view that Kezer and Genghis Khan are the same person.[2] This has hardly happened in the Mongolian region.

How did such a phenomenon occur? I believe that it is due to the close ties in politics, economy and culture between Tyva and Mongolia in the course of history. The Tyva are a trans-boundary ethnicity with most people inhabiting the fron-

---

① Ibid. 7.
② Ibid. 10.

tier of the Tyva Republic of the Russion Federation, some in the western part of Mongolia, and a small part in the Altay region of Xinjiang Uygur Autonomous Region of China. Ever since the founding of the Mongolian Empire, the Tyva have had a close relation with Mongolians. They fought shoulder to shoulder with the Mongolians on political, military and other fronts and established a profound friendship. As regards religion, both believe in Lamaism; economically speaking, the Tyva live a nomadic life like the Mongolians. Moreover, they had been using Mongolian up to the 1930s. This close relationship has not only greatly influenced the mutual exchange of the two nations' oral literature, but also has brought the Tyva language, which formally belongs to the Turkic language family, closer to Mongolian in terms of its basic vocabulary. Nowadays, in the Tyva vocabulary, Mongolian words make up quite a big proportion. With regard to oral epics, Tyva epics are surprisingly similar to Mongolian ones in subject matter, themes and creative formulas. The two nations possess common epics. There are more than three hundred Tyva epics among which epics like *Fifteen-year-old Altai-Sumbür and Boraldai-Mergen*[①] *circulate among Mongolian people. The Tyva like Mongolian epics and many collect the hand-written copies. It was in the city* of Kyzyl that the hand-written copy of the famous epic *Khan Kharangui* was discovered.

Such close historical and cultural ties have facilitated the transmission of the works of oral literature between the two nations. On this basis, we assume that there was a separate legend, or perhaps an epic, about Genghis Khan who conquered Tangut in history, which may constitute the possible route by which the legend of Genghis Khan entered into the Tyva *Kezer*. The legend or the epic once spread widely in both Tyva and Mongolia. On the Mongolian part, historians incorporated the story into historical documents in the 17th century, while in Tyva, the story spread orally and gradually got interwoven with their epic *Kezer*. In fact, the oral Mongolian edition of Genghis Khan's conquest of Tangut didn't

---

① 　Y.L. Aranjin, *Tyva's Epics*, Kyzyl: Tyva Publishing House, 1990: 4.

vanish among Mongolians. A legend was found in the sung text of *Geser* recorded from a contemporary epic artist called Jimhaiamtsu. It tells of Genghis Khan who orders Khasar to shoot Sidurgu Khan's epidemic-spreading witch during the expedition against Tangut.[①] This further illustrates the possibility that the story of Genghis Khan's conquest of Tangut has been circulating orally among the Tyva to this day.

References:

Aranjin, Y. L. *Tyva Epics*. Kyzyl: Tyva Publishing House, 1990.

Chinese Version of 'Compendium of Mongolian Golden History'. Translated by Zhu Feng and Jiajingyan. Huhhot: Inner Mongolian Publishing House, 1985.

Dharm-a. *Alran Khurdum minan Khegegesu*. Annotated by Choiji. Huhhot: Inner Mongolian People's Publishing House, 1987.

History of Ancient Mongolian Khans' Origin. Annotated by Uljiit. Beijing: Ethnicity Publishing House, 1983.

History of Asaragchi. Annotated by B. Bagana. Beijing: Ethnicity Publishing House, 1984.

Jimbadorji. *Crystal Mirror*. Annotated by Liu Jinsuo. Beijing: Ethnicity Publishing House, 1984.

Kozin, S. A. *The Epic of the Mongolian People*. Moscow: Academy of Sciences of the USSR, 1948.

Kuular, D.S. *Achiti Kezer-Mergen*. Kyzyl: Tyva Publishing House, 1963.

——*The Biography of Geser*. Kyzyl: Tyva Publishing House, 1963.

Nekliudov, S.Yu. *Epics of the Mongolian People*. Translated by Xu Changhan, Gao Wenfeng and Zhang Zizhi Huhhot: Inner Mongolian University Publishing House, 1991.

Originally published as: *Geroicheskyépos mongol' skich narodov: Ustnye i literaturnye tradicii*. Moskva: Glavnaja redakcija Vostochnoj literatury, 1984.

Rinchindorji, "An Important Discovery of the *Copy Geser* – Neglected Genius Performer Jimhaiamtsu." *Ethnicity Literature Study* 1 (2002): 4-5.

---

① Rinchindorji, "An Important Discovery of the *Copy Geser* – Neglected Genius Performer Jimhaiamtsu," *Ethnicity Literature Study* 1 (2002): 4-5.

Sagang Sechen. *Origin of Mongolia*. Annotated by Khukhe-undur. Beijing: Ethnicity Publishing House, Beijing, 1987.

Secret History of Mongolia. Edited and annotated by Eldengtei and Oyundalai. Huhhot: Inner Mongolian People's Publishing House, 1980.

VI

The Oral Characteristics of the *Manas* Epic

Adil Zhumaturdi

Abstract: The *Manas* epic is the oldest and most classical part of the oral literary tradition of the Kirghiz. We can get a picture of the Kirghiz oral tradition by closely studying the *Manas* epic in its ancient form, as it is still being performed today by bards – *manaschi*. This paper attempts to explain and explore some of the basic characteristics of this full-length oral heroic epic through a discussion of its formulaic features, through the performance by singers and through the contexts that both determine and inform the "creation in performance".

Both the structure of *Manas* and its content are formulaic. European epics center on events, whereas *Manas* puts heroes at its core. The formulaic structure is an important factor ensuring the stability of *Manas* and formulaic semantics and syntax are the main elements to be creatively employed by singers.

Manas is a representative work emerging from a long, ancient tradition. The performance of *Manas* is a complicated and comprehensive artistic process; a printed version of the text is but an incomplete substitute for the traditional oral form performed live.

Key words: *Manas* epic, orality, formulas

The Kirghiz oral tradition comprises various verse forms,[①] and the epic is one of the oldest forms. The performance tradition of the *Manas* epic can be traced back to more than a thousand years ago and it is the oldest and most classical part of the oral literary tradition of the Kirghiz.[②] With regard to the Kirghiz intellectual and cultural characteristics, especially the Kirghiz legacy of oral poetry, Chingiz Aytmatov,[③] the most famous writer from contemporary Kyrgyzstan pointed out: 'If other ethnic groups preserve their past cultures and histories in the forms of written literature, architecture, sculpture, drama and painting, the Kirghiz preserve all their ideologies, national honors and humiliations, struggles for freedom and independence, ideals and national history and life in the form of the oral epic.'[④]

Epics have been created and orally disseminated by *manaschi* through the ages.[⑤] We can get insights into the Kirghiz oral tradition only by closely studying the *Manas* epic today or by attending the epic performances of its most famous

---

① Verse forms of the Kirghiz oral tradition are: heroic epics (*jomok*), tribal geneology (*sanjira*), ancient ritual songs (*aytimdar*), songs to mourn the dead (*koshok*), love songs (*süyüü ir*), life songs (*turmush ir*), children's songs (*baldar ir*) and proverbs (*makal-lakap*). Prose forms are: myths (*apsana*), legends (*ulamish*), tales (*jöö jomok*), riddles (*tabishmak*) and jokes (*shakaba*).

② According to the *Manas* epic itself, the first epic singer was Irchi-uul, one of the forty warriors of the hero Manas. In Kirghiz, the name Irchi means "singer". The epic has matured and improved through the repeated singing and performing by *manaschi* of various periods. Because we are dealing with an oral epic, it is very complicated to determine its time of appearance, but, guided by the research results of scholars from various countries, UNESCO proclaimed 1995 to be the year of the *Manas* epic and organized activities and an international conference in Bishkek (the capital of Kyrgyzstan) to celebrate the one millennium anniversary of the epic.

③ Chingiz Aytmatov was born in 1928. The work that established his reputation, *Jamilia*, was published in 1958. Later, he also published *Farewell Gulsary*! (1960), *The White Ship* (1970), *The Day Lasts More Than a Hundred Years* (1980), *Execution Block* (1986) and several other works. It is estimated by UNESCO that his works have been translated into 127 languages in the world, among which also Chinese and English, and that Aytmatov is one of the writers with the largest readership.

④ Chingiz Aytmatov, "The Beaming Height of the Ancient Kirghiz Spirit," Said Aliev, Raikul Sarypbekov, Kadyrbek Matiev, eds., *Encyclopaedical Phenomenon of Epos 'Manas'*, Bishkek: Encyclopedia Press, 1995: 15.

⑤ In Kirghiz, *manaschi* refers to those bards who make a living on the singing and performing of *Manas*.

manaschi.

Manas tells of the legendary story about the heroic deeds of Manas and his seven generations of descendants, and extols their heroic spirit. The epic has been wideley circulating among the people for nearly ten centuries, but its first version was recorded from singers only in the second half of the 19th century by the Russian Kazak soldier Ch. Valikhanov[1] and the Russian expert in Turkic studies V. Radlov.[2] Since then, scholars and readers across the world have gradually come to know *Manas* and it has become a subject of international scholarship nowadays. By now, over 150 transcripts of *Manas* have been collected from Xinjiang in China and from the living areas of the Kirghiz in Kyrgyzstan, Kazakhstan, Afghanistan, and so on.[3] The Kirghiz preserve their history in an oral form. It is impossible to list the names of all talented *manaschi* contributing to the dissemination and development of the epic tradition. However, the names of some singers will be passed down on the pages of history, for example Irchiuul – a contemporary of Manas and one of the forty brave warriors who followed Man-

---

[1] Chogan Valikhanov (1835-1865) is the first scholar who collected the *Manas* epic. In 1856 and 1857, he went to the area of Lake Issyk-Kul and the Kirghiz living in Yili and Tekes in China to conduct surveys, and recorded there the traditional chapter of *Manas* "The Memorial Feast for Kökötöy", which consists of 3.319 lines.

[2] Vasilii Radlov (1837-1918) carried out fruitful fieldwork in the Kirghiz area in 1862 and 1869, and recorded a large amount of oral epics, including *Manas*. His version of *Manas* includes all the traditional chapters of the first episode of Manas and some parts of the second episode *Semetey*, totaling 12. 454 lines. In 1885, he included these versions in the fifth volume of *Examples of Folk Literature of the Turkic Tribes*, a book series he compiled. The volume per se was published in German in St. Petersburg in 1885 under the title *The Dialect of the Kara-Kirghiz*.

[3] See Said Aliev, Raikul Sarypbekov, Kadyrbek Matiev, eds., *Encyclopaedical Phenomenon of Epos 'Manas'*, Bishkek: Encyclopedia Press, 1995; Lang Ying, On '*Manas*', Huhhot: Inner Mongolian University Publishing House, 1999; Said Aliev and Turusbek Kulmatov, *Manaschi and Researchers of 'Manas'*, Bishkek: Sham, 1995; Manbet, *All Kinds of Variations of the 'Manas' Epic and Its Performance Art*, Urumqi: Xinjiang People's Publishing House, 1997; Adil Zhumaturdi and Tohan Ysak, *Critical Biography of Jusup Mamay, the Contemporary Living Homer and Great Singer of 'Manas'*, Huhhot: Inner Mongolian University Publishing House, 2002.

*as all the time,*① *Tinibek Japiy,*② *Sagimbay Orozbak,*③ *Sayakbay Karalayev;*④

---

① All transcripts of the epic tell that Irchi-uul was the first to turn Manas's heroic deeds into songs and to sing these songs. In the transcript by Jusup Mamay, Irchi-uul is described as follows: After Manas attacked and captured with his troops Bejin, the capital of Kidan, he falls into a plot by Kongurbay, the leader of the enemy, with his head struck by a poisonous axe. He is persuaded by Almambet to return to Talas (the place where Manas' castle was located) to cure his wounds. Kökchö, a Kazak general was also killed by the enemy. The chief commander Almambet entrusts assignments to his generals and bids them farewell. This is what he says to Irchi-uul:
...

　Uruxka, you should not go to battle, / You should hold tight your pen, / The spirit of Manas, the hero, / Cannot be forgotten. / The history from Mamay, the Khan, to the present, / You have heard of. / Since the troops mounted horses and started their journey, / You have been accompanying him all the time / And accomplished today's glory. / Heroic deeds and glories / You cannot forget, / And should always reflect. / The things he has not done / You do not have to exaggerate intentionally. / My own deeds / I Have written down on paper, / You may ask Aruke for it, / And compile it in ⋯
　(See for the original text the Chinese part of this book).

② Tinibek Japiy (1846-1902) was born by the side of Lake Issyk-Kul in Kyrgyzstan and was one of the most outstanding representatives of all the Kirghiz *manaschi*. His performance style has exerted great impact on the *manaschi* of later generations. The most well-known *manaschi* of the 20th century, such as Jüsüpakun Apay, Eshmat Manbetjüsüp in China and Sagimbay Orozbak in Kyrgyzstan, were all students of Japiy when they began to learn to sing the epic. Japiy's transcript, the second part of the epic Semetey was partially recorded and published as a separate edition in 1898 and 1925 respectively in Kazan and Moscow.

③ Sagimbay Orozbak (1867-1930) was a famous *manaschi* in Kyrgyzstan. He could sing the contents of the first three episodes of the epic with strong traditional characteristics. For various reasons, only the content of the first episode, 180.378 lines in total, was recorded and published between 1981 and 1984. Orozbak fled from Kyrgyzstan to Akqi county of Kizilsu Kirghiz Autonomous Prefecture in Xinjiang before the civil war of 1918-1920.

④ Sayakbay Karalayev (1894-1971) was a famous *manaschi* in Kyrgyzstan. He sang the longest variant of the epic known in the 20th century. His transcripts include the first episode of *Manas*, the second episode *Semetey*, the third episode *Seytek*, the fourth episode *Kenenim* and the fifth episode *Alymsarik and Kulansarik*, totaling 500.553 lines.

and the Chinese singers Jüsüpakun Apay,[1] Ibrayim Akunbek[2] and Eshmat Manbetjüsüp.[3] Among the living manaschi, the most outstanding representative is no doubt Jusup Mamay[4] who was born in Akqi (Aheqi) county of Kizilsu Kirghiz Autonomous Prefecture in Xinjiang and is nicknamed "the contemporary Homer" and "the living Homer".

The oral language of *Manas* has at least the following three characteristics:

---

[1] Jüsüpakun Apay died in 1920. He was born in Akqi county of the Kizilsu Kirghiz Autonomous Prefecture in Xinjiang. He studied under the supervision of Tinibek Japiy, together with Sagimbay Orozbak and Eshmat Manbetjüsüp. In the spring of 1917, he competed with Sagimbay Orozbak at a singing contest to demonstrate his talent. The contest became widely known. The contents of the first three parts of the epic Apay sang were recorded by Balbay, the elder brother of Jusup Mamay. The recordings were handed down to the latter and became a main source of his transcripts.

[2] Ibrayim Akunbek (1882-1959) was born in Uluuqat (Wuqia) county of the Kizilsu Kirghiz Autonomous Prefecture in Xinjiang, China. His singing activities were scarce, but according to Jusup Mamay, his elder brother Balbay recorded from Akunbek's oral performances the fourth episode of the epic, *Kenenim*, the fifth episode Seyitim, the sixth episode *Asilbacha and Bekbacha*, the seventh episode *Sombilek* and the eighth episode *Chigitey* and handed them over to him. After he carefully studied and absorbed them, they constituted an important source for his transcripts.

[3] Eshmat Manbetjüsüp (1880-1963) was born in Akqi county of the Kizilsu Kirghiz Autonomous Prefecture in Xinjiang, China. He was one of the representatives of the *manaschi* of the 20th century in China. The contents of the first three episodes of *Manas*, *Semetey* and *Seyitim* were recorded and translated into Chinese by Lang Ying and Useyin-aji (not published yet). The original recording of the first part was lost during the Cultural Revolution; the Kirghiz version of the second and third parts of *Semetey*, containing 11,070 lines in total, were published in 2003 in Kizilsu under the title *Kart Dastan* (Ancient Epic). Besides the Manas epic, Manbetjüsüp also sang other Kirghiz traditional epics such as *Er-Töshtük*, *Budayik*, *Kurmanbek*, *Janish and Bayish* and others.

[4] Jusup Mamay was born in April 1918. He was well-known in his hometown and in 1961 he attracted the attention of the folklorist circles in China and began to sing Manas for them. He began to learn singing at the age of eight, and by the time he was a teenager, he had already learned the whole epic. His transcripts include the eight episodes of *Manas*, *Semetey*, *Seytek*, *Kenenim*, *Seyitim*, *Asilbacha and Bekbacha*, *Sombilek and Chigitey*, totaling over 232,200 lines. The Kirghiz versions were published between 1984 and 1995 in eighteen volumes. Apart from *Manas*, he also sang and published more than a dozen Kirghiz traditional epics such as *Er-Töshtük* and *Bagish and Toltoy*.

(1) traditional formulaic structures (including themes and narrative patterns), ①
traditional formulaic syntax and formulaic semantics; (2) "creation in performance" – the only effective means to create, preserve, and transmit oral epics
(see below); (3) the contexts of epic creation, interactions between *manaschi*
and audience, and *manaschi's* relations with the orally disseminated version of
the epic. These factors need to be dealt with in research on oral epics. This paper will explain and explore some of the fundamental features of the grand oral
Manas epic by discussing its formulaic characteristics.

Both the structure of *Manas* and its content are formulaic. A formulaic structure is highly functional in: (1) the overall structural composition of the epic;
(2) the unfolding of the epic's contents. According to Albert Lord, there are
many narrative models in oral traditions; these models exist in the creation and
transmission process of oral stories as functionally significant and dynamic constitutive elements regardless of the degree of variations of stories structured on the
models per se. ②

In terms of the overall structure, *Manas* is totally different from the Greek *Ili-
ad*, the British *Beowulf*, the French *Chanson* de Roland, the Spanish *Cantar de*

---

① According to Albert B. Lord, one of the founders of the *oral-formulaic theory*, when singers tell stories
in accordance with formulaic versions, they use small-scale formulas composed of phrases as well as narrative units composed of some repeatedly used words and phrases, such as a gathering, a feast, a battle
and descriptions of horses, heroes and heroines, and so on. This kind of so-called themes also exists in
the Kirghiz oral tradition. The themes are presented with basically the same words and sentences, but
they may be expanded and shortened by different singers during their performance. The more information
the theme conveys, the greater the variation; less information would result in more stability. Lord thinks
that there exists a basic narrative pattern (i. e. story pattern) in the oral tradition which has great vitality
regardless of how many story variations there are and plays a constitutive role in the creation and transmission of folktales. For instance, the story model of the Homeric epic *Odyssey* includes five elements:
departure, disaster, return, judgment and wedding. In Kirghiz traditional oral epics, the story pattern
covers a comparatively wider range of themes.

② See Albert B. Lord, *The Singer of Tales*, Cambridge, Mass.: Harvard University Press, 1960; John
Miles Foley, *The Theory of Oral Composition*: *History and Methodology*, Bloomington, Ind.: Indiana
University Press, 1988; Yin Hubin, *Ancient Classics and Oral Tradition*, Beijing: China Social Sci-
ences Publishing House, 2002.

Mio Cid and the German *Nibelungenlied*. The above-mentioned European epics are basically structured around events, whereas *Manas* is an epic structurally centering on the heroes. It follows a chronological narrative thread about the life of the hero from birth to death. After years of comparative studies, China's famous epic expert Lang Ying points out that the national epics of the Turkic speaking ethnic groups basically follow such a narrative model: unusual birth of the hero – his miserable childhood – his youthful accomplishments – his marriage and settling down – his going on expedition – his going to the netherworld (or coming back to life) – his encounter with catastrophes in his hometown (or his being usurped) – his enemy being killed (or the usurper punished) – his triumphant return (or his heroic death). [1] In the Kirghiz oral tradition, this narrative macro structure of epics applies not only to the epic clusters, like *Manas*, which retell of the heroic deeds of several generations of heroes, but also to dozens of other epics, and they are even widely used by other Turkic language-speaking nations, including the Karakalpak. [2] The open formulaic structure of oral epics enables singers to select suitable words, motifs and themes at their free will and to expand or streamline any theme within a permitted scope. This is the principle of variation within limits formulated by Lord. During the performance, thematic adjustments spring from within the tradition, are also restricted by the tradition, and guarantee the overall stability of the epic's content and structure despite moderate variations. Performers make use of various epic materials to make up stories modeled on the traditional formulaic structure. Word formulas and themes are variable to some extent, but the epic's overall structure remains unchanged. The formulaic structure is the most stable factor in the oral *Manas* epic.

Formulaic syntax constitutes another formulaic unit of the Kirghiz oral epics,

---

[1]   Lang Ying, On '*Manas*', Huhhot: Inner Mongolian University Publishing House, 1999: 21.

[2]   See Nora K. Chadwick and Victor Zhirmunsky, *Oral Epics of Central Asia*, London: Cambridge University Press, 1960; Karl Reichl, *Turkic Oral Epic Poetry*: *Traditions*, *Forms*, *Poetic Structure*, New York/London: Garland Publishing, 1992.

including epic meter, verse foot, rhyme scheme and parallelism. Formulaic syntax sits squarely in the domain of sophisticated poetry-writing techniques that ask for an in-depth analysis and are thus beyond the scope of this paper. I will explore these syntactic formulas in another paper. According to the *oral-formulaic theory* (or the *Parry-Lord theory*), the term "formula" refers to a cluster of words or phrases or even to a poem stanza composed of specific words and phrases, the so-called *run* of Albert Lord. This type of formulas is used in case that the meter be the same, and expresses a relatively stable meaning. However, one of its important prerequisites is that this type of formulas or *run* must reoccur with high frequency as a particular unit in the oral texts, thus facilitating the singing and performing of the epic. [①] Its relatively fixed rhythm and form are shared and disseminated by groups of singers, and feature repeatedly in the texts for performance. [②] In the long Kirghiz oral epic tradition, formulas have not only provided very effective and convenient methods for *manaschi* to memorize and sing the epic's themes and contents and to create new epic sung texts, but also to link up the previous concept with another new one during the performance in the vein of the traditional legacies, so as to guide the audience and draw their attention. For instance, 'Let's put aside this part and return to the hero Manas...'; 'Let's put aside this paragraph and now talk about Aydarkan, son of Kökchö....'; 'Let's stop here and see what's going on with Kanikey, daughter of Karakan...' and so on. This type of formulas is used freely by *manaschi* in different contexts. The most stable word formulas are those that express the most commonplace meanings. Names of heroes, names of steeds and names of special places all become special "signs" to guide singers' thinking and spark off their imagination. Following these "signs", singers can soon find clues and information related to the objects they are describing. Under the leverage of these

---

① John Miles Foley, *The Theory of Oral Composition: History and Methodology*, Bloomington, Ind.: Indiana University Press, 1988.

② Chao Gejin, *Oral Poetics: Formulaic Diction of Arimpil's 'Jangar' Singing*, Nanning: Guangxi People's Publishing House, 2000: 204.

"signs", a great number of readymade formulas will emerge repeatedly to represent the hero's appearance and character, for example his looks, facial expression, costume, unswerving willpower, courage and bravery, extraordinary power and his horse, weaponry, various battles, one-to-one fights, the cruelty of battlefields, natural scenery and other supernatural things. [1]

As for the use of formulas, we can best listen to what the *manaschi* says himself. [2]

A (asks): [In the performance] when describing a hero, such as when Almambet[3] is to appear on the stage, what comes to your mind first?

Jusup Mamay: I first think of his heroic deeds if Almambet appears on the scene.

---

[1]   See Vasilii Radlov, Preface to *The Dialect of the Kara-Kirghiz*, vol. 5 of *Examples of Folk Literature of the Turkic Tribes*, St. Petersburg: Eggers und Schmitzdorff, 1885: 25-34. The English version of the Preface can be found in Said Aliev, Raikul Sarypbekov, Kadyrbek Matiev, eds., *Encyclopaedical Phenomenon of Epos 'Manas'*, Bishkek: Encyclopedia Press, 1995: 25-34. It is in this long and detailed preface that Radlov proposes enlightening views on the traditional features of the performance of Kirghiz oral epics, the recording of oral narrations, creation impromptu, basic narrative units of the oral tradition (i.e. stereotyped expressions), the role played by the audience, complete stories and their multiple component parts (i.e. themes), the mixture of new and old narrative elements in oral poetry (i.e. performance and tradition), the significance of paradoxes in the narration, the impact of the on-the-spot contexts on the singer's creation, the rhyming, melody and tone that accompany the narrative during the performance.

[2]   This is an interview Jusup Mamay conducted on August 26th, 2001 when I was carrying out a field investigation on Jusup Mamay in Akqi county of the Kizilsu Kirghiz Autonomous Prefecture of Xinjiang. This interview was done at Mamay's home. It is published under the title "An Inquiry into the Secret of the Performing of the *Manas* Epic," in *Kizilsuu Literature* 2 (2002): 60-75

[3]   Almambet is one of the main heroes in the first part of the epic *Manas*. He was a Khitan (Qi Dan) prince and left home because of family conflicts. He first went to the Kazak Khan Kökchö and later to Manas. He was a sworn brother of Manas, followed Manas all the time, accomplished remarkable heroic deeds, and became a hero revered by the Kirghiz people. (Khitan or Qi Dan: a group in ancient China that was a branch of the Eastern Hus inhabiting the valley of the Xar Murun River in the upper reaches of the Liaohe river. In the 10th century, Yelu Abaoji (Apao-chi) unified all the Khitan tribes and established the kingdom of Khitan).

A: How do you describe him?

Jusup Mamay: I first want to describe his appearance, such as 'his golden face is radiating, his face is spotless and he is verbally straightforward, Azizkan's Almambet...' all of which are used to describe his looks. There may be some changes in the wording or additions at the time. When singing about Kanikey① it is enough to depict her with the following four lines: 'Kanikey, daughter of the Khan, beauty of beauties, sage of those with long hair, cleverer among women, purer among those wearing loose skirts② and queen among heroines.'

A: These set and vivid words reflect the basic characteristics of every figure. How is Aychürök③ described then?

Jusup Mamay: The lines such as 'flying in the sky and glowing with golden light all over her body', 'how beautiful she is', and 'even the sun and the moon admire...' are used to visualize her beauty which is otherwise beyond description.

A: Are there these kinds of set descriptive words and sentences to depict other heroes such as Bakay and Külchoro?④

Jusup Mamay: To depict Bakay, I would use 'the extraordinarily wise old man Bakay with a gray, shining, long beard' and his own words to mirror his remarkable wisdom. His integrity is the most conspicuous quality of his personality. He speaks out whatever comes to his mind regarding his own hometown without exaggeration or concealment.

A: Apart from these heroic figures, are there any set poetic lines to depict Manas' steed and weaponry?

Jusup Mamay: Yes, I use set lines.

---

① Kanikey is the wife and helpful assistant of Manas, and is both intelligent and courageous.

② Loose skirt is a synecdoche for women.

③ Aychürök is the daughter-in-law of Manas. She is a fairy maiden, an outcome of the marriage between human being and god, can metamorphose into a white goose and fly in the sky. She is the wife of Semetey, the hero in the second episode of the epic.

④ Bakay is a main hero in the first episode of *Manas*. Külchoro is a main hero in the second episode of the epic.

A: How can you recall these words during the performance?

Jusup Mamay: They come to the tip of my tongue by themselves. For example, when a brave warrior goes on fighting on the battlefield, the lines that have been sung in the past about spears and rifles come to the tip of my tongue.

A: When you began to learn to sing *Manas*, what did you remember first, these set lines or the contents of the stories?

Jusup Mamay: Stories.

A: Then?

Jusup Mamay: The opening words.

A: What are the opening words?

Jusup Mamay: Those names of heroes such as Manas, Almambet, Kökchö and Külchoro. No matter where and when they feature, the stories will come along these words.

A: That is, the set lines you've talked about a moment ago that draw forth the story?

Jusup Mamay: Yes. That is to say that they come to your mouth immediately. It is difficult to sing out the verbal layouts if these words are skipped, or it is impossible to continue singing. I sing *Manas* in this way.

This interview provides us with at least the following insights. During his skilful performance before an audience, a *manaschi* can fulfill with ease his mission and win the audience's applause as long as he stores enough formulas in his mind. Without doubt, these set and recurrent lines, i.e. the formulaic words, constitute an important clue for the singer to tap into his memory for the epic's contents and to accumulate themes.

This kinds of formulas spread out in the whole performing process, huge in number and diverse in form, which makes efforts to classify them meaningless and futile. But it is crucial for us to understand the two most important representational forms. First, these formulas, transmitted orally for generations, are very old; in the performing process, they always maintain their old forms and remain unchanged. Into this category fall many repeatedly used words and sentences such as 'courageous warrior Manas', 'Ayköl Manas', 'brave warrior Manas', 'blue-haired wolf Manas', 'Aychürök, daughter of Akunbatyr', 'red battle flag embroidered with a golden crescent moon', 'sagacious Bakay', as well as the formulas made up of a few poem lines , such as:

Like gold and silver	Altin menen kümüxtu
Made of the cream part.	Xiröösünon bütkondoy.
As if made up of the propping-up pil-lars	Asman menen jeringdin
That lift up earth and sky.	Tiröösünon bütkondoy.
As if made up of the brilliant rays	Aying menen künündün
Of the sun and the moon themselves.	Birözünön bütkondoy.
Only the deep earth	Aldi kaling karajer
Can support Manas.	Manaska jerdiginen tütköndöy.

Another kind of formulas also expresses given meanings, and has relatively stable forms, but these formulas may change more or less in different contexts. This kind of formulas appears, and is mainly used in the form of *runs*.

The narrative structure, themes, and words of the *Manas* epic all tend to be formulaic. The overall external structure of the epic is in fact one large-scale formula, whereas lexical and syntactic formulas are internal ones pertaining to the epic's contents. A formula is not a yoke, but rather is like the blood that flows through the dissemination and performance of the epic. In the creative process of performance, 'the formula is used to construct poems; it often follows certain rhyme schemes and grammar rules, and the theme guides the singer to speed up his creative thinking to construct larger structures.'①

For a *manaschi*, to create and to sing are merely the two sides of the same coin. The manaschi's performance before an audience means that, to sing the epic's content, he should mobilize all the internalized formulas familiar to himself and the audience and that he should arouse the enthusiasm of the audience with vivid facial expressions, gestures, body language and fluctuating rhymes and tones in order to help the audience to understand and appreciate the epic. The performance of the *Manas* epic constitutes a comprehensive process of artistic presentation and a complicated form of artistic performance. Only in a process as such can the singer and the audience partake in the creation of the epic, play their respective roles in the performance, and enjoy much joy from such an interactive relationship.

This is the real mode of epic creation, i.e. "creation in performance". The more traditional formulas remembered by singers, the richer the content and the more improvisations during the performance, the more likely a singer's performance will strike a sympathetic chord with and get a warmer applause from the audience and be highly appreciated and admired by the audience. This is typical of how live oral epics are being performed. The printed version of the oral *Manas* epic is an incomplete substitute for its traditional live performance. This substitute can unfold the plot of the epic, but it fails to capture the richer and more colorful things behind the stories that are akin to the long evolution of oral epics. For instance, through the printed version of the sung text of Jusup Mamay, we can appreciate the poems and stories of *Manas*, but we are not able to appreciate this outstanding singer's performing skills and manners, i.e. his "creation in performance" in the traditional linguistic contexts. Singing (or performing) is the lifeblood of oral epics. Only through live performances under a given context can we capture the essence of oral epics, each performance being a renewal of the

---

① Yin Hubin, *Ancient Classics and Oral Tradition*, Beijing: China Social Sciences Publishing House, 2002: 112.

old oral epic tradition. 'The expression "oral tradition" applies both to a process and to its products.'① As a representative work of the Kirghiz oral tradition, *Manas* transmits oral messages from an ancient source, while its creation is a process of repeated singing by *manaschi*, one generation after another, of constant renovation and recreation, of handing down these messages through oral transmission in the interaction with the audience. Therefore, each singing is but one performance at a given time and in a given context during the long evolution of the epic – a process of the development of oral traditional communication. Though originating from within the oral tradition, 'the characteristics of each rendering will differ according to its position in the whole process.'② We must remember that the singing and performance of the epic is never a one-way process of message transmission. Epic singers and audience are both participants in the epic tradition. 'They share a great amount of "inner knowledge" and there is also a great quantity of very complicated exchanges and interactive processes.'③ For a *manaschi*, this process is a good opportunity to create his own new epic variation, to show his performing ability, to disseminate his own works to the audience, to broaden his influence on the audience and to win their compliments. For the audience, this is an opportunity to take part in the creation of the epic with their own viewpoints and aesthetic interests and to appreciate once more this old tradition. 'Each performance is the specific song, and at the same time it is the generic song. The song we are listening to is "the song"; for each performance is more than a performance; it is a re-creation.'④ The performance and transmission of the epic *Manas* also follow this law.

A particular song refers to a process in which each performance means for the

---

①   Jan Vansina, *Oral Tradition as History*, Madison, Wisc.: University of Wisconsin Press, 1985: 3.

②   Ibid. 3.

③   Chao Gejin, *Oral Poetics*: *Formulaic Diction of Arimpil's 'Jangar' Singing*, Nanning: Guangxi People's Publishing House, 2000: 98.

④   Albert B. Lord, as quoted in John Miles Foley, *The Theory of Oral Composition*: *History and Methodology*, Bloomington, Ind.: Indiana University Press, 1988: 42-43.

singer, in a new context, to create a text of his own, consisting of reworked and readjusted motifs, themes, and structures of an ancient epic and modeled on the ready-made formulas, by drawing on the tradition, his own capacities, and new results. In fact, for both the singer and the audience, such a performance is just one event in traditional life. The performance has in it irreversibility, and cannot be accurately and fully represented and recalled. 'Modes of variation include e-laboration, simplification, change in order within a series, addition or omission of material, substitution of themes, and, frequently, different ways of ending the song.'[1] An oral epic narrative is a complicated system mixed with simplicity and complexity, flexibility and openness; variations lie in the arrangement of impor-tant plots, or in the decorative depiction of details.

An ordinary song means that there are close links between numerous perfor-mances, each performed text sharing with one another the backgrounds from the same tradition. 'According to Foley, it is a "map" that guides the singer and the audience to tell an old story whose beginning and end are already known to them, following the set traditional patterns and the rules long familiar to the au-dience.'[2] At any rate, we are always amazed by the stability of the Kirghiz oral epic. All epic texts, regardless of the timing and place of their documentation, have doubtlessly developed from a shared tradition, are branches of the same riv-er, and a big tree growing out of the same root. Generations of audiences and singers have made their contributions to this stability.

Oral performance forms a complicated, yet interesting mixture of singers' body language, the demonstration of their performing skills, and the textual composi-tion. We can hardly imagine how to sum up the essential characteristics of *Man-as* when it is de-contextualized.

From the viewpoint of Prof. Lang Ying, we must attach importance to the fol-lowing four aspects in epic studies: (1) text; (2) singer (performer) as the

---

[1]   Ibid. 43.

[2]   Chao Gejin, *Oral Poetics: Formulaic Diction of Arimpil's 'Jangar' Singing*, Nanning: Guangxi Peo-ple's Publishing House, 2000: 243.

epic's creator and disseminator; (3) audience; and (4) social reality.[①] To come to a full, accurate, and concrete understanding of the creative performance of the Manas epic, we must observe the state of "creation in performance" in a given context and learn about the interaction between the singer and the audience through meticulous fieldwork. The artistic level of the oral text is not only directly related to the quantity of memorized formulas, a singer's lived experience and his accumulation of traditional knowledge, but also closely to the singer's state of mind, audience's moods, the surroundings of the performance, as well as the identity of the audience. At the end of the 19th century, Radlov noted that to please the audience, Kirghiz *manaschi* tried their best to exaggerate the contents of what they were singing, to mobilize their passion in accordance with the audience's moods and to try to involve the audience in the process of performance.[②] During the performance, the interactive relations between the *manaschi* and the audience are always the most important element. The best epic text emerges in a context most fitting for the singer to bring his talent into full play when both the singer and the audience are excited, enthusiastic, and passionate.

In short, *Manas* is representative of the Kirghiz long oral tradition. Formulaic structures, formulaic words, and formulaic text mark its external features. "Creation in performance" is not only a mode of epic creation but also a means to preserve and transmit the epic.

References:

Adil Zhumaturdi. "An Enquiry into the Secret of the Performing of the *Manas* Epic." *Kizilsuu Literature* 2 (2002): 60-75.

——and Tohan Ysak. *Critical Biography of Jusup Mamay, the Contemporary Living Homer and Great Singer of Manas*. Huhhot: Inner Mongolian University Publishing House, 2002.

---

① Lang Ying, *On 'Manas'*, Huhhot: Inner Mongolian University Publishing House, 1999: 192.

② See Vasilii Radlov, *The Dialect of the Kara-Kirhiz*, vol. 5 of *Examples of Folk Literature of the Turkic Tribes*, St. Petersburg: Eggers und Schmitzdorff, 1885.

Aliev, Said, Raikul Sarypbekov, Kadyrbek Matiev, eds. *Encyclopaedical Phenomenon of Epos 'Manas'*. Bishkek: Encyclopedia Press, 1995.

Aliev, Said and Turusbek Kulmatov. *Manaschi and Researchers of 'Manas'*. Bishkek: Sham, 1995.

Aytmatov, Chingiz. "The Beaming Height of the Ancient Kirghiz Spirit." Said Aliev, Raikul Sarypbekov, Kadyrbek Matiev, eds. *Encyclopaedical Phenomenon of Epos 'Manas'*. Bishkek: Encyclopedia Press, 1995: 25-34.

Chadwick, Nora K. and Victor Zhirmunsky. *Oral Epics of Central Asia*. London: Cambridge University Press, 1992.

Chao Gejin. *Oral Poetics: Formulaic Diction of Arimpil's 'Jangar' Singing*. Nanning: Guangxi People's Publishing House, 2000.

Foley, John Miles. "Oral-Formulaic Theory: Summary of Studies of Oral Tradition." Translated by Chao Gejin. *Studies of Minority Literature* 2 (1997): 86-90.

——*The Theory of Oral Composition: History and Methodology*. Bloomington, Ind.: Indiana University Press, 1988.

Chinese translation by Chao Gejin. Beijing, Social Science Documentation Publishing House, 2000.

Kart Dastan [Ancient Epic]. Artush: Kizilsuu Kirghiz Language Publishing House, 2003.

Lang Ying. *On 'Manas'*. Huhhot: Inner Mongolian University Publishing House, 1999.

Lord, Albert B. *The Singer of Tales*. Cambridge, Mass.: Harvard University Press, 1960.

Mamay, Jusup. *Manas, Semetey, Seytek, Kenenim, Seyit, Asylbacha and Bekbacha*. Urumqi: Xinjiang People's Publishing House, 1984-1995.

Manbet. *All Kinds of Variations of the 'Manas' Epic and Its Performance Art*. Urumqi: Xinjiang People's Publishing House, 1997.

Radlov, Vasilii. *The Dialect of the Kara-Kirghiz*. Vol. 5 of *Examples of Folk Literature of the Turkic Tribes*. St. Petersburg: Eggers und Schmitzdorff, 1885.

Reichl, Karl. *Turkic Oral Epic Poetry: Traditions, Forms, Poetic Structure*. New York/London: Garland Publishing, 1992.

Vansina, Jan. *Oral Tradition as History*. Madison, Wisc.: University of Wisconsin Press, 1985.

Yin Hubin. *Ancient Classics and Oral Tradition*. Beijing: China Social Sciences Publishing House, 2002.

Appendix 1
Excerpt form *Manas*[1]

...

The young and vigorous people are separated from the others,

They kill mares and share the meat every day.

The opponent they will fight with weapons is hero Köngtöy,[2]

The battlefield is in Belsaz.

Headed by Balta[3] and Jakip,[4]

The Kirghiz people gather in the field.

The grand red army flag of Orozdu[5]

Is decorated with the pattern of the golden crescent moon,

On it is written the name of Manas.[6]

'You shoulder it to go out to battle',

The flag is handed over to Kirgilchal.[7]

There are more than thirty thousand people

---

[1] This is the orally dictated sung text performed by singer Jusup Mamay in the early 1980s. In 1984 this text was printed in *Manas* (first episode, vol. 1: 83-90) by the Society for Folk Literature and Arts in Xinjiang Uygur Autonomous Region. As reference material for restricted circulation, this text was published in Kirghiz according to the original transcription of the dictated song. This episode provides us with an account of the first campaign of young hero Manas in which he defeats his opponent, famous hero Köngtöy of the Kalmak. See for the Kirghiz text the Chinese part of the present book.

[2] Köngtöy: hero from the tribe of the Kalmak. He was defeated by the young hero Manas during his first campaign.

[3] Balta: uncle of Manas. The singer sometimes uses epithets such as *Ak Balta* (white-faced Balta) and *Balta döö* (Giant Balta) to meet rhythmic and metric needs.

[4] Jakip: father of Manas. Noun-epithets include *Bay Jakip* (Noble Jakip) and *Khan Jakip*.

[5] Orozdu: grandfather of Manas.

[6] Manas: the hero of *Manas* in the first episode. The title of the whole epic cycle is also in his name.

[7] Kirgilchal: main warlord of Manas, commander of forty brave warriors.

Gathered in the field,.

They cover the land, shouting battle cries.

The news is passed on to hero Köngtöy,

On hearing it his mind saddens.

The Kalmak[①] have quite a large force,

The troups are sixty thousand in total.

The news spreads among the people,

Köngtöy comes to the battlefield disregarding all this.

Warrior Köngtöy goes to the front,

Prior to this he had been lying on his sickbed.

He selects warriors from his subordinates,

Ten extraordinarily strong and brave men are found.

Leading his army of sixty thousand men,

The strong and vigorous Köngtöy comes out to the battlefield.

The place where they gather

Is the grassland exposed to the sun in Belsazdin.

In the vast grassland above Kökoydung,

The people of the Kirghiz and Kalmak tribes crowd together and bustle about.

The stream of people rolls onto the vast battleground,

The time for battle and blood has come.

Like the waves surging on the lake,

The Kirghiz tribes

Are quite excited and without fear,

Each of them, filled with happiness,

Rolls up his sleeves for the battle;

Loud .and deafening cries and roars

Resound across the sky.

---

① Kalmak: tribal name, main enemy of hero Manas, his sons and grandsons. This relatively ambiguous name does not denote exactly the dominant population of the Kalmuk Republic of the Russian Federation.

Aged people straighten their backs,

Young ones are irritable and restless;

The sturdy men with broad chests and shoulders

Are eager to have a try.

Aged people with snow-white beards

Ride skillfully on fine horses.

People from the Kalmak come to the battlefield one after another,

Just like a dark mass of lice covering the ground.

Among Bakay,[①] Balta and Jamgirchi[②]

Who is actually the commander?

Bay Jakip, who enjoys high prestige and commands universal respect,

Is the first to speak:

'People say we should have brains in our heads,

And to give a banquet a host is needed.'

'Who will command this powerful army?'

'Without a leader to command us

The whole army cannot fight with one will nor act in unison.'

'What he said is reasonable, it is reasonable,'

People stop walking and start shouting,

Rapidly and indistinctly.

They choose Bakaydi to take the position of Khan.

Bakaydi, from this time on,

Receives the respectful title "Khan".

From then on till present times,

This title of Bakaydi Khan has remained unchanged.

Young hero Manas is in the prime of his life.

When the time has come to take revenge,

① Bakay: Manas' uncle and consultant.

② Jamgirchi: uncle and consultant of Manas. The singer sometimes uses Jamgir as substitute for the name of the hero.

Bakay Khan takes the lead to confront the Kalmak,

Against whom the Kirghiz bear much resentment.

People open their eyes to see

A very fierce Kalmak warrior

Come out of the camp ready to fight.

This is warrior Tatay,[1]

A very famous hero

In his army;

He lives among the Kalmak

Although from Manju[2] lineage.

His saddle horse is prancing about,

It looks as if it will smash the whole world;

He wears a silk cloak

Shining in the sun.

Holding a spear tightly in his hand, he adjusts his body position

Just like a one-humped camel dropping to the ground

With an unusually ferocious appearance.

This very strong warrior

Fiercely rushes out of the camp by himself.

Giant Jamgirchi wants to go to the battlefield,

Wishing to chop off the head of the enemy.

Bakay doesn't grant his wish, instead,

He gives an order to stop him.

There is another warrior named Semet,[3]

Once in a struggle to seize horses,

He defeated one after another the eighty people

Who jointly attacked him.

---

①   Tatay: a Kalmak hero.

②   Manju: the name of a tribe or territory. It might refer to the Manchu and their inhabitant areas.

③   Semet: a brave Kazak warrior.

He is a Kazak warrior named

Hero Semet by the people.

'Please let me go to fight against him,'

He comes to Bakay Khan asking eagerly for a battle assignment.

Although he is very eager to fight his request is turned down

Since Bakay Khan has a different plan in mind.

Chubak,[1] the young boy of nine years old,

Not being able to control himself,

Also comes to the Khan to ask for a battle assignment.

'Go now, Chubak, have good luck and realize the wishes your heart long
    cherished.'

'My son is too young to fight,'

These are the words Balta can never speak out loud.

The young Hero Chubak

Puts on his armor suit and gets all things in order;

Kök-teke[2] is the name of the riding horse

That suits him very well.

With the helmet worn tightly on his head

He rushes onto the battlefield and shouts angrily.

Nine years old,

Chubak is a brave and unmatched hero,

In the times of hero Manas

He becomes his lifelong partner and repeatedly performs outstanding deeds;

He will win today's honor,

And this is why Bakay gives him the assignment.

Chubak has grown up already,

He is going to the battlefield to fight against Manju Tatay.

---

[1]   Chubak: son of Balta, Manas' main warlord.

[2]   Kök-teke: the name of hero Chubak's steed meaning "black blue goat".

Tatay, the Manju hero,

Whose heroic name all people know.

He has defeated countless very capable warriors before

And has won great glories.

He doesn't know that in the past,

The Manggul① destroyed the hometowns of the Kirghiz and other oriental people

And forced them to escape their homes,

With heads covered in blood and too horrible to look at.

According to what people say,

Tatay defeated all his opponents in the fight,

He is wellknown everywhere.

Even a great warrior like Köngtöy

Relies on his support.

The nine years old powerful warrior Chubak

Encounters him at this very moment.

When Tatay faces Chubak

He pulls the reins to turn around his horse's head,

Looking at Köngtöy behind him

He asks the following questions:

'Sir Köngtöy, my respected leader,

I myself, Tatay, have killed

Countless enemies on the battlefield;

I am now a well-known warrior,

How can a Kirghiz young boy riding on the back of a baby horse

Be on an equal footing with me?

People will put me to shame if they know

That I fight with a young boy in front of the battle array.

---

①   Manggul: tribal name, might refer to the Mongols.

Please send someone else onto the battlefield

Instead of me, I will go back to my own army.'

He talks loudly and endlessly.

Kirghiz and Kalmak people live and pasture

Together on the same grassland;

They can basically understand from each other the words and expressions

For everyday use, such as 'come', 'go', 'walk' and 'stop'.

When understanding what the words mean,

Young man Ak-Baltanin

Feels humiliation and is burning with anger;

When getting nearer to Tatay

The quick-witted Chubak stabs at him with his spear.

Tatay, who is arrogant and unwilling to fight with Chubak

Is forced to move his bottom away from the saddle.

Swaying for a second he balances himself at last and turns his head

To glare at Chubak;

Fuming with anger,

Shaking his body and urging his horse,

Tatay charges towards Chubak.

'Damn you, Burut, [①]

You are like a dying goat scratching wilfully

Against the herdsman's stick,

It will lead you to death in the end,

This truth everyone knows.

You scratch yourself against the stick like the goat,

It seems that you want to kill yourself.

He shouts loudly and endlessly,

---

① Burut: tribal name, given to the Kirghiz by the Oriat Mongols. It continued to be used by the Qing government. The Minguo (Republic government) used the word "Kirghiz", which was claimed by the Kirghiz nationality itself.

Resembling fierce floods;

He shakes the spear in his hand

And charges ahead ferociously.

Hero Chubak, although he has never gone through a battle

And lacks the experience of fighting with the enemy,

Is young and smart,

Forceful and quick-witted.

He appears quite experienced,

Just as if he has gone through countless furious fights.

He strikes away Tatay's spear

And severely stabs him,

The arrogant Tatay.

That Manju, who is shouting endlessly,

Is killed by him on the ground without mercy.

Manju warrior Köbögön[1] refuses to accept this outcome,

Crying loudly with anger,

He charges towards Chubak.

Being attracted to Death

And calling loudly the heroic name of Tatay,

He cannot restrain his fury;

He cries endlessly like a mad dog,

And is burning with anger;

He rushes out to Chubak,

Bravely and fiercely.

Warrior Chubak, who is not found among the Oyrot,[2]

Concentrates all his energy;

---

[1] Köbögön: a brave warrior from Manchuria.

[2] Oyrot: in the epic, the Kirghiz people use the word *Oyrot* to refer the Oriat Mongols and their inhabitant areas.

Heroic eagle Chubak
Shakes the red-tasselled spear;
He strikes away
The spear of the shouting Manju
And severely pokes his own into that Manju's rib.
Can a man survive if stabbed by Chubak?
Can he stand up again once has fallen to the ground?
How can Chubak let him go while he is lying on his side
And supporting himself with his hand?
Two of the Manju
Died on the ground.
The destiny of the Kirghiz becomes promising.
Witnessing this scene
Köngtöy is in a towering rage and can impossibly calm down.
Giant Köngtöy, unlike the the others
Who can swallow the insult,
Is rocking his own body and whipping and spurring his horse
To rush forward.
Shouldering a shield
And swaying his two legs,
Köngtöy fiercely rushes on
Without any halts.
With the wolf-tongued spear in his hand,
Made of special steel,
Köngtöy, the unmatched warrior,
Has killed quite a lot of enemies.
His shield is made of black iron,
His giant body
Is like a black mountain.
He has fought many powerful warriors before

And has never been defeated by any of them.

He charges at the enemies' lines

And drinks the enemy's blood mixed with sugars.

In the past the Kara-Kitay[①] and Kalmak

Have never worried about their own fate;

Once danger and disaster appear,

They all believe that Köngtöy will make vigorous efforts to save them.

He is aggressive

And boldly marching forward,

It is obvious that he is bloodthirsty.

He charges at Chubak with all his efforts

And by just one stroke with his spear he beats Chubak down from the horse-
　　back.

Semeti, a Kazak,

Whips his horse immediately

To catch the escaping horse Kök-teke

And holds tightly its reins.

He throws the reins back to his master Chubak

And then rushes to the Kalmak to fight.

Kazak warrior Semet

Fights bravely with Köngtöy.

The Kazak Semet is killed

And hung by Köngtöy's spear-head.

'This is your Kirghiz warrior,'

Köngtöy shouts and throws Semet away,

'Don't waste my time,

Send me quickly your real warrior.'

Trembling with rage

---

① 　Kara-Kitay: a tribal name, referring to the black Qidan.

And burning with anger

Chong-jindi,[1] grasping the Sir- nayza[2] tightly,

Gets on his horse at once.

With the Sir-nayza in his hand

He charges to the front as swift as the wind and as quick as the lighting.

Ak-Balta opens his mouth at once:

'Respected Bakay and Jakip Khan,

Jamgirchi and Kirgilchal,

Please look and listen.

My son Chubak,

You too please come to me;

Elders, you all

May have seen and known

That I had applied to go to battle

But Bakay didn't give me the chance

To go to the front,

My son Chubak, however, he gave permission.

To escort Manas his whole life,

Going through fire and water,

Is his real cherished wish.

Since my father King Orozdu passed away,

Although we have ten brothers

And the congregation of Alash,[3]

We haven't been in any battles

With the Kara-Kalmak and Manjuga.

You were born for the honour of Alash

And for our happiness.

---

[1]   Chong-jindi: a name given to Manas after his birth by his uncle Ak-Balta in order to deceive the people.

[2]   Sir-nayza: spear of hero Manas.

[3]   Alash: the name of the tribal alliance of Kazak and Kirghiz.

Out of fear for Kalmak inspection
I have to change your real name
And give you the name Chong-jindi instead as a temporary one.
Your real name given by Allam
Was Manas.
Today is your first time to go to battle,
You will surely set the world on fire.
Your name "Manas" is being shouted as a slogan,
It is now your time to advance bravely.
Come on, Manas, you can go to the battlefield at once.
I wish you a smooth march.
Our people are being insulted and forced to swallow the humiliation,
You should fight the enemy bravely and take revenge on him for us.'
People raise their hands to pray for him
And watch him go to the battlefield.
The hero is marching
And I'd like to depict the scene at the time for you listening to.
If you don't pay attention,
You'd better stand aside as a deaf-mute.
Immortal hero Manas
Has some unforgettable portents and characteristics
That we should keep in mind forever.
Look! A young hero, fierce tiger and
Mighty army are marching forward,
The people watching are amazed at that scene:
Hanging from his forehead is a red mole
As big as a finger print,
His feet and head bare,
Wearing not a stitch of clothes on his body,
The child prodigy,

Seven or eight years old,

Holds the reins of the hero's horse to lead the way.

Beneath the two stirrups

Are two grey immortal rabbits,

They prick up their ears

And run quickly forward at the two sides of the horse;

They jump and run non-stop,

Their looks and posture are so moving.

The Kirghiz who witness this scene

Pray behind the backs of the others

And mention the name of Baabedin.①

A pair of tigers of black and white color accompanies them,

Running at the sides, people cannot escape

If they are confronted with them;

They are the companions of Manas and very loyal to him.

A thing even more miraculous

Is the moving giant python

As thick as a reel of splendid needlegrass;

Seized with terror

Some cannot help

Passing water in his trousers.

The two ears of the riding horse Kula②

Shine as candlelight

And its forehead shows luck.

---

① Baabedin: a famous 14th-century Islamic priest and craftsman in Central Asia, a propeller of Islamic mysticism. He travelled to many countries such as Arabia and Persia. He is regarded as a sage, and worshipped by Central Asian people such as the Kirghiz. People offer sacrifices to him and shout his name when they are in danger.

② Kulu-at: the name of Manas' horse. The singer always uses *Ak-kula* instead of *Kulu-at* to match the meter and rhythm.

This is an immortal horse coming from the wind.

On the behind of horse Kula

Five fingerprints were left

By the touch of the Kambar deity.[①]

On the back of the *ayköldün*[②] *horse*

A fairy maiden, wearing a *shökülö*[③] *hat*,

Is standing behind Manas;

Looking at her, everybody gasps in admiration.

The rare jewelry on her head

Is shining on the ground.

If we gaze at her from the front

We can see her tall and beautiful *shökülöhat*

Rising above the head of the hero.

The red-faced girl

Is pretty and tall,

People gaze at her and exclaim in admiration:

'Let's enjoy to the full,

How wonderful it is if she appears again.'

The sixty sheep are divided equally

Into two groups and are running

At both sides of the hero;

The hoofbeat of Kula

Sounds like the ones of the sixty riding horses,

Such a sight is so grand and exciting.

---

① Kambar ata: a guardian god and the first person who raised and trained the steeds in myths of the Kirghiz and other Turkic-speaking nationalities.

② Ayköl: honorific title for Manas, meaning "moon lake". The word expresses the auspicious moral of an ancient hero who is broad-minded, bold and unconstrained by nature.

③ Shökülö: an old style hat worn by Kirghiz girls. It is made of expensive silk, adorned with pearls, agate and cornelian. The top and brim of the hat, adorned with mink coat and a strip of gauze serve as a pearl to the beauty of the girl, having a strong Kirghiz cultural flavor.

Among the people watching from the sidelines
There are aged ones brimming with tears,
None of them can conceal the excitement in his heart;
The crowds of people pour about and hold up their heads to watch,
Nobody can hear what they are saying from the bottom of their hearts.
The resourceful young ones,
In front of Bakay and aged Jakip,
Ak-Balta and giant Jamgir,
As well as the group of silky-and-white-bearded elders,
Pick up the *komuz*① *to play beautiful music*
And open their mouth to sing songs;
Using the songs to express their feeling,
They win camels with humpbacks,
Fine horses with reins
As well as people's best wishes;
They win cloaks they take off at once
And countless money;
They shake their heads and reveal their real sentiments,
They become more excited obtaining all this wealth
And cannot calm down.
Casting glances here and there
And wearing the silver belt around the waist,
The black-haired wolf whips on his horse,
His face is shining like the sun.
Looking at him from behind,
People admire the ayköl army greatly.
Looking at his back,
People find his appearance like a white tiger.

---

①　*Komuz*: Kirghiz traditional music instrument, played by folk artists.

Looking at him from the front,

People find his invincible might like a giant dragon.

Looking at him from above,

People find his imposing manner like the immortal bird *alip kara*.[1]

Once he roars in anger

Or cries out loudly to intimidate,

His voice is as strong as that of forty-one mighty armies.

As an eagle born among the Kirghiz,

His appearance is like this.

When he bravely marches forward

People drive up the yellow-foreheaded livestock

And kill sheep to bless him.

Others follow soon after them

And select the lilac horse as sacrifice;

What people say covers all kind of things,

The silky-bearded elders are not absent.

Sitting steadfastly on the back of horse Ak-kula,

The mighty army knows peace of mind;

He leaves his own camp for the battlefield,

Like the Ala-too mountains[2]

His tall and sturdy figure is towering into the sky.

This warrior is fighting with the hero,

The mountains thunder and the earth shakes,

Köngtöy cries out 'Kangay',[3]

The people watching the fight tremble with terror.

The brave warrior rushes ahead with an indomitable will,

---

[1] *Alip kara kush*: the king of birds and beasts in myths of the Kirghiz and other Turkic-speaking ethnic groups. It always is a guardian god of epic heroes.

[2] Ala-too: mountains in the border area of Xinjiang, China, and Kyrgystan.

[3] Kangay: territory inhabited by tribes such as the Kalmak.

162

Riding horse Kula keeps on jumping;
Behind the back of Ak-kula
A cloud of dust is rising up to obscure the sun.
Holding tightly the spear in their hands
They stint no one's life
As if they hang them on a thread of horsehair.
They strike out their spears
To fight each other.
They come and go, strike and poke,
Kalday Köngtöy comes from the Kalmak
Whereas the brave Manas represents the Kirghiz.
The two fight a life-and-death struggle without concessions,
People are touched by such a scene of fierce fighting;
The shields break into pieces
And the armors are torn;
They fight and fight, never give in,
It is a real fierce battle.
Turning the horses
And picking up again the bloody spears,
They strike directly at the chest of the opponent.
They push away the striking spears
And dodge the fatal attacks;
None of them is jabbed nor sheding blood,
Their martial arts are really admirable.
Köngtöy thinks to himself:
'On my body is layer upon layer
Of iron armors,
In my hand is the sharp spear
That can stab everything through,
In the sheath is the sharp sabre

That can cut everything in the world;

I also have the crescent moon axe hanging at my waist

That can cut a stone into two pieces

With just one strike, no matter how hard it is;

Under my thigh is a hammer,

It can break the mountain

And make rocks fly around;

My riding horse knows nothing about hunger and thirst,

Neither does he

Get tired galloping;

I have all of these,

Including the well-known name "General Köngtöy";

That boy, a nobody, is not worth mentioning,

He is too young and not strong,

Only eleven or twelve years old,

Still smells of his mother's milk;

I will stab him to death without mercy,

His blood will pour out mixed with stool

And his chest will be cut open.

To fight with him is a waste of time

And a damage for Köngtöy's reputation.'

This pig plucks up his courage and is puffed up with pride,

Looking like the haze in the sky,

His anger shows on his face:

'Just like the poisonous spider, scorpion and snake,

I will give out all my venom;

I'd rather give up my name of Köngtöy

If I cannot stab him immediately.'

Flying into a rage

He turns his horse.

Seeing the figure of the Kalmak,

Hero Manas heads towards him without fear;

Escorted by the deities in front and behind,

The army of Manas is marching forward;

'I will certainly beat him.'

The escorting army is also dashing ahead disregarding its own safety;

Manas pulls the reins and whips the horse,

A cloud of dust is rising behind him;

The miraculous horse Kula

Runs as swift as the whirlwind,

Its beautiful hair and long tail are waving in the air

And its strong chest is just like an argali;[①]

Shouting his own name "Manas",

The young hero heads on.

Hearing the name of Manas,

Giant Köngtöy panics.

Köntöy comes over to challenge him,

The spear he pokes is struck away by Manas;

Warrior Manas, pulling the reins of horse Kula

And seeking the opportunity,

Makes a flank attack

By stabbing his spear into Köngtöy's rib,

The enemy shakes his body and falls down on the ground.

As a young tiger and daring general

He defeats most famous warrior Köngtöy

The first time he goes to battle.

Being frightened out of their lives,

The troops of Köngtöy have come to a dead end.

---

① Argali: large Asian sheep with large horns.

Trembling, with no one to lead and guide,

They recoil in fear.

Those warriors under the guidance of Köngtöy,

Witnessing the dignified manner of the black-haired wolf,

Having their hearts in their mouths, dare not step forward to battle;

They try their best to hide their heads in their collars

And show the bearing of those who consider themselves no ordinary beings;

The Kalmak who used to show off their strength

Have now lost their courage to respond.

The Kalmak feel quite helpless,

Experience great panic and see no future.

...

VII
The Sanctity of Epics and Their
Singing Ceremonies

Lang Ying

Abstract: Epics in China are mainly oral. The idea of divine power and custom in epics and their performing ceremonies and taboos still exist among many cultures. Oral epics differ from ordinary oral narrative literature. Popular ballads and legends are mainly secular, while the singing performance of oral epics has a sacred character. In some areas in China, an epic is not just to be sung by everyone or by whoever happens to be a singer. Among the singers in southern China who perform epics, it is quite normal that magicians also act as singers. The widespread featuring of this phenomenon has become one of the most important characteristics of the ethnic culture in the southern part of the country, and has incarnated the antiquity and distinctiveness of oral epics of ethnicities in the south. Parallels take place when it comes to the singing of the three major heroic epics in northern China. Be it the traditional belief in magic among ethnicities in the south or shamanism among those in the north, from an ancestral point of view, what magicians and shamans differ in from ordinary people is their unusual ability of receiving explicit instructions from divine beings.
Key words: singing ceremonies, epic singer, oral epic

An epic is the symbol of a nation's culture and the embodiment of a nation's spirit, which holds a sacred place in the nation's spiritual life and in people's hearts. The epics in China are mainly oral. The idea of divine power and custom in epics and their performing ceremonies and taboos still exist among many peoples. The singers' statement of 'being instructed in dreams' and their status of being sacrificial priests or magicians ensure epic singing's mystical and consecrated character.

1
Being a Magician as well as a Singer

Oral epics differ from other oral narrative literature. The bulk of popular ballads and legends are secular, while the singing performance of oral epics has a sacred character. In some areas in China, an epic is not just to be sung by everyone or by whoever happens to be a singer. Only priests can perform on special occasions or during certain ceremonies. Among the singers who perform and present epics, it is quite normal that magicians act as singers of epics, especially in the southern part of the country. Let us take Zhao Anxian of the Achang, singer of the *Zhepama and Zhemima* epic as an example. A priest himself, he takes charge of the ceremony of offering sacrifices, and practices sorcery to drive away devils and to cure patients besides being an excellent epic singer. Yang Gouyan, singer of Miao *Ancient Songs*, is both a magician and epic singer. The *byuqma* (a religious practitioner) of the Hani culture likewise practices sorcery and acts as a singer. Zhu Xiaohua, singer of *Haqniq aqpyuq colpol pol* (Grandfather Colpol pol of the Hanis), is a third-generation *byuqma* within his family. The singer of the Nuosu (a sub-group of the Yi) *Hnewo* epic is a *bimo* (religious priest), Naxi epics are sung by a *domba* (religious priest), the singer of the Wa *Sigangli* epic is a *bei zaix* (magician) and the singer of the Jingpo *Manau Jaiwa* epic is a *jaiwa* (magician-scripture master).[①] The singers of the Zhuang epics

---

① *Manau means* "group singing and dancing" in the Jingpo language. The most ceremonious festival of the Jingpo is the Manau Carnival. Manau is a large gathering intended to celebrate good harvests, to drive out evil spirits and to pray for happiness, success in cultivation and healthy crops to harvest.

Bouxluegduz and *Bouxbwk* and the Yao *Miloto* epic are almost all magicians as well. [①]

When Yi *bimo*, Naxi *domba*, Hani *byuqma*, Jingbo *dumsa*, Wa *bei zaix* and magicians of the Zhuang and Yao cultures preside over the ceremony of offering sacrifices or perform sorcery to dispel evil, they are priests and magicians. But when they sing the epics, they function as singers. The widespread featuring of such a combined function has become one of the most important characteristics of various cultures in the southern part of the country, and has incarnated the antiquity and distinctiveness of oral epics of cultures in the south.

The contents of the epics of those cultures are related to ancient times, notably epics about the genesis, migration and homage to heroes. Some of the epics are to be sung only at very special ceremonies. For instance, the Naxi Genesis is sung by a domba at the ceremony of offering sacrifices to Heaven, and the chapter about the "Origin of Offering Sacrifices to Heavenly Devils" in the Dulong Genesis by the priest at the ceremony of offering sacrifices to devils. At funerals among the Yi living in the areas of Dayao and Yao'an in Yunnan province, a bimo will sing the Meige epic. At the sacrificial ceremony held by the Yi living in Xinping and Shuangbai, the priest will sing the mythological Chamu epic, and, similarly, a shaman will sing the famous Hnewo epic at funerals among the Yi living in the Daliangshang and Xiaoliangshan areas. In addition, during the cao qi or bow-dancing festival, [②] the bimo will solemnly sing the Yi heroic epic King

---

① Liu Yahu, *On Southern Epics*, Huhhot: Inner Mongolian University Publishing House, 1999: 12-15, 297-298. Meng Guanxiong, Meng Haiqing and Meng Songyi, eds. and trans., "Appendix Ⅱ Brief Introduction to the Singers of *Miloto*," *Miloto*, Nanning: Guangxi People's Publishing House, 1998: 433-434: among the ten singers of *Miloto*, five are sorcerers. Lan Huaichang, Lan Shujing and Meng Tongshun, eds. and trans., *Miloto*, Beijing: China Folk Arts Publishing House, 1988: 544. According to the "Reading Notes of *Miloto*", the singers have absolutely played an important role in passing the epic singing.

② A traditional festival celebrating victories by the Lolo, a sub-group of the Yi living in Guangxi and Yunnan.

of the Bronze Drum.[1] The singing performance of Miloto is closely linked to the Bunu people who belong to the Yao.[2] The Yao have a ceremony for redeeming the vow made to the Lotoxi, mother-creator of the world. The Bunu ceremony as well as the ceremony meant to redeem a vow made to the twenty four male and female divinities are quite spectacular. On both occasions, animal sacrifices are offered, and a performance is executed by a priest who sings an epic pleading the case for redeeming a vow to the divinities and invoking the epic hero Miloto for protection from various deities. The Wa[3] hold a solemn ceremony to offer sacrifices to Moik   the genesis hero   before the spring sowing. At the ceremony, the bei zaix will sing the Sigangli epic, which extols Moik's deeds of creating human beings and the world to appeal for Moik to bless the Wa with good weather for crops. At the funeral ceremony held by the Achang people, the magician will sing the Zhepama and Zhemima epic to extol the Achang primogenitors, as well as a song of migration to lead the spirits of the dead to return to the land of their ancestors.

The Zhuang Bouxbwk epic describes Bouxbwk's heroic deeds of fighting against the god of thunder. Therefore, at the ceremony of appealing for rain, the magician will sing the epic. In the past, the Dong would hold a grand ceremony to offer sacrifices to the heroine Sax Sis (also called Sax, Sax Mags, Sax Laox, Sax Siis) before going to battle, and the magician would sing The Song of the Heroine Sax Sis to encourage people to fight bravely.[4] The ceremony to offer sacrifices is a very solemn and sacred event among the people concerned. At the ceremonies of offering sacrifices to Heaven, the divines, devils and ancestors or bidding farewell to the spirits of the dead, all the tribe members will listen with awe and piety to priests' or magicians' singing about the history of each tribe's

---

[1]   Bamoqubumo, *Literature of Ceremonies* (not yet published).

[2]   The Bunu are a branch of the Yao, with a population of 0.4 million people, scattered in the Du'an, Bama and Dahua Yao nationality automous counties in Guangxi prefecture.

[3]   Awa, Va, or Kawa in the Wa language.

[4]   Liu Yahu, *On Southern Epics*, Huhhot: Inner Mongolian University Publishing House, 1999: 12-15.

origin and migration as well as the deeds of its heroes. Among some cultures in the southern part of the country, priests and magicians have made great contributions to the preservation of their traditions and epics.

Parallels can be found when it comes to the singing of the three major epics of heroes in northern China. Adar, singer of Gesar from Naqu county in Tibet is a typical example. He can not only sing Gesar, but also treats patients with magical power.① Mabetale Alaman from Akqi county in Xinjiang is not only an influential Manas singer but also a well-known Tölölchü (augur). He excels in the traditional Kirghiz way of laying forty one-stone (a ritual of laying out forty stones to look into the future) or observing the line of one's blade bone. Those who have their children or anything missing, or want to know whether it is suitable for them to travel consult such singer-magicians.② Jusup Mamay, singer of Kirghiz epics, who has the reputation of a "living Homer", has successfully treated some patients and magically appealed for some sterile women to become pregnant. Among the Turkic language-speaking groups, the same person assumes the triple role of being a singer, a shaman and head of a clan all at once.

Take Dede Korkut for example. He is a well-known singer, an exceedingly powerful bakshi (shaman) and a tribal chieftain. Dede Korkut kitabi (The Book of Dede Korkut), with many editions circulating among groups speaking Turkic languages has become a classic, and in Uzbekistan and Turkmenistan the word bakshi is still being used to refer to both "singer" and "shaman". This linguistic phenomenon merits attention, because it proves that in the ancient Turkic soci-

---

① Yang Enghong, *Folk God of Poetry: A Study on the Ballad Singers of 'Gesar'*, Beijing: China Tibetology Publishing House, 1995: 57-59.

② In September 1998 I carried out field work in Akqi county, and interviewed Mabetale Alaman, who was then 59 years old. He could sing epic songs such as the adventures of *Manas*, Seytek, the fifth episode of the Manas epic, and the Kirghiz *Kurmanbek* epic. During festivals or ceremonies, he was always invited to sing an epic song from *Manas*. He is also famous as a divinatory practitioner. It is said that he had given a divination by the blade bone of a sheep and successfully located the place where a lost girl was found. He used forty pieces of stone to give us a divination and predicted the weather during the interview.

ety, a shaman also acted as a singer. Magicians and shamans have been regarded as the messengers between divine and human beings. There are various explanations of how epics have come into being. Source-tracing takes us back to the ancestral thinking and beliefs. Poetry was believed to have magic power: a singing magician or a shaman could invoke divines in the human world; their song of incantation had the supernatural power to dispel devils and cure illness. The development of ancient epic singing can be traced back on the basis of a large amount of data, that is, the earliest epic singers were mostly magicians, or shamans believed to possess a divine being who then conferred on them the ability to sing epics.

When talking about their personal experience, those artistic singers often argue that they have received the ability of singing epics from some bizarre dreams. The expression of 'being instructed in dream' still prevails among epic singers. Zhao Anxian, singer of the Achang Zhepama and Zhemima epic, recalled that he became very ill one day when he was twenty-one and fell into a coma on the same afternoon, as if he rose up to the sky and fought against various demons. He then met Zhepama and Zhemima, the ancestors of all human beings and the deity-creators. The divine beings taught him sorcery and the story of the creation of the world. After he came to back to the human world, i.e. regained consciousness, he knew not only how to recite scriptures and perform magic, but also the art of singing an epic. Yang Gouyan, singer of the Miao epic Ancient Songs, remarked that he fell seriously ill at the age of fifteen and was raving incessantly for days. On the fourth day, he fell into a coma and felt he arrived at a place he had never visited before, where many people were playing the lusheng (a reed-pipe wind instrument, used among the Miao, Yao and Dong) and singing ancient songs. His dead grandfather taught him how to sing as well as the secret to dispel devils. After he regained consciousness, he had at his disposal endless songs to sing and also had obtained the ability to perform sorcery.[1]

---

[1]   Liu Yahu, *On Southern Epics*, Huhhot: Inner Mongolian University Publishing House, 1999: 300-301.

It is quite normal for the singers of the Manas epic to believe in the saying of 'being instructed in dream'. Tinibek was a singer with a high reputation. When he was away from home, he had a dream about hero Manas and superiors Bakay and Almambet and Manas' forty warriors. One of them asked him to sing a song about Manas. The second day he agreed to sing the epic and began to sing, thinking of the silhouette of the heroes in his dream without knowing what he had sung. After he sang madly for hours, he fainted, foaming with saliva. The next day, he returned to his hometown and began to sing Manas unconsciously. Since then he had acquired the ability of singing the epic and became a well-known epic singer. [1]

In the early 20th century, Jusubakun, a famous epic singer living in Akqi county, Xinjiang, gained his ability to sing Manas thanks to a dream. According to his niece Marjek, the yak herded by her uncle Jusubakun ran across the borderline. Her uncle chased the yak into Kyrgyzstan and fell asleep by the roadside out of utter exhaustion. He found some millet in his mouth when an old man woke him up. After he swallowed the millet down, he couldn't help singing Manas. People set up a yurt (tent) and slew sixty horses for him. He sang for three days in a row and since then became a well-known singer of Manas far and near. Jusup Mamay, who enjoyed the name of "Homer in the contemporary era", said he dreamed of hero Manas, his superior Bakay and warriors Almambet, Chubak and Ajybay. All these heroes disappeared, as soon as he woke up from his dream. His parents at once slew a goat after they heard of his dream, and exhorted him not to tell anyone about his dream. Since then, he became extremely clever and learned Manas by heart after he read the hand copied epic only once. [2] It is impossible to list all the singers of Manas here, but they all claimed to have learned the epic in their dreams.

The saying of 'being instructed in dream' is quite common among singers of

---

[1]   Adil Zhumaturdi and Tohan Ysak, *Critical Biography of Jusup Mamay, the Contemporary Living Homer and Great Singer of 'Manas'*, Huhhot: Inner Mongolian University Publishing House, 2002: 43.

[2]   Lang Ying, On *'Manas'*, Huhhot: Inner Mongolian University Publishing House, 1999: 17, 153-157.

Gesar. The senior singer Grags pa said he dreamed at the age of seven that Vdan-ma, the general of King Gesar cut his belly, took out his bowels and put inside the book of Gesar. After he woke up from the dream, he was subjected to a serious illness. Since then he could sing the number of lines from Gesar that e-quals more than thirty volumes of a written text. Another singer Gyu-sman recollected that when she was sixteen, she dreamed that a fairy and a devil vied for her. The fairy asked her to report back to the villagers the heroic deeds of Gesar, who had subdued the devil in the best interests of the people. She also suffered from a serious illness after the dream and since then she could perform the singing of Gesar.[1] The singer Rin-chen-dar-rgyas from Qinghai can sing many written volumes of Gesar. He said he had a dream before he reached the age of twenty. He dreamed that he followed King Gesar and triumphed over the Roc Kingdom (Khyunf Rdzong) in Dgav Sde (now Yushu prefecture of Qing-hai). He and his troops seized many rocs and returned in triumph. He then dreamed for three days and could sing Dgav sde khyung rdzong (an episode of the Gesar epic). A Buddhist called A-kya-ra-mu-ni-sha-sa, who is well known for his writing of Gesar, said he met with difficulties when writing Competing for Being the Ruler by Horse Race; he then prayed to Gesar and dreamed about the heroes of the Gesar epic. He got some inspirations after he woke up and could keep on writing the epic.[2]

The formation of the saying of 'being instructed in dream' is very complicated, which invites various interpretations in academic circles. But from the perspective of the epic's sanctity, this saying comes down in one continuous line with the idea of 'being instructed by a deity' constituted by traditional thinking and consciousness. Be it the traditional belief in magic among the southern cultures or in northern shamanism, from an ancestral point of view, what magicians and shamans differ in from ordinary people is their unusual ability of receiving

---

[1] Yang Enhong, *Folk God of Poetry: A Study on the Ballad Singers of ' Gesar'*, Beijing: China Tibetology Publishing House, 1995: 147-157.

[2] Xu Guoqiong, "Gesar's Singers," *Forum of Folk Literature* 1 (1986): 73-75.

explicit instructions from deities. As mentioned before, there are still some sacrificial priests and magicians singing epics at ceremonies offering sacrifices. The
influence of traditional culture is so strong that it permeates into the bloodline of
a nation. A nation's cultural tradition has taken shape over a long period of
time, hence constituting the nation's collective sub-consciousness, thinking patterns and collective psychology. Neither the singer nor the audience of the epics
can entirely break with the nation's cultural tradition and collective sub-consciousness. This is the existential basis of the saying 'being instructed in
dream'.

From a psychological perspective, the epic singers grew up in a context akin
to the one as sung in their respective epics. Ever since they learned to sing and
perform the singing of the epic, their thinking has been connected with the plot
and characters of the epic. It is quite natural that one dreams at night about what
one thinks at daytime. Jusup Mamay, a great Kirghiz singer, remarked at the
"Symposium on China's Manas Epic": [1] 'Manas singers think about the scenar-
ios from the epic day and night and are intent on singing the epic well, how
could the plot and characters of the epic not enter into their dreams?' In response to the questions posed by a visiting scholar from abroad he said: 'I recite
Manas every day, and, after a considerable period of time, it is natural for me to
dream of the characters from Manas.' [2] This explanation is convincing. Moreover, some excellent epic singers' memory is indeed incredibly remarkable. Let
us take Jusup Mamay as an example. He can not only sing perfectly a large number of Manas epic verses, comparable to eight volumes of a written text with
230.000 lines, but also eleven "volumes" of Kirghiz heroic epics on end. The

---

[1]   This symposium was held on December 26-28, 1990 in Urumqi, Xinjiang. The title of of Mamay's presentation is "How Did I Begin to Perform the *Manas* Epic". The presentation was translated by Adil
Zhumaturdi from Kirghiz into Chinese and published in the book *Study on 'Manas'*, edited by the Xinjiang Society of Folk Literature and Arts, Urumqi: Xinjiang People's Publishing House, 1994: 234-
239.

[2]   Lang Ying, *On 'Manas'*, Huhhot: Inner Mongolian University Publishing House, 1999: 157-160.

most amazing thing is that he can sing out of his memory the Kazak Seven Khans, which, in written form, contains 140. 000 lines in the first volume alone. After the epic was published in Kazak, it aroused great response among the Kazak. Jusup Mamay said that he had once read the manuscript when he was young and stored it in his memory and remembers it freshly in his old age. The Kazak regard him as a sage and a divine. Parents ask him to touch their newly-born babies and herdsmen strive to get and wear the clothes he has worn, believing that Jusup Mamay's excellent wisdom can be transmitted through his hands and clothes. Given such circumstances, the Kazak are not at all amazed about his claim of 'being instructed in his dream'.

2
Worship to the Supernatural: Magic in Epics

Epics are sacred and endowed with supernatural power in some peoples' eyes. The supernatural and magic are believed to be able to emerge through excellent epic singers' performance. So in the time of natural and man-made disasters, they usually invite a singer to sing a section of an epic, because they believe the epic retains the supernatural magical power to dispel evil. According to the Manas chapter of The Turkic Heroic Epic authored by the Russian scholar Zhirmunsky, a singer called Keldibek from the 19th century was said to sing Manas in a yurt for herdsmen when the wind became gusty all of sudden and rain was pouring down without interval, which threatened the safety of the people and their livestock. At that critical moment, Keldibek sang Manas loudly and skillfully, and the clattering of hoofs could be heard from outside the yurt, which was so loud that the earth started shaking. Manas and his forty warriors appeared and then disappeared again in a glimpse. The wind and rain let up; the disaster was dispelled. [1] The Kirghiz believe that the Manas epic continues to retain supernat-

---

[1] Victor Zhirmunsky, The Turkic Heroic Epic, Leningrad: Science, 1974: 29.

ural magic forces and that these will help them to gain protection from Manas' spirit when the epic is being sung. Therefore, some Kirghiz herdsmen will invite a manaschi (a singer of the Manas epic) to their home to sing a section of Manas when their family members or livestock fall ill, or when a woman is giving birth to a child, so as to cure illness and avoid disaster, dispel evil and subdue demons.

The worship of magic and the belief in the supernatural power of epics is manifest most prominently in Mongolian epic singing. According to the collected verses of the Mongolian singer Sulfongga, once a plague hit the area of Balinyouqi Banner and a large number of cattle and goats died of illness. Believing the Geser epic enjoys the power to cure illness, avert disaster, dispel evil and suppress devils, the villagers invited the folk singer Purong who sang Geser for three days and nights. Abeilmede, a famous singer from Wulianghai, said:

Villagers would invite the singer to their home to sing the epic at any time when they encountered disasters, i.e. their livestock died by large numbers; the old and the young constantly fell ill; they frequently confronted disasters or other causes necessitating the need to dispel evil. The singer might not be able to keep on singing because of a sore or swollen throat. If this were the case, both sides would feel that the circumstances were inauspicious. The family that invited the singer was convinced that it would be impossible to dispel evil in one or two days because of the mounting disasters in the family and would not let the singer leave until he was finished with the whole section. [①]

In some areas of Xinjiang, famous singers would be invited to the residence of influential people to sing Janger from the first day to the third or fifth day of the lunar year. Festive cultural entertainment aside, the most important objective

---

①   Sarengerle, *On the Ethnic Feature of the Formation of the Mongolian Epic*, doctorial dissertation, Department of Ethnic Literature, Graduate Institute attached to the Chinese Academy of Social Sciences, 1998: 47.

was to dispel demons. The Mongolian in Buryatia in the Russian Federation venerate epics very much. A singer once said: 'The so called epic is no more than a means to extol the great achievements that the god of mountain had made when he was still a human being. Therefore, when an epic is sung, mountain divinities will be present among the audience.' If the singing of the epic impresses the divinities, they will dispel the fierce cold winter and bring in the warm spring to exempt human beings and their livestock from decease and enable the pasture to flourish.[1] The Tibetans firmly believe that their Gesar epic has the magic power to dispel evil and drive away devils. Wherever disasters strike, inviting a singer to sing a section of Gesar will help to drive away the disasters. In the area of Bama of Guangxi, the magician will sing the chapter "Creation of Human Beings" which belongs to the epic Bouxluegduz when treating a patient, and the chapter "Creation of Cattle" when treating cattle illness.[2]

Because the epic is sacred and has the magic of supernatural power, there are some taboos for singers at the time of singing. For instance the Yao magician will be forbidden to have sexual intercourse, and will take a bath and fast for twenty days before he sings the epic Miloto. The livestock that will be slain at the singing ceremony will be separated from and forbidden to mate with those non-sacrificial ones for twenty days before the ceremony.[3] In some areas, it is forbidden to sing all chapters of Janger at one performance, for it is believed that this would bring misfortune, or even cause the singer's death. Whereas in some other areas people believe that once the singer begins to sing a chapter, he must finish it. If not, or if someone in the audience would leave in the middle of the performance, both the singer and the audience would be subjected to a shortened lifespan. To sing Janger is an important event, so full preparation should be

---

[1] Siqinbatu, 'Janger' and the Mongolian Religious Belief, Huhhot: Inner Mongolian University Publishing House, 1999: 39.

[2] Liu Yahu, On Southern Epics, Huhhot: Inner Mongolian University Publishing House, 1999: 41.

[3] Lan Huaichang, Lan Shujing and Meng Tongshun, eds. and trans., Miloto, Beijing: China Folk Arts Publishing House, 1988: 545-546.

made beforehand. If otherwise, the singer may have trouble in singing it fluently, hence inducing misfortune, e. g. a hurricane. Some singers sing Janger on their knees to show their reverence to the supernatural power and their respect to the heroes from the epic. [1] Similar taboos are still be observed by the singers of Manas. Let us take Jusup Mamay as an example. He could sing Manas at the age of eight, but his father cautioned him not to sing it in public before he reached the age of forty, for he believed Manas was sacred and misfortune would fall upon the singer if he would begin singing the epic at a young age.

In some areas and among some ethnicities, grand ceremonies will be held before kicking off the singing of the epic. Singers of Achang will light altar lamps and pray to Zhepama and Zhemima, the two divinities in the epic, before they start singing the epic. A Tibetan singer will set an incense burner table or hang the pictures of King Gesar or of other heroes from the epic and burn with respect incense to honour Gesar before he dares perform the singing. [2] The same ritual is in place when performing the Mongolian Janger epic. For instance, in some areas, before singing Janger, a ceremony of burning incense and lighting up altar lamps is needed in order to offer sacrifices to Janger. In Wenquan county, Xinjiang, the singer will shut tight roof windows and doors of the yurt, respectfully burn incense and pray. Some singers will hold a ceremony in which they fire guns to dispel devils before singing the epic. [3] The singing of the epic being sacred, devils should be driven away so as to guarantee the environmental sanctity for singing the epic.

All the above-mentioned phenomena indicate that reverence for the epics'

[1]   Siqinbatu, '*Janger*' and the Mongolian Religious Belief, Huhhot: Inner Mongolian University Publishing House, 1999: 36.

[2]   Jiangbian Jiacuo, On '*Gesar*', Xining: Qinghai People's Publishing House, 1986: 79; Yang Enhong, *Folk God of Poetry: A Study on the Ballad Singers of 'Gesar'*, Beijing: China Tibetology Publishing House, 1995: 147-157.

[3]   Rinchindorji, On '*Janger*', Huhhot: Inner Mongolian University Publishing House, 1999: 14; Siqinbatu, '*Janger*' and the Mongolian Religious Belief, Huhhot: Inner Mongolian University Publishing House, 1999: 32-38.

sanctity is still on hold in the country's oral culture, through which we can look into the traditional features of the sanctity, stateliness, and mystique conveyed by ancient epics, which provide precious data for studying the formation and development of epics. We, however, should also note that the sanctity as a feature of epic singing has been abating along with the passage of time and the speeding up of modernization, while secularity is on the increase. When epic singers are growing older and frail and the number of youngsters among the audience is decreasing, we are facing the threat that there will be no epic singing anymore in the future if those aged singers die. Therefore, saving oral epics and the knowledge of their orally transmitted traditions through modern technology is a pressing task.

3

Jusup Mamay and the Manas Epic He Sings

I would like to pay some more attention to Jusup Mamay (1918-   ), the only one in the world who can sing the whole eight episodes of the Manas epic. He was born into a herdsman's family in Akqi (in a remote and cold mountainous area to the south of Tianshan Mountain). His father had a great passion for Manas, his mother and elder sister were both well-known local folk singers and his elder brother Balbay was a famous collector of oral literature. Balbay's greatest contribution to the Manas epic is his documentation of the first three episodes of the version of Manas sung by the great epic singer Jusubakun, and the last five parts sung by Eblayin, both coming from the county of Akqi. Balbay artistically reworked and recreated the contents sung by the two artists and turned them into a complete sung text of Manas in verse. Balbay entrusted this epic text to his eight- year-old brother Jusup Mamay and taught him the tune and techniques. From then on Jusup Mamay kept memorizing the more than 230.000 lines long epic until he turned sixteen. Balbay lost his text during the war in 1937, but Jusup Mamay incorporated Balbay's version in his own singing, and began his career as a singer of the Manas epic by relying solely on his memory. From 1961 to 1964 he sang the first six episodes of Manas, and from 1979 to 1981 also the seventh and eight episode of the epic. All eight episodes of Jusup Mamay's Manas sung text were published in 1995 in the form of eighteen volumes. [1]

Jusup Mamay has a strong memory. Apart from the Manas epic, he has also sung ten other epics, eight of which have been published (Er Töshtük, Kurmanbek, Bagish, Toltoy, Saykal, Mamake Shopok, Koban and Jet kahan (Seven Khans)); the other two (Aybay and Jangar murza) will be published soon. It is surprising that Jet kahan is a Kazak epic and its publication has evoked many reactions. Jusup Mamay can also relate folk stories. The stories he narrates are rich in content and marked with distinct characteristics. They have become an important chapter in A Collection of Folk Stories of the Kirghiz. [2] Jusup Mamay enjoys the reputation of a "living Homer" and "a treasure house of the folk literature of the Kirghiz".

References:

Adil Zhumaturdi and Tohan Ysak. *Critical Biography of Jusup Mamay, the Contemporary Living Homer and Great Singer of 'Manas'*. Huhhot: Inner Mongolian University Publishing House, 2002.

Bamoqubumo. *Literature of Ceremonies*. Not yet published.

Collection of Folk Stories of the Kirghiz [Kirghiz]. Urumqi: Xinjiang People's Press, 1996. Vol. 4.

Jiangbian Jiacuo. *On 'Gesar'*. Xining: Qinghai People's Publishing House, 1986.

Lan Huaichang, Lan Shujing and Meng Tongshun, eds. and trans. *Miloto*. Beijing: China Folk Arts Publishing House, 1988.

Lang Ying. *On 'Manas'*. Huhhot: Inner Mongolian University Publishing House, 1999.

Liu Yahu. *On Southern Epics*. Huhhot: Inner Mongolian University Publishing House, 1999.

---

[1]　*Manas* [Kirghiz], 18 vols, Urumqi: Xinjiang People's Publishing House, 1984-1995.

[2]　*A Collection of Folk Stories of the Kirghiz* [Kirghiz], Urumqi: Xinjiang People's Press, 1996, vol. 4.

Mamay, Jusup. "How Did I Begin to Perform the Manas Epic". Translated by Adil Zhu-
    maturdi. *Study on 'Manas'*. Edited by the Xinjiang Society of Folk Literature and
    Arts. Urumqi: Xinjiang People's Publishing House, 1994: 234-239.

——*Manas* [Kirghiz]. 18 Vols. Urumqi: Xinjiang People's Publishing House, 1984-
    1995.

Meng Guanxiong, Meng Haiqing and Meng Songyi, eds. and trans. *Miloto*. Nanning:
    Guangxi People's Publishing House, 1998.

Rinchindorji. *On 'Janger'*. Huhhot: Inner Mongolian University Publishing House, 1999.

Sarengerle. *On the Ethnic Feature of the Formation of the Mongolian Epic*. Doctorial disser-
    tation. Department of Ethnic Literature, Graduate Institute attached to the Chinese A-
    cademy of Social Sciences, 1998.

Siqinbatu. *'Janger' and the Mongolian Religious Belief*. Huhhot: Inner Mongolian Univer-
    sity Publishing House, 1999.

Xu Guoqiong. "Gesar's Singers." *Forum of Folk Literature* 1 (1986): 73-75.

Yang Enhong. *Folk God of Poetry: A Study on the Ballad Singers of 'Gesar'*. Beijing:
    China Tibetology Publishing House, 1995.

Zhirmunsky, Victor. *The Turkic Heroic Epic*. Leningrad: Science, 1974.

——and Nora K. Chadwick. *Oral Epics of Central Asia*. London: Cambridge University
    Press, 1969.

VIII

A Comparative Study of Kazak Heroic Epics and Fairy Tales

Huang Zhongxiang

Abstract: Kazak heroic epics bear a close relation to Kazak fairy tales. Fairy tales came into existence earlier than heroic epics and quantatively surpass heroic epics. In the present thesis, a comparative study of Kazak epics and tales about crack shots and heroes leads to the conclusion that tales and heroic epics share the same motifs as well as the same genealogy, which opens up a brand new way for the study of heroic epics and provides a basis for the study of nomadic pasture culture.

Key words: heroic epics, fairy tales, comparative approaches

With a population of over a hundred million, the Kazak mainly reside in the Republic of Kazakhstan in Central Asia and in China. The more than 1.300.000 Kazak in China mainly populate Ile Kazak Autonomous Prefecture, Changji Hui Autonomous Prefecture, Buratala Mongolia Autonomous Prefecture, Barkol Kazak Autonomous County in Hami region of Xinjiang Uygur Autonomous Region in China's northwest, while a small number of Kazak lives in Gansu Province and Qinghai Province. Being an ancient nomadic tribe, the Kazak live on husbandry production. The distinct agglutinative language used by the Kazak belongs to the Kipchak or northwestern branch of the Turkic language family, a sub-family of the Altaic languages. The Kazak living environment as well as its special culture background provides a fertile land for the creation and enrichment of oral literature. As a result, various genres, such as fables, legends, stories, and songs, especially folktales and heroic epics, have developed. A multitude of heroic epics are still spread among the Kazak.[①] These heroic epics, created across time and space, are appreciated for their rich contents and profound cultural connotations.

All the Kazak folktales, myths and legends form a huge system of prose works. Folktales combine imaginary and realistic features, which truly reflect social changes. These folktales are not exactly a copy of the social reality of the Kazak but a conjectural representation of their life. The creation of the protagonists in those folktales, including human beings, animals, plants, inanimate things as well as imaginary fairies and ghosts, has never been temporally or spatially restricted. There is a wide range of tales with rich contents, which constitute the large bulk of this orally transmitted liteature. Classification is therefore a complex issue. With the help of the popular Aarne-Thompson classification system, the tales concerned can be categorized into different groups. Chinese scholars usually make classifications in terms of content. Thus, the Kazak stories are categorized as animal and plant stories, fairy tales, secular stories, stories about quick-witted persons and humor. Among those narratives, fairy tales are most closely related to heroic epics. The present paper attempts to analyze the tales in order to discover their connections with heroic epics.

Kazak fairy tales, like those of other nations, make up the plot of motifs with rich imagination and unusual composition. Kazak fairy tales are composed of stories that have been passed down from ancient Turkic clans, stories that the Kazak themselves created later as well as stories borrowed from other ethnic groups. Kazak fairy tales are primarily concerned with crack shots, heroes, shamanism and so on. The first two categories are meant to eulogize heroes' bravery, which is genealogically related to heroic epics.

---

① Examples of epics and information about their various editions can be found in Appendix I.

1

Features of Heroic Epics as Manifest in Crack Shot Tales

Kazak crack shot tales have a very long history and play a dominant role in Kazak fantasy stories. Tales like *Khula Mergen*,[①] *Sur Mergen*, *Han Mergen*, *Hunter Kharlibay* (Angshi Kharlibay) and *Alaman and Jolaman* are all concerned with crack shots. In spite of the various plots and contents, all the stories illustrate ancient hunting life. A well of fantasy is employed in this kind of stories to help express the ancient hunter's struggle against Mother Nature. The crack shots are extraordinarily capable, valiant, indomitable, wise and inventive, and people thus multiply on their preys. The theme of those fantasy stories concerns the eulogization of the brave spirit that crack shots have displayed in their fighting against nature and wild animals. The most representative example is *Arikh Mergen*.[②]

Once upon a time, a super crack shot named Arikh lives on hunting and offers consultations to people around him in order to help them make a living. He distributes to them all the preys he hunted, not allowing a single person to be tormented by hunger or to wear shabby clothes. Tramping over hills and dales, passing through the sand and wading across rivers, Arikh goes hunting by himself. One day, when he is boiling meat, a beauty – the incarnation of a copper-clawed goblin – spies on him from behind. He immediately shoots her twice and finds the corpse the next day. He wrestles with a fierce tiger and manages to kill it with difficulty. He walkes on and shoots the single-eyed devil that he comes

---

[①]   All the fairy tales in the present paper are taken from *Kazak Folktales*, Urumqi: Xinjian People's Press, 1981; and *Kazak Folktales*, Alma-Ata: Writers Press, 1988.

[②]   Arikh Mergen *was issued in* Shalghin *in 1980 sponsored by Xinjiang People's Press. In 1987, the second volume of* Kazak Folktales *published by Xinjiang Ile People's Press included the Khusayin Jumadil version. The verse edition, edited by Makhsut Mughut, was collected in the fifth volume of* Epics of the Kazak, *Beijing: Minzu Publishing House, 1986.*

across in a remote valley. Just then, people from the *awil* (village) come and find him. He generously hands out to them all his preys, as well as the properties and livestock of the single-eyed devil.

The characteristics of the hero embodied in Arikh are in line with the theme of Kazak heroic epics. Crack shot Arikh is a super hunter and wise hero. The fact that he goes hunting alone can be regarded as a great progress over the more usual group hunting and gathering in a clan society. Not only Arikh in *Arikh Mergen* but also the hunters in other ancient stories hunt on their own. For instance, Kharlibay in *Hunter Kharlibay* hunts outside by himself all year long. Khala in *Khala Mergen* lives alone in the wilderness by hunting deer. These hunters hunt for fun or simply to protect the livestock. In this respect, they differ greatly from those hunters in the time of developing animal husbandry vis-à-vis shrinking hunting as a subordinate means of production. Arikh hunts not only for himself but also for the people around him. After he has killed the copper-clawed goblin and the single-eyed devil, he unconditionally distributes all the grains, livestock and treasures to others. The villagers will go out to look for Arikh if he stays out a little bit longer than usual, for they cannot live without him. Arikh never takes hold of the results of other people's labor; he is not a ruler but a self-reliant man. To guarantee security in his area, he battles against beasts and devils, which is characteristic of heroic epics. Similar heroic characteristics are vividly described in the tale *Hunter Kharlibay*. Kharlibay hunts all year long and looks after the people around him. He generously distributes every single piece of gold he receives after he has mastered the language of the birds. At the cost of his own life, he spreads to the villagers the news he hears from the birds about a severe flood, an intensive earthquake and an avalanche. As a result, he is transformed into a black stone.

Another characteristic of crack shot Arikh is his struggle against devils, for example his encounter with the single-eyed devil. The single-eyed devil is a peculiar creature that lives on livestock, wild animals and even human beings; he lives in a huge cave and can easily move a giant stone to block the entrance. The single-eyed devil features in early oral literature and it was widely spread among the Altay clan societies such as the Turks and Mongolians. Later on, the image was incorporated into the plots of various stories and heroic epics. He is described as a devil attempting to eat the princess in *Gülkhizhan*, a giant killing the hero Jayikh in the story *Edil and Jayikh*, a cruel single-eyed goblin in Er *Dodan* and *Alaman* and *Jolaman*, and a vicious devil in the heroic epics *Khula Mergen* and *Joyan Mergen* and *Khorkhit Ata Kitabi*.

2
Features of Heroic Epics as Manifest in Heroic Tales

Heroic stories, centering on extolling the uncommon experiences of heroes and narrating the crusades and fights among ancient clan societies, form an important component of Kazak tales. Ancient heroic stories and crack shot tales crisscross and intersect in terms of content. Stories praising the heroic spirit of a main character take up a considerable proportion of ancient fantasy stories. Compared with crack shot tales, heroic stories are more complicated in terms of plot and structure and richer in terms of content. Therefore, stories about heroes are more similar to heroic epics. The basic motifs in both heroic stories and heroic epics cover: the plight of the parents, request for a child and blessing by divinities, the mother's pregnancy, unusual birth and growth of the hero, battle steed, hometown, tent, information about the enemy, confirmation of the offensive enemy, preparing the steed, bow and word, going out to confront the enemy, the might of the hero, discovering the enemy and meeting them up, notifying each other's names, fight, the enemy's failure and begging for mercy, killing the enemy and return in triumph. As a matter of fact, heroic stories are just the rudiments of heroic epics.

The hero's unusual birth and growth: The hero's birth is often unusual. He is either the youngest of the brothers like Töstik in Hero Töstik (Er Töstik) or a son born after the prays of an old couple as Dildash in *Hero Born for the People* (Eliüshin Tuwghan Er). In other stories, the hero's birth is even more unusual. For instance, Nan in Nan *Batir* is born only because his mother has eaten some special food. The premonitions of the special fate of the hero appear at his birth. 'The head is as big as a pan and the eyes are as big as wooden bowls', is the way in which Dildash in *Hero Born for the People* is described. In *Hero Kendibay Riding a White-Spotted Yellow Horse* (Ker Khula Atti Kendibay), Kendibay grows up at an amazing speed which is not counted by the year but by the day: 'He is able to laugh on the sixth day, to walk on the sixtieth day and in the sixth year he has grown up into a robust and stalwart young man who can easily tackle the people who come to challenge him.'

The hero's battle horse: Heroes are likely to be blessed by deities with miraculous steeds. For instance, the light maroon steed Kendibay rides on is given birth to by a horse bitten to death by a wolf. The steed of the hero Dildash is originally a lame, yellow-spotted horse left behind by the enemies who came to steal the horses and is raised by Dildash's father with a wooden basin of water and a lump of grass. Thus, the steed gets the name "Yellow Spots and Wooden Basin". The battle steeds of heroes are horses able to speed up like flying or heavenly horses able to catch the feather of a bird. Like the battle horses in heroic epics, they can speak, offer suggestions to the hero and foretell the future at crucial moments. The steed is approachable to no one other than its master and may even sacrifice its own life for him.

The hero's expedition: Some heroes go on an expedition to look for brothers and livestock lost in remote herding areas. For example, Töstik looks for his eight elder brothers and their bulk of livestock. Some heroes depart to look for their parents and for the livestock the enemy looted at the young age of the heroes, in order to take revenge, and to eradicate the old disgrace and hatred. For example, the hero Dildash goes on an expedition to look for his mother and get revenge for the villagers. Kendibay expedites to save the hero Marghanbay and the villagers, and eventually rescues them and goes back to his own home-town. The heroes usually travel at a rapid speed: a six months' journey can be completed within six steps. They can jump over a bird before it stirs to get off the ground. To them, oceans, lakes, rivers and mountains look no different from flat ground. After obtaining his own steed, the hero carefully prepares his five weapons – the *kurbash* (a leather whip used for punishment), the wand, the bigheaded stick, the spear, the bow and the arrows – and embarks on his expedition. The heroes arrive at their destination after a month or a year. Finally, the hero saves his mother, other heroes, and the villagers trapped in a far away country, and returns to his own hometown with the rescued flock of livestock. The expeditions the heroes make are due to the needs of nomadic life; their fight against nature and the conflicts between clans resemble those in ancient heroic epics. Like the protagonists in hunter stories and crack shot tales, the heroes in the fairy tales are not only hunters but also heroes who play an important role in the hunting life of clan societies.

The hero's marriage: Heroes are destined to come across beauties during their expeditions. At the request of the Khan (or sometimes the beauty herself), the hero needs to travel across oceans of fire and mountains of ice. He will encounter devils, huge hawks and fairies and makes every effort to beat them down. Among them are crafty goblins, devilish dragons that eat humans and livestock, cruel giants who are hard to deal with, and the human-shaped devil who is only as tall as a fist but wears a beard as long as forty feet. However, there are angels who assist the hero, like Jelayakh who runs at an incredibly fast speed, Koltawisar who can move a mountain as if he is playing with little stones, Sakhkhulakh who sees and hears whatever happens in any corner of the world and the huge hawk who rewards people for their good deeds. It is thanks to their help that heroes ultimately win. Marriage tests aim to check to what extent the heroes are brave. Apart from arrow shooting, wrestling and horseracing, they need to pass tests given by the girl's parents: eliminating enemies and devils, fetching for them a gold-headed and silver-tailed steed, a rare treasure or magic drug. Usually, heroes will be sent to a place from which one can hardly return. However, heroes never turn down these requests, because the outcome of such tests conditions their marriage. And passing these tests, the heroes will be admired and applauded. In *Hero Born for the People*, the three daughters of the Khan choose their respective husbands by throwing apples. When the youngest daughter throws an apple to Dildash who is dressed up as a bald man, the Khan disagrees. Not before long, the heavily sick Khan recoveres from his illness by eating the magic deer hunted by Dildash. Apart from that, Dildash fetches for the Khan the gold-headed and silver-tailed steed taken away by the huge hawk. Under these circumstances, the Khan consents to the marriage between Dildash and his youngest daughter. This reflects not only the sort of transition from the consanguinity marriage to intermarriage with other tribes, but also the fact that marriage still takes place within the confines of a clan society. This can also be exemplified by Töstik's marriage.

Hero Töstik can be regarded as the most representative among all Kazak tales. It combines the traditional features of hero stories, crack shot tales and heroic epics. Notably, he motif composition of birth, growth, expedition, marriage is precisely in line with that of heroic epics.

This is the framework of Hero Töstik:

I. Birth and childhood of Töstik:

(1) Once upon a time, there is a rich man named Ernazar who has eight sons and owns countless livestock. One winter, a big disaster happens and his eight sons have to go herding in remote areas from which they never come back.

(2) Just at the moment when Ernazar and his wife cannot endure the hunger any more, they see a piece of horse brisket and eat it up. The old lady gets pregnant and gives birth to a baby whose given name is Töstik ("Horse Brisket").

(3) Töstik grows up at an amazing speed: He is like a one year-old child when he is only one month; when he is two months old, he looks like a two year old child and after one year he looks like a fifteen year old youngster and he is able to tackle all the young challengers and shoot through a nine-layered coat.

Ⅱ. Töstik's expedition:

(1) The first expedition

(a) Töstik leaves to look for his eight elder brothers.

(b) He tramps over hills and dales day in and day out. He suffers various kinds of hardship, but does not find his brothers nor the herd until the worn out sole of his boot is as thin as a silver coin. Eventually he finds his eight brothers in a remote tribe.

(c) The only maroon steed the brothers brought there has by then multiplied into a large herd of horses.

(d) Töstik and his brothers get ready to return to their *awil*, but the horses refuse to move forward. Töstik tames the wild maroon steed and leads the herd back to his hometown.

(2) The second expedition

(a) Töstik cheats the old goblin and takes away the magic stone. The old goblin follows Töstik and never gives up chasing him.

(b) Not being able to bear the gallop of Shalkhuyrikh (Töstik's steed), the earth splits open. Both Töstik and his steed fall into the netherworld.

(c) Suddenly Shalkhuyrikh speaks and tells his master an idea to get away.

(d) Töstik comes to Snake King Babi's tribe and is admitted after a severe test.

(e) Babi makes Töstik look for the daughter of Khan Temir. Töstik has to set out for the netherworld, a journey of seven months.

(f) On his way to the netherworld, he meets such giants as the above-mentioned Jelayakh, Sakhkhulakh, Köregen, Tawsoghar who can shake the mountains, Koltawisar who can dry up the water in the lakes, and others. He makes friends with those giants and travels along with them.

(g) At last, Töstik finds the tribe of Khan Temir and fights various battles against Khan Keshi who intends to marry the daughter of Khan Temir. Khan Keshi plans to poison Töstik and his helpers secretly, but Sakhkhulakh comes up with a small trick after hearing the scheme and, instead, Khan Keshi's own people are poisoned to death. In the wrestling competition, Koltawisar defeats all his opponents. In the seven-day horsing race, Shalkhuyrikh turns out to be the first horse to reach the finish. In the hiking race, Jelayakh sees through the goblin's tricks and becomes the first to reach the finish line. Shalkhuyrikh successfully pulls out of the lake Khan Temir's huge pan which has a diameter of forty *chi*.[1] Koltawisar saves Töstik's and other people's lives when Khan Keshi plots to lock them up in a palace and burn them. Ultimately, Khan Keshi has no alternatives but to agree to let the daughter of Khan Temir be engaged with Snake King Babi. Töstik says farewell to the giants on his way back to the Snake King's tribe. The Snake King gives Töstik permission to marry his daughter, who unfortunately dies on the way back to Töstik's hometown because she

---

[1] One *chi* is approximately 0.3 meter.

is unable to bear the hardship of the long journey.

Seeing a hawk being eaten by a dragon, Töstik kills the dragon and saves the life of the hawk. To reward him, the huge hawk carries Töstik back to the earth. Bektori's guard Shoyinkhulakh ("Iron Ear") ties Töstik up and throws him into a dungeon while he is sleeping and takes Töstik's maid as his wife. Shoyinkhulakh sends Töstik a torch, with which he burns a feather of the huge hawk that then carries Töstik out of the dungeon. The maid tells Töstik that the soul of Shoyinkhu-lakh are the nine birds locked in the wooden box inside the stomach of a black goat among the forty wild goats that live near the spring called Borikhti Bulakh. Töstik shoots the black goat and the nine birds, and returns safely to his hometown.

(3) Töstik's marriage and his steed

(a) Only after many setbacks does Ernazar finally succeed in looking out for a family with nine daughters and makes Töstik marry the youngest daughter, Kenjegey.

(b) Kenjegey is beautiful and intelligent. She gives Töstik her dowry: a steed named Sarikhuyrikh, a white male camel and a silver armor. After the wedding of his nine sons, Ernazar returns to his own *awil*.

(c) Taking no notice of Kenjegey's warning, Ernazar sleeps near the alka-line well and is caught by the old goblin.

(d) The old goblin threatens to kill Ernazar who has no other choice but to promise to send both Töstik and the magic stone to her.

(e) On hearing this news, Kenjegey asks Töstik not to approach her but to get rid of the old goblin.

(f) When Töstik gets ready to look for the magic stone, Kenjegey gives him the steed Sarikhuyrikh and the silver armor.

(4) Töstik's return to his hometown

(a) Töstik's people are in deep despair, for he has been away for many years.

(b) On the moment to part, Kenjegey has already foretold that the day when the old white camel would breed and her silk belt would loosen automatically, Töstik would return or be killed.

(c) The old white camel breads. Her silk belt loosens automatically. Kenjegey grieves deeply for she thinks that Töstik has died.

(d) A grey-bearded old man on the back of a white steed comes near. It is Töstik.

(e) Both Kenjegey and Töstik are by now an old couple.

(f) They regain their youth and Sarikhuyrikh turns into a horse in its prime. Ernazar throws a grand and crowded banquet to celebrate their togetherness.

As listed above, this heroic story illustrates the life of the hero as perceived by ancient nomadic people, an unusual life fraught with ups and downs. It is one of the traditional ways of herding of the Kazak to lead the livestock, especially horses, into remote areas in years of famine. The ancient nomads often needed to migrate to places with good pastures and water. In order to save their lives in a year of famine, Töstik's eight elder brothers go herding the horses into a remote pasture. However, they still fail to avert the attack of natural disasters: Of all the livestock only one brown mare survives. This is reminiscent of the arduousness of ancient nomads' hard struggles against nature.

The fairy Bektori tries her utmost to interfere in the marriage of Töstik and Kenjegey, against which Töstik carries on fearless struggles. The old goblin sent by the fairy chases Töstik to the netherworld. After winning the life-or-death struggle against the poisonous snake and the giant dragon and defeating the fiendish and fraudulent Khan Temir, Töstik returns to the earth sound and save. The fairy intervenes again and sends Giant Shoyinkhulakh (son of the old goblin) to throw Töstik into a horrible dungeon. The conflict between the fairy Bektori and Töstik reveals the transition of a praire clan from matriarchy to patriarchy. Töstik belongs to the patriarchal society, whereas his enemies, including the old goblin, the fairy and Shoyinkhulakh, are products of a matriarchal society. The marriage of Töstik and Kenjegey is not based on affection, which is typical of marriage in heroic times or of antithesis wedding. [①] Although Kenjegey hasn't met Töstik before the proposal, she is willing to select for Töstik a saddle horse and armor to help him turn danger into safety. All these plots belong to the domain of a patriarchal society, as also visible in Kazak heroic epics.

Töstik's marriage reflects the customs of an ancient clan society: Ernazar lets his nine sons marry the nine daughters of one family. After a long search, he finally finds a family with nine daughters, judging from the nine earrings in the family. He then holds a wedding ceremony for all his nine sons and leads his nine daughters-in-law back to his hometown. From this extinct marriage custom, the traditional concept of the "big family" can be traced. The objective of the custom according to which the parent of the big family (Ernazar) makes all his sons marry all the daughters of one family, is to safeguard the authority of the big family.

The image of the old goblin usually seen in Kazak fairy tales bears great resemblance to that same character in heroic epics. In spite of the different names in various stories, the essence of this personage remains the same. It is named "old goblin" in *Malhuwan Suluw*, *Treat Equally the Bad and the Good* (Jakhsi men Jamandi Birdey Körüw), *The Homeless* (Khangghirghan Adam) and *Rebellious Relatives* (Opasiz Tuwis); "sharp nosed goblin" in *Son of Onershibay* (Onershibayding uli); "magic witch" in *Sazan and Marjan*; "sorceress" in *The Dreaming King and the Clever Child* (Tüs Körgen Patsha men Zerek Jigit), "black-faced old woman" in *The Noble Jabay and the Beauty Kharghasha* (Jabay Ata men Kharghasha suluw). They all have the appearance of a thin and weak

---

① Mariage within one clan forming a matriarchal family structure. The pedigree of the family is traced back through the maternal line, and children live with the mother. The woman is the head of the family, and the property is passed to the children through the mother, or to the nephews through the mother's brothers.

woman, but, in fact, the old goblin is a sinister and ruthless, cruel and merciless devil. She suddenly turns into a strong beast, attacking the bald shepherd who is walking on a dangerous road; she lures fragile women, degrades them and sucks the blood from their knees; she locks people up in her home and eats them slowly. Lured by the high reward, she helps fiendish kings, greedy and rich persons and envious concubines to execute conspiracies. When the Khan attempts to have another man's beautiful wife, she advises the king to send the husband to a place from which he will never return. When the concubine of the king or of the rich man gives birth to a gold-headed and silver-hipped boy or a blue eyed and golden-haired baby girl, the wife, who is jealous and hateful instigates the old goblin to secretly replace the baby with a dog or throw the baby into a river or wasteland. As a result, the concubine is driven out of the family. The old goblin makes the woman at home betray her husband, the younger sister betray the elder brother. She steals the magic ring that can bring shepherds happiness. In short, as for the goblins in Kazak fairy tales, there is no end to their evil activities on the one hand, whereas, on the other hand, they will eventually be defeated and punished, however crafty and wicked they are.

All goblins in both hero stories and heroic epics feature as the opponents of the heroes. For instance, in the heroic epic *Alpamis*, when the protagonist is invincible, Khan Taykesh appears under the instruction of the old goblin. With forty *yurt* (tents) and forty girls on her side, she lies to Alpamis that her forty sons have died in the war to get back the horses of the family, leaving all the forty girls behind as widows. She tells Alpamis that she would be rather happy if he would get off the horse and greet them in person. The guardless Alpamis gets off his horse and enters the *yurts*. As a result, Alpamis, made drunk by the girls, is thrown into a dark dungeon which is as deep as forty strings. Alpamis couldn't have been caught if it hadn't been for the old goblin. However, the image of Alpamis would have been too idealistic if there hadn't been the old goblin.

Totem worship can also be traced in Kazak tales. The totems are closely related to mythology. The most common totem to be worshipped is the poplar. In

Sazan and Marjan, one branch of the poplar that grows into the sky breaks off. The earth shakes and splitters, the sky is covered with clouds, and even the devils in the forest clamor endlessly. A *domra* (string instrument) made out of poplar branches can play automatically. In the story *Three Children* (üsh Bala), the daughter lives in a *yurt* on top of a big poplar out of reach. Countless men who have a crush on her attempt to climb up the tree and bring her down, but they fail and fall down one by one. As a result, their blood flows like a river; the bones of the dead pile up into a mountain. Eventually, a vagabond successfully gets the girl down from the tree and marries her. In many stories, it is usually under the poplar that the magic incident takes place. For example, a hero sees the bear he has been looking for under the big poplar along the lake and finally defeats it. The astray girl comes across her boy or a protector under the poplar tree, etc. In addition, in *Bald Child* (Tazsha Bala) and *Flower of Gülhakhhan* (Gülhakhhanning Güli) the love story takes place under the poplar.

One of the remarkable plots in Kazak tales is the deification of soil, which will surely become a sacred weapon or miraculous cure whenever there are fights between positive characters and evil forces. For instance, hero Nan is trapped in a deep dungeon, badly injured. Seeing that injured ants recover immediately after rolling in soil, he rolls just as the ants did with the expected result that his wound is healed. The worship of earth is often linked to beliefs regarding the soul. For example, in stories like *Oral*, the Khan, jealous of the bald man who married a beauty, sends him away to fetch the livestock already slaughtered for his parents' memorial ceremony. With the help of a sage, the bald man encounters the souls of the Khan's parents, who return the livestock and ask the bald man to give their own son and daughter-in-law a handful of soil. When the bald man scatters the soil after he returns home, the Khan turns into a boar and the Queen into a sow. Usually, holy soil is used to deal with the unjust, the arbitrary as well as the crafty. In *Story of a Witch*, a hunter rescues a woman and offers her happiness. But this woman actually has hidden motives and is extremely crafty. With a handful of soil, the hunter succeeds in turning the woman into forty donkeys and a wolf. This proves that no greedy person can avoid death and burial in the earth. He will be covered by soil, for in Kazak myths and legends, a kind man is said to be created out of soil.

Bird worship is another common plot of Kazak tales. One of the very popular bird totems is the huge hawk (also called big roc sometimes). Its wings can bring blasts when it hovers. Its tears can turn into torrential rain and it eats people just like eating a tiny piece of meat. In the stories, it carries on its back the protagonist, flying over the most dangerous places. In Sazan and Marjan, the bird marries Sazan. In *Better than Anyone Else* (Bärinan Äbzal) the bird gets married to the bald young man who saw it taking a bath in the river. In *Two Brothers Turap and Turash* (Aghayindi Turap pen Turash), it carries the kindhearted and industrious Turash to the gold mountain at last. One of the birds worshiped by the Kazak people is the swan, a highly revered bird in day-to-day life. Even today, no Kazak would shoot a swan.

Many stories include the image of the "happy bird" which was said to be the pet of the Khan. The "happy bird" will be released after the death of the king. Whoever the bird perches on will be crowned as king. This also embodies bird worship, although there is no clear explanation as to what the "happy bird" exactly is. In Ghipsha, it perches on the sold girl Ghipsha. In Jüsip, it perches on Jüsip who has been bullied. In *Looking for the Strange Khan* (Ghajayipti Izdegen Han), it perches on a wronged person. In *Impartial Khan* (Adil Han), it perches on an orphan. In *Happy Bird* (Bakhit Khusi), it perches on the hired worker Khanzankhap. Clearly, the supernatural bird is a positive figure and a symbol of justice.

Compared with birds and beasts, more respect is being paid to livestock. This is a concrete reminder of the economic development of ancient clan societies. Evidence of the worship of male camels and male horses among the ancient Hun and Usen can be found in wreathed relics. The horses, goats and camels which occur in *Hero Töstik* also illustrate the high respect livestock enjoys. The custom of worshiping the she-camel, the maroon and the brown mare has been passed down to the present day. In Hero Töstik, the white she-camel is worshipped as a holy animal throughout the story. Kenjegey asks her father for the white she-camel and Sarikhuyrikh, and her father hesitates because livestock is a symbol of fortune. Töstik sets out on his adventurous journey because Ernazar has been caught by the old goblin while looking for the white she-camel. All this reveals the special affection in the tradition of people towards the camel.

Regarding livestock worship, the horse is worshipped and deified to a much greater degree in tales than in heroic epics. As the brain box which can speak, the steed can always save its master from danger. In the story of *Skin of Flea*, Gülbadan helps his master to fight against the single-eyed giant. After its death, its bones and fur turn into a garden and palace with flowers and trees in full bloom. In *Flower of Gülhakhhan* and *Shelter of Black Colt*, there are plots in which the bladder of the horse turns into a small boat to rescue a woman in danger. In the story *Piebald Mare*, Piebald Mare can turn into a white horse when looking at the moon at night whereas in the daytime it can give birth to baby horses by looking at the sun. Whenever it encounters a fierce beast, it erects its tail and goes swiftly to the bleak and desolate mountains to turn into a herd of horses so that no beast dares to approach. The custom of worshipping livestock is also clearly reflected in *Töstik*, for the very one who helps Töstik overcome all the difficulties is just his pal – the steed Sarikhuyrikh. The image of Sarikhuyrikh is special. Just as Subar in *Alpamis* and Buril in *Khoblandi*, it helps its master at any time. It saves Töstik from the old goblin. But the image of the steed is enriched with much fantasy when Töstik runs away in order to get rid of the old goblin. It then accomplishes what its master could not and teaches Töstik how to cope with the snake. In the seven-day competition in Khan Temir's tribe, it faints at the finish line for not being able to curb its enormous inertia and it even pulls from the lakebed a huge iron pan the diameter of which equals forty arms. It brings Töstik the fire sickle after he has been locked up in the dungeon. In this story, the image of the steed is continuously enriched in the same way as the hero himself is constantly changing. In this respect, the image of the horse in fairy tales is quite similar to that in heroic epics, both in descriptive means and in figures of speech.

The component of traditional shamanism, which is mainly displayed as soul worship, has already been traceable in fairy tales. In the stories related to beliefs regarding the soul, contents and plots such as exchanging visits and making friends between the souls and the living occur often. In *Bozjigit Akhkhuba*, a young man, who observes a fight between a man and a soul over a gold coin, pays off debts for the soul. Then the dead soul, who turns out to be Akhkhuba, befriends the young man. The two do business together and never leave each other. Akhkhuba kills the old goblin, who lives in the polar cave and her seven giant sons by poisoning them to death. He takes the life of the dragon that eats forty black sheep and forty girls every year. With great wisdom, he defeats the seven robbers who bully the people. He cures a young man's father from blindness. When coveting a beauty, the Khan usually sends her husband away to look for sacrificial animals for the spirits of his dead parents. In *Oral*, a young man is ordered to meet the Khan's dead father to fetch a sacrificed stallion. The young man first revives the stallion and then leads it back to the Khan. Such kinds of plots find echo in *Bald Child*, *The Boy Looking for a Dream* (Tüsin Izdegen Jigit), *Happy Boy* (Bakhitti Baskha Tepken Jigit), and *The Boy Returning from the Netherworld* (O Dülniyege Barip Kelgen Jigit). It is not easy for the protagonists to meet the dead souls. Sometimes they need to hold the tombs tight; sometimes they need to shake the skeletons in a cradle for days. The souls of the parents of kings who often sputter, are by no means easy to deal with. The souls are inclined to return the livestock and offer a handful of soil only after long negotiations. When the handful of soil is scattered by the protagonist, the prince will turn into animals or burn to death. What is revealing here is the belief in souls which can communicate with people as living beings do. Souls will never die even though man is mortal. Thus, a human should not irritate souls, otherwise he is going to suffer. More blessings will be given if more good deeds are accomplished and more sacrifices are offered to the soul. All those ideas that the dead souls are powerful, superb and can foresee the future echo the concepts of traditional shamanism. The stories often end as the tyrannical Khans and fiendish ruffians are punished and the prosecuted protagonist gets rid of the fierce king and finally obtains freedom.

Soul worship in heroic epics resembles such worship in real life, whereas no such kind of reflection can be traced in stories as the ones discussed here. In heroic epics, when the souls of the ancestors are worshipped, they are addressed directly by their names. By contrast, tales only tell of the process of meeting, making friends, man's benevolence imposed on souls, and souls' blessing on man through their own magic power and crafts. In heroic epics, no direct contact takes place between man and souls. Man worships them as gods second only to the God of Heaven. No similar form can be found in tales. All in all, the features of shamanism in fairy tales are related to traditional ideology and customs and are reminiscent of emerging shamanism, whereas in heroic epics these features are much more closely related to real life. In spite of the differences between heroic epics and tales, the two bear a close relation and share the same roots and lineage. Compared with the souls in heroic epics, those in stories are much more imaginary; they are pre-epic products. Apparently, the soul worship in heroic epics is built on the basis of fairy tales.

The protagonists in fairy tales tend to get help from magical sages. In one of the images the sage wears a white beard. He/she is the *Khidir* ("sage") 'traveling around the world by wind'. The protagonist often meets with the sages emerging out of illusion during his tedious and risky journey. For example, in the story *Three Children*, a homeless boy encounters the sage in an illusive state. With the help of the sword the sage has given him, he stabs the dragon that eats forty girls each year. The heroes meet a sage whenever they run into trouble, sometimes for other reasons, or even when they are in the service of the Khan. In *Ancestor Jabay and Kharkhasha* (Jabay Ata men Kharkhasha), Jabay chances upon the sage twice and receives instructions from him. In the story *The Homeless*, Khalash who is looking for his lost three thousand horses, approaches a river and a white-bearded sage suddenly appears, telling him that the herd of horses has been stolen by the devil. At last, Kalash successfully gets the herd back from the hands of the devil. In *Devil's Design Cannot Succeed*, the sage wakes up the child sleeping in the wasteland and tells him that the horse he has been looking for is actually a stealthy dragon, and asks him to find his mother who parted from him years ago. In *Treat Equally the Bad and the Good*, the sage Khidir offers five suggestions and a dagger to the child so that he is able to avenge the ruffian who bullied him. In *One Thousand Black-Headed Sheep* (Ming Khara Bas Khoy), under the instruction of the Khan, the child shepherd goes searching three times, first for the milk of a bear, next for the excrements of the snow cock, and last for the milk of the fairy maiden in a place called Ghayip. He comes across the sage who shows him the way for all three times. Eventually he defeats the arbitrary Khan, returns in triumph, and realizes his own long-cherished wish.

Sages and old men are also among the common images in Kazak oral poetry, especially in heroic epics. But historic and realistic qualities distinguish heroic epics from other tales. The magic sages in fairy tales mainly help the heroes to find the right way and achieve their goals, whereas in heroic epics the sage asks the God of Heaven to grant the hero a descendant. The sages that appear in heroic epics bear a certain relation to historical characters, whereas no realistic basis can be found in such characters from tales. Sages and old men in heroic epics have such names as Shashti Aziz, Angel Ghayip (Ghayip Peri), Kökshe and Sage. In stories, sages have got no fixed names though. Viewed from the surface, no connection can be drawn between heroic epics and fairy tales, but heroic epics are, as a matter of fact the very continuation of fairy tales. The difficulty confronting the protagonist in fairy tales is the hardship in production and life. Under this condition, he must get help from a sage. In heroic epics, the life of the hero, who possesses a large number of cattle and sheep and has a treasure house is tormented only by the fact that he does not have a descendant yet. Therefore, he turns to sage for help. In fact: There would be no concept of traditional religion and sage worship in heroic epics if it were not for the soul and sage worship in stories.

3
Conclusion

Almost two hundred years have past since the Frenchman A. F. Villemain first employed the term "comparative literature" (*littérature comparée*)[①] when he was lecturing at the univerity of Paris in 1827. However, comparative literature studies can be dated back to the Middle Ages. Comparative literature studies were originally conducted between literary works across national boundaries. Later on, comparative literary research was employed in the study of the literature of different nationalities within the same country. The present paper has demonstrated that different genres of intracultural literature can be studied from a comparative perspective. In this light, we can not only lay bare the intrinsic logic and the cultural background of texts, but also explore the stylistic characteristics of a work and its links with other works, thus generating a full view of a literary genre.

Heroic epics and other tales are closely related. They overlap and intermingle in many ways. An overview of all the motifs and plots in both heroic epics and fairy tales informs us that most stories came into being earlier than heroic epics. This is especially clear in the case of tales that can be classified as both folktales and heroic stories. A comparison between Kazak tales and heroic epics reveals that there are many more tales than heroic epics; that there are plenty of tales without verse form; and that few heroic epics without prose form are widespread. Dozens of heroic epics which are currently widely circulating among the Kazak all take the form of prose narratives, while few of the hundreds of the tales passed

---

① No Kami Toyoichiro, *Comparative Literature Studies*, translated by Liu Jiemin. Changsha: Hunan People's Press, 1984: 24.

down to this day are in verse form. A comparison between heroic epics, crack shot tales and other heroic tales brings to light that heroic tales and heroic epics share the same motif-series and the same genealogy, as manifest in shared elements such as the worship of livestock, the character of the sage and nature worship which feature prominently in both heroic epics and tales. The comparison between the two can help us to explore the roots of certain cultural phenomena so as to shed light on the nomadic culture concerned.

References:

Altay Uyasi [*Altay Spring*] [Kazak] 2 (1980).

Epics of the Kazak. Edited by M. Auezov. Alma-Ata: Kazakhstan National Literature Publishing House, 1958.

Epics of the Kazak [Kazak]. Beijing: Minzu Publishing House, 1984- 1986.

Hero Khoblandi. Alma-Ata: Kazakhstan National Press, 1948.

Kazak Folktales. Urumqi: Xinjian People's Press, 1981.

Kazak Folktales. Alma-Ata: Writers Press, 1988.

Khazakh Shalek Ertegileri [*Kazak Folktales*]. Yining: Xinjiang Ile People's Press, 1977 and 1987.

Khazakh Eposi. Alma-Ata: Kazakhastan National Art Publishing House , 1958.

Kazak Keysalare [*Collection of Kazak Narrative Poems*][Kazak]. Beijing: Nationality Publishing House, 1984. Vol. 2.

Kazak Keysalar. Beijing: Minzu Publishing House, 1985. Vol. 4.

Kazak Keyslarae [*Kazak Long Narrarative Folk Poems*]. Beijing: Minzu Publishing House, 1991. Vol. 11.

Majit Äbuzar, ed. *Epics of the Kazak*. Beijing: Minzu Publishing House, 1987. Vol. 6.

Mura [*Heritage*] [Kazak] 1 (1983), 1 and 2 (1986), 2 (1989).

Murin, ed. *Heroic epics*. Alma – Ata: Kazakhstan Alma – Ata Press, 1989. Vols. 6, 7.

No Kami Toyoichiro. *Comparative Literature Studies* [Japanese]. Translated by Liu Jiemin. Changsha: Hunan People's Press, 1984.

Sawranbayev, N. *Khirimning Khirikh Batirding*. Edited by Dawetbay Muren. Alma-Ata: Institute of Historical Literature of Kazakhstan Science Academy, 1942.

Shalghin [*Green Grass*]1 (1981).

Appendix 1
Various Editions of Epics Currently
Spread among the Kazak

Khorkhit Ata Kitabi

Around the 10th century, during his journey in Ile and around the Sir river valley, Arab traveler Iahal heard of the legends about Khorkhit from Turkic tribes as the Uguz, Kipchak and others. It was the first time that the stories of Khorkhit were written down and became known to the outside world. By the 12th century there had existed a written rudiment of *Khorkhit Ata Kitabi* (*Book of Ancestor Khorkhit*). From then on, the book was continuously copied, supplemented, abridged and even distorted or falsified. Around the 14th and 15th centuries the book appeared under the title *Ancestor Khorkhit as Seen through the Great Languages of the Uguz Tribes*. Today, there is a large number of copies of *Khorkhit Ata Kitabi*. Among them, two copies are most authorative. One copy is treasured in the library of Dresden in German. It contains twelve chapters. The cover says 'Khorkhit Ata Kitabi' on the top and 'Languages of Uguz tribes' at the bottom. Another copy is currently stored in the Vatican library. It is made up of six chapters and annotated by Kazan Bek and others with information about Uguz legends. Some think that the language employed in the former copy is Kipchak, while the latter one is written in an Uguz based language. That is to say, the book was originally completed by Kipchak-speakers and was later translated in Uguz, albeit not in full. Other versions such as *Khorkhit and the Dead Gods* (Khorkhit pen Azrayil), *Songs of Khorkhit* (Khorkhit Jiri), *Khorkhit and the Forty Girls* (Khorkhit men Khirikh Khiz) and *Khorkhit's Fight With Angel Azreyil* (Khorkhit pen Äzreyilding Küresuw) can only be considered variants of the two copies mentioned above. In 1815, Friedrich Guentz (1751-1817) introduced the chapter of "Basat Killed One-Eyed Giant Töbeköz" to the academic world and translated it into German. In 1910, the first five chapters of the Dresden copy were translated into Turkish and published. In 1916, the Turkish scholar Kilisli Rifat completed the Arabic version of this copy. Theodor Nöldeke (1836-1930) translated several chapters of the Dresden copy into German, but the Russian Oriental studies scholar V. V. Bartold finished the complete version of this epic in 1922. In 1938, the Turkish scholar Orhan Saik Gokyay published the Latin version of this copy. In 1950, the Azerbaijan scholars Arasli and Takhmasib jointly published the Azerbaijan, i.e Baku version. In 1962, another version was published in Russia. The second handwritten version of the epic was discovered by an Italian scholar in Vatican who published the original text of the handwritten version in 1925 in Helsinki, appended with a list of words. In 1980, Muharrem Ergin from Istanbul University in Turkey published this copy a second time. So far, *Khorkhit Ata Kitabi* has been published in Turkey, Britain, Germany, Russia, and several countries in Central Asia. In 1986, Kazakhstan got the Kazak version translated from Russian. In 1988, China published the Kazak version translated from Turkish by Majit Anewar. In 1987, a version of *Khorkhit* compiled by Majit Anewar was included in the 6th volume of *Epics of the Kazak*. When viewed from its length, which is only 210 lines, it is possible that Majit Anewar collected this version of Khorkhit from a local *akin* (singer).

Alpamis

Alpamis is an ancient and typical heroic epic that has been passed down for more than ten centuries. It came into being in the Turkish Austronesian period in the Kongirat tribe. It was not only popular among Kazak people but also among other nationalities such as the Uzbek, Kirghiz, Tatar, Uygur, Azerbaijan, Khakas and Karakalpak. According to Turkish scholar J. N. Paksoy, the Tajik inhabiting the Pamir plateau, once sang *Alpamis* in Persian Tajik. The extemporization version has been published in Tajikistan. In the 15th century, *Bamis Bölök* – an abridged version of *Alpamis* – was widely spread in the Anatoliya mountain areas in Turkey. *Bamis Bölök* shares plots and structures with *Alpamis*. *Many different copies are extant today. Among them, the following versions are the most popular ones*:

1. Jüsipbek Hoja Shayhislam version: In 1899, Jüsipbek Hoja Shayhislam for the first time published *Alpamis* in Kazan, Russia, under the title *Epos Alpamis*. The book was reprinted many times between 1901-1914 because of its popularity.

2. Abubakir Divayev version: In 1916, Abubakir Divayev recorded and collected a prose version of *Erkinbek Akhinbek*. He published it under the heading *Six Year Old Alpamis* (Alti Jasar Alpamis) and translated it into Russian.

3. Sirdihan Shangkerey version: The text sung by singer Sirdihan Shangkerey in 1962 is a combination of verse and prose. This text was recorded and annotated by Däwletbek Khangbakh. It was discovered and collected in Nelke county of Ile Prefecture, Xinjiang in 1990. In 1991, the sung text was printed in the eleventh volume of *Kazak Keyslarae* (Kazak Long Narrarative Folk Poems) in Kazak.

In recent years, several versions of *Alpamis* in prose have been collected and annotated in the areas inhabited by the Kazak in China. Among these versions, the one collected and annotated by Maralbek Sawran is preserved relatively intact. In 1977, this version was printed in the second volume of *Khazakh Shalek Ertegileri* (Kazak Folktales) in Kazak. Since the 1940s, Kazak scholars have collected and recorded sung texts by singers such as Sultankhul Akhkhoja and Süyinshal Jangbershi. The sung text by Sultankhul Akhkhoja recorded in 1948 is regarded as the longest and the most complete text. This conclusion results from comparisions with many other versions. At the time of recording, Sultankhul Akhkhoja was above 80 years old. According to the singer himself, he had learned his songs from famous 19th-century singer Maykut Saydebayev. The sung text was printed in *Khazakh Eposi* in 1958 and reprinted in Kazak in the second volume of *Kazak Keysalare* in 1984.

Khobilandi (Koblandy)

Khobilandi is one of the most ancient Kazak heroic epics. It came out in the Kipchak tribe in the 12th century. The epic is also known as *Kharakhip-shakhting Batiri Khobilandi*. Kharakhipshakh (Kara-Kipchak) is the name of a tribe that forms part of the Kazak ethnic group, while Khobilandi is the name of the hero in the epic. Of all ancient Kazak heroic epics, Khobilandi is noteworthy for its length. Some versions have a length of over a thousand lines. The version of *Hero Khobilandi* sung by Marghanbay, sorted out by Malik Khabidolla and published in Kazakhstan in 1948 contains 3.330 lines. The second volume of *Epics of the Kazak* (China, 1984) includes a 6.650-line version of the epic, which is developed on the basis of a chapter called *Khobilandi* in *Epics of the Kazak* (Kazakhstan, 1958). Currently there are fifteen versions of the epic, among which the Maralbay version is considered the earliest colleted, sorted out and published, while the most complete, rich and complicated is the version that was published in China in the second volume of *Epics of the Kazak*. This last version is twice as long as the Malik Khabidolla one. It is said that the Chinese version has been completed on the basis of the Malik Khabidolla version. The textual body aside, the accompanying music and singing procedures have also been documented.

Khirimning Khirikh Batiri

Khirimning Khirikh Batiri belongs to the category of series heroic epics, composed of many single pieces of epics. Some of its separate pieces had already been collected, sorted out and published before the series edition appeared. For instance, the poem *Orakh-Mamay Batir* was noted down as early as 1905 and an edition under the title *Orakh men Mamay Batirding Riywayati* was published in 1908 in Kazan. The complex edition started to be collected in the 1940s and was documented. The credits must be given to Tilegen (Murin), the son of the well-known epic singer Senggirbek. Murin's grandfather is Khulkhara. Khulkhara has two sons, one is Ayghir, the other is Dangghir. Ayghir's son is Senggirbek.

Senggirbek has two sons, one is Tilegen (Murin), the other is Tölegen. Khulkhara, Ayghir and Tölegen are all famous iron- or silversmiths. Although Murin had never received professional training in schools, he was a born musician and grew up in an environment of music and epics. Murin learned from singer Nurim – son of the famous epic singer Shirshighul – the chapters of *Anhshibay*, *Parpariya*, *Khuttikhiya*, *Edige*, *Nuradin*, *Musahan*, *Orakh and Mamay*, *Karasay and Khaziy*. Under the guidance of Khashaghan – son of the famous singer Khurjiman – he mastered *Khoblandi*, *Torehan*, *Ämet*, *Oral*, *Kökshe*, *Khasay*, *Abat*, *Toghan*, *Manash*, *Tuyakhbay*, *Ahimet*, *Khargha Boyli*, *Khaztuwghan*, etc. The chapters of *Kharadong*, *Jubanish*, *Süyinish*, *Tegis*, *Tama*, *Tana*, *Närik*, *Shora*, *Khulinshakh*, *Akhjonas*, *Kenges*, *Jangbirshi* and *Telghis* were instructed by Murat. Murin was born in 1859 and died in 1954 at the age of 96. At the invitation of N. Sawranbayev, director of the Institute of Historical Literature of the Kazakhstan Science Academy, and E. Simayilov, chair of the Institute of Folk Tales, Murin came to Alma-Ata (now Almaty) from Mangghistaw in 1942 and wrote *Khirimning Khirikh Batiri down*. He had treasured the epic in his memory for 60 years. People participating in the recording and compiling include Mariyam Hakimjan, Mariyam Iysa, Boztay Jakhipbay and Dawitbay Murin. In 1989, the entire epic was published under the name of Murin in the sixth and seventh volume of *Heroic Epics* in Kazakhstan. In October 2000, this epic was published in China in two books in old Kazak.

Khambar

Khambar, also refered to as *Khambar Batir*, is an ancient Kazak heroic epic of which more than twenty editions exist. The epic was recorded in 1865 and the printed version came out for the first time in 1888. In 1903 a rather small-scale edition of this epic was printed entitled *The Men Who Erect Ninety Tents* (Tokhsan üyli Tobir). In 1922, a complete version of the epic came out in Tashkent, Uzbekistan. In 1933 and 1939, the epic was collected in *Classical Epics*. In 1959, a scientific version combining four editions was published in

Kazakhstan. In 1958, the epic came out as a combined publication of the Kazak and the Russian versions, under the heading *Stories of the Kazak*. In 1968, a separate edition of the epic came out. *Khambar* appeared in Epics of the Kazak in China in 1984; it was based on *Khazakh Eposi* published in Kazakhstan in 1958. This version in verse form contains 1.900 lines and is a relatively complete edition.

Er Targhin

Er Targhin was spread in the Altin Orda (Golden Horde) Kahanne in the 14th century. Several editions of the epic are now extant. The Kazan edition printed in 1962, which was recorded and sorted out on the basis of the lyrics sung by the epic singer Maralbay, is referred to as the original edition. The *Er Targhin* we are talking about today mainly covers the hero's flight after he had killed many people. The verse and prose edition were combined in the second volume of *Kazak Keysalare* published in China in 1984. This 1.700-line version was adapted on the basis of *Khazakh Eposi* published in Kazakhstan in 1958. In addition, another edition dealing with the hero's birth and growing-up prior to his flight was collected in *Kazak Keysalare* published in China in 1987 under the title *Er Targhinning Alghi Khiysasi*. This edition with 940 lines was based on the handwritten compilation by Mukhatay Aday from Toli, Tarbagatay, Xinjiang.

Ablayhan

Ablay is originally named Abilmänsur and nicknamed Sabalakh. Ablay is the name of his grandfather who was once the ruler of Turkestan. His grandfather earned the name "bloodsucker" for his ferocity and invincibleness in battles. Wäli, son of Ablay, failed to defend his father's territory and was even killed by people from another tribe. Thanks to a loyal servant, Abilmänsur was saved. The 13-year old Abilmänsur lived under other people's roof; he earned a living by grazing camels for others. He suffered from hunger and wore shabby clothes. Tore Biy of the Jüz tribe called him Sabalakh ("Disheveled-Haired Man"), and from then on Sabalakh became his nickname. During a fight between three main hordes and Jungar landlords,[①] Abilmänsur decided, at the crucial moment, to ask permission to join the battle. He demonstrated extraordinary valour during the battle. Shouting "Ablay, Ablay", he rushed into the enemy. When asked by Khan Abilmanbet why he kept shouting "Ablay, Ablay..." while assaulting, he explained that he wanted to frighten the enemy and invoke a heroic spirit in the warriors in honour of his grandfather's *jinnee* (a spirit with supernatural power). Knowing that he was the grandson of the famous "bloodsucker" alias Ablay, the Khan entrusted him with decision-making in major issues and later with his throne. Since then, *Ablay* became the hero's own name. *Ablay* has many versions. The three most popular ones are:

1. Sabalakh edition: this 360-line edition was collected and edited by folk singer Änwar Khongkhakh Uli from Tarbagatay, China. It was included in the second Volume of *Epics of the Kazak* published in China in 1984. According to the beginning of the narration, the first singer of this version was Khaliy Adilbek.

2. Ablay edition: this edition has 1.600 lines and was included in the fourth volume of *Kazak Keysalar* published in China in 1985. Folk singer Sheriyazdan Sultanbay Uli from Altay collected the work. This edition contains the main plot of the Sabalakh edition as well as many supplements and variations.

3. Ablay Nan Akh Atan edition: this edition was collected by Ä. Näbiy from Togeztaraw county, Ile Prefecture, Xinjiang, China. The 708-line epic was collected in the 11th volume of *Kazak Keyslarare* and published in China in 1991.

Those editions have been sung, and later edited, on the basis of popular legends and story plots in Kazak. The plot, structure, rhyme scheme and singing style bear much resemblance to the semi-written and semi-oral form that arose in the 19th century and was widely spread in the 20th century. According to the

---

① Jungar is the tribal name given to the Mongols in Xinjiang area in the Qing dynasty (1368-1644). In the Qing dynasty some Jungar feudal lords of the Elutes staged rebellions against the central government.

records, Khökhbay Jantay (1863-1927), a friend and student of the great poet Abay once sung this epic. *Jüsip Köbeyev* (1858-1931), a well-known poet and writer published *Stories of Ablay* in Kazan, Russia in 1910.

Khabanbay Khojaghul

Khabanbay Khojaghul is a Kazak hero of the 18th century who was ranked among the strategists and generals in the battles against foreign troops as the bravest and most erudite hero. In spite of the scarcity of historical records about him, legends, poems and folktales about Khabanbay Kojagul lacked in no way. Khabanbay was born into the Kazak Juz Nayman tribe. Legends, folk songs and poems related to him are widespread among the Kazak, especially among the Nayman and Kharakerey residents in Tarbagatay and Bortala in Xinjiang, China. The longest piece related to Khabanbay was published in the first issue of *Shalghin* [*Green Grass*] and was later republished in the second volume of *Kazak Keysalare* in China in 1984. This edition of *Khabanbay* is the result of the comparison, supplementation and sorting out of six editions that are similar in terms of content and scope. Besides, the first and second issue of the journal *Mura* [*Heritage*] presented in 1986 *Khubas at Khiysasi*, which praises the steed of Khabanbay. This poem was sung by famous singer Beysenghaliy Sadikhan from Tarbagatay, Xinjiang, China, who initially heard it from Mawsimbay and made further supplements after visiting Akhbiyik, wife of Khabanbay's descendant Bulanbay. Chinese scholars conducted research, presented studies of *Khabanbay* and published several editions, for example, in the two Kazak literary journals *Shalghin* and *Mura*. Some of the largest editions include the 170-line *akin* Bitimbay version and the 80-line Kharlibay version.

Janibek

Janibek is a heroic epic narrating the story of Janibek, a great 18th-century Kazak hero. The epic is mainly spread in the Altay and Tarbagatay areas in China. It has been edited, sung and passed down in the form of legends and pedigree poems. Several editions of this epic in China include:

1. Ibray Botay edition: first sung in 1927 by Ibray Botay, a descendant of the folk artist Janibek. Later, the *akin* Baybolsin recorded and refined Ibray Botay's lyric (1964) and published it in 760 lines in the second issue of *Mura* (1989).

2. Mawgesh edition: collected by Mawgesh in Kaba county in Altay, Xinjiang and first edited and published by Ghalibek in the second issue of *Altay Uyasi* in 1980. Later, it was included in 460 lines in the second volume of *Epics of the Kazak* (Kazak version) in China in 1984.

Esenkeldi

The various editions of *Esenkeldi* are:

1. Dosber Sawlek edition: Sung by folk singer Dosber Sawlek according to legends. It was initially printed in *Ile aydenge* in 1981. In 1984, it was included in the second volume of the Chinese *Epics of the Kazak*. This edition of the epic consists of 1.630 lines.

2. Awkat Shariphan edition: An entire lyric sung by singer Dosber Sawlekand and preserved by his relative Awkat Shariphan. It has been published in a poem collection in which the epic consists of 1.750 lines.

Arkhalikh

Although it is an ordinary heroic epic, *Arkhalikh* has two distinctive features. First, it is the most recent of Kazak heroic epics. Second, it is widely spread among the Chinese Kazak. In spite of the fact that it is a relatively new epic (it came into existence after the foundation of the Kazak Khanate[①]), it has got many versions, for example:

[①]   The Kazak Khanate was established at the end of 15th century and the beginning of the 16th century. In this period, as the population grew, the Kazak extended their pastures to the northwest of Lake Balkhash, the Chu River valley and to Tashkent, Andizan and Samarkand in Central Asia, gradually evolving into the Kazak nationality.

1. Askhar Tatanay version: Folk artist Askhar Tatanay collected and sorted out this poem in the early 20th century and transcribed it into a drama script in 1958. This 720-line version was published in the first issue of *Shalghin* in 1981.

2. Iybray and Jumajan version: The handwritten version of this edition, which was copied in 1937 without an identified author or singer, was accidentally found by Iybray in Jemeney county of Xinjiang. Jumajan Abilkhazi edited it and published it in *Mura* in 1983. In 1985, it was collected in the fourth Chinese edition of *Epics of the Kazak* with 3.500 lines. It is said to be the longest edition of this epic.

3. Abdikhaliy Batirbay version: Abdikhaliy mastered this heroic epic in the 1930s and it was recorded and edited on the basis of his 1981 performance at the age of 71. This 1.720-line edition is now preserved in the office of the Xinjiang Ethnic Minority Affairs Commission.

4. Sultan Mejit version: Sultan Mejit learned the epic from the famous singer Aripjan Januzakh in the early 20th century and printed it in the first issue of *Shalghin* in 1981 in 2.580 lines.

5. Erjan Akhmetov version: Erjan Akhmetov (1879-1959) emmigrated from Xinjiang to Kazakhstan. He performed a rather small variant of the epic, which was later recorded and edited by Bekmuhamet into a 200-line text.

6. Ertay Khursayev edition: Kursayev started collecting materials from 1939 on. His version is now stored in Kazakhstan Science Academy. In 1961, this 1.520- line edition was included in the second volume Epics of the *Kazak* published in Kazakhstan in 1961.

7. Dawit Ibrayemov version: this 350-line edition mainly focuses on the accounts of the hero's first combat against the enemy.

Appendix 2
Excerpts from *Khoblandi*

Khoblandi (Khobilandi, Koblandy) also called *Hero Khoblandi of the Kara-Kipchak* (Khara Khipshakhting Batiri Khobilandi) is one of the old heroic epics of the Kazaks. Kipchak is the name of one of the main tribes that make up the Kazak. *Khoblandi* is the name of the main character in the epic. Among the Kazak ancient heroic epics, *Khoblandi* is a relatively large piece. Some editions even reach more than ten thousand lines. The edition named *Hero Khoblandi* is sung by Marghanbay, recorded and sorted out by Malik Khabidolla and published in Kazakhstan in 1948, and has 3.330 lines. The second volume of *Epics of the Kazak* that was published in 1984 in China included this edition. It was adapted according to the version of *Khoblandi* in *Epics of the Kazak* with 6.650 lines, published in 1958 in Kazakhstan. Presently, the epic has fifteen editions. The earliest edition that was collected and sorted out is the one sung by Maralbay. The edition in the second volume of *Epics of the Kazak*, published in China, which was adapted on the basis of the edition published in 1958 in Kazakhstan, has the most complete structure, the richest content and the most interesting plot. The latter is almost twice as long as that of the edition sung by Marghanbay. It is said that it is based on the Marghanbay edition.

Summary of the story:

In remote, ancient times, there is a man named Tokhtarbay who is a famous millionaire owning countless wealth. In his eighties, Tokhtarbay still has no son. He prays for the blessings of the gods and eventually his dream comes true. He gets a son named Khoblandi and a daughter named Karlighash. At the age of six, Khoblandi can already herd the livestock along the borders. When Khoblandi is twelve, Khan Köktim of the neighboring Red Cap tribe sponsors a martial art competion to choose a husband for princess Khurtkha. Anyone who can quiver the golden plate under the moon is allowed to marry the princess. Regardless of the dissuasions of Estemis, the ringleader of his slaves, Khoblandi barges into the palace on his own. Among the twenty princes participating in the martial art competition, only Khoblandi quivers the golden plate.

Köktim keeps his promise and spends thirty days holding games and forty days holding a banquet. However, the marriage meets strongly objection from a famous red-haired Hero. In the end, Khoblandi kills him and his two sons Kharasay and Khaziy, and goes back to his own tribe with princess Khurtkha. On their way back, they meet by chance the cousin of Khoblandi and his herds of horses. Khurtkha gives her a skinny horse she likes at first sight. Not before long, the horse gives birth to a baby horse. Khurtkha feeds it and begins to tame it carefully. This horse becomes the divine horse that accompanies Khoblandi through fire and water.

Khazan, Hero of Red Cap tribe considers it a great shame to let Khoblandi marry the princess, and dispatches his troops to rob and slaughter him. Hero Kharaman invites Khoblandi to fight against Khazan together. Khurtkha says that the battle steed will be tamed within forty-three days and that Khoblandi will surely be up to any hardship or danger. Kharaman jeers at Khoblandi for obeying his wife, which he considers a shame for heroes. He decides to kill Khurtkha so as to force Khoblandi to go onto the battlefield. Khurtkha cleverly avoids the catastrophe. But Khoblandi cannot withstand the inciting words of Kharaman and leaves with the steed that has not as yet been fully tamed. Khoblandi himself defeats Khazan in the presence of Kharaman, but Kharaman gets the credit for the victory. Kharaman then incites Khoblandi to attack Khan Köbikti of the Kalmak. As a result, Khoblandi is utterly defeated and locked in a deep dungeon. Kharligha, daughter of Khan Köbikti falls in love with Khoblandi at first sight. She kills her father and her brothers and saves Khoblandi. Following Khoblandi and Kharaman, Kharligha leaves the Kalmak tribe. Kharaman asks Khoblandi for his reward – Kharligha. At that time, Khoblandi has a dream that the enemy is invading his hometown. So, he immediately starts to fight the enemy, Khan Alshaghir who has robbed the prairie and livestock, enslaved the people there and even forced Khurtkha to marry him. From Kharligha, Khoblandi knows the positions of the enemy troops. Together with Kharaman he defeats Alshaghir and saves the whole tribe. From then on, the people live a peaceful and prosperous life on the Kizdikhul steppe. A segment of the hero epic goes as follows: [1]

In times gone by,
[Lives] Khoblandi from the Kara-Kipchak,
His father is Tokhtarbay,
A rich man, distinguished among the people.
His wealth is countless,
Spreading over the mountains are herds of livestock
Of all four varieties. [2]
The summer pasture is located along Lake Közdi,
Where the livestock is grazing
And the Kipchak settle down in the summer.
The wealth of Tokhtarbay –
Whoever drinks becomes drunk, whoever eats becomes satisfied,
Both the rich and the poor are happy.
The winter pasture is in Kharaspan,
Kharaspan fights with the sky.
The horse loses its herd, [3]
Many Kipchak people live there
Where they seem to live in a garden of flowers.
The seal of the Kipchak

---

[1]   See for the Kazak original the paper in Chinese in this book.
[2]   I.e. horses, camels, cows and sheep.
[3]   I.e. there are so many herds in the pastures that horses often stray from their own herd.

Is even more famous than that of Alash.

Tokhtarbay reaches the age of eighty,

And he has still no son.

Out of misery he cries tears of blood,

He looses his sound mind.

No longer like a robust haws,

He wonders whether he will leave this cold and cheerless world

Without a little hoof. ①

The countless Kipchak feel sorry for

The misery of Tokhtarbay.

They pray to every god,

By seizing the garments in their hands,

They visit seven gods.

They sacrifice horses praying for the blessings of the gods,

They sacrifice sheep to the holy place Khorasan.

And then his dream comes true,

His heart almost bursts,

His old wife Analikh's

Ribs curve. ②

When she reaches the age of fifty,

She thinks she can probably not expect the birth of a child.

Will she live such a life?

At that moment a lion appears.

A son and a daughter are born,

The name of the daughter is Karlighash,

The sister of Khoblandi. ③

---

① I.e. without a heir.

② I.e. she becomes pregnant.

③ *Kazak Keysalare* [*Collection of Kazak Narrative Poems*] [Kazak], Beijing: Minzu Publishing House, 1984: II 701-703.

...

In the tribe of Khizilbas

Grows up a hero named Khazan,

Who is an unpredictable trouble.

He wantonly robbs, imprisons and humiliates

Most of the people in the Nogay tribe.

Those who refuse to obey him

He kills without exception.

He robbs them of their land and livestock

And makes them suffer from serious torture.

Leaving all possessions and cattle behind,

The Nogay people flee in all directions.

Most of the Nogay people wear out their pair of toughened feet,

Drifting from place to place, homeless and miserable.

Taking with force

The castles of Khirli and Sirli,

Hero Khazan rages like a flood.

The castle named Sirli,

No longer fortified, lays open.

In the castle named Khirli

The ringleader and his underlings

Assemble and gain strength.

Saying that no enemy will come

Near the castle Khirli,

Everybody's spirits rise.[1]

...

People gather around, crying,

All thinking that things happen so suddenly,

---

[1]   Ibid. 723-724.

They refuse to leave.
Having dressed himself
The youthful Khoblandi walks out.
The people gather around him.
After having said goodbye to the crowd,
Hero Khoblandi
Mounts his fierce horse Buril,
Hangs the sharp sword around his waist,
Puts on his white armor
And the fur cap of the Nogay,
On a Monday, he embarks on his journey
Over the Kharaspan mountain.
Hero Khoblandi
Follows after the Khiyat[1]
Who left yesterday.
Running after him are
Ninety-year old Tokhtarbay,
Sixty-year old Analikh,
His sister Kharligha
And his wife Khürtkha,
Crying all four,
Unwilling to stop,
They ride quickly,
Following Khoblandi.
When midday sets in,
His sister starts to speak.
What she says is as follows:
Bearing the great trust of the people,

---

[1] Khiyat: A Kazak tribe.

You will do everything,

My only brother,

Prop of my life.

You set out on your journey to realize the long-cherished wish.

With confidence can the white hawk fly

With the help of its wings and tail feather.

I am a little piece of grass in the valley,

I am a pinch of feather on the fur cap.

As long as you don't return in triumph,

As long as you don't see the people live in prosperity,

I will be like a dark-gray lamb,

That is offered as a sacrifice to God.

The enemy is up to all dodges and often plays tricks,

Thinking of which I cannot help crying.

As long as you don't return in triumph, my dear prop,

As long as you don't see your people live in prosperity,

Take me, helpless, left behind without you,

As alm or donation.

Prop of my life, tears cloud our eyes,

Brother, as long as you don't return in triumph,

I, unhappy, left behind without you,

Would rather be a sacrifice.

Five golden flowers grow on my hat.

Brother, without you

The world is just like a pile of waste.

We are stepping on burning coals.

The arrow of death that God predestined for you,

Let it hit us!

You are the locks on my white forehead,

The horse, born together with me,

The blade bone proven to be usefull

My brother, born together with me,

My support, my prop,

You are the reed, towering above the water,

You are the fast horse, riding ahead.

What your parents-in-law urge and behest,

I am willing to take upon myself!

Like the twinborn sheep,

Like the sheep that drink the milk of the same mother sheep

We were born together, we grew up together,

The umbilical cord was cut at the same time.

We are ravens of the same single color,

We are ducks of a purified color,

We were born together, our roots are connected.

If not trapped in the plight,

The forest is full of your camels,

The enclosure is full of your sheep,

In whose care do you leave them?

The horses spreading over the hill,

Your sixty-year old mother Analikh,

In whose care do you leave them?

Born at the same time as you,

Happy like young horses,

Born together with you, grown up together with you,

Whose umbilical cord was cut at the same time,

Me, unhappy one, in whose care do you leave me?

Sharing your pain in this world,

Your fellow-traveller in eternity,

With whom you share your innermost thoughts in bed,

Your wife, united with you by God,

The daughter of Köktim – Khürtkha,

My sister-in-law, in whose care do you leave her?[①]

…

We will end our long story,

Let me tell it straight away.

They enjoy themselves thirty days on end,

Such a beauty as Kharligha,

Such a hero as Khoblandi

Such a relative by marriage as Kharaman

[…]

Thus beauty Kharligha,

Living in the mountains for eight years,

Makes her dreams come true!

If you do not hurry, if you show endurance,

If you try and strive forward,

In the end you will make your dreams come true.

Khoblandi, Khürtkha and Kharligha

No mutual jealousy between each other,

Cherish a broad mind even if jealousy does exist.

Beauty Kharligha has become acquainted

With the sweet fruits of life.

Kharligha and Khürtha have shown

To the numerous Kipchak

This is a sign of harmonious existence,

Only in this way can dreams come true.

They have set an example for the people.

To all this still follows an end:

Kharligha gives birth to a son,

---

① Ibid. 746-750.

Who is named Kiyikbay.
He cherishes a great ideal,
When Kiyikbay will mount his horse,
For the numerous Kipchak the sun will rise,
For Khizilbas the night will set in.
But this is another story
About such a hero as Kiyikbay is.
And thus I end my tale.
Let your words be eloquent if you want to speak,
Just like us akin. [1]

---

[1] Ibid. 965-966.

IX

Tests as Seen Through Epics of
Ethnic Minorities in South China

Liu Yahu

Abstract: The test motif in myths and epics of southern Chinese ethnic groups constitutes an important type of plot, which exhibits the inherent qualities of heroes. The test in southern Chinese ethnic epics has many forms such as the hero or god being abadoned after birth, the testing of a suitor or of a man who wants to be the "great" chief. Their prototypes in real life are all kinds of ceremonies at the early stage of the nationalities in southern China; their narrative models deeply reflect upon the characteristics of agriculture civilization, ethnic group oriented culture, and shamanism in southern China. The Chinese archetype of test and that of Greek myths and epics reflect the differences between the two cultures.

Key words: tale type of test, epic, ethnic minorities of south China

In the myths and epics of nationalities all over the world, the test motif constitutes an important type of plot reflecting the nature of heroes and revealing heroes' character. The most familiar form is the birth test. Zeus in Greek myths was abandoned in a cave on Crete after his birth, surviving the ordeal by drinking goat's milk; Romulus, king of the first generation in Roman myths, and his little brother Remus were put in a basket and thrown into a river. They were saved and fed by a she-wolf after being washed ashore; Herakles and Oedipus in Greek myths, Mosheh in Hebrew oral literature, Karna in Indian epics, and many others, were all abandoned in the hills, fields or rivers.

There are some test stories in ancient Chinese books. After his birth, Houji, the ancestor of the Zhou dynasty had been abandoned and adopted three times. *Biography of Zhou* in *History Annals* records: Houji, called Qi, is a man of the Zhou dynasty. His mother is a daughter from the clan of Youtai; her name is Jiang Yuan. Jiang Yuan walks outdoors, she finds herself happy and satisfied when seeing the footprints of a giant; she can't help stepping on the footprints. After her stepping on the footprints, she feels something moving inside her body just as if she is pregnant. A considerable length of time passes. Jiang Yuan gives birth to a baby boy. Jiang Yuan, considering the baby inauspicious, abandons the newly born baby in a narrow alley. Horses and cows pass by without trampling on him; while the boy was removed to the forest, where crowds often see him; being abandoned in the channel and on the ice, wings of birds cover him. Jiang Yuan then regards Houji as a divinity, and adopts him.

These are examples of the birth test, namely abandoning the newborn baby and testifying if he (she) is a "saint baby". There are other kinds of test models, such as the courtship test: Rama in the Indian *Rāmāyana* epic must undraw a divinity's bow to gain the love of Sita, a princess and daughter of king Janaka; or the test of succeeding to the throne: Jason in the Greek story must bring the Golden Fleece in order to restore his kingship.

There are plenty of test stories in the epics originating from southern Chinese ethnic groups, rich in kind and plot, as well as distinctive in content and form.

1
Detailed Content of the Test

The prototypes of the test stories in the epics of southern China spring from various test ceremonies at the early stage of southern nationalities. Folklorist data indicate that the ethnic group cultures frequently used tests in order to formalize and ritualize the process of individual growth such as birth, manhood and marriage, and in social communication and other important aspects of social life.

Most of these test ceremonies have disappeared due to the changing circumstances, while some remnants lingered on until the forties and fifties of the last century in ceremonies of manhood or marriage in some cultures in southern China. Among the Yao, for example, in the ceremony of "disciplining", a young boy at the advent of his manhood has to undergo the test of "climbing knife ladders", "passing through fire chains" and "jumping off the cloud (high) platform". It was believed that the tests promise new meanings and qualities to the young men's lives afterwards, which enabled them to formally become new members of the society and to take the post of village headman, gain religious protection and have a chance to ascend to Heaven. The manhood ceremony among the Miao also requires that young men climb up and down the knife ladder, tumble over the "oil-fire platform" (a platform with a pan of scalding oil on it), and dance on a red-baked furrow with bare feet. It is the shaman who leads all those rituals. People of other cultures, such as the Zhuang and the Yi usually test the knowledge and capability of the candidates by "song conversations" and song contests, during courtship and the ceremonies of seeing the bride and her escorts in or out. All these are remnants of the test ceremonies from ancient times.

The test ceremonies as manifest in the epics of southern Chinese ethnic groups qualify the hero as superb or even divine. The tests set up a major barrier for the hero to overcome: He has to pass the test when he comes into the world and hopes to be ultimately recognized, in his courtship, or in his quest for leadership or kingship.

The most basic form of the test model in southern Chinese epics is the so called "obstacles and conquest". There are various hurdles: being thrown away, being attacked or being entrusted with dangerous and tough tasks, including such games as quizzes and athletics and such tender means of temptation and urging the hero to stay on as alluring and detainment. Their aims are all the same, i.e. preventing the main character from achieving his goal. The test is meant to explore the hero's qualities and talents.

In stories, infant desertion is an important test of the "sanctity" of the baby in case. In epics, many heroes are confronted with the early experience of being a-bandoned as a newly born baby. In *Hnewo Teyy*, a Yi epic, the pregnancy of Purmo Hniyyr is caused by three drops of dragon-eagle blood, and she delivers Zhyge Alu. After his birth, Zhyge Alu refuses to drink his mother's milk, sleep close to his mother or wear the clothes his mother prepares for him. His mother 'took him for a demon embryo' and throws him down a cliff.

There is a dragon living down the cliff. Zhyge Alu 'ate the dragon's food when he felt hungry, drank the dragon's milk when he felt thirsty, wore the dragon's cloth when he felt cold'. He grows up thanks to the good care of the dragon and eventually becomes a hero.[1] Another hero named High Han under-goes the same experience, as recorded in *Lai Pheng*, a Dai epic. High Han is the incarnation of the god of Heaven, Bar Ring. Bar Ring puts him into an egg and lets nine dragons incubate for nine years, but in vain. High Han is given birth to by a woman who picks up the egg and eats it and then becomes preg-nant. High Han brings a golden sword and is able to speak as soon as he is born. His mother is so scared that she throws him out of the bamboo house to let cows trample on him. But a deity cow keeps him in her mouth to protect him. The cow disgorges him when the cowherd takes the cow to a grazing field. The boy gets the name High Han (transliteration of the Dai language, meaning "cow deity" or "gold cow"). High Han passes the test and later becomes king of the Mengjingha.[2]

This type of test stories in which a baby is abandoned, as in *Hnewo Teyy* and *Lai Pheng* has a profound symbolic meaning. The hero is the son of Nature. He is born after breathing the spirit of the universe; he possesses divine wisdom and strength in the disguise of a human embryo. Nevertheless, he will go back to na-

---

[1] Feng Yuanwei, *Hnewo Teyy* [Chinese], Chengdu: Sichuan Nationality Publishing House, 1986: 49-54.

[2] Dao Yongming, Xue Xian and Zhou Fengxiang, eds. and trans., *Lai Pheng* [Chinese], Kunming: Yunnan Nationality Publishing House, 1979: 591-592.

ture and be submitted to tests. In addition, he needs to hold a ceremony to be transformed from son of humankind to son of Nature, thus achieving his rebirth in a ritual sense. He gets protection from various deities of nature, such as the dragon in *Hnewo Teyy*, and cows in *Lai Pheng*, as a testimony of his sanctity as the son of nature. Some cases can be interpreted as totems.

In the epics of southern Chinese ethnic groups, there are also test stories related to marriage. The most well-known model is "courtship through difficult tests". The tests are of two types: they are either related to farming or to fighting.

In the Naxi epic *Coq pper tv* (*Genesis*),[①] Coq Ssi Leel Ee's courtship test concerning his going out into the outer space, is an example of the first type. In the epic, Coq Ssi Leel Ee is the only person left on the earth in the wake of a flood. He wants to marry the fairy Cel Huq Bu Beq so as to perpetuate humankind. He travels to Heaven and begs the son of Heaven Ccee Laq A Pu for the hand of Cel Huq Bu Beq and for the seeds of all plants to decorate the earthly world. He must go through a series of tests in Heaven.

First, he has to go up and down nine ladders, the steps of which are made of the edges of knives, but he overcomes, 'with no blooddrop in his hands' and 'no knife-wound on his feet'. Ccee Laq A Pu requires him to chop ninety-nine patches of forest in one day and one night. Coq Ssi Leel Ee chops all trees with the help of all the butterflies and all the ants in the forests. Ccee Laq A Pu requires him to burn all the cut-down trees. Coq Ssi Leel Ee does so with the help of the butterflies and the ants, and scorches every tree. Ccee Laq A Pu requires him to spread the seeds all over those ninety-nine pieces of land in one day and one night and then collect all the seeds spread out, a task Coq Ssi Leel Ee finishes also with the help of the butter-flies and the ants. Ccee Laq A Pu asks him to catch blue sheep on the cliff and fish in the river, in order to seize a chance to kick him off the cliff or into the river. Coq Ssi Leel Ee sees through the tricks

① *Coq* means humans or ethnicity, *pper* means migration or branch, *tv* means origination.

and accomplishes the thorny tasks successfully. At last, Ccee Laq A Pu asks him to milk a tiger; Coq Ssi Leel Ee 'went to the tiger's cave in the shade slope, picked up a big rock, killed a baby-tiger, skinned it and wrapped its fur around himself'. At that time 'the tigress came back, and jumped three times, Coq Ssi Leel Ee jumped three times too. Then the tigress roared three times, Coq Ssi Leel Ee also roared three times. The tigress shook its body three times, Coq Ssi Leel Ee also shook three times. The tigress' tail shook three times, Coq Ssi Leel Ee also shook himself three times... Finally, Coq Ssi Leel Ee pretended to be the baby-tiger to suck milk, he squeezed the tigress' breasts and brought back three drops of tiger milk.' Thus, Coq Ssi Leel Ee succeeds in executing all the difficult tasks imposed by Ccee Laq A Pu.[1]

In these tests, the whole process of the antique production of furrowing, kindling and fishing among farming cultures of the country is incorporated, thus reflecting the process of how the Naxi developed from nomadism and migration to farming. According to historical data, the ancestors of the Naxi were linked to the nomadic Qiang people from northwestern China. After migrating to the south into the Jinsha drainage area, the Naxi gradually settled down and engaged in farming. In this process, they may very well have communicated with, become related to by marriage, and begged for corn seeds or even have fought against the aboriginal populations who had already been engaged in farming. As a result, they have gradually merged into a united Naxi ethnic group. The epic is a symbolic rendering of this complex history.

As to the specific form of such testing, it may be related to the backdrop of the transition from polygamy to monogamy, from the custom of living with the wife to the custom of living with the husband during which matriarchal tradition defied the marriage institution of the debutting patriarchy. The old matriarchal custom is still alive in the convention in some cultures of southern China that a

---

[1] Lijiang Folklore Investigation Team of Yunnan Province, ed. and trans., *Coq pper tv* [*Genesis*][Chinese], Kunming: Yunnan People's Publishing Company, 1960:34-68.

husband lives with his wife in her place for a period of time after marriage, and the wife does not live at her husband's home for several years. During this period, the husband must chop firewood and plough the land for his wife's family. This is a form of compensation to the wife's family for their upbringing of the girl. This custom exists in many southern Chinese cultures.

The tale type of tests is traceable in many southern Chinese myths and epics, as, for example, in the myths and epics of the Qiang (an ancient group in China) who also live in the mountain areas. The myths and epics of some coast area people usually prefer testing the hero by means of building bridges or shooting arrows.

In addition, testing tends to be associated with puberty rites. Among some peoples, boys who grow up to sixteen-years-old need to hold a puberty rite, in which they pass physical tests in order to become qualified for social activities, such as dating and marriage. They believe that such ceremonies have religious implications, and these tests have a divine connotation. The tests promise the examinee a new life. This is probably one of the backgrounds of stories about difficult tests to be passed.

The second type of testing is represented in the Dai epic *Nang Gar See Hall* concerning the story of the courtship by Prince Joe Lang Mar of the kingdom Meng Tang Dar Lar Tar. The epic illustrates that princess Nang see Lar, daughter of king Meng Gan Na Ge, is famous for her beauty and that the one hundred and one princes all approach her at the same time. King Meng Gan Na Ge asks the advice of the deity Bar Ring. Bar Ring gives him a bow named "Gang Har Sing" and three divine arrows and suggests that 'Nang see Lar should marry the prince who can pull the bow and shoot out the three arrows.'[1]

The competition begins, and the one hundred and one princes go up the platform by turns, but none of them can raise the bow. The ten-headed king of the

---

[1] Dao Xingping and Yan Wenbian, eds. and trans., *Nang Gar See Hall* [Chinese], Kunming: Yunnan People's Publishing Company, 1984: 164-171.

kingdom Meng Nang Gar succeeds in raising the bow two times, but he can not pull the string and put up the arrow. He tries a third time, but has no strength left. Finally, it is Joe Lang Mar's turn. Joe Lang Mar prays silently: 'I hope that God can give me a hand.' Then he gently raises the divine bow, pulls the string and shoots out the three divine arrows and eventually marries Nang see Lar. Here, Joe Lang Mar's supernatural ability is highly emphasized.

Another test motif connected with marriage in southern Chinese epics is the divination test for a brother-sister marriage after a flood has destroyed all other humans. *Song of King Pan* tells the following story: The only survivors after a flood, a brother and a sister of the Fu Xi family discuss the issues of their marriage. The sister puts forward five tests for her brother: 'to burn incense across the river while the smoke joins', 'to comb their hair across the river while their hair is connected', 'to grow bamboo across the river while the trail intersects', 'to roll the grinder across the river while the grinder folds', 'to chase around the trees, while two persons meet'. The brother finishes the five tasks one by one so that the sister and brother marry and multiply the human race.[1]

Similar plots about brother-sister marriages exist in the epics of many cultures. In *Brother Fu and Sister Xi Create the World*, a Buoyei epic, the difficult tasks manifest themselves as rolling the grinder and passing the thread through the needle. In *Gal ongs bux (Songs of the Ancestor)*, it concerns rolling the grinder. In the *Waving Hands Song*, the requirements concern rolling the grinder, growing calabashes (the two combined into one), rolling the sieve and the dustpan, chasing, etc. These plots mix the model of marrital contract with that of testing. If the brother wants to marry his sister, he must catch up with the sister in a running match, or have the strength to climb a mountain with a big stone grinder on his back and let the two pieces of the stone grinder stick together when they roll down from the mountain, etc. Other tasks consist of testing providence through

---

[1] Zheng Dehong and Li Bengao, eds. and trans., *Song of King Pan* [Chinese], Changsha: Yuelu Book Association, 1988: 149-156.

divination. The marriage between brothers and sisters needs to be confirmed by all kinds of auguries, thus proving itself as providence, i. e., as divine marriage.

The plot of Jangx Vangb becoming the "big brother" in *Old Miao Songs* can serve as an example. The ancient song narrates: 'Birds usually make noise in the forest; people usually strive to become chamberlains.' The brothers of Jangx Vangb, Thunder and Dragon, 'all vie for being the big brother; one will not a-gree for another to become the big brother'. So, Jangx Vangb proposes: 'Who-ever wants to become the big brother must show his abilities. On the edge of the sky, there is a bridge named Nan Ha, eleven spans long, eleven feet wide. The person who can make the loudest noise and move it with his steps is the greatest and will become the big brother.'

The test begins. Dragon is 'rushing onto the bridge swinging his tail'. But the Nan Ha bridge makes no sound and does not move; Thunder is 'turning over the bridge with a flip', and the Nan Ha Bridge still does not sound nor move. Whereas Jangx Vangb captures a *Ke Ke* bird which he hides in his sleeve and walks onto the Nan Ha bridge with a smile on his face. He pinches the bird and makes it shriek with each stepping. Jangx Vangb claims that 'the bridge has sounded with his steps' and 'the bridge has moved with his steps': and there-fore he should become the big brother. But 'no one is convinced' and they still ask for his 'fighting capability' and for 'martial arts competition'. Thunder 'jumps onto the sky', shaking his iron hammer and 'striking the drum loudly'. 'Lightning is flashing, and rain and wind dominate the sky.'

Water Dragon 'glides down the hill', 'shaking his horns and prying open half of the hill'. The three brothers all claim: 'My capability is the greatest.' Jangx Vangb then 'chopps nine shoulder poles of firewood and shears nine shoulder poles of grass', and then demonstrates to Thunder and Dragon his ability in the room. He lights the fire and fans it. 'The smoke is black, the fire is red, eyes cannot be opened, and all directions are obscured. Thunder and Dragon, the one irritated, the other flustered. One calls to Jangx Vangb, the other also calls to Jangx Vangb: "Your ability is the greatest and your skill is the best..." "①

Jangx Vangb thus becomes the "big brother" thanks to his wisdom and tricks. The above-mentioned account is reminiscent of the ancient test ceremony of choosing a chief and provides a metaphorical narrative about how humans are victorious over nature.

2
Cultural Connotation of the Test Models

The characters' behavioral pattern and the narrative mode of epics all embody cultural models, and contain culture-specific features. The aforesaid plots of test models are no exception. Besides the Dai epic, which is deeply influenced by Indian epics, the narrative modes in Miao, Naxi and Yi epics are strongly marked by farming culture, group oriented culture and shamanistic culture in the mountain areas of southern China.

To a large extent, the characters' behavioral pattern in epics corresponds to that of people in real life. People's real-life behavior is not purely "natural" behavior; to a large extent it is conditioned by a specific cultural background and a particular culture's spirit. As a collective creation of a people over the centuries, the epic accumulates many cultural elements. As a result, the concrete scenes as manifest in the works may considerably differ from real life, but the behavioral pattern abstracted out of real life shares considerable generality. Fundamentally, the behavioral pattern is determined by real life.

Most of the test items of various ceremonies in southern China are connected with farming life in the mountain regions. The ceremonies of "climbing up the knife ladder", "passing through the fire chain" and "jumping off the cloud platform" for young men at the "manhood" ceremony among the Yao, all include

---

①   Tian Bing, ed., *Old Miao Songs* [Chinese], collected by the Folklore Team of Guizhou, Guiyang: People's Publishing Company of Guizhou Province, 1979: 211-215.

this people's traditional skills in knife furrowing and fire farming in the mountain regions. The practice of knife furrowing and fire farming in real life requires the Yao people to run, chop firewood, burn grass, step on the scorching soil after grass-burning, dig holes, sow and leap up and down on the steep slope. All these basic skills transform into tests such as "climbing up the knife ladder", "passing through the fire chain" and "jumping off the cloud platform" in the epics. They are deep-seated in the farming culture of mountainous areas.

Both the participants and the form of the tests reflect the customs of farming culture in mountain regions, as regards test-related epic plots. In *Old Miao Songs*, Jangx Vangb is the clan's chief in this ancient agriculture society. His main competitors in the tests are Thunder Father, Water Dragon, etc., who are all natural spirits dominating rain and water, and have close relations with farming. In the test "martial arts competition", the Thunder Father flips, thunders, lights, rains and storms, and the Water Dragon pries the slope to collapse, which all symbolically reflects the bearing on farming of disastrous weather. As a result, a test symbolically represents the ongoing struggle of humankind against catastrophic weather conditions in farming life.

The test procedures reflect as well the essence of farming culture in mountain regions. In the Naxi epic *Coq pper tv* (*Genesis*), Coq Ssi Leel Ee flies to the sky to ask God Ccee Laq A Pu for the hand of the fairy Cel Huq Bu Beq and for seeds of all earthly plants. His tests in Heaven include chopping forests, burning wood, choosing and planting seeds, catching a rock goat, grasping fish and shrimp, etc. Actually, these activities represent farming and fishing life in the mountain regions.

The test also represents qualities of collective cultures. Coq Ssi Leel Ee takes the tests in Heaven not for his own ardor or material rewards, but for a spouse and seeds to perpetuate humankind and decorate the earthly world respectively. After the various tests Ccee Laq A Pu asks him: 'Whose offspring are you?' Coq Ssi Leel Ee responds with the following powerful words:

I'm the offspring of the nine brothers opening the nine-layered sky,

I'm the offspring of the seven sisters hacking the seven-layered earth,

I'm the offspring of the white whelk lion,

I'm the offspring of the golden elephant,

I'm the offspring of a man of unusual strength, Jiugao Nabu,

I'm the race with greater strengh crossing ninety-nine mountains,

I'm the race with hearty spirit crossing ninety-nine slopes,

I'm the race of the deathless not to be killed by all those who can kill,

I'm the race of the unbreakable not to be broken by all those who can break![①]

These remarks are filled with pride and affection for one's ethnic group and are highly characteristic of ethnic consciousness and a collective culture.

Finally, testing contains attributes of a shamanistic culture hidden in the act of the protagonist's acceptance of tests. In *Old Miao Songs*, in his contest with Thunder Father and Water Dragon, 'chopping nine shoulder poles of firewood, shearing nine shoulder poles of grass', Jangx Vangb places them all in a room. Thunder Father and Water Dragon admit their defeat and recognize: 'Your skill is the greatest, we give up'.[②] Here, simulated shamanism features, or in other words, the smoke from burning firewood and grass symbolizes the effort to dispel rain and waterlogging for the purpose of controlling natural disasters.

In the Naxi epic *Coq pper tv* (*Genesis*), Coq Ssi Leel Ee's appearance and behavior are characteristic of traditional shamans and shamanism. When Coq Ssi Leel Ee first meets the god Ccee Laq A Pu, he is put to hard tests. Coq Ssi Leel Ee sings: 'White butterfly ah, quickly fly, fly here and help me. Black ants ah, quickly run, run here and help me!' As a result, the next morning, 'in the

---

① Lijiang Folklore Investigation Team of Yunnan Province, ed. and trans., *Coq pper tv* [Genesis] [Chinese], Kunming: Yunnan People's Publishing Company, 1960: 61-62.

② Tian Bing, ed., *Old Miao Songs* [Chinese], collected by the Folklore Team of Guizhou, Guigyang: People's Publishing Company of Guizhou Province, 1979: 214-215.

ninety-nine pieces of forest, oh, all trees have been laid down'.[①] Here, the protagonist relies completely on the incantation that enjoys magic power and can mobilize all forces of nature, which is exemplary of shamanism.

3
Comparison of the Test Models

The characters' behavioral patterns in epics are limited by the respective cultural models of various ethnic groups as the products of cultural and historical life and eventually determined and affected by historical life. It is historically induced differences that lead to differences in various cultural models and in the different characters' behavioral patterns in various epics.

The creators of Greek fables and epics were the Aryans who once lived in Central Asia in the remote age of antiquity. Aryans experienced a large-scale split-up and migration in their evolution process, in which one branch emigrated to the hinterland of Europe and reached the Greek Peninsula by the Aegean Sea. They destroyed the very developed local Mycenaean culture and established their own rule.

The history of the Aryan migration and evolution is one of expedition, adventure and robbery. One branch of Aryans settled down after entering Greece and constantly travelled far to conquer, adventure and loot. Their culture was extroverted; they tended to be more appreciative of force, foray and conquest, which asked for more venturesome spirits and individual wisdom.

Differing from the Aryans who settled down on the Greek Peninsula by the Aegean Sea, part of the ethnic groups who inhabited the mountain regions of southern China were aboriginals, while others migrated from northern China, most of which were losers and escapers of war, instead of being conquerers as the

---

①   Lijiang Folklore Investigation Team of Yunnan Province, ed. and trans., *Coq pper tv* [Genesis] [Chinese], Kunming: Yunnan People's Publishing Company, 1960: 38-43.

Aryans were. They embarked on an agricultural economy at a rather early stage. Living in the mountain areas vulnerable to flood and drought, they were first confronted with the needs of utilizing collective strength to adapt to or reform the e-cological environment to meet the needs of the survival and perpetuation of the group. In a farming society, people live and cultivate the land with contentment, and clans peacefully co-exist. They enjoy a life of stability, peace, amity, and equity, so that their cultures are inward, and their values group orientated.

The differences between two cultural models lead to different contents of culture-specific test plots. The well-known story of Jason seeking the Golden Fleece in Greek myth and epic is a test story. Jason goes back home as his father's successor. However, his uncle who had pilfered the throne, puts forward a condition to return power to Jason: Jason must lead the army to attack the distant country of Colchis, and acquire the precious Golden Fleece from brutal King Aeetes. Jason accepts the challenge and together with a group of heroes he embarks on the risky journey by boat Argo. This condition is a kind of test, a difficult task, an obstacle, which the hero must fulfill and overcome. It includes a long journey, crusade and treasure-looting and represents the cultural model of the Greek.

The content of the tests in southern Chinese epics is mostly introvert, characteristic of mountain farming culture. The Coq Ssi Leel Ee story in *Coq pper tv* (*Genesis*) is a typical one. It contains the whole procedure of farming and fishing activities of the farming population in mountain areas, which manifest themselves as chopping ninety-nine forests, burning the woods of the ninety-nine forests, scattering seeds on the ninety-nine pieces of land, harvesting the seeds from the ninety-nine pieces of land, hunting goats on cliffs, and fishing in the rivers. [1] The differences in cultural models bring about huge differences in the protagonists' behavioral patterns in test-related stories.

The more obvious difference lies in the heroes' accomplishments in their

---

[1] Ibid. 41-58.

adulthood as a logical outcome of the passing of tests upon their birth. When the hero is born and passes the test, it attests to his divinity and heralds the hero's uncommon way of life and experience. Almost all the heroes in Greek myths and epics choose the life style of taking risks, going on expedition and changing the ruling order when they grow up. When Zeus grows up, he overthrows his father Cronos' rule, leads the gods on the Olympus, putting down the rebelling Titans and establishes his supreme status. Taking risks and conquering were the utmost survival principles and value pursuits of people from this culture.

Extraordinary performances of the heroes during their youth in southern Chinese epics represent the farming life in the mountain regions. Zhyge Alu in Yi *Hnewo tepyy*, can 'follow ranchers to pasture pigs' when he is one year old, he can 'follow herds to pasture sheep' when he is two years old. Moreover, his greatest achievement is the shooting down of the extra suns and moons that were closely related to farming and herding. At that time, 'there are six suns rising up in the day time and seven moons coming out in the night time', which made the river dry up, the grass and wood die away, birds and animals fall victim, and people suffer. Hnewo Teyy 'pulls the divine curve bow, lifts up the divine arrow', intending to shoot suns and moons. He stands on the grass, on the vine, on top of a bamboo and on top of a pine, in order to 'shoot the sun but failed, and shoot the moon but failed'. He is not frustrated and continues to try. He then stands on top of a cypress on top of Mountain Turlurbbo. Eventually, he 'shoots at the sun and succeeds, and shoots at the moon and succeeds', and accomplishes the most splendid feat of his lifetime.[①] Working for the group's growing and facilitating farming represent the heroes' utmost pursuit in southern Chinese epics.

References:

Dao Xingping and Yan Wenbian, eds. and trans. *Nang Gar See Hall*. [Chinese]. Kun-

---

① Feng Yuanwei, *Hnewo Teyy* [Chinese], Chengdu: Sichuan Nationality Publishing House, 1986: 53-60.

ming: Yunnan People's Publishing Company, 1984.

Dao Yongming, Xue Xian and Zhou Fengxiang, eds. and trans. *Lai Pheng* [Chinese]. Kunming: Yunnan Nationality Publishing House, 1979.

Feng Yuanwei. *Hnewo Teyy* [Chinese]. Chengdu: Sichuan Nationality Publishing House, 1986.

Lijiang Folklore Investigation Team of Yunnan Province, ed. and trans. *Coq pper tv* [Genesis][Chinese]. Kunming: Yunnan People's Publishing Company, 1960.

Tian Bing, ed. *Old Miao Songs* [Chinese]. Collected by the Folklore Team of Guizhou. Guiyang: People's Publishing Company of Guizhou Province, 1979.

Zheng Dehong and Li Bengao, eds. and trans. *Song of King Pan* [Chinese]. Changsha: Yuelu Book Association, 1988.

X
Precious Volumes and Their Ritual Context. A Case – Study of Houtu Cult and Oral Tradition in North China

Yin Hubin

Abstract: This paper provides a case study of the cult of the Houtu deity and of the oral narrative tradition in the folk society of Hebei province. The data of my fieldwork are primarily concerned with the temples of Houtu, music and religious associations and their rites, and narrative texts of oral traditions. All of these materials have been existent in the local activities of the Houtu cult, as well as in local recordings of inscriptions on stone tablets and oral narratives. My theoretical hypothesis is that the cult of Houtu is some kind of on-spot activities which draw on myth and ritual. At the center of the seasonal recurrence of sacrificial offerings to the deities and spirits lies the Houtu deity. As for the actual performance of precious volumes and the narrative of Houtu mythology, the core belief is that singing the Houtu deity's story summons her as a goddess whose power is then actualized to protect the community. Precious volumes and the related folk narrative tradition in Hebei areas have been evolving from the cult of the Houtu deity.

Key words: the cult of the Houtu deity, precious volumes, oral tradition

Hongya Mountain, located at the place where Yi county and Laishui county of Heibei province join, has played a central role in the cult of the Houtu deity since the end of the Qing dynasty and the beginning of the Republic period (1912-1949). The regional cult of Houtu has been evolving in the areas surrounding Hongya Mountain. At the seasonal recurrence of ceremonies held in temples and tents, the Houtu deity was regarded as the highest goddess. Compared to the polytheism of Chinese folk religion, the local tradition of Houtu worship has taken on attributes of some kind of monotheism. A community that shares a common belief in Houtu as its spiritual foundation took shape on the basis of the traditional cult of the Houtu deity. The Houtu temple fair on a yearly basis constituted a spiritual bond, which enabled regular pilgrimages to a mountain temple and incense-burnings for the Houtu deity, sacrificial offerings and money-raising for the reconstruction of the temples as a sacred obligation. The tradition of Houtu worship on a local level has exerted a great impact on related folk narratives including the precious volumes.

Houtu used to be a natural spirit, cultural hero and ancestral deity. It had evolved into the spiritual system of Taoism from a god in Chinese mythology and became one of *siyu* (four deities in Taoism). It used to be the goddess of Laomu (venerable mother of Chinese folk religion), and was later on accepted as a goddess into folk belief. The cult of Houtu in folk society has its own typological features. It took the temple as its prop, religious associations as its entity and sacrificial offerings and village festival activities as the media through which people could communicate with the goddess. The cult per se fit in with local people's psychological needs, and drew on mythological narratives to embody the diffusion of religious inheritance.

Religious associations, such as Buddhist affairs associations and music associations, scattered across the areas of the Jizhong plain surrounding the capital city of Beijing. These associations have been responsible for village festival activities in the local farming society. They acted on traditional ideological spirits to worship the gods of Heaven and Earth, to revere ancestors – both of which were deeply seated in the patriarchal clan – and to fulfill the mission of preserving the local tradition. The precious volumes have been their sacred texts constituting the legacy of their ancestors, including the performance tradition.

The precious volumes and their performances have been part of the sacrificial ceremony for the Houtu deity. The precious volumes have been spread and propelled by the ritual activities practiced by village associations. The transmission of *Precious Volumes for the Houtu Deity* belongs to the living tradition of local areas. The precious volumes bear diachronic links with traditional artistic forms.

The living oral tradition lies right behind the precious volumes. Mythological narratives about the cult of the Houtu deity have been continuously reproduced up to date, and they have become part of Chinese farming ideology. Folktales and legends related to the efficacious effect of the Houtu deity have been told and transmitted as historically true events. These kinds of narratives are actually the re-interpretation and appraisal of those social events by the people. The narratives pertaining to the efficacious effects of the Houtu deity liken the myths. They are live performances and re-tellings and closely related to the specific belief, morality, ethics and behavioral patterns. More importantly, it is exemplary of traditional myths about the Houtu deity.

When examining the materials from the living oral tradition, we should pay special attention to the interaction between the cult of Houtu and oral traditional literature in the local areas of Hongya Mountain. First, as we proceed to consider in some detail the evidence of living oral traditions in contemporary local areas of Hongya Mountain, it is important to stress the explicit function of religion in the folk narratives. A working definition of religion will suffice in this study, that is, the interaction between myth and ritual. I take Gregory Nagy's line of argument to specify "religion" in terms of cult, or in more precise terms, as a set of practices combining elements of ritual as well as myth.[①] The precious volumes and their performance give prominence to on-spot cult activities. As for the actu-

---

① See Gregory Nagy, *Greek Mythology and Poetics*, Ithaca/London: Cornell University Press, 1990: 8-10. When the author proceeds to consider in some detail the evidence of living oral epic traditions in contemporary India, he stresses the explicit role of religion in the very function of epic. As one of the most powerful illustrations of the role of religion in the performance of the Indian epic, he points to those situations where the performer presupposes the presence of an audience of gods, waching out for errors in the performance.

al performance of the precious volumes, the central belief is that singing the Houtu's story summons her as a goddess whose power is then actualized to protect the community. The cult of the Houtu deity on the regional level leaves a great impact on the precious volumes and folk narrative tradition. The Houtu deity lies at the center of a ritual held in seasonally recurring activities.

At the shrine of the Houtu temple in Hongya Mountain, the deity was placed at the center of a cult. The spirit manifests herself through a medium, usually a nun or an old lady (i.e. grandmother, *nainai* in Chinese). The shrine becomes active through this medium; the spirit begins to solve problems for the local people. An effective and truthful disposition by the possessed medium of the grandmother will attract people from far and wide, and the shrine may become an important ritual site where the scripture reciting is also performed.

In the precious volumes of Emperor Houtu, the deity features as a village girl in the Han dynasty (named Han Zhangu). The girl left her family, came to Hongya Mountain, and carried on ascetic practice for forty years. Her death works to confer on her ultimate power; the event functions as a "generative point" for narratives in the local contexts. It leads to deification, to worship, to a cult, and eventually to a narrative, which is ritually performed to invoke the spirits of the dead.

1
The cult of Houtu and Its Local Tradition

I. Houtu and Belief in the Houtu Deity

Early earth worship was dedicated to the square mound (*fangqiu*) or altar of the earth (*tutan*). The cult of earth and grains later evolved into the cult of human beings who were in charge of earth and grains. At that point, the worship of natural gods evolved into a personality cult. In primitive times, ancestor worship and heroic worship were mingled together.[①] The ceremony of the Houtu deity had undergone a downward evolution from a national level to a local level. The state-sponsored ceremony of Houtu began to decline since the Jin and Yuan dynasties, and in the meantime, the universality of the deity was challenged. The ceremony of Houtu was only practiced in north China, e. g. Hebei, Shanxi and Shaanxi since the Qing dynasty.[②] There were hundreds of Taoist and Buddhist temples scattered across the areas surrounding Hongya Mountain in Hebei province, most of which were built before the Ming dynasty. The earlier Buddhist temples were built in Tang times. In the Yuan dynasty, the Yao ethnic group migrated to north China, and built the Pangu temple in Hongya. In Song and Jin times, the Taoist priests entered the mountains. The Zhengyi sect of the Complete Pure Taoism entered the mountains. While in Yuan times, the Complete Pure Taoist sect entered the northern side of the mountains. For example, there were Taoist temples in Baoquan village. After the Tang dynasty, Hongya Mountain has become a religious and cultural center in the local areas of Hebei province.

II. The Regional Level of Houtu Ceremonies

Hongya Mountain, offshoot of Mountain Taihang located in the east of Yi county, Hebei province, earned its name as a famous Taoist site. It is called *houshan* (hills behind the village) on the grassroots level. Among the variety of folk beliefs prevailing in Yi county, the belief of Emperor Houtu is age-old and sustainable. On top of Hongya Mountain there is a temple of Emperor Houtu as recorded in *Yixian Zhigao* (*Yixian Gazetteer*):

The temple of Emperor Houtu, popularly called the *shengnu miao* [temple of the female deity], is located on Hongya Mountain, which is thirty-five *li*

---

① Cao Fulin, *Xian Qin Minsu Shi* [*History of Folklore in the Pre-Qin Era*], Shanghai: Shanghai People's Publishing House, 2001: 318.

② Xue Yinbing and Tsao Pen-ye, "The Cult of Houtu and the Folk Music Associations in Yi and Laishui Counties," *Zhongguo Yinyuexue* [*Musicology in China*] 1 (2000): 79-98.

away from the northern county, at a height of ten *li*, with the mountain paths twisting and zigzagging. According to editorial notes, the temple has been making ceremonial offerings to the female deity. To this day, the folk beliefs have been mingled with teratology (oral traditions about gods and spirits). There is a popular saying that the goddess is an old woman who saved Emperor Guangwu of the Han dynasty from disaster. According to *Commentary on the Waterways* [a classic work of geography written by Li Daoyuan of the Northern Wei dynasty, 386-534], Emperor Guangwu chased the burglars Tongma and Wufan in Xushui, the southern areas of Yi prefecture. The emperor was defeated and later saved; he retreated to and safeguarded Fanyang. However, the man who saved the emperor was a cavalryman named Wangfeng. The legends about the woman do not have sufficient evidence. That is why the temple was named after Emperor Houtu. It is supposed to serve sacrifices to the Yellow Emperor Xuanyuan [surname of the Yellow emperor, legendary first Chinese ancestor]. According to *Shiji* [*Historical Records* by Simaqian, c. 145-? BC of the Western Han dynasty], Chi You, the legendary leader of the Jiuli tribes living in the eastern part of what is now the North China plain, fought the Yellow Emperor at Zhuolu in present Hebei province and was defeated and killed by the Yellow Emperor. The Yellow Emperor fought Chi You at Zhuolu, and then met with dukes or princes at Fushan, located in the southern area of present day Yixian, fifty *li* away from the county. Since then, Fushan has been seen as the place where the Yellow Emperor met with dukes or princes. It is reasonable that the Yellow Emperor had his temple in Yi area. The temple fair is extremely prevalent nowadays. In the third month of the Chinese lunar year, thousands of villagers from the nearby areas flock to the temple fair, which has become the most spectacular affair in town. [1]

---

[1] Shou Pengfei, ed., *Yixian Zhigao* [*Annals of Yi County*], reprint, Beijing: Xueyuan Publishing House, 1990: 298-299.

According to inscriptions on a stone tablet recording the sixteenth year of the Hongzhi reign in Ming times (*Chong xiu shouyangyuan zhi ji* [*Renovated Record for the Shouyang Courtyard*]):

Thirty *li* away from the northern Yi prefecture, there was a mountain called Hongya where the Shouyang courtyard is located. It is the place in which Liu Zhenren [Taoist practitioner] lived in seclusion during the second year of the Taihe reign in the Jin dynasty. The three rooms of the Yuhuang temple are renovated; the temple is lofty and wide, and looks grand and splendid. The statue of Yuhuangdadi [Jade Emperor of Heaven, the supreme deity of Taoism] stands in the middle, guarded by the twenty-eight constellations (*er' shibaxiu*).

Another stone tablet says: 'The Baiyun Temple and Phoenix Mountains of Yi county have been in full cooperation for the same cause, maintaining a long-standing friendship for numerous generations.'

2
Folk Associations : Their Ritual Activities and Scripture Recitation

There have been many names for the music associations, for example, *nandenghui* (Southern Lantern Society), *nandengshenshe* (Southern Lantern Holy Society), or *nandeng shenghui* (Southern Lantern Sacred Society). The musicians are generally known as *xueshi* (pupils). Those who are proficient in music and are capable of teaching are called *shifu* (master). The head of the music association is called *huishou* (association head) who is usually in charge of everything concerning the association. The person who presides over the whole ritual is often called *Xiangshou* (incense head). There are about thirty persons in a music association, among whom twenty are *xueshi*, one is *huishou*, and one is *xiangshou*. [1]

The music by the association has its specific scope. Music includes thirteen large pieces (*daqu*) composed of solemn melodic instrumental music and about thirty small pieces (*xiaoqu*). Furthermore, the music must be played by this specific association, other genres played by other associations are not called "music". [2] The melodic repertory and instruments of the music association are fixed, and the mode of the performance follows strictly the inherited regulation.

The traditional function of the music association is to serve village rituals. The function of the music is to please the spirits to whom the vow is made. In Laishui and Yi counties, the music association would accompany pilgrimages to pray for *Houtu nainai* (the goddess Houtu). Traditional ceremonies involve making and fulfilling vows, offering incense, reciting scriptures, and singing hymns. [3] Some old music score books have prefaces in verse, one of which reads: 'The traditional music association handed down and transmitted from the Ming to the Qing dynasties highly regards the gods and sacrificial ceremonies dedicated to heaven and earth from generation to generation.'

It is exclusively male musicians who perform the instrumental music in the village's ritual activities, most of them coming from the big family (*dahu*) of the village, thus maintaining their ancestral heritage on the foundation of kinship and genealogy. The association pays tribute to heaven and earth and historical courtesy to earth on the basis of ancestral worship. The cultural background of the same clan system of a village lays ground for preserving the tradition. In southern Gaoluo of Laishui county, there are four large clans, San, Li, Yan, and He.

---

[1] Xue Yibing, "The Types and Humane Background of the Folk Music of Wind and Percussion Instruments," *Studies on the Folk Music of Drums and Wind Instruments: A Collection of the Research Papers from the First Symposium on Chinese Folk Music of Drums and Wind Instruments*, edited by Qiao Jianzhong and Xue Yibing, Jinan: Shandong Friendship Publishing House, 1999: 57.

[2] Stephen Jones, *Folk Music of China: Living Instrumental Traditions*, Oxford: Clarendon Press, 1995: 189.

[3] Ibid, p.189.

Music is still often handed down from father to son in a traditional society. Musical knowledge, instruments, instrumental techniques, scores and score reading are handed down within the institution of the family. Some families have a lineage of five generations of musicians. Membership of the music society of a village is a socially cohesive form of music education.[①] The all-male tradition constitutes a partriarchal line of knowledge transmission in the local areas.

The music association and the Buddhist affairs society usually have their own property such as instruments, scriptures, the place of training or performance, and always make use of village temples for their ritual activities. If there is more than one society within a village, each of them may have its own well-defined territory and a certain number of supporters from the villagers. Music associations preserve notated scores, which have been handed down for many generations. In terms of melodic notation, some villages use the standard *gongche* notation, the signs of which vary somewhat from village to village, but in whatever form they may have been written, they are pronounced as standard *gongche*. The musicians sing these note-names when chanting the score (*yunpu*) to rehearse a piece. According to Stephen Jones, villagers often say that their music was acquired from Buddhist temples or from Buddhist monks. This line of transmission has a history of approximately 500 years.[②]

---

① Qiao Jianzhong, Xue Yibing, Stephen Jones and Zhang Zhentao, "General Investigation Report on the Folk Music Society in Jizhong Plain, Beijing, Tianjin", *Zhongguo Yinyue Nianjian* [*Year Book of Chinese Music*], edited by Tian Qing, Jinan: Shandong Friendship Publishing House, 1985: 293.

② Ibid. 293.

3

The Text of Precious Volumes of Emperor Houtu

Ⅰ. Origins of the Text

(ⅰ) Precious Volumes of Taoist Origin about Emperor Houtu Who Shows Gratitude to Heaven and Follows Law, Releases Souls from Purgatory (Hanjiazhuang text)

This edition was preserved by Fu Xihua, but was later edited and published in
Precious Volumes, *First Collection* (*Baojuan Chuji*) in 1994. At the end of the
precious volumes there are names of benefactors whose efforts had marked the
printing of the text: Liu Hao, Guo Yu, Zhang Wenguang and Wang Lianyou.
There are five folk religious paintings on the back cover. Four of them are related
to Taoism or the Hongyang religious sect, one being that of Buddha. On the final
page of the text there is a painting of a memorial tablet, in which there is an inscription: in memorial of merits and virtues of the benefactors who effected the
printing of the portraits of Buddha in Hanjiazhuang: Wei Tianfu, Chang Rui.[①]
The mixings of Taoism and Buddhism are characteristic of the Houtu cult.

This edition was originally divided into twenty-four *pin* (chapters), but the
first 12 *pin* of the edition are missing. The thirteenth *pin* of the precious volumes
reads: 'As the story goes, the goddess Houtu, who, by decree of Buddha, set
up the gateway to the law [dharma door] on the hilltop of Loessland, opened the
altar and taught the doctrine, elaborated the sectarian teaching and released the
souls from purgatory.'

---

①   *Baojuan Chuji* [*Precious Volumes*, *First Collection*], 43 vols., edited by Zhang Xisun, Pu Wenqi,
    GaoKe and Song Jun, Taiyuan: Shanxi People's Press, 1994, vol. 11.

The thirteenth *pin* tells about the obligation of the female deity Houtu: I myself am the deity proper in charge of earth in this world. All human beings and things on earth are born out of soil. It is this female deity Houtu who spread the sectarian teachings at the grand temple on the hilltop of Hongya Mountain located in the northern area of Yi county.

The sixteenth *pin* concerns the story of how the Houtu deity guided an official called Zhang Bin to Taoism and how she granted Zhang Bin a son. This episode portrays Zhang Bin praying for a child which is similar to the textual accounts in the precious volumes preserved by Matou village in Yi county. The Houtu precious volumes tell: It so happened that there was a benefactor in Luoyang county, Henan prefecture. His surname was Zhang, his given name Bin, and his wife was Madam Wang. The couple had no child. One day Zhang Bin suddenly remembered that last year when he passed the Yi prefecture, he met a pilgrim who said that *songzi niangniang* (son-granting female deity) could send children to human beings and guaranteed its effect. When Madam Wang, the wife of Zhang Bin, prayed for a child to the female deity, the Houtu deity transformed into a nun and begged a meal from Zhang's house. The deity introduced herself like this: 'I am from the northern side of Yi city, Baoding prefecture, very near the Houtu temple.' And then, Zhang Bin and his wife asked for a portrait of the female deity, using it for incense burning. The divine picture was like this: The head of Houtu was adorned with brilliant jewels and pearls, and several other goddesses all wore necklaces of pearls and jade, with their faces plated in gold.

(ii) Precious Volumes about the Houtu Deity Preserved by the Temple of Goddess Houtu (Matou text)

Matou village of Liujing township in Yi county used to have a music association which preserved both *dengke* and *yike* religious scriptures, including the volume of Houtu and the volume of ten kings, most of which were lost. There are a lot of religious scriptures extant at the temple of Houtu, one of which are the volumes of Houtu in possession of Shangfang village, Xingtang county, Zhending prefecture. According to this edition, the female deity disciplined herself in the Danxia cave and eventually became immortal. The second part of the volumes tells of the official Liu Yong's praying for a child. According to the local legends, Zhang Qi composed this precious scripture at the end of the Yuan dynasty. Yet no evidence points to Zhang Qi's authorship.

Liang Shuming, a villager of Matou village, preserved several precious volumes, which used to be the treasure of the Houtu temple located on hills behind the village. During the Cultural Revolution, young red guards damaged the temple. Liang saved the scriptures and has preserved them up till now. He has preserved two versions of the precious volumes of the Houtu deity. The first version might be composed at the end of Qing times, as indicated by the condition and the legends of the volume. The whole book contains three volumes and thirty-two chapters, all hand written in big Li-style characters, folded in the form of sutra and having illustrations. The main contents concern praying for a child.

The front cover is entitled: "Precious Volumes about the Source and Course of Goddess Houtu, Her Being Mercyful and Efficacious." The first page is entitled: "Precious Volumes about Emperor Houtu, the Earth Deity Who Shows Gratitude to Heaven and Follows Law." Prior to the textual body there are eight "divine invocations" for purifying the body, mouth and mind, blessing water, dispelling pollution and purifying Heaven and Earth. There were incantations, names, title incantation, incense offering incantation, opening scripture incantation, you're the name of Yuqing divinity, the name of Shangqing divinity, the honorary title of Maitreya divinity, the honorary title of Gouchen divinity, the name of star master Ziwei divinity, the name of emperor Houtu, the honorary title of Wanglingguan divinity. What follows is the main text, entitled "Precious Volumes about the Mercyful Houtu Deity". In between the title and chapter one are "Incense-holding Hymn", "Scripture-opening Hymn", and "Divinity-inviting Hymn".

(ⅲ) The second version of Precious Volumes about the Houtu Deity Preserved by Liang Shuming (Manuscript of Liang)

This edition originally had four volumes (*yuan*, *heng*, *li*, *zhen*) and forty-eight chapters. Only the first three volumes with thirty-six chapters are extant, with the last volume missing. These precious volumes were composed during Qing times, handwritten in large characters, bound between cardboard rectangles in accordion style, and folded in the form of sutra (*jing zhe zhuang*). On the front cover is the title written top-down in a red stripe: "Precious Volumes about Emperor Houtu, the Earth Deity Who Shows Gratitude to Heaven and Follows Law". These precious volumes have been transmitted by the goddess Houtu temple in the hills behind the Matou village in Yi county. This site used to be a Taoist temple where Taoist abbots affiliated with the Ten-Directional Complete Pure Sect once resided. Liang's precious volumes contain some Taoist incantations, mostly printed in the Taoist canons, from which we can tell that the Taoist priest sung the ordinary Taoist scriptures and chanted the precious volumes like the Houtu precious volumes in earlier times. The Taoist rites began with the chanting of the "opening scripture and solacing the gods", "incantation of purifying the mouth", "invocation of purifying the body", "incantation of incense offering", "opening altar incantation" and "the goddess Houtu precious volumes". As the Taoist practitioners of the Houtu Temple recall, the Houtu precious volumes consisted of two parts: the first part telling of the goddess Houtu, and her ascetic practice; the second part recording the legend of Liu Xiu as well as his flee from the country. The two parts combined could be seen as a local history of the origin of the temple, and as an orally transmitted local history of Yi prefecture. The mural paintings evidence the legendary history of goddess Houtu and Emperor Liu Xiu. The mural paintings in the main hall called Taining mirror the contents of the two parts of the precious volumes and the content of widespread local myths and stories. According to the legend, the great artist Cui Zhizhong had painted the mural paintings during the Ming dynasty.

(iv) *Precious Volumes about Emperor Houtu* Preserved by South Gaoluo Village (Gaoluo Text)

This edition has been preserved by the music association of South Gaoluo village, Yi'an township in Laishui county. It is printed in large characters, bound between cardboard retangles in accordion style and folded in the form of sutra. This edition is 14 inches (36cm) high and 5 inches (13cm) wide. It has two volumes (juan), composed of twenty-four chapters and 19.000 characters. There are fifteen illustrations. The front cover reads: "Precious Volumes about Emperor Houtu" and the inside front cover: "The Greatest Earth". The inscription at the bottom records the completion by Ma Xiantu on the first day of the first month of the lunar year of Guiwei (1943). From page one to page three, there is a paragraph written by the inscriber Mr. Ma: "Casual notes on the accomplishment of transcribing the precious volume."

Emperor Houtu, since the revival in the Eastern Han dynasty, has lasted for 2.000 years up to date. The deity has been very efficacious and attracting an ever-increasing number of worshippers and pilgrims, especially during the grand sacrificial ceremony in spring and autumn and on the birthday of the deity. Its historical continuity came to a halt in the Republic Period. Since superstition was subjected to suppression under the guidance of the Three Principles of the People (nationalism, democracy, and the people's livelihood), all the temple fairs were on the gradual decline. Furthermore, since the Marco Polo Bridge Incident of 1937, the people were in shock several times each day, and were thus in no mood for a pilgrimage to the deity. Every year on the fifteenth day of the third month, people could just face the north-west, paying tribute to the goddess, repaying her Majesty's kindness. People were recollecting that goddess Houtu had experienced painstaking self-cultivation and eventually achieved perfect virtues and merits. The goddess had protected the unity of the Han dynasty. Besides, she responded favorably to every plea of men and women from the human world. The second volume records Mr. Zhang's prayer for a child and the return to Heaven of the four sages who invoke admiration and conviction.

I acted on impulse to bring the precious volumes of Houtu from Gaoluo village, washed my hands and copied it, so as to repay the goddess' kindness, and simultaneously to make up the shortage of the scripture box of the Hongyang association in our village, and to sustain commemoration. By the way, after my completion of copying, Shan Fuhong, my sister's husband, bought paper from Beijing, and asked me to write another copy for preservation by his village. I appreciated the conviction in the goddess, that is, in the cause of Hongfu's readiness to effect good and kind deeds, I was pleased to satisfy his kindness. I re-set my brushes and ink, copying with clean hands and respectfulness, and painting the pictures, all in my spare time after my daily teaching. Best Regards with respect.

For Gaoluo Benevolent Society as a supplement to the scripture box.

Faithful believer Ma Xiantu from Hubenyi village wrote with respect at North school. The thirty-second year of the Republic of China, the Year of Guiwei, on the auspicious day of the first month of the lunar year.

In addition to the versions we mentioned above, Buddhist affairs associations and music associations around Hongya Mountain have preserved the other versions of Houtu precious volumes. Most of these editions are copies of the original texts of Liang Shuming from Matou village in Yi county. Most of these copies constitute only half of the original text. The volumes of the Matou musical association were copied from fellow villager Liang Shuming's half edition in 1994, and have been preserved by the head of the association Jia Yutian. Xibaoquan also copied Liang's version in 1990. In 1992, the Buddhist association at Lijiafen of Laishui county brought the copy from Xibaoquan. So did the Nanlaoping village. The above-mentioned village associations brought and copied the volumes in response to the revision of the temple faire in Hongya Mountain and the revival of the ceremonial activities regarding goddess Houtu. The significance of this phenomenon lies in that we can have an overview of the spreading of the precious volumes in close relation to the cult of Houtu in the local areas. The phenomenon that village associations only preserve half of the complete text indicates that these precious volumes are meant to cope with ritual performance in the service of inviting the female deity Houtu at sacrificial ceremonies. [1]

II. The Classification of the Texts

The earlier precious volumes have directly absorbed elements of the Buddhist scripture, such as meter, formulas, syntax, notably some borrowings from *Ji* (songs for the ritual of praying to gods), *Zhan* (tune name, six-verse, a hymn for the gods). This is because, first of all, the precious volumes were a kind of scripture, created and used by the religious sects, and their first objective was to elucidate the doctrines. Therefore, the precious volumes must have been modeled on the Buddhist scripture, and were alike in spirit. In the course of their development, the precious volumes have taken on a more complex look through absorbing elements of preaching Buddhist sutra by way of story-telling, transformed text and drama (e.g. such local opera as southern and northern tunes). The precious volumes portrayed, in the first place, two categories of Buddhist subject matter, i.e. the performance of the sectarian scripture elaborating on the Buddhist canons and the talking and singing of Buddhist tales. Later on, there appeared the precious volumes, folk religion and folk precious volumes. The task of performance was transferred from Taoist and Buddhist monks to the folk artists. The ways of performance liken preaching Buddhist sutras by way of story-

---

[1]   Xue Yibing, "*The Precious Volumes of Houtu* in Yi and Laishui Counties of Hebei Province," *Yinyue Yishu* [*The Arts of Music*] 2 (2000): 31-37.

telling, primarily in terms of the formula of performance and the system of combining pictures with talking and singing.[1]

The formatting of precious volumes has taken shape in accordance with the requirement of performance and by drawing on given traditional elements.[2] Firstly, the units of *pin* and *fen* are actually the performance episodes or the music episodes. Each chapter has a standardized format, and manifests itself as a sequential aggregate of multiple paragraphs. All separate chapters adopt the same format. In terms of contents, chapters are divided on the basis of themes or large narrative paragraphs, which is meant to meet the need of paragraph-based performance.

Secondly, precious volumes are composed of some fixed paragraphs or sections that have certain names, coming from the Buddhist scriptures. The beginning part of the book usually is *juxiangzhan*, a tune name, six verses, and a hymn to the gods, rehearsed by all members. The subsequent part is *kaijingji*, containing songs for the ritual of praying to gods; *foutou*, the first line of the verse, meaning chorus. The subsequent part is structured on twenty-four paragraphs each of which is similar in form. There are five elements in each paragraph.

In the 1990s, Chinese music scholars carried out fieldwork concerning the music associations in rural Hebei areas. They have provided the ethnography of folk music, which is closely related to the performances of precious volumes. The village music associations in today's Hebei province still preserve and perform instrumental music for ritual purposes at the calendrical ceremonies. The precious volumes are the texts collectively performed by the musicians.

"Precious Volumes about Emperor Houtu, the Earth Deity Who Shows Grati-

---

[1]   Huang Yupian, *Po Xie Xiang Bian* [*A Detailed Refutation of Heresies*], reprinted in *Historical Document of Qing Dynasty*, vol. 3, edited by the Institute of History, Chinese Academy of Social Sciences, Beijing: Zhonghua Book Company, 1982: 4.

[2]   Daniel L. Overmyer, *Folk Buddhist Religion: Dissenting Sects in Late Traditional China*, Cambridge, Mass./London: Harvard University Press, 1976. Chinese edition: Shanghai: Shanghai Guji Press, 1993: 292-293.

tude to Heaven and Follows Law," preserved and transmitted by the Houtu temple on the hills behind Matou village, Yi county, embodies the themes of Taoist sectarian doctrines, related to the experience of the village girl Zhang Shengxiang, who underwent painstaking religious practice, saved Emperor Guangwu from disasters and sent children to human beings.

"Precious Volumes about Emperor Houtu", preserved by music associations of south Gaoluo village is a handwritten text of the Republic Period. Still another version of precious volumes about the Houtu deity entitled *Houshan Precious Volumes* (Precious Volumes of Houshan Mountain) incorporates the oral tradition of the folktales about Zhang Shengxiang, and belongs to the category of folk tale precious volumes.

These precious volumes concerning the goddess Houtu preserved by the temple and music associations in Hebei belong to the texts of folk religions. In terms of style, these texts belong to the narrative texts as defined by Sawada Mizuho.[1] In general, the typological features of the Houtu precious volumes have undergone a long period of historical evolution, ranging from earlier precious volumes, to folk belief versions emerging in the Republic Period, and to the pure folk tale precious volumes. A comparative study of these precious volumes and oral traditions such as myths, legends, and folktales has illustrated that a variety of folklore genres has provided us with very different images of the Houtu deity.

4
Thematic Studies of Precious Volumes for Emperor Houtu

I. Precious Volumes and Stories

The narrative texts for our textual analysis here include precious volumes, stories

---

[1] Sawada Mizuho, *Zoho Hokan no Kenkyu* [*A Study of Baojuan*], revised and enlarged edition, Tokyo: Kokuso Kankokai, 1975: 40-41.

and paintings of the Houtu deity. The painting under scrutiny here has been pre-
served in the main hall of the temple of Emperor Houtu with twenty-four episodes
(i. e. twenty-four scenes). *Precious Volumes of Taoist Origin about Emperor
Houtu Who Shows Gratitude to Heaven and Follows Law*, *Releases Souls from
Purgatory* (Hanjiazhuang text) with two volumes, and twenty four *pin* (divi-
sions) is preserved by Fu Xihua and dated back to the transition of the Ming-
Qing dynasties. *Precious Volumes about the Source and Course of Goddess Houtu*,
Her Being Merciful and Efficacious is preserved and transmitted by the temple of
the goddess Houtu (Matou text), has three volumes, thirty six *pin*, and is dated
back to the Qing dynasty (text A). The second version of "*Precious Volumes
about Emperor Houtu*, " preserved by Liang Shuming (Manuscript of Liang),
contains three volumes and thirty six *pin* and is dated back to the Qing dynasty;
it is written in large characters, bound between cardboard rectangles in accordion
style and folded in the sutra form (*jing zhe zhuang*). Here it is refered to as
"text B". The fourth Matou version of the same name of precious volumes, entitled *Precious Volumes of Emperor Houtu*, is in the hands of south Gaoluo village.
It has two volumes (*juan*), is divided into twenty-four chapters and copied by
Ma Xiantu in 1943. It is shortened as Gaoluo text, or "text C".

The mural paintings of the Houtu deity story, the precious volumes of the
Hanjiazhuang text, Matou text, the manuscript of Liang Shuming and the Gaoluo
text can all be seen as narrative texts about the Houtu deity. The Houtu narratives subsume the following four categories: the story of Houtu, her experience of
self-teaching, legends of Liu Xiu's flee from the country, the story of Houtu
granting a child to Zhang Bin in Henan, and that of the Houtu deity granting a
child to Liu Yong in Shandong. Among them, the self-cultivating experience of
the Houtu deity and her granting children to human beings are widespread narrative texts. The legend of Liu Xiu's fleeing the country is a main narrative context
as manifest in the mural paintings in the Houtu temple and the Houtu precious
volumes. The legends of Liu Xiu have not been widely accepted with the diffusion of the precious volumes. This conclusion is backed up by the traditional

folktales. A comparison of the aforesaid five texts is shown in the following chart:

Text \ Theme	Houtu's self-cultivation	Liu Xiu's fleeing the country	Zhang Bin's praying for a child	LiuYong's praying for a child
Hanjiazhuang text	1	×	1	×
Matou text	4	1	11	11
Gaoluo text	5	4	12	×
Liang manuscript	9	9	9	×
Wall paintings	12	12	×	×

(Note: The figures here refer to the number of chapters dedicated to the given themes)

In the above four specific stories, the stories of Houtu's self-cultivation and of Houtu's granting a child to human beings are narrated most fully, structurally well-organized with a set of clear-cut themes, and even correspondences between formulaic phrases, names of tunes and the above-mentioned themes. All this indicates that these themes have been preserved, transmitted, and eventually standardized in the oral tradition. The narrative of the precious volumes is archetypal, standardized and formulaic, all of which can be examined in terms of themes, formulaic phraseology, narration in combined verse and prose, and performance combining talking with singing.

The common themes concerning the experience of Zhang Shengxiang's self-cultivation in different texts of precious volumes and mural paintings of the Houtu temple can be listed as follows: 1. Zhang Shengxiang leaves home and is seen off by the neighbors; 2. Zhang Shengxioang enteres the deep mountains and cultivates herself; 3. The old mother cultivates her nature; 4. The old mother engages in introspection and perceives the true nature of her being and eventually attains consumation and becomes a deity; 5. The Houtu deity designs a scheme and rescues Liu Xiu; 6. The old mother sells firewood and converts Jing Geng; 7. Jing Geng collects alms for the temple's renovation; 8. Pious believers build the Taining hall for the Houtu deity. Corresponding to the eight themes there are eight labeled melodies (tune names), each expressing essential meanings in verse, which indicates the close relations between themes and formulas. These tunes are named *Bang zhuang tai* [Beside the Dressing Table], *Chao tianzi* [An Audience with the Son of Heaven], *Jin zi jing* [Golden Characters], *Shan po yang* [Sheep on the Slope], *Lang tao sha* [Wave-shifted Sand], *Gua jin suo* [Wearing a Golden Lock], *Zhu yun fei* [Stopping the Clouds from Flying], *Zhao luo pao* [Black Gauze Robe].

Both the precious volumes about the Houtu deity (text B) and the mural paintings of granny Houshan have drawn on such oral traditions as the legends concerning Wang Mang's overthrowing Liu Xiu, which have undergone a long process of evolution. The narrative patterns of these legends can be summed up as: calamity → rescue → reward. The large number of folktales and legends differ from each other only in details, for example, the specific context where Liu Xiu meets with catastrophe, his endurance of hunger, his failure to escape his ill fate, specific rescue efforts, and the identity of the rescuer. The only way in which Liu Xiu rewarded his rescuer was to confer a title on the rescuer by imperial order.

The folk narration of Liu Xiu is illustrative of the following cyclic legends concerning Liu Xiu's fleeing the country: Liu Xiu is chased by Wang Mang → a farmer saves the emperor from danger → the mole cricket helps the emperor out of distress → Liu Xiu eats mulberry fruits to stave off hunger (survives on herbs) → climbs hills on the back of a tiger → drinks water by a slant well → Han Zhanggu rescues the emperor → Liu Xiu rewards, confers a title on his rescuer → builds a temple by imperial edict.

The legends of Liu Xiu being chased by Wang Mang are represented in the mural paintings of the granny Houshan story. In the mural paintings there are the following narrative events: 1. Wang Mang kills Ping Di of the Han dynasty and usurps supreme state power; 2. Liu Xiu flees the country to rejuvenate it; 3. Liu Xiu sleeps at Maoxiashui at night; 4. The tiger helps Liu Xiu out of distress; 5. Farmer Jia Fu rescues Liu Xiu; 6. Liu Xiu eats mulberry fruits to dispel hunger; 7. Zhang Shengxiang rescues Liu Xiu at Danxiadong; 8. Liu Xiu acknowledges Zhang Shengxiang as his mother; 9. Liu Xiu kills Wang Mang and founds the Eastern Han dynasty; 10. Liu Xiu mounts the throne, and confers a title on his adoptive mother; 11. The adoptive mother dies, Liu Xiu holds a sacrificial ceremony to the mountains; 12. The temple of Houshan has attracted numerous believers since then.

The legends about Liu Xiu, very remote in origins and widely spread, are closely related to the life of Chinese farmers in specific geographical contexts. For example, the village, the temples, and the well, all of which were typical scenes in these oral traditions and have become symbolic of local traditions in northern China. The legends about the historical figures have been drawing on the stories about Chinese villages and farmers.

These local narratives were included in the precious volumes to interpret the history of the temple of the Houtu deity, and to make a draw a forced analogy with emperor Liu Xiu. People believed that it was Liu Xiu who built the temple in the Han dynasty. All this expresses the local people's intention to attribute a kind of authority to their own beliefs. In the course of history, Yi prefecture used to be dominated by alien rulers in the Liao, Jin, and Yuan dynasties. In modern times, many great incidents happened in Yi prefecture such as fights against the eight allied foreign nations, Japanese invaders, etc. "The emperor returns to his native village" has been a story pattern in the folk narrative tradition. According to the legends, Liu Xiu acknowledged the goddess Houtu as his adoptive mother. In this way the imperial power and the power of gods merged into one single entity.[1] The folktales also tell that the Houtu deity is a great aunt of the Wang family in Xingao village of Dingxing county. This is the assumed blood lineage. Liu Xiu could be seen as a god whose divine power was transformed from imperial power. This kind of god is quite different from those natural gods or cultural

---

[1]   Dong Xiaoping and R. David Arkush, *Northern Country Opera Performance and Modern Chinese People*, Beijing: Beijing Normal University, 2000: 149-150.

heroes, which have never been subjected to change in the local tradition. This phenomenon has proven that the farmers not only need the natural spirits, religious gods and cultural heroes, but also need a supreme god whose power, transformed from imperial power, could protect the people. The two stories – Houtu rescues the emperor and Liu Xiu confers a title on the goddess Houtu by imperial order – point to this combined need by the local people: the worship of divine power and the worship of imperial power.

II. General Themes in Precious Volumes

According to folklore studies, the concept of theme refers to the unit of contents, which recur in different texts, for example the same events, scenes and passages. In this study I define "theme" as the essential ideas which have deep roots in the tradition, repetitively used by different texts of the precious volumes. The common themes in precious volumes include: autobiographical statements attributed to the patriarch that transmits the texts; the individual understanding of these books as divine revelation; references to the names of the sects and congregations; creation myths, salvation, reincarnation; meditation; rituals; ethical teachings; descriptions of purgatory; and social perspectives. [1] Closely related to religious belief are ritual practices that facilitate acceptance by ordinary people, memorials and passports to Heaven, exercising names of Buddhas and deities and relevant scriptures, meditation, and fasting, all of which emerged long ago but were actualized and practiced by people in a specific context. The thematic scope of the precious volumes lies in the middle ground between popular religious belief and orthodox Buddhism, in a given context of their own. [2]

It is also important to note what these precious volumes do not emphasize. There is nothing about divination or *Fengshui*, animal sacrifices except for pilgrimages on a yearly basis (excluding pilgrimages to Mount Tai), nothing about

---

[1] Daniel L. Overmyer, *Precious Volumes*: *An Introduction to Chinese Sectarian Scriptures from the Sixteenth and Seventeenth Centuries*, Cambridge, Mass.: Harvard University Press, 1999: 6.

[2] Ibid. 281.

shamanist healing practice, and little about ancestral worship (except the theme of filial duty).

Ⅲ. Some Essential Ideas Expressed by Houtu Precious Volumes

Precious Volumes about the Houtu Deity begins with the theme of Zhang Shengxiang's cutting off the family ties in her quest for masters and companions to cultivate her physical and mental capabilities according to Buddhist rules. At the age of three, she lost her father and mother; her three brothers had left home and set out to practice asceticism.

The next theme is the blocking of the way by the sea of misery from the world of bliss. According to Buddhism, the human world is the sea of misery. The merciful Buddha could deliver the lay people out of it with the Dharma boat (ferry boat). [1] In the precious volumes, there is a scene in which the Yuhuangdadi dispatches the golden star to act as a fisherman, helping Zhang Shengxiang across the sea. The scene can be seen as a religious symbol.

The theme that Houtu Laomu practices asceticism inside a cave draws on the Taoist symbols of fairyland (dwelling place of immortals). [2]

The theme of the white monkey presenting peaches stems from Taoist tradition. In the local area of Yi prefecture, a legend goes thus: Wang Tuan, the old ancestor in the Yunmeng Mountains, was in possession of a white monkey that guarded a peach garden at Matou village, at the foot of the Qianfeng Mountains, and presented peaches to the Houtu deity on time.

The theme of introspection and perception of the true nature of one's being.

The theme of transcending the worldly and becoming immortal. Taoism encourages people to obtain ascetical perfectionism. Folk sectarian religion emphasizes the idea of the lay orientation of eschatology. The sectarian master can save

---

[1]　Yu Songqing, *Mimi Zongjiao Jingjuan Yanjiu* [*A Study of the Scriptures of Secret Folk Religions*], Tai bei: Taiwan Lianjing Press Company, 1994: 326.

[2]　Gan Chunsong, *Shen Xian Zhuan* [*Biography of the Immortals*], Beijing: Publishing House of the Chinese Academy of Social Sciences, 1998: 129.

mankind from the sea of misery; people can go to Heaven after death, avoid the misery of the eternal cycle of birth and death, and never descend to the earthly world again.

The theme of enlightening the astray, the wise and the stupid: the Hunyuan patriarch devotes a first-person narrative about his quest for enlightenment and his first missionary work to this theme. The narratives around this theme are composed of several elements such as disguise, a deceptive story often employed by precious volumes. When the deity enters the earthly world, it must get rid of its image, and thus become an everyday woman. The patriarch tells the deceptive story in the first person, thus these seemingly autobiographical narratives are actually hagiographic in tone, with mythological elements.

The theme of sending a child to human beings, in which the deity incarnates as a poor woman, tells of deceptive stories about her life, and sends a child to a human being to display her prowess.

The theme of patriarchs transmitting the texts.

The theme of begging for alms, which was closely related to folk customs. In northern Chinese villages, during the Ming and Qing dynasties, villagers often raised and collected gold and silver for charity's sake, such as setting up temples, printing scriptures, carrying out congregations, carving stone tablets, buying religious paintings, and so on.

Other themes such as child education, imperial civil examination, official promotion, loyalty to emperors, all pointing to folk Confucianism that combines the principles of "the two saints" (Confucius and Mencius), value the highest goal of sectarian teaching and emphasize the utmost importance of relationships in families, villages, and prefectures.

IV. Some Typical Passages in Precious Volumes of the Houtu Deity

The thematics of the precious volumes reveal that form and content are unified and form two sides of the same coin. The precious volumes often employ traditional, regularly used methods to express some themes, and thus the so-called typical passages actually convey particular themes by means of particular styles. When it comes to representations of contents related to space and time, the precious volumes often take on a chronological order. Some catalogue verses feature particularly in long passages in the form of *dafo*,[①] depicting typical scenes, e. g. gatherings of gods, grand ceremonies, artefacts in particular geographical contexts. Things suitable for genealogical accounts are mostly exemplified, expanded, and broadened in a highly rhythmic and striking way. The most typical passages contain a variety of catalogues, such as the catalogue of place names, assemblies, deities, scriptures, purgatory, as well as the hymns to the gods and the songs for ten rewards (*shi bao ge*).

Examples in the precious volumes include style (alternative prose and verse), structure, typical scenes, and thematic significance, all of which are discernable in tradition. Thus, the making of volumes puts in order the ready-made, prefabricated components according to a fixed structure and format. The verse lines of the volumes are reminiscent of Buddhist sutras, abounding in clichés, expressed in standard form. In general, the themes of precious volumes are traditional both in form and in content.

The precious volumes have taken on both semantic and structural characteristics of religious sutras, assimilated the artistic means of classical Chinese poetry, and been strongly influenced by the local, oral tradition in the light of their narrative patterns. On the textual level, the precious volumes and local narrative texts form an interactive, intertextual, and dynamic relationship in which they borrow from each other through a constant process asking for insights into the specificity of cultural contexts. Local knowledge constitutes the context of the precious volumes, as confirmed by our fieldwork.

---

①   *Dafo* is a sub-genre of the precious volumes, mainly used for the narration of the main plot or events in the precious volumes. *Dafo* is generally written ten-syllable lines.

5

Myth as Examples of Narratives Concerning the Efficacious Houtu Deity

Diachronically speaking, the belief in the Houtu deity has inherited historical legacies. Oral narrative texts concerning the efficacious Houtu deity have been continuously created, even in contemporary contexts. This proves the stability and the inheritance of the cult of the Houtu deity. The populace always resorts to traditional formulaic modes of expressions to represent their convictions.

I . The Image of the Houtu Deity in Oral Tradition

Earth worship has been institutionalized, abstracted, and ritualized. By contrast, the contents of nature or ancestor worshipping have never changed in oral tradition. In the course of history, Houtu has adopted different images, such as the deity of earth, a cultural hero, a woman farmer, and a village girl who pursues love. Villagers address the deity by different names, from old grandmother to village girl of the Han dynasty, from firewood seller to a girl named Shengxiang, from a spinning and weaving old lady to the inventor of some manual skills who engages in some kind of laboring. The legends about the Houshan grandmother briefly depict her family background, experience of self-cultivation, work, her experience of saving Liu Xiu from disaster, and the populace's memorials after her departure from this world.

It is a common practice to attribute major achievements of a society, even if these achievements have been realized only through a long period of social evolution, to the episodic individual accomplishment of a cultural hero as dipicted in an earlier era of the given society. The legends about granny Houtu, for example, tend to reconstruct this figure as the originator of the sum total of customs that have been evolving through the ages. She is portrayed as a food maker, even the initiator of such natural phenomena as the natural attributes of plants.

The image of granny Houtu in local legends has inherited the core tradition that foregrounds Houtu as the great deity of earth. In the precious volumes, Houtu reveals some characteristics of an earth deity. For example, the goddess scared away demons, subdued the dragon and tamed the tiger. She has been regarded as the creator of many tools. The Houtu deity's prowess reflects Taoist influences. She could incarnate as a poor lady, begging for alms down the street, exempted the emperor from danger, and brought the stone monkey back to life after hundreds of years.

The secularization of the Houtu deity is visible in the legends about this figure. She may be depicted as a virtuous wife, a woman practitioner of folk religion or an incense-creating girl in addition to the images mentioned earlier. In the mural paintings of the Houtu temple, there is a love story about Zhang Shengxiang and the herd boy Shiniu. For example, the legends about Shiniu and his weaving machines, Zhang Shengxiang's planting of poplar trees, the origin of the Qianfu mountains are all related to love stories. [1]

II. The Efficacious Houtu Deity and Relevant Narratives

The narratives about the efficacious Houtu deity have been closely related to rituals in memory of the deity. Most of these narratives are based on historical events and exhibit the storytellers' positive or negative attitudes towards these events. The narrative events are closely associated with everyday life in the local area. Meanwhile, they convey traditional social values. The narratives are modeled on traditional myths, and express local and popular ideologies. These narratives carry cross-references to events that actually happened. By way of divine intervention, they play a part in preserving the social order. They share the precious volumes' thematics. However, these narratives also include some kinds of superstition, witchcraft, fortunetelling or *fengshui*. They are tinted with myths and rituals. All this differentiates the Houtu narratives from commonplace legends.

---

[1]　Gong Li, *Houshan Shenhua* [*Houshan Myths*], Beijing: Chinese Folk Literature and Arts Press, 1998.

The labeling of tales about the efficacious deity is a local product, but these tales do not appear to be fictional. They are marked by authenticity, presence, and cult, and should thus be considered serious. These narratives work to carve out a cultural space to accommodate the populace's beliefs and behavior. The tales of the efficacious Houtu deity are a local terminology, which indicates insiders' opinions about the category of the genre. The essential idea of the tales is to tell the story about the Houtu deity. In general, the narratives about the Houtu deity and the cult mirror each other.

Myth and legend are closely related to folk religions. The most important issues of the sacrificial offerings concern the praying for rain and praying for children. These are primitive religious beliefs to propel human reproduction. To some extent, Confucianism finds its roots in the worship of procreation. Chinese culture originated in consanguinity on the basis of which the national psychology has been developed. The traditional regulations of rituals pay special attention to human reproduction; to have many sons is to have many blessings.

The folk narratives often tell of gods who interfere with the social order and human relations. These folk narratives work to regulate human behavior, and are closely related to local knowledge. The idea of retribution for sin is based on traditional social and moral institutions. The gods will punish whoever violates the institutions.

The sins listed in the precious volumes include: vilifying the scripture, destroying the temple and divine statues and breaking a religious precept. Those who have sinned are depicted in the volume of ten kings in purgatory. They are accused of being jealous of capable and virtuous people, slandering, offending elders' pride, running amok in the country and setting fire to the mountains. The precious volumes call on people to avoid the destruction of people's lives, stealing, blaspheming the gods and offending the intention of the gods.

The function of the Houtu deity was supposed to protect the land, territory, nation and state. She could allegedly drive away the invaders of alien forces, and help heroes fight against the enemy.

The deity could fight against the barbarians in ancient times; in modern times, she can force the invaders of alien forces to retreat so as to safeguard and promote the friendship of ethnic minorities and maintain the unity of the country. Therefore, the legends of the Houtu deity, as well as its mercifulness and efficacious effects, are actually legends about human beings. Furthermore, the aforesaid legends present persepectives and typical legendary scenes about how the Houtu deity fights against Korea and Daweiguo and safeguards the local area around Hongya Mountain. These legends tell us that Houtu is a deity of earth, a deity of the national territory. These modern interpretations of the politicized role of the Houtu deity come as a logical outcome of the deity's alleged connection with imperial power in legends.

6
Conclusion

Different folklore genres, e. g. the precious volumes, the narrative about the Houtu deity and her efficacious effects, legends about Liu Xiu, Emperor Guangwu of the Han dynasty and the local myths and legends, are all based on the common ground of historical origins and shared essential ideas. The intertextuality of these folklore genres manifests itself as follows: They belong to local folk traditions, express the essential idea of the Houtu worship, and take the myth as their archetype.

The tradition of the precious volumes and folk narratives has originated and been propelled by the cult of Houtu in local areas. Throughout the long historical development of the Houtu worship, the deity used to be highly regarded at imperial ceremonies of the Han dynasty. Since the Yuan dynasty, the cult of Houtu has been gradually localized, and the deity has become a village girl and later on a goddess attracting many pilgrims. She eventually features as a main goddess in the shrine of folk society, because merits and virtues have been attributed to her.

The Houtu deity has been occupying the center of the shrine of folk society. The goddess in the precious volumes and legends is the incarnation of a Taoist nun. The goddess manifests herself as a poor village woman, and through this medium the goddess solves problems for the local people. The cult of the Houtu deity has attracted people from a large area, and the shrine has become an important ritual site where the Houtu deity's story is sung.

As for the actual performance of the precious volumes, the central belief is that singing the invocation summons the Houtu as a goddess, whose power is then actualized to protect the community. What grants Houtu ultimate power is the actual fact of her death: The death event operates as a generative point for stories in local traditions. It leads to deification, to worship, to a cult, and eventually to a narrative that is ritually performed to invoke the spirits of the dead.

References:

Arkush, R. David. *Zhongguo Minzhong Sixiang Shi* [*North Chinese Folk Materials and Popular Mentality*]. Translated by Dong Xiaoping, Beijing: Central University for Nationalities Press, 1995.

Cao Fulin. *Xianqin Minsu Shi* [*History of Folklore in the Pre-Qin Era*]. Shanghai: Shanghai People's Press, 2001.

Dong Xiaoping and R. David Arkush. *Northern Country Opera Performance and Modern Chinese People*. Beijing: Beijing Normal University, 2000.

Gan Chunsong. *Shenxian Zhuan* [*Biography of the Immortals*]. Beijing: Publishing House of the Chinese Academy of Social Sciences, 1998.

Gong Li. *Houshan Shenhua* [*Houshan Myths*]. Beijing: Chinese Folk Literature and Arts Press. 1998.

Jones, Stephen. *Folk Music of China*: *Living Instrumental Traditions*, Oxford: Clarendon Press, 1995.

Mizuho, Sawada. *Kochu haja shoben* [*A Detailed Refutation of Heresies*, *with Correction and Commentary*]. Tokyo: Dokyo kanko kai, 1972.

Nagy, Gregory. *Greek Mythology and Poetics*. Ithaca/London: Cornell University Press,

1990.

Overmyer, Daniel L. *Zhongguo Minjian Zongjiao Jiaopai Yanjiu*. Translated by Zhou Yu-min. Shanghai: Shanghai Guji Press, 1993.

Originally published as: *Folk Buddhist Religion: Dissenting Sects in Late Traditional China*. Cambridge, Mass.: Harvard University Press, 1976.

——*Precious volumes: An Introduction to Chinese sectarian scriptures from the Sixteenth and Seventeenth Centuries*. Cambridge, Mass.: Harvard University Press, 1999.

Pu Wenqi and Song Jun, eds. *Baojuan Chuji* [*Precious Volumes, First Collection*]. 43 Vols. Taiyuan: Shanxi People's Publishing House, 1994. Vol.11.

Qiao Jianzhong, Xue Yibing, Stephen Jones and Zhang Zhentao, "General Investigation Report on the Folk Music Society in Jizhong Plain, Beijing, Tianjin." *Zhongguo Yinyue Nianjian* [*Year Book of Chinese Music*] Edited by Tian Qing. Jinan: Shandong Friendship Publishing House, 1985: 293.

Shou Pengfei, editor in chief. *Yixian Zhigao* [*Annals of Yi County*]. Reprint. Beijing: Xueyuan Publishing House, 1990.

Xue Yibing. "*The Precious Volumes of Houtu* in Yi and Laishui Counties of Hebei Province." *The Arts of Music* 2 (2000): 31-37.

Xue Yibing. "The Types and Humane background of the Folk Music of Wind and Percussion Instruments." *Studies on the Folk Music of Drums and Wind Instruments: A Collection of the Research Papers from the First Symposium on Chinese Folk Music of Drums and Wind Intruments*. Edited by Qiao Jianzhong and Xue Yibing. Jinan: Shandong Friendship Publishing House, 1999: 57.

Xue Yinbing and Tsao Pen-ye. "The Cult of Houtu and the Folk Music Associations in Yi and Laishui Counties." *Musicology in China* 1 (2000): 31-37.

Yu Songqing. *Minjian Mimi zongjiao Jingjuan Yanjiu* [*A Study of the Scriptures of Secret Folk Religions*], Taibei: Taiwan Lianjing Press Company. 1994.

中国少数民族文化中的

史诗与英雄

主　编

［荷］米尼克·希珀　尹虎彬

广西师范大学出版社

目 录

序

在此,谨向在本书撰稿和编辑过程中参加工作并付出努力的诸位同仁致以谢意,感谢诸位使该合作项目得以完成。关于本书的缘起,我不禁要回溯 1999—2000 年度,那一年适逢杨恩洪教授来到荷兰,在国际亚洲研究所莱顿基地做访问学者。那时,她介绍我初识了时任中国社会科学院文学研究所所长的杨义教授。早在访问莱顿大学期间,杨义教授便提出双方开展合作研究的意向。关于在中国社会科学院和荷兰学者之间,就跨文化比较文学研究领域的合作研究意向,杨义表示鼎力支持。可以说,我随后应邀访问中国社会科学院,是该合作意向的延续。作为这一跨文化研究项目的撰稿人和参与者,我们大家对杨义都怀有感激之情。

这一以"史诗与英雄"冠名的合作项目的首倡者是杨恩洪教授,我们对她深表谢意。1999 年杨恩洪教授在莱顿的国际亚洲研究所做访问学者,该项目正是由她提出的。杨教授当时正在莱顿与人合作筹备并组织国际藏学家会议,我们来往密切,她邀请我参加那次大会的一个专题研讨,题目是"跨文化的文学研究与口头文学"。很显然,绝大多数的藏学专家还不能适应从跨文化的角度开展研究,还不能在更广泛的比较背景下,去反映他们所研究的具体文学的相似性和差异性。他们对此有所领悟,请我将这方面的研究继续下去。他们这样做是因为,跨文化研究不仅可以给藏族文学提供新的视野,而且可以丰富我们的比较文学研究。藏族史诗研究将会给世界史诗的比较研究增添一道亮色,反之亦然。这种互惠互利的关系同样适用于研究其他样式的口头文学,如创世神话、谚语、动物故事等。

多年来,中国社会科学院民族文学研究所在搜集和整理少数民族口头文学资料方面付出了极大的努力。但是,研究人员较少将其相关的研究成果与熟悉其他文化的国内专家开展交流,较少把自己的研究与世界其他地方正在进行或业已付梓的成果进行比较。我们这一新的研究项目,其目的首先在于,我们要为中国少数民族文学的跨文化研究提供新的尝试;其次,要把他们的研究成果介绍给国际比较文学的学界同行。杨恩洪教授对于此举给双方所带来的重要收获是深有领悟的。

杨恩洪教授访学莱顿期间,我们经常沟通思想,切磋学术,引以为乐。在此期间,她问我是否愿意到北京,在中国社会科学院民族文学研究所作讲演,为进一步对中国丰富多样的口头文学和文化的比较研究作准备。起初我很犹豫,因为我并非汉学家。然而,杨恩洪教授丝毫没有动摇初衷。她指出,我对口头传统现象,对口头传统与相关的迻译或书写文本之间的联系,以及两者的相互联系和辩证关系,发表了许多重要见解。这些见解得益于我的理论修养,得益于我在跨文化的文学研究领域的训练和实践,得益于我多年来在非洲口头传统与书面文学方面所作的专门研究。鉴于此,中国社会科学院民族文学研究所向我发出邀请,希望我与中国同行共享这份"局外人"的知识。希望我加盟新的合作项目,并以此作为该研究所进一步关注跨文化研究的启动项目的一部分,而这一领域也是我过去数年来所一直从事的工作。

民族文学研究所建议,在该合作项目里,我的任务包括2001年9月为有关跨文化视野下口头文学领域的研究提供信息,为下一年度扩大的学术研讨的计划和筹备提供指导。我应邀参加了2002年10月北京举办的"中国少数民族文化中的史诗与英雄"的学术研讨会议,担任会议论文的评议人。

自本项目启动伊始,中国社会科学院及其民族文学研究所和荷兰皇家科学院及其中国委员会两方一直给予全力支持,对此,我们由衷地表示感谢。我的中国之行,以及我的中国同行杨恩洪和尹虎彬以访问学者身份来访荷兰,都要归功于中荷双方的研究机构所提供的道义支持和经济资助。对此,我要表示深深的谢意。如果没有双方研究机构既已达成的有关协议,这一富有成果的合作几乎不可能实现。

感谢荷兰皇家科学院为书稿翻译和编辑慷慨提供的专项资助。这使我们有可能聘请两位关键性的人物,她们为此殚精竭虑。我们在这里有必要隆重地推出这两位的名字:首先是刚在莱顿完成了博士学位论文的张晓红,她在英文论文的语言润色和书稿的编辑方面显示出非凡的才能;其次是泰拉·吉尔森(Thera Giezen),她对书稿的编排竭尽全力,认真核对脚注和参考文献,纠正其中涉及作者、书名、出版地和出版日期等方面的讹误,她聪慧伶俐,作用至关重要。两位女士,特别感谢你们,感谢你们出色的工作、你们付出的心血,感谢你们克服了时间紧、任务重的压力,身心疲惫还保持乐观精神。感谢毕桪教授,他孜孜不倦,为我们提供了十分珍贵的哈萨克文转写的材料。在此,特别感谢周翔和宋颖两位女士,她们为中文版论文集的编辑作出了不懈努力。

朝戈金博士曾经共同参与组织了2002年在北京举办的第二届学术研讨会议,那时我们还讨论过本书的筹划问题。很遗憾,由于他要务缠身,没有能够与我合编本书。他委派尹虎彬博士代劳,于 2004 年春前来荷兰。我们的合作富有成效,与他合作也令人愉快,尽管书稿英译,其表达殊难信达,不得不解决大量的问题。这本论文集,中文部分的编辑工作由尹虎彬博士负责,英文部分的编辑工作由我负责。我们两人谨再次感谢本书的各位撰稿人,尽管由于地域上的距离,语言迻译带来的诸多麻烦,各种始料未及而又迫在眉睫的俗务的搅扰,以及其他许多压力,作者们为自己的论文付出了艰辛的劳动。我们希望借助大家共同努力,那些来自中国灿烂文化、来自不同语言的妙不可言的史诗,那些史诗歌手和讲述者连同他们的雄辩才能,将日益受到世人关注,必将为比较视野下的世界史诗研究增添一道新的风景。

米尼克·希珀于莱顿

2004 年 5 月 7 日

撰稿人简介

米尼克·希珀(Mineke Schipper),荷兰莱顿大学(The University of Leiden)跨文化文学研究(Intercultural Literary Studies)教授,著述甚丰,主要有:《大脚女人不能娶:世界各地谚语中的妇女》(*Never Marry a Woman with Big Feet Women in Proverbs from Around the World* , 2004)、《想像的局内者》(*Imagining Insiders*)、《非洲与归属问题》(*Africa & the Question of Belonging* , 1999)、《未曾听见的词语》(*Unheard Words*)、《女性与非洲、阿拉伯、亚洲、加勒比、拉美文学》(*Women and Literature in Africa* , *The Arab World* , *Asia* , *The Caribbean* , *and Latin America* ,1985)、《现实主义:文学中现实的幻想》(*Realism. The Illusion of Reality in Literature* ,1979)。她还发表过两部小说。

杨恩洪,中国社会科学院民族文学研究所研究员,藏族文学研究室主任。主要从事藏族史诗研究,长期深入西藏、四川、青海等边疆地区调查《格萨尔王传》史诗艺人及其演唱,并在该领域发表过许多论文。主要著作有:《中国少数民族史诗〈格萨尔王传〉》(1990)、《民间诗神——〈格萨尔王传〉艺人研究》(1995)。

李连荣(华瑞·宗哲迦措),藏族,文学博士,助理研究员。现在中国社会科学院民族文学研究所藏族文学研究室工作,目前主要从事《格萨尔王传》史诗的文本和表演研究。主要论文有:《〈格萨尔王传〉研究的理论建构》(2003)、《中国早期的史诗学》(2001)、《历史与西藏的〈格萨尔王传〉史诗》(2001)。

扎拉嘎,蒙古族,中国社会科学院民族文学研究所研究员。主要从事蒙古文学研究、蒙汉文学关系研究以及中国各民族文学关系研究。著有《比较文学:文学平行本质的比较研究——清代蒙汉文学关系论稿》(2002)、《尹湛纳希评传》(1994)、《尹湛纳希年谱》(1991)、《〈一层楼〉、〈泣红亭〉与〈红楼梦〉》(1984)。

斯钦巴图,蒙古族,文学博士,中国社会科学院民族文学研究所副研究员。专业领域为蒙古文学与宗教。主要成果有:专著《〈江格尔〉与蒙古族宗教文化》(1999),论文《蒙古神话研究三题》(1992)、《阿尔泰语民族树木崇拜概略》(1990)、《蒙古佛教神话功能问题研究》(1989)、《江格尔汗宫与萨满教》(1999)等。

阿地里·居玛吐尔地,柯尔克孜族,文学博士,副研究员。现在新疆维吾尔自治区文联民间文艺家协会工作,长期从事《玛纳斯》史诗和柯尔克孜族民间文学研究。主要著作有:《柯尔克孜族民俗志》(2004)、《〈玛纳斯〉演唱大师居素普·玛玛依评传》(2002);论文有:《〈玛纳斯〉的萨满面孔》(2004)、《神话史诗〈艾尔托西吐克〉比较研究》(2003)、《16世纪波斯文史集及其与〈玛纳斯〉史诗的关系》(2002)、《居素普·玛玛依演唱本〈玛纳斯〉的艺术特色》(2000)等。

郎樱,中国社会科学院民族文学研究所研究员。长期从事维吾尔族以及突厥语民族文学研究,在中国北方民族史诗尤其是柯尔克孜族史诗《玛纳斯》研究领域做过大量工作。主要著作有:《〈玛纳斯〉论》(1999)、《〈福乐智慧〉与东西方文化》(1992)、《〈玛纳斯〉史诗论析》(1991)、《中国少数民族史诗〈玛纳斯〉》(1990)。

黄中祥,中国社会科学院民族文学研究所副研究员,文学博士。主要研究领域为新疆突厥语民族的民间文学。自1980年代起就突厥语民族的语言和文化深入新疆、青海、甘肃、河南等地区做田野调查,获得大量资料。主要论文有《哈萨克族史诗中的萨满教观念》(2002)、《哈萨克族谚语特点与狩猎文化》(1999)、《哈萨克族谚语与饮食文化》(1997)。

刘亚虎,中国社会科学院民族文学研究所研究员。主要从事中国南方史诗和各民族文学关系史研究。主要著作有《南方史诗论》(1999)、《中华民族文学关系史·南方卷》(1997)、《广西山水传说探美集》(1994)。

尹虎彬,朝鲜族,中国社会科学院民族文学研究所研究员,主要从事口头诗学、口头传统与民间宗教研究。最近的成果有:专著《古代经典与口头传统》(2002),论文《荷马与我们时代的故事歌手》(2003)、《20世纪史诗学述评》(2002)、《口头诗学与民族志》(2002)。

史诗及其英雄

——口头文学的跨文化研究

[荷兰]米尼克·希珀　著

叶舒宪　译

摘　要　理论的框架、概念、工具，文学的分析、描述，这些都与比较密不可分。比较文学可以划分为两类：其一是具有历史相关性的传统(有接触关系，单向的或相互的影响)；其二是没有历史相关性的传统(只有类型学的关系)。在后一种情形中，人们可以认识文化现象的相对独立特性和普遍性，例如像创世神话、史诗、悲剧和小说这样的文本类型。跨文化研究是涉及一种文化以上的诸多要素的研究。史诗跨文化研究中一些最为常见的事宜和问题有：与文本相关联的形式和主题的要素，文本中涉及的与文化语境相关的一些特征。

关键词　比较文学，跨文化研究，体裁样式分类，史诗样式

一、理解对方的文化

我们可以假定(虽然不能确证)全世界所有的文化都具有诗歌和讲故事这样的文学形式。更确切地说，所有不同文化的人们都使用起源神话(origin myths)来寻求对周围的隐秘和神秘的解释，那是我们在全球范围里均可以看到的一种文类。神话处于变化中，它们能够激起争论、对抗和和解。它们产生新的神话或神话变体，也使老的神话复活。在争论中，发展出有利于神话的或反对神话的各种观点。争论还可以催生出与原初形式相反的神话叙事来。

这种情况也发生在史诗中。人们为了生存而创制出有益策略，在特定的境遇中支配自己的传统以便达成最佳的生活状态。文化规范确实通过口头传统而传播下来，不过也会随着历史而发生变化。这些文化规范从不同的方面反映出来，有时

也遭到质疑和挑战。文化规范和法则并不是在僵硬的过去永远固定的东西。但是,在文学的遗产中得到表现的那种过去是需要反复地加以学习的。

从文化上讲,如果我们想知道在世界范围内我们作为人类是怎样的一个物种,那就需要知道我们的男女先祖是谁。我们还要知道先祖们所讲述的故事和所吟唱的歌,以便从我们共同的遗产中选择出我们准备传给下一代的口头与书面文学,选择出我们质疑的或者干脆抛弃和遗忘的东西。作为来自不同文化的人群,我们正是从过去流传下来的口头的与书面的故事中了解到,我们作为男人和女人是从哪里来的。人们通过挑选、誊录或传递他们所喜爱的故事,来选定他们自己的先祖。于是,人们不只是讲故事者和作者,也是听众和读者,是文化批评者和学者。

在何种程度上那些故事可以标示出人类的相似性和文化的差异性呢? 为了回答这个问题,我们必须用比较的方法研究文学。跨文化的比较涉及大量的不同的文化和语言。我们如何能够理解来源于所有不同种类的"外国"文化中的文本呢? 我在世界不同地方的研究和教学过程中,就经常惊奇地看到观众能够轻而易举地理解来自另一个文化、国家和大陆的口头文本,甚至不亚于理解本文化的文本。比如在中国,当我引述非洲或欧洲的谚语和创世神话时,听者毫无困难地就理会了,尽管有巨大的背景差异,反之亦然。

个人和社会持有关于生活和事件的理想观念,即关于人应该如何行动和理想的事物应该是怎样的观念。这样的理想通过语言来表现,文学教会人们这些理想如何能实现。文本——不论是口头的还是书写的,也表现出偏离这些理想的情形,比如一些有问题的和那些常常该受谴责的理想。有三个相关的领域就这样联结起来:社会规范与价值,语言,人们的心灵。人们的普遍理想观念作为某种具体的理想在某一具体的文本中,通过具体的语词和句法得到表现。其普遍性来源于人们在生理的、心理的和文化的层面上的同一性。一种理想观念在其文化语境中变成特殊的,因为它代表着得到普遍理想观念的一种特殊的和地方的形式。这一普遍观念潜藏在所考察文本之中并为该文本提供推动力量。理想观念要利用对照和比较。大部分的口头文本可以划分为两类信息:确认理想的(ideal-confirming)和不确认理想的(ideal-disconfirming)。前者表现理想是什么,或者如何获得理想;后者只是通过描绘对理想观念的某种背离而间接地表达理想。理想观念及其对立面常常表现在同一个文本之中。例如在史诗中,不同的形象代表着理想及其对立面。当讲述者告诉人们什么是不应该去想和做的事,或者什么是不应该期望的东西时,理想就变得更加明确了。在口头传统中,从叙述者的观点中出现的那些被指认为"不要做"的事,必然会导致一种可受责备的情况。叙述者要把这样的信息传达给他的听众。

虽然实际情况比我在这里所说的要复杂得多,但是在口头文学中与普遍的超文化的理想相联系的信息还是为跨文化地理解口头文本提供了基础。人们怀抱的理想可以是人们集体记忆的一部分,尽管在许多时候人们不再明确地意识到这些理想。

接下来的问题是,那些理想是从哪里来的呢? 它们是否像文化论的观点所认为的那样,是通过社会化的过程而学来的呢? 当然,确实存在着这种学习,不过文化论的观点忽略了生物的因素和个体对物质世界的体验。

日常知识是在社会文化背景之中发展而来的,社会现实表现在人们的语言文化之中。另一方面,人们天生就有人类的认知能力。这两个方面的因素,认知的和文化的,就成为理想发生的源头。主要理想则看起来更加具有普遍性,而不是局限于哪一种文化。

比较研究具有相当的复杂性,而跨文化的比较也是一个争议颇多的话题。我所生活于其中的西方世界的大多数论述比较文学的书,都是只局限于西方文学与文化传统。

理论的框架、概念和工具,对文学的分析、描述,这些都与比较密不可分。如果这些理论是来自某一特殊的文化背景,那么应用于别处时,就需要仔细地检验和权衡(或者干脆放弃它)。

比较研究可以划分为两类:其一是具有历史相关性的传统(有接触关系,单向的或相互的影响),其二没有历史相关性的传统(只有类型学的关系)。在后一种情形中,人们可以认识文化现象的相对独特性和普遍性,例如像创世神话、史诗、悲剧和小说这样的文本类型。

跨文化比较的用途和可能性(不可能性)是什么? 随之而来的还有其他一些问题。我们是不是具有太多的偏见,乃至不能理解他者文化呢? 有没有一种普遍的模型呢? 或者这些东西只是我们自己的视野和假说的产物? 寻求文学创作的普遍法则是可能的吗?[①] 一般而言,有两种极端的态度:或者作为一种原则,拒绝任何一种形式的比较;或者是天真的比较者,根本看不到任何问题。介于这两种极端态度

---

① 我在其他场合曾就其中的问题发表过见解。参见 Mineke Schipper, *Beyond the Boundaries*: *African Literature and Literary Theory*. London: Allison and Busby, 1989.

之间的是这样一种人,他们了解到比较的方法是必要的和有效的,他们也从研究中体会到这一点。进行跨文化比较的方法最好是与个别文化内部的专家或者研究个别文化的专家进行合作,而且不论何时,只要有可能,就应该与属于该文化成员的学者进行合作。

跨文化研究是涉及一种以上的文化因素的研究。这包括,用一种文化的概念和方法来研究另一种文化。这立刻产生如下问题:他者文化是从哪里开始的? 文化的界限是随着研究者的视野而发生变化的。文化的内部成员和局外人之间的文化界限的判定是非常主观的,在我们今天的全球化时代,它们要比以往更加成问题。在每一种情形中,研究者都有必要仔细权衡他所要遵循的文化标准。跨文化研究是研究者不得不重新考虑他们自己所习惯的处理事物的方式,同时还要不断地提出问题,即对其自身视野和知识的可能的文化限制发出疑问。权威科学在主体和客体之间、在描述者和被描述者之间所建立的那种有害的等级关系正在受到挑战,因为一种强烈的跨学科的研究正在兴起。这种等级关系虽然成问题,却发生在人类科学的所有学科之中,从历史学到人类学,从社会学到文学理论和比较文学。目前还没有现成的解决办法。

二、史诗传统的比较观:若干纲领

本研究项目的目的在于研讨中国少数民族文化中作为既定文类的史诗。本书所面对的读者对那些少数民族文化并不熟悉,不论是在中国还是外国。讲故事是传播文化价值并满足细节要求的一种方式。如何对大不相同的不同文化的文本进行比较研究呢? 比较需要有可比的资料。因而,让我们审视一下在全世界范围里研究史诗都要关注的最常见的事宜和问题。史诗可以被粗略地定义为最初由讲述者、游吟诗人或歌手在口头表演中表现的长篇英雄诗。在这样的口头"文本"中,我们可以识别与文本本身相关的要素与特征,还有与文化背景相关的特征。

讲故事是传播文化价值并满足细节要求的一种方式。我们怎样知道文本是否在指导或操控着我们想当然地接受某些种类的信息呢? 我们是怎样确定一种认识他者而不是认识自己的方式呢? 为了回答这两个问题,我们需要集中关注文本并提出几个问题:在相关文本中谁是英雄? 他的职能和他的行为是什么? 英雄是荣耀的还是不名誉的呢? 由谁来断定,为什么? 其他人物的作为是什么? 他们的行动是个人的还是集体的? 他们彼此配合还是彼此对立?

这样的问题有助于我们在两个方面获得洞见：一是跨文化的一般性比较的复杂性，二是人类关系的文化建构。如何对来自差异极大的不同文化的文本做比较研究呢？比较需要可比的资料。我们如何找到可比的资料？我们可以识别与文本本身相关的要素与特征（在文本中涉及的）。以下的几点可以成为口头文本的跨文化比较研究的有用框架。在这里，也就是史诗的跨文化研究之框架。首先，我们要将史诗当作一种书写文本（transcribed texts）。*

（一）史诗文本

1.形式特征。文本在语言使用或特定语言表达手段上具有鲜明的特征。一个文本可能包含一些固定的程式，例如在开头和结尾（"很久以前"等），或者其他的程式，一组诗句或者某种特征鲜明的表达；谚语、谜语、隐喻、重复、歌唱、词汇游戏、韵律、节奏；一种显而易见的"散文"叙事与"诗歌"的交替使用。

2.书写文本所指明的与听众的关系。一个叙述者可以直接向全体听众发话，也可以向听众中部分特定的人发话（文本中的一位巫师、一位客人或某个异邦人，或者是随行的乐师）。还有，要注意听众方面的反应、评论与介入，看看文本是不是留下了这方面的痕迹？或是在书写过程中被删去或忽略了？

3.文类与故事类型。它是一部史诗吗？它为什么被认定为是史诗？英雄的作用对于史诗这一文类的故事有哪些贡献？在特定文化中是否存在某种地方性分类（参看下文"文学领域之语境中的史诗"）？

4.主题。有没有与特定文类相关的传统主题呢？主题的循环又是怎样的情况？史诗的地方背景或英雄主人公是否表现着统一的主题？

5.人物。首先，有一个英雄或几个英雄。在世界不同地区的史诗之中可以找到一种模型，这是许多学者所探讨过和揭示过的。该范型的要点如下：

在比较史诗的文本方面，英雄的生活是一个重要的普遍因素。需要检验的要点如下：诞生，生命，或许还有英雄之死。不寻常的出身（贵族或皇族？）和奇异的诞生。英雄有非同寻常的童年，极端的困苦经历或令人惊异的奇迹；他从这样的童年经历中获得免受伤害的特质，或者相反，他要解决许多个人的难题以便应付敌手。英雄做出惊世的举动，克服可怕的危险。重要的英雄有强大的敌手：他们是谁，又

---

* 书写文本（transcribed texts），它不是书面创作的文本，而是人们以文字等书写符号对口头叙事的一种记录。——译者注

做了什么？在英雄的冒险生涯中宗教和法术发挥什么功能？英雄是否依靠某种仪式或药物而变得免受伤害呢？英雄对阴间下界的访问值得特别关注。经历冒险之后的英雄常常注定要登基为王。

与史诗文本相关的其他特殊形象是怎样的（比如说：神灵、妖魔、萨满、男人、女人、儿童、动物——如一匹马，魔法物体或其他物体所发挥的重要作用如何，等等）？

以上这些形象——特别是英雄主人公，在他们的各种职能角色中是如何被表现的？文本之中对于两性都适用的规范和社会的可能性（或不可能性）是什么？英雄同其他形象的关系是怎样的，比如和他的兄弟，他的母亲或继母，他的妻子，一位萨满巫师，等等，这种关系是正面的还是反面的？是英雄性的还是普通的？遵守社会规范还是打破规范？主宰的还是服从的？还有诸如此类的问题。所有这些要点都可以从世界范围的史诗作品中验证其表现及诗学的效果。

6.时间。作品提到的时间是哪一类的？是神话的时间（比如时间之开端，创造之中的时间，世界之初始等），人类的时间，魔幻的时间（如时间停滞或者延迟），还是未可知的时间？创世的结束意味着人类的时间秩序得以建立。神话中的人类祖先不同于神灵之处在于，在创世过程中或者之后，死亡被带进了人类的世界，或者注定为人类时间秩序的组成部分。神灵则是不死的。在每个文本中都可以看到对时间的暗示，诸如"开辟之时"或"很久很久以前"一类的说法。

7.空间。在一个故事中，一个事件总是要在"某处"发生。一个事件总是意味着跨越两种空间或情境之界线。该空间或地点是如何描绘的？是熟悉的还是陌生的？是善的还是恶的？是舒适的还是危险的？故事中的行为与形象是否从一个空间转换到另一个空间？比如，从神灵居住的地方转移到人类的凡尘世界？或是从天堂转向地狱？或者，假如行动发生在尘世之中，那就从城市转到荒野或遥远的大山里，以及从远处荒野转到城市？

在史诗中，把秩序带给一个由混沌所统治的空间或一个国家，这样一种过程并不比在其他故事、传说、动物故事和童话中要少。混沌的统治通常是由一个邪恶形象所创造出的。

一个空间的实际表现要么是熟悉的，要么是陌生的：我们的村庄，森林，草原，沙漠，水面（海，河流），天空（空气），一株（空心）树，一座山峰，一所房屋或茅舍，一座神庙。还有熟悉的或陌生的景观——另一个彼岸世界，死后世界或下界，以及中间空间（地上的天堂，童话界等）。

重要的是注意到哪一种史诗的形象被准许进入哪一种空间或地点，还有哪一种行动与特殊的地点相关联。进入某些空间将会部分地决定人物的英雄属性和特异行为。

8.物件。熟悉的或陌生的？可以从几个层面上回答这个问题：在史诗中，人物可以将一个物件视为"特别"，因为它包含着超自然力，也可以是对故事所由产生的那个文化背景而言较生疏的物件。

(二)文学领域之语境中的史诗

有两种语境要加以区分：文学的语境和社会的语境。在这里，文学的背景指一个文本同该文化中其他文本的关系网络。一个口头的或书写文本通常与同一个时间/空间中的同一文本的其他版本有关联，或是与同一文本代代相传的早先形式有关联，而不论它是否被前人书写下来。一个文本总是处在同文本的其他版本和各种变体的关联之中。关于这一问题并非总有可能找到确凿的材料。有时，同一故事的变体也存在一个邻近的或遥远的文化中，就像本书所讨论到的藏族史诗《格萨尔王传》那样。研究一个变体版本会是极为有趣和具有启发性的。另一方面，在地方背景之中，同一村庄不同的讲故事人会按照不同方式来讲一个故事或唱一首歌，引出不同的作品人物，对原有情节加以增删。对于同一个歌手来说，这样的情况也会发生。

一个口头文本不仅同该史诗的各种形式相关联，而且也同其他史诗和文类相关联。如果我们把文类界定为具有共同特征的一系列作品，那么我们就应当考虑到口头与书写文本的分类是在文化之内和文化之间做出的。一个故事可以吞并和消化其他的文类，如谜语或谚语。一部史诗可以借用起源故事或历史编年，等等。一个文本的表演有时保留在一个特殊的讲故事人的群体中(职业歌手，祭司，猎手，男人或女人一方)。有时一个文本具有特殊性，因为讲述的场合具有封闭性：比如在一种葬礼上或在丰收之后。地方性分类可以建立在这样的标准之上：猎人的故事，丰收的故事，等等。跨文化的文类之划分从来都是棘手的问题。

同一文化之中的不同文本是互相补充的。在文化之内和之间的分类比较给各种文类之间的相似与差异提供更清楚的观照。一种来自本文化之外的分类可能有帮助，也可能造成混乱，因为学者们有时不加分析地认可某一标准，不管它来自本文化还是外来文化。

(三)社会文化语境中的史诗

口头文学有一种社会功能。在故事的进程中，某些人物打破了既定的社会与文化规范,但是接近故事结尾处,这种规范通常得到重新确认。社会与文化的背景因素是建构故事房屋的砖石。这些因素涉及日常生活的现实、地理环境和社会组织等。另一方面,故事也可以成为掌控听众的手段,以便为了某种利益而服务。故事之中总是有一些符号暗示所要满足的利益,尤其当我们提出早先提到的批判性问题时,这些利益就更加凸显出来。然而,故事不能照字面去理解。它们大部分是出于虚构,尽管人们将某些神话、传说或谱系理解为"真实的事件"。故事虽也指涉现实,但不是直接的。获取有关地方背景的信息,对习俗、传统、事件、社会关系等的解释,是非常重要的,正如本书中的某些学者所细心留意的那样。另一方面,故事中也总有一些与背景相异的成分,在日常的现实中罕见的或不存在的成分,以及为了吸引和迷惑地方听众而特意渲染的成分。

(四)跨越文化语境的史诗

跨文化语境的史诗享有一种特殊的构成风格,以及惊人的主题相似性。正如印度学者那巴尼塔·德森(Nabaneeta Dev Sen)在她的著作《对位》中所指出的那样。①实际上,固定的程式、歌曲和主题的运用,诸如集会、离去、庆典、挑战、战争和胜利,用作长故事展开的线索,这是世界各地口头文学的特征和常用的手段。当然,这种手段也用于书写文本中,不过在书写文学中,变化的可能性更加广阔,更少具有强制性。

人们讨论的较多的一点是,一部被打造成诗歌的史诗是否只是一部史诗呢?这里的问题是:如何定义诗歌。截然区分散文与诗歌是不可能的,或者至少是成问题的。在一般的口头文学中,通过韵律、音乐和歌唱,散体与诗体相遇、结合、交织。在一种口头表演的散体、诗体和戏剧体之间,具有一种过渡性的而不是一种根本性的区别。这个观念改变了西方世界中对散文或诗歌进行定义的观点。回溯欧洲中世纪的情况,诗歌(poetry)是用于文学中的一般性的术语。只有到了18世纪的英格兰,有韵的诗歌和无韵的散文才彼此区分并相互对立起来。我不知道在中国文学中,尤其是在我们的案例——对中国少数民族史诗的界定中,这种散文与诗歌的区分是怎样做出的,或者应该怎样做出?

在口头表演中,音乐常常起到关键的作用。在不同的文化中,史诗的表演往往是讲唱结合。伴奏音乐极为密切地联系着情感,那是由诗歌之魂激发出来的情感。

---

① Nabanita Dev Sen, *Counterpoints*: *Essays in Comparative Literature*. Calcutta: Prajña, 1985.

歌手通常强调,他们发现没有音乐的表演是非常困难的,甚至是不可能的。讲述与音乐是一种活的统一体,它在今天得到更为认真的研究,这种研究必将开启新的视野,并且引起人们对散文与诗歌之间的人为区分进行重新反思。

不论何时史诗被书写成文字,人们有时会发现这样一些提示:"嘿,竖琴师,你跟不上我的词了",或者:"如果你弹得太快的话,我就跟不上说了",或者:"睡眠让你的眼睛沉重,注意节奏啊"。①这样的警告是对与叙事相伴的乐师发出的。它们表明,节奏对于叙事者保持故事的顺畅叙述是必不可少的。音乐支持了表演,统合了叙述上的枝蔓。

长篇创作的史诗常常有数千行之多,没有程式是不可能的。实际上,它们由固定的结构因素所组成,诸如,程式随着即兴表演而变化。在《罗摩衍那》中,那巴尼塔·德森发现了与西方史诗中同样的程式技巧。西方史诗中的这种技巧是由帕里(M. Parry)、洛德(A. B. Lord)和鲍勒(C. M. Bowra)发现的。②有时,同一主题的两个或三个变体构成重复以便形成故事的张力(例如在《贝奥武甫》中;有两场针对邪恶的战斗;或者在《吉尔伽美什》中,英雄得到两次机会获取永生之草。同样的事情发生在奥德修斯的探险中,他相继遭遇了卡鲁普索和塞壬)。这些都是用主题的重复构成故事张力的手段的例子。从本书关于蒙古族、藏族、柯尔克孜族史诗的论述中我们可以看到类似的手段。

虽然在时间上和文化上有所不同,英雄的生与死总是位于史诗叙述的中心。如果我们要把握史诗英雄的主要特征,那么,我们就要发问,英雄是否总是一个男人,或者还是有女英雄?起源与出生的细节不可避免地强调英雄的杰出人格,英雄之死也是这样。矛盾的是,一位史诗英雄在人类之中似乎最容易得到永生,正是因为他的不合时宜的戏剧性死亡。

最后的两个提示是:首先,就史诗而言,在口头表达中,人们会发现几种风格,最重要的是言语模式,其次还有背诵模式和歌唱模式。感情越强烈,音乐也越强烈,看来是个规则。在刚果的南嘎人(Nyanga)史诗中,英雄名字叫作珉多(Mwindo)。有一种程式按照下面的情形而展开:"珉多把甜蜜的语词丢进自己的嘴里,然后歌

---

① Isidore Okpewho, *The Epic in Africa*: *Toward a Poetics of the Oral Performance*. New York: Columbia University Press, 1979.

② Albert B. Lord, *The Singer of Tales*, Cambridge, Mass.: Harvard University Press, 1960; Cecil Maurice Bowra, *Heroic poetry*, London: Macmillan, 1961; Milman Parry, *The Making of HomericVerse*: *The Collected Papers of Milman Parry*, edited by Adam Milman Parry, Oxford: Clarendon Press, 1971.

唱。"歌唱总是出现在故事的戏剧性场合。

其次,现在要比过去更加关注游吟歌手(bards),歌手通常是具有高度天赋的表演者,尽管他们中也有一些普通的艺术家,研究者需要研究和比较他们的品格和个性,采访他们,试图发现他们的艺术背景的奥秘:在何种程度上,他们的品格是由他们的文化传统所决定的,或者由他们的个人才能所决定的。为本书撰稿的藏学教授杨恩洪对我讲述了德高望重的藏族老歌手桑珠(Sam-grubb)的特殊才能。

跨文化比较的领域是丰富和多变的,深度地方性研究的丰硕成果正在汇聚起来,对这一笔艺术财富的比较研究的时代已经到来。通过细心搜集整理而收获的中国少数民族史诗已经被学者们多年耐心地记录下来。他们的分析将为理解这一笔天才的史诗叙述者和演唱者的非凡的艺术遗产带来新的契机。

三、全球化时代的跨文化比较

比较需要有可比的资料,在进入这个问题之前,我们必须首先了解比较文学中"细读"和"远观"的利与弊。二者均有所长,二者相互依赖。没有必要再去解决两者之间的矛盾。"细读"的优势在于,近距离地考察一个特定文化背景中的口头或书写文本。"远观"——

> 使你能够集中考察比文本更小得多或大得多的单位:构思、主题、比喻,或者文类和系统。况且,在非常小和非常大之间,文本自身消失了。这正是那样一种场合,人们可以公正地说,越少即越多。如果我们要理解系统的整体,我们不得不接受部分的损失。①

为了使资料具有可比性,一个简短而实际的规则应该是"所要研究的地理空间越大,那么分析的单位就应该越小"②。换言之,如果我们要对一部史诗进行深入研究,我们可以透彻地考察整个文本,但是我们不能提出关于英雄及其对手的跨文化的问题,我们不能比较史诗主题或者史诗中的重要旅行,或者通常地,我们不能研究存在于大不相同文化中的史诗这一文类。史诗中英雄这一统一性主题使之特别

---

① Franco Moretti, "Conjectures on World Literature," *New Left Review* Jan. – Feb. 2000: 57.
② 同上,第61页。

适合于进行跨文化的比较。

文学理论拥有很长的研究西方书写文本的经验,但是,除了某些个别的研究者以外,只是在相对晚近的阶段,人们的眼光才开始看到西方世界之外。在 20 世纪 60 年代末期,文化相对主义的概念被带入文学研究,但是今天我们需要坚实的努力,从全球的观点去把握比较文学的对象。

在文学理论中,某些对待来自他文化文学的态度非常盛行。最为谨慎的态度是一种极端的相对主义:我远离其他的文化是因为对它们而言,我是一个局外者。这一态度也许是出于相反的动机:或者是由于漠不关心,或是由于极度谦虚所引起的。相反的,研究自身文化的独有的权利,也可以由该文化之内的人提出。理由是,局外人不能做到这一点。这是一种令人遗憾的反应,表现的是同样令人遗憾的等级次序的错误观念和不光彩的言论。上述两种情形结果都导致某种形式的种族隔离。

跨文化的文学理论要研究来自不同文化的口头与书写文学。另外,文本、文类或者文学变异,或者是与一种以上文化相关的特定的文学观念,这些都可以进行比较研究。这里涉及的各种关系和不同的观念是复杂的,但是它们的存在不能被否认,否则我们就不能公正地审视所要考察的文学。

对我来说,研究非洲文学并在非洲居住数年,已经成就了一种对跨文化的文学研究非凡的眼光。首先,它让我明白了,我们先入为主的关于文化的观念是多么成问题。我开始意识到,我本人在普遍世界观方面的文化偏见是多么严重。我开始向自己发问,这些新的问题是非常具有启发性的,无论对我研究一般性文学问题,还是对我的特殊的比较文学的跨文化研究都是这样。对于从事少数民族文化研究的中国学者也是这样。他们拥有不止一种文化的知识,这样的知识为他们增添了考察我们人类文化世界的新层面。

在所有的背景中,需要小心翼翼地建立研究中使用的文化标准。在这些方面,把文化看成是一种建构是非常重要的,这种建构性从来不阻止有些人将文化视为生活现实,一种对他们自己有效的现实。对于少数民族文化而言,这一点尤其适用。

依照人们的兴趣,并且依照他们心目中的现实,每一种历史都要开始于一种特殊的时间和空间。当然这包括文学史和比较文学。

文学作品中的和关于文学作品的文化观点包含着有关文化与社会的丰富信息。不论作者、读者和研究者表示赞同或是反对,在所有场合下,他们的反应引发出文化的意义,这些文化意义反映着这些作者、读者和研究者的观点及文化背景。

口头文学在文学研究之中已经开始扮演一种非常重要的角色,因而也是一种更为体制化的角色。国际比较文学学会的跨文化研究委员会只是在非常晚近的时候(2000年8月在南非的比勒陀利亚)才要求更加关注口头文学,而该学会在过去完全忽略了这一研究领域。在今天全球化背景中,新的文类,例如,流行歌曲,很容易被融会贯通,一有需要就可以进入到现存的传统形式中。而且,只要口头文学一旦被誊录或迻译,人们马上就会面临跨文化问题的限制;在口头文学领域中,跨文化的文学理论的确具有一种重要的使命。再次试问,这在中国的跨文化研究背景中会意味着什么呢?

在何种程度上,不同的学科能够解决研究与学术中的文化差异问题呢?我们取得了何种程度的进步,使得我们为开展跨文化学术争论扫清道路呢?作为批判的读者,我们的任务是批判性的确认文本。我们怎样能够知道文本是否在操控我们接受某种信息,仅仅是因为这些信息和我们自己的背景知识相协调?我们怎么样能够知道其他的认知方式呢?在寻求解答这样的问题时,我们有必要集中关注文本的主体。

简单的问题,诸如谁在讲话,谁在看,谁在行动。在这一文本中,仍然是相关的,而且需要在所有的语境中用批判眼光对待所考察的文本。这三个问题可以按照几种方式加以修正,它们可以用否定的形式发问:谁没有讲话?谁在文本之中没有讲话的权利?谁没有看或被禁止看(这是否意味着:他的观点没有得到表现?)?谁没有行动?谁在一开始就是被动的或是无力行动的?谁必须顺从于他人的行动?下一个问题集中于三个基本的行为对象:讲话人在说什么?他/她正在采取什么样行动?在故事中,他/她认为有价值的东西是什么?什么东西从中被"自然"地省略掉?何种观点被表达出来,在何种程度上这些观点与其他的观点(表达出来的或没有表达的)相一致?作品中的人物在做什么?他们的行为是个人的还是集体的?他们的行动彼此配合呢还是彼此对立?这样的问题使我们能够获得关于主导话语之权利效应的认识。这样的问题同样与理论、与文学、与在印刷媒体或在电视中报道的日常新闻相关。当我们为理解跨文化关系的复杂性做出种种尝试时,这些问题仍然是相关的,还有那些性别、阶级或种族关系的问题也同样具有相关性。

选择跨文化的比较,我们丢失了某些东西——尤其是地方文本将提供给我们的隐含意义,但是我们也获得了某些东西。我们所获得的是,在文学类别中关于人类的普遍性与差异性的新认识,还有,关于人类文化所孕育的文学形式和观念在何种程度上具有相似性的认识。

随之而来的,在比较文学的跨文化研究中有两种主要的现象需要加以考虑:一方面,存在着以跨文化的接触中所产生的相互影响为标记的文学;另一方面,还存在类型学的比较,审视文类之中的相似性与差异性(没有文化间的接触):神话、史诗、谚语、传说,以及所有这些可以从全球视野加以考察的对象。

在我们时代的学术村落中,新的挑战是,不再限制我们仅仅研究那个属于自己的学术领地或文化花园。在文本研究、理论和学科研究中,最广泛意义的跨文化交流已不可避免。正因为如此,真正同来自不同文化背景的研究者们进行合作和对话才是最基本的。地方性深度研究法和跨文化比较法都是重要的和必需的。所有那些以研究一种文化或亚文化为专长的人都需要虚心学习。不过,研究者没有必要成为在一种与他自己的文化不同的文化之水中游泳的鳄鱼,正如他没有必要成为一个女人以便从事女性研究那样,或者没有必要成为那个他所要研究的文化中的一名成员。

作为一个局外者,并不一定就是消极的。实际上,米·巴赫金(Michael Bakhtin)已经强调过局外者身份可以成为理解过程中强有力的因素:

> 一种意义只有当他与另外的意义相遇和相接触的时候才显示其深度:它们加入了一种对话,这就超越了这些特殊意义和特定文化的封闭性与单一性。我们对一种外来文化提出新的问题,这样的问题是不会自己提出的。我们在其中寻求对我们自己问题的答案。外来文化对我们的反应是,向我们揭示其新的方面和新的语义深度。①

反过来也是一样,作为一种对话,跨文化的相遇就其本质而言也是一种相互充实。就跨文化的文学研究而言,我们可以引用一句东非的斯瓦希里谚语:"知识如海洋,它需要众多的手臂来拥抱它。"或者,如同一句中国古话所言:"智慧不会随着时光的流逝增减毫厘。"

---

① M.M.Bakhtin, *Speech Genres and Other Late Essays*. Translated by vern W. McGee; edited by Caryl Emerson and Michael Holquist. Austim: University of Texas Press, 1986.

参考书目

Bakhtin, Michail M. *Speech Genres and Other Late Essays*. Translated by Vern W. McGee; edited by Caryl Emerson and Michael Holquist. Austin: University of Texas Press, 1986.

Bowra, Cecil Maurice. *Heroic poetry*, London: Macmillan, 1961.

Dev Sen, Nabaneeta. *Counterpoints*: *Essays in Comparative Literature*. Calcutta: Prajña, 1985.

Lord, Albert B. *The Singer of Tales*, Cambridge, Mass.: Harvard University Press, 1960.

Moretti, Franco. "Conjectures on World Literature," *New Left Review* Jan. – Feb. 2000: 54—68.

Okpewho, Isidore. *The Epic in Africa*: *Toward a Poetics of the Oral Performance*. New York: Columbia University Press, 1979.

Parry, Milman. *The Making of HomericVerse*: *The Collected Papers of Milman Parry*, edited by Adam Milman parry, Oxford: Clarendon Press, 1971.

Schipper, Mineke. *Beyond the Boundaries*: *African Literature and Literary Theory*. London: Allison and Busby, 1989.

藏族口头传统的特性

——以史诗《格萨尔王传》为例

杨恩洪

摘　要　藏族自吐蕃时代始有文字。与此同时,佛教传入我国西藏,在藏族社会逐渐占据统治地位,最终形成了政教合一的地方政权。由于受宗教典籍的影响,这时期的文人创作形成了一种穷源溯流的顺时叙述模式。散韵合体被认为是藏族叙事传统中的主要形式,它在史诗、叙事诗、故事和藏戏中至今仍被广泛采用。藏族传统文化的传承除了用文字记载的典籍以外,口传是一种最早的而且极具生命力的方式。即使文字发明以后,这种口耳相传的方式仍一直被沿用。史诗《格萨尔王传》继承了藏族传统的格律特点。藏族口头传统历史悠久,这对于我们理解说唱艺人记忆长篇史诗的奥秘是有所启示的。

关键词　口头传统,《格萨尔王传》,说唱艺人

生活在青藏高原独特环境中的藏族有着自己悠久的历史与深厚的文化传统。1500 年有文字记载的历史以及长约 5000 年的人类繁衍的进程,为这个民族的文化奠定了坚实而丰厚的基础。让我们循着历史与文化的血脉,去探寻史诗《格萨尔王传》的说唱传统,探寻这一藏族口头传统的历史根基吧。

藏族是一个勤劳、骁勇的民族,自远古时代起,他们的祖先就生活在青藏高原。据近年来在西藏的考古发现,在广阔的青藏高原,如那曲地区申扎、阿里地区的扎布和普兰县以及后藏日喀则地区的定日县均有旧石器文明的遗存分布,而中石器文化遗存、新石器文化遗存则遍及西藏的广大地域。① 人们在与恶劣的自然环境艰苦卓绝的斗争以及与周边部族长期交往融合的过程中形成了今天的藏族。

---

① 丹珠昂奔:《藏族文化发展史》,第 64—143 页。

藏族在与大自然的长期搏斗与抗争中,乐观向上,积极进取,以他们独特的历史积淀、社会阅历和精神感受,创造了自立于世界民族之林的高原文化——博大精深的藏文化。按照藏族传统的分类,藏文化分为大五明和小五明,大小五明统称为rig gnas che chung lnga。大五明即工艺学、医学、声律学、正理学、佛学,小五明即修辞学、辞藻学、韵律学、戏剧学、星象学。文学虽未独立设类,但涵盖其中,这是由于藏族历史文献记载大都具有文史哲合璧的特点所致。

藏族社会自吐蕃创制文字以来,其文学发展的脉络是:吐蕃时期(7—9世纪)是藏族古典文学酝酿、萌发阶段;分裂割据时期(9—13世纪)是古典文学正式兴起、形成阶段;元朝统一以后(13世纪以后)是兴盛发展阶段。[1] 佛教自吐蕃时期传入藏族社会,经过与本土宗教苯教的长期斗争,最终占据统治地位,在西藏建立了政教合一的地方政权。佛教势力强大,寺院星罗棋布,僧人在寺院不但学习宗教知识,还学习天文历算、医药、哲学、逻辑、历史、语言、文学等知识,很多僧人成为身兼医生、历史学家、语言学家、天文学家、文学家的知识分子。自11世纪后,僧人兼文学家的现象成为当时作家文坛的一大特点。至17世纪,藏族作家几乎全部由僧人组成。由于僧人长期在寺院中受教育,他们的知识获得以及人生观、价值观、审美取向及创作的方法均受到佛教的制约,因此,他们的作品多为文史哲不分,或文学、哲学合璧的形式,这是西藏古典作家文学的一个重要的特点。

由于受到宗教典籍的影响,这一时期的文人创作还形成了一种穷源溯流的顺时叙述模式,即任何古籍的叙述均从讲述宇宙、天地形成开始,继而是印度先王、释迦牟尼、藏族族源、赞普史、蒙古王史、中原王史等内容的叙述。

西藏古典文学的另一个特点是,不论是传记、诗歌、道歌、寓言故事还是后来产生的小说、戏剧,其形式均为散韵相间的文体,即说唱体。不同的只是各种体裁的散文体和韵文体所占的比例有一些差异。这一特点在藏族民间文学作品中也普遍存在。在故事的叙述中穿插韵文以抒发情感,而长诗、抒情诗中以散文体解释或交代情节。因此,这种散韵合体可以认为是藏族叙事传统中的最主要并经常使用的一种形式。

一、藏族叙事传统的渊源

上述散韵合体的例证可以追溯到敦煌所保存的藏文历史文书,在敦煌古文献

---

[1] 佟锦华:《藏族古典文学》,第5页。

中，从《赞普传略》到卜辞，散韵相间的形式已经得到了很好的运用。说明这一文体远在吐蕃时期就已在民间广泛流传，如《赞普传略》中可以看到松赞干布赞普与大臣唱和的诗歌。

盟誓毕，赞普高歌：

> 自今天至以后，
> 你不要背弃我啊，
> 我将不舍弃你！
> 我若是抛弃你啊，
> 苍天定会保佑你！
> 你若是抛弃我啊，
> 我会进行惩罚也！

歌毕，韦义策和歌作答。歌云：

> 吾之属官长上是赞普你，
> 我虽小也要把王放在肩上。①

在敦煌写卷中发现的卜辞约有 30 段，每段均由两部分组成，第一部分是韵文体的卜辞正文，第二部分是这段卜辞将应验的内容的散文体解释，如：

> 啊！
> 子嗣呢如金宝，
> 金水呢流滔滔，
> 流水呢弯又曲，
> 仇敌呢纷纷逃，
> 地位呢日日升，
> 这是呢幸福兆。

---

① 王尧、陈践：《敦煌吐蕃历史文书》，第 63 页。

在卜辞的后边,有对卜辞诗行的散文体解释:"此卦应的是游览风景之卦。若卜家宅和寿命,善神或女神们在游玩山水和欣赏风景,好好供奉之,有求必应。卜经商则获利,卜游子则归,卜病者则愈,卜财者大发,卜敌人则无,卜子嗣则有。此卦无论占卜何事皆吉。"①

此后,以藏传佛教噶举派僧人米拉日巴(1040—1123)道歌为代表的,在藏族文学史上具有重要影响的"道歌体"诗在民间广为流传。道歌虽名为诗歌,却是由诗歌咏唱与散文体叙述交替组成,诗歌部分采用藏族民歌的多段回环格律和自由体格律咏唱噶举教派的教义、修法途径,劝诫人们出世修法,走上解脱之路。散文体部分承担叙述情节发展的任务。这一文体继承了吐蕃时期《赞普传略》散韵结合的传统。在诗歌格律方面在原来四句六言形式的基础上发展成为多段回环,即每段句数相同,每句音节数多为六、七、八,每段各句的音节数也相同的新形式。

历史名著《贤者喜宴》(作者为巴俄·组拉陈,1504—1566)史料丰富,旁征博引,立论比较公允,书中所记载的历史掺杂了神话、传说、故事等,也可视为文史合著。正文为诗歌体,每句为九个音节,诗歌后附以散文解释,全书形成了散韵结合的文体。

17世纪时五世达赖喇嘛罗桑嘉措(1617—1682)撰写的历史著作《西藏王臣记》,虽为阐述历史的作品,仍然采用了散韵相间的文体,作者为年阿体(sngan ngag)② 名家。受《诗镜》的影响,文中除了优美典雅的诗章外,还有一些散文体叙述夹杂其间。其后产生于17世纪的传记文学作品《颇罗鼐传》以及18世纪产生的藏族第一部长篇小说《勋努达美》,均受到传记文学的影响,虽然摆脱了长期以来文史哲不分的状态,走上了"纯文学"之路,但仍然采用藏族传统的叙事形式——散韵合体。

具有古老传统的散韵结合体,在藏族民间文学与戏剧中是十分常见的形式,它在史诗、叙事诗、故事和藏戏中至今仍被广泛采用。它综合了散文体富于故事性、简洁明了和韵文体富于乐感、便于抒情的特点。史诗以散文铺叙故事,承上启下,而韵文因其韵律产生的乐感效应,在烘托人物心理活动、渲染战争的激烈与场面的恢弘等方面产生了强烈的艺术效果。

---

① 佟锦华:《藏族民间文学》,第193页。
② 13世纪以来,许多藏族学者把印度学者檀丁(7世纪印度宫廷诗人)创作的诗歌修辞理论著作《诗镜》(藏语为"年阿美隆","年阿"意为"雅语"或"美文","美隆"意为"镜子")进行翻译、解释以及修改补充后,成为藏族自己的文学与修辞的理论著作,按照这一理论创作的诗称为"年阿体"诗。

散韵合体这一形式是藏族文学重要的,同时也是主要的表现形式,它产生于民间,经过不同时期文人的创造,不断丰富并出现了一定的变化,从而形成了各具特点的文体,进而又对民间文学产生一定的影响。这种古老的叙事模式在西藏传承近两千年而经久不衰,对后世的文学创作也产生了巨大的影响。

二、藏族传统诗词格律与《格萨尔王传》的韵律

藏族有浩如烟海的历史典籍及丰富多彩的民间文学样式和作品,在这极其丰厚的文学土壤里,史诗《格萨尔王传》就像一棵深深扎根于藏族传统文化沃土的禾苗,在汲取了充足的营养后拔地而起,成为枝繁叶茂的参天大树。我们完全有理由说,《格萨尔王传》是产生于青藏高原这片广袤土地上的本土之作,无论从形式到内容,从叙事传统到修辞方式,均与藏族文学一脉相承。我们可以在众多作品中看到二者的内在关联。

头尾相连的顺时叙事方式是藏族历代名师撰写文史著作共同遵循的规律,古典名著在叙述历史时,都从叙述宇宙形成开始。印度佛教的传入使古代的人们有"藏族南来之说",所以首先讲述印度先王、释迦牟尼创建佛教的历史,继而叙述藏族赞普的世袭、佛苯斗争、蒙古王史、中原王史等,这种叙述方式在藏族社会成为一种模式,并为后人所延续。史诗《格萨尔王传》也遵循了这一规律,史诗各部的安排以及艺人的说唱均从天地形成(或叫岭国形成)开始,叙述的顺序是按照主人公格萨尔王的年龄由小到大顺时推进,如出生、成长、赛马称王、征战四方以及后来完成人间使命返回天界。史诗分若干部,每部又可独立成章,拿出来单独说唱,但在各部中故事的讲述仍是顺时叙述。敦煌文献的赞普传记中,人物的叙述往往以自我介绍及介绍地名、马名、歌曲曲调名开始。

> kye rje vi ni mtshan ba vdi?
>
> 噫嘻！若问赞普(btsan po)是何名?
>
> khri vi ni srong btsan zhig。
>
> 我乃埤松赞是也。
>
> blon gyi ni mying ba vdi?
>
> 这位大臣是何名?
>
> stong rtsan ni yul zung zhig。

乃东赞域松是也。

chibs kyi ni mying ba vdi?

若问骏马是何名？

rngul bu ni gtsang gtsang lta;

乃玉布藏藏是也；

gtsang gtsang ni yang yang lta。

藏藏为驯良之马也。①

史诗《格萨尔王传》中，这种自我介绍是唱词中不可或缺的部分之一，如：

sa vdi dang sa ngo ma shes na,

此地你若不认识，

rma klung dal vbebs gyas zur dang,

这是缓流黄河右一角，

ri sbrul mgo vdra bavi gyon zur na,

蛇头山的左山侧，

dpon jo ru sprul bavi srin gling red。

是觉如神变的罗刹国。

bu nga dang nga ngo ma shes na,

汉子我你若不认识，

blon tsha zhang vdan ma spyang khra zer。

大臣江查擦香丹玛就是我。

gling chung rgyud mu bavi blon chung yin。

是幼系木哇(mu ba)部落小首领。②

藏族诗歌极为发达，从最早的敦煌文献中就可以看到四句六言的工整对仗的形式。吐蕃时期，这种被称为"协体"(gzhas)的民歌已经在民间广为流传。第六世

---

① 王尧、陈践：《敦煌吐蕃历史文书》，第 79 页。

② 《降伏妖魔》(藏文)，贡却才旦编，第 117—118 页（汉文参见王沂暖译《降伏妖魔之部》，第 109 页）。

达赖喇嘛仓央嘉措（1683—1706）创作的情歌采用协体民歌形式,在民间产生了深远的影响。在此基础上产生的被称为"鲁体"（glu）的多段回环体诗歌形式以及由宗教僧人米拉日巴采用"鲁体"形式创作的道歌的产生与流传,对后世的诗歌也产生了极大的影响。上述藏族诗歌的固有形式在藏戏、长篇叙事诗甚至在故事中均被广泛运用,在《格萨尔王传》中也得到了很好的体现。

多段回环体道歌汲取了民歌中的许多素材,如白雄狮居雪山、鹫鹰盘旋岩峰、猛虎盘踞森林、金眼鱼游大海等,用以作为比喻,前几段为设喻,最后一段为写实。《米拉日巴传及其道歌》中有这样一段:

gangs stod kyi seng ge dkar mo nga,	雪山顶上的白狮我,
gangs stod yongs la mi vphyo ru,	如不游遍大雪山,
gyu ral legs po rgyas dus med,	狮鬃难以长丰满,
ras chung mi sdod dbus la vgro,	日琼不留要去卫,
da res bla mas bkav gnang zhu .	请求上师恩准俺;
brag stod kyi bya rgyal rgod po nga,	岩峰顶上的鹫鹰我,
nam vphang mthon po mi gcod du,	如不凌翅翔蓝天,
gshog drug legs po rgyas dus med,	鹰翅难以长劲健,
ras chung mi sdod dbus la vgro,	日琼不留要去卫,
da res bla mas bkav gnang zhu .	请求上师恩准俺;
nags gseb kyi stag gu ri bkra nga,	森林之间的斑虎我,
nags khrod yong la mi vphyo ru,	如不游遍森林边,
gra vdzum legs po rgyas dus med,	虎纹难以变斑斓,
ras chung mi sdod dbus su vgro,	日琼不留要去卫,
da res bla mas bkav gnang zhu .	请求上师恩准俺;
mtsho dkyil gyi nya mo gser mig nga,	大海之中的金鱼我,
mtsho mthav yong la mi rgyu ru,	如不游遍大海湾,
gser mig legs po rgyas dus med,	金眼难以长周全,
ras chung mi sdod dbus su vgro,	日琼不留要去卫,

da res bla mas bkav gnang zhu.　　请求上师恩准俺；

gung thang ras chung rdor grags nga,　贡塘的日琼多扎我，

rgyal khams yong la mi vgro ru,　　如不游遍各地盘，

nyams rtogs bzang po rgyas dus med,　证悟难以收效验，

ras chung mistod dbus su vgro,　　日琼不留要去卫，

da res bla mas bkav gnang zhu.　　请求上师恩准俺。①

　　以上道歌为五段，每段五行，每行七个音节。前四段以白狮、鹫鹰、斑虎、金鱼设喻，最后一段为写实。每一段中的第一行的末尾均为"我"（nga），第三行的最后三个音节均为"难周全"（rgyas dus med）；各段的第四、五行均相同，以"日琼不留要去卫，请求上师恩准俺"结尾，既压韵脚，易于上口，同时反复咏唱，加强感染力。

　　这种多段回环的诗句在史诗《格萨尔王传》中也有极其相似的表述。

stod gangs dkar rtse movi seng ge de,

白雪山顶的白狮子，

mgo gyu ras sngon po rgyas yod na,

若要玉鬃长得好，

khyod thang la ma vbab gangs stod zungs。

别下平原住山里。

Nag rgya rdzong dkyil gyi stag phrug de,

森林中间的斑毛虎，

Stag vdzum drug ri mo rgyas yod na,

若要笑纹长得好，

Phyi gzan la ma chastshang sgo zungs。

不要外出住洞里。

Dmav rgyal mtshovi klong gi gser nya de,

---

① 《米拉日巴传及其道歌》（藏文），西宁：青海民族出版社，1981年，第736页。

大海深处的金眼鱼，

Nya gser mdog khrab ri rgyas yod na,

若要金甲长得好，

Chu mtsho mthav ma bskor mtsho dkyil bsdod。

别到海边住海里。①

在这首三段体的诗歌中，每段三行，每行为八个音节，较之道歌有所发展。每段第一、二行均押尾韵：第一行的最后一个音节均为"那"(de)，第二行的最后三个音节相同均为"长得好"(rgyas yod na)。

对比上述两段诗歌，可以看到二者相同并且相互影响的一面，同时也可看到出自作家之手的诗歌的工整对仗与来自民间说唱的诗歌的自由变异的鲜明对照。道歌产生的时间(11—12 世纪)与《格萨尔王传》在民间开始流传的时间基本处于同一时代，二者产生于同一文化背景之下，受到的民歌的影响以及二者间的相互影响，都是显而易见的。②

仅以甘肃本《降伏妖魔》(藏文)为例，除上述多段回环式的唱词外，类似设喻的唱段还有五处，每处都有变化。唱段一为三段每段八行(第 13—14 页)，以狮、虎作比喻；唱段二为三段每段四行(第 19 页)，以狮、虎、金眼鱼作比喻；唱段三为五段每段两行(第 88 页)，以狮、野牛、鹰、虎、鲸鱼作比喻；唱段四为三段每段五行(第 89 页)，以玉龙、雄狮、野牛作比喻；唱段五为五段每段四行(第 134—135 页)，以大鹏鸟、绿鬃狮、花斑虎作比喻。③

在格萨尔王即将出征魔国时，他把国事一一交付给爱妃珠牡(vbrug mo)。他唱道，要将绸缎库、珠宝库、城堡、珍贵佛像、宝幢、佛经、马场、牛场、羊场、账房等一一交给珠牡，在九段的唱词中，每段的后两句都采用相同的句子："交付时完全来交付，收回时也要全数收。"(ngas bcol dus kha tshang cha tshang yin, tshur len dus sprod rgyu yod ni gyis)④继承了多段回环、反复咏唱的传统诗歌形式，便于上口。

自 13 世纪《诗镜》以译述的方式被介绍到藏族地区以后，众多藏族学者纷纷对

---

① 王沂暖译《降伏妖魔之部》，第 7—8 页。
② 一般学者认为《格萨尔王传》产生于 11 世纪，后经过长时间在民间的流传，不断丰富才形成今天的规模。艺人认为格萨尔王诞生于 1038 年，其时间与米拉日巴(1040—1123)接近。
③ 藏文拉丁转写与汉译诗行见附录一。
④ 《降伏妖魔》(藏文)，贡却才旦编，第 33—36 页。藏文拉丁转写与译文见附录二。

其进行研究并撰写专著对《诗镜》原文加以注释,而且在此基础上进一步发展,淘汰了一些根据梵文的结构和语音特点归纳出来的不符合藏语特点、结构的修辞手法,补充、归纳了藏族诗歌的韵律特点。这些诗词格律在史诗《格萨尔王传》中得到了很好的运用和发展。如重叠格律:年阿体是在一首不分段的诗歌中各句的相同位置或同句的不同位置上出现重叠;而《格萨尔王传》所采用的多段体回环形式是在各种位置上发生整个字或词组乃至句子的重复。"这种重叠格律,在音韵和节奏方面,出现反复回环,显得和谐悠扬,抑扬顿挫,铿锵有力,给诗歌增添无限的音乐美;在意境上产生加强思想深度,浓化感情色彩,给人以回味无穷的感受。还因为它琅琅上口,容易诵记而便于流传,影响广,成为藏族诗歌中最富民族特色、最占优势的格律。"①这种重叠格律包括句首重叠、句中重叠、句尾重叠、隔句重叠或全句重叠(如上文中所列举的每段最后两句重叠的例子)等。这里仅作一简略介绍。

句尾单音节重叠的如:

lam drang bor ston pavi dam pa <u>dkon</u>, 指示正路的善人少,

sems gcig tu gnas pavi sgom pa <u>dkon</u>, 心不外骛的修行者少,

khrel phyi thag ring bavi grogs po <u>dkon</u>, 永远知耻的朋友少,

tshong drang por gtam pavi khe ba <u>dkon</u>, 买卖正直的商人少,

sems mos pa mi vgyur slob ma <u>dkon</u>, 信仰不变的徒弟少,

gnas gcig tu mthun pavi bzav tshang <u>dkon</u>, 和睦相处的夫妻少。②

句尾多音节重叠的如:

shar nyi zla <u>da la la</u>, 东方日月达拉拉,

lho na char sprin <u>da la la</u>, 南方雨云达拉拉,

nub na gribs so <u>da la la</u>, 西方阴影达拉拉,

byang na skyi ser <u>da la la</u>, 北方冷风达拉拉,

pha bla mavi gsum chos <u>da la la</u>, 喇嘛念经达拉拉,

---

① 佟锦华:《藏族文学研究》,第 381 页。

② 《降伏妖魔》(藏文),贡却才旦编,第 85—86 页。(汉文参见王沂暖译《降伏妖魔之部》,第 82—83 页)

dpon bzang povi zhal gsung <u>da la la</u>。好官说话达拉拉。①

句首隔句重叠的如：

<u>ha cang</u> shes rab che mkhan po，绝顶聪明大智者，

bya ba mang na rang nyid vphung，乱事过多害自家，

<u>ha cang</u> rgyal po grags chen po，赫赫有名大国王，

dran rgyu mang na rgyal srid nyams，乱想过多害国家，

<u>ha cang</u> longs spyod sgrub mkhan po，过于享受的修法人，

gsog ma shes na rang gi gshes，不知积蓄会受苦，

<u>ha cang</u> zas la dad che bas，过于暴饮暴食的人，

za ma shes na dug du vgyur。不自节制会中毒。②

史诗诗词中还出现了顶真格的形式，一般是前一句结尾的词语作后一句的开头，使语言递进紧凑，生动畅达，易于上口。如：

phu gsum dkar yag <u>gang</u> kyi ri，山谷上部的白雪山，

<u>gang</u> la dung <u>seng</u> vkhor bavi ri，雪山中雄狮常眷恋，

<u>seng</u> la gyul ral rgyal bavi ri，雄狮抖动绿鬃在雪山。

Sked gsum tsan dan <u>nags</u> kyi ri，缠绕檀香林的青山，

<u>Nags</u> la rgua <u>stag</u> vkhor bavi ri，檀香林中猛虎多眷恋，

<u>Stag</u> la vdzum drug rgyas pavi ri，猛虎显示花纹兴旺之山。

Mdav gsum chu ma <u>zhing</u> gi ri，沟口水田环绕的山，

<u>Zhing</u> la <u>vbras</u> drug smin pavi ri，良田谷物多丰收，

<u>Vbras</u> la dbu nag vkhor bavi ri，谷物是黑头人眷恋之山。

---

① 达拉拉是一种形容词，把上文形容得更形象，其意为：东方日月明亮亮，南方雨云乱蓬蓬，西方阴影黑呼呼，北方冷风冷飕飕，喇嘛念经声琅琅，好官说话温柔柔。

② 《降伏北方鲁赞王》(扎巴说唱本)，第15页。这里为了表现诗中的顶真格，笔者采取直译，以便看出其规律。

Mthal gsum chu bo chab kyi ri, 缓缓河水环绕之山，

Chu la gser nya vkhor bavi ri, 水中金鱼多眷恋，

Nya la gser gshog rgyas bavi ri, 金鱼跳跃环绕之山。

Gling la sde gsum chags pavi ri, 岭国三部落形成之山，

sde la dpav brtul vkhor bavi ri, 部落英雄眷恋之山，

Dpav la rtsal dtug cdzoms pavi ri, 英雄显示武功之山。①

以上顶真的修辞手法为：每段第一行的第五或第二、第三、第四音节，即为下一行的起始；同样，第二行的第三或第四音节，又是第三行的起始。其次，在五段回环的15句中，每句都以山（ri）作结尾，有着同一韵脚。第三，每段第二行的结尾均为"环绕之山"（vkhor bavi ri），第三行的结尾均为"兴旺之山"（rgyal〈rgyas〉bavi〈pavi〉ri）结尾，构成句尾的三音节重叠。

在《格萨尔王传》中，动物被拟人化，如仙鹤（藏语仙鹤的音译为虫虫）与命命鸟（藏语命命鸟的音译为香香）的对话很有特点，每句的结尾都有"虫虫"与"香香"作为歌曲的衬音出现，更趋于戏剧化。如：

sa vdi yi sa ngo ma shes na khrung khrung,

此地你若是不认识，虫虫

bdud kyi bla ri mthon po nas khrung khrung,

这是魔国命根子山，虫虫

lcags ra rtse dguvi rtse mo red khrung khrung,

这是九尖城顶尖。虫虫

Bya nga dang nga ngo ma shes na khrung khrung,

鸟儿我你若是不认识，虫虫

Ri rgyal lhun povi khang rdzong nas khrung khrung。

我从须弥山城来。虫虫

Bya khyung chen rgyal povi sring mo red khrung khrung,

是大鹏金翅鸟亲姐妹，虫虫

---

① 同前注。

Shar khra mo gling gi sa cha naskhrung khrung,

是从东方花岭来,虫虫

Rma rdzong shel dkar lhun po nas khrung khrun。

是从黄河白水晶城来。虫虫

Bya vdab chags khrung khrung dkar mo yin khrung khrung,

我是鸟类白仙鹤,虫虫

Sman me bzav a vbum bla bya yin khrung khrung。

我是梅萨的命根子鸟。虫虫①

在仙鹤唱完长达 114 行的虫虫歌后,命命鸟王唱了一首回答的歌,每行歌都以"香香"作结尾(共 143 行):

bya nga dang nga ngo ma shes na ni shang shang,

鸟儿我你若是不认识,香香

nub phyogs rgya gar yul chen na ni shang shang,

在西方印度大地方,香香

mtsho rab lha chen po yi dkyil ni shang shang,

汪洋神海正当中,香香

dwang bsil gyu yi lha chab nang ni shang shang ,

清凉美玉仙境里,香香

ma dros klu yi gzal med khang ni shang shang。

有无热龙王越量宫。香香

pho brang mdzes sdug khang bzang dbus ni shang shang,

这个美丽的好宫殿,香香

shang shang tevu rgyal bzhugs sa yod ni shang shang。

我命命鸟王住其中。香香②

史诗《格萨尔王传》的诗词格律继承了藏族传统的格律特点,由于长期在民间广泛流传,众多的民间艺人为其注入了多姿多彩的民间说唱特色,使其更加生动活

---

① 《降伏妖魔》(藏文),贡却才旦编,第 140—146 页。
② 同上书,第 146—153 页。

泼,更加贴近民众,受到普通百姓的欢迎,因而具有强大的生命力。

三、藏族口传知识的历史与传统

口头传承是藏族延续传统文化最早的且极具生命力的方式。即或是在发明了文字以后,出现了用文字记载的典籍,口传的方式仍一直被沿用。这一形式可追溯到苯教经文的传授,其方式均为师徒相传或父子相传,也称"单传"。尤其是在佛苯斗争以后,苯教遭到迫害,为了保存其教义,苯教徒更广泛地使用了这种传承方式。传承至今的一些苯教主要经典如《象雄儿续》、《光荣经》等,都是首先通过口传被苯教僧人代代铭记,而后才被记录成文字保存下来的。

口传记忆佛教经典的例子也不少,如赤德祖赞时期,曾派大臣郑噶木来果卡和业童智二人到印度取经,当二人到达冈底斯山时,遇到在这座山中修行打坐的印度高僧佛密和佛寂,他们将两高僧铭记的《经藏说分别部》、《金光明经》、《珈怛特罗》、《事续》等经典牢记心中,然后回来献给了结波(国王)。①

产生于12世纪的噶举派,其"噶"(bkav)意为佛语,"举"(rgyud)意为传承。该派主张依靠师徒口耳相传,着重修习密法。著名的噶举派大师米拉日巴曾在该派创始人玛尔巴的座前修习口传密法,《米拉日巴传》形象地介绍了这位高僧由于施咒伤害无辜,自己悔罪修行,在得道前遭到玛尔巴上师的百般折磨而不与传法,最后修成后传法的经历。其中多次记录了玛尔巴上师给众弟子口传授受的经过。

该传记的作者桑吉坚赞(1452—1507)还撰写了《玛尔巴传》,作者在传记的最后特作说明,介绍了玛尔巴的生平事迹由口传到记录成书的经过:最初是由玛尔巴的亲授弟子米拉日巴和玛尔巴果勒二人口述给米拉日巴的弟子安宗顿巴,米拉日巴又讲述给得意门徒日琼巴。之后,日琼巴和安宗顿巴二人共同商量编写成传。桑吉坚赞以此书为基础,又吸收玛尔巴其他弟子口传下来的记述,综合贯通后加工写成。这说明在噶举派的传承中,口传是一种很重要的授受方式。

据传,印度密乘之法,特别是无上瑜珈之法是通过以下三种途径从天界传到人间的,即:诸佛密意传、持明标传和常人耳闻传。佛密意传者是一切佛法的起点和终极根据,它指的是法身佛普贤如来在清净佛土内所开示的密法;标传指不直接用平常易懂的口语,而是通过标示、符号或象征等为中介而进行的教法授受;常人耳闻传

---

① 东嘎活佛:《论西藏政教合一制度》,北京:民族出版社,1981年,第17页。

则指师徒口耳相传,用口语应对来完成教法传承之使命。

此后在藏族地区又有亲承语旨的授记传、有缘的掘藏传和发愿的付印传三种传承方式,后被宁玛派接受并传播。

至今广为流传的《甚深法寂忿尊密意自解脱》,也称《西藏死书》,据说是由普贤如来亲自讲授,由莲花生埋藏,后于14世纪被伏藏师事业洲发现。伏藏师事业洲之后,三代之内单传,三代以后才向外传。① 莲花生是8世纪后半叶来西藏传教的,从他埋下经典到伏藏师掘藏,三代单传直至最后公开流传于世,经历了六七百年。在这漫长的岁月中,甚至直到14世纪,这种口耳相传的传承方式仍然被人们使用。

说唱艺人中掘藏艺人的产生,则完全与宁玛派有关,目前我们发现的一位掘藏艺人——青海果洛的格日坚赞即为宁玛派僧人。② 掘藏艺人运用了宁玛派经典传承的传统来传承史诗。由于宁玛派把格萨尔王视为莲花生大师的转世,故而以掘藏的手法来传承《格萨尔王传》自然是天经地义的事了。

这种口耳相传保存经典的传承方式至今仍然存在。口传传统的悠久历史以及由此培养出来的一个民族的极强记忆能力,对于我们理解今天藏族《格萨尔王传》说唱艺人能够记忆长篇史诗的奥秘是有所启示的。

史诗《格萨尔王传》在民间传承千余年,其主要传播形式依然是口耳相传。仅以民间说唱艺人中最杰出的所谓"神授艺人"为例,均是口耳传承。他们都生活在史诗广泛流传地区——青藏高原的牧区,如西藏的那曲、阿里、昌都专区,青海的果洛、玉树、海南藏族自治州,甘肃的甘南藏族自治州,四川的甘孜、阿坝藏族自治州以及云南的迪庆藏族自治州。上述地区目前虽分属不同的省区,但在地图上我们可以看出具有共同的地域特点,即地处西藏、青海、甘肃、四川交界地带。这些地区的共同点为:(1)这些地区正是史诗广泛流传的地域,同时也是操康方言和安多方言人们生活的地区;(2)这里远离西藏腹地拉萨,属于边远的藏族地区,远离由格鲁派控制的政教合一政权,多为宁玛派、噶举派或苯教流传地区,在意识形态方面具有相对的自由度;(3)这一地区又是藏族人民赴拉萨圣地及西藏腹心地带,以及朝佛、朝圣的必经之地,也是藏族人民与祖国内地各民族交往的重要地区,人口具有流动性。因此,古老的口耳传承方式得以生存、发展并保存至今。

---

① 参见沈卫荣《伏藏师事业洲和〈甚深法寂忿尊密意自解脱〉》。
② 四川甘孜州色达县已故的著名掘藏大师更桑尼玛活跃于20世纪初的藏区,他是宁玛派世袭的掘藏师,发掘了不少经典,同时又是史诗《格萨尔王传》的说唱艺人。

史诗《格萨尔王传》作为藏民族民间文化精髓的载体,它不但集中、凝聚了一个民族的传统与智慧,而且是藏族口头叙事传统的典型代表,人们从中可以探寻藏族口头传统发展与流变的历史,通过它追溯青藏高原古老的文化之源。

藏族地区独特的口头传统的产生与发展仰赖于独特的人文、自然环境,尤为重要的是广大藏族牧民的精神需求以及千百年来形成的审美取向与标准。这一传统并不是一成不变的,它随着时代的前进也在发生着变化,这些论题笔者将另著文探讨。

参考书目

丹珠昂奔:《藏族文化发展史》,兰州:甘肃教育出版社,2001 年。

东嘎活佛:《论西藏政教合一制度》,北京:民族出版社,1981 年。

佟锦华:《藏族古典文学》,长春:吉林教育出版社,1989 年。

佟锦华:《藏族民间文学》,拉萨:西藏人民出版社,1991 年。

佟锦华:《藏族文学研究》,北京:中国藏学出版社,1992 年。

《降伏北方鲁赞王》(扎巴说唱本),北京:民族出版社,1997 年。

王尧、陈践:《敦煌吐蕃历史文书》,北京:民族出版社,1980 年。

王沂暖译《降伏妖魔之部》,兰州:甘肃人民出版社,1980 年。

沈卫荣:《伏藏师事业洲和〈甚深法寂忿尊密意自解脱〉》,原载《贤者新宴》第 2 册,石家庄:河北教育出版社,2000 年。

附录一

《降伏妖魔之部》唱段一,三段每段八句,每句八音节(第 13—14 页):

Stod gangs ri shel gyi lding khang na, 上边雪山水晶宫,

Seng dkar mo gyu yi ral ba can, 雪白狮子绿玉发,

Khyod gcan gzan mang povi rgyal po red, 它是世上百兽王,

Lus rtsal gsum rdzogs povi dpav po red, 好似英雄力量大,

Spyin smug povi gseng la yar ltos dang, 但是仰看云层中,

Lho gyu vbrug zer bavi ngar skad can, 青龙吼叫惊天下,

Vdi ma thub klad la shor song na, 如果敌不过青龙丧性命,

Seng gyu ral rgyas pa ngo re tsha。 头上白白长了绿玉发。

Dmav tsan dan nags kyi skyid tshal na, 下边檀香碧树林,

Stag dmar yag me lcevi vdzum ri can, 猛虎笑纹如火焰，

Khyed sder bzhi kun gyi rgal po red, 它是四爪兽中王，

Bkra thig le vdzum pavi dpav po red, 如花笑纹多灿烂，

Yul grong sde dkyil la mar ltod dang, 但是往下看村中，

Khyi bdav lu rgya bo rnga ring bo, 长尾巴老狗须满面，

Vdi ma thub klad la shor song na, 如果敌不过老狗丧性命，

Stagv dzum drug rgyas pa ngo re tsha. 长了六种笑纹也羞愧。

Gling seng vbrug stag rtse pho brang na, 岭丞僧珠达孜宫，

Gling seng chen gser gyi kgrab can, 雄狮王金甲光灿烂，

Khyod mgo nag yongs kyi rgyal po red, 你是黑头人类王，

Phyogs dgra bzhi vdul bavi dpav po red, 能降四魔是好汉，

Nub bdud yul lung nag phar ltos dang, 请你往西看魔国，

Bdud tshe zad klu btsan sdig can kho, 命尽的老妖是鲁赞。

Vdi ma thub klad la shor song na, 你如敌他不过丧性命，

Rgyab khrab dkar gyon pa ngo re tsha. 穿着黄金铠甲也丢脸。

唱段二,三段每段四句。每句八音节(第19页)：

stod gangs dkar zur gyi pho thung seng, 白雪山顶雄狮王，

mgo gyu ras rgyas dus ma ngoms na, 绿发盛时不显示，

phyis lung gzhung shod la babs pa na, 等到下山到平原，

mgo gyu ras vdi yang vtshor nyen che. 绿发恐怕受损失。

Nags rgya rdzong dkyil gyi dmar yags stag, 大森林中斑斓虎，

Stag vdzum drug rgyas dus ma ngoms na, 笑纹丰满不显示，

Gzan za vdod lung gsum vgrim pavi dus, 等到觅食出森林，

Stag vdzum drug ri mo nog nyen che. 笑纹恐怕受损失。

Mar rgya mtshovi gting gi gser mig nya, 大海深处金眼鱼，

Nya gshog drug rgyas dus ma ngoms na, 六鳍丰满不显示，

Phyis mtsho mthav bskor nas rgyal bavi dus, 等到浮游到海边，
Nya gser mig yag dang vbral nyen che. 恐怕金眼受损失。

唱段三，五段每段两句，每句八音节(藏文版第88页)：

Shel dkar povi gangs mthav bskor dus su, 在转水晶般的白雪山时，
Seng dkar po gcig gis bskor na mdzes. 有一只白狮子来转才美丽。

Rdza khra bo edza mthav bskor dus su , 在转花花的石岩时，
Vbrong ru dmar gcig gis bskor na rgyan. 一头红角野牛来转才是好装饰。

Dgung a sngon nam vphang gcod dus su, 在飞翔在高高青天时，
Rgod thang dkar gcig gis bcad na mtho. 有一只白胸鹰才显山高峻。

Nags rgya edzong vthug po bskor dus su, 在转无边的大森林时，
Stag dmar yag gcig gis bskor na ngar. 有一只红虎才显威风。

Phyi rgya mtsho chu mthav bskor dus su, 在转汪洋大海时，
Stobs chu srin gcig gis bskor na vjigs. 有一条大鲸鱼才令人畏惧。

唱段四，三段每段五句，每句八音节(第89—90页)：

dgung a sngon mthongs ki gyu vbrug de,高高的青天上有玉龙，
sprin stug povi klong nas btsan rdzong vdzin,住在厚厚的紫云城，
skad drag po ldir nas vjigs vjigs ston, 发出猛烈吼声示威武，
lce glog zhags vphangs nas thog mdav vpgen, 抛出赤电长舌像箭锋，
brag dmar po gtor nas rgod tshang vjoms. 击碎红岩捣鹰巢。

Gangs dkar povi zur na pho thung seng, 白白雪山一角有雄狮，
Mtho gangs rivi rtse nas btsan rdzong vdzin, 住在白雪山顶守坚城，
Mgo gyu ral gsig pas vjigs vjigs ston, 头披玉发示威武，

Skad nga rovi gdangs kyis sa gsum vdar，猛烈吼声大地动，
So mche sder bgrad nas gcan gzan za. 张牙舞爪食猛兽。

Rdza mthon povi vgrim pavi bre se vbrong，高高的花石山上有野牛，
Rdza mthon povi rtse nas btsan rdzong vdzin，住在花石山顶守坚城，
Rawa spang la brdar nas du ba vphyur，角磨草山起烟雾，
Rawa rmig paq enon pos vjigs vjigs ston，角利蹄坚显威风，
Dgra gar byung thal kar phug nas gsod. 敌人出现即丧生。

唱段五，五段每段四句，每句七音节(藏文版第 134—135 页)：

Dkar povi phyogs kyi spav rtsal de，白方英勇大力士，
Dgra lhavi dung mkhar nang na rgyal，在保护神白螺城中得胜利，
Nags povi phyong kyi bdud rigs de，黑方一切众妖魔，
Ngam yul sa mkhar nang du pham. 在昂地魔城败到底。

Mkhav lding bya khyung dmar po de，红色空翔大鹏鸟，
Ri rab lhun povi rtse na rgyal，在须弥山顶得胜利，
Gnyis skyes gdug pavi sbrul nag de，两栖动物黑毒蛇，
Pha nag mchin pavi gting na pham. 在黑黑深处败到底。

Rtsal ldan seng ge gyu ras can，有力的绿鬃白狮子，
Gang ri dkar povi etse na rgyal，在白雪山顶得胜利，
Gshog sgro zad pavi ltas ngan go，两翅无力的猫头鹰，
Khog rul shing gi khong na pham. 在枯树中间败到底。

Rgya stag vdzum khravi ri mo can，笑纹斑斓的花老虎，
Tsan dan nags kyi dkyil na rgyal，在檀香林中得胜利，
Khab ltar spu gzengs sgang chung de，皮毛针一样的硬刺猬，
Chu nag vkhyags pavi vgram na pham. 在冰冻黑水旁败到底。

Rdzu vphrul bu egod seng chen nga, 神变小伙格萨尔王我，

Mgo nag mi yi yul na rgyal, 在黑头人地方得胜利，

Bdud blon khyi nag srog rtsa de, 魔大臣牧羊老黑狗，

Mi gtsang vdam gyi khrod na gcod. 在肮脏泥潭里败到底。

附录二

藏文《降伏妖魔》第33—36页：

Rtsis len rtsis sprod de ring byed, 今天我要交国事，

Chung ma vbrug mo rtsis len mdzod, 珠牡妃子来接受。

Phyi kha dog sna mang gos mdzod yod, 我外有各色绸缎宝，

Nang vdod vbyung nor buvi lcags kyu yod, 内有如意珠宝钩，

Ngas bcol dus kha tshang cha tshang sprod, 交付时我要全交付，

Tshur len dus sprod rgyu yod ni gyis。收回时也要全数收。

Cha ma bcu sum rtsis len mdzod, 库存沱茶十三垛，

Phyi mu tig gyu byur sgrom gyi mdzod, 外有珍珠、松石、玛瑙库，

Nang rgya cha bzhir brtsigs pavi mdod, 还有四方汉茶堆满库，

Ngas bcol dus kha tshang cha tshang yin, 交付时我要全交付，

Phyir len dus sprod rgyu yod ni gyis。日后收回时也要全数收。

Mkhar mthon po seng vbrug stag rtse bcas, 高高的狮龙虎官殿，

Gling dkar povi lha mkhar drug po rnams, 另有白岭神城共六座，

Phyi phreng rdog tsam zhig vthor ba med, 要外不散失如念珠，

Nang sgong shun tsam shig lhung ba med, 内不打破如蛋壳，

Ngas bcod dus a vgrig cha vgrig yin, 交付时完好来交付，

Tshur len dus sprod rgyu yod ni gyis。收回时也要原样收。

Mdzod bar mavi phug gi yang phug na, 在中仓库的最后边，

Gser bzang thub pa rang byon dang, 有黄金自现的释迦像，

Gyu yi sgrol ma sngon mo dang, 有碧玉雕成的绿度母，

Dung gi thugs rje chen po yod, 有白螺做成的观音像，

Ngas bcol dus kha tshang cha tshang yin, 我交付时完全来交付，

Tshur len dus sprod rgyu yod ni gyis。收回时也要全数收。

Mdzod gong mavi phug gi yang phug na, 在上仓库的最后边，

Byu ruvi tshe dpag med mgon dang, 有珊瑚做成的无量寿，

Gdugs dkar rin chen rgyal mtshan dang, 更有白伞盖和宝幢，

Khrim mdung dar khra phyug mo dang, 有法矛达叉曲莫，

Chos dung lha rten dkar po dang, 有法螺拉丹尕波，

Tham ka nor bu vod vbar yod, 有放光国玺稀世宝，

Ngas bcol dus gtsang ma yang ma yin, 交付时完全来交付，

Tshur len dus sprod rgyu yod ni gyis。收回时也要全数收。

Mdzod vgab mavi phug gi yang phug na, 秘密库的最里边，

Zas vbras dkar spungsbavi shel gar dang, 有盛白饭用的水晶碗，

Gser bum chung bdud rtsi vkhyil ba dang, 有盛甘露的小金瓶，

Dbyig stag sgam rnam sras bang mdzod yod,有多闻天王的宝虎箱，

Ngas bcol dus kha tshang cha tshang yin, 交付时完全来交付，

Tshur len dus sprod rgyu yod ni gyis。收回时也要全数收。

Cha mkhar yang steng lha kang na,在茶城上边的神殿里，

Vdod dgu gter gyi bum bzang yod, 有随欲即得的好宝瓶，

Gser dngul rin chen mtshal snag gis, 用金粉、银粉、朱砂粉，

Bzheng bavi bkav vgyur bstan vgyur dang, 写就的甘珠尔、丹珠尔大藏经，

Chos srid gter sgrom sna tshogs yod, 装满各种政文、教令的百宝箱，

Ngas bcol dus kha tshang cha tshang yin, 交付时完全来交付，

Tshur len dus kha tshang yod ni gyis。收回时也要全数收。

Gyas lung dang po rta yi rdzong, 左边沟口是马场，

Gyon lung dang po nor gyi rdzong,右边沟口是牛场，

Bar lung gyang dkar lug gi edzong, 中间沟口是羊场，

Ngas bcol dus grangs ka tshang mo yin，交付时全数来交付，
Tshur len dus sprod rgyu yod ni gyis。收回时也要全数收。

Gling bra chen thang shom gong dgu de，岭国塘雄巩谷大帐篷，
Mi la las bsam vgrub vkhyil ba zer，人叫心想事成大帐篷，
Mi la las khyung gshog lding ba zer，也叫大鹏展翅飞翔帐，
Spra khyon thag phur ba cha tshang yin，所有的帐绳与帐橛，
Phyi nang bar gsum yo byad rnams，内外中用具一件件，
Ngas bcol dus kha tshang cha tshang yin，交付时全部来交付，
Tshur len dus sprod rgyu yod ni gyis。收回时也要全数收。

《格萨尔王传》史诗在西藏的传播特点

李连荣

摘　要　本文试图探讨藏族史诗的传播问题。流传区和传播形式的研究是解决该史诗流变问题之关键所在。文章首先从敦煌文献中寻找史诗中提到的有关氏族的传说和历史,认证史诗的传播区域;其次,将史诗的演唱传统与西藏的其他演唱传统进行比较,从而认识史诗的传播特点;最后,从史诗主体结构的形成,说明史诗传播地区与传播形态扩大化的原因。作者从上述三个方面进行分析,试图说明史诗在西藏南部缺乏演唱形态的原因。

关键词　《格萨尔王传》,表演传统,传播

一、问题的背景与探讨思路

新世纪之初,关于《格萨尔王传》史诗传承和传播区的问题,又成为我国《格萨尔王传》史诗研究领域中的新话题。这与我国《格萨尔王传》研究的自身规律有关,还与当前我国开发西部的现状有关。尤其是 2002 年联合国教科文组织将这部史诗列为 2002—2003 周年纪念项目后,我国开展非物质文化遗产的保护行动和西部地区借文化求发展的需要结合起来,客观上推动了这个研究课题的进程。①

从 20 世纪 40 年代起我国学者就开始关注这个问题,有人提出了史诗起源和流传于西藏东部的看法,甚至推测史诗在卫藏地区不能传承的原因是受到黄教的

---

① 2002 年一系列庆祝和纪念《格萨尔王传》史诗活动是明显的例证,它们引起了各种媒体的广泛关注。最引人注目的一条消息是"专家学者已经确定东部藏区为史诗的发祥地"。

限制。① 到80年代,关于它的讨论异常热烈,人们最终赞同史诗从东部起源并向四方传播开。② 近年来新一代《格萨尔王传》研究者也将目光集中到目前仍然传唱史诗的东部藏区。得出的结论概括起来有以下三点:(1)格萨尔王是历史人物,生活在藏历纪年的第一个绕迥(即11世纪);(2)《格萨尔王传》史诗传承于东部藏区;(3)关于史诗的产生年代:一种认为是11世纪;一种认为在吐蕃时期甚至更早。③

2002年8月,我进入藏族主要居住区西藏④ 进行调查、了解《格萨尔王传》史诗的抢救和搜集状况。经过一段时间,我发现了一个有趣的现象:概而言之,以北纬30度为界,西藏的南北生产生活模式有明显差异,即北部为以牧业为主的生产生活模式,而南部则为以农业为主兼顾林业的生产生活模式。与此同时,演唱形态的《格萨尔王传》史诗也只流传和分布在北部地带,特别是现今的昌都、那曲和阿里三个行政区。那么南部,尤其作为藏族文化摇篮的雅鲁藏布江流域即今天的山南、日喀则和林芝地区,也包括拉萨市在内,为什么没有《格萨尔王传》史诗的演唱呢? 除了演唱形式外,在南部还有其他形式的传承和传播吗?

实际上这不是什么新发现,而应该是整个《格萨尔王传》研究学界早已熟知的情况。⑤只不过人们已经习惯于这样一种说法,即这部史诗是一部广泛流传在整个藏族居住区,乃至北至西伯利亚、南至珠峰周边、西至喀什米尔、东至我国西南诸民族等广大地区的中亚史诗。

这种说法在一定程度上掩盖或忽略了史诗主要流传区和主要流传形式的细微

---

① 参见任乃强《〈蛮三国〉的初步介绍》,《边政公论》1944年第4卷第4、5、6期;徐国琼:《藏族史诗〈格萨尔王传〉》,北京:《文学评论》1959年第6期。
② 参见王沂暖《藏族的〈格萨尔王传〉史诗》;降边嘉措《〈格萨尔王传〉初探》;杨恩洪《略论〈格萨尔王传〉的流传》。
③ 参见洛哲加措《〈格萨尔王传〉遗迹传说》(藏文);角巴东主、旦正《〈格萨尔王传〉新论》(藏文);保罗《岭国早期地理及其相关历史问题新探》;尊胜《〈格萨尔王传〉史诗的源头及其历史内涵》;尊胜《坚持唯物史观 深化〈格萨尔王传〉研究》。
④ 文中凡提到"西藏"一词均指现行的行政区划。
⑤ 对于史诗流传区的探寻,自从这部史诗被国外学者"发现"以来,就一直被想当然地与史诗的起源、形成等一系列的问题纠合在一起。从最早(18世纪末)介绍到国外学界的蒙语和蒙文本《格萨尔王传》史诗,到20世纪初弗兰克在拉达克地区记录了这部史诗的藏语本,以及30年代达维-尼尔和庸登喇嘛记录了西藏东部康区流传的比较完整的《格萨尔王传》史诗,再到策·达木丁苏荣《〈格萨尔王传〉史诗的历史源流》(俄文,莫斯科,1957年)和石泰安《西藏史诗与说唱艺人的研究》(法文,巴黎,1959年)的出版。国外学者的认识逐渐趋于一致:史诗主要流传区或起源地为西藏地区,尤其是西藏的东部地区。最近的探讨更有代表性:

差别。我认为考察史诗的主要流传区和流传形式是解决史诗传承、发展的关键所在,是我们解析藏族文化组成结构的关键所在,同时也是找到西藏南部不演唱这部史诗的根源所在。

由于本人"发现"西藏南部——藏族文化的发祥地并不传唱史诗的现状后,我也被引回到关注史诗的传承和传播这一"古老"问题上来。在这里我不准备讨论史诗的产生和形成等问题。史诗的产生和形成是一个非常复杂的问题,我们不能像瞎子摸象一样只就史诗中的某一点或某一部历史文献来确定。我国在五六十年代的热闹争执中,已有学者指出要综合考虑此问题,并认为它是在其他问题的研究取得一定成果的基础上才能去考虑的问题。①

学者确定史诗流传区的基本依据来自两个方面:(1)有关史诗或史诗主人公的后期文献;(2)依据史诗中提到的地望、族群等内容。另外,在一些学者的文章中也指出了演唱艺人在其中的作用,但对艺人与传承区的关系似乎并没有给予足够的注意。

根据上述的研究成果,我觉得我们现在关注这个课题,应该在思路上有所改变,需要从三个方面入手进行考察,以求能够带来新的认识:首先,应该将敦煌文献作为具有一定历史真实性的材料(而不是从后期文献中寻找它的历史根源),从中寻找史诗中提到的氏族的传说和历史,进而查找史诗的主要传播区域和路线;其次,将史诗的演唱传统与西藏的其他演唱传统进行比较,找到史诗演唱传统的特点及其传播特点;最后,应该从史诗的内容结构出发,找到史诗中神话与氏族之间的联系,同时从史诗主体结构的形成说明史诗传承和传播地区与传播形态扩大化的原因。从以上三个方面进行分析,或许能使我们发现史诗在西藏南部没有演唱形态的原因。但限于篇幅,本文仅将史诗的演唱传统与西藏的其他的演唱传统进行比较,就此问题作一次尝试探讨。

(接上页)参见萨缪尔(Geoffrey Samuel),"The Gesar Epic of East Tibet," *Tibetan Literature*:*Studies in Genre*, Ed. by Jose Ignacia Cabezon and Roger R. Jackson, New York, Snow Lion Publications of USA,1996.pp.358—367;卡尔梅·桑木旦《〈格萨尔王传〉:藏族人民的史诗传统》,"Study on the History, Myth and Ritual of Tibet," *The Arrow and Spindle*, By Karmay Samten Gentsen. Kathmandu, Mandala Book Point, 1998 年. p.465。

① 黄静涛:《〈格萨尔王传〉四——霍岭大战(上)》"序言"。

二、演唱传统与史诗传播

普罗普在讨论史诗的一般特点时说:"音乐、演唱表演对史诗来说如此重要,以至于对这些作品而言,不唱就意味着没有史诗的品质。"[①]演唱是史诗的生命,因此,史诗的音乐构成了史诗不可分割的重要部分。那么,西藏南部没有演唱形态的《格萨尔王传》史诗的存在说明了什么呢?

(一)引子

每个民族的演唱传统均有自己的特点,这种特点不是一下子形成的,而且至今仍处在不断的变化之中。但是有一点我们必须承认,就像人类和其他生物均有自己独特的基因组一样,民族的文化也有自己一些稳固的基因组。说到藏族演唱传统的基因组,我认为由于藏族文化和历史形成的繁杂性,因此在其基因组中既有共同的东西,也有差异的东西,或者说在共同的基因组下面,仍有许多地方文化基因组的存在。但现在看来,由于长久的历史文化的混合,这种共同的东西所占比例要大得多。

藏族文化主要由四大或六大氏族部落文化组合而成,[②] 当然青藏高原上的古氏族绝不仅仅是这六大氏族。有学者认为,藏族的文化和演唱有三千多年的历史。他所依据的资料是组成藏族文化的两个主要氏族的历史:雅砻王统和象雄王统。[③]那么其他四个氏族就没有文化和演唱,乃至没有历史吗? 而文献资料在这一点上却并没有显得那么沉默。因此,我认为认识西藏的文化应该扩大视野,而不应该仅限于冈底斯雪山周围及雅鲁藏布江流域。

以下就史诗中出现的英雄和其氏族属于藏族历史上的四大或六大氏族之一的"董"(Ldong)氏族,试作一点介绍。"董"氏族的记载最早出现在敦煌藏文文献中,

---

[①] Vladimir Propp, *Theory and History of Folklore*, ed. by Anatoly Liberman, trans. Ariadna Y. Martin &Richatd P. Martin, Minneapolis: University of Minnesota Press, 1993. p. 150.

[②] 关于四大或六大氏族有多种不同说法,一般认为四氏族为:塞(se)、木(rmu)、董(ldong)、东(stong),再加上扎(dbra)和珠(adru),就成了六氏族。参见南卡诺布《藏族远古史》(藏文),第121页。

[③] 雪康·索南达杰认为,西藏悉普野王统的第一代国王聂赤赞普已经有2100年的历史,而象雄王统十八代就有800多年的历史(雪康·索南达杰1992:48)。

据目前所能见到的敦煌文献来看,记载"董"氏族的文献是 P.T.1287。在此文献的第四段讲到赤论赞(khri slon btsan)征服了北方的森波杰(zing po rje)后,占领了相当广阔的地域。并下令将森波杰所在的"岩波"(ngas po)改名为"彭域"(vphan yul)。①接着文献讲到了赞普大宴群臣,席间琼保邦赛(khyung po spung sad)唱了一首歌,其中鼓吹了自己的功勋,并说:"洛族和埃族被彭所压服,色族和琼族被彭所安置。"(Lho rngegs ni vphan gyi snon, se khyung ni vphan gyis btab.)②唱毕后,赞普希望大臣洛埃两族能够出来应对,但是谁也没有出来。这时候尚囊白乌苏正波(zhang snang pe vu zur vbreng po)经赞普要求也唱了一首歌。歌中赞美了对征服森波杰有功的娘氏(myang)和韦氏(dbavs)功臣以及雅砻部落的雄强,并说:"洛族和埃族被彭所压服,董族和东族被彭所安置。"(Lho rngegs ni vphan gyi snon, ldong tong ni vphan gyis btab.)③而在另一段有关嫁到象雄的松赞干布(srong btsan sgam po)妹妹的唱词中说:"哎!北方的牧区有一头野牦牛,它是一头种公牛,若要杀死北方的这头野牦牛,上谷脑里要有人大声喊呀,董和东乃是彭所征服,从下谷口摇旗招集者,畿曲河的夏和布,从中心地区投石者,雅砻的洛和埃……"(Kye byang vbrog ni ya bi na, pho mvi ni gchig pa, byang vbrog ni vbrong dgum na, pu nas ni kus vdebs pav, ldong thong ni vpan gyis thob, mdav nas ni gyab vdor ba, skyivi ni sha dangs spug, dbus nas ni dpor vphen ba, yar gyi ni lho dang rngegs……)④这些唱词的"作者"大约是六七世纪的人,但唱词所反映的内容并不完全是当时的情况。实际上这些"历史"就是雅砻部落逐渐兴盛、发达起来的历史,其中带着浓厚的传说性质和诸多隐喻。

松赞妹妹的唱词从整体上看,是鼓舞士气、树立雄心,希望赞普像征服北方野牦牛部落那样,再次征服象雄的麋鹿和野马部落。就像麦克唐纳所说那样,用猎获野牦牛的办法去征服象雄。但我认为这里的野牦牛更可能指北方的董、东两部落,而不是隐喻象雄部落。从当时文献的比喻和后期文献中可见,一般均将冈底斯雪山周围看作是麋鹿和野马出没的地方,而北方则是野牦牛的故乡。因此,上述松赞妹妹的唱词,其中心意思讲的就是彭怎样征服了董和东两部落。彭指的是雅砻部

---

① 王尧、陈践:《敦煌本吐蕃历史文书》(增订本),附录2,P.I.563,第184—185行。
② 同上书,附录2,P.I.565,第227—228行。
③ 同上书,附录2,P.I.565,第239行。
④ 王尧、陈践:《敦煌本吐蕃历史文书》(增订本),附录2,P.I.573,第412—414行。上述译文参考了王尧、陈践译文与 A.麦克唐纳译文,同时请教了西藏社科院的诺布加措和关却加两位副研究员。

落,这是很多学者所赞同的。那么董、东两部落的地理位置在哪里呢? 很多人认为也在雅砻地区,但是从上述的歌词中可以看到,他们更可能是在畿曲河(拉萨河)的上游,那就是念青唐古拉山周围地区或唐古拉山地区。也就是说在北方广阔的羌塘草原上有两个强大的部落:董和东。他们应该是号称野牦牛部落的氏族。这样一来,这种推测刚好吻合了上述尚囊的唱词:"唐古拉山山巅被削平了,并垫在了香波山山基;域那堡寨已被征服,成为了琼瓦的补充。"(Thang la ni rtse bchad ching, sham po ni rmed duva bsnan,yu sna vi ni mkhar pab,pying ba vi ni snon du bgyis.)① 因此,学界一般认为居于年噶尔(nyen kar)的森波杰·达嘉沃(stag ska bo)和居于域那(yu sna)的森波杰·赤邦松(khri pangs sum)② 均为苏毗(孙波 sum pa)的部落。③ 但是也有人认为这种观点值得商榷。不管怎样,可以确定的是董、东两部落就是在唐古拉山附近游牧的部落,并且被雅砻部落征服。因为从文献来看,当赤伦赞征服森波杰后,森波杰逃向了更北方的祝古(dru gru)地区。由此可见,一方面森波杰和祝古关系密切,另一方面还可看到在雅砻视野中的北方是一个广阔的地域,可能包括了今天的昆仑山南北。

也有一些学者认为,汉文文献中提到的"党项"对应藏文文献就是"董羌"或"董项"。④ 这种观点有一定的道理。但我认为"党项"一词并不是依据后期康巴人的称呼,而应该来自吐蕃时代甚或更早一些。从赤伦赞时期的尚囊的唱词来看,雅砻部落征服董、东两部落可能指的就是对森波杰的胜利。新旧《唐书》在《西域传》中,将"党项"列在比较重要的位置,又说:"汉西羌别种,魏、晋后微甚。周灭宕昌、邓至,而党项始疆。其地古析支也,东距松洲,西叶护,南春桑、米桑等羌,北吐谷浑。"⑤ 更早一些的《北史》和《隋书》中的《党项传》说:"党项羌者,三苗之后也,其种有宕昌、白狼,皆自称猕猴种。"从上述记载来看,党项活动的范围最早与昆仑山、析支水有关。也就是说他以昆仑山为其西部出发点(甚至新疆地区的叶护),北距吐谷浑(环青海湖地区以及青海湖东北部),南至唐古拉山或念青唐古拉山(唐古拉山以

---

① A.麦克唐纳(Macdonald, Ariane)著,耿昇译《敦煌吐蕃历史文书考释》,第71页。这段原文没有收录在王尧、陈践的《敦煌本吐蕃历史文书》中。

② 王尧、陈践:《敦煌本吐蕃历史文书》(增订本),附录2,P.I.561,第118—119行。

③ 同上书,第188页注68;宗喀·杨正刚布:《苏毗与吐蕃及其他临近政权的关系》,第51页。

④ 南卡诺布认为,"董项"一词是康巴人对他们北部的"董巴"人的称呼。这与卫藏地区称"董羌"在发音上有所不同,而汉族史书则依此称"董巴"为"党项羌"。参见南卡诺布:《藏族远古史》(藏文),第127页。

⑤ 欧阳修、宋祁:《新唐书》卷一二一《西域·党项上》。

南,念青唐拉以北的东西走向的那学[Nag shod]走廊或那曲河流域可能是东·苏毗的部落在游牧),然后沿通天河、析支河(黄河上游)向东游牧,一直绵延到松潘。最后在玛域(即果洛)具有了一定的实力,并且兴盛起来。后来其中的一部继续沿玛曲河(黄河)东上建立了西夏王朝。[①] 甚至也有可能它曾向西游牧与阿里的象雄文化发生了关系,如敦煌文献中出现的野马和野牦牛的战争,[②] 在一定程度上具有两个部落之间的隐喻意义。

在整个藏族居住区内,冈底斯雪山、玛旁雍措湖是象雄文化的代表,雅拉香波山、雅鲁藏布江是雅砻文化的代表,而唐古拉山则是董、东两部落文化的标志等。我们相信董、东两部落具有与雅砻、象雄一样悠久的演唱传统。如果能够将董、党项、木雅的演唱传统和《格萨尔王传》史诗的演唱直接进行比较,就可以解决有关史诗的诸多问题。但是,目前我们所能见到的关于这两氏族的纯粹的古代文献资料却少之又少。我们只能对以记载雅砻部落为主的文献以及演唱传统进行分析。当然,这些文献中必然也有董、东两部落的演唱传统所作出的贡献。

(二)西藏的演唱传统

早期雅砻部落时代,施政方面主要依靠"仲(sgrung)、弟吴(ldevu)和本(bon)"[③],其中并没有提到"歌"。而从文学的发展规律来看,"歌"往往是走在最前面的品种。因此,我认为上述三种的表达方式肯定是"歌"的形式,或者是"歌和白"相结合的形式。实际上从后期有关上述三者的记载来看,基本上均具有"歌"的特点。"仲"中有"歌"有"白",包括《格萨尔王传》史诗在内的史诗(故事)传统;"弟吴"据说有点像谜语歌,总结人生经验的积累;而"本"的表达形式也具有"歌"的特点——念诵,它是早期的宗教信仰。因此,可以说"歌"是普遍运用在了各个方面。

除了上述三者具有"歌"的形式以外,在记载雅砻—吐蕃王朝的敦煌文献中,除了记述活动外,人物的对话基本上是大量地运用了演唱的方式,即以"歌尔鲁"

---

① 在后期藏文文献中均将"董"和"弥药"联系在一起,称弥药是董的一个部落。建立西夏国的党项是其中的木雅部,汉文献称之为"弥药"。在西夏演唱祖先歌的《颂祖先诗》也将故土追到了弥药,如《夏圣根赞歌》中唱到:"黔首石城漠水边,赤面父冢白河上,高弥药国在彼方。"参见白滨《党项史研究》,长春:吉林教育出版社,1989 年,第 89—90 页。这也是归属吐蕃的一部,"地乃入吐蕃,其处皆为吐蕃役属,更号弥药"。参见欧阳修、宋祁:新唐书》卷一二一《西域·党项上》。

② 参见托马斯著,李有义、王青山译《东北藏古代民间文学》第一章。

③ 巴俄·祖拉陈瓦:《智者喜筵》(藏文),第 165 页。

(mgur glu)的形式表达。据学者端智加研究,"歌尔"(mgur)和"鲁"(glu)最初是原始社会民众的创作,但它也与宗教有密切的关系,由于赞颂各种神祉就要用"歌尔鲁"来表达,因此"歌尔鲁"也有自己的"歌神"。[①]"歌尔鲁"最初发源于雅砻地区,那时"歌尔"、"鲁"和"奇"(mchid)的含义基本一致,到了后期由于宗教人士为了宣传宗教的需要,将这些民歌进行了加工,由此"歌尔"和"鲁"的含义发生了变化。"歌尔"成了"鲁"的敬称,而且"歌尔"成为了宗教界专用的"歌",特别是经噶举派的玛尔巴和米拉日巴的加工和广泛运用后,"歌尔"的宗教性得以确立。而"鲁"则依旧在民间广泛运用,代表了民歌。他同时分析指出,后期民歌的发展发生了分化:(1)卫藏中心地区传承着六言四句一段体的"谐"(gzhas)和六言四句对歌体的"册甲"(tshig rgyag);(2)多麦地区传承着八言四句三段体的"鲁"和八言四句对歌体的"鲁霞"(glu shags);(3)多康地区传承着七或八言四句两段体的表达男女爱情的"拉叶"(la gzhas)。[②]

敦煌文献中的"歌尔鲁"和后期卫藏地区的"谐"体民歌之间有密切关系。从字数上来看两者一致,而且节奏和表达方式也比较相似。但与多麦和多康地区的"鲁"体等民歌的距离就比较远一些。造成这种差异的原因,很可能是它们具有不同氏族的文化源头。多麦和多康地区的民歌固然和卫藏地区的民歌有千丝万缕的联系,毕竟在吐蕃时期已经经过了几百年甚至上千年的文化互动。但是就像上面提到的民族文化的基因组一样,两者在根本上有质的差异。民歌虽然始终在发展着,字句在不断变化,但它是一个民族心律波动的体现,其中的节奏、字数和韵律是其外在表现的关键形式,如同源自民歌的汉族古诗的五言和七言、绝句和律诗代表着汉民族的文化心律一样。因此它最终将会形成一种适应其表现的比较稳定的结构,即表现其民族心律的结构。我们可以推测,卫藏地区广泛流传的"谐"体民歌演唱更多地继承了雅砻王统的节奏和表达方式,是其部落心律结构的体现,甚至可以说是一种农业文化的典型表现;而多麦和多康地区的民歌则更多的是游牧的董、东两部落的心律的写照。这些稳定的成分就是组成我们文化的基因组。从这方面也可以说,藏族文化具有多元的特色。

西藏境内代表性的两种民歌传统的"谐"体民歌和"鲁"体民歌的分布状况如下:"鲁"体民歌明显地占据了北部牧业区的广阔天地,如"山歌"、"果卓"等;"谐"体

---

① 端智加:《道歌源流》(藏文),第9—11页。
② 同上书,第一章。

形式的多种民歌如"谐青"、"果谐"、"囊玛"、"堆谐"、"酒歌"等基本上分布在拉萨及其以南的广大农业区。①这也恰好说明了西藏地区不同的生产生活方式与相应的文化特点:北部是以牧业为主的生产生活方式,演唱着"鲁"体民歌;南部则是以农业为主的生产生活方式,演唱着"谐"体民歌。

(三)《格萨尔王传》史诗在西藏的流传特点

学者们已经指出,《格萨尔王传》史诗的演唱基础是"鲁"体民歌。我们上面已经说过,"鲁"体民歌是北部游牧部落中传承的民歌。这也与《格萨尔王传》史诗至今传唱于游牧部落地区的事实相一致。

从演唱形态的史诗在整个藏区的传承和传播情况来看,刚好印证了我们上面所说的史诗在北部乃至多麦和多康地区传唱的分析,这些地区同样也是"鲁"体民歌最为盛行的地区。以唐古拉山和念青唐古拉山为中心(特别是沿唐古拉山山脉的走向),形成了演唱史诗的一个东西走廊,这也和我们上面提到的董、东两部落游牧的路线图基本吻合,特别与董部落的游牧图和向东的发展路线图吻合。从念青唐古拉山和唐古拉山口出发,向东一直到今青海省玉树县的三江源碑附近分成两路,一路沿金沙江南下,一路沿玛曲河北上直到今天的宁夏境内。向西则沿开阔的昆仑山山脉和冈底斯雪山山脉之间的羌塘草原,直到巴尔蒂人居住的拉达克境内。这部史诗在整个流布区域的演唱形态的生存图,基本上是我们现今的调查资料所证实的。同时这也说明我们上面关于董、东两部落及其演唱传统的推测具有一定的合理性。

从这部史诗的演唱艺人在现今西藏境内的分布情况来看,其特点也很明显,同样在北部游牧地区传承着演唱形式的《格萨尔王传》史诗,在北部的唐古拉山山脉和南部的念青唐古拉山脉之间的游牧走廊上(再向西延伸就是昆仑山山脉和冈底斯山脉之间),广泛地分布着演唱这部伟大史诗的民间艺人。目前了解到的能够完

---

① 据中国歌谣集成·西藏卷组委会编《中国歌谣集成·西藏卷》,它将西藏现行民歌分为了12种:果谐、谐青、果卓、热巴舞、囊玛、堆谐、酒歌、山歌(情歌)、儿歌、生活歌、劳动歌、《格萨尔王传》史诗及说唱。需要补充说明的是:(1)"果谐"和"果卓"形式的民歌,是典型的藏族文化中的"歌、舞、乐"三者统一的艺术。这种艺术可能是青藏高原上所有氏族共享的艺术门类(包括后来东迁已经成为其他的民族)。从北部的吐谷浑人的后代即现在的土族到西南部的纳西、羌、普米等诸多民族都有相同的传承。但在演唱的"歌"方面,就像西藏南北有明显的差异一样,这些民族均按自己的民歌特点进行着发挥。(2)关于"鲁"体民歌和"谐"体民歌之间的许多差异,在本书中有更多的论述,可参阅本书"前言"。

整演唱 10 部以上史诗的民间艺人有 40 多位,^① 其中能够演唱 40 部以上史诗的著名民间艺人基本上来自昌都边巴县(扎巴)、丁青县(桑珠)和那曲索县(玉梅、曲扎)等地,这正是从古至今董、东两部落氏族最为活跃的地区。

《格萨尔王传》史诗除了演唱形式传承和传播以外,在西藏也有别的传承和传播方式,比如风物遗迹、传说、舞蹈、民歌等。需要说明的两点是:首先,除演唱以外的上述其他流传形式广泛分布在西藏全境。其次,"传说"、"风物遗迹"这种传播形式仍然在北部游牧地区占有较大的比重。史诗在西藏的传承和传播是多方面的,但作为史诗主要流传形式的演唱却仅仅在北部地区广泛流传,南部地区虽然也有史诗的流传,但在流传形态上却明显发生了本质的变化。因此,从这些现象我们同样可以肯定北部游牧地区是史诗最早的传承和传播地区,而南部地区则是后来的传承和传播区。

另外,就史诗本身的音乐特色来看,虽然我们在后期文献记录中可以看到,吐蕃王朝时期为庆祝桑耶寺竣工,从国王到佛教论师、译师再到王后、王子、大臣,都演唱了代表各自身份的具有调名的歌。有人指出这种调名很像《格萨尔王传》史诗中的各种人物的演唱调名,并依此来断定史诗产生年代等有关问题。^②这些推测是值得商榷的,首先这些记载发现在史诗已经广泛传播开来的 14 世纪及之后,它们之间有互相借用的可能性;再者,即便在早期存在这些调名,也正像一些研究者所说的似乎仅仅是用来表达感情的一个唱腔,并没有一种独特的曲牌之类的东西。^③特别是近年来经过对安多地区和康巴地区史诗演唱特色的研究,学者们指出《格萨尔王传》的演唱曲调特征是由一个基本曲式结构数次或无限反复的方式来进行。比较固定的结构形式是乐句乐段结构的单一部曲式。它是由上下乐句相互对比、

---

① 次旺俊美:《西藏〈格萨尔王传〉抢救工作及其研究前瞻概述》。

② 参见边多有关史诗音乐的论著:《当代西藏乐论》;《浅谈〈格萨尔王传〉说唱音乐艺术》。他在这些论文中引用并指出了《五部遗教·后妃遗教》中桑耶寺建成后唱的 13 调名与《西藏王统记》中的 20 个调名,并在《格萨尔王传·赛马称王》中发现了 50 多个调名等。

③ M.艾尔费说:"对《赛马篇》中出现的曲名提出了一些解释,虽然藏人自己也提供了一些注解,但仍然晦涩难解……"参见 M.艾尔费《藏族〈格萨尔王传·赛马篇〉的歌曲研究》,第 3565 页。马成富认为,所谓的演唱史诗的曲牌是不存在的,即史诗没有像戏剧那样固定的曲牌,它只是一些表达感情的形容词,但史诗的唱腔确实是史诗演唱中的主要特点。起初它可能只是语言音调高度夸张近似吟诵的强调,甚至只有一个乐句。它的独特之处在于,无论唱腔如何变化,总突不破《格萨尔王传》唱腔的基本结构形态,即"鲁阿拉拉莫阿拉岭"与"鲁塔拉拉莫拉拉岭"所起的作用。参见马成富《〈格萨尔王传〉史诗唱腔音乐探秘》,第 30—31 页。

应答、补充达到共同完成音乐内容的结构整体。其音乐唱腔原始,音程由四个音符作一度上下级进,只有三小节末尾与四小节第一个音为三度音,属于典型的吟诵腔。[①]

综上所述,西藏的演唱传统中史诗具有藏区北部游牧文化的典型特征,乃至于这种以北部民歌为基础形成的演唱传统,由于民族心律或文化特征的差异,在史诗向南部传播时受到了限制,并不能在南部的田野上广泛普及,而只能以其内容在这里悄悄地滋长,因而在传播形式上发生了变化。

三、小结

现在我们回到最初的疑问上,我提出这个问题的初衷只是希望通过对藏族文献和现状的调查,得到一个简单的回答。但是随着翻检毫无头绪的历史文献和种种弥漫着各种偏见的宗教"源流",我越来越发现这个问题牵扯到许多问题,而且这些问题被前人编织的美丽"神话"掩盖了起来,甚至当代人也不愿意揭开明明已经暴露出来的事实真相。就拿藏族文化的多元起源或多元组成来说,它直接联系着过去我们对藏族起源的争论:北来说—羌族起源说与南来说—印度起源说,最后大家比较一致认可的是雅砻地区起源说等。这些讨论或文献记载夹杂着许多学术以外或客观事实以外的各种感情。同样在藏族文化的起源上,也明显地编制了美丽的"猴子生六族"的神话。在后期文献中提到的所谓四族或六族的论点,不一定形成于吐蕃时代,而更可能是在由分裂走向统一的9—12世纪的文化重建中(这种将原始氏族家族化的做法同样可见于佛教文献《释迦谱》中"瞿昙仙人"的故事所讲的印度四个种姓的来历)形成的,这也隐约地指出了藏族文化的多元起源观。因此只将雅砻河谷的王统作为藏族文化的历史原点,这怎么可能覆盖整个青藏高原上的藏族文化呢? 所以,我认为只有将敦煌文献的记载仔细地研究,并以后期文献(苯教与佛教)作为参照,加上汉文献和其他民族文献特别是那些从青藏高原上迁移出去的民族的神话传说,再结合考古发现,我们或许才能较清楚地了解藏族文化的源头以及青藏高原上的早期文化史。

具体说到雅砻地区不演唱《格萨尔王传》史诗的问题,似乎在许多学者尤其是

---

① 参见张春梅:《安多〈格萨尔王传〉说唱音乐的单一部曲式结构》;马成富:《〈格萨尔王传〉史诗唱腔音乐探秘》。

那些靠藏文献分析的学者看来,这是一个毫无价值甚至有点幼稚的问题。很多情况下个中原因在于他们很不情愿打破雅砻王统以及宗教信仰所制造的种种"神话"。在我看来这近似民族的狭隘主义了。比如石泰安对于"格萨尔王"一名的外来说,我们学界就采取了极端的否定态度,事实上我们也没有找到什么充分的理由来驳斥这种观点,仅仅是由于受到了某种民族主义情绪的左右,甚或一些学者更大的问题可能在于眼界所限。

现在从藏族文献记载来看,"格萨尔王"这个称号或许就是来自拂林的恺撒,这从文献记载上进行对比是有一定的相似性的,或者岭·格萨尔王就是"格萨尔军王"、"冲木·格萨尔王"。因为从文献记载来看"董"部落在北方;汉文献说"党项"地界西至叶护,三苗后裔;拉萨河上游的森波杰失败后逃向了北方的祝古,而祝古和冲木在很多情况下指的是同一个地方——北方,甚至在后期的文献中也将"董"称为异族,① 难道这一切似乎在告诉我们,这个"格萨尔军王"、"冲木·格萨尔王"就是后来的"岭·格萨尔王",它们原来就可能是青藏高原上乃至包括新疆地区的一个能够和雅砻部落抗衡的异族部落,只不过后来被发达起来的雅砻部落所征服,因而在地界上进行了向东的迁移、改变了原来的地域或族群称呼,才从"冲木"变成了"岭"。再从语言学上做点补充的话,"冲木"一词在安多口语中除了具有市场的意思外,更多是指公羊。据有的学者考察,在新疆库车(龟兹)的许多早期壁画中可以看到公羊头的崇拜,② 而在今天安多和康巴藏区甚至在卫藏地区均有公羊头的吉祥装饰。另外,牛头的装饰也在这些地区非常盛行。因此,北方强大的格萨尔军王部落也可能与"董"氏族甚至"岭·格萨尔王"具有亲缘关系。

但是不管怎样,我提出的史诗不在雅砻部落传唱的问题,讨论了史诗所提到的"董"氏族的早期历史或传说,基本上得出了史诗中的"董"氏族是位于北方的一个强大的游牧部落。它曾被南部农业发达的雅砻部落征服和安置。如果史诗没有被后来的学者和艺人们加工得面目全非,那么史诗中的"董"部落可能就是最早传唱这部史诗的族群。它们最先开创了这部古老史诗江河之源头。也可以说,这部史诗起初的源头可能仅仅是颂扬"董"氏族祖先的英雄歌。

从西藏的演唱传统特点出发,可以发现雅砻河谷以北的游牧地区的演唱传统和敦煌文献乃至后期雅砻地区的演唱之间具有一些本质的差异。后期雅砻地区的

① [法]石泰安:《川甘青藏走廊的古部族》,第53—54页。
② 诺布加措:《语言学新探》(藏文),第45—46页。

演唱明显地继承了敦煌文献上有关吐蕃王朝的演唱特点,这就是至今仍然盛传于南部地区的"谐"体民歌以及相关的其他演唱。而北部包括多麦和多康地区则流传着以"鲁"体民歌为主的多种演唱传统,《格萨尔王传》史诗是其中的一个代表,它们明显地具有其他部族尤其是游牧部落文化的特点。由此,我更加肯定,两种演唱传统的差异在一定程度上限制了史诗演唱形式在南部地区的流传。而有关史诗的其他形式的传承和传播在南部依然清晰可见。同样的例子也可在史诗盛传的安多地区发现,在安多的农区,特别是民族交界地区,史诗则更多的不是以讲唱形式而是以口头讲述的形式存在。① 总之,史诗传播的形式或者说文化传播的形式,要比其内容的传播受到的局限更多。这从我们对西藏地区的《格萨尔王传》史诗流传地区和流传形式的考察中可见一斑。

参考书目

M.艾尔费:《藏族〈格萨尔王传·赛马篇〉的歌曲研究》,赵秉理编《格萨尔王传学研究》第5集,兰州:甘肃民族出版社,1998年。

巴俄·祖拉陈瓦:《智者喜筵》(藏文),北京:民族出版社,1986年。

保罗:《岭国早期地理及其相关历史问题新探》,拉萨:《西藏研究》1999年第4期。

白滨:《党项史研究》,长春:吉林教育出版社,1989年。

边多:《当代西藏乐论》,拉萨:西藏人民出版社,1993年。

边多:《浅谈〈格萨尔王传〉说唱音乐艺术》,《西藏研究》2002年第4期。

次旺俊美:《西藏〈格萨尔王传〉抢救工作及其研究前瞻概述》,《西藏研究》2002年4期。

端智加:《道歌源流》(藏文),北京:民族出版社,1985年。

恩格斯:《家庭、私有制和国家的起源》,北京:人民出版社,1972年。

黄静涛:《〈格萨尔王传〉四——霍岭大战(上)》,上海:上海文艺出版社,1962年。

降边嘉措:《〈格萨尔王传〉初探》,西宁:青海人民出版社,1986年。

角巴东主、旦正:《〈格萨尔王传〉新论》(藏文),西宁:青海民族出版社,1995年。

卡尔梅·桑木旦:《〈格萨尔王传〉:藏族人民的史诗传统》,原载 The Arrow and Spindle: Study on the History, Myth and Ritual of Tibet. By Karmay Samten Gentsen. Kathmandu: Mandala Book Point, 1998.

刘志群:《藏戏与藏俗》,拉萨:西藏人民出版社,石家庄:河北少儿出版社,1999年。

洛哲加措:《〈格萨尔王传〉遗迹传说》(藏文),拉萨:西藏民族出版社,1994年。

马成富:《〈格萨尔王传〉史诗唱腔音乐探秘》,《西藏艺术研究》2002年第4期。

---

① 徐国琼:《〈格萨尔王传〉考察纪实》,第60页。

A.麦克唐纳(Macdonald, Ariane):《敦煌吐蕃历史文书考释》,耿昇译,西宁:青海人民出版社,1991年。

南卡诺布:《藏族远古史》(藏文),成都:四川民族出版社,1990年。

诺布加措:《语言学新探》(藏文),北京:民族出版社,2002年。

欧阳修、宋祁:《新唐书》。

Propp, Vladimir. *Theory and History of Folklore*, ed. by Anatoly Liberman, trans. Ariadna Y. Martin & Richatd P. Martin, Minneapolis: University of Minnessota Press, 1993.

任乃强:《〈蛮三国〉的初步介绍》,《边政公论》1944年第4卷第4、5、6期。

Samuel, Geoffrey. "The Gesar Epic of East Tibet," In *Tibetan Literature*: *Studies in Genre*. Ed. by Jose Ignacia Cabezon and Roger R. Jackson. New York: Snow Lion Publications of USA, 1996.

石泰安:《西藏史诗与说唱艺人的研究》,耿昇译,拉萨:西藏人民出版社,1993年。

石泰安:《川甘青藏走廊的古部族》,耿昇译,成都:四川民族出版社,1992年。

托马斯:《东北藏古代民间文学》,李有义、王青山译,成都:四川民族出版社,1986年。

王尧、陈践:《敦煌本吐蕃历史文书》(增订本),北京:民族出版社,1992年。

王沂暖:《藏族的〈格萨尔王传〉史诗》,北京:《中央民族学院学报》1983年第1期。

徐国琼:《藏族史诗〈格萨尔王传〉》,《文学评论》1959年第6期。

徐国琼:《〈格萨尔王传〉考察纪实》,昆明:云南人民出版社,1989年。

雪康·索南达杰:《西藏音乐简史》(藏文),拉萨:西藏人民出版社,1992年。

杨恩洪:《略论〈格萨尔王传〉的流传》,《民族文学研究》1989年第5期。

杨恩洪:《民间诗神》,北京:中国藏学中心出版社,1995年。

张春梅:《安多〈格萨尔王传〉说唱音乐的单一部曲式结构》,第5届国际《格萨尔王传》学术讨论会论文,2002年。

中国歌谣集成·西藏卷组委会编《中国歌谣集成·西藏卷》,北京:中国ISBN中心,2001年。

宗喀·杨正刚布:《苏毗与吐蕃及其他临近政权的关系》,见《西藏研究》1992年第3期。

尊胜:《〈格萨尔王传〉史诗的源头及其历史内涵》,拉萨:《西藏研究》2001年第2期。

尊胜:《坚持唯物史观 深化〈格萨尔王传〉研究》,拉萨:《西藏研究》2002年第4期。

《格斯尔》与《格萨尔王传》^①

——关于三个文本的比较研究

扎拉嘎

摘 要 蒙藏两个民族中流传的《格斯（萨）尔》史诗文本，虽然具有共同的起源和故事题材，却不能因此而否定它们各自所具有的独立价值。本文拟以具有一定代表性的三种文本，藏族贵德分章本《格萨尔王传》，蒙古族北京版《格斯尔》和蒙古族琶杰本《格斯尔》进行比较研究，进而深入研究史诗的文化内涵，发现各民族史诗所寄托的独特民族精神和独特的审美理想。

关键词 《格萨（斯）尔》史诗，蒙藏文化，比较研究

在中国各民族文学关系研究中，蒙古族《格斯尔》与藏族《格萨尔王传》之间的关系，是一个引人注目课题。《格斯尔》与《格萨尔王传》，不仅主要人物相同，而且故事的基本框架也基本相同。这使人们相信，《格斯尔》与《格萨尔王传》是有同一故事起源的史诗。在《格斯（萨）尔》的流传过程中，体现出蒙藏两个民族之间存在着历史悠久的文学与文化联系。

蒙藏两个民族中流传的《格斯（萨）尔》史诗文本，虽然具有共同的起源和故事题材，却不能因此而否定它们各自所具有的独立价值。史诗是各个民族的民族精神体现。无论各个民族的史诗采取何种形式，或者在题材上出现何等相同，只要它们曾经经过每个民族民间艺人，或者文化人的创作或者再创作，它们就具有了本民族的文化内涵，它们所歌颂的就是本民族的民族精神。史诗主要人物的相同，史诗故事结构的类似，在与史诗的民族精神相比较时，都只是事物的表象。只要透过这

---

① 蒙古族史诗《格斯尔》与藏族史诗《格萨尔王传》，又合称为《格斯（萨）尔》，或者《格萨（斯）尔》。

表象,深入研究史诗的文化内涵,就会发现各民族史诗所寄托的独特民族精神和独特的审美理想。

本文拟以具有一定代表性的三种文本为主,对蒙藏《格斯(萨)尔》进行比较研究。这三种文本是:藏族贵德分章本《格萨尔王传》,蒙古族北京版《格斯尔》和蒙古族芭杰本《格斯尔》。① 藏文贵德分章本《格萨尔王传》,是一部手抄本,因最初发现于青海贵德而得名。全书共分五章。已故的著名藏学家王沂暖教授说:"根据这个分章本原文中,曾不止一次地提到西藏的黄教,可能这个本子成书于15世纪黄教创立以后。"② 蒙古文北京版《格斯尔》,又称《格斯尔可汗传》,1716年在北京木刻刊行。全书共计七章,是目前发现的《格斯尔》的最早印刷版本,在《格斯尔》传播史上具有特别重要意义。芭杰是20世纪蒙古族著名的民间艺人。他说唱的《格斯尔》,在蒙古族史诗发展史上占有重要地位,也可以认为是蒙古《格斯尔》说唱文本的代表作。芭杰是一位极富天才的语言大师。他在说唱《格斯尔》的同时,还说唱诸如《说唐五传》、《水浒传》、《三国演义》等,被称为"蒙古本子故事"的长篇叙事故事。③

一

包括贵德分章本《格萨尔王传》在内的藏文《格萨尔王传》,一个重要特点是在叙述故事时,人物对话经常采用歌唱的形式。研究者认为这是来源于戏剧的影响,并称为"史诗说唱的戏剧化倾向"④。这种戏剧化的倾向,在贵德分章本《格萨尔王传》中,是非常显著地存在的。同时,根据对其他几部翻译成为汉文本的藏文《格萨尔王传》的考察,还可以发现藏文《格萨尔王传》在叙说故事情节时,通常采用散文的形式,很少用韵文的形式。

---

① 关于以上三部《格斯(萨)尔》的书名,引用者常有一些异同。本文为了简明方便,在正文中统一为贵德分章本《格萨尔王传》、北京版《格斯尔》和芭杰本《格斯尔》。
② 王沂暖、华甲译《格萨尔王传(贵德分章本)》"译者前言",第3页。
③ 这里所要作比较的三部作品,是如下几种版本:藏族贵德分章本《格萨尔王传》,以甘肃省人民出版社1981年3月第1版,王沂暖、华甲译文本《格萨尔王传(贵德分章本)》作为比较的底本;蒙古族北京版《格斯尔》,以内蒙古人民出版社1993年5月第1版《十方圣主格斯尔可汗传》为底本(汉文引文参考了人民出版社1960年4月第1版,桑杰扎布译文本);芭杰本《格斯尔》,以民族出版社1989年8月第1版,道荣尕整理本为底本。
④ 杨恩洪:《民间诗神——〈格萨尔王传〉艺人研究》。

蒙古文《格斯尔》，在文体上可以分成三种形式。其一，是散文体，只有少量的韵文。北京版《格斯尔》即属于此类。其二，是韵文体，基本不出现散文的叙述。琶杰本《格斯尔》以及布里亚特《阿拜格斯尔》即属于此类。其三，散韵结合体。《南赡部洲雄狮大王传》即属于此类。相比之下，书面文本多数是散文体，艺人说唱多为韵体或者散韵结合体。蒙古艺人在说唱《格斯尔》时，人物对话也经常采用韵文形式。而且，在说唱到韵文体的对话时，艺人也经常会一展歌喉。但是，这只是艺人在"唱"，不是史诗中的人物在"唱"，并不包含戏剧因素。用韵文形式对话的传统，在蒙古文学中具有十分悠久的历史。还在 13 世纪，蒙古族的伟大作品《蒙古秘史》中，就已经熟练地使用韵文形式表达人物之间的对话。蒙古艺人在叙述《格斯尔》的故事情节时，也经常采用韵文的形式。在艺人说唱的《格斯尔》中，有大量的祝颂词、赞美诗以及民间谚语等。这些也都只有采用韵文形式，才能引起较好的美感效应。在蒙古文《格斯尔》中，以上文体的不同，具有特别重要的意义。例如，蒙古文《南赡部洲雄狮大王传》，[①] 所采用的仍然是雷同于藏文本的散韵结合体：在叙说故事时，采用散文体，在涉及人物对话时，大多采用韵文体。而且，对于这些韵文体的人物对话，在蒙文《南赡部洲雄狮大王传》中也称之为"唱"。这个看似简单的称谓文字，却说明了该抄本乃是源于藏文《格萨尔王传》的翻译。

北京版《格斯尔》采用散文体，琶杰本《格斯尔》则采用韵文体，与藏族贵德分章本《格萨尔王传》的散韵结合体，形成明显的区别。

在口头传播形式方面，蒙藏《格斯（萨）尔》之间，也是各有特征。蒙古族《格斯尔》，主要靠师承关系传播。每一个艺人都有自己的师傅。他从自己的师傅那里，学习说唱活动所需要的基本技能，包括拉、弹乐器，学唱曲调，各类故事的故事梗概，以及将故事梗概现场发挥成史诗的大量程式。藏族《格萨尔王传》的口头流传过程，却是另一番情景。藏族艺人通常没有明确的师承关系。他们是在史诗说唱活动得以产生和发展的广阔的文化背景之中，经过长期熏陶，自己"悟"得史诗说唱技能的。根据艺人的自述，研究者们将艺人按获得说唱技能途径的不同，划分为五种类型，即："神授"艺人、"闻知"艺人、"掘藏"艺人、"吟诵"艺人、"圆光"艺人。

根据现有资料，可以确认历史上藏族《格萨尔王传》的说唱中心，在青海东南和西藏东北一带。蒙古族《格斯尔》的说唱中心，则在清代东部三盟，即哲里木盟、昭

---

① 《南赡部洲雄狮大王传》（蒙文），乌·新巴雅尔校勘注释，内蒙古科学技术出版社 1988 年 8 月第 1 版。

乌达盟和卓索图盟一带。说唱传统和传播形式的截然不同,加之两个民族历史上《格斯(萨)尔》说唱中心相距遥远,可以相信过去两个民族的艺人,不可能形成说唱形态,即史诗的本体形态的直接而广泛的交流。两个民族在《格斯(萨)尔》史诗方面的联系,主要是通过史诗的非本体状态,即史诗的书面文本形式建立起来的。

二

　　这里也不准备对上述三个文本进行全面比较。本文拟比较的只是其中的一段故事,即关于格斯(萨)尔与茹格慕·高娃(即王沂暖等译文中作"珠毛")订婚的一段故事。本文选择有限的例证,对两部史诗进行探讨式的比较,意在经过这有限的比较,形成关于两部史诗联系与区别的具有实证性的初步认识。比较按如下两个步骤进行:第一步,比较贵德分章本《格萨尔王传》与北京版《格斯尔》;第二步,比较北京版《格斯尔》与琶杰本《格斯尔》。

　　首先介绍贵德分章本《格萨尔王传》的故事梗概:

　　小头人夹罗顿巴的三个女儿,分别许给了大食财王、班达霍尔王和古古玉王。一天,三位姑娘到岭地的蕨麻海挖蕨麻,在过一条河的时候,被躺在小桥上的台贝达朗挡住了去路。这台贝达朗也就是格萨尔王的化身。当时,他还是一个穷孩子,叔叔们刚给了他这片蕨麻海。三位姑娘为过河,先将带的酥油糌粑送给他,他没有同意她们过河。三位姑娘没有办法,只好手拉手向河里走去,想从水中走过去。台贝达朗朝水中扔一块石头,那水便涨到姑娘们的腰部。在妹妹们的要求下,大姐珠毛提出将自己的一件衣服送给台贝达朗,请他同意她们过河。台贝达朗又向河中扔一块石头,河水涨到姑娘们的肩膀。在妹妹们的要求下,大姐珠毛提出将自己头上戴的松耳石送给台贝达朗,请他同意她们过河。台贝达朗又向河中扔一块石头,河水涨到姑娘们的脖颈。三位姑娘到了不能进也不能退的地步。在妹妹们的要求下,大姐珠毛提出将自己许给台贝达朗,请他同意她们过河。这次,台贝达朗才让她们过了河。

　　姑娘们的父母,听说大女儿将自己许给了穷孩子台贝达朗,非常愤怒。但是,珠毛却不懊悔。妈妈说:"走到半路上,私自把身许。不选核桃仁,却要核桃皮。珠毛你这傻丫头,断送了今生好福气。"珠毛说:"走在半路上,自愿把身许。选了核桃仁,没要核桃皮。我夹罗珠毛啊,才算真有好福气。"大食财王前来迎亲,珠毛提出了一个条件,要他将一瓢酒,不碰五指,不碰舌头,不碰嘴唇,不碰牙齿地喝下去。大食财王无法做到,台贝达朗却做到了。于是,珠毛让台贝达朗骑在自己的马后背上,将他带回家中。那天夜里,台贝达朗把自己的靴子扯成碎块,伪装被狼吃掉了。然后,便离开珠毛的家,在众多天兵天将的拥戴下现出了格萨尔王的真身。珠毛醒来后,以为丈夫被狼吃了,便在母亲的说服下,到寺庙出家了。格萨尔王登上王位后,命令部下又将珠毛迎接回来。

以下是北京版《格斯尔》中的对应故事情节:

那时,僧格斯鲁可汗的女儿茹格慕·高娃,到立身的年龄,却还是没有找到呼必勒罕(转世)好丈夫。所以召集三位神箭手,三位高超的摔跤手,一位有大智慧的喇嘛以及众随从,听说吐伯特那里有三十位呼必勒罕英雄,想必会有好男子,便带领这众人而来。说要举行一万人的聚会。于是集合了一万人。格斯尔的化身侏儒也到会上。在来的路上,步行的侏儒要求骑马的叔叔楚通能够让他骑在马的后胯上,楚通没有同意。当聚集万人之后,茹格慕·高娃站起来说:"在我出生的时候,右檐上有犀牛欢腾,左檐上有角鹿欢腾。没有太阳的时候也充满光明,没有云彩的时候也降落雨露……圆满这九种吉祥的天仙,就是我茹格慕·高娃姑娘。"然后,她介绍了自己带来的摔跤手和神箭手,并说谁能胜过他们,自己就嫁给那个人。但是,那三十位呼必勒罕英雄,没有谁能胜过茹格慕·高娃带来的勇士。这时候,侏儒站出来,提出要比试比试。茹格慕·高娃带来的喇嘛说:"三十位呼必勒罕都没有取胜。啊!你能如何。"在侏儒的要求下,才同意了他比试。侏儒将头一名摔跤手扔到目之所及的千倍以外,将第二位摔跤手扔到目之所及的两千倍以外,将第三位摔跤手扔到目之所及的三千倍以外。随后,他又在比试射箭中获得胜利。茹格慕·高娃看着侏儒那挂在脸上的两道黄鼻涕,心中生厌,于是又提出新的条件:看谁能一只手抓住七十只羊的肋骨,另一只手提着一缸酒,在她转身的瞬间,将这些肋骨和酒分给在场的一万人,就嫁给那个人。众人都未能做到。侏儒要试一试时,茹格慕·高娃厌恶他的大鼻涕,不说可否,在众人的坚持下才同意他试一试。但是在她转身的瞬间,侏儒却早已经完成了要求。茹格慕·高娃想赖婚,带着随从逃走。她一边逃,一边让随从看是否有侏儒的踪影,随从说没有看到侏儒的踪影。但是,茹格慕·高娃正想松一口气的时候,随从却说:"啊呀,原来在你的马后胯上。"

回到家中之后,茹格慕·高娃的父母也都抱怨她,为什么领回来这样一位女婿。父亲拿起鞭子去看马群,哥哥拿起弓箭去看羊群,母亲生气走了出去,仆人们也表示不满。侏儒说了许多好话。晚上,父母都回来后,又对茹格慕·高娃发脾气,并将侏儒扣在锅底下。夜间,侏儒推开锅走出来,杀了一只羊,自己吃过后,把一部分给了狗。又将羊血涂在自己的牛犊皮衣上,然后躺到野外。早上,茹格慕·高娃的父母看到后说:"你的好丈夫被狗吃了,以后的灾难你自己承担吧!"茹格慕·高娃心中悲伤。又想:我身多有罪孽,不知是死是活。于是,去找侏儒。那时,侏儒却变作放马人。茹格慕·高娃向他询问是否见到侏儒。他说没有看到侏儒,但是却听说岭国的人们,得知茹格慕·高娃一家将侏儒喂狗之后,正要来报仇呢。茹格慕·高娃哭着向前走,又遇到变化为牧羊人的侏儒。牧羊人也重说牧马人的那番话。茹格慕·高娃想,已经闯下大祸,与其回家受到父母谴责后死去,莫如自己现在就死。于是,放开马向一条河冲过去。那时,却被人抓住了马尾巴,茹格慕·高娃回头看时,正是淌着金黄鼻涕的侏儒。侏儒也骑到马上,茹格慕·高娃厌恶他的鼻涕,让他面朝后骑。侏儒只好跟在后面步行。马奔跑时,侏儒被马踢倒,躺在地上装死。茹格慕·高娃要他起来,侏儒提出不能反向骑马。茹格慕·高娃同意了他的要求。二人回到家中后,恰逢茹格慕·高娃的舅父舅母也来了。他们说,我们的外甥女是天仙,不知找了一个何等女婿。茹格慕·高娃的父母,给侏儒一碗炒麦子,将他藏起来。可是侏儒一听到人们说到他,就淌着黄鼻涕,还故意在鼻涕上粘着麦粒走出来。茹格慕·高娃的舅父舅母看到侏儒后,怒气冲天地赶着马群走了。侏儒追上去枪回了马群。几天后,侏儒对茹格慕·高娃讲自己要回去。到外面后,他却先后变化为楚通诺彦和巴达玛里的儿子,回来试探茹格慕·高娃。茹格慕·高娃默许他们害死侏儒,然后嫁给他们。侏儒批评茹格慕·高娃,不该对自己不忠。第三天,侏儒变化为吐伯特的三十位勇士,挥舞着刀枪,问茹格慕·高娃的父亲到底嫁不嫁女儿。茹格慕·高娃的父母惧怕三十位勇士,不仅同意嫁女儿,而且举家搬到吐伯特。

以上分别是贵德分章本《格萨尔王传》与北京版《格斯尔》中,格斯(萨)尔娶茹格慕·高娃(珠毛)的故事梗概。这里用较大的篇幅,叙述两部史诗同一段故事,主要是为了进行比较时的方便。事实上,即使不曾读过原著的人,在看到如上的故事梗概之后,也能够对两部作品之间的异同形成初步的印象。

三

比较贵德分章本《格萨尔王传》与北京版《格斯尔》的前述对应故事,可以发现其间存在一定联系的同时,确实还存在着不小的差别。

首先,从联系角度考察,诸如主要人物名字相同,故事情节的大框架相同,以及故事发生的地点大致相同等,都是明显的例证。其中,故事大框架之相同,可以包括如下几点:其一,故事所要说的都是格斯(萨)尔与茹格慕·高娃(珠毛)的婚姻大事;其二,对这桩婚姻,姑娘的父母都不满意;其三,经过格斯(萨)尔的努力,最终这婚姻都成为现实。

其次,相比之下,不同之处要更多一些:

其一,故事的起因不尽相同。在贵德分章本《格萨尔王传》中,故事的直接起因不是婚姻,而是珠毛姐妹们要过河挖蕨麻。在北京版《格斯尔》中,故事直接起因于茹格慕·高娃要选丈夫。

其二,在贵德分章本《格萨尔王传》中,珠毛答应嫁给格萨尔王的原因是被迫的,其目的是为了救出姐妹三人的性命。如果姐妹三人没有被河水淹到脖颈,珠毛的妹妹不可能建议姐姐嫁给格萨尔王,已经许配给大食财王的珠毛,也不会提出嫁给穷孩子格萨尔王。北京版《格斯尔》中,没有出现贵德分章本《格萨尔王传》中的上述情节。在北京版《格斯尔》中,茹格慕·高娃同意嫁给格斯尔,也是出于被迫。但是,此前茹格慕·高娃还尚未许配人。为着嫁给一位理想的丈夫,茹格慕·高娃自己提出了具体的条件。茹格慕·高娃被迫嫁给格斯尔,是因为格斯尔赢得了摔跤和射箭比赛的胜利,完成了茹格慕·高娃提出的条件。这个细节的不同,包含着深刻的文化内容。摔跤、射箭和赛马,是古代蒙古族著名的"男子三项游戏",具有悠久的历史传统。男子通过在摔跤和射箭比赛中获胜,赢得女孩子的欢喜,实现二人之间的婚姻,这在过去是常有的事情。

其三,北京版《格斯尔》中,没有贵德分章本《格萨尔王传》中,珠毛回家后用对唱方式与母亲争论是否该许给格萨尔王的情节,也没有大食财王等各带十万人马迎亲,珠毛巧妙拒绝大食财王,以及珠毛热情地将格萨尔王带回家并款待他等情节。在北京版《格斯尔》中,却出现了贵德分章本《格萨尔王传》中不存在的,如茹格慕·高娃自己提出择夫的条件,又带领神箭手等游历诸方,在比赛之前她还自我介绍等情节,再如格斯尔的叔叔楚通也欲参加比赛,格斯尔拖着黄鼻涕出现在茹格慕·高娃面前,在格斯尔比赛胜利后茹格慕·高娃欲逃婚,茹格慕·高娃的舅父母看望外甥女的丈夫,以及格斯尔两次考验茹格慕·高娃等情节。

其四,上述对应情节中的区别,还显示出两部史诗人物形象方面的不同。

在贵德分章本《格萨尔王传》中,珠毛这个人物形象,以贤惠善良为主要特征。上述情节,也显示出她的这个特征。她能够为姐妹的利益牺牲自己。在妹妹们的要求下,她能用自己的衣服,用自己的首饰,一直到将自己作为交换条件,请求格萨尔王让她们过河。在婚姻的选择上,她不嫌贫爱富。在爱情上,她能坚持初衷。正因为如此,在母亲批评她,不该将自己许配给穷孩子格萨尔王时,她能够坚持自己的诺言。在大食财王前来娶亲时,她能够提出使对方无法做到的条件,从而拒绝了父母为她说定的婚姻,并终于将格萨尔王带回家中。

在北京版《格斯尔》中,茹格慕·高娃的形象,更具有女中豪杰的特征。这同样也反映在上述情节中。茹格慕·高娃是一位汗王的女儿,在出生的时候显现出九种吉祥的征兆。为了嫁给理想的丈夫,她没有在家中等待父母的安排,而是自己带上三位摔跤能手和三位神箭手,游历各地,寻找无人可敌的英雄。在比赛前,茹格慕·高娃所讲的一番话,气度不凡,更显出她的魅力出众。

即使从上述对应情节,也可以发现茹格慕·高娃与珠毛显然不是一类人物。茹格慕·高娃比较矜持自得,不是安分守己的女子。茹格慕·高娃也不是很忠于格斯尔。格斯尔两次变幻着考验她,她都没有经得住考验。这为后来的相关情节留下了伏笔。在北京版《格斯尔》第六章中,蟒古斯变化为呼必勒汗喇嘛,前来谋害格斯尔时,茹格慕·高娃为蟒古斯的珠宝所诱惑,曾经背叛格斯尔,帮助蟒古斯将格斯尔变幻为毛驴。①

在上述对应情节中,北京版《格斯尔》中的格斯尔形象,也显出不同于贵德分章本《格萨尔王传》中格萨尔王的个性特征。北京版《格斯尔》这段故事中的格斯尔,

---

① 王沂暖教授在他的《蒙文北京本〈格斯尔传〉读后记》一文中,曾经通过比较《北京版〈格斯尔〉》与贵德分章本《格萨尔王传》之间的同异,探讨蒙藏《格斯(萨)尔》的关系。他在该文中说:"北京本第一章包括贵德本第一章、第二章、第三章的三章主要情节……北京本第二章格斯尔斩除北方魔虎,贵德本与拉达克本均无此类情节……北京本第六章格斯尔被妖魔化身的喇嘛变成驴子,我见到的藏文分章本和分部本,尚未发现过这样情节。"该文原载《民间文学论坛》1982年第2期第15—19页。本文转引自赵秉理编《〈格萨尔王传〉学集成》第2卷第1097—1098页。

突出表现了幽默、诙谐、滑稽的特征。他总是在脸上挂着黄色的鼻涕,这是令茹格慕·高娃讨厌的主要原因;当茹格慕·高娃骑马逃走时,他不动声色地坐在她的马后胯上;当茹格慕·高娃的舅父母到来时,他不仅不按吩咐藏在暗处,反而挂着黄鼻涕走出来,那鼻涕上竟还粘着几粒炒熟的麦粒;当岳父岳母将他扣在锅下时,他却在半夜跑出来,偷杀羊吃,又伪造现场,骗他们自己被狗吃了;茹格慕·高娃找到他,要他一起回家时,他因为不让他正骑在马上,于是假装被马踢死,躺在地上耍赖……在这不长的文字中,格斯尔确实多次表现出滑稽、风趣的性格特征。

如果进一步比较两部作品的其他情节,还会发现更多的不同之处。这里不妨再举两个例证。

其一,是决定格斯(萨)尔从天国下凡一节。在贵德分章本《格萨尔王传》中,格萨尔王是天帝最小的儿子,在三个皇子中让他下凡,是由弟兄们之间的比赛决定的。在北京版《格斯尔》中,格斯尔是天帝的次子,在三个皇子中让他下凡,是因为他具有高超的射箭和摔跤本领。天帝的长子阿敏萨黑格奇(汉译为"惜命者",或"守己者"),首先推荐他的弟弟威勒布特格奇(汉译为"成功业绩者",是格斯尔在天界的名字)说:"不是在说弟弟的坏话,威勒布特格奇能够成功所有的事情。在梵天举行的有 17 位天神参加的那达慕上,比赛射箭和摔跤,没有一个人能够胜过这位威勒布特格奇。他最有本事。在这里有 33 位天神参加的那达慕上,比赛射箭和摔跤,也没有谁胜过他。在下界,诸龙王也曾召集那达慕,比赛竞技,又如何呢,还是没有人胜过他。这威勒布特格奇学到了诸如此类的一切本领,我们怎么能因为自己是天的儿子就去呢!"[1] 这样,在茹格玛·高娃举行那达慕时,书中提到有格斯尔参加的那达慕已经有四次之多。其中,天界两次,海中一次,地上人间一次。在《北京版〈格斯尔〉》撰写者的眼中,蒙古族喜爱的那达慕,成为天上、地上、海中无处不存在的竞技娱乐活动。对那达慕如此偏爱,当然只能出自蒙古族的文化心理。北京版《格斯尔》构思出那达慕和比赛摔跤、射箭的情节,一方面反映出其中的蒙古文化底蕴,另一方面又与格斯尔来到人间之后,擅长射箭、摔跤的情节遥相呼应。在争夺与茹格慕·高娃结亲的情节中,格斯尔夺取摔跤和射箭比赛的胜利,就有了在天界的基础。

其二,在北京版《格斯尔》中,格斯尔是天帝的次子,不同于贵德分章本《格萨尔王传》中格萨尔王是天帝的最小儿子,这也与蒙古族民族文化传统及其发展变化有

---

① 王沂暖、华甲译《十方圣主格斯尔可汗传》,第 4 页。

关。在古代,蒙古族是幼子继承制,即父母的家产由最小的儿子继承。幼子也被称为"斡惕赤斤"。在《蒙古秘史》中,成吉思汗分封时,总是特别照顾自己弟兄中的"斡惕赤斤",以及自己儿子中的"斡惕赤斤"。后来受到其他民族的影响,有些地区也实行长子继承制。在北京版《格斯尔》中,天帝要在三个儿子中间,派遣一个儿子到凡间的时候,如果按着蒙古族的古老传统,应该派遣长子或者次子去。如果按照后来的习俗,则应该派遣次子或者第三子去。帝的使者第一次征求威勒布特格奇,即格斯尔的意见时,他曾经说:"我难道不是天帝的儿子吗?并非行走在凡间的活物,世间的人类。就是去了,我也不能坐上皇帝的座位。皇位属于成为我哥哥的阿敏萨黑格奇的吧!要说比我年幼的,还有特古斯朝格图吧?与我有什么相干呢!"①从这话中,也可以看出,上有兄长,下有弟弟的威勒布特格奇即格斯尔,对自己在家庭中的处境,还是有着满腹牢骚的。这说明,史诗的作者是注意到蒙古族家庭关系中的传统的。但是如果既考虑古老的传统,又要兼顾后来的习俗,那么应该派遣的恰好是第二子威勒布特格奇,即后来的格斯尔。

以上这些例证说明,北京版《格斯尔》与贵德分章本《格萨尔王传》之间,虽然在故事情节的基本框架方面存在联系,但是在故事的文化内涵,大量情节处理方式,以及人物形象的特征方面,又存在着重要的区别。这些区别,说明贵德分章本《格萨尔王传》与北京版《格斯尔》,都是在文学与文化上显示出各自民族特征的作品。

四

芭杰本《格斯尔》共计 13 章,在故事情节的来源方面,前面的 7 章取之于北京版《格斯尔》,后面的 6 章取之于隆福寺版《格斯尔》。关于茹格慕·高娃与格斯尔结为夫妻的一段故事,在芭杰本《格斯尔》中包括三节文字,即第一章中的第 22 节、第23 节和第 24 节。其标题分别为《请茹格慕·高娃做夫人》、《现丑的茹格慕·高娃》和《试探茹格慕·高娃的心情》。以上三节,总计 1900 多诗行。《芭杰本〈格斯尔〉》的这段故事,虽然来源《北京版〈格斯尔〉》,其间也略有改动。例如,删去底本里茹格慕·高娃讲自己出生时汇聚九种瑞祥征兆的文字,增加了说唱者对她美丽容貌的直接赞美。对其他故事情节,几乎没有作什么改动。这使上述这段故事,从梗概上很难发现艺人说唱本与书面底本之间的区别。因此,只得从中摘译若干文字如下,作

---

① 　王沂暖、华甲译《十方圣主格斯尔可汗传》,第 3 页。

为比较的具体例证：

　　金色的世界，//巨大而广阔。//百姓万民，//纷纭众多。//楚通的宴席已尽，//楚里斯通喇嘛已归。//如今我讲的故事，//要从别处开始。//在英雄侏儒的家乡，//向西向北的方向，//还有一个小国家的人民，//生活得幸福安详。//国主唤僧格斯鲁，//王后是巴达玛嘎丽。//国主与夫人，//有一位姑娘十分可爱。//她超过所有的姑娘，//她是真正的天上仙女。//金色的世界罕见，//听说是观音菩萨的转世。//宇宙人间少有，//乃是罕迪玛的化身。//父亲与母亲，//唤她为茹格慕·高娃。//将这位姑娘的容颜，//这里稍稍说一番：她那美丽圆润的脸颊，//令一万个太阳失色。//她那端庄温柔的性情，能使钢铁感化。//她那娇嫩倩丽的容貌，//令十万个太阳失色。//她那文雅的热心，//会使金石熔化。//人人看到生爱慕，//老人看到会怜悯，//孩子们看了会喜欢，//少男看了会爱恋。//真是有德行有本事的，//这样一位好姑娘。

　　这姑娘已经成长到，//思想未来的年龄。//她不听父亲的话，//她不按母亲的意愿行事。//她如今一定要嫁给：能够战败那三位摔跤手，//能够超过那三位神射手，//能够被年长喇嘛看中的，//容貌出众德才兼备，//体魄强健智勇双全，//有福分有运气的一位人。//她要将己身托付他，//她要与他结为伴侣。//那年少的茹格慕·高娃，//她现在为此：带上汗父僧格斯鲁那，//扬名大千世界的，//三位大摔跤手，//三位神射手，//在预知一切的，//年长喇嘛的保护下，//还有那所有的丫环，//众多的侍从用人，//还有那行装帐篷，//要出门远行啊。

　　附近的各国各地，//都已经走遍，//随行前住，//举行着竞赛和欢宴。//思念欲找的那个人，//却还是没有找到啊。//即使天仙又如何，//不停地这样走也要败坏名声吧？//娇嫩的孩子茹格慕·高娃计穷心灰，//朝着家乡如今走上归程。//但凡那诸类事情，//谁能知道何种奇特。//正在行程之际，//遇到旅客数人，//常言道："路上遇到的人，//也有百日的缘分。"//正在谈论着，//怎样奔波，//如此这般之际，//有一位旅客说："听人们的议论，//正朝东方而去，//走上十日五日，//就到三个部所在，//有三十位英雄。//神奇的才能力量，//在宇宙世间，//真是罕见又罕见。//您三位出众的摔跤手，//您三位神射手，//到那三个部的家乡，//与三十位英雄比试比试，//难道不行吗？"//说者无意而去，//听者生疑住下。//娇嫩的茹格慕·高娃姑娘，//听后便说"那现在就去"。//旅行的目标不是家乡，//正朝东方走去。//十天九天不算久，//已经走到三部住地。//如今来到三部的附近，//俊俏漂亮的茹格慕·高娃姑娘远眺看去：驻扎在广阔美丽的草原中间，//建起一座座雄伟壮丽的蒙古包。//那美丽富饶的牧场真是肥美啊！//五种畜群布满草原。//勇士英雄穿梭往来，//各种武器闪烁着光芒。//欢聚的乐曲悠扬悦耳，//欢乐幸福的地方却在这里！//先哲喇嘛看到后已然发呆，//三位神射手望见后惊奇万分，//莽撞的三位摔跤手也羡慕不已，//当即在河边扎下了营盘。//那少女茹格慕·高娃不倦地在眺望，//内心深处波涛滚滚。//一路怀着择夫的愿望而来，//想着要在人们中发布告示。//远方的旅客驻扎本地，//次日早晨人们都已知晓。//昨日看到的那部落的几位青年，//清晨便赶来询问这旅客。//到老喇嘛身边讨得阿底萨佛，//听到姑娘来的意图便向回跑去。//众人的口舌不是快得很吗？//用男儿的竞技选择丈夫还不新奇吗？//三天未到的两天里，//三部的家乡人们已被轰动。①

这是芭杰本《格斯尔》中，茹格慕·高娃要通过比赛摔跤、射箭，选择丈夫那段故事开始时的若干文字。芭杰本《格斯尔》的上述这段引文，无论是叙述故事，或者人物对话，都由韵文组成。它在文体方面，可以认为也代表着全书的特征。芭杰本《格斯尔》总计4万多诗行。将篇幅如此长的史诗，全部用韵文传达出来，绝非易事。其风格与传统蒙古英雄史诗，可谓一脉相承。这一方面反映出说唱者的语言天赋，另一方面也说明该史诗在长久的流传过程中，可能经过了几代艺人的反复锤炼。

在北京版《格斯尔》中，上述芭杰本《格斯尔》引文所对应的是如下的一节文字：

> 那时，僧格斯鲁可汗的女儿茹格慕·高娃，到如今的年龄，却还是没有找到转世的好丈夫。所以召集三位神箭手，三位高超的摔跤手，一位有大智慧的喇嘛，以及众随从，听说吐伯特那里有三十位转世英雄，想必会有好男子，于是带领这众人而来。说要举行一万人的聚会。于是集合了一万人。②

---

① 道荣尕整理本芭杰本《格斯尔》，第205—210页。
② 王沂暖、华甲译《十方圣主格斯尔可汗传》，第51页。

芭杰本《格斯尔》的上述引文，总计 138 诗行。北京版《格斯尔》中对应的这段情节，翻译为汉文却只有 128 个字。可见二者之间在篇幅上差距之悬殊。也可以说，这差距中所展示的，也就是史诗书面文本与史诗口头说唱文本之间的主要区别。

艺人说唱本在篇幅上，比较史诗底本的大量扩充，主要是由以下方面造成的。

其一，是说唱中间顺延书面文本留下的空间，所做的细节内容之充实。经过比较可以发现，在说唱本中增加了许多细节。例如遇到路上旅行的客人，经客人的讲述，引导他们由返回的路程，又转而去吐伯特，在北京版《格斯尔》是没有的。同时，在北京版《格斯尔》中，也没有说在去吐伯特之前，他们已经周游附近的"各国各地"。这样一些细节的增加，会使故事在内容上丰富起来，不再是比较单调的梗概，典雅庄重却又显得缺少生活气息和风俗趣闻。在到达吐伯特三部时，艺人还用一些诗句描绘当地的富饶美好，以及茹格慕·高娃和随行人员，看到当地景色后的惊奇神态。这不仅增加了篇幅，同样也可以认为是艺人对自己家乡，即蒙古草原的间接赞颂。再如，在茹格慕·高娃所带领的人们来到吐伯特三部时，还增加了头一天看到他们的当地青年人，次日早晨前来探望的情节。无论在什么时代，青年人都最活跃，最容易接触新人新事。吐伯特三部的青年人，首先前来接近这些外来的人们，也是十分合乎情理的。蒙古草原，地广人稀，热心待客。头一天看到有客人到来，次日清晨便急冲冲地去接近，这也反映出人们的好客习俗。艺人很善于通过各种机会，向史诗的故事中插入自己由生活中提炼出的细节。芭杰本《格斯尔》增加的这些细节，也可以认为是艺人对史诗的独特理解和独特阐释。这种理解和阐释，来源于哺育艺人的蒙古文化传统，来源于艺人对生活的艺术洞察，来源于艺人的天赋。

其二，是增加赞美、比喻、形容的诗句。例如，北京版《格斯尔》书面文本中，在这里并没有描写茹格慕·高娃容貌和气质的情节。但是，艺人说唱时，却增加了 20 多行诗文字，用来赞美茹格慕·高娃美丽无比的容貌和高贵的气质。艺人在这里，用了诸如"观音菩萨的转世"、"令太阳失色"、"使金石熔化"等大量的形容和比喻，使听众对茹格慕·高娃的美丽非凡和高贵气质，形成深刻的印象。再如，说到茹格慕·高娃欲找的丈夫时，所用的"容貌出众"、"体魄强健"、"有福分有运气"等词语，也属于形容类词语。

其三，重复也是使篇幅得以扩充的重要原因。例如，形容茹格慕·高娃的容貌令"一万个太阳失色"后，艺人认为这还不够，又说茹格慕·高娃的容貌令"十万颗太阳失色"。在说茹格慕·高娃的性情,"能使钢铁感化"后,又说"会使金石熔化"。这些都属于重复的比喻。前后比喻的诗句之间虽然有加强的作用,但在气质和容貌内容上并没有重要的区别。再如,用"观音菩萨的转世"和"罕迪玛的化身",比喻茹格慕·高娃,在内容上也十分相近,属于重复的比喻。这类重复的形容和比喻,如果是书面的散文创作,很难产生美的感觉。但是,由于是艺人的说唱,是韵文体,加上艺人说唱时的起伏情绪,以及悦耳的歌声和乐器声,就产生完全不同的感觉。这也是欣赏史诗说唱活动,与阅读史诗本子的根本区别。阅读史诗本子,要靠读者自身的理解和发挥取得审美效果。欣赏艺人说唱史诗,使单一的书面文本走向立体,成为多重的审美艺术。在优秀的艺人那里,史诗的书面文本只是为他提供了一种形式,一种将他所承继的有关史诗的各种信息组织到一起的形式。由他口中说唱出来的,才是真正可以被称为"史诗"的那种艺术。

按着早已形成的审美定势,稍加改动甚至不加改动,重复某些具有悠久历史的固定程式,是蒙古史诗的重要特征。这些程式,包含着听众的审美心理模式,即听众对某些事物的独特理解方式。史诗作为一种产生在没有文字时代的艺术,只有适应听众的审美心理模式,才能够被特定的听众群体所理解所接受。在当代人们的眼中被视为重复的那些诗句,常常是最清楚地反映出史诗早期特征的部分。

经过以上比较可以发现:第一,蒙藏两个民族的英雄史诗《格斯(萨)尔》,其间的主要联系建立在书面文本的范围,而在口头说唱活动范围内,两个民族的《格斯(萨)尔》,在历史上是各自独立发展的,并且是建立在每个民族自己的文学艺术传统之上的;第二,贵德分章本《格萨尔王传》与北京版《格斯尔》之间,在故事的基本框架上有较多的雷同之处,但是同时也有不小的区别;第三,在北京版《格斯尔》向琶杰本《格斯尔》转变的过程中,无论在艺术形式上,或者是审美理想方面,《格斯尔》史诗同样发生了质的变化。

因此,无论是书面文本之间的比较,或者是书面文本与艺人说唱本之间的比较,无论是故事内容方面的比较,或者是艺术形式方面的比较,都说明蒙文《格斯尔》与藏文《格萨尔王传》之间,既存在着无法分隔的联系,又存在着分属不同民族文化,因而具有不同民族文化特征的根本区别。单纯从故事基本框架方面考察,或者从故事来源角度考察,很容易将它们归为同一部作品,或是同一作品的不同支系。但是,如果从文化传统角度考察,或从史诗的审美底蕴,史诗的说唱风格角度考察,那么就不能不指出,它们并不是同一部作品。这样的认识,不仅符合事物的本来面目,同时也更加显示出《格斯(萨)尔》整体的辉煌伟大和浩瀚丰富。

参考书目

道荣尕整理本《琶杰本〈格斯尔〉》,北京:民族出版社,1989年。

杨恩洪:《民间诗神——〈格萨尔王传〉艺人研究》,北京:中国藏学出版社,1995年。

乌·新巴雅尔校勘注释《南赡部洲雄狮大王传》(蒙文),赤峰:内蒙古科学技术出版社,1988年。

王沂暖、华甲译《格萨尔王传(贵德分章本)》"译者前言",兰州:甘肃人民出版社,1981年。

王沂暖、华甲译《十方圣主格斯尔可汗传》,呼和浩特:内蒙古人民出版社,1993年。

王沂暖:《蒙文北京本〈格斯尔传〉读后记》,北京:《民间文学论坛》1982年第2期。

赵秉理编《〈格萨尔王传〉学集成》第2卷,兰州:甘肃民族出版社,1990年。

图瓦《克孜尔》与成吉思汗征伐西夏的传说

斯钦巴图

摘　要　图瓦《克孜尔》[①]与蒙古族《格斯尔》很接近,但也有很多差异,尤其是第九章在《格斯尔》中没有对应的故事。本文比较了图瓦《克孜尔》与成吉思汗征伐西夏的传说,认为《格斯尔》流传到图瓦并形成《克孜尔》有近三百年的历史,这可能是图瓦与蒙古族政治、历史、文化密切联系的结果。成吉思汗的故事进入《克孜尔》的途径可能是:过去曾有独立的传说或史诗,并在图瓦和蒙古流传。在蒙古,它于17世纪被史料化;在图瓦,它仍然口头流传并逐渐融入《克孜尔》。

关键词　图瓦《克孜尔》,蒙古族《格斯尔》,跨文化比较研究

一

产生于蒙古族和藏族民间的世界著名史诗《格斯(萨)尔》,不仅在中国各民族中流传并深受喜爱,而且还流传到蒙古国、阿富汗、巴基斯坦、俄罗斯等国家各民族当中,成为当地国家和民族精神财富的一个重要组成部分。毫无疑问,那些从故乡传播到海外的《格斯(萨)尔》故事,在当地民族和国家的独特历史文化中重新生根发芽,在新的文化环境中形成了不同的思想内容和艺术特色,在《格斯(萨)尔》研究领域中具有独特的价值。

2002年9月至2003年2月,我以高级访问学者身份留学蒙古国国立大学期间,有幸得到一本采自俄罗斯联邦图瓦共和国民间的《格斯尔传》,原书名叫《阿齐

---

① 图瓦人把格斯(萨)尔的名字叫作"克孜尔(Kezer)"。

图·克孜尔·篾尔根》。① 由于在国内,无论是学术界还是普通百姓,都不甚知晓图瓦《克孜尔》,于是我就把它翻译成了蒙古文。全书共九章,其中从第一章至第五章,第七章至第八章,是俄联邦图瓦共和国陶竹地方的著名史诗艺人巴彦·巴里巴尔(Bayan Balbyr)于1953年讲述的;第六章是东克木其克(Chöön khemchik)地方的著名艺人翁达尔·丹达尔(Ondar Dandar)于1961年讲述的;第九章是乌鲁克·克木(Ulug khem)地方的著名艺人图鲁士·巴奘盖(Tülüsh Baazanggai)于1951年讲述的。这九章分别是:

第一章,阿齐图·克孜尔·篾尔根下凡尘世之部;

第二章,阿齐图·克孜尔·篾尔根铲除北方的黑斑虎蟒古思之部;;

第三章,阿齐图·克孜尔·篾尔根到乞台国劝说贡布汗之部;

第四章,阿齐图·克孜尔·篾尔根铲除12个头的奥伦扎—蟒古思之部;

第五章,沙拉阔里地方的黄帐汗、白帐汗、黑帐汗三汗之部;

第六章,阿齐图·克孜尔·篾尔根斩除15个头的郎多里巴汗(Lang Dolba khan)之部;

第七章,阿齐图·克孜尔·篾尔根镇压阿达噶尔·哈日·蟒古思之部;

第八章,十方之主阿齐图·克孜尔·篾尔根到阎王(Erlik Lovung khan)处救母之部;

第九章,阔尔布斯塔(Kurbustu)天神之子阿齐图·克孜尔·篾尔根可汗之部。

据说,图瓦的史诗艺人们都承认,他们讲述的有关克孜尔可汗的故事是从蒙古人那里传播过来的。他们有的以散文形式讲述《克孜尔》故事;有的以韵文形式演唱《克孜尔》;有的则手里拿着蒙古文《格斯尔》,翻译给大家听。② 可想而知,图瓦《克孜尔》与蒙古《格斯尔》之间的关系是多么密切。然而在翻译的过程中,我感觉它们之间也存在诸多不同之处,表现在相同故事中的不同情节,相同情节之间的繁简差异,乃至出现完全不同的故事等方面。尤其是其中的第九章,也就是乌鲁克·克木地方的著名艺人图鲁士·巴奘盖于1951年讲述的故事很特别,它在蒙古《格斯尔》中没有相对应的故事。其中的主要情节倒使我想起了一个关于成吉思汗的传说故事。在此,我把图瓦《克孜尔》与蒙古《格斯尔》之间的大规模比较研究留待将来,先对图瓦《克孜尔》中的阔尔布斯塔天神之子阿齐图·克孜尔·篾尔根可汗之部

---

① 库拉尔(Kuular, D. S.)整理、注释:《阿齐图·克孜尔·篾尔根》。

② 同上书,第10页。

和成吉思汗征伐唐古特国(Tangut,西夏)的传说故事进行一番比较。

我们知道,在《格斯(萨)尔》学研究历史上,曾经有过把历史人物成吉思汗和史诗人物格斯尔可汗等同起来的观点。俄罗斯著名蒙古学家科津(S. A. Kozin)院士就曾提出过蒙古卫拉特史诗《江格尔》中的英雄江格尔、史诗《格斯尔》中的英雄格斯尔和《蒙古秘史》中的历史人物成吉思汗是同一个人物的观点。他认为,《蒙古秘史》是关于成吉思汗的叙事长诗,在 14 世纪下半叶,关于成吉思汗的叙事传说应该已经逐渐成为史诗,但是,这一过程由于帝国的迅速解体和蒙古社会僧侣势力的迅速膨胀而一度停顿,正在形成的成吉思汗的史诗在蒙古的东部形成为《格斯尔》英雄史诗,而在西部,则形成为《江格尔》英雄史诗。① 这种观点遭到了学术界猛烈的批评。科津院士也接受了学界的批评。我在这里提到这些是想说明,我的研究不同于科津的研究,我不准备证明整个《克孜尔》史诗是关于成吉思汗的史诗,而仅仅想证明,《克孜尔》中的一个故事与蒙古文古代历史文献中记载的关于成吉思汗征伐西夏的故事之间,存在着一些具体的母题和故事情节上的对应关系。

二

事实上,我们将要研究的图瓦《克孜尔》中的这个故事,它在艺术上并没有什么更突出的特点,倒显得有一些粗糙,情节也很简单。但就是这么一个简单而又显得比较粗糙的故事,却给我们提出了一个有着很重要意义的研究课题。为了让读者更具体地了解,也为了给后面的比较研究提供方便,我们先将图鲁士·巴奘盖讲述的《阔尔布斯塔天神之子阿齐图·克孜尔·篾尔根可汗之部》的故事梗概归纳如下:

阔尔布斯塔天神的儿子阿齐图·克孜尔·篾尔根向全国发出命令,禁止国人吸烟、喝酒。然而,从此阿齐图·克孜尔·篾尔根的国度遭受了史无前例的干旱,河流干枯,寸草不生,牲畜和财产耗费殆尽。一天,克孜尔·篾尔根出去打猎,遇见一个老人。这老人住的地方水草丰美,还养着 60 多只山羊。问他是哪个可汗的臣民,老人说是阿齐图·克孜尔·篾尔根可汗的臣民;问为什么只有他这里不遭干旱,水草丰美,老人回答是因为他背地里一天也没有停止吸烟、喝酒之故。克孜尔听了,就宣布废除禁烟禁酒令。果然见效,从此,他的国家风调雨顺,人民安居乐业。克孜尔任命老人为大臣,叫他处理 336 位大臣三年都没能处理的事务,老人只用了三个

---

① 涅克留朵夫(Nekliudov, S. Yu.):《蒙古人民的英雄史诗》,第 32—34 页。

小时就全处理妥当了。

一天,克孜尔可汗和老人一起打猎,看见猎物鲜红的血洒在雪地上是那么的美,就问老人:世界上有没有雪白的皮肤血红的脸蛋的美女? 老人说有。他说,住在西方的库格都里汗的通拉克察汗哈屯有此娇美。问老人那可汗的力气和意志如何,老者说,那可汗的力气和意志都不可怕,倒是有七条红狗,都有从遥远的地方预知敌人的踪迹并扑而灭之的本领。克孜尔决定去抢夺那个美夫人,带着336位大臣和老人出发了。

途中在一个地方驻营,克孜尔可汗察看了良久,赞叹道:"富有的人居住着,过瘾,穷苦的人把尸骨安葬着,过瘾,真是一个美丽富饶的地方啊(Bay kiji jurttap maga khanmas jer – dir, bagay kiji sook salip maga khanmas ondur jaagay oran – dir)。"

众大臣赞许,唯独老人沉默。到了库格都里可汗的领土上,库格都里可汗的七条红狗从很远的地方发现了克孜尔可汗,猛扑过来,克孜尔可汗把它们全部消灭了。克孜尔可汗攻入库格都里可汗的汗宫里,不理睬他的苦苦哀求,结束了库格都里可汗的生命,夺取了他的通拉克察汗哈屯。在归途中,又来到那个大加赞赏的美丽富饶的地方驻营。是夜,克孜尔可汗试图与夫人做爱,不料,那夫人却用剪刀把克孜尔可汗的阳物连根剪掉,将克孜尔可汗杀害。库格都里可汗的臣民和克孜尔可汗的臣民各自回乡去了。这时,克孜尔可汗的三个姐姐来了,在弟弟的尸体上洒了圣水,克孜尔苏醒过来,说:"睡得怎么这样厉害。"

克孜尔欣赏老人的智慧,赐名为萨如拉·乌甘(Saryyl Ugaan,意为智者),让他去察看这个国家还缺什么。萨如拉·乌甘老人察看的结果是,其他什么都不缺,只缺如意树。克孜尔命令种植如意树。如意树越长越高,人民的生活一天比一天幸福。

这个故事在内容上可分为三部分,分属于三个主题。第一部分讲述克孜尔可汗发布和撤销禁烟禁酒令的故事;第二部分讲述克孜尔可汗征服库格都里可汗,夺取库格都里可汗的妻子,却被她所害,死而复生的故事;第三部分讲述克孜尔可汗令全国种植如意树,让全国人民安居乐业的故事。

这个故事有两个鲜明的特点:第一,这是一个相当独特而新鲜的故事。虽然说图瓦《克孜尔》是从蒙古人那里来的,但这个故事在已知蒙古《格斯尔》古今版本和口传版本(包括卫拉特《格斯尔》和布里亚特《格斯尔》在内)中都是没有的。第二,在这个故事里,智者老人的形象似乎更加突出了一些,盖过了克孜尔可汗。尽管如此,克孜尔可汗的业绩仍然是连接整个故事的线索,这也是这个故事的一大特点。故事的第二部分,即克孜尔征服库格都里可汗,接纳他的夫人为妻的故事,是整个

故事的主线索。以下几点构成了故事的核心:

1. 有人向克孜尔可汗推荐库格都里可汗的妻子,说她的容貌举世无双,建议克孜尔可汗前去夺取;

2. 库格都里可汗有七条红狗,都有从遥远的地方预知敌人的踪迹并扑而灭之的本领;

3. 克孜尔可汗在征途中驻营,赞美那个地方;

4. 克孜尔可汗不顾库格都里可汗的苦苦哀求,杀其身,夺其妻;

5. 在归途中,库格都里可汗的夫人通拉克察汗哈屯用剪刀连根剪掉克孜尔可汗的阳物;

6. 克孜尔可汗在自己曾经羡慕和赞叹过的地方遇害身亡。

其中第一个情节,即老人向克孜尔可汗推荐库格都里可汗的妻子,说她的容貌举世无双,建议克孜尔可汗前去夺取,成为故事发展的线索,而夺取美女成为克孜尔可汗发动战争的唯一理由。

三

现在我们看一看与上述故事非常相似的蒙古故事。这个故事就是蒙古古代历史文献所载成吉思汗征服唐古特(西夏)国的传说故事。这个故事在各个时代的不同文献中不尽相同,形成了一个故事的多种版本。为了便于读者更直接地感受它们与图瓦故事之间的相似性,也为了节约篇幅,我们先对与图瓦故事最近似的故事予以介绍,然后对其他版本作简略的介绍。这样,既简单明了,也可以展现成吉思汗传说在各个不同时期流传演变的特点。

在蒙古历代历史文献中,与上述图瓦《克孜尔》故事相似的故事最早出现在佚名氏的《蒙古黄金史纲》,后见之于罗卜桑丹津的《蒙古黄金史》、萨囊-彻辰的《蒙古源流》、《古代蒙古诸汗源流大黄史》、《阿萨拉克齐史》、《金轮千辐》、《水晶鉴》等众多蒙古历史文献中。下面是《蒙古黄金史纲》中的故事:

> 圣主征服了汉地,取了金主的大位,西夏的失都儿忽汗得知后,惧怕了,派伯颜萨儿塔固尔之子多儿通为使,誓言:"做您的右翼,向您输纳贡赋。"该使者奏事既毕,陛辞之际,说道:"圣主诚乃天子,皇后也胜过我们的皇后夜不秉烛

而光艳射人。"① 说完走了。原来圣主选定泰赤乌部的雅布噶之妻蒙郭伦郭斡作妃子,雅布噶听了多儿通的话,禀告主上:"比起我妻蒙郭伦郭斡来,汉人张家尼薛禅欧密台之女、西夏失都儿忽汗的称作古尔伯勒津郭斡的妃子,光彩夜不秉烛,愿主上聘她何如?"主上乃派了使者,对失都儿忽汗说:"我将征伐回回,你须出兵!"失都儿忽汗却对那使臣说:"既没有占领一切,何以称汗;既已称汗,何需友助?"拒不出征。主上闻得此语,发誓:"我宁肯舍此黄金之躯,也不放过你!"……② 乃宣谕:"往征夏国。"

失都儿忽汗的名为库伯勒克的黑嘴黄毛狗,能预知征兆。如果吠得太平、宁谧、吉祥、安泰,便无敌人;倘若嚎叫,就表明有敌人了。圣主建立九游白纛,征伐驻跸三年之久。这狗知道主上出征,嚎叫了三年。"我的狗已经老了,没有这种征兆了。"失都儿忽汗这样说过以后,未加防范。猪年(丁亥,1227 年)偕也遂哈屯起驾,率兵出征。主圣望见穆纳山咀,降旨道:"丧乱之时,可以隐遁;太平之时,可以驻牧。当在此猎捕麋鹿,以游豫晚年。"……③ 传令大狩,行围于杭爱山,敕言:"若有苍狼、花鹿入围,不许杀戮;卷毛黑人骑铁青马入围,要生擒他。"果有苍狼、花鹿入围,而放走未杀。骑铁青马的进来,被活捉了。问:"你是属于谁的?"〈对方〉没作声,因此送于主上。主上讯问时,奏道:"闻得蒙古圣主发兵,失都儿忽汗派出探子,所有的马都追不上的库斯博勒特铁青马,〈到如今〉被追上了,四蹄似乎脱落了;我就是战胜一切人的啮食哈喇布通,都败在你们手下,我的头颅怕是要掉了。"回奏已毕,圣主问道:"据闻,你们的汗是'呼毕勒罕',据实说来!"哈喇布通说:"早晨〈他会〉变成黑花毒蛇,那时捉不得;中午变成斑斓之虎,那时捉不得;夜晚睡觉时,变成漂亮而略带稚气的幼童,坐下来与妃子欢聚,那时才能捉得。"奏毕,随被赦免。其后来到西夏境内……④ 当失都儿忽汗变作毒蛇的时候,主上化为凤凰;变作老虎的时候,主上化为狮子;变作幼童的时候,主上化为老人,捉住了他。失都儿忽汗被捉以后,对主上说道:"且不要杀我,捉得金星,〈为你〉禳除不祥;捉得彗星,〈为你〉消灭灾荒。如果定要杀我,必会危及你的寿命;不杀将要祸及你的子孙。"其奏,未获允许。〈然而〉射、砍皆不能入,〈于是〉失都儿忽汗说道:"砍、射都不能

---

① 此处蒙古文原文有误,其他蒙古历史文献中是:圣主诚乃天子,皇后倒不如我们的皇后。
② 此处省略了上帝赐甘露酒与成吉思汗的神话。
③ 此处省略了圣主让哈萨尔(成吉思汗的弟弟)射恶鹗的传说。
④ 此处省略了成吉思汗让哈萨尔射杀失都儿忽汗的传播瘟疫的巫婆的传说。

损伤我的身体,我的靴腰里藏着三折斑纹肚带,用它绞死吧!"于是取出那肚带缢杀的时候,失都儿忽汗说:"今若勒毙我,你的后人将会像我一样被勒死。对于我的古尔伯勒津郭斡哈屯,从手指甲到全身,都要搜遍!"言毕,死去。圣主取了古尔伯勒津郭斡哈屯。从主上以至普土大国,无不诧异她的美色。古尔伯勒津郭斡哈屯说:"我的容颜已为您的兵尘污染,先前较此,更为绚丽,现今若能在水中沐浴一番,就会更加俊秀了。"此话,圣主信以为真,打发她去水里沐浴。这位哈屯行至水边,书写信息于兰雀之尾:"我将死于此水,我的尸体,莫顺流相寻,可逆流去找。"这样通知其父以后,投水自尽了。父亲依照女儿的言语,逆流而来,找见了,每人拿上一个皮袋,撒土埋葬了。遂名坟墓为特穆尔鄂勒呼,河水为哈屯郭勒(Khadun gool 河)。降服了西夏国,杀死了失都儿忽汗,摧毁了灵州城(Turimekhei balgasun),纳取了古尔伯勒津郭斡哈屯。

那次大守,主上避暑于六盘山,患重病于灵州城……① 于丙亥(丁亥,公元1227 年)年,六十七岁,七月十二日殂天。

当灵车套上衡轭奉载汗的金枢归来之际……② 行至穆纳之泥淖处,灵车之毂陷住,深达辐轴而移动不得,套上各色牲畜都拽不出……因为圣主途经此地之时,表示过赞美与欣赏,所以灵车深没轮毂;据说,向众臣庶降下了疑似之诏,把身穿的衫子、居住的房子和一只袜子留在那里。而其真身,有人讲,葬于不而罕哈里敦;有人说,葬在阿尔泰山之阴、肯特山之阳、名为大鄂托克的地方。③

这段关于成吉思汗征服西夏的历史事件的记载穿插了很多相关的传说故事。这些传说故事在成吉思汗辞世后不久成书的《蒙古秘史》中大多是没有的。为了比较的方便,我们在这里省略了其中一部分。这样我们能够清晰地看到成吉思汗征服西夏国的完整的故事。分析上引故事,可归纳出构成故事核心的内容有以下几点:

1.成吉思汗征服西夏的原因有两条:其一是唐古特国的失都儿忽汗出尔反尔,违抗成吉思汗的指令;其二是有人向他推荐了失都儿忽汗的妻子古尔伯勒津郭斡

---

① 此处省略了成吉思汗病重期间与众臣的一段谈话。
② 此处和下一个省略号处,是省略了护送成吉思汗的灵车途中吉鲁格台勇士对成吉思汗的悼念和赞美诗。
③ 朱风、贾敬颜译:《汉译蒙古黄金史纲》,第23—35 页。

哈屯的美貌,夺取这个美女是成吉思汗出兵的另一个重要原因。

2.失都儿忽汗有名为库伯勒克的黑嘴黄毛狗,能预知征兆;失都儿忽汗有各种奇异的法力;失都儿忽汗拥有恶鹊、传播瘟疫的巫婆(这两个,我们因篇幅原因省略了)等,都凸显失都儿忽汗的非凡能力,实际上,这些都是在把失都儿忽汗魔鬼化,拥有这些的失都儿忽汗更像蒙古史诗中的恶魔——蟒古思。

3.成吉思汗在征伐唐古特途中望见穆纳山咀,降旨道:"丧乱之时,可以隐遁;太平之时,可以驻牧。当在此猎捕麋鹿,以游豫晚年。"

4.成吉思汗不顾失都儿忽汗的苦苦哀求,杀其身,夺其妻。

5.失都儿忽汗临死,提醒成吉思汗,要仔细检查其妻子的身体。

6.成吉思汗在征服唐古特的争战途中驾崩,其灵车通过他生前经过并赞美的地方时陷住,于是在那里营建了永世坚固的八白室(Naiman Tsagan Ordon)。①

四

对两个故事进行比较,它们之间的区别是显而易见的。首先,图瓦《克孜尔》中的故事是纯粹的史诗故事,而蒙古文历史文献中的这个故事则是作为历史来叙述的"历史故事"。叙述者在开头和结尾的处理方式上完全不同。在故事的开头,《克孜尔》中克孜尔征伐库格都里可汗的理由只有一个:抢美丽的夫人。这是阿尔泰语系诸民族的史诗中常见的一种开头方式。而在蒙古文历史文献中,成吉思汗征伐失都儿忽汗的理由,最主要是失都儿忽汗归顺了成吉思汗,却又一再违抗成吉思汗的命令。虽然也提到了库格都里可汗的美丽的通拉克察汗哈屯夫人,也暗含抢夺这个夫人的意思,但是叙述的时候还是没有把这个当作重要的理由。这是史诗故事和"历史故事"之间最大的区别。在故事的结尾方式上,《克孜尔》中克孜尔可汗遇害身亡后,他的三位神仙姐姐用圣水让他复活了,他和他的臣民又开始过上了幸福的生活。这也是阿尔泰语系诸民族英雄史诗普遍的结尾方式;而在蒙古文历史文献中的成吉思汗征服西夏的传说故事,则没有这样的结尾。

开头和结尾的不同,使得两个故事在主题上有了根本的区别。《克孜尔》故事的主题是阿尔泰语民族史诗中常见的抢婚主题;而蒙古文历史文献中的故事的主

---

① 供奉成吉思汗生前所用马具等遗物、成吉思汗的旗纛、成吉思汗后妃,并进行成吉思汗祭奠的地方,在今鄂尔多斯。现今称之为"成吉思汗陵",不当。

题,则是军事上的征服主题。

如果按故事情节的划分来进行比较的话,它们之间的相似点也是显而易见的。我们在这里列出的关于成吉思汗征伐唐古特国的故事的六个主要情节,与上面的图瓦《克孜尔》故事的六个情节,虽然人物不同且在细节上有所差别,但从叙事的整体上说是完全对应的。

就第一个情节来说,图瓦《克孜尔》中智者老人向克孜尔可汗报告西方的库格都里可汗的通拉克察汗哈屯夫人貌美举世无双;而在成吉思汗的传说中,是失都儿忽汗的使者多儿通向雅布噶,雅布噶又向成吉思汗报告了失都儿忽汗的夫人貌美举世无双。并且,这一点都成为克孜尔可汗或成吉思汗发动战争的重要原因。所不同的是,在图瓦《克孜尔》中,这是战争的唯一原因;而在成吉思汗的历史传说中这仅仅是重要原因之一,而不是唯一原因。根据古代蒙古文历史文献记载,成吉思汗发动战争还有更重要的历史原因,那就是,唐古特的失都儿忽汗不遵守协议,不履行誓言,出尔反尔,公然向成吉思汗挑战。古代蒙古文历史文献中为什么会出现这样的情况,是耐人寻味的。我们在后面还要讨论这一点。

就第二点来说,克孜尔的敌人和成吉思汗的敌人都以拥有能预知征兆的狗为特征。虽然狗的名字和关于它们的叙述在细节上有所不同,但这仍然是两个故事非常抢眼的一个共同点。两个故事中都用不凡的狗来预示库格都里可汗或失都儿忽汗的国度充满危险。在这方面,蒙古历史文献中的成吉思汗征服唐古特国的传说表现得更胜一筹,失都儿忽汗不仅有能预知征兆的狗,而且还拥有恶鹦和传播瘟疫的巫婆。

就第三点来说,两个故事之间的对应性也是显而易见的。尤其把第三点和第六点联系起来看,它们之间的共通性更加明显。在第三个情节上,克孜尔可汗或成吉思汗在远征途中,看见一个地方,并非常喜欢且赞美了这个地方。而在第六个情节上,恰巧他们在归途中都到了这个地方,克孜尔可汗遇害身亡,其意思就是在这里葬身;而成吉思汗的灵车到了这里就陷住不动,从而在这里营建了永世坚固的八白室,象征把成吉思汗葬在这里,以示尊重成吉思汗的意愿。不仅如此,克孜尔对那个地方的赞美词和成吉思汗对穆纳山咀的赞美词,在表达的意思上也非常一致。请看:

富有的人居住着,过瘾,穷苦的人把尸骨安葬着,过瘾,真是一个美丽富饶的地方啊(Bay kiji jurttap maga khanmas jer – dir, bagai kiji sook salip maga khanmas ondur jaagay oran – dir)（引自图瓦《克孜尔》）。

丧乱之时，可以隐遁；太平之时，可以驻牧。当在此猎捕麋鹿，以游豫晚年（Ebderegsen turu – tor khorkholaltai/ Enkhe turu – tor odoglaltai/ Udegu bukhu udegleltei）（引自佚名氏《蒙古黄金史纲》、罗卜桑丹津《蒙古黄金史》、《阿萨拉克齐史》）。

上述各种蒙古历史文献中，这首诗的意思不太好理解。我们参看《蒙古源流》中的记载，意思就非常明白了：

丧乱之时，可以隐遁；太平之时，可以驻牧。麋鹿当在此繁衍，老人当在此歇息（Ebderkhei turu – tor khoorgalaltai/ Enkhe turu – tor nuduglaltai/ Ule bugu – dor udegeleltei/ Utegu humun – dor amuraltai gajar bololu）（引自《蒙古源流》）。

原来这首诗对穆纳山咀赞美之余，流露出将来把自己的尸骨安葬在这里的意愿。图瓦《克孜尔》中的那首诗，应该说表达的意思与此相同。这与故事中克孜尔在他曾经赞美的地方死亡和成吉思汗的灵车在他曾经赞美的地方陷住不动，因而在那里营建八白室这些情节，是前后呼应的。

就第四个情节来说，尽管图瓦《克孜尔》的故事在细节上简略了许多，而蒙古成吉思汗的传说又很繁杂，但它们的基本情节是一致的：克孜尔可汗不顾库格都里可汗的苦苦哀求，杀其身，夺其妻；而成吉思汗也不顾失都儿忽汗的苦苦哀求，杀其身，夺其妻。

关于第五个情节，从《蒙古黄金史纲》摘录的故事中，看不出与图瓦《克孜尔》相对应的情节。然而有趣的是，失都儿忽汗在临死时提醒成吉思汗，要仔细搜遍其妻子的身体。搜遍失都儿忽汗的夫人的身体究竟有什么意义，其身体中藏着什么，故事没有交代。失都儿忽汗死了，也就没有了下文。这句话似乎很有意思，但就这样很神秘地留在那里。如果不查看其他的蒙古历史文献，还真弄不清是什么意思。然而《古代蒙古诸汗源流大黄史》等一些蒙古历史文献已经揭开了这个谜。根据《大黄史》中的故事，当成吉思汗结束失都儿忽汗的性命时，失都儿忽汗提醒成吉思汗，要搜遍古尔伯勒津郭斡夫人的身体。成吉思汗接纳了古尔伯勒津郭斡夫人。后来这位夫人到哈喇沐连（Khara muren）沐浴之际，给自己的父亲写了一封信，告知他自己将投河自尽,她的尸体要逆流而寻,不可顺流而找,把信系在其父使唤的一只鸟的脖子上寄走了。她回到成吉思汗身边,将一把剪刀藏在自己身体的最隐秘之处,伤了主上的阳物,出逃到哈喇沐连河边,投河而尽。从此,蒙古人将哈喇沐连改称哈屯郭勒。① 与这个版本的故事相近的还有萨囊－彻辰的《蒙古源流》中的故事,② 金巴道尔吉的《水晶鉴》中的故事,③ 达尔玛的《金轮千辐》中的故事④ 等。

我认为,《古代蒙古诸汗源流大黄史》、《蒙古源流》、《水晶鉴》和《金轮千辐》等文献中的故事,就这一故事情节来说是完整的。而佚名氏的《蒙古黄金史纲》、罗卜桑丹津的《蒙古黄金史》是故意删除了这个情节。其原因我认为有三条:第一,这些文献的作者可能认为,这样的事情有损于圣主成吉思汗的形象,于是他们认为有必要删除;第二,他们可能还怀疑这个故事情节的真实性,于是作了删除处理。蒙古人中间对成吉思汗的死因还有另一种说法,说他是在一次狩猎中从马上摔伤而死的;⑤ 第三,这些作者在写成吉思汗征服唐古特国的历史时利用的史料来源有两种,一种是古代的历史文献,另一种是民间流传的历史传说故事,当两种史料相互发生冲突时,他们只好对其中一个采取删除处理。而这样处理的过程中很容易出现衔接不连贯等这样那样的问题。我们也确实感觉到,这些文献中叙述成吉思汗患病、逝世的部分,在前后衔接上是不够理想的。

到这里,我们清楚地看到,图瓦《克孜尔》的故事和成吉思汗征服唐古特国的传说故事之间在第五个情节上也是完全相同的。图瓦《克孜尔》中克孜尔可汗征服库格都里汗的故事和蒙古历史文献中成吉思汗征服唐古特国的故事,在很多重要的情节上相同或相似,甚至在人物所说的具体话语上都存在相似性。这一事实明白无误地告诉我们,这两个故事具有同源性,也就是说,关于成吉思汗的历史传说融入到图瓦《克孜尔》故事中去了。

---

① 乌力吉图校注《大黄史》,第89—90页。哈喇沐连(Khara muren),直译作黑河,古代蒙古人叫黄河为哈喇沐连;哈屯郭勒(Khadun gool),哈屯(khadun)为夫人之意,郭勒(gool),即河,哈屯郭勒可直译作夫人河。蒙古人至今叫黄河为哈屯郭勒。
② 萨囊－彻辰撰,呼和温都尔校注:《蒙古源流》,第101—130页。
③ 金巴道尔吉撰,留金锁校注:《水晶鉴》,第419页。
④ 达尔玛撰,乔吉校注:《金轮千辐》,第82—83页。
⑤ 巴根校注:《阿萨拉克齐史》,第57—58页。

五

《克孜尔》的故事与成吉思汗征伐西夏的传说之间的对应性已经由上面的讨论中得到确认。那么,成吉思汗的传说是怎么进入到图瓦《克孜尔》中去的呢? 是否曾经流传过成吉思汗征服西夏的英雄史诗? 带着这个问题我们再次分析了成吉思汗的传说故事。我们的分析是从两个方面进行的。在对 17 世纪以后的蒙古文历史文献中有关成吉思汗征服西夏的传说进行分析后发现,这个传说本身具有英雄史诗的很多特征,包括具有史诗的传统题材、情节、母题;在对 13、14 世纪的蒙古历史文献和 17 世纪以后的蒙古文历史文献进行比较以后发现,所有这些具有史诗特征的题材、情节和母题绝大部分在 13、14 世纪的文献中则没有,说明它们是在成吉思汗去世以后很久,大约在 15—17 世纪形成,并被蒙古历史文献所吸收的。

成吉思汗征服西夏国,是历史上发生过的真实事件。这个历史事件被成吉思汗去世后不久成书的《蒙古秘史》所记载。根据《蒙古秘史》的记载,成吉思汗先后两次出征西夏。第一次,在征伐金国返回途中进攻了西夏。当时西夏的国王布尔汗向成吉思汗投降,誓言要向成吉思汗称臣,成吉思汗退兵。后来,成吉思汗征伐回回时,派使者命令布尔汗作为右翼一同出兵。但是布尔汗不但拒绝出兵,还出言不逊藐视成吉思汗。于是成吉思汗完成了征服中亚和欧洲的七年远征后又出兵征伐西夏。在进军途中,成吉思汗行猎,坐骑受到惊吓,成吉思汗从马上摔下受伤。成吉思汗劝布尔汗投降,布尔汗的一个部下不从,被成吉思汗击溃。布尔汗见势不妙,要求投降,成吉思汗受降,并给布尔汗赐名叫失都儿忽汗。成吉思汗命令杀死布尔汗,西夏灭亡,成吉思汗伤重去世。[①] 波斯历史学家拉施特于 14 世纪初主编完成的《史集》对这个历史事件的记载已经开始增加一些民间传说的内容,但基本上与《蒙古秘史》的记载相吻合。其中最引人注目的是增加了征伐西夏的途中成吉思汗梦中得到启示,知道自己死期将至,留下了遗嘱。按照《蒙古秘史》的记载,成吉思汗是在此之前,远征回回途中听从一位爱妃的劝告才立下遗嘱指定自己的接班人的。[②]

---

① 额尔登泰、乌云达赉校勘本:《蒙古秘史》,呼和浩特:内蒙古人民出版社,1980 年,第 249、256、265、267、268 节。

② 同上书,第 254、255 节。

　　这么一个历史事件,到了 17 世纪的蒙古文历史文献中完全变了样。首先,在征战主题被保留的前提下又加入了抢婚主题,这是传统的史诗主题。成吉思汗形象更具有史诗英雄的色彩(会变幻术)。如前所述,失都儿忽汗的形象则更具有史诗中的蟒古思形象的特征。失都儿忽汗有能预知未来的狗和恶鹦、巫婆,以及成吉思汗消灭恶鹦和巫婆的情节,也是蒙古史诗中常见的母题和情节。杀死失都儿忽汗时,射、砍皆不能入,于是失都儿忽汗说道:"砍、射都不能损伤我的身体,我的靴腰里藏着三折斑纹肚带,用它绞死吧!"蒙古史诗中英雄的敌人也是这样刀枪不入,敌人自己说出杀死自己的办法,甚至连一些具体的诗句,也保留着浓重的史诗味道。比如说,失都儿忽汗的探子被捕后说的话就是这样:所有的马都追不上的库斯博勒特铁青马,〈到如今〉被追上了,四蹄似乎脱落了;我就是战胜一切人的啮食哈喇布通,都败在你们手下,我的头颅怕是要掉了。这句话,我们通常只有从史诗中听到。

　　这一切都显示出,历史上,取材于成吉思汗征服西夏的历史事件的英雄史诗似乎很流行。这样的史诗可能产生于 14—16 世纪之间,到了 17 世纪的时候,蒙古历史学家们编纂史书时,把这个史诗作为史料吸收到自己的著作中。

　　这点有特别重要的意义。它不仅反映了蒙古史诗产生、发展和流传方面的一些轨迹,同时也反映了蒙古史诗与历史的相互关系。我们过去只是在理论上承认蒙古历史文献与蒙古史诗有体裁和题材上的传承关系,并没有能够证明我们的历史文献直接引用具体的史诗材料。如果我们的研究将来能进一步证明是正确的,那么,对认识草原的蒙古游牧民族的历史学家怎样编写史书这一问题将有重要的意义。

六

　　最后,我想谈谈关于成吉思汗的史诗为什么会传入图瓦人中的问题。

　　回答这个问题的关键,还是在于进一步了解图瓦《克孜尔》及其传统,以及图瓦人和蒙古人之间的历史文化联系。图瓦的史诗艺人们普遍认为,《克孜尔》是蒙古史诗。[①] 这种说法大概是可信的。因为,在我们翻译出的九部故事中,除了现在讨论的这个之外,其他的都在蒙古《格斯尔》里有相应的故事。并且,它们之间的差异

---

① 　库拉尔整理、注释:《阿齐图·克孜尔·箧尔根》,第 6 页。

不是很大。其中有的还与蒙古《格斯尔》的相应故事几乎一样。因此,可以认定蒙古《格斯尔》流传到图瓦人中间,成为了图瓦《克孜尔》。那么,蒙古《格斯尔》什么时候传播到图瓦人中间的呢？关于这个问题,库拉尔认为,可分两个阶段。第一个阶段,是 1716 年北京木刻版《格斯尔》刊行之前,由于图瓦与蒙古两个民族在文化上的密切联系,蒙古《格斯尔》故事以口耳相传的方式流传到图瓦人中间。第二个阶段,是 1716 年北京木刻版《格斯尔》刊行之后,《克孜尔》在图瓦地区广泛传播。1861 年 B. B. 拉德洛夫从图瓦最边远、最偏僻的被崇山峻岭包围的卡拉阔勒(Khara kul, 黑湖之意)地区发现的《格斯尔》的印刷本残卷,可以证明这一点。① 因此,可以肯定,《克孜尔》在图瓦地区传播至少已经有近 300 年的历史了。

蒙古《格斯尔》传播到图瓦人中间成为图瓦《克孜尔》,并且在那里就与图瓦传统文化相结合,形成了非常独特的图瓦《克孜尔》文化。最令人惊奇的是,格斯尔的名字在那里与历史人物成吉思汗的名字紧密地联系在一起了。在图瓦地区,有很多人认为克孜尔和成吉思汗就是一个人,认为他们的故事是历史上曾经发生过的真实事件,因此,有的人干脆把《克孜尔》史诗叫做《克孜尔·成吉思汗传》。同时,图瓦地区广为流传的《克孜尔·成吉思汗的水渠》、《克孜尔坝》等历史传说,更为克孜尔和成吉思汗是一个人这样的观念提供了依据。② 这是蒙古地区所不曾有的。

历史上图瓦和蒙古两个民族在政治、经济、文化等方面都有密切联系。图瓦族是一个跨国界的民族。其中大多数居住在俄罗斯联邦图瓦共和国境内,一部分居住在蒙古国西部,另有一小部分居住在我国新疆的阿勒泰地区。从蒙古帝国时期起,图瓦人同蒙古人的关系就非常密切,他们在政治、军事各方面与蒙古人并肩作战,建立了深厚的友谊。在宗教信仰方面,他们同蒙古人一样信仰喇嘛教。在经济方面,他们同蒙古人一样过着游牧生活。到上个世纪 30 年代为止,图瓦人还在使用蒙古文。这种亲密的关系,不仅强烈地影响了两个民族的口头文学的相互交流,更使得原本属于突厥语族的图瓦语在基本词汇方面更接近于蒙古语。现在,图瓦语的基本词汇中蒙古语词汇占据相当的分量。在口头史诗这方面,图瓦英雄史诗和蒙古英雄史诗不仅在题材、主题、母题和创作程式等方面存在着惊人的相似性,而且两个民族还拥有共同的史诗作品。图瓦英雄史诗有三百多部,其中,《十五岁

---

① 库拉尔整理、注释:《阿齐图·克孜尔·篾尔根》,第 9 页。
② 同上,第 10 页。

的阿勒泰·孙布尔》、《宝日勒岱·莫尔根》等史诗在蒙古民族民间也有流传。① 图瓦人喜欢蒙古英雄史诗,他们中有很多人收藏蒙古史诗手抄本。蒙古著名的英雄史诗《汗哈冉贵》的一个手抄本,就是在图瓦的克孜勒市发现的。

历史、文化上如此密切的联系,为包括史诗在内的一些口头文学作品在两个民族之间传播提供了便利。于是,我们就找到了成吉思汗的传说进入图瓦《克孜尔》的一种可能的途径——历史上曾经有过关于成吉思汗征服唐古特国的独立的传说,它或许是英雄史诗。这个故事或史诗在蒙古族和图瓦族中都曾广泛流传。在蒙古族这边,这个故事到了 17 世纪就被蒙古族史学家们当作史料收入到他们编纂的蒙古文历史文献当中;而在图瓦那边,这个故事仍然口头流传,并逐渐融入到了《克孜尔》史诗中。事实上,关于成吉思汗征服唐古特国的传说的蒙古口头版本并没有在蒙古民间消失,人们从内蒙古当代著名的史诗艺人金巴扎木苏那里记录下来的《格斯尔》说唱本中,发现了一个来源于成吉思汗征服唐古特国途中命哈萨尔射杀失都儿忽汗的传播瘟疫的巫婆的故事。② 这更表明了有关成吉思汗征伐唐古特的故事在图瓦人中以口头形式流传至今的可能性。

参考书目

阿兰金(Aranjin, Y. L.):《图瓦英雄史诗》,克孜勒:图瓦文出版社,1990 年。

巴根(Bagana, B.)校注:《阿萨拉克齐史》,北京:民族出版社,1984 年。

达尔玛(Dharm - a)撰,乔吉(Choiji)校注:《金轮千辐》,呼和浩特:内蒙古人民出版社,1987 年。

金巴道尔基(Jimbadorji)撰,留金锁校注:《水晶鉴》,北京:民族出版社,1984 年。

库拉尔(Kuular, D.S.)整理、注释:《阿齐图·克孜尔·篾尔根》,克孜勒:图瓦文出版社,1963 年。

涅克留朵夫(Nekliudov, S.Y.):《蒙古人民的英雄史诗》,呼和浩特:内蒙古大学出版社,1991 年。

仁钦道尔吉:《〈格斯尔〉文本的一项重大发现——被埋没的天才艺人金巴扎木苏》,北京:《民族文学研究》2002 年第 1 期,第 4—5 页。

萨囊 - 彻辰撰,呼和温都尔校注:《蒙古源流》,北京:民族出版社,1987 年。

乌力吉图(Uljiitu)校注:《大黄史》,北京:民族出版社,1983 年。

朱风、贾敬颜译:《汉译蒙古黄金史纲》,呼和浩特:内蒙古人民出版社,1985 年。

---

① 阿兰金:《图瓦英雄史诗》,克孜勒:图瓦文出版社,1990 年,第 4 页。

② 仁钦道尔吉:《〈格斯尔〉文本的一项重大发现——被埋没的天才艺人金巴扎木苏》,北京:《民族文学研究》2002 年第 1 期,第 4—5 页。

《玛纳斯》史诗的口头特征

阿地里·居玛吐尔地

摘　要　本文将通过讨论《玛纳斯》史诗的程式特征、歌手的"表演中的创作"和语境，来探讨这部规模宏大的口头史诗的一些最基本特征。要想了解柯尔克孜族口头传统，就要从英雄史诗《玛纳斯》的演唱活动中了解，去现场观察天才的民间歌手玛纳斯奇的传承和表演。这种演唱在今天仍然保持着它的古老形态。《玛纳斯》史诗的结构和内容，具有程式化的特点。程式化结构是《玛纳斯》史诗最稳定的一个因素，而程式化语词则是史诗能够被歌手自如调配和运用的主要因素。《玛纳斯》史诗的表演是一个综合性的展示过程，具有复杂的艺术表演形式。对于口传史诗《玛纳斯》来说，印刷文本只是传统的、活形态表演形式的一种不完整的替代品。总之，《玛纳斯》是在漫长的口头传统中产生的，是柯尔克孜族最具代表性的史诗。

关键词　《玛纳斯》史诗，口头性，程式

柯尔克孜族的口头传统包括韵文形式的英雄史诗(jomok)、部落系谱(sanjira)、古老的仪式歌(aytidar)、哭悼歌(koshok)、情歌(süyüüir)、生活歌(turmux ir)、儿歌(baldar ir)、谚语(makal－lakap)和散文形式的神话(apsana)、传说(ulamish)、故事(juööjomok)、谜语(tabishmak)、笑话(shakaba)等。其中，《玛纳斯》史诗的表演可以追溯到一千多年以前，它是柯尔克孜族口头文学传统中最古老最经典的部分。① 吉尔

---

① 根据《玛纳斯》史诗的内容，史诗的最初演唱者是主人公英雄玛纳斯的40勇士之一——额尔奇吾勒。他的名字"额尔奇"在柯尔克孜语中就是歌手的意思。史诗是在漫长的发展过程中，经过各个年代玛纳斯奇的反复演唱不断成熟和完善的。作为一部口头史诗，其产生年代的考证是一个十分复杂的课题。联合国教科文组织根据各国学者的研究成果，把1995年定为《玛纳斯》史诗年，并在吉尔吉斯(柯尔克孜)斯坦首都彼什凯克举办了史诗诞生1000周年纪念活动和世界性的学术研讨会。

吉斯(柯尔克孜)当代最著名作家钦吉斯·艾特玛托夫(Chingiz Aytmatov)① 针对柯尔克孜精神文化特点,特别是针对柯尔克孜的口头诗歌遗产指出:"如果其他民族将自己过去的文化和历史用书面文学、建筑、雕塑、戏剧和绘画艺术保存的话,柯尔克孜族则将自己所有的思想意识、民族的荣辱,为自由和独立而进行的抗争、理想以及民族的历史和生活均用口头史诗的形式进行展现。"②史诗的创作者、口头传承者都是各个不同时代的玛纳斯奇(Manaschi)。③ 对于柯尔克孜族的口头传统,我们只能通过现场观察天才的民间歌手玛纳斯奇的传承和表演,通过今天仍然保持着自己古老形态的英雄史诗《玛纳斯》的演唱活动去寻找答案。

《玛纳斯》史诗讲述的是以玛纳斯及其七代子孙的英雄业绩为内容的传奇故事,赞颂的是他们的英雄主义精神。史诗虽然在民间传承了近 10 个世纪,但直到 19 世纪下半叶才由俄国哈萨克军官乔坎·瓦里汗诺夫(C. Valikhanov)④ 和俄国突厥学家拉德洛夫(V. V. Radlov)⑤ 从民间歌手口中第一次记录下它的文本。从那以后,《玛纳斯》史诗开始逐渐被世界各国学者和读者所认识,并发展成为当前这样的国际性学科。到目前为止,从我国的新疆维吾尔自治区以及吉尔吉斯斯坦、哈萨克斯坦、阿富汗等国的柯尔克孜族聚居区搜集到的《玛纳斯》史诗的各类唱本有 150

---

① 钦吉斯·艾特玛托夫于 1928 年出生,是当代世界文坛上享有盛誉的著名的吉尔吉斯斯坦作家。他的成名作《查密利雅》发表于 1958 年。此后他又先后发表了《白轮船》、《再见,古里萨勒》、《一日长于百年》、《断头台》等名作。根据联合国教科文组织 1997 年的统计,艾特玛托夫的作品被译成 127 种语言,是世界上拥有读者最多的作家之一。他的作品几乎全部被译成了汉语,深受中国读者喜爱。

② Chingiz, Aytmatov. "Beaming Height of Ancient Kirghiz Spirit," Said Aliev, Raikul Sarypbekov, Kadyrbek Matiev, eds., *Encyclopaedical Phenomenon of Epos' Manas'*, Bishkek: Encyclopedia Press, 1995. p. 15.

③ "玛纳斯奇"为柯尔克孜语,指专门以《玛纳斯》史诗演唱为职业的民间艺人。

④ 乔坎·瓦里汗诺夫(1835—1865)是最早对《玛纳斯》史诗进行搜集的学者。他于 1856 年、1857 年数次对吉尔吉斯斯坦的伊塞克湖地区和我国的伊犁、特克斯等地的柯尔克孜族聚居区进行调查,并在那里记录下了《玛纳斯》史诗的传统章节"阔阔托依的祭奠",共计 3319 行。

⑤ 拉德洛夫(1837—1918)于 1862 年和 1869 年在柯尔克孜地区进行了卓有成效的田野调查工作,记录了包括《玛纳斯》在内的大量传统口头诗文本。其中,《玛纳斯》史诗文本包括史诗第一部《玛纳斯》的全部传统章节以及第二部《赛麦台》的部分章节,共计 12454 行。1885 年,他将这些文本编入自己的系列丛书《北方诸突厥语民族的民间文学典范》第 5 卷中,以《卡拉—柯尔克孜(吉尔吉斯)的方言》(*The Dialect of the Kara – Kirghiz*)为题在圣彼得堡出版。

多个。① 柯尔克孜族是用口头形式保存自己的历史记忆的民族,要想——列举对史诗的传承和发展做出过重要贡献的每一个天才玛纳斯奇的名字是不可能的。但是有些玛纳斯奇的名字将永远载入史册。如与玛纳斯生活在同一个英雄时代、成为英雄的 40 勇士之一、跟随玛纳斯东征西战的额尔奇吾勒(Irqi‐Uul);②吉尔吉斯斯

---

① 见《〈玛纳斯〉百科全书》,共两卷,吉尔吉斯斯坦彼什凯克,1995 年;郎樱:《〈玛纳斯〉论》;斯·阿里耶夫,特·库勒玛托夫,《玛纳斯奇与〈玛纳斯〉研究者》;曼拜特,《〈玛纳斯〉史诗的多种变体及其说唱艺术》;阿地里·居玛吐尔地,托汗·依萨克,《当代荷马〈玛纳斯〉演唱大师居素普·玛玛依评传》,呼和浩特:内蒙古大学出版社,2002 年。

② 在史诗的各个唱本中,都有关于额尔奇吾勒的内容,他是第一位将玛纳斯的英雄业绩创编成歌进行演唱的人。在居素普·玛玛依唱本中,对于额尔奇吾勒的身份有如下描述:玛纳斯率领大军远征,攻入契丹的首都别依京,后遭到敌首领空吾尔拜的暗算,头部被毒斧劈中,在阿勒曼别特的劝说下回塔拉斯养伤。哈萨克将领阔克确也被敌人杀死。以下诗行叙述全军统帅阿勒曼别特向各位将领强调各自的任务,并与他们话别。他对玛纳斯 40 勇士之一的额尔奇吾勒说:

额尔奇吾勒你不要去参战,	Uruxka irqi barbaghen,
你要紧握你的笔杆,	Kalemdi kolgo karmaghen,
英雄玛纳斯的英灵,	El unutup kalbasen,
决不能被人们遗忘。	Aykol Manas arbaghen.
从汗王玛玛依至今的历史,	Han Mamaydan berjaka,
你都曾亲耳听说。	Eldin gebin ukkanseng,
自从雄狮跨马登程,	Aristan atka mingeli,
你与他同吃同住紧紧相随,	Birge jatip bir turup,
成长为今天这份年龄。	Uxul jaxka qikkanseng.
英雄的光辉业绩,	Oyronumdun jumuxun,
你可不能有点滴的遗忘,	Unutuptaxtap koybogun,
要时时刻刻回想思索。	Jatsang‐Tursang oylogun,
他未干的事情,	Kilbagande kildi dep,
你不必有意夸张渲染。	Apirtip aytsang bolbodong.
与我相关的业绩,	Men ozum kilgan ixterim,
早已被我记在纸上,	Ak kagazga butkomun,
你可从阿茹凯手中索取,	Arukeden surap al,
把它也编入其中……	Irqim, sozgo ulap al.

坦的19—20世纪之交的玛纳斯奇特尼别克·加皮(Tinibek Japiy)、① 20世纪的玛纳斯奇萨恩拜·奥诺孜巴克(Sagimbay Orozbak)② 和萨雅克拜·卡拉卡拉耶夫(Sayakbay Karalayev)等;③ 中国20世纪的玛纳斯奇居素朴阿昆·阿帕依(Jüsüpakhun Apay)④、额布拉音·阿昆别克(Ibirayim Akunbek)⑤ 和艾什玛特·玛木别特居素普(Eshmat Mambetjüsüp)⑥ 等。在当代玛纳斯奇中,出生于我国新疆阿合奇县哈拉不拉克乡米尔开其村被国内外学者尊称为"当代荷马"、"活着的荷马"的居素普·玛玛依

---

① 特尼别克·加皮(1846—1902)出生在吉尔吉斯斯坦伊塞克湖边,是当时整个柯尔克孜族玛纳斯奇中最杰出的代表人物。他的演唱对后代玛纳斯奇产生了广泛的影响。20世纪最著名的几位玛纳斯奇如我国的居素朴阿昆·阿帕依(Jüsüpakhun Apay)、艾什玛特·玛木别特居素普(Eshmat Mambet jüsüp),吉尔吉斯斯坦的萨恩拜·奥诺孜巴克(Sagimbay Orozbak)曾在学艺初期一同来到他们下,拜他为师,跟随他数年学习史诗的演唱技艺。其唱本史诗第二部《塞麦台》的一部分曾被记录下来并于1898年和1925年分别在喀山和莫斯科以单行本形式出版。

② 萨恩拜·奥诺孜巴克(1867—1930),吉尔吉斯斯坦著名玛纳斯奇。他能够演唱史诗前三部的内容,具有浓郁的传统特色,但是由于各种原因从他口中只记录下了史诗第一部的内容,已出版共计180 378行。

③ 萨雅克拜·卡拉耶夫(1894—1971),吉尔吉斯斯坦著名玛纳斯奇,是20世纪玛纳斯奇中演唱内容最长的一位。他的唱本包括史诗第一部《玛纳斯》、第二部《塞麦台》、第三部《赛依铁克》以及第四部《凯南》、第五部《阿勒木萨热克和库兰萨热克》等,共计500 553行。

④ 居素朴阿昆·阿帕依于1920年去世。出生在中国新疆阿合奇县。他曾于少年时代与萨恩拜·奥诺孜巴克、艾什玛特·玛木别特居素普等师从当时名扬四方的大玛纳斯奇特尼别克·加皮学艺。1917年春,他与萨恩拜·奥诺孜巴克进行《玛纳斯》演唱比赛,展示自己的才能。他们两人的史诗演唱比赛成为佳话传扬四方。在此期间萨恩拜·奥诺孜巴克因战乱从吉尔吉斯斯坦逃亡到中国新疆阿合奇县。由他演唱的史诗前三部的内容曾由居素普·玛玛依的兄长巴勒瓦依记录下来传给居素普·玛玛依,成为后者唱本的一个主要来源。

⑤ 额布拉音·阿昆别克(Ibirayim Akunbek 1882—1959),出生在中国新疆阿合奇县。他在民间的演唱活动比较少,但根据居素普·玛玛依本人的讲述,他的兄长巴勒瓦依从额布拉音·阿昆别克口中记录下史诗第四部《凯耐尼木》、第五部《塞依特》、第六部《阿斯勒巴恰 – 别克巴恰》、第七部《索木比莱克》、第八部《奇格台》的内容,并且把这些篇目传给居素普·玛玛依,居素普·玛玛依经过学习吸收,成为他唱本的另一重要来源。

⑥ 艾什玛特·玛木别特居素普(Eshmat Mambetjüsüp, 1880—1963),出生在中国新疆乌恰县。他是中国20世纪玛纳斯奇的代表人物之一。他演唱的史诗前三部《玛纳斯》、《塞麦台》、《赛依铁克》的内容曾于1961年被记录下来,并由郎樱和玉塞音阿吉翻译成汉文,但在"文革"中第一部的原始记录稿丢失,第二部和第三部的柯尔克孜文版于2003年由克孜勒苏柯尔克孜文出版社出版,共计11 070行。除了史诗《玛纳斯》之外,他还曾演唱过柯尔克孜其他民间传统史诗《艾尔托西图克》、《禽王布达依克》、《库尔曼别克》、《加尼西和巴依西》等。

(Jusup Mamay)① 无疑是其中最杰出的代表。

从口头语言艺术的角度观察,《玛纳斯》史诗至少有以下三个特征:(1)程式化传统结构(包括主题和故事范型②),程式化传统句法和程式化的语词;(2)"表演中的创作"——口头史诗创作、保存和传播唯一有效的方式;(3)史诗创作的语境——玛纳斯奇和听(观)众的互动关系以及他们与史诗口承文本之间的关系。本文将通过对《玛纳斯》史诗的程式特征(尽管没能充分讨论史诗的程式化句法构成过程)、歌手的表演以及表演的语境的分析,探讨这部规模宏大的口头史诗的一些最基本特征。

《玛纳斯》史诗的结构和内容之中都具有程式化的特点。程式化结构具有很强的功能。在歌手创编史诗时,这种功能在以下两方面具有显著的作用:第一是在史诗整体结构的构造方面;第二是在史诗内容的铺展方面。根据洛德的观点,在口头传统中存在着诸多故事范型,无论围绕着它们而建构的故事有多大程度的变化,它们作为具有重要功能并充满着巨大活力的组织要素,存在于口头故事文本的创作和传播之中。③

在整体结构方面,《玛纳斯》与古希腊的《伊利亚特》、英国的《贝奥武甫》、法国

---

① 居素普·玛玛依,1918 年 4 月出生,在当地早已声名远扬,从 1961 年起,受到我国民俗学界的关注。他从 8 岁开始学唱,到十几岁时已经掌握了完整的史诗。他的唱本包括《玛纳斯》、《赛麦台》、《赛依铁克》、《凯耐尼木》、《赛依特》、《阿斯勒巴恰 – 别克巴恰》、《索木比莱克》、《奇格台》等 8 部,232 200 多行。其柯尔克孜文版在 1984 年至 1995 年由新疆人民出版社出版,共计 18 卷。除了《玛纳斯》之外,他还演唱并出版了《艾尔托西图克》、《库尔曼别克》、《巴额西》、《托勒托依》等十几部柯尔克孜族传统史诗。

② "口头程式理论"的创立者之一美国学者洛德(Albert B. Lord)认为,歌手在按照程式化文本形式讲述故事时,除了由词组组成的规模较小的程式外,还有一个由一些反复使用的一组意义构成的叙述单元,如一次集会、宴会、一次战斗以及对马匹、男女主人公的描绘等。在柯尔克孜口头传统中也存在这一类主题,与南斯拉夫克罗地亚人的史诗相类似。这些主题虽然用基本相同的词语来表述,但在不同的歌手表演时具有一定的伸缩性和差异性。主题所容纳的信息量越大,其变异性就越大,反之则相对稳定。洛德认为在口头传统中存在着故事范型(story pattern),不管围绕着它有多少故事的变体,它仍具有伟大的生命力,在口头故事文本的创作和传递中起组织功能。比如,荷马史诗《奥德赛》的故事模式有五个成分:离去、劫难、回归、果报、婚礼。对于柯尔克孜族口头传统史诗歌手而言,故事模式具有更大规模的涵盖面,绝大多数口头史诗作品都遵循:诞生、苦难童年、少年立功、婚姻、出征、死而复生(或进入地下)、家乡遭劫、回归等主题序列。

③ 有关论述见 *The Singer of Tales*,Albert B. Lord,1960;[美]约翰·迈尔斯·弗里《口头诗学:帕里—洛德理论》;尹虎彬《古代经典与口头传统》。

的《罗兰之歌》、西班牙的《熙德之歌》、德国的《尼伯龙根之歌》等欧洲史诗截然不同。上述欧洲史诗基本上都是以事件为结构中心，而《玛纳斯》则是典型的以人物为结构中心的史诗。它基本上是按照英雄主人公从出生到死亡的人生轨迹来叙述故事。我国著名史诗专家郎樱教授经过多年的比较研究后指出，突厥语民族史诗在叙事结构上遵循以下模式：英雄的特异诞生—苦难的童年—少年立功—娶妻成家—外出征战—进入地下（或死而复生）—家乡遭劫（或被篡权）—敌人被杀（或篡权者受惩处）—英雄凯旋（或牺牲）。[①] 这种叙述方式或史诗的宏观结构，在柯尔克孜口头传统中，不仅属于像《玛纳斯》那样讲述数代英雄人物事迹的史诗集群，而且也属于数以十计的其他史诗作品，甚至也被哈萨克、维吾尔、乌兹别克、土库曼、卡拉卡勒帕克等其他突厥语民族广泛采用。[②]

作为一种与书面文学不同的语言艺术形式，口头史诗开放式的程式结构使得演唱者在演唱过程中能够自由地从古老的口头传统中撷取任何一个合适的语词、母题或者主题运用到自己的演唱之中，也可以将任何一个主题在允许的范围内扩展和精简，这也正是洛德所谓的"限度之内变化的原则"。在表演中对于主题的这种调整来自于传统，因此也受传统的制约，在适度的变异中保持整部史诗的内容和结构的稳定性。表演者只是在传统的程式化结构中运用各种史诗材料创编故事。语词程式和主题具有一定限度的可变性，而史诗的整体结构框架则是不可变的。程式化结构是《玛纳斯》史诗最稳定的一个因素。

程式化句法作为柯尔克孜口头史诗中的另一个程式单元，包含史诗步格、韵律以及平行式。它属于难度较大的需要进行专门的深入细致分析的作诗法范畴。考虑到它的特殊性，在本文中暂不讨论。

根据口头程式理论（或帕里－洛德理论），程式是一组词或短语，甚至是类似于洛德所说的"大词"（large words）的那种由特定的词组和短语组成的一节诗。这类程式通常是在相同的步格条件下被运用，表达一个相对稳定的意义。但是，它的一个重要的先决条件是，这类程式或"大词"，作为一个特定的单元，必须反复出现在口头文本当中，为史诗歌手的演唱和表演提供便利条件。[③] 它有相对固定的韵式和

① 郎樱：《〈玛纳斯〉论》，第21页。

② See Nora K. Chadwick and Victor Zhirmunsky, *Oral Epics of Central Asia*, London: Cambridge University Press, 1960; Karl Reichl, *Turkic Oral Epics Poetry*: *Traditions*, *Forms*, *Poetic Structure*, New York & London: Garland Publishing INC., 1992.

③ 参见［美］约翰·迈尔斯·弗里：《口头程式理论：口头传统研究概述》。

相对固定的形态,它由歌手群体所共享和传承,并反复地出现在演唱文本中。① 在柯尔克孜族漫长的口头史诗传统中,程式不仅为玛纳斯奇记忆和演唱史诗的主题、内容,创造史诗的新唱本提供了极为有效的便利方法,而且在演唱中按照传统脉络,把前一个概念同另一个新的概念关联起来,以此来引导听众的思维,吸引他们的注意力。比如:"让我们放下这一段,回到英雄玛纳斯身边……""让我们把这一段放一放,讲一讲阔克确之子阿依达尔汗……""我们在此停一停,听一听卡拉汗之子卡妮凯的情况如何……"等。这类程式在不同的语境之下被玛纳斯奇们自由灵活地运用。最稳定的语词程式是那些表现最常见意义的程式。英雄的名字、骏马的名称、一些特殊的地名等都会成为引导歌手思维、激发史诗歌手想像的特殊"标示",顺着这些"标示",歌手们在表演中很快找到与自己的描述对象相关的线索和信息。在这些"标示"的作用下,表现英雄的外表、性格,如面貌、表情、服装、坚忍不拔的毅力、勇气和胆量、超人的力量等,以及坐骑、武器、各种战斗、一对一的搏斗、战场的残酷、自然景色以及其他各种超自然的事物的大量程式会反复出现。② 对于程式的运用,让我们还是听一听玛纳斯奇自己的说法吧:③

    阿:(在演唱中)需要描述一位英雄时,比如在阿勒曼别特④ 要出场时,您首先想到的是什么?

---

① 朝戈金:《口头史诗诗学:冉皮勒〈江格尔〉程式句法研究》,第 204 页。

② 见拉德洛夫于 1885 年在圣彼德堡出版的《北方诸突厥语民族民间文学典范》丛书第 5 卷《卡拉-吉尔吉斯人的方言》(*The Dialect of the Kara - Kirghiz*)前言部分,该前言的英文部分见 *Encyclopaedical Phenomenon of Epos 'Manas'*, Bishkek: Encyclopedia Press, 1995. P. 25—34。在前言中,拉德洛夫对柯尔克孜族口头史诗表演的传统特征如口头叙述的记录,即兴创作,口头传统的基本叙事单元即陈词滥调,听众在表演中的作用,完整故事及其组成部件的多重构件(即主题),口头诗作中新旧叙事因素的混杂(即表演与传统),叙事中前后矛盾所具有的意义,现场语境对歌手创作的影响,表演中与叙事相伴随的韵律、旋律、调式等都提出了对后人具有很大启发作用的见解。

③ 根据本文作者 2001 年 8 月 26 日在阿合奇县进行田野调查时对居素普·玛玛依老人的访谈。此次访谈在居素普·玛玛依家中进行,访谈录以柯尔克孜文发表在《克孜勒苏文学》的柯尔克孜文版 2002 年第 2 期上。访谈对话中的"阿"表示访谈者阿地里·居玛吐尔地,"居"表示接受访谈者居素普·玛玛依老人。

④ 阿勒曼别特是《玛纳斯》史诗第一部中主要人物之一,是因家庭内讧而离家出走的契丹王子。他先投奔哈萨克汗王阔克确,后投奔玛纳斯,与他盟誓结为同乳兄弟,随同他东征西战,立下赫赫战功,为柯尔克孜人民崇拜的人物。

居:当阿勒曼别特出场时,我首先想到的是他的英雄事迹。

阿:那您怎么描述他呢?

居:首先要描述他的外貌。比如用这些话"金色的容颜光芒四射,洁白的脸上没有斑点。说话直率没有曲折,阿则孜汗的阿勒曼别特……"来描述他的容貌。这时,可能会有个别词语上的变化或者增加。当演唱卡妮凯时,① 只要有下面四行诗"汗王之女卡妮凯,是女人中的美女,是长头发中的贤能,是妇女中的巧者,是宽裙子② 中的纯洁者,是巾帼中的王者"就足够了。

阿:这些固定而且形象的诗句表现出了每一个人物的基本性格特征。那么,阿依曲莱克③ 又是怎样描述的呢?

居:描述阿依曲莱克要用"在天空飞翔,镀着一身金子的光芒,'她是多么的美丽啊',太阳和月亮也发出赞叹"这样的诗句来表现她的美貌,让太阳和月亮都为她而发出赞叹。如果不这样唱,阿依曲莱克的美丽就不能体现出来。

阿:其他英雄人物,如巴卡依、古里巧绕④ 也都有这样固定的描述诗句吗?

居:说到巴卡依,我会用"银白的长须闪闪发光,智慧超群的巴卡依老人"来描述他并用他自己的话来表现他出众的智慧。阿勒曼别特的性格中最引人注目的是他的正直。他甚至对自己的故乡也有什么说什么,没有丝毫的夸张和掩饰。

阿:除了这些英雄人物外,描述玛纳斯的骏马阿克库拉,他的武器装备等是不是也有固定的诗句呢?

居:是,是用固定的诗句来演唱。

阿:在演唱时您怎么就能想起这些诗句呢?

居:它们自己就会跑到我嘴边来。比如一个勇士冲上战场拼杀时,以前唱过的那些有关矛枪的诗句自己就会到你舌尖来。

阿:那么,您最初学唱(《玛纳斯》)时,先记住的是这些固定的诗行,还是故事内容的呢?

---

① 卡妮凯是主人公英雄玛纳斯的智勇双全的妻子和有力助手。

② 宽裙子:此指女人。

③ 阿依曲莱克是玛纳斯的儿媳,是人神结合而生的仙女,能够幻化成白天鹅在天空中飞翔,为史诗第二部主人公赛麦台的妻子。

④ 巴卡依为《玛纳斯》史诗第一部的主要英雄人物。古里巧绕为史诗第二部中的主要英雄人物。

居:先记住故事。

阿:然后呢?

居:开头的词。

阿:什么是开头的词呢?

居:开头的词就是像玛纳斯、阿勒曼别特、阔克确、古里巧绕这样的英雄人物的名字。无论他们在什么时候什么地方出现,只要有这些开头的词就会把故事引出来。

阿:也就是把那些您刚才说的那些固定的诗句引出来吗?

居:对。就是它们马上引到你嘴边来。如果想跳过这些词,就很难把后面的诗句排列演唱出来了,也可能根本就唱不下去。我演唱《玛纳斯》的方法就是这样。

这段访谈至少会给我们一些这样的启发,那就是对于口头表演已经驾轻就熟的玛纳斯奇面对听众,在表演中创编史诗时,只要他脑海中储存有足够的程式,他就会轻松地完成自己的使命,赢得观众的喝彩。这些固定的反复出现的诗句,即程式化语词,无疑是歌手对史诗内容进行记忆的重要线索,也是主题积累的一个重要组成部分。

这类程式弥漫于表演的全过程,数量多、形式繁杂,试图对它们进行分类是毫无意义的,也是徒劳的。但是,弄清它们最重要的两种表现形式对我们来说是至关重要的。第一是这些程式十分古老,在口头传统中经过数代人的传承,依然顽强地保持着它们原始的形态。在表演过程中,这类程式必然总是按其原始状态出现并保持不变。它们数量极多、在文本中反复使用的诸如"雄狮玛纳斯"、"阿依阔勒玛纳斯"、"勇士玛纳斯"、"青鬃狼玛纳斯"、"阿昆汗之女阿依曲莱克"、"绣着金色月牙的红色战旗"、"睿智的巴卡依"之类的程式,以及像以下由数句诗行构成的程式均属于这一类。

犹如金子和银子	Alten menen kumuxtun
最精华的部分组成。	Xiroosunon butkondoy.
就像由支撑大地和天空的	Asman menen jeringdin
擎天大柱组成。	Tiroosunon butkondoy.
像是由太阳和月亮,	Ayingmenen kunongdun

本身的光芒组成。	Bir ozunon butkondoy.
只有深厚的大地,	Alde kaleng karajer
才能够把玛纳斯支撑。	Manaska jerdiginen tutkondoy.

　　另一种语词程式虽然也表达特定的意义并且有相对固定的形态,但它们却能够在不同的语境中或多或少地得到变异。这类程式在大多数情况下都以"大词"的形态出现和运用。

　　《玛纳斯》史诗的叙事结构、主题以及语词均具有程式化的特点,史诗的外部整体结构是史诗结构规模较大的程式,而与史诗内容相关的内部程式则为语词和句法上的程式。程式不是一个羁绊,而是像血液一般流动在史诗传承和表演中。在"表演中的创作"中,"程式用于构筑诗行,常常遵循一种韵律——语法上的规则,主题则引导歌手快速创作过程的思考,去建构更大的结构"[1]。

　　对于玛纳斯奇来说,创编和演唱只是同一事物的两个方面。玛纳斯奇面对观众进行表演,意味着他们要调动自己长期以来储存在脑海中所有的对于自己和观众来说也都十分熟悉的程式来演唱史诗内容,并以生动的眼神、丰富的面部表情、手势、身体动作和变化起伏的韵律、音调调动观众的热情,帮助他们更好地理解和欣赏史诗。也就是说,《玛纳斯》史诗的表演是一个综合性艺术展示过程,是一个十分复杂的艺术表演形式。在这样的表演过程中,歌手和观众才能同时参与史诗的创作,在创作中发挥各自的作用,并在这样的互动关系中找到无穷的乐趣。这就是口头史诗的真正创作方式,即"表演中的创作"。歌手储存在脑海中的传统程式数量越多、内容越丰富,并能在表演中运用自如,他的表演就越能够引起观众的共鸣和喝彩,得到观众的赞赏和推崇。这是活形态口头史诗最典型的表演场面。对于口头史诗《玛纳斯》来说,印刷文本只是传统的活形态表演形式的一种不完整的替代品。这种替代品只能展示史诗的故事情节而不能包含伴随着史诗走过同样漫长岁月的与口头史诗文本血肉相依的故事背后的更加丰富多彩的事物。比如说我们通过阅读居素普·玛玛依唱本的印刷文本形式,只能够欣赏《玛纳斯》史诗的诗句和故事,但却不能够欣赏这位杰出的史诗歌手(玛纳斯奇)的表演风采,即他在传统语境当中的"表演中的创作"。表演是口头史诗的生命,我们只能通过特定语境下的表演才能全面理解口头史诗的本质。

---

① 尹虎彬:《古代经典与口头传统》。

另外,在观众面前演唱《玛纳斯》,是在特定语境下重新创作这部史诗的过程,也是对古老的口头史诗传统的一次翻新。"口头传统"不仅属于创作过程,而且属于所创作的作品本身。①《玛纳斯》史诗作为柯尔克孜族口头传统的代表作,它传递着来自古老源头的口头信息,而它的创作过程正好是一代又一代的玛纳斯奇反复演唱,不断翻新和再创作,在与观众的互动中口耳相传,用口头形式传承这些信息的过程。因此,每一次的演唱仅仅是漫长的史诗发展进程中,在当时特定时间和语境中的一次表演,是原始交流以口头形式发展的一个过程。虽然源自传统,但"每一次表演的性质都会因它所处的在整个过程中位置的不同而有所区别"②。我们必须牢记,史诗的演唱,从来都不是单向度的信息传递过程。史诗的歌手和听众都是史诗传统的参与者。"他们共享着大量的'内部知识',而且还存在着大量的极为复杂的交流和互动过程。"③ 对于玛纳斯奇来说,这个过程是他创造自己新的史诗变体、展示自己的表演才能、向观众传播自己的作品、在听众中扩大自己的影响、赢得听众们的赞誉的好机会。而对于听众们来讲,这是他们以各自的观点和审美情趣与玛纳斯奇共同参与史诗的创作,以极大的热情再一次欣赏这一古老的传统的机会。"每一次表演都是一首特定的歌,而同时又是一首一般的歌。我们正在聆听的歌是'这一首歌',因为每一次表演都不仅仅是一次表演;而是一次再创作。"④《玛纳斯》史诗的表演和传承也遵循这样的规律。

一首特定的歌,指的是一个过程。在这个过程里,歌手的每一次演唱,都是在传统基础上,根据自己的能力和新收获,在新的语境当中运用现成的程式,对古老的史诗的母题、主题和结构重新加以审视并进行适当调整,从而创编出一个属于自己的文本。实际上,不论是对于歌手还是对于听众,这样的一次演唱,只是传统生活中的一次事件。它具有不可重复性,绝对不可能原原本本地再现和回忆。"变异的模式包括细节的精雕细琢、删繁就简、某一序列中次序的改变和颠倒、材料的添加或省略、主题的置换更替,以及常常出现的不同的结尾方式等。"⑤ 口头史诗的叙事是一个繁简夹杂、灵活开放的复杂体系,其中的变异既可能发生在重大情节的安

---

① Jan Vansina, *Oral Tradition as History*, Madison, Wisc.: University of Wisconsin Press, 1985, p.3.
② Jan Vansina, *Oral Tradition as History*, Madison, Wisc.: University of Wisconsin Press, 1985, p.3.
③ 朝戈金:《口传史诗诗学:冉皮勒〈江格尔〉程式句法研究》,南宁:广西人民出版社,2000年,第98页。
④ [美]约翰·迈尔斯·弗里:《口头诗学:帕里—洛德理论》,第100页。
⑤ 同上,第101页。

排方面,也可能发生在修饰性的细节描述方面。

一般意义的歌,指无数次的演唱之间存在千丝万缕的联系,在每一次演唱的文本之间,共享来自同一个传统的背景。"按照弗里的话说,是'地图'——引导歌手和听众双方沿着固定的传统图式,沿着听众所早已熟悉的规程,讲述一个他们早已经知道开端和结局的古老故事。"① 无论如何,我们总是会对柯尔克孜口头史诗那牢固的稳定性感到惊奇。无论在什么时间从什么地方搜集的史诗文本中,它们都无疑是从一个共同的古老传统中发展而来,是从一个源头流出的溪水,是从一个根基上长成的大树。对于这种稳定性,世世代代的听众和歌手都做出了自己的贡献。

在口头表演中,演唱者的身体动作、演唱技能的展示与文本构成形成一个复杂而有趣的融合,我们无法想像脱离表演语境情况如何总结《玛纳斯》史诗的本质特征。

根据史诗专家郎樱的观点,在研究口头史诗时,我们必须关注以下四个方面的因素:文本、作为史诗创造和传播者的歌手(演唱者)、听众、社会现实。② 我们要想对《玛纳斯》史诗的演唱创作过程有一个完整、准确和具体的认识,就必须通过认真仔细的田野调查工作,观察其在特定语境下的"表演中的创作"状态,了解歌手与听众在互动状态下的实践。表演中的口头文本的艺术水平不仅与表演者所储存的程式数量、生活经历和他对传统知识的积累有直接的关系,而且与演唱者当时的心情、观众的情绪、演唱环境以及听众的身份都有密切联系。拉德洛夫早在19世纪末就注意到了柯尔克孜族的玛纳斯奇为了取悦听众而尽力渲染自己所演唱的内容,根据听众的情绪不断调动自己的演唱激情,努力将听众也融入到自己的演唱活动当中的情景。在表演中,玛纳斯奇和听众之间的互动关系总是其最重要的有机活动因素。史诗最优秀的文本只有在歌手和听众都处在兴奋、热烈、激动的情绪下,在最适合歌手发挥才能的语境下,在歌手与听众互动配合之中产生。

总之,《玛纳斯》是柯尔克孜族漫长的口头传统中产生的代表作。程式化的结构、程式化的语词、程式化的文本是其典型的外观;"表演中的创作"不仅是创作史诗的方法,而且是保存和传播这部史诗的手段。

参考书目

阿地里·居玛吐尔地,托汗·依萨克,《当代荷马〈玛纳斯〉演唱大师居素普·玛玛依评传》,内

---

① 朝戈金:《口传史诗诗学:冉皮勒〈江格尔〉程式句法研究》,第243页。
② 郎樱:《〈玛纳斯〉论》,第192页。

蒙古大学出版社,2002年。

Aitmatov, Chinggiz. "Beaming Height of Ancient Kirghiz Spirit," *Encyclopaedical Phenomenon of Epos 'Manas'*, Bishkek: Encyclopedia Press. 1995.

斯·阿里耶夫(S. Aliev),特·库勒玛托夫(T. Kulmatov):《玛纳斯奇与〈玛纳斯〉研究者》,彼什凯克,1995年。

Chadwick, Nora K. and Victor Zhirmunsky, *Oral Epics of Central Asia*, London: Cambridge University Press. 1960.

朝戈金:《口头史诗诗学:冉皮勒〈江格尔〉程式句法研究》,南宁:广西人民出版社,2000年。

约翰·迈尔斯·弗里:《口头程式理论:口头传统研究概述》,朝戈金译,《民族文学研究》1997年第2期。

[美]约翰·迈尔斯·弗里:《口头诗学:帕里-洛德理论》,朝戈金译,北京:社会科学文献出版社,2000年。

郎樱:《〈玛纳斯〉论》,呼和浩特:内蒙古大学出版社,1999年。

Lord, Albert B. *The Singer of Tales*, Cambidge, Mass.: Harvard University Press. 1960.

曼拜特:《〈玛纳斯〉史诗的多种变体及其说唱艺术》,乌鲁木齐:新疆人民出版社,1997年。

Radlov, Vasilii V. *The Dialect of the Kara - Kirghiz. Vol*. 5 *of Examples of Folk Literature of the Turkic Tribes. St*. Petersburg: Eggers und Schmitzdorff, 1885.

Reichl, Karl. *Turkic Oral Epics Poetry*: *Traditions*, *Forms*, *Poetic structure*, New York & London: Garland Publishing, 1992.

Vansina, Jan. *Oral Tradition As History*, Madison, Wisc., : University of Wisconsin Press. 1985.

尹虎彬:《古代经典与口头传统》,北京:中国社会科学出版社,2002年。

附录

《玛纳斯》史诗的文本①

柯尔克孜文拉丁转写：汉文译文：

---

① 这段文本摘自居素普·玛玛依在20世纪80年代初的一次演唱,并由中国民间文艺家协会新疆分会(现为新疆民间文艺家协会)根据柯尔克孜文原始记录稿出版的《玛纳斯》史诗内部参考资料本第一部第一卷,第83—90页。描述的是史诗主人公玛纳斯少年第一次出征,战胜卡勒马克著名英雄空托依的故事。

Tiñduunun baari bölüdü, 年轻力壮的人们分离出来，

soygonu kündö bee boldu. 每天宰杀牝马分享。

Betteşeri er Köñtöy,① 要搏杀的对手是英雄空托依，

turgani bel saz jer boldu. 战场摆在别勒撒孜地方。

Balta,② Jakip③ baçtagan, 巴勒塔、加克普为首领，

kelip Kirghiz el toldu. 柯尔克孜人聚集到了这里。

Orozdu④ nun kizil tuu, 奥诺孜都的红色大纛，

ay? igin altin taktirdi, 用金色的月牙形图案装饰，

Manas⑤ tin atin jazgirdi. 将玛纳斯的大名写在上面。

Kötörup joogo bargin dep, "你要扛着它上战场"，

Kirgilçal⑥ ga tapşirdi. 大纛被交到克尔额勒手上。

Sanati boldu otuzmiñ, 到达的人有三万多，

sapirilip el toldu. 呐喊喧嚣，铺满大地。

Er Köñtöygö ayttirdi, 消息传给英雄空托依，

ugup Köñtöy kam kildi. 空托依听后心中悲伤。

Kalmak⑦ ta asker ötö köp, 卡勒马克的人马极为众多，

altimiş miñ boldudep, 总共达到六万人，

aytip elge dañ kildi, 这话在人们中间宣扬，

oolugup Köñtöy attandi. 空托依不顾一切来到战场。

Köñtöy baatir atanip, 空托依勇士走上战场，

---

① Köñtöy：人名。汉语音译为"空托依"，《玛纳斯》史诗第一部中，少年英雄主人公玛纳斯第一次骑马出征战胜的卡勒马克英雄。

② Balta：人名。汉语可音译为"巴勒塔"。史诗中为玛纳斯的叔父。歌手在演唱时为了诗歌押韵和步格的需要，有时还用"Ak Balta"（白脸庞的巴勒塔）、"Balta döö"（巴勒塔巨人）等表示。

③ Jakip：人名。汉语音译为"加克甫"。为玛纳斯的父亲。"bay Jakip"（富翁加克甫）、"han Jakip"（汗王加克甫）等指的也是这个人物。

④ Orozdu：人名。汉语音译为"奥诺孜都"，为玛纳斯的爷爷。

⑤ Manas：人名。汉语音译为"玛纳斯"，为《玛纳斯》史诗第一部的主人公，整个史诗系列也以他的名字命名。

⑥ Kirgilçal：人名。汉语音译为"克尔额勒恰勒"。为玛纳斯的主要战将之一，40名勇士的首领。

⑦ Kalmak：部族名称。《玛纳斯》史诗中，英雄玛纳斯及其子孙的主要敌人。是一个比较模糊的概念，并不一定指现在俄罗斯境内卡尔梅克自治共和国的主体民族。

oorukta murun jatkanbu. 此前他一直躺在病榻上。

Elinen balban ilgadi, 从手下挑选战将,

epsiz çoñdon ondu aldi, 选中了十位超大的壮士,

altimiş miñ koldu aldi, 带领着六万大军,

opsuz Köñtöy çoñ bardi. 身体强壮的空托依来到了战场。

Çoguluşkan jerleri, 他们的聚集之地,

belsazdin berki kerüüsü. 是别勒撒孜的阳面草场。

Kök oyduñ üstu kök jayit, 阔克奥依墩上面的广阔草地上,

Kalmak, Kirghiz el toldu, 柯尔克孜和卡勒马克人熙熙攘攘。

keñiri jerge jaykalip, 广阔的战场人流滚滚,

kan tögülör kez boldu. 正好是拼杀流血的时光。

Tolkugan köldöy çaykalip, 就像湖水掀起的波浪,

Kirghiz uruu degender, 属于柯尔克孜的部落,

korkboy baari kubanip, 毫不惊慌却兴奋异常,

koş boluşup duulanip, 各个心里欢喜摩拳擦掌;

kulak – murun tundurup, 嘈杂的喊声与吼叫声,

aç kiykirik çuu salip. 响彻云天,震耳欲聋。

Çaldardin bari bakçañdap, 老人们挺直腰杆,

jaştardin baari çakçañdap, 年轻人暴躁不安;

keñ kökürök som dali, 宽胸厚肩的壮汉,

balbandin baari dakdañdap. 敞胸露怀跃跃欲试。

Sakali aktar jaykalat, 胡须雪白的老人轻微摇晃,

mingeni jorgo çaypalat. 骑的是平稳走马极为舒畅。

Çigip jatat kalmaktar, 卡勒马克人纷纷走来,

örgön bittey samsaalap. 就像黑压压的虱子铺满地上。

Bakay[①], Balta, Jamgirçi,[②] 巴卡依、巴勒塔、加木额尔奇,

kimisi eldi başkarat, 到底由谁坐镇指挥,

[①] Bakay: 人名。汉语音译为"巴卡依",为玛纳斯的叔父和谋士。有时用"han Bakay"(汗王巴卡依)表示。

[②] Jamgirçi: 人名。汉语音译为"加木额尔奇",为玛纳斯的叔父。有时用"Jamgir"(加木额尔)表示。

bay Jakip uluu kari üçün, 巴依加克甫德高望重，

eñ aldinda gepsalat: 首先由他打开话腔：

Baştin meesi degen bar, 人们说头中要有脑子，

aştin eesi degen bar, 设宴也得有个主人，

eliñdi kimiñ başkarar? 千军万马有谁率领？

el başkargan bolboso, 如果无人统领全局，

eliñdin çeti çaçilar. 就会造成人心不齐行动不一。

'Aytsa – aytbasa iras' dep, "说得有理，说得有理。"

jalpi toktoy kilişti, 人们纷纷停下步履，

Çurkuratip – çuuldatip, 唧唧喳喳你叫我喊，

Bakaydi şaylay sılışti. 将巴卡依推到汗位。

Oşo bolot Bakaydin, 巴卡依正是从这时起，

handik atti alişi, 得到了汗王的尊名；

emgiçekti Bakaydin, 从那时起直到如今，

öçpöy ati kalişi. 巴卡依的王号没有更名。

Baatir Manas jaş bolup, 英雄玛纳斯正当少年，

badişa Bakay baş bopup, 汗王巴卡依统领全面，

kekteşe turgan kez boldu, 报仇的日子已经来临，

Kalmak, Kirghiz kas bolup. 卡勒马克、柯尔克孜积怨已深。

Karap tursa erdemsip, 人们纷纷睁大眼睛，

Kalmaktan çikti bölünüp, 卡勒马克的一员战将已冲出了阵营，

karaanduu biröö derdeñşip. 看他的身影十分威猛。

Tatay① degen neme eken, 那是名叫塔塔依的勇士，

öz içinde kalmaka, 在自己的军队中，

taanimal çikkan er eken, 也算是赫赫有名的英雄；

Kalmaktin jürgön içinde, 他在卡勒马克人中生活，

tübü Manju② neme eken. 却具有满洲的血统。

Mingen atin bulkuntup, 坐骑腾跳不停，

---

① Tatay：人名。汉语音译为"塔塔依"。卡勒马克英雄。

② Manju：部族名和地名。可能是指满族及其生活的地域。

tepsetçüdöy julkuntup，欲将世界踏平；

tişinan kiygen kirmizi，披在身上的丝绸大氅，

kün çagiltip kulpuntup．在阳光下熠熠闪光。

Nayzasin karmap oñdonup，他紧握长矛调整身体，

çögörgön narday komdonup，如同卧地的单峰驼，

bendeden başka neme eken．面目狰狞不同寻常。

Kak oşondoy çoñoyup，他就是这样体格粗壮，

b? lünüp çikti Kalmaktan，冲出卡勒马克的阵营，

jalgiz özü goroyup．独自一人气势汹汹。

Alip Jamgirçi attandi，巨人加木额尔奇准备出征，

alamin dep komorup．欲砍下敌人的首级。

Jiberbey Bakay koygonu，巴卡依下令制止了他，

Jamgirçiga jolkoyup．没有遵从他的意愿。

Semet① degen bar ele，有一个名叫塞买特的勇士，

jilki alişkan çabuulda，在抢夺马群的搏斗中，

sekśenge kalsa betteşip，遇到八十人的围攻，

sayip alçy er ele．他会将他们一一战胜。

Özü Kazak② urugu，他是来自哈萨克的勇士，

Semet baatir deer ele．人称他是塞买特英雄。

'men baram' dep jeldenet，"让我去吧"他前来请战十分积极，

han Bakaydin aldina．站在了汗王巴卡依的面前。

Uruksat surap keldi emi，他请战的态度如此积极，

aga dagi er Bakay，汗王巴卡依另有打算，

uruksatti berbedi．对他出征也没有同意。

Toktono albay Çubagiñ③，楚瓦克已经不能自已，

toguzdagi ? unagiñ，这位年方九岁的少年，

uruksat surap kelgeni．也上前来要求出战。

---

① Semet：人名。汉语音译为"塞买特"。哈萨克族勇士。
② Kazak：部族名。即为今天的哈萨克人。
③ çubak：人名。汉语音译为"楚瓦克"。玛纳斯身边的主要战将。为巴勒塔的儿子。

'bolsun joluň şar' dedi, "祝你一路顺风,

'jolborsum Çubak bar' dedi.你去吧,楚瓦克,祝你心想事成。"

'Barbayt' dep uulum aytuuga, "我儿现在还不能出征,"

Baltanin oozu kelbedi.巴勒塔没法说出这话。

Bala jolbors Çubaktin, 少年英雄楚瓦克,

bar jaragi teldelüü, 武装齐备,准备停当;

jaraşiktuu ilayik, 骑着骏马合适又得体,

Kök – teke① anin mingeni, 阔克铁开是他的骏骑;

kömörö kiyip tuulgani, 头盔紧扣在头上,

kykirip Çubak jurdu emi.高声怒吼着冲向战场。

Toguzda Çubak jaşi bar, 楚瓦克正是九岁的年龄,

jetkir baatir çagi bar, 具有无敌英雄的神勇,

baatir Manas tuşunda, 在英雄玛纳斯的时代,

baştan – ayak dagi bar, 成为终身伙伴屡建奇功;

bügündön baştap at alsin, 从今天起赢得功名,

jibergen Bakay çagi bar. 这正是巴卡依派他的原因。

Koşuldu Çubak katarga, 楚瓦克已经长大成人,

bettesti Manju Tatayga. 上场与满洲人塔塔依对阵。

Tatay Manju degeni, 这位满洲英雄塔塔依,

taanimal elge muruntan.英名盖世人人知晓;

Talkalap neçen er alip, 曾战胜无数强手,

taanilgan elge boluçu. 赢得了无数荣耀。

Körgön emes Kirghizdan, 他不曾见过柯尔克孜人,

batiştin elin Mañguldar②, 东方的各族被蒙古人,

talkalap şaarin mañ kilip, 毁坏城市流离失所,

başi – közün kan kilip, 满头鲜血不堪入目;

aytip elge kelgende, 在人们的口碑中,

---

① kök – teke: 英雄楚瓦克的坐骑名称。汉语意译为"青色的公山羊"。音译为"阔克铁开骏马"。

② Mañgul: 部族名称,可能与蒙古人对应。

Tatay jeñdi baarin dep, 都说是塔塔依战胜所有人，

atin anin uguçu, 他的名声无人不知，

Köñtöy degen kaldayi, 空托依这个大将领，

Tataydi jölök kiliçu, 也把塔塔依当靠山；

toguzda Çubak jolborsuñ, 年方九岁的楚瓦克雄狮，

jolukkan jeri mina uşu. 正好与他相遇在此时。

Çubakti körüp Tatay kul, 奴仆塔塔依看到楚瓦克，

atinin ba？in buruptur, 拉住缰绳掉转马头，

arkasinda Köñtöygö, 面向身后的空托依，

kilçayip karap turuptur. 注目而视发出疑问。

'Ulugum Köñtöy sen eleñ, "你空托依是我尊敬的首领，

uypalap neñen erdi algan, 战场上捏死无数敌人，

uruşta Tatay men elem, 正是我塔塔依本人；

taanilgan elge Tatayga, 塔塔依我声名显赫，

tay minip jürgön jarişip, 一个骑着马驹的柯尔克孜小孩，

mina bu Kirghiz teñ bele？怎能与我平起平坐？

Balaga Tatay çikti dep 塔塔依与小孩上阵对杀，

barlik el uksa uyat gep. 谁听了都会羞辱我。

Başka biröön jibergin, 还是派出另外的人吧，

koşuma kayra ketem' dep, 我要回到自己的阵营。"

koburap Tatay kalgani. 他叽里呱啦说了一通，

Kirghiz, Kalmak aralaş, 柯尔克孜语和卡勒马克语夹杂，

mal bakkanda çamalaş, 一同在草原上放牧，

bardi－keldi bas－tur du, 来去走停等日常语，

tilin Kalmak bile alat. 基本上都能听得懂。

Aytkanin uga bariptir, 明白了他说的话之后，

Ak－Baltanin çunagi, 阿克巴勒塔这小子，

ardanip buga kaliptir. 倍感羞辱怒火中烧；

Jetken jerde Tataydi, 刚刚靠近塔塔依，

jetkileñ çubak bir saydi, 机智的楚瓦克刺出矛枪。

maktanip jatkan barbayim dep, 高傲自负不愿上阵，

eerden kötü kiyşaydi.臀部却离开了马鞍。

Oop barip oñolup, 摇晃着身体最后坐正，

arkasin karap oloyup, 回过头来怒目圆睁；

ormoloñdop aliptir,气势汹汹怒发冲顶，

oydu – kayki çapkilap, 左右摇晃催马拉缰，

Çubakka Tatay bariptir.塔塔依冲到楚瓦克身旁。

Atañden körü Burut[①] dep, "你这该死的布鲁特，

ölör eçki koyçunun,话说死到临头的山羊，

tayagina söykönüp,故意蹭靠牧人的棍棒，

ölüp alat eken – dep, 最终遭致自己的死亡，

ugup jürgön bu bir gep.这话流传广泛人人知晓。

Eçkiden beter söykönüp, 你就像山羊一样蹭身，

ölmökçü eken Kirghiz dep, 想必是自寻死亡。"

eñ ele jaman süylönüp, 他叽里呱啦滔滔不绝，

kirgin suuday türdönüp, 那神态犹如暴发的洪水，

bulgap alip nayzasin, 挥动着手中的矛枪，

katuu tiydi güülönü.冲上前来十分凶狂。

Karmaşti murun körbögön, 从没经历过搏杀的场面，

karmaşip joogo könbögön, 没有与敌交手的经验，

antken menen er çubak, 但是那英雄楚瓦克，

balada bolso eñ çiyrak.年少气盛机灵敏捷。

Kakşita jürüp köngöndöy, 他显得十分老练，

dalaydi murun körgöndö, 就像经历了无数恶战，

kagip – iyip nayzasin, 拨开迎面刺来的矛枪，

tamiljigan Tataydi,对准那自命不凡的塔塔依，

taamay çubak sayiptir, 楚瓦克狠狠地刺中对方。

tatalagan Manjunu, 把那滔滔不绝的满洲人，

añtara sayip saliptir.刺翻在地毫不留情。

---

① **Burut:** 部族名称。最初为卫拉特蒙古人对柯尔克孜族的称呼,清朝政府也沿用了这个地方性称呼。民国政府则又改用柯尔克孜族的自称"kirghiz"的音译。

Körüp turup çidabay, 目睹此景心里不服，

Köbögön① degen bir Manju, 名叫阔波干的满洲勇士，

kürküröp jete bariptir. 大声怒吼着冲杀而来。

Ajal aydap turalbay, 定是死神将他招引，

al Tataylap bakirip, 他大喊着塔塔依的英名，

ayabay jani açinip, 心中的怒火难以平静；

kabagan ittey karsildap, 如同狂犬叫个不停，

açuulanip arsildap, 满腔的怒火无法平静，

jetip keldi çubakka, 冲杀至楚瓦克身旁，

tüz kaçirip jakindap. 毫无恐惧气势威猛。

Oyrotto② jok er çubak, 在卫拉特中找不到的勇士楚瓦克，

kara boyun çiñdadi, 集中了浑身的精力；

kizil tüpök nayzani, 那带有红樱的矛枪，

kiraan çubak irgadi, 被雄鹰楚瓦克挥舞；

kiykirip bargan Majunun, 把那怒吼而来的满洲人，

kagip iyip nayzasin, 刺来的矛枪拨到一边，

kiy süböögö bir saydi. 狠狠地戳进了他的软肋。

Çubak saygan oñobu? 楚瓦克刺中的人还能活吗？

Jigilgan ödö bolobu? 既然倒地还能站吗？

Jer tayanip jigilsa, 如果他侧身倒地用手支撑，

tirüü Çubak koyobu? 楚瓦克怎会让他活命？

Jer kuçaktap Manjudan, 满洲已有两个人，

eköö ölüp jok boldu, 抱着大地走向死亡。

Kirghizdin işi oñoldu. 柯尔克孜人的命运有了希望。

Karap turup çidabay, 目睹此情忍无可忍，

kaardanip turalbay, 怒气冲天难以平静，

kaar boyuna siyalbay, 心中的怒火喷发不停，

karbalastap çoñ Köñtöy, 巨人空托依挥鞭催马，

---

① Köbögön：人名。汉语音译为"阔波干"，来自满洲的勇士。

② Oyrot：史诗中柯尔克孜人对卫拉特蒙古人和他们生活地域的称呼。

kalgandin baari jönököy, 其他人均属一般,

kantip turup alalsin, 他又怎能忍气吞声,

kaldayip özü jönöböy. 只好晃动着身体亲自出征。

Karbalastap kaldañdap, 他风风火火一刻不停,

kalkani jondo daldadap, 盾牌在肩背上摇摆不停;

kaçirip Köñtöy keletat, 空托依直冲而来十分凶猛,

karasa butu salpañdap. 两条腿摆动一刻不停。

Karmagani kara til, 手中握着狼舌矛枪,

kara kurçtan nayzasi, 是用特殊的利钢打成,

kara jer maylap jatiçu, 多少英雄抱地死亡,

kaçirganda kançasi. 他是一个无敌的战将。

Kalkani kara temirden, 盾牌用黑铁做成,

kara boyu kem emes, 他那巨大的身体,

kara toonun señirden, 如同黑色的山冈。

karsildaşkan duşmandan, 与强敌拼杀无数,

kaçan Köñtöy jeñilgen. 空托依哪一次有过失败。

Kaçirganda kan içken, 冲锋陷阵他饱喝人血,

kanga koşup kant jegen, 并将糖块掺和在一起。

Kara – Kitay① Kalmaktar, 黑契丹和卡勒马克,

kalgandan kaçan kam jeşken, 何时曾为自己的命运担忧;

kaçan kiyin kun bolso, 危难的日子一旦出现,

kaarduu Köñtöy bar deşken. 都相信空托依会力挽狂澜。

Katuu jönöp kaliptir, 他气焰嚣张勇猛向前,

kadimkidey kan iççü, 嗜血的习性,

kazabina aliptir. 暴露无遗。

Kaçirgan jerde Çubakti, 他面对楚瓦克奋力向前,

kañtara koyup saliptir. 一枪就将他从马背上掀翻。

Kazaktardin Semeti, 哈萨克的塞买特,

at koygon boydon jetti emi, 挥鞭催马不敢迟缓,

---

① Kara – Kitay: 部族名,指黑契丹。

jelip çikkan Kök – teke，把逃离战场的阔克铁开骏马，

çilbirinan karmadi，从缰绳上紧紧拉住；

irgitip çilbir Çubakka，把缰绳扔给楚瓦克主人，

Kalmakka saldi jañjaldi．直冲卡勒马克进行搏杀。

Kazaktardin er Semet，哈萨克勇士塞买特，

karsildaşip kalgani．砰砰嘣嘣展开交锋。

Kazaktardin Semetin，哈萨克的塞买特，

nayzaga Köñtöy ilgeni，被空托依戳在矛尖；

minake Kirghiz eriñ dep，"这就是柯尔克孜的勇士，"

irgitip munu jiberdi，说着将他扔到一边，

ubara kilba kaljañday，"不要浪费我的时间，

eriñden birööñ kel dedi．真正的勇士赶紧上来。"

Estenip turgan kararip，早就气得脸色发青，

kaar boyana taralip，怒火早在心中升腾，

Çoñ – jindi① mindi atina，大疯子立刻飞身上马，

Sir – nayzani② kolgoalip．色尔矛枪紧握在手上。

Sir – nayza kolgo ilgende，色尔矛枪端在手中，

sizdirip jolgo kirerde，风驰电掣冲杀战场，

Ak – balta turdu munu aytip：阿克巴勒塔立刻开了腔：

abañ Bakay Jakip han，尊敬的巴卡依和加克普汗，

Jamgirçi menen Kirgilçal，加木额尔奇和克尔额勒恰勒，

karap turdu tiñşaşip．放眼注目，侧耳细听。

'Balam？ubak sen dedi，"我的儿子楚瓦克，

janima jakin kel dedi，你也到我身边来；

bildiñerbi karilar，各位长老你们是否知晓，

karap turduñ bariñar，你们已经亲眼看到，

barayin desem aldinda，我先前就想出征，

---

① çoç – jindi：汉语意译为"大疯子"。史诗中，玛纳斯出生后，为了掩人耳目而由其叔父阿克巴勒塔暂时为他起的别名。

② sir nayza：英雄玛纳斯的矛枪。汉语一般采用音译和意译混合的形式，译为"色尔矛枪"。

uruksat Bakay berbedi. 巴卡依却没有给我战机；

Maga berbey uruksat, 没有给我上阵的机会，

Uulum Çubak saa berdi. 我儿楚瓦克你却得到了允许。

Ömürünçö Manaska, 一生跟随玛纳斯，

ölgünçö birge bolot dep, 出生入死与他相伴，

saa uruksat bergeni. 这才是他真正的心愿。

Orozdu atam ölgölü, 自父王奥诺孜都仙逝，

on uulu aman biz turup, 尽管有我们十兄弟，

bütün Alaş[①] el turup, 尽管有阿拉什大众，

Kara Kalmak Manjuga, 对于喀喇卡勒马克和满洲，

alibiz kaçan kelgeni. 我们何时有过对阵出击。

Atagi Alaş el üçün, 为了阿拉什的荣誉，

iriska seni bergeni, 你的降生是我们的福气；

Kalmaktan korkup aytalbay, 因为害怕卡勒马克的巡查，

atiñdi senin kotorup, 只好将你的大名改动，

Çoñ – jindi koydum men dedi. 大疯子的暂名是我给起。

Allam süyüp saa koygon, 安拉给你起的名，

atiñ Manas boluçu, 本来是叫玛纳斯。

attanip çiktiñ jañidan, 如今你首次披挂出征，

bolosuñ elge taanimal. 定会一鸣惊人扬名四方。

Manas dep uraan çakirip, 高喊着'玛纳斯'的口号，

baraturgan jol uşu. 这正是勇往直前的征程。

Bargin Manas bar dedi, 你去吧玛纳斯，立刻出征，

bolsun joluñ şar dedi, 祝你征途顺利，一路前行，

elge salgan bülüktü, 人民忍气吞声遭受凌辱，

duşmandan öçüñ al dedi.' 你要勇敢杀敌报仇雪恨。"

Bata berip dürküröp, 人们举起双掌为他祝福，

baarisi turup kaldi emi. 目送着他出征而去。

Bastirganda baatirdin, 英雄踏上征程，

---

① Alaş：为柯尔克孜和哈萨克部落联合体的名称。汉语音译为"阿拉什"。

bayanin aytam ugup kal，我要说一说那时的情景你要听清，

kulagiñdi salbasañ，心不在焉不侧耳细听，

dülöy bolup özüñ kal. 你变成聋子呆在一旁。

Oluya Manas baatirdan，神仙英雄玛纳斯，

unutbas dalay sözü bar，有一些难忘的征兆和特征，

unutup iybey estep al. 应该记在心里永世不忘。

Bastirganda karasa，关注他上路时的情形，

bala jolbors aristandi，少年猛虎和雄狮，

baykagan baari tañ kaldi. 看到的人们惊叹不已：

Barmaktay kizil meñi bar，一块指印大小的红痣，

mañdayinda salañdap，悬挂在前额上，

jilañ ayak jilañ baş，光着脚丫光着脑袋，

kiyimsiz özü jilañaç，光着身体没有衣裳，

çilbirlap ketip baratat，牵着英雄的马缰引领，

jeti menen segizdin，七至八岁的年龄，

ortosunda balajaş. 有这样一个神童。

Eki üzöñgü aldinda，在两个马镫下面，

eki tügöy sur böjök，两个灰色的神兔，

kulagin tiktep japirip，竖着耳朵十分灵敏，

ketip barat çoçoñdop，伴随左右向前奔腾；

böjöñ – böjöñ jelişip，一蹦一跳瞬间不停，

bölökçö sonun kelişip，那神情姿态十分动人。

körüp turgan Kirghizdar，目睹此景的柯尔克孜人，

bir – birine tuyguzbay，瞒着别人进行祈祷，

Baabedin[1] aytip iyişti. 暗暗提及巴别丁的大名。

Kizil çaar jup jolbors 一双花色斑点的老虎，

jolukkan bende soo bolbos，与它相遇的人绝不能生还；

---

[1] Baabedin：中亚著名的伊斯兰教僧人民间工艺家，生活在 14 世纪，是伊斯兰神秘主义的推广者。曾周游阿拉伯、波斯等地，被柯尔克孜族等中亚民族视为圣人而加以崇拜，在危难时呼唤其名或用牲畜为他献祭。

jandap çurkap aliptir, 伴随左右一路狂奔，

Manaska bolup al joldoş. 成为玛纳斯的伙伴十分忠诚。

Sonun işi dagi bar, 还有更神奇的事情，

türgön çiydey joondugu, 与卷起的茇茇草帘一般粗壮，

soylop barat ajidaar, 巨大的蟒蛇蠕动向前，

korkkonuna çidabay, 止不住心里的惊恐，

iştanina dalaylar, 直接在自己的裤子里小便的，

siyip iygen çagibar. 大有人在。

Aldinda mingen kula① attin, 坐下的库拉骏马，

kulaginda şami bar, 双耳上烛光闪亮，

mañdayinda bagi bar, 前额透出吉祥，

kuyundan bütkön janibar, 这匹由风生成的神物，

soorusunda kula attin, 在库拉骏马的后臀，

Kambar ata② silagan, 康巴尔神曾经触摸，

beş kolunun tagi bar. 留下了五指印痕。

Arkasinda ayköldün,③ 在阿依阔勒的马背，

uçkaşkan kizi dagi bar, 还有一位仙女站立身后，

şökülö④ kiygen başina, 头上戴着雪库略帽；

körüp ayran kolişti, 看着让人无不赞叹，

tagingan şuru başina. 那头上的珠宝极为罕见，

Bermeti jerge tögülüp, 珠光宝气映射地面。

utur kelse mañdayga, 从正面仔细注视，

tuulgadan aşip koykoyup, 可见到她的高出英雄的头盔，

---

① kulu at: 英雄玛纳斯的坐骑。汉译时一般采用音译和意译混合的形式译为"库拉骏马"。歌手在演唱时为了音律及步格的需要，还用"ak－kula"（阿克库拉）表示。

② Kambar ata: 柯尔克孜族和其他突厥语民族神话中骏马的第一位驯养者和守护神。汉语翻译时普遍采用音译的方式译为"康巴尔阿塔"。

③ ayköl: 史诗中对于玛纳斯专用的隐喻尊称，意为"月亮湖"。汉语音译为"阿依阔勒"，以此表现英雄玛纳斯心胸宽广、豪爽无私的原始英雄美德。

④ şökülö: 柯尔克孜族未婚少女戴的一种传统帽子。用华丽的红色锦缎等贵重布料缝制而成，表面修饰有各种珍珠、玛瑙等珠宝。尖顶，帽子下沿用四指宽的水貂皮等修饰，帽顶上垂直盖下一个薄纱，透出姑娘的妩媚，具有浓郁的民族特色。

şökülösü körünüp. 高高的雪库略帽十分鲜艳。

Ötö körköm kizil kiz, 娇艳妩媚的红脸姑娘

özü jandan uzun kiz, 身材修长亭亭玉立，

dürküröşüp el kaldi, 人们竞相观望发出赞叹：

dagi birden körünüp, "让我们饱饱眼福，

koyso deşip uşul kiz. 再出现一次该多好啊。"

Otuzdan kulja altimiş, 六十只盘羊分成均等，

tepe – teñ eke bölünüp, 不多不少分在两旁，

derdeñdeşip aliptir, 伴随英雄向前奔腾；

bir kula attin dabirti, 一匹库拉骏马的蹄声，

altimiş attay dabirap, 就像六十匹骏马起步狂奔，

mana mintip kalip tir. 如此壮观令人兴奋。

Karap turgan kalayik, 在一旁观望的人们，

karilar közgö jaş alip, 老者均泪湿衣襟，

karagan baari tañ kalip, 无人能掩饰内心的激动；

dürküröşüp jar salip, 人群涌动翘首观望，

güñgürönüp aliptir. 发自内心深处的言语无人听清。

Mal tabuuçu şiluundar, 反应机敏的年轻人，

Bakay, Jakip kariga, 面对巴卡依和加克甫老人，

Ak – Balta, Jamgir zalina, 面对阿克巴勒塔和加木额尔奇巨人，

aksakaldin baarina, 面对众多白胡须长老，

komuzun① tolgop kolgo alip, 拿起考姆兹奏出妙曲，

jagimduu irdap un salip, 敞开歌喉唱起歌；

irdap barip irçilar, 用歌声表达心情，

komu menen töö alip, 赢得了带驼子的骆驼，

eeri menen at alip, 得到了备有马鞍的骏马，

aga koşup bata alip, 外加一句句美好的祝福；

çeçtirip bergen tondu alip, 赢得了即时脱下的氅袍，

çenebey bergen puldu alip, 得到了不计其数的金钱；

---

① komuz: 柯尔克孜族传统民间乐器"考姆兹琴"。

jagaldanip kirdanip, 摇头晃脑真情涌动，

mal tabişip jaldanip, 得到了财富更为兴奋，

süyünüşüp tinç alip. 喜悦的心情久久难平。

Eki jagin karanip, 两眼不停地左顾右盼，

kümüştön kemer kurçanip, 纯银的腰带束在腰间；

kök jaliñ çikti attanip, 青鬃狼策马出征，

kündöy beti nur çalip. 太阳般的脸庞闪烁光芒。

Artinan karap baykaşip, 从背后将他望去，

ayköl şerge tañkalip. 人们对阿依阔勒雄师大加赞赏。

Arkasinan karasa, 从后背上望去，

ak jolborstun sini bar, 他有白虎般的气质。

mañdayinan karasa, 从正面仔细审视，

ajidaardin sürü bar, 他有巨龙般的神威。

töbösünön karasa, 从头顶进行俯瞰，

alip kara kuş① türü bar, 他有阿勒普卡拉神鸟的气派。

açuusu kelip akirsa, 如若他发出一声怒吼，

aybattanip bakirsa, 如若他发威高声喊叫，

kirk bir şerdin ünü bar, 声音与四十一头雄狮的一样。

Kirghizdan çikkan kiraandin, 柯尔克孜中诞生的雄鹰，

tişki sini uşular. 他的外貌就是这样。

Bastirip jönöy bergende, 当他勇敢无畏冲向前方，

ak sarbaşil mal aytip, 人们赶来了黄额头的牲畜，

atap atin koy aytip, 有人宰杀绵羊为他祝福，

aga koşup turgan el, 众人随后齐声呼应，

ak boz beeni koşo aytip, 点出了雪青马作为牺牲；

aytbagani kalbadi, 人们说出的无所不包，

aksakaldar kalgani. 白胡须老人们也没空缺。

---

① Alip kara kuş: 柯尔克孜族和其他突厥语民族神话中的飞禽之王，在危难时常常成为英雄的守护神和帮手。汉语可采用音译和意译混合形式译为"阿勒普神鸟"。有一些人直接将此神鸟译为"大鹏"或"鹏鸟"。

Ak – kula minip bolkoyup, 稳坐在阿克库拉背上，

şañdanip aristan kaliptir, 雄狮的心情十分舒畅；

Ala-too① doy zoñkoyup, 如同阿拉套山那样高高耸立，

topton çikti bölünüp, 离开阵地冲向战场，

tetigi çoñ opoldoy körünüp. 身体高大犹如入云的峰峦。

Betteşti kalday baatirga, 那战将与英雄交手，

too köçköndöy kürküröp, 山体轰鸣大地摇晃，

Kañgay② lap Köñtöy bakirsa, 空托依发出"抗嗳"的呐喊，

karagan baari tañ kaldi. 观战的人们心惊胆战。

Kaçirip kirgen baatirga, 勇士冲杀一往无前，

mingeni kula şañdanip; 坐下的库拉骏马腾跳不停；

Ak – kulanin artinda, 在阿克库拉的背后，

burulgup çikkan çañ kalip. 升起翻滚的尘云蔽日遮天。

Çiñdap nayza karmaşip, 紧握着手中的矛枪，

çiminday jandi ayabay, 毫不吝惜苍蝇一样的生命，

kilga baylap taştaşip. 把它仅用细细的马鬃吊栓。

Nayzalarin suuruşup, 伸出各自的长矛，

küülöp alip uruşup. 不断挥动奋力搏杀。

Kaçirişip sayişip, 你冲我戳有来有往，

kalday Köñtöy Kalmaktan, 卡勒达依空托依来自卡勒马克，

kaarduu Manas Kirghizdan, 勇猛的玛纳斯出自柯尔克孜一方；

kalbalaşip bul ököö, 两人搏杀毫不相让，

katuu jaman uruştu, 激烈的场面动人心魄；

kalkandarin kiyratip, 盾牌碎裂不知去向，

zoottorun juluştu, 铠甲被撕扯得不成模样；

kaçbay turup uruştu, 奋力拼杀毫不退让，

katuu kiyin jumuş bu. 这真是惊心动魄的鏖战。

Kayta aylanip salişti, 回转马头重又开战，

---

① 横贯我国新疆和吉尔吉斯斯坦的一座高山。

② 史诗中指卡勒马克等氏族的世居地。

kanduu nayza alişti, 把血染的矛枪重又紧握手上，

kan jürökkö malişti. 直接戳向对方的胸膛。

Kagip nayza sayganda, 矛枪戳来你推我挡，

Saydirbastan kagişti, 设法躲过致命的刺伤；

Saydirip nayza kan akbay, 没有被戳中没有鲜血流淌，

Mununda jolun tabişti. 他们的武功让人赞赏。

Köñtöy oyloyt oyunda, 空托依暗暗地将这些猜想：

'kabat – kabat temirler, "一层层铁衣，

kiyip tursam boyumda, 穿了我的通身，

sayganin teşbey kalbagan, 将任何东西都能戳通，

nayzam tursa kolumda, 这样的长矛握在我手上，

çapkanin kesbey kalbagan, 世间的一切都能劈开，

kiliçim tursa kininda, 锋利的战刀放在鞘中，

taşti çapsam kaytbagan, 劈向坚石从不反弹，

jara çaap taştagan, 多硬的石头都要劈成两半，

aybalta tursa belimde, 月牙斧放在我腰间，

toonu ursam tomorgon, 砸向高山能够将它粉碎，

tomorulup jogolgon, 飞沙走石不知去向何方，

çokmorum tursa takimda, 战锤就压在我大腿下；

çalikkansip kalbagan, 从来没有饥渴的忧烦，

çaap jürsom arbagan, 奔跑时从不知疲倦，

atim tursa arbagan, 这样的骏马就在我下面；

naamim kalday er Köñtöy, 我还有空托依将军的大名，

uşunun baari turganda, 所有这些都属我所有；

alda kança menden pas, 不值一提的无名小子，

jaşi kiçüü küçü az, 年龄偏小力气薄弱，

on bir menen on eki, 仅在十一二岁之间，

ortosunda balajaş, 这个小子乳臭还未干，

öltürö sayip albasam, 我要将他戳死毫不手软，

kani – jini aralaş, 让他的鲜血和大便混合流淌，

özögünön jarbasam, 我要剖开他的胸膛，

eregişip uşintip, 与他进行搏杀浪费时间

özüm Köñtöy nee turam.'我空托依的名声会受损伤。"

Öçöşüp çoçko kamindi, 这头猪猡鼓足勇气非常嚣张,

kayra jaaçu buluttay, 就像天上的阴霾一样,

kaar betine jabildi, 恶气冲天涌现在脸上:

'böyön – çayan jilanday, "我要像毒蜘、蝎子和毒蛇那样,

zaarimdi salbasam'; 把所有的毒性爆发出来;

Köñtöy bolboy kalayin, 我要放弃空托依之名,

komoro sayip albasam. 如果不把他即刻戳翻。"

Kazabina algani, 他暴跳如雷大发雷霆,

kayta artina aylandi. 掉转马头回过头来。

Karaanin körüp Kalmaktin, 看到卡勒马克的身影,

aldinan toso jönödü; 迎面而上毫不畏惧;

aldi – artinda jürgönü, 簇拥在左右的神灵,

kalbay koşo jönödü; 也都紧密伴随一同前行;

'Kañtara sayip alam' dep, "我一定要把他戳翻。"

aristaniñ dagi kögördü. 你的雄狮也奋不顾身;

Atiriltip argitip, 扯缰催马腾越狂奔,

artinan çañdi bargitip; 尘雾在背后升腾;

tulpar gülük kula atti, 奇骏神骑库拉骏马,

kuyunday kilip kargitip, 风驰电掣犹如旋风

jal kuyrugun jayiltip, 美鬃长尾在风中飘逸

kuljaday töşün salintip; 胸部健壮如同盘羊;

Manastap uraan çakirip, 高喊着"玛纳斯"的口号,

jaş Manas kirdi kaçirip. 年轻的玛纳斯迎头而上。

Manstin atin ukkanda, 听到玛纳斯的名字,

çoñ Köñtöy kaldi şaşilip. 空托依巨人也心慌意乱。

Öçöşüp kelgen Köñtöydün, 前来讨战的空托依,

nayzasin kagip jiberdi; 矛枪被拨打到一边;

Kirinan tiydi batiriñ, 勇士从侧旁出击,

Kulanin oozun imerip, 拉扯着库拉骏马的衔缰,

kiyamina keltirip, 瞅准机会把握时机，

kiy süböödön bir saydi, 对准软肋戳出矛枪，

tomorulup kiyşaydi. 敌人摇晃着身体滚落到地上。

Bala jolbors kara kök, 少年猛虎无畏的闯将，

betteşip çikkan jerinde, 初次上阵第一次亮相，

beldüüdön Köñtöy erdi aldi. 就把大名鼎鼎的空托依勇士战胜。

Esi ketip temtirep, 心惊肉跳失魂落魄，

Köñtöydün eli sandaldi. 空托依的人马穷途末路。

Akil aytaar adam jok, 无人指挥无人引导，

çigalbay baary titirep, 畏畏缩缩浑身发颤。

Köñtöygö jölök balbani, 空托依手下的好汉们，

sürün körüp kök jaldin, 目睹青鬃狼的威严，

sürdöp basa albadi, 提心吊胆不敢上前；

başin katip şilkiyip, 把头尽量往衣领里缩，

balbansip jürgön çandani; 这就是那些自命不凡者的神态；

akimsingen Kalmaktar, 耀武扬威的卡勒马克人，

a deerge ali kalbadi. 没有了任何回应的勇气。

aylasi ketip Kalmaktin, 卡勒马克人束手无策，

alapayi kuuruldu. 前途渺茫惊恐万状。

史诗的神圣性与史诗演唱仪式

郎　樱

摘　要　史诗的神圣性与表演者的独特地位和史诗演唱活动的仪式与禁忌密切相关。歌谣、传说、故事的传承,具有群众性与世俗性特点,而口传史诗的演唱活动则具有神圣性,在我国南方一些少数民族中,只有祭司、巫师在特定的场合、特定的仪式上才能演唱史诗,成为南方民族文化的重要特征之一,也是南方民族史诗传承古老性与独特性的体现。类似的情况在我国北方三大英雄史诗中也存在着。

关键词　史诗,神圣性,仪式

史诗是民族文化的象征,民族精神的体现。史诗在民族精神生活与民众心目中占有神圣的地位。我国的史诗基本上是口承史诗,史诗的神力崇拜观念与习俗、史诗的演唱活动仪式与禁忌,在许多民族中至今犹存。歌手的"梦授说"及其祭祀、神巫的身份,使史诗演唱活动具有神圣性与神秘性。

一、巫师兼史诗歌手

口承史诗与一般的口承叙事文学有所不同。民间歌谣、传说、故事的传承具有群众性与世俗性的特点,而口承史诗的演唱活动则具有神圣性的特点。不是任何人、任何歌手都可以演唱史诗,在我国有些地区,只有祭司、巫师在特定的场合、特定的仪式上才能演唱史诗。在南方少数民族的史诗演唱者中,巫师兼史诗歌手的现象至今还很常见。如云南阿昌族史诗《遮帕麻和遮米麻》的演唱者赵安贤,他既是主持祭祀仪式、行巫术驱鬼治病的祭司,又是出色的史诗演唱者。《苗族古歌》的演唱者杨勾炎,他是巫师,既行巫术,又唱史诗。《哈尼阿培聪坡坡》的演唱者朱小华祖孙三代是哈尼族的"贝玛",既是专职祭司,又是歌手。彝族史诗《勒俄特依》的演唱者是"毕摩"(宗教祭司),纳西族史诗一般也是由"东巴"(宗教祭司)来演唱。佤族史诗《司岗里》的演唱者是"大魔巴(巫师)",景颇族史诗《穆瑙斋瓦》的演唱者是"斋瓦(巫师)",壮族史诗《布洛陀》、《布伯》以及瑶族史诗《密洛陀》的演唱者多为"师公(巫师)"。①

　　彝族的"毕摩"、纳西族的"东巴"、哈尼族的"贝玛"、景颇族的"董萨"、佤族的"大魔巴"、壮族与瑶族的"师公"是神巫,在主持祭祀仪式、行巫术驱邪活动之时,他们是祭司、巫师;在演唱史诗时,他们的身份又成为歌手。巫师兼歌手的现象大量存在,成为南方民族文化的重要特征之一,也是南方民族史诗传承的古老性与独特性的体现。

　　南方民族史诗的内容比较古老,以创世史诗、迁徙史诗为主,也有歌颂英雄的史诗。其中有些史诗,平日是不允许演唱的,只有在族群的重大仪典上才可以演唱。例如,纳西族的《创世纪》是在祭天仪式上由祭司东巴来演唱,独龙族《创世纪》的一章"祭鬼的由来",是在祭祀天鬼的仪式上由祭司演唱。云南大姚、姚安一带的彝族为亡者举行安灵和送灵仪式时,由毕摩演唱创世史诗《梅葛》;生活于新平、双柏的彝族在祭祀仪式上,祭司要演唱神话史诗《查姆》;大小凉山的彝族在丧葬祭祀仪式上,祭司要庄严地演唱著名的史诗《勒俄特伊》。此外,滇桂彝族的罗罗支,在每年"跳宫节"期间,由祭司毕摩演唱英雄史诗《铜鼓王》。②《密洛陀》的演唱活动与布努瑶的"还愿"仪式密不可分,③ 布努人举行的洛陀洛西(创世之母)与24位男女大神的"还愿"仪式相当隆重,杀牲宰畜,由师公演唱"还愿"的缘由和《密洛陀》,祈求诸神灵保佑平安。佤族在春播以前要举行祭祀创世英雄木依吉的庄严仪式。仪式上,由主祭者大魔巴(巫师)演唱歌颂木吉依创造人类与万物的事迹的史诗《司岗里》,祈求木吉依保佑族人一年风调雨顺。阿昌族在老人去世的葬礼上,巫师演唱歌颂始祖功绩的史诗《遮帕麻和遮米麻》与迁徙歌,引导亡灵返回祖先的故地。壮族史诗《布伯》描写了布伯敢斗雷公的事迹,因此,在壮族的祈雨仪式上由师公(巫师)演唱这部史诗。过去,侗族人民在出征前,要举行祭祀女英雄萨岁的庄严仪式,

---

① 　参见刘亚虎:《南方史诗论》,第12—15、297—298 页;蒙冠雄、蒙海清、蒙松毅搜集翻译整理:《密洛陀》,第433—434 页;蓝怀昌、蓝书京、蒙通顺搜集翻译整理:《密洛陀》,第554 页。

② 　巴嫚曲布嫚:"仪式文学",未刊稿。

③ 　布努瑶是瑶族的一个支系,40 多万人口,主要分布于广西都安、巴马、大化三个瑶族自治县。

巫师演唱《萨岁之歌》，激励人民英勇奋战。① 祭祀仪式，对于一个民族来说，是相当庄严而神圣的。在祭天、祭祀鬼神、祭祀祖先、为亡者送魂的仪式上，参加祭祀仪式的部落、部族成员，怀着敬畏与虔诚之心，倾听着祭司、巫师神圣地演唱记述民族起源与迁徙的历史，讲述着民族英雄的事迹。在我国南方少数民族中，祭司与巫师在传承民族文化、保存史诗方面是卓有贡献的。

类似的情况在我国北方三大英雄史诗中也存在着。西藏那曲县的《格萨尔王传》演唱艺人阿达尔，亦是一位民间艺人兼巫师的典型人物。他既会演唱《格萨尔王传》，又会以巫术给人治病。②新疆阿合奇县的曼拜特阿勒·拉合曼既是有影响的《玛纳斯》演唱歌手，又是当地有名的托略克奇占卜师。他用柯尔克孜族传统的 41 个石子布阵和观看羊肩胛骨纹路进行占卜，孩子丢了、东西丢了、出行凶吉等都去找他问卜。③ 被誉为"活着的荷马"的柯尔克孜史诗演唱大师居素普·玛玛依也曾给人治过病，并曾为不孕的妇女求子。

在突厥语民族中，集歌手、萨满、部落首领于一身的情况也曾存在，如广为人知的阔尔库特，他是著名的歌手，神力通天的巴克西（萨满），又是部落首领。《先祖阔尔库特书》在突厥语各民族广为流传，有多种版本，成为经典之作。至今在乌兹别克斯坦、土库曼斯坦，"歌手"与"萨满"仍使用同一词汇"巴克西"，这种语言现象很值得重视，这是古代突厥社会萨满兼歌手的有力例证。巫师、萨满被视为人神之间交通的使者。关于史诗的形成，有各种各样的说法。如果追根溯源，可以发现史诗最初始的演唱活动与先民的原始思维及原始信仰有着密切的关联。先民相信诗歌具有魔力：巫师或萨满诵唱请神歌，便能把神请到人界；巫师和萨满所念唱的咒语歌，具有驱魔祛病的神力。依据大量的资料，我们可以推测出古代史诗演唱活动的发展轨迹：即最初的史诗演唱者多由巫师或萨满担任，人们相信他们通过巫术仪式使神附体，是"神授"使他们获得演唱史诗的本领。

民间艺人在叙述自己经历时，往往会说因为做了一个异梦而获得演唱史诗的本

---

① 刘亚虎：《南方史诗论》，第 12—15 页。
② 杨恩洪：《民间诗神——〈格萨尔王传〉艺人研究》，第 57—59 页。
③ 笔者 1998 年 9 月赴新疆阿合奇县田野调查时，在哈拉奇乡三小队访问过曼拜特阿勒·拉合曼，他当年 59 岁，会演唱《玛纳斯远征》、《玛纳斯》的第五部《赛依特》以及柯尔克孜史诗《库尔曼别克》。遇到喜庆之事，他经常被邀请去演唱《玛纳斯》。他作为占卜师，在当地也有些名气。据说，他曾用羊肩胛骨占卜出一个失踪女孩的方位。他还用 41 个黑石子为我们占卜了出行的天气。

领。这种"梦授"说,在史诗说唱艺人中至今仍相当盛行。云南阿昌族史诗《遮帕麻和遮米麻》的演唱者赵安贤,自述 21 岁时曾得了一场大病,每天下午昏迷不醒,仿佛飞升上天,与各种妖魔搏斗,并见到了创世天神、人类的祖先遮帕麻和遮米麻,天神还教他巫经、巫术以及造天地的故事。他醒后,不仅能诵经、通巫术,而且还会演唱史诗。贵州苗族史诗演唱者杨勾炎则说自己 15 岁时曾经大病一场,天天说胡话,到了第四天昏睡过去,来到一个没有到过的地方,许多人在吹芦笙,唱古歌,死去的爷爷教他唱歌以及驱除恶魔的秘诀。他醒了以后,心里有唱不完的歌和兴巫的本领。[①]

史诗《玛纳斯》的演唱者中,持"梦授说"的现象非常普遍。特尼别克是 19 世纪末享有盛誉的玛纳斯奇,他外出时做了一个梦,梦见英雄玛纳斯、长者巴卡依、阿勒曼别特以及玛纳斯的 40 名勇士。其中一人让他演唱英雄玛纳斯的事迹。第二天,他在众人面前答应演唱《玛纳斯》,他心里默想着梦中英雄们的身影就开了口,但不知自己在唱什么。他疯狂演唱了数小时后便不知不觉口吐白沫昏了过去。第二天他骑马返回故乡,在马背上又不知不觉地唱起《玛纳斯》。从此,他获得了演唱《玛纳斯》的本领,成为著名的史诗演唱大师。[②] 20 世纪初期,生活于新疆阿合奇县著名的史诗演唱艺人居素普阿洪演唱《玛纳斯》的本领也是通过梦授获得的。据他的侄女玛尔捷克说,居素普阿洪放牧的牦牛奔跑越境,他追赶至吉尔吉斯斯坦,由于太劳累了便在路上睡着了。一位老人将他唤醒,他发现自己嘴里有黑粟米,咽下去后便情不自禁地唱起了《玛纳斯》。人们为他支起毡房,宰杀 60 匹马,他在那里连续演唱了三天三夜,后来成为远近闻名的《玛纳斯》演唱家。有"当代荷马"之称的居素甫·玛玛依对人说,他 13 岁时在梦中见到了英雄玛纳斯、长者巴卡依、勇士阿勒曼别特、楚瓦克和阿吉巴依,这些英雄一现即逝。居素普·玛玛依从梦中惊醒,他的父母得知他所做的梦,立即宰了羊,并叮嘱他 40 岁以前不要把做梦的事传出去。自做梦之后,他聪慧异常,《玛纳斯》抄本读一遍便牢记心间。[③] 玛纳斯奇一般都持"梦授说",这里不再一一列举。

说唱《格萨尔王传》的民间艺人中,"梦授说"也很普遍。扎巴老人说,他 7 岁时曾梦见格萨尔王的大将丹玛将他的腹部切开,掏出内脏,把《格萨尔王传》之书放入他的腹内。梦醒后他大病一场,从此能唱出三十多部《格萨尔王传》。玉梅则说她

---

① 刘亚虎:《南方史诗论》,第 300—301 页。
② 阿地力·朱玛吐尔地,托汗·依莎克:《居素普·玛玛依评传》,第 43 页。
③ 郎樱:《玛纳斯论》,第 17、153—157 页。

在 16 岁那年,梦见仙女与妖魔争夺她,仙女让她把格萨尔王降服妖魔、造福百姓的英雄事迹告诉乡亲们。玉梅梦醒后亦大病一场,从此便会说唱《格萨尔王传》。① 青海艺人仁青达吉会演唱多部《格萨尔王传》,他说自己在 20 岁以前做过一个梦,梦中跟随格萨尔大王在嘎迪(青海玉树地区)大胜大鹏国,俘获许多只大鹏鸟,最终凯旋。此梦做了三天,醒后就会演唱《嘎迪穹宗》了。还有一位名叫阿恰热牟尼霞撒的僧人,他以写作《格萨尔王传》著称,他在写作《赛马称王》时遇到困难,便向格萨尔王祈祷,并在梦中遇到了《格萨尔王传》中的一些英雄,醒后便获灵感,将史诗顺利写下去。②

"梦授说"的形成,是个十分复杂的问题,学术界有多种阐释。但是,从史诗神圣性的角度去考察,"梦授"与"神授"是一脉相承的,它是原始思维和意识的积淀。无论是南方民族的原始巫信仰,或是北方民族的萨满教信仰,在其祖先的心目中,巫师与萨满区别于常人之处,是他们具有接受神喻的特殊本领。如前文所说,目前,仍有祭司、巫师在祭祀仪式上演唱史诗的现实存在。文化传统的影响力是十分强大的,且具有极强的渗透力。它已深深地渗入到民族的血脉之中,历经漫长的岁月,逐渐成为民族的集体潜意识、内在的思维定势以及民族文化的心理积淀。无论是史诗演唱艺人,或是史诗的听众,都很难彻底摆脱渗入民族血脉之中的民族文化传统与民族的集体潜意识。这是"梦授说"存在的传统文化基础。

从心理层面考察,史诗演唱艺人从小生活在史诗演唱的语境中,自己学唱史诗与演唱史诗以后,所思所想均与史诗情节和人物有关。日有所想,夜有所梦,也是很自然的。柯尔克孜族史诗演唱大师居素普·玛玛依在研讨会的发言中说:"玛纳斯奇日夜思考史诗情节,一心一意为演唱好史诗而努力,史诗的情节和人物怎么可能不进入梦乡呢?"他在回答国外来访学者的提问时,也说"我每天背诵《玛纳斯》,天长日久,自然会梦见《玛纳斯》中的人物"。③ 这种解释是令人信服的。此外,一些杰出史诗演唱艺人有超常的记忆力,也确实令人惊奇,甚至不可思议。居素普·玛玛依不仅能够完整地演唱 8 部 23 万多行的史诗《玛纳斯》,还能连续演唱 11 部柯尔克孜英雄史诗,最令人惊异的是,他还自唱自记了一部哈萨克族史诗《七个可汗》,仅第一部就有 14 000 多行。这部史诗用哈萨克文出版以后,引起哈萨克人巨大的

① 杨恩洪:《民间诗神——〈格萨尔王传〉艺人研究》,第 147—157 页。
② 徐国琼:《试论〈格萨尔王传〉"仲肯"的"博仲"》,第 73—75 页。
③ 郎樱:《玛纳斯论》,第 157—160 页。

反响。他说年轻时,曾看过这部史诗的手稿,仅看过一遍便储存在他的记忆中,到了古稀之年仍记忆犹新。柯尔克孜人视他为圣人、神人。婴儿让他触额,他穿过的衣服,牧民争相抢穿,他们相信居素普·玛玛依过人的聪慧会通过他的手、他的衣服而传递。在这样的背景下,柯尔克孜民众对于玛纳斯奇的"梦授说",深信不疑。

二、史诗的神力崇拜

在群众的心目中,史诗是神圣的,而且具有神力。通过杰出史诗演唱家的演唱活动,史诗的神力就会显现出来。因此,遇到天灾人祸,他们往往请歌手来演唱一段史诗,相信史诗具有驱邪的神力。据俄国学者日尔蒙斯基在《突厥史诗》的《玛纳斯》篇章中记载,相传19世纪有位名叫奇克里迪别克的玛纳斯奇在毡房里为牧民演唱《玛纳斯》,突然间狂风大作,暴雨不止,威胁着人畜的安全。这时,奇克里迪别克用高超的技法,高声演唱《玛纳斯》,毡房外突然响起马蹄声,蹄声之大,震得大地抖动,只见玛纳斯和他的40名勇士显现,一闪即逝。奇迹出现了,风停雨止,灾消难祛。柯尔克孜人相信史诗《玛纳斯》具有神力,唱起它就能得到玛纳斯灵魂的保佑。因此,过去有些柯尔克孜牧民家里的人或畜生病了,或是妇女要分娩,便去请玛纳斯奇来家里演唱一段《玛纳斯》,以祛病消灾、驱邪镇魔。

史诗的神力崇拜在蒙古族史诗的演唱活动中体现得最为突出。据蒙古族艺人苏鲁丰嘎回忆,巴林右旗一带发生了瘟疫,牛羊大量病死,乡亲们相信史诗《格斯尔》具有驱妖降魔、驱邪祛病的神力,于是请来了民间艺人普荣。这位艺人在村子里唱了三天三夜的《格斯尔》。据乌梁海著名艺人阿贝尔梅德说"有些人家里灾难多的时候,比如畜群死亡多了,家里老人、孩子生病了,惨遭种种不幸或者由于某种原因需要驱邪避难时,就请艺人到家里演唱史诗,以此避邪。有时,在一些人家演唱,会喉咙积血,嗓子哑而唱不下去了。如果出现这种情况,双方都觉得不吉利。请去的人家会认为他们家里的灾难多,一两天之内邪恶除不尽,所以更不让艺人离开家,一定要唱完后才能走"。①

新疆一些地方,以前每年自正月初三或初五开始到正月底,在汗宫王府里请著名的艺人来演唱《江格尔》。这一活动的目的除了节日文化娱乐、欣赏之外,还有一

---

① 萨仁格日勒:《论蒙古史诗生成的民族志特征》,第47页。

个重要的目的,就是驱除、消灭恶魔,祈求全年平安。① 俄罗斯布里亚特的蒙古人对史诗非常崇拜,一位歌手曾说"所谓史诗,无非就是诵唱当山神曾经还是人的时候所建立的伟大功绩。因此,当演唱史诗的时候,聚集的不仅是人,还有诸山神"。听完史诗演唱的山神会对人类产生好感,会驱除寒冷的冬天,带来温暖的春天,使人畜免遭疾病的危害,使牧草长得茂盛。② 藏族人民亦十分相信《格萨尔王传》具有驱邪除魔的神力。哪里有灾有难,只要请艺人来说唱一段《格萨尔王传》,便能起到消灾避难的作用。在广西巴马地区,巫师给人看病时,要唱史诗《布洛陀》的"造人"章,给牛看病时,则要唱史诗《布洛陀》的"造牛"章。③

　　史诗是神圣的、具有神力的,因此,民间艺人演唱史诗有一些禁忌。如瑶族的师公(巫师)在演唱史诗《密洛陀》,要在十二天前禁止房事、净身吃斋。演唱仪式上宰杀的贡神牲畜也要在十二天前将其隔离,严禁它们与非贡祭畜群交配。④ 一些地区的江格尔奇忌讳在一个场次里演唱完《江格尔》的所有章节,认为那将带来不幸,甚至有可能招致江格尔奇的死亡。然而,另外一些地区的人们认为,江格尔奇一旦开始演唱《江格尔》中的一章,就一定要把这一章演唱完。歌手中断演唱,或是听众中途退场,都会折寿的。演唱《江格尔》是一件重要的大事,演唱前要做好充分的准备,演唱困难、不流畅,甚至还会给周围带来不幸的后果——可能会招致一场旋风等。有的歌手跪着演唱《江格尔》,敬畏史诗的神力,也是对史诗中英雄们的无比尊敬。⑤ 在《玛纳斯》的说唱艺人中也存在着类似的禁忌,例如,居素甫·玛玛依8岁开始会演唱《玛纳斯》,但是,他父亲告诫他,40岁以前不能公开演唱,因为《玛纳斯》是神圣的,年轻时演唱会招来不幸。

　　在有些地区与民族中,演唱史诗前要举行隆重的仪式。阿昌族史诗演唱者在演唱史诗《遮帕麻与遮米麻》前,要点燃长明灯,虔诚地向史诗中的两位神——遮帕麻与遮米麻祈祷之后才能开始演唱。藏族民间艺人演唱史诗《格萨尔王传》之前,要设香案,摆挂格萨尔王(或史诗中其他英雄人物)的画像,虔诚地焚香敬拜后才开

---

① 　仁钦道尔吉:《〈江格尔〉论》,第14页。
② 　斯钦巴图:《〈江格尔〉与蒙古族宗教信仰》,第39页。
③ 　刘亚虎:《南方史诗论》,第41页。
④ 　蓝怀昌、蓝书京、蒙通顺搜集翻译整理:《密洛陀》,第545—546页。
⑤ 　斯钦巴图:《〈江格尔〉与蒙古族宗教信仰》,第36页。

始演唱《格萨尔王传》。① 这种情况在蒙古族史诗《江格尔》的演唱活动中也存在,如有的地区演唱《江格尔》之前亦举行焚香、点佛灯、祭拜江格尔的仪式。新疆温泉县,江格尔奇演唱《江格尔》前,要把蒙古包的天窗和门关严,虔诚地焚香、祈祷之后,才开始演唱史诗。有的江格尔奇演唱史诗前,要举行鸣枪驱鬼仪式。② 由于史诗演唱活动是神圣的,演唱之前要祛邪驱鬼,保证史诗演唱环境的圣洁。

上述种种现象表明,史诗的神圣性特点至今仍在我国的口承史诗中有所遗存。我们可以从中窥视到古代史诗传承的神圣、庄严、充满神秘性的原始面貌,为史诗形成与发展的研究提供极为宝贵的资料。但是我们也应注意到,随着岁月的流逝、现代化进程的加快,史诗演唱活动的神圣性特点正在逐渐减弱,世俗性特点日渐增强;随着演唱歌手的年迈多病、年轻听众的日渐减少,史诗也面临着"人亡歌息"的险境。因此,利用现代科技手段抢救口承史诗的任务迫在眉睫。

参考书目

阿地力·朱玛吐尔地,托汗·依莎克:《居素普·玛玛依评传》,呼和浩特:内蒙古大学出版社,2002 年。

巴嫫曲布嫫:"仪式文学",未刊稿。

降边嘉措:《〈格萨尔王传〉初探》,西宁:青海人民出版社,1986 年。

蓝怀昌、蓝书京、蒙通顺搜集翻译整理《密洛陀》,北京:中国民间文艺出版社,1988 年。

郎樱:《玛纳斯论》,呼和浩特:内蒙古大学出版社,1999 年。

刘亚虎:《南方史诗论》,呼和浩特:内蒙古大学出版社,1999 年。

蒙冠雄、蒙海清、蒙松毅搜集翻译整理《密洛陀》,南宁:广西人民出版社,1998 年。

仁钦道尔吉:《〈江格尔〉论》,呼和浩特:内蒙古大学出版社,1994 年。

斯钦巴图:《〈江格尔〉与蒙古族宗教信仰》,呼和浩特:内蒙古大学出版社,1999 年。

萨仁格日勒:《论蒙古史诗生成的民族志特征》(博士论文),北京:中国社会科学院研究生院少数民族文学系,1998 年 5 月,北京。

徐国琼:《试论〈格萨尔王传〉"仲肯"的"博仲"》,北京:《民间文学论坛》1986 年第 1 期。

杨恩洪:《民间诗神——格萨尔王传艺人研究》,北京:中国藏学出版社,1995 年。

---

① 降边嘉措:《〈格萨尔王传〉初探》,西宁:青海人民出版社,1986 年,第 79 页;杨恩洪:《民间诗神——〈格萨尔王传〉艺人研究》,北京:中国藏学出版社,1995 年,第 57—59 页。

② 仁钦道尔吉:《〈江格尔〉论》,呼和浩特:内蒙古大学出版社,1994 年,第 14 页;斯钦巴图:《〈江格尔〉与蒙古族宗教信仰》,呼和浩特:内蒙古大学出版社,1999 年,第 32—38 页。

哈萨克族英雄史诗与幻想故事的比较研究

黄中祥

摘　要　哈萨克族英雄史诗与其幻想故事的关系比较密切,幻想故事的形成时间早于英雄史诗,数量多于英雄史诗。本文对哈萨克族英雄史诗与神箭手故事及英雄幻想故事进行了比较研究,探讨了英雄人物形象及其诞生、远征等成长经历及婚姻考验,分析了故事中出现的恶魔、圣人等形象以及对土、飞禽、牲畜的神化与崇拜等观念,认为二者在情节单元上基本一致,具有一定的渊源关系,为研究英雄史诗开辟了新的途径。

关键词　英雄史诗,幻想故事,比较研究

全世界哈萨克族的人口已经超过 1000 万,主要居住在中亚哈萨克斯坦共和国和中国。中国的哈萨克族有 130 多万人,主要分布在中国西北部新疆维吾尔自治区北部的伊犁哈萨克自治州、昌吉回族自治州、博尔塔拉蒙古自治州及哈密地区的巴里坤哈萨克自治县等地,另有少部分居住在甘肃和青海两省。哈萨克族主要从事畜牧业生产,是古老的游牧民族之一,其语言属于阿尔泰语系突厥语族,是典型的粘着语。哈萨克族所处的人文地理环境为其口头文学的产生和发展提供了肥沃的土壤,形成了大量的寓言、传说、故事和歌谣,其中民间故事和英雄史诗尤为丰富。如产生于 10 世纪前后流传在锡尔(sir)河流域的《先祖阔尔库特书》(*khorkit ata kitabi*),产生于 10 世纪弘吉剌剔(khongirat)部落的《阿勒帕米斯》(*alpamis*),产生于 12 世纪克普恰克(khipshak)部落的《库布兰德》(*Khoblandi*),产生于 14 世纪金帐(altin orda)汗国的《克里木的四十位勇士》(*khirimning khirikh batiri*)、《康巴尔》(*Khambar*)、《英雄塔尔根》(*er targhin*)以及形成于哈萨克汗国(khazakk handighi)建立之后的《阿布赉汗》(*ablayhan*)、《卡班拜》(*Khabanbay*)、《贾尼别克》(*janibek*)、《叶先坎尔

迪》(*esenkeldi*)、《阿尔卡勒克》(*arkhalikh*)等英雄史诗,它们至今仍然在哈萨克族的民间传承。① 在如此大的时空跨度背景下产生的英雄史诗,其内容极其丰富,文化底蕴十分深邃。

哈萨克族的民间故事与神话、传说一同构成了散文体作品的庞大体系。民间故事是指既有某种假想性,又与现实生活有着密切联系的民间口头散文体作品。故事的假想性和现实性使哈萨克族的民间故事真实地反映了社会生活的变化。它不是对现实生活的照搬,而是通过虚拟方式去表现真实的生活。民间故事中的主人公可以是人、动物、植物和无生物,也可以是假想中的神仙和鬼怪,在创作上不受时间和空间的限制。在哈萨克民间文学中,民间故事占有重要的地位。依据内容进行划分,哈萨克族的故事可分为动植物故事、幻想故事、世俗故事、机智人物故事和笑话等,其中幻想故事与英雄史诗的关系较密切。本文拟从哈萨克族幻想故事入手去探讨其与英雄史诗的关系。

哈萨克族的幻想故事与其他民族的幻想故事一样,是通过丰富的想像力和奇特的构思来编织故事情节的。它既包括古代突厥氏族、部落时代产生和传承的故事,又包括后来哈萨克人民自己创作的故事,也包括从外族吸纳过来的故事。哈萨克幻想故事主要包括神箭手、英雄、巫术等方面的内容,其中前两类故事主要赞颂英雄们的英勇精神,与英雄史诗同宗同源。

一、神箭手故事所反映的史诗特征

哈萨克族有关神箭手的故事十分古老,在其幻想故事中占有主要的地位。神箭手的故事主要反映了哈萨克先祖的狩猎生活。如《库拉神箭手》(*khula mergen*)、《苏尔神箭手》(*sur mergen*)、《汗王神箭手》(*han mergen*)、《猎人哈尔勒拜》(*angshi kharlibay*)、《阿拉曼与卓拉曼》(*alaman men jolaman*)等故事中的主人公大都与神箭手相关。② 1尽管故事的情节和内容各不相同,但都与古代狩猎生活密切相关。这类故事的幻想成分较多,反映了古代猎人与大自然进行斗争的愿望。神箭手们本领超凡、足智多谋、英勇顽强,是乡亲们的靠山,大家靠其捕获的猎物繁衍生息。这

---

① 关于以上英雄史诗的内容概要及版本介绍详见附录一。

② 本文的哈萨克族幻想故事主要参考《哈萨克民间故事》(哈萨克文,乌鲁木齐:新疆人民出版社,1981 年)和《哈萨克民间故事》(哈萨克文,阿拉木图:作家出版社,1988 年)第 1—2 集。

一类幻想故事的思想内容基本上是赞扬神箭手在与大自然和野兽搏斗中所表现的英勇精神，其中最具代表性的是神箭手故事《阿尔克神箭手》(*arikh mergen*)。[①]

在很久很久以前，有一个名叫阿尔克的猎人，他是一个本领高超的神箭手。他靠打猎生活，能给周围的人拿主意、指点谋生之路。他把自己获取的猎物分给大家，不让一个人忍饥挨饿、衣不蔽体。阿尔克独身骑马，跋山涉水去打猎。一天，他正在煮肉时，铜爪妖婆变成美女前来窥伺，他立刻射了两箭，翌日发现了铜爪妖婆的尸体。之后，他又与一只扑来的猛虎搏斗，十分艰难地杀死了它。他继续前行，在一座遥远的山谷里与一个独目恶魔相遇。独目恶魔力大无比，他巧妙地用烧红的铁钎戳瞎恶魔的独目，然后用箭射死了它。此时，阿吾勒(awil，意即牧村)的人们前来寻找他，他毫不吝啬地把自己获取的所有猎物及独目恶魔的牲畜和财产都分给了乡亲们。

故事中阿尔克身上所显现的英雄特征，正是哈萨克英雄史诗所要表现的主题。阿尔克神箭手既是一位超凡的猎人，又是一位足智多谋的英雄。英雄的这一特征，较之氏族社会时期人们共同采集、狩猎，具有一定的进步意义。不仅《阿尔克神箭手》中的阿尔克独自打猎，其他古老故事中的猎人也是独自打猎。如《猎人哈尔勒拜》中的哈尔勒拜，不分春夏秋冬，独自一人外出狩猎；《哈拉神箭手》(*khala mergen*)中的哈拉也是独自一人，主要靠猎鹿在荒野生活。这些猎人不同于后来畜牧业有所发展、狩猎业处于附属地位时期的猎人，后者狩猎的目的只是为了保护家中的牲畜或游乐开心而已。阿尔克不单为自己出猎，而是为了众人的温饱出猎。当他杀死铜爪妖婆和独目恶魔后，把自己在山洞里找到的粮食、牲畜和财宝都无条件地分给了众人。如果阿尔克在外打猎时间过得略久些，乡亲们就会去找他，因为大家离不开他。阿尔克不是统治者，不占有他人的劳动果实，而是一个地地道道的自食其力的人。他为了一方平安，与猛兽、恶魔搏斗，这正是史诗中英雄的特征。幻想故事中的英雄特征在神箭手故事《猎人哈尔勒拜》中也有生动的描绘。哈尔勒拜常年外出打猎，照顾周围的人。他学会鸟语之后，获得了很多金子，把它们毫不吝啬地分给了大家。他甚至不惜牺牲生命，把从鸟那里听到的即将洪水泛滥、山崩地

---

① 《阿勒克篾尔干》(*arikh mergen*)1980 年发表于中国新疆人民出版社主办的《绿草》(*shalghin*，哈萨克文，季刊)；1987 年新疆伊犁人民出版社出版的《哈萨克族民间故事》(哈萨克文)第 2 集，收入了由库赛音·居玛迪尔(Khusayin Jumadil)搜集的版本；1986 年中国民族出版社出版的《哈萨克族民间长诗》(哈萨克文)第 5 集，又收入了由玛克苏特·穆合特(Makhsut Mughut)根据情节改编的韵文体版本。

裂的消息透露给众人,结果自己变成了一块黑石。

在阿尔克神箭手的故事中有主人公外出打猎与独目恶魔相遇的情节。独目恶魔是一个十分独特的形象,它吃人畜和野兽,住在非常大的山洞里,而且力大无比,能够轻易搬起巨石堵住洞口。独目恶魔这一民间文学形象产生的时间较早,在突厥、蒙古等阿尔泰语系诸民族的氏族、部落时代曾经广泛流传,后来逐渐被移入故事和英雄史诗的情节之中,并有不同的表现。它在故事《古丽克孜罕》(gul khizhan)中是企图吞吃公主的恶魔;在故事《叶迪力与贾依克》(edil men jayikh)中被描绘成在芦苇丛中杀死英雄贾依克的巨人;在故事《英雄杜坦》(er dodan)和《阿拉曼与卓拉曼》中是一个心狠手辣的独目妖婆;在英雄史诗《库拉神箭手与卓彦神箭手》(khula mergen men joyan mergen)和《先祖阔尔库特书》中是一个穷凶极恶的恶魔。

二、英雄故事中所反映的史诗特征

英雄故事是哈萨克族幻想故事的另一重要组成部分,它主要是颂扬英雄的非凡经历,在幻想的世界中讲述古代氏族和部落间的讨伐与征战。在内容上,古老的英雄故事与神箭手故事相互包容、彼此交叉。较之神箭手故事,英雄故事的情节结构更复杂,内容更丰富。与神箭手故事相比,英雄故事更接近于英雄史诗,它们有着基本相似的情节单元。如父母求子并得到神灵的许诺、母亲怀孕、英雄的特异诞生及成长、战马、故乡、宫帐、敌人的信息、证实来犯、英雄备马、携带弓箭和宝剑、出征迎战、英雄的威力、发现敌人、与敌人相遇、互相通报姓名、搏斗、敌人战败、求饶、杀死敌人、凯旋等。实际上,英雄故事就是英雄史诗早期的雏形。

英雄特异诞生及成长:英雄的诞生很奇特,他或者是众兄弟中最小的弟弟,如《英雄托斯提克》(er töstik)中的托斯提克;或者是一对老年夫妻苦苦祈求而生的儿子,如《为人民而生的勇士》(eli üshin tuwghan er)中的迪力达西(dildash)。在有些英雄故事中,英雄的诞生更是奇特,如《英雄馕》(nan batir)中的馕,他原本是发面做的娃娃,他的母亲当初吃了特殊的食物而怀孕,后来生下了他。这些孩子一出生就有英雄的征兆,如《为人民而生的勇士》中的迪力达西"头像锅一样大,眼睛像木碗一样大"。又比如《骑黄骠马的坎迪拜》(ker khula atti kendibay)中的坎迪拜成长神速,"不是以月计,而是以日计,六天就会笑,六十天就会走路,六年长成腰圆背宽的魁梧小伙子,能把前来挑战的人都摔倒在地"。

英雄的坐骑:英雄的面前出现天神赐予的神驹,如英雄坎迪拜所骑的浅栗色骏马,当时是在一匹被狼咬死的骒马腹中得到的;英雄迪力达西的神驹是当初敌人抢掠马匹时剩下的一匹不起眼的跛腿黄斑马驹,是由英雄的父亲一把青草、一木盆水把它饲养大的,因此起名为"黄斑木盆"。英雄们的这些坐骑都是疾驰如飞的神驹,是"用嘴能咬住飞鸟羽毛的天马"。它们在危急关头,能像史诗中英雄的神驹一样会说话,给英雄出主意,预卜未来。除了主人之外,它们不让其他任何人接近,甚至愿意为主人牺牲生命。

英雄的远征:有些英雄到远方去寻找他们的兄长和牲畜,兄长们通常是去非常遥远的地方放牧而迷了路的,如托斯提克寻找自己的八个长兄和大批牲畜;有些英雄寻找在自己幼年时被敌人掳掠的英雄、父母和牲畜以报仇雪恨,如迪力达西远行去寻找被敌人掳掠的母亲,并且为乡亲们报仇;坎迪拜远行去寻找被敌人抓走的英雄麦尔干拜和乡亲们,最后把他们解救出来,返回故乡。英雄徒步远征的速度非常快,视大海、湖泊、江河和高山为平地。六个月的路程只需跨跃六步。眼前的鸟还没有来得及从地面上拍翅飞起,英雄就已从它们的上面一跃而过。骑马的英雄在得到自己的伙伴神驹之后,便备好英雄的五件武器(皮鞭、棍、大头棒、矛、弓箭)开始远征。他们的行程一般为一个月或一年,到达目的地后,英雄在异乡解救被困的母亲、英雄和乡亲,赶着牲畜群凯旋。英雄远征是出于某种需要,比如在游牧生活中人们与大自然的抗争,氏族、部落之间的冲突等。幻想故事在这一点上与古老的英雄史诗十分相似。这类幻想故事中的主人公与猎人、神箭手故事中的主人公一样,不仅是猎人,而且是在氏族部落的狩猎和游牧生活中起着重要作用的英雄。

英雄的婚姻考验:英雄在途中会遇到美女,为了满足汗王(有时是姑娘)的要求,英雄要过火海、越冰山,与恶魔、善魔、巨鹰、妖魔相遇,并千方百计地战胜它们。恶魔有阴险毒辣的老妖婆,有活吞人畜的恶龙,有凡人难以对付的凶恶巨人,有身体一拳高、胡子四十档子的人形魔鬼。而善魔中有飞毛腿吉尔阿亚克(jelayakh),有一口喝光湖水的阔里塔吾沙尔(koltawisar),有把山抓起像玩石子一样的塔吾索哈尔(tawsoghar),有眼观六路、耳听八方的萨克库拉克(sakhkhulakh)和知恩图报的巨鹰等。英雄要得到它们的帮助,攻克艰难险阻。这些婚姻考验情节,主要是为了考验英雄的勇敢程度。像英雄史诗一样,英雄在射箭、角力、赛马、摔跤的同时,还要经受女方父母的考验。即替女方的父母去消灭敌人,降妖伏魔,寻找被巨鹰叼走的金头银尾马驹、稀世之宝或灵丹妙药。派英雄去的地方一般是"一去难返"的地方。对这些委派,英雄绝不推辞,因为这是对英雄婚姻的考验。若不经过这些考验,英雄即使与自己所爱的美女成亲,众人也不会折服。在《为人民而生的勇士》中,汗王的三个女儿投苹果挑选未婚夫,小女儿选中了装扮成"秃头"的迪力达西,但汗王不同意。不久,汗王身患重病,迪力达西猎来神奇的狍子,汗王吃后就痊愈了。迪力达西又为汗王找回了被巨鹰叼走的金头银尾马驹。汗王这才同意迪力达西和小公主的婚事。这既反映了当时氏族部落不再局限于血缘婚姻,出现了与氏族、部落以外的人通婚的现象,但婚姻依然没有超出氏族、部落范围的事实。英雄托斯提克的婚姻就颇具代表性。总之,英雄故事中已经显现出英雄史诗的特征。

在哈萨克英雄幻想故事中,最具代表性的故事是《英雄托斯提克》(er tostik),它汇集了英雄故事、神箭手故事和英雄史诗的传统特征,尤其是主人公的出生、成长、征战、婚姻等情节与英雄史诗基本如出一辙。《英雄托斯提克》的结构如下:

(一)托斯提克的出生成长

(1)很早很早以前,有一个名叫叶尔纳扎尔(ernazar)的富翁,他有八个儿子和不计其数的牲畜。

(2)有一年冬季发生了大灾,八个儿子赶着牲畜去遥远的地方放牧,长年未归。当叶尔纳扎尔和老伴饥饿难忍时,抬头看到了挂在毡房天窗上的一块马胸肉,于是饱餐了一顿。老伴怀孕生子,起名托斯提克(意即胸脯肉)。

(3)托斯提克成长神速,一个月时像一岁的孩子,两个月时像两岁的孩子,一年后像15岁的孩子。他能摔倒所有前来挑战的小伙子,能射穿九层厚的毛织外衣。

(二)托斯提克的出征

(1)初次出征

(a) 徒步去寻找在远方放牧未归的八个长兄。

(b) 他翻山越岭不分昼夜地走,终于在一个遥远的部落找到了八个长兄。

(c) 长兄们带来的唯一的一匹棕色骒马,已经繁殖了一大群马。

(d) 他们准备返回自己的阿吾勒(意即牧村),但赶不动马群。托斯提克制服暴烈的棕色骒马,带领马群返回故乡。

(2)二次出征

(a) 托斯提克欺骗老妖婆,拿上魔石逃跑,老妖婆穷追不舍。

(b) 大地经不住夏勒库依勒克(shalkhuyrikh,意即老尾神驹)的疾驰而裂开一道缝,主人和坐骑掉进地下界。

(c) 夏勒库依勒克突然会说话,为主人献出了脱身之计。

(d) 来到蛇王巴布(babi)的部落,经过严格考验后被接纳了。

(e) 蛇王巴布让托斯提克去找铁米尔(temir)汗王的女儿,托斯提克只好向有七个月路程的下界进发。

(f) 托斯提克在途中遇见吉勒阿亚克(jelayakh,意即飞毛腿)、萨克库拉克(sakhkhulakh,意即顺风耳)、阔列干(koregen,意即有预见的人)、塔吾索哈尔(tawsoghar,意即能震动群山的人)、阔里塔吾沙尔(koltawisar,意即能使湖水干竭的人)等巨人,与他们交友结伴而行。

(g) 在荒无人烟的地方,他找到铁米尔汗王的部落,并与准备娶铁米尔汗王女儿的克谢(kexe)汗王进行各种较量。克谢汗王企图暗中毒死他们,但萨克库拉克听到后,掉包毒死了克谢汗王的手下人;在摔跤较量中,塔吾索哈尔战胜所有的对手;在赛程为七天的赛马较量中,神驹夏勒库依勒克遥遥领先,冲到了终点;在徒步长跑比赛中,吉勒阿亚克揭穿老妖婆的诡计,第一个跑到了终点;铁米尔汗王有一口直径为40度的大锅沉在湖底,当阔里塔吾沙尔都无法捞出它时,夏勒库依勒克把它拉了出来;当克谢汗王企图把托斯提克他们关在铁宫里烧死时,阔里塔吾沙尔救了他们;克谢汗王万般无奈只好让铁米尔汗王的女儿嫁给蛇王巴布的部落;在返回蛇王巴布部落的途中,托斯提克与各位巨人告别。蛇王巴布把自己的女儿许配给托斯提克。托斯提克在返回故乡时,蛇王巴布的女儿经不住长途跋涉而死去。

托斯提克看到一条龙欲吃雏鹰,杀死龙救出雏鹰;巨鹰回报他的恩德,驮着托斯提克飞回地界;别克托丽(bektori)的守卫绍因库拉克(shyinkhulakh,意为铁耳)在托斯提克沉睡时,把他捆绑起来扔进地牢,并把夏勒库依勒克拴牢,将跟随托斯提克的女仆抢占为妻;夏勒库依勒克送给托斯提克一个火镰,托斯提克用它点燃巨鹰的翎毛,巨鹰驮着托斯提克飞出地牢;女仆告诉托斯提克,布鲁克(borikhti bulakh)泉边有40只野羊,其中一只歪角黑野羊的腹中有一只木匣,里面的九只小鸟是绍因库拉克的灵魂;托斯提克射死那只野羊,杀死九只小鸟,摆脱绍因库拉克返回了故乡。

(三)托斯提克的婚姻和骏马

(a) 叶尔纳扎尔(ernazar)几经周折为自己的九个儿子物色到一家的九个女儿,让托斯提克和最小的女儿坎吉凯(kenjekey)成亲。

(b) 坎吉凯姑娘美丽又聪慧,她把陪嫁的沙里库依勒克骏马、白母驼和白银铠甲送给托斯提克,叶尔纳扎尔同时操办了九个儿子的婚事,上路返回故乡。

(c) 叶尔纳扎尔不顾坎吉凯的提醒,夜宿碱水井旁,结果落入老妖婆手里。

(d) 老妖婆以死胁迫叶尔纳扎尔,叶尔纳扎尔无奈,答应交出托斯提克,并把他的魔石交给老妖婆。

(e) 坎吉凯得知此事,不让托斯提克接近自己,要他摆脱老妖婆。

(f) 托斯提克准备寻找魔石时,坎吉凯把沙尔库依勒克骏马和白银铠甲交给了他。

(四)托斯提克返回家乡

(a) 托斯提克长年不归,部落的人们深感绝望。

(b) 坎吉凯和托斯提克分别时,就预卜到托斯提克返回或遇难的那一天,白母驼会产羔,自己的绸腰带会自动松开。

(c) 白母驼产羔,绸腰带自动松开,坎吉凯认为托斯提克已经遇难,悲痛欲绝。

(d) 一位胡子花白的老翁骑着白骏马跑来,原来是托斯提克。

(e) 托斯提克和坎吉凯两人都已经衰老。

(f) 他们恢复了青春,沙里库依勒克也变成一匹牙口正好的神驹,叶尔纳扎尔为他们举行了隆重热闹的庆宴。

这一英雄故事描绘了古代游牧部落英雄的非凡生平和坎坷经历。托斯提克为了寻找去远方放牧未归的哥哥们,历经了艰难险阻,终于找到了自己的兄长和马群。他为了心上人奋不顾身,与违背众人意愿的非正义势力进行无畏的斗争,体现了他的英勇精神和聪明机智。叶尔纳扎尔的八个儿子为了在灾年保全牲畜,去遥远的地方放牧,在那里马群倒毙,只剩下一匹棕色骒马。几年后这匹骒马繁殖了几千匹马,无法赶回来。托斯提克饱受艰辛,徒步而行,铁靴子的底儿都磨得像银元那样薄,终于找到了哥哥们,赶着马群返回了故乡。为了度过荒年,需要把牲畜,特别是把马群赶到比较远的地方去牧放,这是哈萨克族传统的放牧方法之一。古代部落根据游牧经济的特点,常年逐水草而迁徙。托斯提克的八个哥哥把马群赶到遥远的牧场去放牧,但还是没能摆脱自然灾害的侵袭。这反映了古代游牧部落与大自然斗争的艰苦性。

仙女别克托丽极力破坏托斯提克与坎吉凯的婚姻,托斯提克与之进行了无畏的斗争。她派老妖婆把托斯提克追得掉进下界,与毒蛇、巨龙进行了殊死搏斗,又战胜凶恶、奸诈的铁米尔汗王之后返回地界。别克托丽又派绍因库拉克巨人(老妖婆之子)把他扔进深不可测的地牢。这里所揭示的是古代草原部落从母系社会向父系社会过渡时期的矛盾。托斯提克等人是父系时代的人物,而他们的敌人——

老妖婆、别克托丽和凶恶的巨人(绍因库拉克)是母系时代的人物。托斯提克与坎吉凯的婚姻并非建立在感情基础上,而是英雄时代的婚姻,具有对偶婚的性质。叶尔纳扎尔为儿子们提亲之前,托斯提克并没有与坎吉凯见过面,而且坎吉凯还为托斯提克挑选坐骑和铠甲,协助他化险为夷。这些情节带有父系社会的印记,在哈萨克英雄史诗中也有所反映。

托斯提克的婚姻反映了古代氏族、部落的婚俗,即叶尔纳扎尔给自己的九个儿子娶了来自一个家庭的九个女儿。他四处奔波,最后发现一个人家有九只耳环,从而得知这家有九位姑娘,并一次为九个儿子举办了婚礼,带着九个儿媳返回家乡。这是现在已经绝迹的古老婚俗,我们从中可见哈萨克族"大家庭"传统观念的遗迹。叶尔纳扎尔作为"大家庭"的家长,亲自为九个儿子迎娶了来自一个家庭的九个女儿,其目的是为了维护"大家庭"的权威性。

在哈萨克族英雄幻想故事中常见的老妖婆形象也与英雄史诗中的比较一致。她的称呼在不同的故事中不同,但本质是一样的。如在《美女玛尔胡莞》(*malhuwan suluw*)、《好与坏一视同仁》(*jakhsi men jamandi birdey koruw*)、《流浪人》(*khangghirghan adam*)、《叛逆的亲戚》(*opasiz tuwis*)等故事中被称为"老妖婆";在《奥尼尔西拜的儿子》(*onershibayding uli*)中被称为"尖鼻妖婆";在《萨赞与玛尔江》(*sazan men marjan*)中被称为"魔术婆";在《做梦的国王与机智的孩子》(*tus korgen patsha men zerek jigit*)中被称为"巫婆";在《阴谋不会得逞》中被称为"铜爪妖婆";在《贾巴依老爷与哈尔卡莎美女》(*jabay ata men kharghasha suluw*)中被称为"黑脸婆"。这些妖婆表面上好似一个处在可怜境地的羸弱女人,但实际上是阴险毒辣、残酷无情的魔鬼。当秃头牧羊人在险恶的路途行走时,她突然变成猛兽扑过来;她诱惑脆弱的妇女,使她们堕落,从其膝盖里吸血;她把人捆绑起来关押在家里,然后慢慢地吞食;为了得到重赏,她帮助凶恶的国王、贪婪的富人和嫉妒妾妇的嫡妻策划阴谋,无恶不作;当汗王企图抢占别人的娇妻时,她献计把其丈夫派到一个"一去难返"的地方;当汗王、富翁的妾妇生下金头银臀的男婴或金发碧眼的女婴时,不生育的嫡妻心怀嫉恨,会指使老妖婆偷偷地用狗崽代替婴儿,把婴儿扔到荒野或江河里,妾妇被赶出家门;她诱惑守在家里的女人背叛丈夫,妹妹背叛哥哥;她偷窃能使牧羊人获得幸福的神奇戒指。总之,哈萨克族英雄幻想故事中的"老妖婆"是无恶不作的恶魔,但不管她的诡计多么阴险、魔法多么高明,最终都会被挫败,甚至受到惩罚。

老妖婆形象在英雄故事和英雄史诗中有着相同的表现,都是以陷害英雄的身份出现的。如英雄史诗《阿尔帕米斯》中的主人公所向披靡、势不可挡时,受塔依西克(taykesh)汗王指使的老妖婆出现了。她携带40顶毡房和40位姑娘对阿尔帕米斯撒谎说:"我的40个儿子为了夺回你们家的马群全部战死在疆场上,你的40个嫂子都成了寡妇。如果你能下马亲自向她们问个安,我会不胜感激。"毫无戒备的阿尔帕米斯下马走进了她们的毡房,结果被她们灌醉捆绑了起来,被塔依西克汗王投进一个有40根绳子深的地牢里。如果没有这个可恶的老妖婆,阿尔帕米斯是不会被抓住的。当然如果没有老妖婆,阿尔帕米斯的形象也就被过分地理想化了。

在哈萨克族英雄幻想故事中,留下了许多图腾崇拜的遗迹。这些图腾崇拜与神话有关,其中最常见的是杨树崇拜。在《萨赞与玛尔江》(sazan men marjan)中,当高耸入云的杨树的一根枝条折断时,大地就震动裂开,天空乌云密布,连森林里的魔鬼都叫嚣不休。用杨树的枝条做成的冬布拉琴可以自动弹奏。在《三个孩子》(ush bala)中,努尔的女儿努尔佩依丝居住在大杨树顶梢上的毡房里。杨树高不可攀,爱上努尔佩依丝的男子数不胜数。他们纷纷爬杨树想把姑娘带下来,但总是被摔下来,鲜血流成河,白骨堆成山。最后,一个流浪汉成功地将姑娘从杨树上接了下来并娶为妻子。在很多故事中,大杨树底下都是神奇事件发生的地点。如一位英雄在湖边的杨树底下看到自己寻找的熊并征服了它,迷路的姑娘在杨树底下碰到了小伙子或庇护者等等。如《秃小子》(tazsha bala)、《古力哈克汗的花》(gülhakhhanning güli)等故事中的爱情就发生在杨树底下。

在哈萨克族幻想故事中,把土神化是突出的一个情节。正面人物与恶势力斗争时,土总是能成为神圣的武器或灵丹妙药。如:英雄镶被暗害掉进深牢时,身负重伤。这时他见受伤的蚂蚁在土里一滚就痊愈了,于是自己也在那堆土里滚了滚,果然伤势痊愈了。对土的崇拜还往往与灵魂信仰联系在一起,如在《奥拉尔》(oral)中,汗王嫉妒秃头有漂亮的妻子,于是派秃头去索取早就为祭奠父母而宰杀的牲畜,秃头在圣人的帮助下,与汗王父母的灵魂相遇,灵魂退还牲畜,并给自己的儿子和儿媳一把土。当秃头回到家撒这一把土时,那恶徒汗王变成了公猪,汗后变成了母猪。这圣土还可用来对付其他奸宄。在《巫师的礼物》中,一个猎人救出一个女人,并给予她幸福,但这个女人居心叵测、诡计多端,于是猎人撒一把土,使这个女人变成了40头驴和一只狼。这说明再贪婪的人也不免一死,会被埋进黄土。在哈萨克族神话传说中,也有人类是由土创造的叙述。

崇拜飞禽也是哈萨克族幻想故事中常见的情节,其中广泛流传的飞禽图腾形象之一是巨鹰(有时亦称大鹏)。它飞翔时,翅膀能扇起狂风,泪水能变成暴雨,吃人就像吃一小块肉。它飞到需六个月行程的地方去觅食,能带回来50只黄羊。它驮着主人公飞过刀山火海,有时飞到九重天界,有时从七层下界飞上来。除了巨鹰之外,"天鹅仙女"的形象在故事中也比较常见。在《萨赞与玛尔江》中,她与萨赞结合;在《比谁都好》(barinen abzal)中,当她在湖中洗澡时遇见了秃头小伙子,于是和他成了亲;在《两兄弟吐拉甫与吐拉什》(aghayindi turap pen turash)中,她把善良、勤劳的吐拉什驮到太阳里的金山,使他达到了目的。天鹅是哈萨克族崇拜的飞禽之一,平时哈萨克族就特别敬重天鹅,直到现在也从不射猎。此外,在很多故事中还可见到"幸福鸟"的形象,据说它是汗王的宠物。汗王死去时,人们要放飞"幸福鸟","幸福鸟"落在谁的头上,谁就能当上汗王。故事中没有说明"幸福鸟"是什么鸟,但这也是特别尊崇飞禽的一种反映。在《赫甫莎》(ghipsha)中,它落在被贩卖的赫甫莎姑娘头上;在《玉素甫》(jusup)中,它落在遭受欺辱的小伙子玉素甫头上;在《寻找"奇怪"的汗王》(ghajayipti izdegen han)中,它落在被冤枉的一个人的头上;在《公正的汗王》(adil han)中,它落在一个流浪儿的头上;在《幸福鸟》(bakhit khusi)中,它落在雇工哈山卡甫的头上。总之,神鸟是正面形象,是正义的象征。

幻想故事更多地反映了人们对牲畜的尊崇,相对而言,比对飞禽走兽的崇拜要多,这也是古代氏族、部落经济发展程度的一个具体反映。在《英雄托斯提克》(er tostik)故事中,托斯提克就是因为母亲吃了栗色骒马的胸脯肉而出生的,他们家的马群是由一匹棕色骒马繁殖的。叶尔纳扎尔看到自己的九个儿子赶着9000匹马平安归来时,宰杀公驼、公马、公羊,准备大量的马奶酒和肉,举办盛大的庆宴,使部落的男女老幼感到无比的自豪。托斯提克上路时,坎吉凯让白母驼与公驼交配,预卜它产羔的那一天就是托斯提克平安返回或遇难的日子。最后,白母驼产羔的那一天,托斯提克果真平安回家了。从许多出土文物中,我们也可找到古代匈奴和乌孙特别尊崇公驼和公马的证据。哈萨克族尊崇母驼、栗色骒马和棕色骒马的习俗一直延续到近代。故事《英雄托斯提克》把白母驼奉为神圣的牲畜,贯穿于整个故事情节的始末。当坎吉凯(kenjekey)想要白母驼和夏勒库依勒克(sarikhuyrikh)骏马时,她的父亲有些犹豫不决,因为他认为牲畜是福分;叶尔纳扎尔因寻找白母驼而落在老妖婆的手里,导致托斯提克走上冒险之路。这些都反映了古代人对骆驼的特殊感情和心理。

在幻想故事的牲畜崇拜中,对马的崇拜和神化程度比在英雄史诗中更高。马是主人的智囊,会说话,在危险关头能拯救主人。如在《跳蚤皮》中,古力巴旦(gülbadan,意即黑灰马)帮助主人与独目巨人展开了搏斗,死后其骨头和皮变成了鲜花盛开、草木繁茂的花园和宫殿。在《古力哈克汗的花》(gülkhakhhanning güli)、

《黑马驹的庇护》等故事中,可见到马的膀胱变成小舟,去解救遭难女人的情节。在《骢骒马》故事中,骢骒马每天夜里望着月亮变成一匹白马,白天望着太阳生马驹;若遇到猛兽就立起颈鬃、伸直尾巴,一溜烟地跑到荒凉的山里变成一群马,使猛兽不敢靠近。尊崇牲畜的习俗在托斯提克身上也有明显反映,如伴随他战胜所有艰难险阻的不是别人,而是他的伙伴——夏勒库依勒克神驹。夏勒库依勒克神驹是一个特殊的形象,起初它像英雄史诗《阿尔帕米斯》(alpamis)中的苏巴尔(subar)及《库布兰德》(khoblandi)中的布尔勒(buril)骏马一样,伴随着托斯提克出生入死。曾从老妖婆那里救出过托斯提克。但是,当托斯提克为了摆脱老妖婆而逃跑时,骏马的形象被赋予了浓厚的幻想成分。它完成了主人无法做到的事情,教会主人与蛇周旋的方法;在铁米尔(temir)汗王部落的七天比赛中,它跑到终点因承受不住自己的巨大惯性而昏倒在地,它甚至独自从湖底拉出直径为40度的大铁锅。当托斯提克被关进地牢时,它又送来火镰等物件。在该故事中,骏马的形象随着英雄形象的变化而不断地丰富。在这一点上,幻想故事中马的形象与英雄史诗中作为英雄伙伴的马的形象基本相似,其描绘手法和比喻手段如出一辙。

幻想故事已经含有原始萨满教的成分,主要表现在灵魂崇拜上。在有关灵魂信仰的故事中,人们可以见到亡灵与活人来往、交友的内容和情节。在《小伙子阿克库巴》(bozjigit akhkhuba)故事中,一个年轻人遇见一个人因一枚金币的债务而与亡灵打架,于是替亡灵还了债务。这个亡灵变成了一个小伙子——阿克库巴,成了年轻人的伙伴。他们俩一起做生意,形影不离。阿克库巴杀死住在杨树洞中企图毒死他们的老妖婆和她的七个身躯庞大的儿子,杀死一条一年能吞食40只黑羊和40个姑娘的龙,又机智勇敢地消灭了祸殃百姓的七个强盗。他使年轻人失明的父亲重见光明。

汗王觊觎美貌之女,一般会将她的丈夫派去索取为早已死去的父母亡灵供献的牲畜。如在《奥拉尔》(oral)故事中,一个小伙子被汗王派去见自己已故的父亲,取回为祭祀而供献的青花公马。小伙子首先让青花公马复活,然后牵回来。类似的情节在《秃小子》(tazsha bala)、《寻找梦的小伙子》(tiisin izdengen jigit)、《享福的小伙子》(bakhitti baskha tepken jigit)、《去另一个世界返回的小伙子》(o düniyege barip kelgen jigit)等幻想故事中也可见到。主人公与亡灵相见并不容易,有时要抱住坟墓,或者把尸骨放在摇篮里摇晃数日,等等。汗王父母的灵魂也不是好伺候的,交涉到了一定的程度时,亡灵才退还祭祀的牲畜,并赐予一把土。当主人公撒出这一把土时,汗王就会遭到惩罚,或变成动物,或被火烧死。这些都反映了古代灵魂信仰观,即认为亡灵也像活人一样可以与人类交往。人虽死了但灵魂不死,依然活着,不能让其生气,否则将遭受祸殃;为亡灵供奉得越多,好事做得越多,所得到的恩赐越多。亡灵的威力强大,魔法高超,未卜先知,这些都是原始萨满教的观念。故事的结局往往是那些使亡灵生气的暴戾汗王、凶恶歹徒遭到应有惩罚,而遭受迫害的主人公得以摆脱凶残的汗王而获得自由。

英雄史诗中的灵魂崇拜反映出了现实生活,而在幻想故事中则没有这方面的直接反映;在史诗中向祖先灵魂崇拜时,直呼其名,具有鲜明的部落特征,而在故事中则只讲述人类与亡灵相见与交友、人类为亡灵行善、亡灵通过自己的威力和法术给人类赐予恩惠的过程;在史诗中人类与亡灵没有这种直接的交往,人类将它们视作仅次于天神的神灵进行崇拜,而故事中几乎没有这种形式。归根结底,故事中的萨满教特征与久远的思想意识和习俗有关,是萨满教最初产生时期的遗迹,而史诗中的灵魂崇拜与现实生活比较接近,现实基础比较明显。虽然幻想故事与英雄史诗中的灵魂崇拜存有差异,但二者毕竟是血脉相连、同出一宗。故事中的灵魂崇拜较之史诗的更具幻想性,是史诗之前的产物。史诗中的灵魂崇拜是在幻想故事的基础上形成的。

幻想故事中的主人公常常会得到神奇圣人的佑助。圣人形象之一是长着白须,"骑风周游世界"的克德尔(khidir,意即圣人)。圣人往往从虚幻中出现,主人公在艰险路途中偶然与他们相遇。如在《三个孩子》(ush bala)中,一个流浪的孩子在虚幻中与一个圣人相遇。他用圣人赠送的短剑杀死每年吞食40位姑娘的龙。故事中的主人公遇到困难时几乎都可以遇见圣人,甚至这些主人公在汗王的委派下或是因为其他原因,每次上路都会遇见圣人。在《贾巴依祖爷与哈尔卡莎》(jabay ata men kharkhasha)中,贾巴依祖爷在两次路途中都遇见圣人,并得到教诲。在《流浪人》(khangghirghan adam)中,哈拉什(khalash)寻找丢失的3000匹马。当他走近河边时,一个白须长老突然出现了,告诉他马群是被魔鬼赶走了。最后,哈拉什战胜凶恶的魔鬼赶着马群凯旋。在《阴谋不会得逞》故事中,圣人叫醒昏睡在荒野的孩子,告诉他自己寻找的骏马不是马而是一条隐了身的龙,并让他去寻找分别多年的母亲。在《好与坏一视同仁》(jakhsi men jamandi birdey koruw)故事中,所讲述的长老是圣人克德尔。他给一个善良的孩子出了五个主意,并送他一把匕首,叫他向欺辱自己的歹徒复仇。在《一千只黑头羊》(ming khara bas khoy)故事中,放羊孩子在汗王的委派下,第一次去寻找熊的奶汁,第二次去寻找雪鸡的粪,第三次去哈依甫(ghayip)这个地方找仙女的乳汁,放羊孩子三次都遇见圣人,圣人给他指明道路。

最后,他胜利归来,战胜专横跋扈的汗王,实现了自己的夙愿。

圣人和长老也是哈萨克民间长诗,特别是英雄史诗中常见的形象之一,但其时代性和现实性与幻想故事有所区别。幻想故事中的神奇圣人、长老主要是在主人公遇到困难时为其指明方向,帮助他们达到目的,而英雄史诗中的则是替主人公向天神求子。史诗中所反映的圣人、长老形象与历史人物有一定的关系,而故事中的这类角色则没有任何具体的现实依据,只是纯粹的幻想;史诗中的这类形象往往有诸如沙什特艾则孜(shashti aziz)、阿依甫佩连(ghayip peri)神、阔克谢(kökshe)圣人等名字。而故事中的这类形象则没有固定的名字。从表面上看幻想故事与英雄史诗中的圣人与长老形象之间的联系不多,实际上后者是前者的继续。幻想故事的主人公所面临的最大困难是生产和生活的艰辛,这时必须求助于圣人;而史诗的主人公一般是牛羊满坡、财宝满仓,唯一揪心的事是膝下无后嗣,只好祈求于具有非凡能力的圣人。总之,倘若没有故事中的灵魂和圣人崇拜,就可能没有史诗中原始宗教观念和圣人、头人崇拜现象。

结　语

如果从 1827 年法国的维勒曼在巴黎大学讲学,第一次使用"比较文学"这个术语算起,[①] 至今已有近 200 年的历史了。实际上朴素的"比较文学"研究并非只有这两个世纪的历史,可追溯到更久远的中世纪。早期学界认为比较文学是国家间的文学比较研究,后来概念发展到同一国家不同民族文学之间的比较研究。本文认为同一民族文学的不同体裁之间也能进行比较研究。这样,既可揭示被比较的不同体裁作品的内在规律和文化内涵,又有利于发现不同体裁作品的内在联系和文体特点,从而全面展现一个民族的文学的全貌。

哈萨克族英雄史诗与幻想故事的关系比较密切,是一种你中有我、我中有你的关系。综观整个哈萨克幻想故事和英雄史诗的母题和情节,不难看出大部分幻想故事早于英雄史诗,尤其是对那些既是民间故事又是英雄史诗的作品而言更是如此。哈萨克族的民间故事与英雄史诗相比,前者数量远远多于后者。没有韵文体形式的故事很多,但没有散文体形式故事流传的英雄史诗几乎没有。目前在哈萨克族民间,传承较广的几十部英雄史诗几乎都有散文体形式的故事,而流传在民间

---

① 　[日]野上丰一郎:《比较文学论要》,刘介民译,长沙:湖南人民出版社,1984 年,第 24 页。

勺近百部幻想故事却很少有韵文体形式。本文通过哈萨克族英雄史诗与神箭手、英雄幻想故事的比较,明显地看出二者情节单元基本一致,具有一定的渊源关系。这就为我们的研究提供了方法,特别是对英雄史诗的研究更为重要,因为故事形成于史诗之前。史诗中对牲畜、圣人、大自然的崇拜现象,可在故事中得到验证。通过对二者的具体比较,可更明确地探寻到一种文化现象的深层根源,从而更深刻地理解这个游牧民族的文化脉络。

参考书目

《阿勒泰春光》(*altay ayasi*,哈萨克文,季刊),1980 年第 2 期,阿勒泰。

《哈萨克族民间长诗》(哈萨克文)第 4 集,北京:民族出版社,1985 年。

《哈萨克民间故事》(哈萨克文)乌鲁木齐:新疆人民出版社,1981 年。

《哈萨克民间故事》(哈萨克文)第 1—2 集,阿拉木图:作家出版社,1988 年。

《哈萨克族民间故事》(哈萨克文)第 2 集,奎屯:伊犁人民出版社,1987 年。

《哈萨克族民间长诗》(哈萨克文)第 5 集,北京:民族出版社,1986 年。

《哈萨克族民间长诗》(哈萨克文)第 2 集(哈萨克文),北京:民族出版社,1984 年。

《哈萨克族民间故事》(*Kazak Xalek Ertegileri*)第 2 集,奎屯:伊犁人民出版社,1987 年。

《哈萨克英雄史诗》(*Kazak Epose*),阿拉木图:哈萨克斯坦国立文艺出版社,1958 年。

《哈萨克史诗》专辑,M.艾维佐夫(M.awazov)和 H.斯米尔诺娃(H.Simirnnova)主编,阿拉木图:哈萨克斯坦国家文化艺术出版社,1958 年。

《哈萨克叙事长诗选》第 2 卷,北京:民族出版社,1984 年。

《哈萨克叙事长诗选》(*Kazak Keysalare*)第 2 卷,北京:民族出版社,1984 年。

《哈萨克叙事长诗选》(哈萨克文)第 6 卷,北京:民族出版社,1987 年。

《哈萨克族叙事长诗选》第 2 卷,北京:民族出版社,1984 年。

《哈萨克叙事长诗选》(*Kazak Keysalare*)第 7 卷,北京:民族出版社,1987 年。

《哈萨克叙事长诗选》第 4 卷,北京:民族出版社,1985 年。

《哈萨克叙事长诗选》第 11 卷,北京:民族出版社,1991 年。

《哈萨克叙事长诗选》第 2 卷,北京:民族出版社,1984 年。

《绿草》(*shalghin*,哈萨克文),新疆人民出版社主办,1981 年第 1 期,乌鲁木齐。

《叙事诗——阿尔帕米斯》,居素甫别克·霍加·沙依赫斯(Jusipbek Koja Xaykeselam)版本,1899 年,喀山。

《遗产》(mura,哈萨克文,季刊),1983 年第 1 期,乌鲁木齐。

《遗产》(mura,哈萨克文,季刊),1986 年 1—2 期合刊,乌鲁木齐。

《遗产》(mura,哈萨克文,季刊),1989 年第 2 期,乌鲁木齐。

《英雄史诗》(哈萨克文)第 2 集,阿拉木图:作家出版社,1961 年。

《英雄史诗》第 6、7 卷,阿拉木图:作家出版社,1989 年。

《英雄史诗》第 11 卷,阿拉木图:作家出版社,1961 年。

《英雄史诗集》,阿拉木图:阿克苏瓦特出版社,1977 年。

附录一

《先祖阔尔库特书》(khorkit ata kitabi)

10 世纪前后,阿拉伯旅行家伊斯哈里(Ishal)在伊犁、锡尔河流域旅行,在乌古孜(Uguz)、克普恰克(Kipchak)等突厥部落里听到了霍尔赫特的传说。这是阔尔库特故事首次流传到外界,并被笔录成文字。至 12 世纪,《先祖阔尔库特书》的雏形已经形成。从此不断地辗转传抄,增删补益,甚至附会篡改,大约在十四五世纪时以《见诸乌古斯诸部伟大语言的先祖阔尔库特》之名成书。目前流传在民间的《先祖阔尔库特书》的抄本很多,比较权威的有两个抄本。一个抄本收藏在德国的德累斯顿图书馆,共 12 章,封面上方写有"先祖阔尔库特书"的字样,下方注有"乌古斯诸部的语言"的字样。另一个抄本收藏在梵蒂冈图书馆,共 6 章,注有"关于喀山别克及其他人的乌古斯传说故事"。有人认为前一个抄本的语言应为克普恰克语,后一个抄本是以乌古孜语为基础的语言。也就是说,当初是由讲克普恰克语的人将其笔录于文字的,后来又有人把其译成乌古孜语,但没能全部译完。其他诸如《阔尔库特与死神》(khorkhit pen azrayil)、《阔尔库特之歌》(khorkhit jiri)、《阔尔库特与四十个姑娘》(khorkhit pen khirikh khiz)、《阔尔库特与阿兹来依勒天使搏斗》(khorkhit pen äzreyilding küresuw)等只能算做是这些抄本的不同变体。1815 年,费里德里希·济慈(Friedrich Guentz,1751—1817)把该诗的"巴撒特(basat)斩除独眼龙铁莱郭孜(töbeköz)"一章介绍给了学术界并译成了德文。1910 年德累斯顿抄本前 5 章被译成土耳其文,并得到了刊布。1916 年土耳其学者克里斯里·日法特(Kirsli Rifat)刊布了该抄本的阿拉伯字母转写本。特·诺尔德凯(Theodor Nöldeke,1836—1930)将德累斯顿抄本的部分章节译成了德文,但史诗的全译本是由俄罗斯的东方学家彼·彼·巴尔托里德(V.V.Bartold)在 1922 年完成的。1938 年土耳其学者沃尔茨·夏依克·高雅依(Orhan Saik Gokyay)又刊布了该抄本的拉丁字母转写本。1950 年阿塞拜疆学者阿拉丝勒(Alasli)和塔合玛西勃(Takhmasib)合作出版了阿塞拜疆本,即巴库本。1962 年在俄国再次出版了俄文本。史诗的第二个手抄本是由意大利学者伊特吐热·罗西在梵蒂冈发现的,并于 1925 年在赫尔辛基出版了附有词语表的手抄本原文。1980 年土耳其的伊斯坦布尔大学穆哈热姆·艾尔肯(Muharrem Ergin)再次刊布了该抄本。现在《先祖阔尔库特书》在土耳其、英国、德国、俄国等几个国家及中亚地区都已出版。1986 年哈萨克斯坦出版了译自俄文的哈萨克文本。1988 年中国出版了由麦吉提·阿布扎尔(Majit Äbuzar)译自土耳其文的哈萨克文本。1987 年由民族出版社出版的多卷本《哈萨克叙事长诗选》(哈萨克文)第 6 卷中刊登了新疆乌鲁木齐市麦吉提·安尼瓦尔(Majit Anewar)搜集整理的《阔尔库特》。这可能是他从当地民间阿肯(akin)那里搜集来的,篇幅很小,只有 210 行。

《阿尔帕米斯》(*alpamis*)

《阿尔帕米斯》是一部古老而典型的英雄史诗,在民间已经流传了十多个世纪了。它形成于突厥语族共同时期,不仅广泛地流传在哈萨克民间,而且在乌孜别克(乌兹别克)、柯尔克孜(吉尔吉斯)、塔塔尔(鞑靼)、维吾尔、阿塞拜疆、哈卡斯和卡拉卡尔帕克等民族中也得到了传承。据土耳其学者帕克索依(J. N. Paksoy)介绍,居住在帕米尔(Pamir)高原的塔吉克(Tajik)族也用波斯—塔吉克语演唱《阿尔帕米斯》,在塔吉克斯坦出版了他们的演唱版本。15 世纪,在土耳其的阿纳托利亚(Anatoliya)山区开始流传着《阿尔帕米斯》的一个短小传说版本——《巴米斯·拜列克传说》(bamis bäläk)。《巴米斯·拜列克》就是《阿尔帕米斯》,故事情节、母题基本相同,是《阿尔帕米斯》的另一个版本。《阿尔帕米斯》在哈萨克民间流传着十几个版本,主要有以下几个较流行的版本:

1. 居素甫别克·霍加·沙依赫斯版本

1899 年居素甫别克·霍加·沙依赫斯拉木(Jüsipbek Hoja Shayhislam)以叙事诗《阿尔帕米斯》为名,将该史诗首次在俄国喀山印刷发表。由于该史诗的这一版本深受广大人民群众的欢迎,1901—1914 年间又连续多次重版发行。

2. 阿布巴克尔·迪瓦耶夫版本

1916 年阿布巴克尔·迪瓦耶夫(Abubakir Diwayev)从叶尔肯别克·阿肯别克那里记录搜集了该史诗的一个散文版本,以《六岁的阿尔帕米斯》(*alti jasar alpamis*)为名发表公布于众,并且译成了俄文。

3. 斯尔迪罕·尚克列版本

1990 年新疆伊犁州尼勒克(Nelke)县发现了斯尔迪罕·尚克列(Sirdihan Shangk-erey)于 1962 年演唱的版本。这是一个散韵结合的版本,由达吾特别克·康巴克(Däwletbek Khangbakh)记录整理,收入《哈萨克族民间长诗》(哈萨克文)一书中。近年来,在中国哈萨克民间搜集整理了几个散文体版本的《阿尔帕米什》(*alpamis*),其中玛拉尔别克·沙玛兰(Maralbek Sawran)搜集整理的版本较为完整,收入《哈萨克族民间故事》(*khazakh shalek ertegileri*)第 2 集(伊犁人民出版社,1987 年)。1940 年以来哈萨克斯坦的学者先后搜集记录了苏尔坦库尔·阿克霍加(Sultankhul Akhkhoja)、克里木别克·色尔哈里(Kelimbet Serhaley)、拉卡特·吉劳吾(Rahat Jeraw)、艾特别克·尼桑(Aytbek Nesan)、苏音沙勒·江布尔什(Süyinshal jangbershi)的唱本。经过整理和比较研究之后,认为篇幅最大、最完整的是 1948 年记录的苏尔坦库尔·阿克霍加的唱本。当时,民间艺人苏尔坦库尔·阿克霍加已经是年过八旬的老人。据他说,这一史诗是他从生活在 19 世纪的一位著名民间歌手玛依阔特·山德巴耶(Maykut Say-debayev)那里学会的。1958 年这一唱本被收入艾维佐夫(M. Awazov)和斯米尔诺娃(H. Simirnnova)主编的《哈萨克史诗》专辑(哈萨克斯坦国家文化艺术出版社,阿拉木图)。1984 年,该唱本收入我国民族出版社出版的多卷本《哈萨克族叙事长诗选》第 2 卷中。

《库布兰德》(*Khobilandi*)

也称《喀剌克普恰克的勇士库布兰德》(*kharakhipshakhting batiri khobilandi*),是哈萨克族古老英雄史诗之一。喀剌克普恰克是部族名,是形成哈萨克族的主要部族之一,而库布兰德是史诗中主人公的名字。在哈萨克古代英雄史诗中,《库布兰德》是篇幅较大的一部,有的版本长达万余行。由麦尔干拜(Marghanbay)演唱、马里克·哈布杜拉(Malik Khabidolla)记录整理、哈萨克斯坦国立出版社于 1948 年出版的名为《英雄库布兰德》的版本共 3330 行。中国民族出版社 1984 年出版的多卷本《哈萨克叙事长诗选》第 2 卷收入了该诗,这个版本是根据哈萨克斯坦国立文艺出版社 1958 年出版的《哈萨克英雄史诗》中《库布兰德》一章转写的,共 6650 行。现在,该诗大约有 15 个版本,其中最早被搜集整理和刊布的是民间史诗演唱家玛拉勒拜(Maralbay)的唱本,而结构最完整、内容最丰富和情节最曲折的是中国出版的《哈萨克叙事长诗选》第 2 卷中从哈萨克斯坦 1958 年版本中转写的版本。这个版本比1948 年出版的民间史诗演唱家麦尔干拜演唱的唱本正好多一倍。据说,这个版本是在麦尔干拜唱本的基础上整理完善的。记录这个唱本时,还记录了它的伴奏曲和演唱程式。

《克里木的四十位英雄》(*khirimning khirikh batiri*)

《克里木的四十位英雄》是由一系列单篇型诗歌组成的一部串联式复合型英雄史诗。它的单篇型诗歌在早期就被搜集整理，并出版发行。如单篇型诗歌《英雄奥拉克和玛玛依》(*oralkh men mamay batirding riywayati*)早在1905年就被搜集记录成了文字，1908年在喀山(Kazan)出版过它的一个名为《奥拉克和玛玛依传奇》(*aralkh men mamayding riywayati*)的版本。该史诗的串联式复合型版本于20世纪40年代开始搜集并整理成文字。这个功劳要归功于史诗演唱家森格尔别克(Sengirbek)之子提列根(Tilegen)，他也叫穆仁(Murin)。穆仁的曾祖父叫库勒卡拉(Khulkhara)。他有两个儿子，一个叫阿依额尔(Ayghir)，一个叫党额尔(Dangghir)。阿依额尔的儿子是森格尔别克，森格尔别克有两个儿子，一个是提列根(即穆仁)，一个是托列根(Tölegen)。穆仁的爷爷阿依额尔、父亲森格尔别克和兄长托列根都是远近出名的打铁镶银的手艺人。虽然穆仁没有进过学堂，但他天生聪颖，伴随着诗歌和乐曲成长。穆仁从著名史诗演唱家齐尔齐吾勒(Shirshighul)之子演唱家奴热木(Nurim)那里学会了该诗昂齐拜(angshibay)、帕尔帕尔亚(parapariya)、库特可亚(khuttikhiya)、叶德盖(edige)、奴拉丁(nuradin)、木萨汗(musahan)、奥拉克(orakh)、玛玛依(mamay)、喀拉赛(karasay)、喀则(khaziy)等篇章。他又从著名演唱家库尔吉曼(Khurjiman)之子演唱家喀夏汗(Khashaghan)那里学会了该诗霍布兰德(khobilandi)、拖列汗(torehan)、艾买提(ämet)、阿劳(alaw)、阔可谢(kökshe)、叶尔活塞(erkosan)、阿巴特(abat)、托汗(toghan)、玛纳什(manash)、图亚克拜(tuyakhbay)、阿合买提(ahimet)、喀尔哈波依勒(khargha boyli)、喀则突兀汗(khaztuwghan)等篇章。他还从演唱家木拉特(murat)那里学会了喀拉冬(karadong)、朱巴尼西(jubanish)、瞿因尼西(suyinish)、铁格斯(tegis)、塔玛(tama)、塔纳(tana)、纳日克(narik)、肖拉(shora)、库仑卡壳(khulishakh)、阿克卓纳司(akhjonas)、肯也司(kenes)、江布尔齐(jangbirshi)、铁拉额司(telaghis)等篇章。穆仁生于1859年，卒于1954年，享年96岁。1942年，穆仁应哈萨克斯坦科学院历史语言文学研究所所长赛乌兰巴也夫(N. Sawranbayev)和民间文学研究室负责人司马依洛娃(E. Simayilov)的邀请从莽格斯套(Mangghistaw)来到阿拉木图(Alma-ata)，把埋藏在心里已经60年的宝贵文化财富——《克里木的四十位英雄》写到了纸上。参加这次录制整理工作的有玛利亚姆·哈克木江(Mariyam Hakhimjan)、玛利亚姆·依萨(Mariyam Iysa)、波孜泰·加克普拜(boztay jakkipbay)和演唱家的儿子达吾提拜·穆仁（dawitbay murin）。1989 年，哈萨克斯坦阿拉木图作家出版社在《英雄史诗》第 6、7 卷里以穆仁的名字刊布了该诗的全部内容。2000 年 10 月，我国新疆伊犁出版社根据该版本并参考哈萨克斯坦阿拉木图 1961 年出版的《英雄史诗》第 11 卷、1964 年出版的《英雄史诗》第 11 卷和 1977 年阿拉木图阿克苏瓦特（Akhsuwat）出版社出版的《英雄史诗集》，用哈萨克老文字（阿拉伯字母）分上下册出版了该诗的全文。

《康巴尔》（Khambar）

也称《勇士康巴尔》（Khambar batir），是哈萨克族的古老英雄史诗之一，有 20 多个版本。1865 年，这部英雄史诗的内容被记录下来，1888 年首次出现了刊印的单行本。1903 年又出现了一个规模较小的版本《扎有九十帐毡房的人们》（tokhsan uyli tobir）。1922 年乌兹别克斯坦的塔什干市出版了该诗的全文。1933 年和 1939 年又将该诗收入《古代英雄史诗》集。1959 年哈萨克斯坦科学出版社出版了该诗的四个唱本合而为一的科学版本。1958 年，该诗被收入用哈萨克文、俄文出版的《哈萨克英雄史诗》专集中。1968 年，该诗的单行本出版。1984 年我国民族出版社出版的多卷本《哈萨克叙事长诗选》第 2 卷中收入的《康巴尔》，是从哈萨克斯坦国立文艺出版社 1958 年出版的《哈萨克英雄史诗》（Kazak epose）中转写的。这个版本全部是韵文，共 1900 行，是一个相对较完整的版本。

《英雄塔尔根》（er targhin）

它有好几个版本，一般认为其原始版本应该是 1862 年刊印的喀山（Kazan）版本。这个版本是根据哈萨克民间史诗演唱家玛拉勒拜（Maralbay）的唱本记录整理的。目前，我们所说的《英雄塔尔根》，主要叙述塔尔根在本部落杀了人逃离以后的经历。中国民族出版社于 1984 年出版的多卷本《哈萨克叙事长诗选》（Kazak Keysalare）第 2 卷收录了韵文体和散文体相间的版本。这个版本共 1700 行，是从哈萨克斯坦国立文艺出版社于 1958 年出版的《哈萨克英雄史诗》（Kazak epose）中转写的。另外，还有一个版本主要描写塔尔根逃离之前出生成长的故事。我国民族出版社于 1987 年出版的多卷本《哈萨克叙事长诗选》（Kazak keysalare）第 7 卷收录了这个版本，名为《英雄塔尔根的序诗》（er targhing alghi khiysasi）。这个版本共 940 行，是根据中国新疆塔城（Tarbagatay）地区托里（Tole）县穆卡泰·阿戴（Mukhatay A-day）搜集的手抄本整理刊印的。

阿布赉汗(*Ablayhan*)

阿布赉(Abilay),本名艾布勒满素尔(Abilmansur),绰号萨巴拉克(Sabalakh)。阿布赉本来是他爷爷的名字,是当年土尔克斯坦(Turkstan)的统治者。他爷爷作战凶猛、所向披靡,因此也被称为"吸血鬼"。他的儿子瓦里(Wali)没能保住父亲的江山,地盘被邻近的部落抢占了,自己也被杀害了。幸亏一位忠诚的佣人保护了艾布勒满素尔,才使他获得了生存的机会。只有13岁的艾布勒满素尔寄人篱下,帮人家放骆驼。他饥一顿饱一顿,衣服破烂不堪,头发蓬乱不齐,乌孙(usen)部落的托列毕官(toli biy,意为千户长)就称他为"萨巴拉克"(即头发蓬乱者)。从此,"萨巴拉克"就成了他的绰号。当时正处于哈萨克的三大玉兹(juz)抵抗准噶尔(Junggar)封建主的紧要关头,艾布勒满素尔主动要求参战,在战斗中异常勇猛,并高喊"阿布赉!阿布赉!……"地冲向敌人。阿布勒满木别特(abilmanbet)汗询问他,为什么要在冲锋时高喊"阿布赉"。他回答说,是为了借助自己的爷爷阿布赉汗的神灵,震慑敌人的威力,鼓舞勇士们的斗志。汗王得知他就是当年威震四方的"吸血鬼"——阿布赉的孙子,就把全军的大权托付给了他,后来把汗位也让给了他。从此,阿布赉就成了他的名字。英雄史诗《阿布赉》的版本很多,目前主要有三个版本。

1.《萨巴拉克》(*sabalakh*)版本。该版本是中国塔城地区(Tarbagatay)民间歌手安瓦尔·弘卡克(Anwar Khongkhap Uli)搜集整理的,篇幅为360行,并收入中国民族出版社1984年出版的《哈萨克叙事长诗选》第2卷中。据该诗开头的叙事程式讲述,该版本的最初演唱者是哈力·阿迪尔别克(Khaliy Adilbek)阿肯。

2.《阿布赉》(*ablay*)版本。该版本的篇幅为1600行,收入中国民族出版社1985年出版的《哈萨克叙事长诗选》第4卷。搜集整理者是中国新疆阿勒泰(Altay)地区的民间演唱家谢力亚孜旦·苏勒坦拜(Sheriyazdan Sultanbay uli)。这一版本包括《萨巴拉克》版本的基本情节,但也有许多补充和差别。

3.《阿布赉与白公驼》(*ablay nan akh atan*)版本。该版本是由中国新疆伊犁州巩留(togeztaraw)县的艾·纳比(A. Nabiy)搜集整理,篇幅为708行,收入民族出版社1991年出版的《哈萨克叙事长诗选》第11卷。

这些版本基本上是根据流传在哈萨克民间的传说和故事的情节改编演唱的,其情节、结构、韵律、演唱风格较之古老英雄史诗,更倾向于19世纪产生、20世纪上半叶广泛流行的半书面半口头文学形式。据记载,哈萨克伟大诗人阿拜(Abay)的挚友和学生阔克拜·江泰(Kokbay Jangtay,1863—1927)也演唱过这部史诗。著名诗人、民间文学家居素甫·阔别耶夫(Jusip Kobeyev,1858—1931)在喀山出版过《阿布赉汗的故事》(1910)。

《卡班拜》(khabanbay)

卡班拜·阔加胡尔(khabanbay khojaghul)是18世纪的哈萨克英雄,是抗击外敌斗争的组织者和哈萨克军队的统帅之一,是当时众多英雄中最勇敢、最博学的英雄。虽然有关卡班拜的历史记载并不多,但流传在哈萨克民间的传说故事、赞歌、长诗和抒情诗中却不少。卡班拜出身于哈萨克中玉兹(juz)乃蛮(nayman)部落,有关他的传说故事、歌谣和长诗,在中国哈萨克民间,尤其是在中国新疆塔城(Tarbagatay)、博尔塔拉(Bortala)等地区的乃蛮、喀喇克烈(Kharakerey)部落民间中广泛流传。有关卡班拜的民间创作,目前搜集到的篇幅最大的是刊登于1981年《绿草》(shalghin)(哈萨克文)季刊第一期上的版本,后来又收入中国民族出版社1984年出版的《哈萨克叙事长诗选》第2卷。《卡班拜》的这个版本是在六个内容相似、篇幅相近唱本的基础上,经过比较、补充和整理的。此外,《遗产》(mura,哈萨克文)季刊于1986年1—2期合刊上发表了歌颂卡班拜骏马的长诗《叙事诗库巴斯骏马》(khubas khiysasi)。该诗是由中国新疆塔城地区的著名民间演唱家别先哈里·萨德汗(Beysenghaliy Sadikhan)演唱。他最初是在1931年从系谱诗人毛斯木拜(Mawsimbay)那里听说了该诗的主要情节,后又到卡班拜的后裔布兰拜(Bulanbay)之孙的妻子阿克比克(akhbiyk)那里进行了补充性调查。20世纪80年代,中国学者围绕着《卡班拜》进行了探讨研究,到民间进行了搜集和整理,先后在《绿草》和《遗产》这两种哈萨克文民间文学刊物上发表了几个唱本。主要有毕特木拜(Bitimbek)阿肯的唱本:该唱本篇幅为170行;卡里拜(Kharibay)唱本:该唱本篇幅较小,只有80行。

《贾尼别克》(janibek)

它是一部反映18世纪哈萨克族贾尼别克英雄事迹的英雄史诗。主要流传在中国新疆阿勒泰(Altay)和塔城(Tarbagatay)地区。该诗多以传说、系谱长诗等形式创作、演唱和传承。该诗在中国主要有以下几个版本:

1.伊布赉·波泰(ibray botay)版本。该版本由中国新疆塔城地区的民间艺人贾尼别克的第五代后裔伊布赉·波泰于1927年开始演唱。后来拜波森(baybolsen)阿肯根据伊布赉·波泰于1964年演唱的唱本进行了记录整理,刊载于《遗产》(mura,哈萨克文,季刊)1989年第2期上,篇幅为760行。由中国新疆塔城地区的民间艺人伊布赍·波泰于 1964 年演唱,拜波森阿肯记录整理。

2. 莫凯什(Mawgesh)版本。该版本是由莫凯什·多勒巴斯在中国新疆阿勒泰地区哈巴(Kaba)河县一带搜集记录,由卡力木别克(Ghalimbek)整理最初发表于《阿勒泰春光》(*altay ayasi*,哈萨克文,季刊)1980 年第 2 期上,后收入《哈萨克族民间长诗》第 2 集(哈萨克文,中国民族出版社,1984 年),篇幅 460 行。

《叶先坎尔迪》(*esenkeldi*)

它是一部具有历史系谱性质的英雄史诗,主要有以下几个版本:

1. 多斯佩尔·萨吾勒克(Dosber Sawlek)版本。该版本是民间艺人多斯佩尔·萨吾勒克根据传说和系谱演唱的,最初刊于《伊犁河》(*Ile aydenge*,哈萨克文,1981 年第 1 期),后收入《哈萨克族民间长诗》第 2 集(民族出版社,1984 年,北京),篇幅 1630 行。

2. 阿吾卡迪·沙里甫汗(Awkat Xariphan)版本。该版本仍然是由多斯佩尔·萨吾勒克民间艺人演唱的,由其后代阿吾卡迪·沙里甫汗保存的一个完整唱本,篇幅为 1750 行,收入新疆伊犁州尼勒克(Elke)县印制的一本诗辑中。

《阿尔卡勒克》(*arkhalikh*)

它虽然是哈萨克族的一部普普通通的英雄史诗,但至少具有两个特点:其一,它是一部形成年代最晚的英雄史诗;其二,它是一部流传于中国哈萨克族民间的英雄史诗。这部史诗形成的年代并不长,但它的版本却相当多:

1. 阿斯卡尔·塔塔乃(Askhar Tatanay)版本。民间艺人阿斯卡尔·塔塔乃在 20世纪上半叶就搜集整理了该诗,并于 1958 年将它改编成剧本。该版本刊于《绿草》(*shalghin*,哈萨克文,1981 年第 1 期),篇幅为 720 行。

2. 伊布来(Iybray)和居玛江(Jumajan)版本。该版本的手抄本是牧民伊布来偶然在中国新疆吉木乃(Jemeney)县的一个山洞里发现的,抄写年代为 1937 年,但演唱者和抄写者不详。由居玛江·阿布尔哈孜(Jumajan Abelkaze)整理,发表于《遗产》(*mura*,哈萨克文,1983 年第 1 期),后收入《哈萨克族民间长诗》(哈萨克文,第 4 集,民族出版社,1985 年),篇幅为 3500 行。该版本是迄今篇幅最大的版本。

3. 阿布德哈力·巴特尔拜(Abdikhaley Batirbay)版本。该版本是阿布德哈力于20 世纪 30 年代学会的,并根据 1981 年他 71 岁时演唱记录整理的。现存于新疆民委古籍办公室,篇幅为 1720 行。

4. 苏尔坦·米吉提(sultan mejit)版本。该版本是著名阿肯苏尔坦·米吉提于 20 世纪上半叶从新疆塔城地区的一位著名民间歌手艾里甫江·坚吾扎克(Aripjan Januzakh)那里学会的，刊于《绿草》(哈萨克文，1981 年第 1 期)，篇幅为 2580 行。

5. 叶尔江·阿合麦托夫(erjan akhmetof)版本。叶尔江·阿合麦托夫(1879—1959)原系中国新疆人，后移居哈萨克斯坦。叶尔江在 1958 年演唱了一个较小的变体，由哈萨克斯坦的别克木哈麦提(bekmuhamet)记录整理，篇幅为 200 行。

6. 叶尔泰·库尔萨耶夫(ertay khursayev)版本。叶尔泰于 1939 年从民间搜集整理，收藏在哈萨克斯坦科学院手抄本收藏室。1961 年收入哈萨克斯坦出版的《英雄史诗》(哈萨克文，第 2 集)，篇幅为 1520 行。

7. 达吾特拜·伊布来莫夫(dawwit ibrayemov)版本。该版本比较小，只有 350 行，只叙述了英雄阿尔卡勒克首次出征抗敌的情景。

附录二：《库布兰德》的片段

《库布兰德》(*qoblandi*)① 也称《喀剌克普恰克的勇士库布兰德》(*qara qïpšaqtïng batïri qoblandï*)，是哈萨克族古老英雄史诗之一。

故事梗概：

在那遥远的时代，有一位名叫托克塔尔拜的显赫富翁。他有无数的财产，牛羊满山遍野，四畜一应俱全。夏牧场是阔孜迪库里湖畔，冬牧场是喀拉斯潘山麓，但他活到 80 岁，仍无后嗣。这使他痛苦得椎心泣血，变得神智痴癫，而且还受人歧视。他决心舍弃财产，与妻子一起去向神灵求子。他们杀马向神灵祭祀，宰羊向霍拉散圣地祭奠，愿望终于实现了。他们有了一个儿子和女儿，儿子的名字叫库布兰德，女儿的名字叫卡尔丽哈西。

库布兰德 6 岁时，就已经能够到部落接壤的地方放牧了。他 12 岁那年，相邻的红帽子部落的汗王阔克提穆举行比武大会为公主库尔特卡择婚。谁能射中高悬于月光之下的金盘，谁就可以娶公主为妻。库布兰德不听随身奴隶头目叶斯铁密斯的劝阻，只身闯入比赛会场。前来参加比武的有 20 个汗王的公子，惟独库布兰德射中了金盘。阔克提穆履行诺言，为女儿的出嫁举行了 30 天游戏和 40 天宴会。这事却遭到手下一位著名红发勇士的坚决反对，于是库布兰德与他刀戈相见，杀死

① 为了便于阅读，本文附录二中出现的哈萨克文一律使用国际通行的突厥语拉丁字母转写。

了这位勇士和他的两个儿子,携带公主库尔特卡返回自己的部落。途中,库布兰德巧遇堂兄萨里木拜富翁的马群,堂兄把库尔特卡一眼看中的一匹枯瘦如柴的灰花骝马作为见面礼送给她。不久,这匹骝马生下了一马驹,库尔特卡精心喂养,亲自调教。这就是后来跟随库布兰德英雄出生入死的神驹布尔勒。

红帽子部的勇士喀赞认为让库布兰德娶走库尔特卡是红帽子部的奇耻大辱,便出兵进行掠杀抢劫。勇士喀拉曼约库布兰德一同去抗击喀赞。库尔特卡说,再过43天,布尔勒战马才能最终调教出来。如果库布兰德现在出征,一定会遇到危险。喀拉曼讥讽库布兰德竟然听凭女人的摆布,是对英雄好汉的污辱。他想杀死库尔特卡,逼迫库布兰德出征。库尔特卡机智地躲过了杀身大祸,库布兰德却经不住喀拉曼的怂恿,强行骑着还没有调教好的布尔勒马随喀拉曼出发了。

库布兰德赶在喀拉曼一行之前,单枪匹马地打败了喀赞,战利品却被后到的喀拉曼不劳而获了。喀拉曼又怂恿库布兰德去攻打卡尔马克的柯波克特汗,结果被对方打得落花流水,一同被关进深深的地牢。柯波克特汗的女儿喀尔勒卡与库布兰德一见钟情,她亲手杀死生父柯波克特和自己的胞兄,救出了他们俩,投奔了库布兰德。喀尔勒卡跟随库布兰德和喀拉曼离开了卡尔马克部。喀拉曼向库布兰德索要战利品——喀尔勒卡。这时,库布兰德梦见自己外出征战时家乡被敌人侵占,立即动身去征讨入侵的敌人阿勒沙合尔汗。阿勒沙合尔强占了牲畜和草场,奴役着家乡的父老乡亲,而且还要逼娶库尔特卡为妻。库布兰德通过喀尔勒卡掌握了敌方的布防,与喀拉曼一道攻打,打败了阿勒沙合尔,拯救了整个部落,从此阔孜迪库里草原的人们过上了和睦繁荣的生活。下面就是这部史诗片段:

kešegi ötken zamanda,	在那个遥远的远古时代,
qara qïpšaq qoblandï,	喀剌克普恰克库布兰德,
atasï munïŋ toqtarbay,	他的父亲叫托克塔尔拜,
xalïqtan asqan boldï bay,	是一位出名的显赫富翁,
baylïyïnda esep joq,	他拥有无以计数的财产,
aydalïp bayïp jayïldï,	牧放着的牲畜遍野漫山,
tört tülik maldïŋ bäri saj.	四类牲畜全都一应俱全。
jaz jaylaw közdi köl,	夏季牧场是阔孜迪湖畔,
közdi köldi jaylayan,	牲畜牧放在阔孜迪湖畔,
qalïŋ qïpšaq jayalay.	克普恰克百姓沿着湖边。

toqtarbaydïŋ däwleti,　　　托克塔尔拜的财富物产，

iškeni mas jegen toq,　　　能酩酊大醉但是吃不完，

bay-kedeydiŋ köngil jay.　　富家穷户全都心满意欢。

qïs qïstawï qaraspan,　　　冬季牧场是喀拉斯潘山，

qaraspan kökke talasqan.　　喀拉斯潘山脉高耸蓝天。

at üyirinen adasqan,　　　马匹多得经常跑错群圈，

qalïŋ qïpšaq tizilip,　　　众多克普恰克聚居在此，

qasïna qonïs jarasqan.　　居住之处好似百花乐园。

älip tangba qïpšaqtïŋ,　　克普恰克部落的大印章，

atayï ozyan alaštan.　　已超过阿拉什名声远扬。

seksenge jasï kelgenše,　　他的年龄已经到八十岁，

bir bala körmey toqtarbay,　托克塔尔拜仍然无后嗣，

qayyïmenen qan jutïp,　　他痛苦得捶胸口吐鲜血，

aqïlïnan adasqan.　　　　变得模糊不清神智痴癫。

šöl iyesi sungqar qïyasïz,　老头已不是矫健的雄鹰，

eš närse körmey düniyeden,　他想过这世界冷冷清清，

ötkenim degen tuyaqsïz,　难道没有后嗣了结一生，

toqtarbaydïng zarïna,　　对于托克塔尔拜的忧伤，

qalïŋ qïpšaq qayïsqan.　　克普恰克百姓万分哀怜。

äwliye qoymay qïdïrïp,　向每一位神仙奔走请求，

etegin šenggel sïdïrïp,　把他们的衣襟抓在手中，

jeti pirge tanïsqan.　　让他们结识了七位神仙。

äwliyege at aytïp,　　杀马匹向神仙祷告祭祀，

qorasanya qoy aytïp,　宰羊向霍拉散圣地祭祀，

qabïl bolyan tilegi,　他们的夙愿终于已实现，

jarïlyanday jüregi,　激动得心一直跳个不断，

analïqtay baybiše,　他的老伴儿阿娜勒克呀，

qabïryası mayïsqan.　　　　　　她悲伤痛苦得回肠九转。

eliwge jası kelgende,　　　　　心想自己已经到五十岁,

közim ašpay düniyeden,　　　　孩儿都见不到就要过世,

ötemin be degende,　　　　　　难道一生就像这样度过,

sonda körgen arïstan.　　　　这时生了雄狮般的好汉。

bir ul,bir qïz atadan,　　　　老人终于有了一女一男,

qïzdïng atï qarelyaš,　　　　女儿的名字叫卡尔丽哈西,

qoblandïya qarïndas.①　　　　这是勇士库布兰德的胞妹。

[⋯⋯⋯]

qïzïlbastïŋ elinen,　　　　　在克孜勒巴斯的部落里面,

qazan degen er šïqtï,　　　　出来一个名叫喀赞的勇士,

jün bilmegen šer šïqtï,　　　是一个无法预测到的祸根,

noyaylïnïŋ köp elin,　　　　把诺盖部落的大部分百姓,

oljalap šawïp janšïptï.　　　肆意抢掠俘虏欺凌和侮辱。

bayïnbayan adamïn,　　　　　他把没有归顺自己的人们,

qïrïp, joyïp tawïsïptï.　　　屠杀、消灭得一个也不留。

jerin, malïn oljalap,　　　　掠夺了他们的土地,牲畜,

qatarïnan asïptï.　　　　　使他们受尽了非人的折磨。

mal-janïna qaramay,　　　　无暇顾及自己的牲畜财产,

noyaylïnïŋ eli qašïptï.　　诺盖部落的百姓四处逃离。

oljalap janïn basïptï,　　　掠夺逼迫得他们纷纷逃难,

noyaylïnïŋ köp elin,　　　　使诺盖部落的大部分百姓,

qarataban desipti,　　　　走破了脚板到处颠沛流离,

qïrlï qala, sïrlï qalasïn,　　已把克尔勒,斯尔勒城堡,

tartïp alïp er qazan,　　　攻克占为己有的喀赞勇士,

① 参见《哈萨克叙事长诗选》(哈萨克文)第 2 辑,北京:民族出版社,1984 年,第 701—703 页。

tasïyan suwday tasïptï.	宛如一泻千里的高山洪水。
sïrlï qala deytin qalasï,	这个名叫斯尔勒的古城堡,
qoryansïz sïrtï ašïq-tï.	失去了屏障成了残垣断壁。
qïrlï qala deytin qalaya,	这个名叫克尔勒的古城堡
atarman da šabarman,	早已经变成了头目和喽啰
bekteri basïn qosïptï.	伯克们聚首相逢的居住处。
qïrlï qala mangïnan,	他们说克尔勒城堡的周围,
jaw jüre almas desipti,	再不会见到敌人的踪迹,
köngili sonday ösipti.①	一个个是那样的疯狂自喜。
[……]	
jïyïlïp jurtï jïladï,	聚集的百姓热泪盈眶,
xalayïq qayran qïladï,	都感到事情有些突然,
jiberiwge qïymaydï,	任何人都舍不得离开,
qoblandïday balanï.	库布兰德这样的孩子。
kiyinip üyden šïqqasïn,	他穿戴好走出了房门,
xalqï ortaya aladï.	人民从四周围住了他。
jïyïlyan jurtpen qoštasïp,	与聚集的乡亲们告别,
qoblandïday batïrïŋ,	库布兰德这样的勇士,
taybuwïrïl atqa minedi,	跃身跨上布鲁勒骏马,
beline semser iledi,	把利剑挎到了他腰间,
aq sawïtïn kiyedi,	把铮白铠甲穿在身上,
toyay börkin kiyedi,	把诺盖皮帽戴在头上,
düysenbi kün säskede,	礼拜的第一天上了路,
qaraspan tawdï bökterip,	他沿着喀拉斯潘山麓
kešegi ketken qïyattïŋ,	昨天离开的克亚特人,

---

① 同上，第 723—724 页。

qoblandïday batïrïng,	库布兰德这样的勇士,
songïnan jelip jöneldi.	紧随着他们策马奔驰。
toqsandayï toqtarbay,	九十岁的托克塔尔拜,
alpïsta šešesi analïq,	六十的母亲阿娜勒克,
qarïndasï qarlïyaš,	他的妹妹卡尔丽哈西,
qosaq jarï qïz qurtqa,	其伴侣库尔特卡姑娘,
törtewi jïlap songïnan,	四个人跟随其后哭泣,
keskiley ket dep qolïngnan,	不忍心强迫他们止步,
qoblandïnïŋ artïnan,	离开库布兰德的后面,
olar da erip jöneldi.	他们都跟在后头奔驰。
tüstik jerge kelgende,	当跑完了半天的路程,
qarïndasï söyledi,	妹妹开头把话说,
söylegende büydeydi:	所说的话是这样的:
xalïq uyyarsa qalmaysïn,	不要辜负人民的重托,
köngiliŋ süymey barmaysïn,	你不会做不情愿的事,
jalyïz ayam,	我的惟一的哥哥呀,
jan kökem,	我的生命支柱呀,
saparlandïŋ talapqa.	为了夙愿开始了征途。
aq sungqar senip ušadï,	白隼有信心方能翱翔,
quyrïyï men qanatqa.	凭借的是尾翎和翅膀。
sayya bitken qoqtïmïn,	我是山谷里的一棵草,
börik üstinde šoqtïmïn.	我是帽子上的一撮毛。
kökejan qaytïp kelgenše,	在哥哥凯旋之前,
el-jurtïn esen körgenše,	平安地见到百姓之前,
aytïp ketken qudayya,	说一声让胡达多保佑,
qongïr šunaq toqtïngmïn.	是割耳尖的褐色羊羔。
men tüsemin qïyalya,	我思绪万千想了很多,

nešik ayla boladï,   敌人诡计多端伎俩多，

közimniŋ jasïn tïyarya.   我想起这些潸然泪下。

kökejan qaytïp kelgenše,   在哥哥凯旋之前，

el-jurtïŋ esen körgenše,   百姓平安见到你之前，

artïngda qalyan men našar,   把我这个没能力的人，

aytïp bir ketši nïyazya.   就当作施舍的布施品。

közge, köke jas aldïq,   哥哥，我们泪流满面，

kökejan, qaytïp kelgenše,   哥哥，凯旋之前，

artïngda qalyan men sorlï,   我这个留下的不幸人，

bolayïn senen tasadtïq.   我情愿为您充当祭品。

basïmda bar altïn šoq,   我帽子上有金色花朵，

kökešim , seni körmesem,   哥哥，不见你的时候，

basïmnan öter düniye boq!   这世界就像一堆粪垛！

tabanïma tiyer šoq.   仿佛踩着烧红的铁戳。

sizge degen qudaydïŋ,   求胡达把射向您的箭，

bizge bolsïn ajalï oq!   转向射到我们的胸部！

aq mangdayda tulïmïm,   是我白额头上的抓髻，

birge tuwyan qulïnïm,   是我一起出生的马驹，

kerekke bitken jawrïn,   是派上用场的肩胛骨，

birge tuwyan bawrïm,   是我一起出生的胞兄，

qolyanatïm, quyrïyïm,   是我的依靠，是支柱，

suwdan šïqqan süyrigim,   是顶出水面上的芦苇，

suwïrïp ozyan jürigim,   是那遥遥领先的骏马，

sizge degen qudanïng,   亲家对您的叮咛吩咐，

qabïl ettim buyrïyïn!   今后由我去接受执行，

qozïday menŋ egizim,   你我犹如孪生的羊羔，

tel qozïday sezimim,   像吃着双母奶的羊羔，

birge tuwïp,birge ösken,	一起出生，一起成长，
kindigimdi bir kesken,	脐带一个时辰被剪掉，
qarγa jündi qattasïm,	犹如一色的乌鸦羽毛，
üyrek jündi ottasïm,	好似没有杂色的野鸭，
birge tuwγan tektesim,	是一天出生根连着根，
qïsïlγan jerde demesim.	如果不陷入艰难困境。
toγay tolγan tüyeŋ bar,	满树林的骆驼是你的，
qora tolγan qoyïŋ bar,	满棚圈的绵羊是你的，
onï kimge tapsïrdïŋ?	把它们交付给谁看管？
jerge sïymas jïlqïŋdï,	把布满了山坡的马群，
alpïsta anaŋ analïq,	把六十岁的阿娜勒克，
jengešemdi,kimge tapsïrdïŋ?	把我嫂子，托付给谁？
özingmen birge tuwïsqan,	和你一起同生在一天，
tay-qulïnday tebisken,	和小马驹一样心欢，
birge tuwïp,birge ösken,	同一天生，一块儿玩，
kindigimdi birge kesken,	脐带割的都是同一天，
men sorlïnï kimge tapsïrdïŋ?	要把我交付给谁照管？
bul düniyede mungdasïŋ,	你今世的知音诉苦者，
axïyrettik joldasïŋ,	你来世的伴侣同路者
tösekte jatsa sïrlasïŋ,	你同床共枕的知情者，
quday qosqan qosayïng,	胡达为你撮合的伴侣，
köktimniŋ qïzï qurtqanï-	阔克提穆之女库尔特卡，
jengešemdi,kimge tapsïrdïŋ?①	我的嫂子，要托付给谁？
[……]	
uzïn sözdi qïsqartïp,	长话短说就唱到这里，

---

① 同上，第 746—750 页。

endi aytayïn tötesin.	让我直接把话来说穿。
otïz kün uday oyïn qïp,	连续举行三十天庆典,
qarlïyaday sulïwdï ŋ,	像喀尔勒卡这样的美人,
qoblandï sïndï batïrya,	像库布兰德这样的英雄,
qaramanday qurdasï,	像喀拉满这样的亲家,
osï jerde qïydï nekesin.	在这儿只好放弃婚姻。
qarlïyaday sulïwdï ŋ,	像喀尔勒卡这样美人,
segiz jïl jatïp bir tawda!	八年同居在一座山里!
muradïn solay ötesin.	理想就这样得到实现。
asïqpasa ŋ sabïr qïp,	不要鲁莽要持之以恒,
talaptansa ŋ umïtïlïp,	要想有出息就要努力,
maqsatïnga aqïr jetesin.	最终能把理想来实现。
qoblandï, qurtqa, qarlïya,	库布兰德,库尔特卡,喀尔勒卡,
kök päweske küymesin,	相互间不要嫉妒红眼,
küymeni ŋ ilip tüymesin,	即使有也要心胸坦荡,
qarlïya sulïw köredi,	喀尔勒卡美人目睹到,
däwirdi ŋ tätti jemisin.	时代的累累硕果成就。
qarlïya, qurtqa körsetip,	喀尔勒卡,库尔特卡,
qalïŋ qïpšaq eline,	展示给克普恰克百姓 ,
tatïwlïqtïŋ belgisin,	这是和睦相处的标志,
maqsatqa jetken osïlay,	这样才把理想来实现,
elge jayïp ülgisin.	为大众百姓作了表率。
ayayï munï ŋ äli bar,	故事并没有到此结束,
qarlïyadan ul tuwar,	喀尔勒卡生了一男孩,
ulïnï ŋ atï kiyikbay,	男孩子名叫克依克拜,
talabï tawday biyikti-ay,	克依克拜的理想宏远,
kiyikbay atqa mingende,	克依克拜跨上骏马时,

köp qïpšaqqa kün tuwar,　　　　　克普恰克百姓见光日，

qïzïlbasqa tün tuwar.　　　　　　克孜勒巴斯的日光尽。

bul özi bölek bir qïyssa,　　　　这个又是另一部史诗，

kiyikbayday batïrtïng.　　　　　像克依克拜似的勇士。

toqtattïm bulay aqïrïn,　　　　　最终我就到此把话停，

söylese sözdiŋ jüyesin,　　　　　要说就要说得成系统，

keltirer bizdey aqïnïŋ.①　　　　就像我们这样的阿肯。

---

① 同上，第 965—966 页。

中国南方民族史诗中的考验型

刘亚虎

摘　要　考验型是神话、史诗中展示英雄人物英雄本色的一个重要的情节类型。中国南方民族史诗中的考验型有出生被弃考验、求婚考验、当"大"（首领）考验等多种形式，它们的生活原型是南方民族早期各种考验仪式。这一叙事模式深刻地反映了南方民族山地农耕文化、群体文化、神巫文化特质。它们与希腊神话、史诗中考验型的差异体现了两种民族文化模式的差异。

关键词　南方民族，史诗，考验型

在世界各民族的神话、史诗中，证明英雄人物英雄本性和展示他们英雄本色有一个重要的情节类型：考验型。最常见的是出生考验。希腊神话中的大神宙斯（Zeus）出生后被抛弃在克里特岛的一个山洞里，靠喝山羊奶长大；罗马神话中的第一代王罗慕洛（Romulus）和他的弟弟瑞穆斯（Remus）出生后被装进篮子里丢入河中，漂至浅滩后为一只母狼救助哺养；希腊神话中的赫拉克勒斯（Herakles）、俄狄浦斯（Oidipous），希伯来神话中的摩西（Mosheh），印度史诗中的迦尔纳（Karna）等，出生后都曾被丢弃于山间田野或河流中。

中国汉文典籍也有一些考验型故事。周人始祖后稷诞生后曾经被"三弃三收"。《史记·周本纪》载："周后稷，名弃。其母有邰氏女，曰姜原。……姜原出野，见巨人迹，心怡然悦，欲践之，践之而身动如孕者。姜原……居期而生子，以为不祥，弃之隘巷，马牛过者，皆辟不践；徙置之平林，适会山林多人；而弃渠中冰上，飞鸟以其翼覆荐之。姜原以为神，遂收养之。"这些，都属于出生考验，即将出生不久的婴儿丢弃以证明其是否是"圣婴"。此外，还有求婚考验，如印度史诗《罗摩衍那》中的罗摩（Rama）要得到遮那竭王（Janaka）的公主悉多（Sita），必须拉开一把神弓；继位考验,希腊神话和史诗中的伊阿宋(Jason)要恢复王位,必须取来金羊毛等。

中国南方各民族史诗里也有不少考验型故事,而且种类多样,情节丰富,无论内容或形式都颇具特色。

一、考验的具体内容

中国南方史诗中考验型故事的生活原型是南方民族早期的各种考验仪式。民俗学的资料表明,处于群体文化状态的早期人类在个体生长历程的许多阶段,例如诞生、成丁、婚嫁等,以及群体交际和社会生活的方方面面,都频繁地使用考验以至将其仪式化、形式化。

这些考验仪式随着时代的变迁大都已消逝,但它们的一些残余形式一直流传到上世纪四五十年代,闪现在南方一些民族成丁(成年)、婚嫁等礼仪中。如瑶族男子在成丁的"度戒"仪式上,要经受"上刀梯"(赤脚攀爬由刀刃向上的刀搭成的梯子)、"过火链"(赤脚踩踏烧红的铁链)、"跳云台"等考验,他们认为经历此考验之后生命才具有新的意义、新的质性,才能成为社会的正式成员,可参加村社活动,选举或担任村寨头人,才能得到宗教庇护,死后升天成仙……一些地方苗族男子成丁,也要在巫师的带领下上刀梯,在"油火台"上翻筋斗,赤足踩烧红的犁口等。壮族、彝族等许多民族在谈情说爱、迎亲送亲等场合,往往以对歌、赛歌方式考察对方或对家的知识或能力,这也是考验仪式的遗存。

在南方民族的史诗里,历史生活中的考验仪式已经成为主体能力、资格以至神性的证明。作为一个人来到世间能否被接纳要考验,求婚要考验,做首领要考验,当国王也要考验。考验成为史诗里英雄前进道路上最常见的难关。

南方史诗中考验类型最基本的结构形式是"阻碍—克服"。阻碍的具体内容多种多样,有被丢弃、被攻击、被赋予某项凶险艰难的任务,也有斗智、竞技等带游戏性质的方式,还有引诱、挽留等温情脉脉的手段。它们的目的都是一个:阻碍主体达到追求的目标。阻碍就是考验,克服就是证明主体的资格、能力、禀赋的过程。考验的具体形式有出生被弃考验、求婚考验、当"大"考验等。

把出生的婴儿以丢弃的行为来证明其神圣性的考验是验证"圣婴"的重要方式。在史诗里,许多英雄都有这种出生被弃的经历。彝族史诗《勒俄特依》(*Hnewo Teyy*)叙述,蒲莫尼衣(Purmo Nniyyr)因龙鹰滴下三滴血而怀孕生下支格阿龙(Zhyge Alu)。支格阿龙生下后不肯吃母奶,不肯同母睡,不肯穿母衣。母亲"以为是个恶魔胎"而把他抛到岩下。岩下有龙住,支格阿龙"饿时吃龙饭,渴时喝龙乳,冷时穿龙衣",在龙的庇护下长大了,成了英雄。① 傣族史诗《厘俸》(Lai Pheng)里的英雄海罕(High Han)出生后,也遭遇到这样的考验。海罕原为天神下凡投胎,被叭英(Bar Ring)放在蛋里让九条母龙孵了九年而不出,后来一个女人把蛋捡去吃了怀孕生下海罕(或说一个女奴捡果食后孕生海罕)。海罕一出世就带着宝刀并能讲话。母亲十分害怕,将他抛下竹楼想让楼下的牛群把它踩死。一条神牛将他含入嘴里保护了他。当牧童把牛赶到野外放牧时,神牛才将他吐出来,因而他得名"海罕"(傣语译音,意即"金牛"或"神牛")。海罕被弃不死,经受了考验,后来当了勐景哈的国王。②

《勒俄特依》、《厘俸》所叙述的这一类弃婴考验型故事具有深刻的象征意义。英雄是大自然之子,吸宇宙天地精华灵气而孕,蕴含超人的智慧和力量,但他借人胎而育,还要回大自然接受验证,还要举行一种仪式从人类之子置换为自然之子,从而获得仪式意义上的再生。他得到大自然种种灵物的保护,如《勒俄特依》里的龙、《厘俸》里的牛,也验证了他作为大自然之子的神圣性。有的还具有一种图腾识别意义。

南方各民族史诗里与婚姻有关系的考验型故事有多种情节,最为人们所熟知的就是"难题求婚"型。其难题又分为两类:与农耕相联系或与征战有关。

纳西族史诗《创世纪》(Coq Pper Tv)的从忍利恩(Coq Ssi Leel Ee)上天求婚经受考验的故事属于前一类。史诗叙述,洪水过后,大地上只剩下从忍利恩一个人。他为了与仙女衬红褒白(Cel Huq Bu Beq)成亲重新繁衍人类,为了要到万物的种子重新装扮人间,毅然上天向天神子劳阿普(Ccee Laq A Pu)求取衬红和万物的种子。他在天上经受了一系列考验。

他首先爬过九座用刀刃做踏杆的梯子,"手上没有一滴血","脚上没有一丝刀痕"。阿普要他一昼夜砍完 99 片森林,他依靠"所有的蝴蝶"、"所有的蚂蚁"的帮助,棵棵都砍光;阿普要他一昼夜烧光 99 片砍倒的树木,他又依靠蝴蝶与蚂蚁的帮助,"棵棵都烧焦";阿普先后要他一昼夜把种子撒遍 99 片地,一昼夜又捡回撒出的种子,他还是依靠蝴蝶、蚂蚁的帮助——做到。

阿普又要他到岩上打岩羊,到江边抓鱼,想乘机把他踢下岩、踢下江,他识破

---

① 冯元蔚译《勒俄特依》,第 49—54 页。
② 刀永明、薛贤、周凤翔翻译整理《厘俸》,第 91—592 页。

了阿普的阴谋,圆满解决难题。最后,阿普要他挤虎奶,他"来到阴坡老虎洞,拣起大石头,打死小老虎,剥下虎皮披身上"。这时候,"母虎食饱回虎洞,母虎跳三跳,利恩跳三跳;母虎吼三吼,利恩吼三吼;母虎扭三扭,利恩扭三扭;母虎尾巴摇三摇,利恩摇三摇……利恩假装小虎去吃奶,三滴虎奶挤回来"。至此,子劳阿普所设置的难题全部解决了。①

这些考验中,山地农耕民族原始刀耕火种、渔猎生产的整个过程都被组织进去,可能反映了纳西族在形成过程中由游牧民族发展成农耕民族的一些情况。根据史料分析,纳西族一部分先民跟原在中国西北部主要从事游牧的羌人有渊源关系。当他们向南迁徙进入金沙江流域以后,逐渐定居下来从事农耕。在这个过程中,他们可能曾与当地原来从事农耕的土著居民交往、联姻、求取谷种甚至斗争,进而逐渐融合为统一的纳西民族。史诗当为这些情况的象征性反映。

至于"难题求婚"考验的具体形式,其背景可能是对偶婚走向一夫一妻制,在"从夫居"代替"从妻居"的过渡阶段,母权制传统反对新出现的父权制婚姻的某种方式。其遗存形式,即在南方一些民族,婚后男方一段时期内"从妻居"和女方几年"不落夫家"等习俗。在"从妻居"期间,男方必须为女方家砍柴、耕地,这在某种意义上也是对女方家抚养女儿做补偿。这些习俗在南方很多民族中存在。

"难题求婚"考验模式也在南方民族不少神话、史诗里有所表现。在同样居于山地的羌族等民族的神话、史诗里,这一模式的情节大致相同;而在居于水滨的一些民族的神话、史诗里,则往往代之以搭桥、射箭等形式,可见其普遍意义。

另外,南方一些民族"难题求婚"考验模式又可能与成年仪式有联系。在这些民族中,男子到十六七岁要举行成年仪式,要进行从身体素质到技能本事等各方面的考验,然后才有资格从事社会、社交活动,才能恋爱、结婚。这些民族认为,这种仪式具有神圣意味,这些考验具有神圣性质,考验的结果是赋予了被考验者一种新的生命形式。这也可能是难题考验模式的背景之一。

傣族史诗《兰嘎西贺》(*Nang Gar See Hall*)里勐沓达腊塔(Meng Tang Dar Lar Tar)王子召朗玛(Joe Lang Mar)求婚考验属于后一类。史诗叙述,勐甘纳嘎国王的公主楠西拉(Nang See Lar)的美丽和名声传遍大地,101个勐(Meng)的王子同时来向她求婚。国王向天神叭英求教,叭英交给他一张"弓阿沙尖"(Gang Har Sing)和三支神箭,说:"谁能挽动弓阿沙尖,并把三支神箭射出去,楠西拉就嫁给谁。"

---

① 云南省民族民间文学丽江调查队搜集整理翻译《创世纪》,第34—68页。

比试开始了，100个勐的王子轮流上台，没有一个能举得动。勐兰嘎（Meng Nang Gar）十头王两次能举起弓，却不能拉弦搭箭。想试第三次，却没有了力气。轮到召朗玛了，召朗玛默默向天祷告："望天神助一臂之力。"便轻轻把神弓高高举起，拉上弦把三支神箭射出去。他终于娶到楠西拉。这样，召朗玛的神奇本领被高高地烘托起来。[①]

南方各民族史诗里与婚姻有关的考验型故事还有洪水后兄妹婚的占卜考验。湖南瑶族《盘王歌·葫芦晓》叙述，洪水后仅存的伏羲兄妹议婚，妹妹提出五点来"考哥哥"，即要他做到"隔岸烧香烟相合"，"隔岸梳头发相绞"，"隔河种竹尾相交"，"隔冲滚磨磨相叠"，"绕树追赶两相逢"，哥哥一一办成，兄妹终于成婚繁衍人类。[②]

与此相类似的情节在许多民族史诗的洪水后兄妹婚部分都有。布依族《赛胡细妹造人烟》是滚磨、穿针，侗族《侗族祖先哪里来》是滚磨，土家族《摆手歌》是滚磨、栽葫芦（两兜合成一兜）、滚筛子簸箕、追赶等。这些情节混合了契约（婚约）和考验两种类型。哥哥要同妹妹结婚，必须有速度在赛跑中追上妹妹，必须有力量背石磨上山，还要让两扇石磨从山上滚下重合在一起等。这些考验也是以占卜方式试测天意，他们的婚姻受到种种占卜方式的肯定，从而证明合乎了天意，因而是神圣的婚姻。

当首领经受考验的故事可以举《苗族古歌》（*Hxak Lul Hxak Ghot*）里姜央（*Jangx Vangb*）当"大"的情节。古歌叙述，"鸟多闹山林，人多争管家"，姜央、雷（*Hob*）、龙（*Vongx*）等各兄弟，"个个争作大，你当我不依，我当你不服"。于是，姜央提出："想要当大哥，就要显本事，在那天边，有座南哈桥，桥长十一孔，桥宽十一庹，哪个踩得响，哪个踏得动，本事他最大，大哥他来当。"

考验开始了，龙"甩尾冲上桥"，南哈桥不响不动；雷"筋斗翻上桥"，南哈桥还是不响不动，而姜央"捉只喀喀鸟，藏在袖子里"，"走上南哈桥，脸上笑眯眯，一步捏一下，雀子喀喀叫"。姜央借此说自己"踩桥就响"，"踏桥就动"，要当大哥。但"大家都不服"，还要"斗法"、"比武"。雷公"跳到半空中"，挥舞铁锤"敲鼓响轰轰"，"电光一闪闪，下雨又刮风"。水龙"忽溜下山冲"，"挥舞头上角，撬垮半山坡"。他们都说"本事我最大，本领我最高"。而姜央"砍来九挑柴，割来九挑草"，然后让雷、龙等在屋里看他显本事。他点着火，扇起风，"火烟黑乌乌，火焰红彤彤，眼睛睁不开，四面

---

① 刀兴平、岩温扁等翻译整理《兰嘎西贺》，第164—171页。
② 郑德宏、李本高翻译整理《盘王大歌》，第149—156页。

看不清,这个心着急,那个心着慌,你也喊姜央,我也喊姜央:本事你最大,本领你最高……"① 姜央就这样凭智慧、凭机灵当上了"大"。这里,有古代遴选氏族、部落或部落联盟首领的考验仪式的影子。这种叙事结构包含了人类战胜自然的隐喻。

二、考验的文化内涵

民族史诗里人物的行为模式,史诗的叙事模式,体现着民族的文化模式,蕴涵着民族的文化特质。上述考验型情节也不例外,除了受印度史诗影响较大的傣族史诗以外,苗族、纳西族、彝族史诗考验型情节的叙事模式都深刻地反映了南方民族山地农耕文化、群体文化、神巫文化的特质。

史诗里人物的行为模式,与生活中人们的行为模式在很大程度上是对应性的。生活中人们的行为模式不是一种纯粹的自然行为,它受民族文化背景的限定,凝聚着民族的文化精神;史诗作为一个民族千百年集体创作的作品,更在深层次积淀着这个民族无意识结构中的东西。因而,尽管作品里所反映的具体生活情景与人们实际生活情景可能会有很大的差异,但抽象出来的人物行为模式则会有很大的共同性。在根本意义上,前者由后者决定。

中国南方民族各种仪式的考验项目,大都与他们山地农耕生活相连。瑶族成丁仪式的"上刀梯"、"过火链"、"跳云台"等,都包含着这个民族在山地刀耕火种所需要的基本技能。瑶族实际生活中的刀耕火种,需要不断地在布满荆棘的山野里奔走、砍草、烧草,在烧过草木的灼热的土地上踏行、挖眼、点种,在陡峭的高坡间跃上、跃下……这些基本技能,凝聚成了"上刀梯"、"过火链"、"跳云台"等考验项目,它们植根于民族山地农耕文化的土壤。

在史诗考验型情节里,无论是参与考验的对手,还是考验的形式,都无不显现出山地农耕文化的特质。《苗族古歌》里的姜央,是苗族原始农业社会的氏族首领;在考验中他的主要竞争对手,是雷公、水龙等,都是人们心目中主宰雨和水、与农耕有密切关系的自然灵物。在考验("比武")中,雷公翻跟斗、响雷、闪电、下雨、刮风,水龙撬垮半边坡,象征性地表现了灾害性的天气对农耕的影响,因而考验也成为人们在农耕中与灾害性天气斗争的象征性显现。

不仅如此,考验的程序也深深地打上了山地农耕文化的烙印。纳西族《创世

---

① 贵州民间文学组整理、田兵选编《苗族古歌》,第211—215页。

纪》里的从忍利恩,为了与仙女衬红褒白成亲重新繁衍人类,为了要到万物的种子重新装扮人间,毅然上天向天神子劳阿普求取衬红褒白与万物的种子。他在天上经受了一系列考验,例如砍森林、烧树木、撒种子、拣种子、打岩羊、抓鱼虾等,而这些,恰恰是山地农耕民族原始刀耕火种、渔猎生产的整个过程。

考验还体现了一种群体文化的特质。从忍利恩到天上去经受考验,是为了求取配偶、种子以繁衍人类、装扮人间,是为了种族的生死存亡,而不是为了个人的情欲、物欲。在他经历了种种考验以后子劳阿普问:"你是什么种族呀,你是谁的子孙?"他回答了一段气势磅礴的话:

> 我是开九重天的九弟兄的后代,
> 我是劈七层地的七姊妹的后代,
> 我是白海螺狮子的后代,
> 我是金黄大象的后代,
> 我是大力士久高那布的后代,
> 是翻越九十九座大山气力更大的种族,
> 是翻过九十九座大坡精神更旺盛的种族,
> 是所有会杀人的人来杀也杀不死的种族,
> 是所有会敲人的人来敲也敲不碎的种族![1]

这一段话,充满了对自己种族的自豪、依恋,反映了强烈的种族意识、群体文化特质。

最后,考验包含了一种神巫文化特质,它隐藏在主人公接受考验的行为里。《苗族古歌》中姜央与雷公、水龙斗法比武,"砍来九挑柴,割来九挑草",摆满一间房子的四围,然后,把雷公、水龙等请进屋里,再点火煽风。于是,"火烟黑糊糊,火焰红彤彤,眼睛睁不开,四面看不清",使雷公、水龙都甘拜下风,承认"本事你最大","我们认输了"。[2]这里闪现着模拟巫术的影子,即在久雨和久涝的日子里烧柴草用火烟象征性地驱雨驱涝,以达到控制自然灾害的目的。

纳西族《创世纪》中从忍利恩的形象和行为更带有原始巫师和巫术的特点。当

---

① 云南省民族民间文学丽江调查队搜集、整理、翻译《创世纪》,第61—62页。
② 贵州民间文学组整理、田兵选编《苗族古歌》,第214—215页。

他第一次见天神子劳阿普的时候，天神要他爬过"九座利刃的梯子"，从忍利恩爬过梯子"手上没出一滴血"，"脚上没有一丝刀痕"，这是很多民族过去的"成年礼"或学巫"拜师礼"的考验仪式——上刀梯。特别当子劳阿普出难题要从忍利恩一昼夜砍完99片大森林来刁难他时，从忍利恩"嘴里喃喃的轻哼：'白蝴蝶啊，快快飞，飞来帮我的忙！黑蚂蚁啊，快快跑，跑来帮我的忙！'"。结果第二天早上，"99片森林呀，棵棵都倒地"。[①] 这里，完全是凭借在原始人心目中具有神奇魔力、可以调动一切自然力量的咒语来起作用，巫术的性质尤其明显。

三、考验的模式比较

史诗里人物的行为模式受民族文化模式的选择和限定，但文化模式说到底是历史生活的产物并最终受历史生活的选择和影响，正是不同民族的历史形态的差异最终决定了文化模式的差异，从而决定了不同民族史诗的人物行为模式的差异。

希腊神话和史诗的创造者是远古时期曾经居于中亚（一说中欧）的雅利安人。雅利安人在发展过程中经历过一次大分化和大迁徙，其中一支向欧洲腹地挺进，最后到达爱琴海边的希腊半岛。他们摧毁了当地相当发达的迈锡尼文化，建立了自己的统治。

雅利安人迁徙壮大的历史在相当意义上是远征、冒险和掠夺的历史，进入希腊的一支定居下来后，仍不断地到远方去征战、冒险、掠夺或进行商业贸易活动，他们的文化是一种外向型的文化，他们更欣赏武力和劫掠、征服的生活方式，更需要冒险的精神，需要个人的才智。

与远征爱琴海边希腊半岛的雅利安人不同，栖息于中国南方山地的少数民族一部分是土著居民，另一部分由北方迁徙而来，但多为战争失败者和逃亡者，与征服者不可同日而语。他们较早地进入了农耕经济。在山岭纵横、易涝易旱的山地生活，人们首先面临的是如何以群体的力量顺应、改造生态环境，以满足群体生存繁衍的需要；同时，在农耕社会，人们定居耕作、自给自足，氏族部落间多和平共处、自然融合。因而，他们更欣赏的是安定、平和、友好和公平交换的生活，他们的文化是一种内守的文化模式，价值取向重群体。

两种不同文化模式的差异，表现在考验型情节上首先是考验内容的不同。希

---

① 云南省民族民间文学丽江调查队搜集、整理、翻译《创世纪》，第38—43页。

腊神话和史诗中著名的伊阿宋寻取金羊毛的故事,就可以看成是一个考验型故事。伊阿宋为了继承父亲的王位,回到自己的故乡;而早已窃据这一位置的叔父提出一个交还王位的条件:要伊阿宋出征远方的科尔基斯国(Colchis),从凶狠的埃厄忒斯(Aeetes)国王那里寻取宝贵的金羊毛。伊阿宋接受了这个条件,带领一群英雄乘坐"阿尔戈"(Argo)号船远航开始了冒险历程。这个条件是一个考验,是某种难题,某种障碍,需要主体去解决,去克服。而这个难题包含了远航、征战、夺取财宝等一系列行为,正是希腊民族文化模式的体现。

中国南方史诗中的考验内容大都是向内的,带有山地农耕民族文化的特点。前述的纳西族《创世纪》里从忍利恩所经受的考验就是一个典型的例子,它的深层包括了山地农耕民族原始刀耕火种、渔猎生产的整个过程,有砍山——砍完九十九片森林,烧地——烧光九十九片砍倒的树木,撒种——把种子撒遍九十九片地,收获——拣回种子,狩猎——到岩上打岩羊,渔捞——到江边抓鱼。① 文化模式的不同,带来考验型故事人物的行为模式巨大的差异。

更明显的差异表现在经历过出生考验的英雄成年阶段的作为。英雄出生,经过考验,证明具有某种神异性,也预示着会有不平凡的生活方式和生命历程。希腊神话和史诗中的英雄,成年后几乎都选择了冒险、远征、改变统治秩序等活动。宙斯长大后,推翻了其父克洛诺斯(Cronos)的统治,并率领奥林匹斯(Olympus)的众神镇压了提坦神(Titans)的反叛,确立了自己至高的地位。赫拉克勒斯在为欧律斯修斯(Eurystheus)服役期间,完成了12项英雄业绩,还参加阿尔戈船英雄的远航,攻打特洛伊王拉奥墨冬……也许,他们只要一息尚存,就要出外漫游冒险,以满足自己;冒险征服是他们最高的甚至唯一的生存原则和价值追求。

中国南方史诗里的英雄,成长起来以后的神奇体现在山地民族农耕畜牧的生活中。彝族《勒俄特依》里的支格阿龙,一岁就能"跟着牧童放猪玩",两岁就能"跟着牧人放羊玩",而他最伟大的功绩是射下与农耕畜牧关系密切的多余的太阳月亮。那时候,"白天六个太阳一起出,晚上七个月亮一起出",江河枯竭,草木枯萎,禽兽受害,人们受难。支格阿龙"扳着神弯弓,搭上神仙箭",要去射日月。他先后站在草上、藤上、竹子顶上、松树顶上,"射日也不中,射月也不中"。他毫不气馁,继续奋斗,最后站在"土尔山"(Turlurbbo)顶的柏树顶上,终于"射日也射中,射月也射

---

① 云南省民族民间文学丽江调查队搜集、整理、翻译《创世纪》,第41—58页。

中",完成了自己一生最辉煌的壮举。① 为群体,利农耕,这是中国南方民族史诗里英雄最大的追求。

参考书目

刀兴平、岩温扁等翻译整理《兰嘎西贺》,昆明:云南人民出版社,1984 年。

刀永明、薛贤、周凤翔翻译整理《厘俸》,昆明:云南民族出版社,1987 年。

冯元蔚译《勒俄特依》,成都:四川民族出版社,1986 年。

贵州民间文学组整理、田兵选编《苗族古歌》,贵阳:贵州人民出版社,1979 年。

云南省民族民间文学丽江调查队搜集整理翻译《创世纪》,昆明:云南人民出版社,1960 年。

郑德宏、李本高翻译整理《盘王大歌》,长沙:岳麓书社,1988 年。

---

① 冯元蔚译《勒俄特依》,成都:四川民族出版社,1986 年,第 53—60 页。

宝卷及其仪式语境

——华北后土信仰与口头传统的个案研究

尹虎彬

摘　要　本文是关于河北民间后土崇拜与口头叙事传统的个案研究。我的田野作业的材料主要涉及后土神庙、音乐会、佛事会及其仪式、口头叙事文本。这些材料存在于地方性的后土崇拜活动中,也见于地方志、碑刻、口头叙事之中。本文的基本理论假设是:后土崇拜是一种含有仪式和神话成分的现场活动。后土在季节性重复出现的神灵祭祀仪式中处于中心地位。对于宝卷的实际表演和后土灵验叙事而言,其核心内容表现为讲述后土的故事,把后土作为一位神祇来召唤,它的力量便可以显现,以庇护共同体的人们。地方性的宝卷和民间叙事传统是在本地的后土祭祀中发展起来的。

关键词　后土崇拜,宝卷,口头传统

河北易县、涞水交界的洪崖山,自清末、民初以来,扮演着后土信仰的中心地角色。后土神祇在民间庙祭、坛祭仪式中处于中心的地位,体现出多神崇拜与一神独尊的特点,形成后土崇拜的民间地方传统。后土祭祀的仪式活动形成了一个信仰共同体,它以共同信奉后土为精神基础,以一年一度的后山庙会为纽带,以定期朝山进香为义务。在河北以洪崖山后土皇帝庙为中心的方圆数百里范围内,后土为民间崇拜的主神。在地方性层次上的后土祭祀传统对宝卷在内的民间叙事产生了重要影响。后山庙自清代以来香火很盛,历史上经历过 1938 年抗战,1949 年解放,1966 年“文革”,以及 1984 年的恢复等历史变迁。农历 3 月 15 日后土庙会,其组织很严密,仪式活动有统一指挥,按照顺序进行,是附近各县各乡民间会统联合组织的后土普祭活动。

后土曾经是自然神、文化英雄和祖先神。它由古代神话里的神进入正统道教

神龛里,变为四御之一,被民间宗教收为老母神,又演变为民间信仰里的娘娘神。河北地方民间后土信仰具有类型化特点,它以庙宇为依托,以神社为实体,以祭祀和社火的仪式为通神的媒介,以适应民众的基本心理需求为旨归,以神话叙事来体现信仰传承的普化性。

河北冀中平原的民间神社如音乐会和佛事会,它们是地方村落社会的社火仪式的承担者,秉承敬神礼地、尊祖追远的传统精神,以血缘宗族为根基,担负传承乡土社会文化的传承使命。宝卷是它们的神圣文本,包括它的表演传统,都被认为是祖先的遗产。

宝卷及其演唱是被包括在民间神灵与祭祀的现场活动中的。宝卷的传播,是由祭祀推动的。河北民间的《后土宝卷》是一种可见的流布过程。《后土宝卷》属于活形态的民间地方传统,它在历时的层面上,继承了传统的艺术形式。

在宝卷传统的背后,存在着活形态的民间口头传统,它今天仍然继续产生着关于后土和后土崇拜的神话叙事,成为地方民间意识形态的一部分。后土灵验叙事是被当作真实的故事来讲述的,每一个故事背后都有过真实的社会事件发生。叙事是人们对这些事件重新讲述和真实的评价。地灵叙事就像神话一样,它是现场的演述,与信仰、行为、伦理道德互为表里。更重要的是,它体现了传统的神话范例。

当我们考察活形态的口头传统材料时,应当强调后土崇拜仪式与洪崖山民间叙事的交互作用。我们可以对后土崇拜作一个最简单的定义:它是一种膜拜仪式(Cult)。我在此进一步以膜拜仪式这一术语来特指民间的神灵与祭祀传统。膜拜仪式是一种含有仪式和神话成分的现场活动。后土在河北民间季节性重复的神灵祭祀活动中处于中心地位,民间社会对神灵的祭奠具有循环的特性。与此相关,我将在以下的论述中说明本文的一个重要的理论假设:神灵与祭祀是民间叙事传统的原动力。在地方性层次上的后土神祇祭祀,它对宝卷、民间叙事传统的影响是很重要的。我们可以在较为广泛的社会历史背景下,通过后土崇拜的地方传统,来了解一个地方性的民间叙事文本的实现过程。①

---

① 参见 Gregory Nagy, *Greek Mythology and Poetics*, Cornell University Press. 1990: 8—10。作者认为膜拜仪式含有神话与仪式的意味,可以替代"宗教"这个术语。他认为印度的一些地方性的神话和史诗的叙事,是围绕当地的神灵崇拜与仪式活动而展开的。他由此类比古代希腊史诗传统也存在一个制度化的宗教祭奠节日——泛雅典娜节。荷马史诗在这样的地域性崇拜仪式中演唱,最终形成了它的城邦意义上的传统。作者的具体结论并不重要,这里主要借鉴他的阐释学的模式。

在民间的万神殿内,后土处于中心的位置,在宝卷或地灵故事中她通常要化为道婆下凡人间,解决一些当地人的困难,这一媒介的效力和真实性吸引了广大人群,后土神殿成为重要的仪式场所,人们在那里吟诵后土的颂歌。

对于宝卷的实际表演而言,核心的信仰表现为讲述神的故事,把她作为一位神祇来召唤,她的力量便可以显现,以庇护共同体的人们。后土在宝卷里是汉张姑,她在后山修炼40年,她的死亡赋予其最终的力量:死亡就是坐化,真性离开凡体,这件事的作用在当地来说就是故事的"生发点"。它导致了神格化,导致了膜拜,导致了祭奠,最终导致了叙事,这种叙事在宝卷来说是伴随仪式而演唱的,以请神降临。

一、后土崇拜及其地方传统

(一) 后土与后土信仰

早期的大地崇拜对象为方丘、土坛。对土地、谷物的崇拜演变为对于整治土地、谷物的人物的信仰。这时自然神崇拜已经发展到人格神的崇拜。在原始时代,祖先神崇拜和英雄崇拜往往是交织在一起的。① 金、元以后,国家正祀后土开始衰落,它的普遍性受到冲击。清代以来仅华北的河北、山西、陕西等地,仍然保留后土祭祀活动。民间乡社祭祀后土成为民间地方文化的一部分,古代旧有的、严格的典章和礼仪制度被破坏,后土信仰的内涵、后土的神格,已经因为各地风土的不同而呈现出多元的特点。② 洪崖山周围佛教、道教寺庙密集,它们大都为明代以前兴建。唐代佛教进山,建设寺庙。元代瑶人北迁,修建盘古庙。宋代、金代道教进山,全真道正一派进入后山北坡,元代全真派进入南坡。如豹泉村就有道教庙宇。唐代以后,洪崖山成为河北地方的一个宗教中心。

(二)地方层次上的后土祭祀仪式

洪崖山,位于河北东北部,道教名山,俗称后山,为太行山余脉。在易县流行之各种民间信仰中,后土皇帝尤为古老,经久而不衰。洪崖山上有后土皇帝庙,对此

---

① 晁福林:《先秦民俗史》,第318页。
② 参见薛艺兵:《河北易县涞水的后土宝卷》,第79—98页。

《易县志稿》有如下记述：

> 后土黄帝庙,俗称圣女庙,在县北三十五里洪崖山上,上山十里,山径九道十八盘。按,今庙祀女神,乡民信仰杂以神怪之说。佥云,女神为山居老妇,曾免汉光武帝于难,故祠祀至今。考光武帝追铜马、五幡贼于县南徐水上,兵败投崖,遇救,退保范阳,见于《水经注》。然救之者为突骑王丰,老妇之说似不足凭。惟既称后土皇帝庙,当为祀黄帝轩辕氏者。《史记》黄帝与蚩尤战于涿鹿,又会诸侯于釜山,今县南五十余里,釜山相传黄帝会诸侯之所,是则黄帝在易有祠理或然也。今乡民望走极盛,每岁三月,远近数县人民麇集进香,为邑中庙会之最盛者。①

明弘治十六年《重修寿阳院之记》碑文载："易郡去北三十里有山,名洪崖。寿阳院,山势异香,景物清奇……有一石室外狭中阔……考大金泰和二年,刘真人隐栖之处……重修玉皇殿三间,巍巍宽敞,金碧辉煌,中塑玉帝,左右二十八宿卫两旁。"另有碑文说："白云观与易县凤凰山同心一气,历古之友,年深悠久,不记辈载。"

二、民间会统仪式活动和经卷表演

音乐会有不少名称,它叫南灯会,也叫南灯神社、南灯圣会、蓝旗圣会。民间乐社亦为神社,它设立神堂,逢年节设坛敬奉神明,拥有神像、经卷、乐器,演奏音乐以娱神灵,逢年节举行踩街、拜庙等仪式活动,所有这些都表明乐社的核心职能是为民间宗教信仰服务的。音乐会内部组织形式比较简单。乐手统称为"学事",乐手中精通乐律并能传授音乐的又称"师傅",掌管音乐会内部事务的人,称作"会首"、"管事的"。负责宗教祭祀活动的主持人,称作"香首"。听从香首、会首调遣,跑腿传话、召集乐手、安排杂务者,取名"攒管"。音乐会一般30人左右,其中约有20人为学事,会首1至3人,香首1人,攒管2至3人。②

在民间乐社局内人的视点来看,音乐会之"音乐",其范围是很确定的:它包括

---

① 民国《易县志稿》,第298—299页。
② 薛艺兵:《民间吹打的乐种类型与人文背景》,第57页。

打击乐在内的 13 套大曲和 30 多首小曲。并且还必须是由这个特定编制的乐队演奏的这些乐曲,用其他编制的乐队演奏别的乐曲就不叫"音乐"。①音乐会的曲目固定,乐器种类不能添加,演奏模式也是严格传承的规矩。

服务于村落的仪式活动是音乐会的传统功能。音乐会以音乐娱神,为神灵颂经、唱赞。易县、涞水县的音乐会每逢年节带领村民朝拜后土奶奶(后土女神)。这些传统的仪式涉及念咒、进香、诵经、唱赞、敬奉神灵。②一些音乐会的乐谱序文开宗明义,提出"古传音乐会,由明至大清,敬神祭天地,流芳百世通"的口号。

在村落仪式活动中,器乐的演奏都是由男性乐手来承担的,这些乐手来自村里的大户人家。音乐会这一祖先的遗产是以血缘和宗族为基础来传承的。音乐会以礼神明、敬天地为宗旨,以敬祖追远为其历史根基。同宗村落的文化背景是民间音乐会保持传统的基础。河北涞水县南高洛村有单、李、何、阎四大姓氏,一般而言,只有男性来演奏乐器,在传统的村落社会里,音乐也通常由父子传承的。音乐知识、乐器、演奏技巧、乐谱识读,这些都是在家族制度之内传承的。有些家族具有五代人的乐手传承历史。村落音乐会及其成员是传授音乐的一种具有凝聚力的社会组织形式。③

音乐会和佛事会拥有自己的财产,如乐器、经卷、演练场所,他们还利用村落里的庙宇作为仪式活动的场所。如果村里有两个以上的会统,那么,各个会统会分别具有自己特定的空间管辖范围和外围的支持者的组织。音乐会拥有世代传承的乐谱。就乐谱而言,一些音乐会使用工尺谱的记音,这些符号在各个村落之间是不同的,尽管如此,它们还是按照标准的工尺谱来发音的。乐手们按照记录的谱子来吟诵(韵谱),以背诵曲调。据钟思第(Stephen Jones)的研究,村民们说他们的音乐来自佛寺或佛教僧人。这种音乐的传承大约有 500 年的历史。④

---

① Stephen Jones, *Folk Music of China*: *Living Instrumental Traditions*, Clarendon Press, Oxford, 1995: 189.

② Ibid. p.189.

③ 乔建中、薛艺兵、[英]钟思第、张振涛:《冀中、京、津地区民间"音乐会"普查实录》,第 293 页。

④ 同上。

三、《后土皇帝宝卷》及其文本

(一)《后土宝卷》的文本来源

1.易州韩家庄《承天效法后土皇帝道源度生宝卷》

《承天效法后土皇帝道源度生宝卷》原为傅惜华所藏,后收入张希舜等编的《宝卷初集》中。[①] 原版于卷末署名燕山化众刊经善士刘浩、郭玉、张文广、王良佑。封底有一画像功德碑,上书"易州韩家庄刊像功德:魏天福、常瑞"。卷末有民间宗教神像5幅,4幅为道教或弘阳教神像,1幅为菩萨像。这部宝卷分为24品,并配有曲牌,前12品缺。

在该宝卷第13品中交代:"夫话说后土圣母奉佛旨在黄土顶上立超升法门,开坛说法演教度生。"第14品更明确了后土圣母之神职:"吾本是,普天下,管土之主。大地人,吃万物,都打土生。"这个后土圣母,就是在易州城北洪崖山黄土坡上的后山大庙里传道的。

宝卷第16品为引渡张斌修道,后土圣母送子给张斌,这一品内容与马头村、南高洛村《后土宝卷》所述张斌求子的内容是一致的。"却说河南府洛阳县有一善人姓张名斌妻王氏……缺后无子……张斌忽然想起,去年从易州所过,遇有一个香客,他说送子娘娘与人间送子,甚是灵应。"张斌妻王氏求子、得子,怀胎十月,这时娘娘化一道婆,来到张员外家化斋。娘娘自称"我是保定府易州城北人氏",离后土娘娘庙很近。接着张斌夫妇又向道婆请了一幅圣母画像,以供烧香报效。这幅神像被描述为,后土母"头戴九流珠冠,众位娘娘都璎珞垂珠,金容金像"。

2.易县后山庙《后土宝卷》

易县流井乡马头村早年有音乐会,他们拥有科仪本经卷和灯科本宝卷,据说曾有《后土卷》和《十王卷》,现已散失。当地人说《后土卷》分为上下两卷,上卷为后土修行故事,下卷为王莽篡汉故事。他说《后土宝卷》为元末张琪所撰。《直隶易州志》卷十五记载:张琪,字廷玉,元末举进士,隐洪崖山不复仕,以诗文名世。此说并无证据,存疑。

据笔者调查马头村后山庙得知,该村村民梁树明先生藏有后山庙经卷,为"文

---

① 张希舜、濮文起、高可、宋军编,《宝卷初集》第11卷,第128页。

革"毁庙时其抢救后私家收藏至今。梁树明藏有后山庙遗留的两种《后土宝卷》。

这里先介绍第一种。该宝卷年代不详,但从卷本和语言来看,最晚也在清末。该宝卷为写本,隶书,大字经折装,有插图。全卷分为上中下3卷,32品。以下为卷本具体内容介绍。

封面题签:《慈悲灵验后土娘娘源流宝卷》。卷首题名:《承天效法后土皇灵地祇宝卷》。宝卷正文开始之前为道士做道场常用的神咒、宝号、号咒:《开经神咒》、《净口神咒》、《净身神咒》、《祝香神咒》、《开经玄蕴神咒》、《玉清天尊宝号》、《上清天尊宝号》、《泰清天尊宝号》、《弥罗天尊宝号》、《勾陈天尊宝号》、《星主紫薇宝号》、《后土皇帝宝号》、《王灵官天尊号咒》。

以下为宝卷正文,卷内题名:《后土娘娘慈悲宝卷》。从题名到第1品开始之前为《举香赞》、《开经偈》、《请神偈》,其后为各品目名称和曲牌名称。

3.梁树明所藏第二种《后土宝卷》(梁写本)

该宝卷原为元、亨、利、贞4卷,共48品,现存3卷36品,即元、亨、利3卷,后一卷散失。该宝卷为大字经折装,蓝底碎花锦缎装帧,红纸竖条封面题签《慈悲灵验后土娘娘源流宝卷》,卷首题名《承天效法后土皇灵地祇宝卷》。原版本为写本。宝卷为后山后土皇帝庙的庙传宝卷。后山庙曾是一处道观,据说为全真道十方丛林,当年曾有住持道人,是一处道教活动场所。梁氏《后土宝卷》正文开始之前有神咒、宝诰,细察其内容,多为道经所载,可见当年后山道士既习诵寻常道经,也习用后土卷。在做道场之始,先念《开经安神咒》、《净口神咒》、《净身神咒》、《祝香神咒》、《开坛玄蕴神咒》以及《后土娘娘宝诰》。梁氏第二种《后土宝卷》原为4卷48品,分为元、亨、利、贞4卷。第4卷缺。第1卷叙述后土圣母修行事,第2卷叙述刘秀走国事,第3卷意在突出后土圣母对于人间善恶的干预,具有劝世思想,充斥着民间宗教的因果报应观念。后土修行故事、后土救主故事,为两大口头传说系列,仍具有活态的性质。

据后山道士们回忆,《后土宝卷》分为前后两部;前部为张姑修真,后部为刘秀走国。前后两部合起来,构成一部完整的后山大庙由来的历史,并由此而构成易州城北一带地方史的口述传统。这一点,可以从后山壁画的叙事传统中得到认证。后山庙正殿太宁宫西面山墙上的壁画,反映了《后土宝卷》前后两部之大致轮廓,同时吸收了当地广为流传的神话、故事的核心内容。后山庙壁画,相传为明代大画家崔自忠所绘制,原件已不存。

4.涞水县南高洛村《后土宝卷》(高洛本)

该宝卷是涞水县义安镇南高洛村音乐会所藏之灯科本,大字经折装,手抄本。该宝卷为上下2卷,共24品,1.9万多字。内有15幅插图。封面题签《后土皇帝宝卷》。封二题字:大哉坤元。下面落款署:癸未年元月一日写完。马献图(人名章)敬。第1至第3页内容有马献图撰写的《宝卷完成随意笔录》,全文如下:

后土皇帝始自东汉重兴,至今二千余年,灵异非常,每逢春秋大祭、圣诞之日香火甚盛。至我民国三民主义实铲除迷信,各庙香火渐衰,又接民国戊寅年中日事变以来,民心一日数惊,民无圣心顾瞻。每逢三月十五日,只可望西北遥拜,以达圣恩。忆昔圣母苦修功完果满后,保汉室江山一统,又应人间男女,有求必应。后卷张公求子,四圣归天之灵,令人钦佩信仰。我因一念之际,由高楼村请来后土卷,净手抄录以达圣恩,又可宜补我村弘阳圣会之簾,又能永存纪念奉诵。因之我妹文单鸿福见我抄毕之时,他由北京买来纸张,令我再抄一卷以补贵村存念。我是很欢迎信仰,即鸿福乐善好施,乐心成其善念,因此,重整笔砚,每日在校课完之裕,净手敬心抄录,图画完成。奉上高楼善会存念以补经箱。

信士弟子虎贲驿村马献图敬书于北学校。中华民国三十二年岁次癸未年正月穀旦。

第4页有插图:灵霄宝殿、三清大殿、观音堂、透灵碑(大定二十八年二月二十三日立)、圣水潭。第5页插图为三郎官。第6至第7页插图为后土奶奶圣像。第8页为御制龙牌。第9页书碑文两通。其一:马献图居于河北保定道新城县南虎贲驿村,于民国三十一年岁次壬午净手抄录敬献高楼善会。其二:单鸿福因敝亲马献图在校与该村抄写后土卷甚堪欣赏,余当由北京购来纸张,敬烦马君重新抄录,存于我会,以备奉诵。特此敬述。民国三十二年癸未正月一日。第10页卷首题名:《后土娘娘慈悲灵验源流宝卷》。卷下终了有马献图题记:

信士弟子马献图于中华民国三十一年即夏历壬午年六月抄录,至来年癸未正月初一日完功,元宵节虔诚开卷,点句丹青完毕,亲身送卷来贵村善会保存。后土宝卷上下二册内容字数一万九千余,文词甚佳,辙韵和平,以及后卷张斌求子,灵异非常。可见老母修成正果,救护万民,不愧为神,能解除痛苦,大众仰望虔诚。

除了上述版本之外,后山庙附近的民间佛事会和音乐会也藏有《后土宝卷》,它们大多数是 1990 年以后从后山梁树明或西豹泉村抄写的卷子,而且,多为半部宝卷。马头村音乐会的后土宝卷就是从本村梁树明那里抄写的,只有上卷,1994 年抄写,由会头贾玉田收藏。西豹泉村的宝卷也来自马头村,上卷,1990 年抄写。涞水县李家坟佛事会的《后土宝卷》是 1992 年从西豹泉村抄来的。涞水县南洛平佛事会的《后土宝卷》1990 年抄写,是从西豹泉村请来的经卷。上述这些宝卷是适应后山庙会或后土祭祀活动的恢复而重新抄录的,这一现象的意义在于,我们可以从中看到宝卷流布的大致情况,它是与民间会统的后土崇拜的仪式活动相关联的现象。只抄写半部宝卷的现象说明,这时的宝卷只是为了应付表演的需要,为了用于后土祭祀活动中请神时使用。①

(二)后土宝卷的归类

初期宝卷从佛经中直接吸取了一些形式上、内容上的要素,在韵式、套语、句法,特别是一些偈、赞、佛等固定形式上的袭用。宝卷首先是经,是教派的经典,以阐发教义为首要特征。因此,它从体例上要尽量符合一般佛经的体例以做到神似。当然宝卷在其发展当中又吸收了俗讲、变文、戏曲甚至地方剧种如南北曲之要素,日趋复杂化。宝卷初始乃为佛教题材,一类为演说佛经的科释经文,一类为讲唱佛教故事,后来又有道教宝卷,民间宗教宝卷以及民间宝卷,演出者也由僧人而转入民间艺人。其表演方式与俗讲相似,这主要指表演的程式以及图像配合说唱的制度。②

若研究宝卷题材样式特点,即它的文本结构、句法结构等诸般要素,15 世纪出现的早期宝卷,可以视为该题材样式的早期模式。

宝卷的篇章结构是适应表演而吸取传统既有之一些成分而形成的。③

首先,宝卷之分"品"、"分",实际上即为演唱之段落,也是音乐的段落。一品之内,篇章体例固定,为多段体之有序组合。各品之间大体遵循相同的篇章体例,从

---

① 薛艺兵:《河北易县涞水的后土宝卷》,第 31—37 页。
② [日]泽田瑞穗:《增补宝卷の研究》,第 274—275 页。
③ [加]欧大年:《中国民间教派研究》(Daniel L Overmyer, *Folk Buddhist Religion: Dissenting Sects in Late Traditional China*, Harvard University Press, 1976),周玉民等译,上海:上海古籍出版社,1993 年,第 292—293 页。

音乐上讲就是重章叠唱。宝卷之分品,从内容上讲是全卷之几个主题或大的叙事段落之划分,从表演上讲是分段演唱的实际需要。

其次,宝卷由一些固定成型的段落(或曰篇章)组成,这些段落有其固定名称,它们来自佛教或道教经典。从卷首题名到第一品开始之前为举香赞、诸佛奉请、开经偈(咒)。这是民间宗教做道场时焚香敬神、请神降临的仪式。

20世纪90年代,中国音乐研究者的田野工作,提供了与宝卷演唱活动关联密切之音乐志报告,现在河北民间乐社里仍然演唱宗教仪式音乐,宝卷是依乐而吟唱的,而且是集体吟诵。

易县马头村后山庙的《承天效法后土皇灵地祇宝卷》体现民间道教的主题,它讲述了一个叫张生香的村姑,出家修行,计救汉光武帝刘秀,与民送子的故事。

南高洛村音乐会的《后土皇帝宝卷》,为民国抄本;另外,还有一部名为《后山宝卷》,它汲取了民间关于张生香的口头传说,属于民间故事宝卷之类。

这些由河北民间音乐会和佛事会保留的有关后土女神的宝卷,都属于民间宗教的文本。同时,它们在文体上属于泽田瑞穗所划分的叙事宝卷。[1] 总之,《后土宝卷》的归类应该视具体的卷本而定。《后土宝卷》经过一个历史的演变过程。至少,从目前的卷本来看,就有前期秘密宗教宝卷,稍后又出现民间信仰的宝卷。最后,还有纯粹的民间故事宝卷。我们从宝卷与后山神话、传说和故事里,可以看出不同类型的民俗学样式对于后土女神的描述,其形象竟是如此不同。

四、《后土宝卷》的主题研究

这里所要分析的后土叙事文本,包括易县城北后土皇帝庙太宁宫(正殿)绘制的《后山奶奶故事图》24品(24幅情节画面)。傅惜华所藏明末清初之《后土皇帝道源渡生宝卷》,上下2卷24品,简称韩家庄本(D本)。后山庙遗留《灵验慈悲后土娘娘源流宝卷》,3卷36品,梁树明所藏清代写本,简称马头本(A本)。另有同名宝卷一部,为梁树明根据后山庙原藏本整理而成,大字竖写,经折装,3卷36品,简称梁写本(B本)。第四部同名宝卷为南高洛音乐会藏本,大字竖写经折装,民国二十三年(1934)马献图手抄本,2卷24品,简称高洛本(C本)。

---

① [日]泽田瑞穗:《增补宝卷の研究》,第40—41页。

(一)宝卷与故事

后山奶奶故事图、韩家庄本、马头本、梁写本和高洛本皆属后土故事叙事文本，主要涉及以下四个系列：后土修行故事、刘秀走国传说、后土与河南张斌送子和刘勇求子故事。其中，后土修行、后土送子为广泛流传的叙事文本；刘秀走国则为后山庙传壁画和宝卷的叙事内容，在宝卷的流传过程中，这一部分内容并未被广泛接受。这可以从民间口承故事研究中加以印证。为了更加清楚地反映上述五种文本的异同，特以图示作如下说明：

图示一

故事 文本	后土修行	刘秀走国	张斌求子	刘勇求子
韩家庄本	1品	×	1品	×
马头本	4品	1品	11品	11品
高洛本	5品	4品	12品	×
梁写本	9品	9品	9品	×
梁写本	12品	12品	×	×

上述四个特定题目的故事中，后土修行故事、后土送子故事在各卷本中叙述最为充分，结构上呈现出明晰的主题的排列组合模式，甚至程式化的套语、曲牌，也与特定主题实现了呼应关系，这说明，这些故事的主题在民间叙事中被长期保存、传播，已趋向于定型。宝卷叙事具有相对固定的形态，具有类型化、模式化、程式化的特点，这从其叙事主题、程式化语言特征、散韵结合的叙述、表演上的说唱结合中都可以看到。

张生香出家修真成正果故事这一的叙述是由传统的主题按照一定的组合方式来进行的。从《后山奶奶故事图》、《后土宝卷》之三个版本（A本、B本和C本）的比较研究中可以看出，它们拥有共同的主题，有相当一部分的叙述语言是重合的。下面将《故事图》、《后土宝卷》中张生香出家修真成正果故事的共同主题展示如下：(1)汉张姑出家众邻相送[上小楼]，(2)张生香入深山修行[清江引]，(3)老母于洞中修真养性[金字经]，(4)老母明心见性成正果[山坡羊]，(5)后土救主[浪淘沙]，(6)娘娘卖柴度化井耕[挂金锁]，(7)井耕化缘重修后土庙[驻云飞]，(8)众善缘修建太宁宫[皂罗袍]。与以上八个主题相呼应的是八个曲牌，它们表达了主题的核心内容，表现出宝卷在主题与程式化语言紧密呼应的特点。

在汗牛充栋的刘秀走国故事中,有一组为刘秀走国系列故事,很有典型性。这一系列可以用下列图示来表示:王莽赶刘秀→耕夫救驾→蝼蛄土里钻孔救主→食桑子充饥→跨虎登山→石井自斜→汉张姑救主→刘秀报恩、敕封、建庙。上述每一个故事都代表一个类型。如耕夫救驾,它可以由人、动物、植物所代替。民众在解释地方文化传统的时候,常常以本地为中心,将普遍流布的传说附会到自己熟悉的地方风物上,按照他们的生活想像和逻辑来再现历史。一个最为朴素的逻辑便是,皇帝为天子,自然可得天助、地助、人助、神助;皇帝报恩的方式也不过就是敕封。

刘秀走国故事可以被划分为以下几个主题:(1)王莽篡汉;(2)刘秀走国;(3)刘秀夜宿帽下水;(4)老母假扮石婆送石饼;(5)食桑子刘秀充饥;(6)猛虎救驾;(7)贾甫耕田救主;(8)后土老母智救刘秀;(9)刘秀登基敕封后土;(10)刘秀建庙报恩;(11)汉光武亲临降香。

宝卷利用这些传说,把后山大庙说成是刘秀建立的,把二者附会到一起。这些都表现为将信仰转化为现实权威的愿望。易州在辽、金、元一度为异族统治。后来的八国联军侵华,反洋教,日本占领,都留下痕迹。民间对皇帝的叙事还有"帝王还家"的模式。刘秀认后土皇帝为干娘,说明皇帝权力与神权的合一。[①] 根据当地传说,后山奶奶又是定兴县辛告村王家的姑奶奶,这是血缘关系的虚拟。刘秀可以被视为皇权转化而来的神。后山一带民间传说却不曾改造过自然神和文化英雄,这说明,由皇帝改造过来的神与其他的神是有区别的。这也说明他们除了自然神、宗教神和文化英雄以外,还需要一种能由皇权转化而来的、能保护平民的最高权力的神。后土救驾,刘秀封神,这两个故事说了一件事:神权和皇权的统一。

后土娘娘为河北易县、涞水县民间普遍信仰的女神,该神主管人间生儿育女,因此后土娘娘香火极盛。围绕求子、送子这一民间宗教信仰而举行的祭祀仪式,是民众所广泛参与的活动。关于后土老母灵验故事也颇为广播,可谓家喻户晓,反映了华北民众浓厚的传统观念。因此,敬奉神明、积德行善,成为民间倡导的道德行为规范,许愿还愿也成为每年一度参加后山庙会的人们广泛参与的活动。我们对《后土宝卷》进行主题分析,无疑会更加透彻地解释上述民俗事象的内涵。

后土娘娘与河南张斌送子故事,它在《后土宝卷》中是一个相对独立、完整的叙

---

① 董晓萍、欧达伟(R. David Arkush):《乡村戏曲表演与现代华北民众》,北京:北京师范大学出版社,2000年,第149—150页。

事段落,一般称这一部分为《送子卷》。A本、B本和C本的送子卷,在基本情节、主题、主题的排列组合上大体一致,表现出明显的对应关系。

(二)宝卷的一般性主题

民俗学所说的主题,它是由不同文本之间的比较中产生的一个概念,它指的是重复出现的内容单元,如相同的事件,场景,段落。欧大年(Daniel L. Overmyer)在他的宝卷研究中,在基本方法上也采用了这样的主题概念。他所说的主题是指,从传统中继承下来的在不同的宝卷文本中重复出现的一些核心观念。这一概念,对了解宝卷在叙事层面上的传统模式是有效的。他所探讨的主题包括:传授经卷的教主自传性陈述,对这些神谕经卷的自悟,列举教派名称及会众,创世、普度、来世神话,禅定,仪式,道德说教,地狱描绘,社会观念。①欧大年认为上述宝卷主题,反映了中国民众的一些宗教观念,这些观念涉及诸般仪式活动,如持斋、念佛、超度、参禅,这些内容以前都有,但宝卷有自己的特定语境。其实,宝卷的主题范围,是介于俗信和经典佛教之间的中间地带。例如,宝卷主题不涉及牺牲献供、一年一度的朝拜圣地活动(泰山进香活动除外)、占卜吉凶或风水,几乎没有人神中介者的巫术祛病之主题,祖先崇拜的主题也不常见(当然宝卷里有孝敬、赡养父母的主题)。欧大年认为宝卷不大讨论这样的民间信仰主题。宝卷具有强烈的神话意识,讲述创世或诸神故事,神明以梦的形式脱离神形变化为凡人。宝卷号召人们脱凡入圣。当然宝卷中渗透了道德伦理观念,这包括儒家伦理、中下层民众的信仰。

(三)宝卷表达的一些基本观念

《后土宝卷》所叙张生香出家修行故事从"弃舍家缘"的主题开始。张生香父母双亡,自叹孤苦,为生活所迫,情愿修行辩道,寻一个出身之路。于是,她告别邻里,出家修行去了。

苦海拦路主题主要是说娘娘在归山修行途中路逢汪洋苦海拦住去路。玉帝差金星,慈航度缘人。佛教把人世间视为苦海,把菩萨发慈悲、救度众生出离苦海,称为慈航。②据喻松青之介绍,明代的民间秘密宗教宝卷中,很早就有法船的说法。③

① Daniel L. Overmyer, *Precious Volumes: An Introduction to Chinese Sectarian Scriptures from the Sixteenth and Seventeenth Centuries*, Harvard University Press, 1999: 6.

② Ibid. p.281.

③ 喻松青:《民间秘密宗教研究》,第 326 页。

后土卷中所述玉帝令金星化渔翁为生香摆渡为一典型场景,这一主题毋宁说是一种色彩强烈的宗教象征。

老母于洞中修真这一主题也是取自道教固有的洞天福地之说法。①

白猿献桃主题,其意象也来自于道教传说,其他宝卷也多有采用,易州当地流行一则传说:云蒙山水帝洞王拚老祖门下有白猿,它在马头口子千峰山下后桃园看桃,按时给老母送桃充饥。后山庙中壁画也有白猿献桃给张生香一品。

明心见性这一主题指明张生香终于修成正果。罗教经典中称教主修成正果为"明心见性"。明代的无为教把无生老母信仰具体化、定型化,塑造出无生老母这位最高女神的形象,出现了老母化为沿街乞讨的贫婆的形象。无生老母成为我国民间继娘娘和观音之后,又一位享有最高信仰者地位的女性神。

归圣主题指的是老母奉玉帝丹诏赴,跨上仙鹤飞升天界的故事。有一日,真人刘若夷于丹霞洞见老母纯阳体性,意识到老母在丹霞洞修炼 32 载之后,真性已经离开凡体,飞升天界。上界玉皇敕封老母为后土正位,永居太宁宫,等到三期劫,龙台赴会,同众圣掌宝筏,普度众生。归圣主题不仅适用于后土老母,也适用于修炼成真的其他圣贤。民间教派宣扬三阳劫变观念,宣称教主能普度众生,号召人们入超生法门,脱轮回之苦,早升天界,永不临凡。

《后土宝卷》讲述了老奶奶卖柴邱家店的故事。这个故事反映了化愚度贤的主题。该主题包括伪装、谎故事等叙事成分,这些成分成为宝卷惯用手法。神明进入凡世必须脱离神形,化作凡人,自述一段谎故事说明身世,以博世人同情。民间宗教教主们常常自称能度化群迷,宣扬法船普度思想,号召世间婴儿姹女脱离生死轮回之苦,早升天界,永不临凡。后土老母脱化一贫婆,这一伪装及其自述身世的谎故事,在宝卷中已成为独立的叙事成分,它反复出现在不同的宝卷当中。

上界神明给人间送子,这也是宝卷常见的主题。《后土宝卷》写后土老母为显化神通,故意脱化贫婆下到人间。老母常常谎称自己为讨饭女流之辈而沿街乞讨。她被主人引入家中之后,会趁机把金丹一粒放入主妇碗中,令其十月怀胎。

造卷主题是说后土老母能够梦里神授经卷。《后土宝卷》渲染了后土老母托梦造卷的故事。一个儒林秀士竟然能够按照神明在梦中的托付制造宝卷。这是民间宗教家为提高其经卷之权威而编造的事实,是人为宗教而非初民的信仰。

在这部宝卷里,化缘主题指的是老母度化井耕、令其发心修庙的故事。该主题

---

① 于春松:《神仙传》,第 129 页。

与民间的俗信活动关系紧密。在明清时代华北乡村,造庙、刊经、作会、树碑、造像等,皆为公德义举,这是乡民积金攒玉,募化钱粮而实现的。在华北乡村类似记载化缘事象的功德碑比比皆是,直至今天民间仍以募集钱款来进行重修庙宇、恢复庙会等民间社火活动。

像教子攻书、登科及第、入仕、效忠皇帝、孝养双亲这样的主题,反映了民间社会传统的儒家伦理道德观念。这些观念也是儒家社会得以运行的保证。宝卷中讲张振先登科及第,荣任翰林,不能孝养双亲,双亲认为这是忤逆声名,因此,夫妇千里赴京城,令儿子振先辞官归家,孝养双亲,上山朝拜后土老母,进香还愿,以求尽忠尽孝敬神,功果圆满。

(四)宝卷的一些典型段落

在分析宝卷的主题时,形式和内容往往是统一的,是一个事物的两个侧面。宝卷在表述某些类型的主题时,它所采用的是一些传统的惯用手法,因此,一些典型段落其实就是以特定文体所表达的特定主题。宝卷在表现与空间、时间相关内容时,总是按顺序来叙述的,尤其在长篇的打佛段落中,出现了一些详表韵文的文体,它们描绘的是一些典型的场景,如神的集会,盛大的仪式场景,特定地理环境中有规律地排列的人工物,一些适合用谱系法交代的事象,大都详加列举、铺张,景象宏大,节奏感强烈,有一定的震撼力。最为典型的是地名详表、集会详表、诸神详表、经卷详表、地狱十殿详表,后土祝赞以及《十报歌》这类特殊文体。

总之,就宝卷主题而言,它的内容和形式都是传统的,具有一定的历史文化底蕴,宝卷是俗文学的一种样式,是一种“固存的艺术”(immanent art)。因为宝卷从其文体(散韵结合)到结构(开经偈、走文、打佛、连枷佛、幺五子、四句交子、曲牌,走马词、了道歌、化缘歌),再到典型场景以及主题意义,这些都可以追溯到传统的历史深处,都可以找到它们的前身或来源。因此,造卷不是创作、原创、杜撰,而是编织,将现成的、固有的预制部件,按照固定的结构、格式排列组合起来;它的诗行充满了佛教经文的遗韵,套语连篇,多为固定的表达方式。它的句式、曲牌就是起一种极大程度的限定作用。

《后土宝卷》继承了传统的教派宝卷主题。早期的后土宝卷,它的主题是宣扬秘密宗教的。如无生老母、八卦教教义。河北易县、涞水民间的《后土宝卷》主题遗留了上述一些内容。但是,后土宝卷的研究价值是它的地方性。后土宝卷提供了地方文化语境。宝卷还记录了当地后土祭祀的历史面貌。

宝卷具备了一般宗教经卷的语言、篇章结构特点,利用了中国古典诗歌的艺术手段,同时也具有地方性、民间性和口头传统的叙事模式。从文本的层面来说,宝卷和民间叙事文本,两者之间是互为文本的,二者存在着借用、传递、标准化、地方化的动态影响过程。对这个过程的认识必须借助于文化语境的认识来完成。地方性知识就是宝卷的语境。它是我们田野工作中反复取证过程中获得的认识。

五、后土灵验叙事的神话范例

从历时的角度来看,我们可以观察到后土老母信仰的历史继承性。这种信仰在当代仍然催化出大量的口头叙事文本,这些文本证明了这种信仰的稳定性,它具有世代传承的特征。当民众把信仰诉诸表达的时候,总是要求助于传统的、类型化的表现形式。

(一)口头传说文本中的后山奶奶形象

国家正祀、道教的后土神曾经被制度化、抽象化、礼教化。民间叙事却不曾改变自然崇拜和祖先崇拜的内容。后土的形象即有大地之神、文化英雄、劳动妇女、追求爱情的村姑等不同的类型。民众对该神的称谓是老奶奶、汉张姑、砍柴女、纺线婆、香姑娘,把她说成某种劳动技能的发明者,从事某种劳动的人。后山的老奶奶传说,大致勾勒了她的身世,修行经历,劳动生活,晚年生活,计救刘秀的业绩,以及她过世以后民众对她的怀念。

人们往往把人类历史上的一些发明创造、在漫长的进化过程中形成的某种制度,当作某一文化英雄个人的、一朝一夕的创造。在老奶奶传说中,人们把制造纺车、发明纺线的技能、打制碾子、发明黑面条儿、3 月 18 日吃素馅饺子的风俗、植物来源甚至酸枣棵不长倒钩这样的自然界现象的起源,都归于她的名下。

后山奶奶的许多传说把她世俗化,把她的形象塑造为邻家的女孩、贤嫂、老婆子,她是求神女、纺线女、给人间送子的贫婆、砍柴女、香姑娘(她发明了香)。除此之外,香姑娘还是追求爱情生活的凡人。后山壁画上有张生香和放牛娃石牛的爱情故事。像《石牛和石纺车》、《香姑栽槐》、《千夫山的缘起》等传说,它们表达了现实生活,反映了民间疾苦和社会矛盾,也充满了地方文化的特色。

(二)后土灵验的民间叙事

民间口头传统中的后土表明,该神曾经是自然神、文化英雄和祖先神。民间传说不曾改变自然崇拜和祖先崇拜神话。后土由古代神话里的神,进入正统道教神龛里,变为四御之一,被民间宗教收为老母神,再到民间信仰里的娘娘神,这一系列语义学上的转变,是中国民间宗教的独有现象。关于祖先和英雄的区别不同于英雄和神的区别,越往后推移,祖先与英雄的界限越模糊。

后土灵验的民间叙事是与后土膜拜仪式相关的口头叙事,它多以历史或现实的事件为背景,讲述后土老母灵验的故事,讲述者对神灵的取态上是严肃和神圣的,所叙述之事与当地社会生活有关,同时也表达一种传统的价值观念。①

它以传统神话为范例,是对传统母题的再利用,表达地方性的民间的观念意识,涉及实际发生的历史事件,以神灵干预的形式来维护现实社会秩序;它与宝卷文本有重合的主题范围,但是,它还包括宝卷一般不常表现的迷信或占验风水、巫术内容;它具有较强的神话和仪式的意味,这是它区别于一般传说的地方。地灵故事这个名称是民间的说法。但是,它不是那种虚构故事,它的特点是真实,带有现场性和膜拜仪式性,具有严肃的意义。总之,它在人们的信仰活动和行为方面划定了一个文化的空间。地灵故事与后土膜拜互为表里。

神话、传说等与地方的宗教信仰有密切的关系。反映在地方传说中的宗教的祈求,不能不以下列二者最为重要:(1)求食料;(2)求子息。神赐子嗣,这是原生性的宗教信仰。它用以解决人的生产问题。儒家的根本思想,生发于生殖崇拜。中国文化的血缘根基,为民族的心理结构,这种传统的礼教文化,重视多子,以此为福。

民间叙事经常表现神灵干预主题的民间叙事。这些神话叙事规定了人们的行为的文化空间。这些故事的数量最大,与地方性知识联系最紧密。神判的主题,反映了因果报应的观念,宣扬作恶必遭惩戒的思想,这是以传统的社会道德规范为基

---

① 参见公李《后山神话》,另外,笔者曾于2003年与河北易县文化馆副研究员公李合作进行了关于后土叙事的搜集工作,编印了田野资料集《后土地祇灵应故事》。在它的后记里编者公李写道:"2001年初尹虎彬到易县搜求《后土宝卷》。他是继英国学者钟思第先生、美国学者欧大年先生、中国艺术研究院音乐研究所薛艺兵先生、香港中文大学陈教授以及曹教授,第六位来洪崖山后土神庙考察的学者。于是由我陪他共同考察一些地方。他也耐心地听取了我对洪崖山大地神庙的部分见解,更对洪崖山大地神庙流传现代灵验神话故事发生了浓厚兴趣。于是,在我的鼓动下,尹虎彬与河北10位长期生活在基层社会的民间文艺工作者,从2002年6月始,到2002年10月结束,历时5个月,进行了尝试性地辛苦搜求和整理。现在摆在你面前的正是我们10人的田野作业。这部分资料本暂定名为《后土地祇灵应故事》。河北易县文化馆公李。2003年2月15日。"

础的。谁违犯禁忌，神就要惩罚谁。宝卷涉及神判的罪名有：毁经谤卷、亵渎神灵、毁像拆庙、开斋破戒等行为。神明会对犯有这些罪名的人施以重罚，把他们打入地狱。民间广泛流行地狱十王图，其中除前述的几条罪名之外，妒贤夸能、诽谤他人、触逆尊长、横行乡里、放火烧山也在惩戒之列。

神话里的后土，能够击退番兵，辅助英雄杀敌。这使得后土神祇具有像古代那样掌建邦国和守护国土的军事职能。后土神在古代能分夷狄，近现代能抵御外来侵略，当代则促进民族团结和国家统一。因此，关于后土神祇慈悲灵验的传说归根到底是人的传说。而且，上述传说时代感极强，具有现实性；当然，它所反映的核心意义、典型场景，仍然继承了传统的类型化、模式化的表达方式。现代传说里的后土显然超越了民族和宗教信仰的界限。传说反映出后土为大地之神，是国土之神，能护国佑民；同时它又超越族群、宗教、地方性文化的界限，从而普济四方。

结　论

后土宝卷、后土灵验叙事、刘秀传说、河北洪崖山神话传说群，它们属于不同的民俗学题材样式，但是，它们互为文本，具有共享意义范围和共同的历史根源。它们都以地方性的民间叙事为文本特征，以后土崇拜为核心内容，以传统的神话为范例。

地方性的宝卷和民间叙事传统，它们是由本地的后土祭奠发展起来的。历史上国家正祀的后土被民间化，又被地方化，成为本地的村姑，由村姑变而为神。

神灵与祭祀是民间叙事传统的原动力。以上这些话，强调了民间叙事文本的地方传统。我们还必须把文本作为文本来看待。现在，我们至少可以在较为广泛的社会历史背景下，了解一个地方性的民间叙事文本的实现过程。

参考书目

曹本冶、薛艺兵：《河北易县涞水两地的后土崇拜与民间乐社》，北京：《中国音乐学》2000年第1期。

晁福林：《先秦民俗史》，上海：上海人民出版社，2001年。

(清)陈杰等撰《涞水县志》，光绪二十一年刊本。

干春松：《神仙传》，北京：中国社会科学出版社，1998年。

公李：《后山神话》，北京：中国民间文艺出版社，1990年。

Jones, Stephen. *Folk Music of China*: *Living Instrumental Traditions*, Oxford: Clarendon Press, 1995.

Jones, Stephen and Xue Yibing, "*The Music Associations of Hebei Province, China: A Preliminary Report*," Ethnomusicology, Vol. 35, No. 1, Winter 1991.

马西沙、韩秉方:《中国民间宗教史》,上海:上海人民出版社,1992 年。

Nagy, Gregory. *Greek Mythology and Poetics*. Ithaca: Cornell University Press, Revised paperback version, 1992.

欧达伟(R. David Arkush):《中国民众思想史》,董晓萍译,北京:中央民族大学出版社,1995 年。

Overmyer, Daniel L. *Folk Buddhist Religion: Dissenting Sects in Late Traditional China*, Harvard University Press, 1976.

Overmyer, Daniel L. *Precious Volumes: An Introduction to Chinese Sectarian Scriptures from the Sixteenth and Seventeenth Centuries*, Harvard University Press, 1999.

乔建中、薛艺兵、[英]钟思第、张振涛:《冀中、京、津地区民间"音乐会"普查实录》,《中国音乐年鉴》,田青主编,济南:山东友谊出版社,1995 年。

乔建中:《民间鼓吹乐研究:首届中国民间鼓吹乐学术研讨会论文集》,济南:山东友谊出版社,1999 年。

民国《易县志稿》,寿鹏飞撰修,北京:学苑出版社,1990 年。

薛艺兵:《屈家营音乐会的调查与研究》,北京:《中国音乐学》1987 年第 2 期。

薛艺兵:《民间吹打的乐种类型与人文背景》,原载《民间鼓吹乐研究》,乔建中、薛艺兵主编,济南:山东友谊出版社,1999 年。

薛艺兵:《河北易县涞水的后土宝卷》,上海:《音乐艺术》2000 年第 2 期。

喻松青:《民间秘密宗教研究》,台北:台湾联经出版事业公司,1994 年。

张希舜、濮文起、高可、宋军编,《宝卷初集》第 11 卷,太原:山西人民出版社,1994 年。

张振涛:《民间乐师研究报告》,济南:《民间鼓吹乐研究》,山东友谊出版社,1999 年。

[日]泽田瑞穗:《增补宝卷の研究》,东京:株式会社国书刊行会,1975 年。

图书在版编目(CIP)数据

史诗与英雄/(荷兰)希珀,尹虎彬主编.—桂林:
广西师范大学出版社,2004.7
　ISBN 7 - 5633 - 4820 - 4

　Ⅰ.史…　Ⅱ.①希…②尹…　Ⅲ.少数民族 - 英雄
史诗 - 文学研究 - 中国 - 文集 - 英、汉
Ⅳ.I207.22 - 53

　中国版本图书馆 CIP 数据核字(2004)第 065296 号

广西师范大学出版社出版发行

(桂林市育才路15号　邮政编码:541004)
(网址:www.bbtpress.com)
出版人:萧启明
全国新华书店经销
发行热线:010 - 64284815
三河盛达印务有限公司
(三河市燕郊中赵甫　邮政编码:065201)
开本:787mm×1 092mm　1/16
印张:30　字数:400 千字
2004 年 7 月第 1 版　2004 年 7 月第 1 次印刷
印数:0 001 ~ 3 000　定价:48.00 元